W9-AFZ-372

COMPILER CONSTRUCTION
Theory and Practice
Second Edition

FOREWORD   *by W. M. McKeeman*

The art of translating programming languages has, in many ways, come of age. From its beginnings in Fortran and Algol and hundreds of other languages, we find the concept of high-level languages well established and the construction of translators routine.

Such progress exists because of the highly developed craft of compiler writers to whom the tools of the trade are well-known and regularly applied. There are few places where that rich craft is recorded altogether in a way that is understandable and immediately applicable. To provide such a source is the purpose served by the following text.

The reader must be a programmer. The terminology comes from that field, and the insights necessary to understand the material do so as well. Assuming that background, the reader should find here the world of automatic translation opening up—from the formalities of language description to the tough details of machine code generation. It is a fascinating subject and well worth the intellectual effort of study.

FOREWORD   *by Harold Stone*

Compiler Construction: Theory and Practice is exactly what the title promises. It is an excellent mix of the mathematical foundations of compilers and the practical considerations required in developing high quality compilers for commercial release. The level of discussion is suitable for college juniors and seniors. The material is readily digested because all of the mathematical prerequisites are included in the book, and they are exposed in a highly palatable fashion.

One of the strengths of the book is that algorithms are normally discussed in high-level Pascal-like language that brings out the structure and flow of the algorithms with great clarity in contrast to similar descriptions in flow-chart language or automation operations used by some earlier texts in the area. The authors do a particularly commendable job on the practical aspects of code generation, code optimization, and syntax error handling, all three of which are still "black arts" by comparison to the topic of parsing where theory and practice have largely merged.

Here is a book that the professional compiler writer can use to create better language translators, that the computer scientist and engineer can use to gain an understanding and appreciation of the process of language translation that is part of his interface with the computer, and that the student can use to further his knowledge of the capabilities of computers and methods for harnessing the power of the computer.

Acquisition Editor	John Levstik
Project Editor	Molly Gardiner
Production Direction	Greg Hubit Bookworks
Technical Art	House of Graphics
Composition	Typothetae and William A. Barrett

Copyright © Science Research Associates, Inc. 1986, 1979. All rights reserved. No part of this publication may be reproduced, stored in a retrieval system, or transmitted, in any form or by any means, electronic, mechanical, photocopying, recording, or otherwise, without the prior written permission of Science Research Associates, Inc.

Printed in the United States of America.

Library of Congress Cataloging in Publication Data

Barrett, William A., 1930–
　Compiler construction.

　Rev. ed. of: Compiler construction / William A. Barrett, John D. Couch. © 1979.
　Bibliography: p.
　Includes index.
　1. Compiling (Electronic computers)　I. Title.
QA76.76.C65B37　1985　　　005.4′53　　　85-14325
ISBN 0-574-21765-7

10　9　8　7　6　5　4　3　2　1

COMPILER CONSTRUCTION
Theory and Practice
Second Edition

WILLIAM A. BARRETT
RODNEY M. BATES
DAVID A. GUSTAFSON
JOHN D. COUCH

 ® SCIENCE RESEARCH ASSOCIATES, INC.
Chicago, Henley-on-Thames, Sydney, Toronto

A Subsidiary of IBM

Preface

Compiler Construction: Theory and Practice is intended as a one- or two-semester course in the fundamentals of compilers and/or language translation. It is designed especially for students with some programming or computer systems background. A background in discrete mathematics is helpful, but not required. This text treats:

- Grammars, trees, and parsing fundamentals.

- Finite-state automata—their relation to regular grammars and regular expressions, their systematic generation, their reduction to minimal form, their representations, and their application to compilers.

- Lexical scanning—general principles and application to several common programming languages.

- Top-down parsing—principles, LL(k) grammars, LL(1), and recursive-descent parsers. A construction and verification algorithm is given for a recursive-descent parser.

- Bottom-up parsing—principles, precedence parsers, and the LR(k) parsers. Construction and conflict resolution are discussed in detail.

- Syntax-directed translation—principles and applications to translation. Data structures and sample programs in Pascal are given and discussed.

- Symbol table access and application—principles, scope rules, type rules, static representation of Pascal data structures. Efficient symbol lookup methods.

- Run-time machine model—a complete abstract stack machine is defined (similar to Pascal PCODE) and shown to be sufficient to support Pascal recursive procedure calls, arithmetic expressions, variable access, and control structures.

- Optimization—efficient register allocation, constant folding, recognition of common subexpressions, and introduction to data-flow analysis.

- Error recovery—an error recovery for each of the major parsing methods and for finite-state machines is given.

The Authors

The authors have both academic and industrial experience in compiler construction. William Barrett taught courses in introductory computer systems and compiler construction at Lehigh University, Bethlehem, Pennsylvania, before accepting a staff position in software development at Hewlett-Packard Company, Cupertino, California. He designed and implemented a systems programming language and a Pascal compiler while there. He most recently designed and wrote the Qparser™ translator writing system, a commercial product offered by his company, Qcad Systems, Inc.

As faculty members in the Computer Science Department at Kansas State University, Manhattan, Kansas, Rodney Bates and David Gustafson have taught many courses on compiler construction, formal languages, and theory of languages. Dr. Bates' areas of research include compilers for object-oriented languages and computer architecture to support compiler construction. Dr. Gustafson's areas of research include program analysis and software engineering. Dr. Bates has recently taken a position with Vitesse Electronics Corporation in Camarillo, California, developing compilers.

John Couch taught compiler construction at California State University, San Jose, for several years. He was responsible for several compiler projects while at Hewlett-Packard and as vice president for software for Apple Computer. He was most recently vice president and general manager for the Personal Office Systems Division at Apple.

As teachers, the authors believe that some language theory is an essential part of compiler construction. However, much of language theory is irrelevant to compiler construction. This text should help bridge the gap between theory and practice.

The authors also believe that a balance should be struck between parsing and code synthesis issues and between top-down and bottom-up methods. Although most of the synthesis material in this text pertains to bottom-up parsing, both parsing approaches are given approximately equal treatment, and many of the synthesis notions are applicable to either approach.

Features

This text contains some standard material, some material that has been brought together under one cover for the first time, and some original material. Most of the algorithms are illustrated through the use of Pascal program fragments. A floppy diskette containing an LALR parser generator and utilities for a small translator are also included with the text for instructors.

The first three chapters present a core treatment of grammars, trees, and parsing finite state automata. We have included only enough language theory and automata theory to understand parsers and compilers. We have omitted such topics as Turing machines and computability. Enough automaton theory is presented to make it possible to develop the commonly used top-down and bottom-up parsers, and to prove that they perform as claimed. We believe that, between the formal descriptions, the proofs, the extensive discussion, and the many examples of machines and machine traces, a student will be able both to understand how a parser works, and to use professional literature on programming languages for additional information.

Chapter 3 discusses finite state automata, their relation to regular grammars and regular expressions, and their reduction to minimal form. As an application, lexical analysis is discussed briefly. A designer must be aware that some languages pose difficult lexical problems. Such problems are discussed in some detail.

The remaining chapters contain much original material. An extensive discussion of recursive-descent parsers will be found in Chapter 5, in which we not only describe this commonly used parsing method, but develop an automatic generator and the conditions under which the parser operates correctly.

The LR(k) parsing methods, often incorporated into commercial compiler systems, are discussed in considerable detail in Chapter 6, which also covers methods of reducing the size of the stored LR tables, and of estimating the size of the tables. Parser reductions based on special grammar properties are described in some detail. The instructor diskette can be used on an IBM or IBM-compatible machine as an interactive instructional tool in LR table generation and bottom-up parsing.

The organization of a symbol table for single and multiple pass compilers with multiple block levels is given in Chapter 8. Efficient access methods are also described there. We show how to organize a symbol table for PL/I structures and Pascal types, and how to resolve partially specified names.

Run-time data structures are presented in Chapter 9. We develop a special abstract machine system similar to the UCSD Pcode that can be used to implement Ada, Fortran, Pascal, and many other languages. The operations of this system must be provided in one form or another in implementing the basic features of any language. The important issues of procedure calls, parameter passing, blocks, and array and structure access are dealt with in considerable detail. The material on the efficient access of multi-dimensional arrays or structures should be of particular interest.

Chapter 10 deals with optimization issues. We have followed a modern school of thought in this area—that of constructing a directed acyclic graph of a program segment, then performing various reductions on that graph. We consider the multi-register allocation problem at some length, following the work of Aho and others in this field. Finally, we develop some fundamental notions of flow analysis, which can be used to reduce code and also to detect subtle programmer errors at the compilation level.

Error recovery is discussed along with each of the major parsers. The most extensive error recovery discussion is related to the LR parsers. Error recovery experiments are reviewed. The instructor diskette carries an error recovery procedure in Pascal for further study.

Designing a Compiler Course

For a one-semester course, some portions of this text should be covered in detail; other sections can be approached tangentially. To concentrate on basic matters in one semester, we recommend Chapters 1, 2, 4, 6, 7, and selected portions of 3, 5, 8, and 9. The material on finite-state machines in Chapter 3 may have been covered in a separate course; if so, it can either be briefly reviewed or omitted. We recommend the material on FSM representation and lexical analysis in Chapter 3, however. Section 5.1 provides an abstract treatment of bottom-up nondeterministic parsing, extending the light survey found toward the end of Chapter 2. The remaining sections in Chapter 5 are of largely historical interest; there is little practical value in precedence parsers.

For a two-semester course, we suggest using Chapters 1–7 for the first semester, then 8-11 for the second semester. Chapters 8–11 will not fill a semester, and should be augmented with additional outside material, or with a class project. Many suggestions for projects are contained in the exercises. A Qparser demonstration diskette is available from QCAD Systems for a modest price. The diskette carries sufficient programs for a number of elementary exercises in grammars, LR table construction, symbol table operations, semantic structures, error recovery experiments, and design of simple languages.

For larger projects, we suggest that the instructor acquire the full Qparser system, which contains complete Pascal source code for most of the fragments discussed in the text, a working assembler and simulator for the machine of Chapter 9, and a Pascal subset compiler. The full system also contains a powerful parser generator capable of implementing a sophisticated compiler or interpreter.

An instructor's guide, containing solutions to the exercises in this text, is available from the publisher.

Major Changes in the Second Edition

Our main goal in this revision is to provide a more contemporary approach to the practical issues of translator construction, and to support more fully the concepts with correct Pascal fragments. We have provided a suite of compiler tools and example programs as a companion to the book. Finally, the exercises have been revised.

We have chosen not to alter the basic abstract treatment of grammars and parsers found in the first edition, except to correct errors and improve clarity. Thus most of Chapters 1, 2, 3, 5, and the first parts of Chapters 4, 6, and 7 have been carried over with little or no change. The recursive-descent material in Chapter 4 has been improved, and a discussion of error recovery can now be found there. Chapter 6 has been reworked, with some material eliminated. The latter part of Chapter 7 has been expanded to contain a more specific treatment of semantics with Pascal declaration and code fragments.

Chapter 9 was completely rewritten. The AOC machine of the first edition has been replaced with a machine very similar to the Pcode interpreter found in the UCSD Pascal compiler. The concepts are the same as in the first edition, but the machine expression is somewhat more modern. This machine is implemented through an assembler and simulator available in the complete Qparser system.

Chapter 10 in the first edition was eliminated. We found that few instructors made use of the detailed description of the three commercial machines. Although those machines are still sold and supported, they are no longer representative of modern computer architectures.

Optimization now appears in Chapter 10. The error recovery material that appeared in Chapter 12 of the first edition has been subdivided and now appears with the appropriate parsers. Some new error recovery material has been added for finite-state machines, recursive-descent, and LL(1) parsers. Material related to LR error recovery will now be found in Chapter 6.

Information on Qparser

For more information about the Qparser translator writing system, please write to QCAD Systems, Inc., 1164 Hyde Avenue, San Jose, CA 95129. Additional information is also contained in the booklet for the instructor diskette.

Acknowledgments

We are very grateful to the many readers and teachers who have sent in corrections and suggestions for improvements in the first edition. In particular, the criticisms of Professor Dr. Reinhard Wilhelm, University of Saarbrucken; Professor Patrick Ho, University of Colorado; and Professor Frank DeRemer of the University of California, Santa Cruz, were most helpful in correcting the first edition.

There were many reviewers of the new second edition material to whom we owe our thanks: Mark Laventhal, Judy Geist, and Dave Graham of Hewlett-Packard Company; Professor Mike Tindall, Seattle State University; Dr. Stephen J. Allan, Colorado State University; Dr. Gordon L. Bailes, East Tennessee State University; Dr. C. K. Cheng, Virginia Commonwealth University; Professor Robert H. Dourson, California Polytechnic State University; Dr. James Gimpel, Lehigh University; Professor Martin G. Keeney, Michigan State University; Professor John T. Korb, Purdue University; Professor Terry LePera, James Madison University; Professor Wing Tam, Harvey Mudd College; and Professor W. Tasi, Polytechnic Institute of New York. Their attention to the details of the text have weeded out numerous errors. Should any errors remain, they are entirely the responsibility of the authors.

Among the SRA staff, we would especially like to thank Alan Lowe, John Levstik, and Molly Gardiner for the persistence and attention to detail that have brought this book onto the market on schedule. Lyn Dupré's copy editing was superb, as was Greg Hubit's handling of the details of production. We'd also like to thank the staff of Typothetae, Inc. for their patience in assisting us with moving this textual material from our small computer into their typesetting system.

Finally, we'd like to thank our wives, Jean, Coni Jo, Karen, and Diana, for their support and understanding. The time spent on this book might otherwise have been spent in their pleasant company.

CONTENTS

CHAPTER 1

INTRODUCTION

1.1. Translators

A *translator* accepts a *source program* and transforms it into an *object program*. The source program is a member of a *source language* and the object program is a member of an *object language*. Both languages are artificial, inasmuch as they are designed for a digital computer, as opposed to a natural language like English or German.

Each program expresses some behavior. We are primarily interested in those translations for which the source and object behaviors are identical. For example, a Fortran program should yield the same results for a given input regardless of the machine language to which it is translated. The result of executing the machine language program should be the same as that expected from the program as expressed in Fortran.

Artificial translation is rapidly becoming a mathematical discipline, whereas natural translation remains rather more an art. Yet the two are somewhat akin. Any student of foreign languages knows that one language cannot be translated to another simply by substituting words. A human translator must first grasp the precise meaning of each source sentence, then compose an equivalent sentence in the object language. So it is with artificial translators. A source program must first be analyzed to uncover its underlying meaning and structure; this process is called *parsing*. Then a number of transformations on the structure are performed, ultimately ending in the object program.

For a given source language, the translation may be carried to several different levels of completeness: to *assembly code,* to *machine code,* or to execution. Assembly code is a sequence of mnemonic instructions and symbolic address references; it is a member of an *assembly language,* and must be translated into machine code by yet another translator, called an *assembler.* Assembly language usually has a very simple structure with a fixed format: a program location field, an instruction field, and an address field. Each line of assembly code usually translates to one machine instruction. There are no nested statements, arithmetic expressions, or procedures as in Fortran or Algol. Machine code is a sequence of binary machine instructions that require little or no modification to be executed.

An *interpreter* accepts a source program, translates it into some intermediate data structure, then executes the algorithm by carrying out each operation given in the intermediate structure. A program can be developed rapidly with an interpreter, because its execution can follow its modification quickly. Most interpreters also provide means of interrupting the program flow and examining variable values by name. The simplest possible interpreter parses the source and immediately executes the result. The speed of execution is poor, because each line must be scanned and parsed prior to execution.

The advantage of a compiler is that it can generate a maximally efficient, short, executable program. It demands fairly heavy computer resources while compiling, but when executing requires only those resources needed by the executing program. The disadvantage of a compiler is the time lag between writing or modifying a program and executing it. For example, many Pascal compilers require that the entire program be recompiled for any change anywhere, however slight. As a program grows in size, so will the number of modifications and the time required for compilation.

Certain new systems combine the advantages of high run-time performance of a compiler and the convenience of an interpreter by providing *incremental compilation*. An incremental compiler permits a programmer to compile just one portion of the text—usually one module or procedure—then execute the program.

Two approaches have been taken to incremental compilation. In one, the source must be decomposed by the program writer into one or more discrete modules, each of which can be compiled separately. The programmer must decide on the decomposition, and arrange the source appropriately. Some Pascal systems are modular. The languages C and Ada require modular support systems. In the other approach, portions of a full program may be incrementally compiled. The Symbolics 3600 series provides such a Pascal compilation system. On the 3600, the Pascal source is incrementally translated into equivalent Lisp source. The Lisp source is in turn incrementally compiled into efficient run-time object code.

A compiler or an interpreter is itself a program written in some language, called the *host* language. We therefore see that three languages are involved in a compiler—source, object, and host. These are often three different languages. A Fortran compiler that runs on an IBM 360 might be written in PL/I, and generate machine code for a 1401. A compiler that generates code for its host machine is called *self-resident;* if, in addition, it is written in its own source language, it is *self-compiling*. If it generates code for a machine other than the host, it is called a *cross compiler*.

1.2. Why Write a Compiler?

A programming language is designed and a compiler written for it for only one reason—to make it easier for human beings to get a computer to carry out some task reliably. If it were possible for us to translate rapidly without error a task description into the long lists of binary numbers that compose a computer's instruction list, then programming languages and compilers would be unnecessary. Unfortunately, human beings make mistakes. They are unable to cope with a big list of binary numbers, and their time is more valuable than machine time.

A computer is well suited to clerical tasks and can handle them cheaply and accurately. One task that a computer can perform is assisting us in programming itself.

Human errors can occur anywhere in a system design. The issue is not whether humans will err—they will—but just how a machine aid such as a compiler can not only detect errors but also help prevent them in the first place.

The most effective error-prevention mechanisms are built into the language's design. An effective language design makes it possible for the human coder to concentrate on writing a concise and clear description of an algorithm. He or she should be completely free of extraneous considerations, such as how memory is to be assigned to variables, how branches are to be resolved to statements, or what machine instructions are to be invoked.

The efficiency of the programmer in producing a reliable program cannot be overlooked. There is the direct cost of software in the salaries and overhead of the programmers, and the computing machinery that they require. However, that direct cost may be considerably less than the cost of missing a delivery deadline.

An important factor in reducing the production time of a software system is *how effectively the task can be partitioned into relatively independent, watertight modular compartments*. The counterpart to partitioning is *integration*—once the modules have been written and tested independently, the whole *system* must pull together efficiently and operate reliably. The development of modular programming languages, such as Ada, now makes it possible for us to produce large, reliable systems in a much shorter time than we could a decade ago.

1.2.1. Modularity

A large program must be divided into small chunks for it to be written and debugged efficiently. This "divide and conquer" principle applies to the development of any large, complex system.

Ideally, the compiler of a modular system should be capable of compiling each module separately. It should not be necessary to compile all the source of the system to deal with one or two simple changes.

Modular partitioning helps in several important ways: (1) the whole programming task can be divided among the members of a programming team, (2) the team members need not understand the whole system in detail, and (3) compilation time can be reduced in proportion to the subdivision of the task.

The division of labor implied by (1) often does not hold for software projects. Given N team members, the task time usually will not be reduced by a factor of N. The time may even be *increased* by adding more people to a team, because members must invariably spend time talking to each other about common issues. Our team of N members has N(N - 1)/2 ways of talking to each other one-to-one: they can easily spend nearly all their time discussing the project!

Division of labor helps only if each task to be performed stands alone and is clearly defined. Team members should spend most of their time concentrating on their particular portion of the task, and not on how all the other parts of the system might affect their part. This demands an effective modularity strategy.

Understanding a task (2) takes time, too. This training time is often overlooked by software managers, who may assume that if members of a team have been trained in, say, operating systems and Pascal, then they should be able to start writing programs for a project immediately. If the whole system concept must be understood in detail before any one team member can start writing his or her part, then training will take time. Training a new member also stops work on the task temporarily, because the rest of the team has to train the new member. When a system is well modularized, each team member does not have to understand all of the system.

A compiler that can compile separately one module or, even better, a single procedure, saves time and computer resources on a large system. Programmers fall into a natural rhythm of (1) noticing a problem, (2) diagnosing the problem, (3) curing the problem by patching the source program, and (4) recompiling. Often, several compilations are needed during diagnosis to get the program to report more details than it normally would. If the time spent by the computer on compilation is more than a few seconds, the compiler will become the dominant consumer of time in developing the software.

The worst situation is that in which *all* the source must be compiled to repair just *one* problem. Not only does this make it almost impossible for several isolated teams to work on the system independently, but the time required to compile a large system can easily run to one hour or longer.

Procedures

The most commonly used partitioning mechanism is the *procedure call*. A procedure or function call performs some more-or-less complicated task in response to a few parametric values. The task preferably can be described in a few lines of comment, although its execution may require many pages of source. The effect is to hide the details of execution of the procedure from the purview of the programmer who calls that procedure.

For example, a *sort* procedure performs a task that is easily understood: given an array of numbers, characters, or whatever, the procedure yields the same or a new array with the same items ordered. However, there are many ways of sorting an array, and some algorithms are hard to understand but are very efficient. A programmer who needs to sort an array *does not have to know how the sort is performed:* he or she need only have confidence that the sort procedure will perform its task.

Program Modules

A *module* is a set of variable declarations associated with a set of procedures. Some of the variables and procedures are intended for internal use only, whereas others may be designated for external use. The internal variables and procedures cannot be affected by any operation of any other module. The external variables may be designated *read-only* or *read-write* in some modular schemes. The module's external procedures can be called from some other module.

The internal variables and procedures are considered *hidden:* they need not be understood or even known about by outsiders. The externally advertised variables and procedures are considered *exported:* people who must use the module will examine them and their definitions. Finally, the module may invoke other modules: it will *import* variables and procedures from the other modules.

These access controls clearly are vital to the decomposition of a large system. The large system is divided like an office building into a number of rooms. The rooms are connected by doors with doorplates in the form of import and export statements. The internal details of a room may be rearranged by its occupants as long as its doorplate continues to describe the room accurately.

Consider the alternative to modularity: any procedure may be called by anyone, and any variable may be changed by anyone. Team members must spend a great deal of time making sure that all the other programmers respect their wishes. Moreover, to be completely safe, they must inspect all of the code in the whole system to make sure that their requirements are met. It is much better to have a suitable compiler enforce the standards of a modular language.

Note that the system ultimately must be brought together and executed as a whole. The machine that executes the system need not know anything about the modular decomposition; it knows only code sequences and data spaces in a large linear memory. It is the *compiler* and a *linking loader* that bring the modules together as a whole. When the compiler is invoked on one module, it produces an *object module;* that module must be connected to other object modules by the loader to yield a complete program.

1.2.2. Static versus Dynamic Interpretation

You must keep in mind the distinction between the sequence of source statements (the *static* or *lexical* interpretation) and the run-time execution of the program (the *dynamic* interpretation) while designing and writing a compiler.

A compiler must operate on the lexical interpretation, which is essentially the sequence of characters as drawn from a source file. It does not "see" the dynamic execution sequence of the source interpreted as a program—yet its translation generally must be an executable program.

Inferring the dynamic behavior of a program is a hard computational problem in general. It is made difficult by the existence of dynamically generated control flags. For example, a WHILE loop is terminated when some Boolean condition becomes true, but that condition may depend on the values of variables influenced or changed within the statements controlled by the WHILE.

Ideally, a compiler should detect and report *all* potential and real errors in the source program. In reality, it can report only those that are detectable within static computability constraints. Thus, the compiler might be able to show that the

Boolean condition of a WHILE loop (that is, WHILE *condition* DO . . .) is not influenced by any state changes in the WHILE statements; although it would be useful to report this to the programmer, it may not in fact be an error. Some programs are written to run forever, or until halted by a system-level interrupt.

As another example, a compiler can detect that two different statements in a CASE form carry the same label. This error can be detected because the CASE labels are bound to integer constant values at compile-time. However, the compiler usually cannot determine whether the CASE selector (that is, CASE *selector* OF . . .) always will yield one of the case labels. The selector usually is an expression containing variables the value of which depends on the dynamic execution environment of the CASE statement.

1.2.3. Machine Independence

A major service provided by a compiler is *machine independence*. A large number of different machine architectures are now provided by manufacturers; there is no standard architecture. This diversity promotes the development of more powerful and cost-effective computers, but can create a serious problem in moving an application software system from one machine to another.

If the system is written in a high-level language, moving it from one machine to another with even a radically different instruction set is much easier than if it is in machine or assembly code. Great strides have been made recently in portable languages, mostly notably in C and Ada. A system is *portable* if it can be made to execute easily on more than one computing system; the source programs probably will have to be recompiled.

Language Standards and Portability

Portability is achieved at the language *design* level, not by clever compiler implementation tricks. Essentially, the language definition must become a *standard,* independent of any particular computing machine's characteristics, and not subject to the whims of any particular compiler implementor.

A language standard can be achieved through publication and general acceptance of a standard document, government fiat, or both. Cobol and Ada were standardized through government fiat, but both were designed through joint efforts by industry, academia, and government. The Fortran standard was achieved after the language was first designed at IBM. Several revisions to the Fortran standard have appeared since then. Pascal was designed by Niklaus Wirth for instructional purposes. There are several serious omissions in the Jensen and Wirth *Pascal User Manual and Report* [Wirth, 1974] that have been filled in different ways by other implementors. There are now several dozen different Pascal implementations, each with its own characteristic features that are unsupported by the others. The C language has become a defacto standard through general acceptance of *The C Programming Language* reference manual by Kernighan and Ritchie [Kernighan, 1973]. Another factor has been the porting of Unix to a variety of machines, which has required a standard C compiler.

A programming language standard is of practical value only if it makes no reference to any specific computing machine's features. Computer feature characteristics can creep into programs through certain combinations of data forms and operations on data.

For example, what is an *integer?* The ANSI Pascal standard [ANSI Pascal, 1983] defines the Pascal integer type as representing a subset of the whole numbers. The *range* of an integer is implementation-dependent. Thus, on a machine in which 36-bit twos-complement arithmetic is the most efficient, a Pascal integer is likely to be implemented with that arithmetic. However, a microcomputer may support only 16-bit numbers. These two ranges are upward compatible—a program that works on the small machine will work on the larger machine, provided that the program never makes any assumptions about the internal form of the number or depends on an overflow condition in 16-bit arithmetic.

A program will be sensitive to the internal representation of numbers through an operation that can access individual bits of the number, or move the bits around in a logical fashion, yet also deal with the number in an arithmetic fashion. For example, a left shift of one will double the value of an integer if the integer is in twos-complement form; it will not if the integer is in sign-magnitude form.

For this reason, ANSI Pascal does not include logical operations that can be applied freely to ordinal numbers. This is an example of a *type restriction* required by the language definition for the sake of achieving a high level of portability.

However, Pascal supports a variant CASE data structure. For example:

```
VCREC= record case boolean of
         true: (I: integer);
         false: (B: packed array [0..3] of char);
       end;
```

Using this variant, it is easy to decompose the internal form of an *integer* into bytes, assuming that (1) an integer spans four bytes (not always the case), (2) a char represents one byte, (3) the packed attribute in fact packs bytes (not always the case), and (4) the compiler aligns the integer I with the array B (it may not). The loss of any one of these conditions will render the decomposition meaningless.

1.2.4. Language Features

In summary, here are some of the services that a high-level language should provide, and that its compiler should support:

1. Support modular partitioning of programs.

2. Support symbolic references to all statement locations and data.

3. Provide structured control statements.

4. Provide structured data statements.

5. Enforce consistent type declaration and usage for variables.

6. Provide automatic type conversion where safe, and require user-defined type conversion otherwise.

7. Be portable, or potentially portable, among a variety of different machines and operating systems.

The compiler writer's task is to provide an accurate implementation of the language's design, and to provide a reasonable programming development environment if possible.

1.3. The Cost of a Compiler

The development of a compiler for a large modern language is a major software project. Depending on the complexity of the language and the target machine, as little as three person-months or as much as 30 person-years may be required to write and debug a compiler. The most complex compiler ever written was probably PL/I for the IBM 360. PL/I is an extraordinarily rich language, containing not only several file access methods but also a large set of data types and operations. Ada is also a rich language and requires several person-years to implement.

Another cost is a loss of machine efficiency for a program written in a high-level language compared to the same algorithm written by a skilled programmer using assembly language. A high-level language imposes various constraints on a programmer that do not exist in assembly language, such as its forms of control structures or limited data types. This loss of efficiency is particularly severe for a high-level language that is not particularly well suited to its target machine. Pascal and PL/I are fairly well suited to a stack architecture. A multiregister machine, such as the 360, generally requires elaborate optimization techniques for a compiler to compete with an assembler. The optimization phase of compiler design for a machine poorly suited to the language can double the compiler cost and size.

A compiler's inefficiency in generating executable code is paid for each time the code is used. If that cost is deemed too high, there are several alternatives, such as recoding in another language or coding portions of the software in assembly language. Often an inefficiency in a programming system stems from a poor choice of algorithm, or a poor peripheral device access strategy, rather than from an inherent inefficiency in the compiler.

1.4. The Compiling Process

The major operations in a compiler are illustrated in figure 1.1. The process begins with a source file at the top of the figure, and ends with optimized object

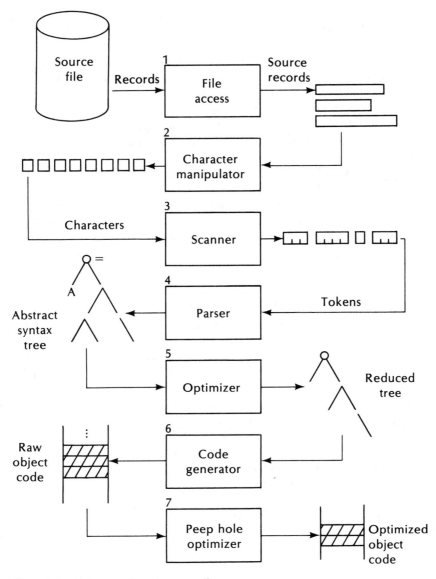

Figure 1.1.   Major operations in a compiler.

code at the bottom. Our description in this section is necessarily highly simplified; many special problems in a real compiler system are overlooked in this review.

A compiler is based on a sequence of transformations that preserve the operational meaning of a program, but not necessarily all the information in it, nor even the exact sequence of operations requested in the source program.

The character of the system in which the compiler resides has a strong influence on the design of a compiler. Most computers have a limited "fast" memory (semiconductor), but have extensive "mass" memory (magnetic disk). A compiler often must process large source programs, so that only a relatively small portion of the source can be processed actively at any one time. That portion is placed in electronic memory, which forms a kind of moving window on the source. A compiler usually is designed such that only the least information necessary is retained in fast memory, and most of the compilation is sequential in character—object code or some intermediate structures are emitted as additional source is read.

Not all translators fit this pattern, nor must a compiler be strictly sequential on all systems. A system with virtual memory, for example, in effect has unlimited memory available, so sequential processing is less important. An interpreter usually has to carry all of the source, symbol tables, and program during editing and execution; however, they need not necessarily all be in fast memory.

Source

Compilation begins with some source form, shown in figure 1.1 as a file. Of course, source can originate in any of a variety of forms, such as a disk file, a terminal, or magnetic tape. The access to different physical source devices is quite different in detail, but the differences usually are of little or no concern to the compiler writer. An operating system almost invariably provides isolation of physical access characteristics from programs such as compilers. The compiler therefore first sees some sequence of source records, emitted by box 1.

In some languages (for example, Fortran and Basic), source record boundaries are important as statement delimiters. In others, source boundaries are of no consequence. Hence, a compiler is likely to contain a section that accepts source records and emits a sequence of characters (box 2). This section might detect and remove comments and special control commands that have nothing to do with the source language. If the language specification is such that blanks are ignored, then blanks are suppressed by the character manipulator (box 2). However, this is not always easy. In Fortran, blanks are crucial in some contexts but not in others, and the necessary distinctions are sometimes difficult to make.

Tokens

The character sequence is next grouped into a sequence of *tokens* by a *lexical scanner* or *screener* (box 3). A token may be a single character, or some special sequence of characters. Comments and blank separators must be removed from the token stream. Examples of tokens are identifiers (names assigned to variables, statement labels, and so on), quoted strings, numbers, and special character sequences (such as := in Pascal).

Boxes 2 and 3 are sometimes called a *lexical analyzer*. The lexical analyzer usually must be tailored to the language and the grammatical description of the language chosen by the compiler implementors. For example, the Fortran source record:

```
6       DO5I   =4,X *( Y -16)     , 16
```

would be translated by a lexical analyzer into the token sequence:

```
6
DO
5
I
=
4
,
X
*
Y
(
—
16
)
,
16
```

Parsing

The token sequence emitted by the lexical analyzer is next processed by a *parser* (box 4), the task of which is to determine the underlying structure of the program. Until the parser is reached, the tokens have been collected with little or no regard to their context within the program as a whole. The parser considers the context of each token and classifies groups of tokens into larger entities such as *declarations, statements,* and *control structures.* The product of the parser usually is an *abstract-syntax tree.* (An example of an abstract-syntax tree for the Fortran DO statement is given in figure 1.2.) A tree is a useful representation of a program or program segment, inasmuch as it facilitates several subsequent transformations designed to minimize the number of machine instructions needed to carry out the required operations.

In addition to the structural interpretation, a *symbol table* is constructed and managed. The symbol table provides an association of identifiers appearing in the source with various attributes.

Source Errors

The parser has the responsibility of ensuring that the token sequence conforms to the requirements of the language. It does so by reporting a *syntax* or *semantic error* on illegal sequences. The distinction between these two forms of error will become apparent as we study the theory and application of parsers, but we can give a rough definition now.

A *syntax error* arises on one token when the parsing algorithm finds that the token is not among the legal subset permitted with respect to the parser's state.

The following Pascal statement contains a syntax error, because the token / does not belong after the := :

I :=/ R;

A *semantic error* usually arises in conjunction with some appearance of a variable the type of which is incompatible within the context of operations applied to it. Thus, the Pascal statement:

I := S;

is syntactically legal, but results in a semantic error if S is type *powerset* whereas I is type *integer*. No meaning within the Pascal language can be attached to such an assignment statement. However, if S were declared type *integer,* the statement would be legal.

An *error recovery system* (not shown in figure 1.1) usually is attached to the parser (box 4), and takes control when a syntax error in the source program is detected. Its purpose is to report and—if possible—diagnose the error, then attempt a correction so that the subsequent source input need not be discarded. The correction may take the form of inserting or discarding tokens in an attempt to patch over the offending section of source.

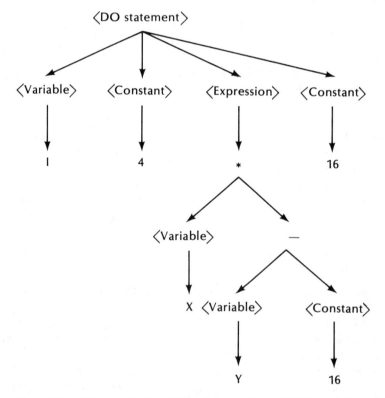

Figure 1.2.   Abstract syntax tree for the Fortran statement DO 1 = 4,X∗(Y − 16), 16.

Optimization

The abstract-syntax tree next can be subjected to a number of optimizations through a tree optimizer (box 5). The result is some reduced tree, possibly rearranged to suit the needs of the machine architecture. Examples of optimization possible at this level include: constant expression evaluation; use of commutativity, associativity, and distributivity of certain operators to collect constant expressions; detection of common subexpressions; or rearrangement to suit special instructions provided by the target machine.

The reduced tree then can be transformed into a sequence of object code instructions by a code generator (box 6). The object code may be of several kinds, depending on the purpose of the compiler: (1) it may be binary machine code for some particular target machine, (2) it may be symbolic assembly code that subsequently must be passed through an assembler, or (3) it may be a special intermediate language that must be further translated or interpreted.

Finally, the object code may be subjected to further optimizations by a *peephole optimizer* (box 7). Such an optimizer examines short sequences of code and determines whether, in certain cases, a sequence can be replaced by a shorter equivalent sequence. For example, the sequence:

```
STOR      A;       {copy accumulator to location A}
LOAD      A;       {copy location to accumulator}
```

could be reduced by removing the LOAD instruction. This sequence will occur if the STOR represents the end of one source statement and LOAD the beginning of another.

1.5. Translator Issues

A simple compiler often can be made by omitting all the optimization steps, even the tree-building step. Many compilers generate machine code directly from each parse step, using simple methods to achieve a crude, inefficient translation.

A compiler may translate a source language to another closely related intermediate language, or to symbolic assembly code. The latter then can be translated by some existing compiler or assembler to machine code. Many of the functions of a full compiler thus can be omitted, considerably reducing the compiler development task. However, such a compiler is likely neither to be very efficient nor to generate particularly efficient object code.

A compiler that generates an intermediate language could be used with several different machines. Of course, a translator from the intermediate language to each machine's code also will be needed, but these often are easier to write than are several complete compilers. For example, a translator from Pascal to PCODE has been used to implement Pascal on several machines. In some of the implementations, PCODE is interpreted rather than further translated.

The steps outlined in figure 1.1 may be carried out in one or several *passes*. A pass is some scan either through the source records, or through some translation of the source. A practical multipass compiler requires sufficient temporary memory to hold the intermediate translation; this can be any read/write medium. The intermediate structures may well be much larger than the final machine code and, in any case, during compilation, the machine's memory must be shared with the compiler program and the compiler's data areas.

In a one-pass compiler, the different sections of the compiler represented in figure 1.1 appear as different procedures in one large compiler program. Whenever a point in some process is complete, a procedure may be called that accomplishes the next step. For example, the parser may be the primary "driver" for the compiler—that is, the main program. It might then call the lexical analyzer to deliver one token; the lexical analyzer in turn may call a file handler to deliver one record, and so on. The parser in turn might then call a tree-builder as the various parts of a source statement are analyzed. The tree could be built in several ways, but when enough is completed, a tree optimizer might be called, which eventually would call the code emitters. In such a system, all of the steps of figure 1.1 are performed repeatedly as the compiler scans the source text, and code is emitted in short segments that correspond to segments of source text.

In a multipass compiler, each of the steps in figure 1.1 might be a separate pass. In practice, some groups of steps are combined. For example, it is feasible to construct a sequence of abstract-syntax trees in one pass, then devote subsequent passes to reducing or transforming the tree. The tree itself can either be stored as a linked-list data structure or represented in some linear form, such as reverse Polish.

The principal advantage of a multipass compiler is its ability to collect information that can be used to allocate storage for variables efficiently and emit instructions, information that is often difficult to obtain in one pass. Some optimizations require several scans over a major source program module. The principal disadvantage is that it is applicable only to a computer system with sufficient intermediate storage. Some small computer systems have rather slow intermediate storage (for example, floppy disks), and hence a multipass compilation is time-consuming.

1.6. Summary

A compiler, a translator from one language to another, can be organized in a variety of ways, depending on the source and target languages used, the degree of optimization desired, the time available to develop the compiler, and the compiler's future value. The characteristic features of a typical compiler include means of translating source records into a sequence of tokens, parsing this sequence to yield a syntax tree, and then transforming the tree to yield the object program. Alternatively, it is often possible to bypass tree-building, and simply emit code directly from the parsing system. Modern practice seems to favor tree construction and multiple passes, because these facilitate a number of optimizations, modularize the compiler design, and often are more efficient than the alternatives.

1.7. Exercises

1. Choose some assembler with which you are familiar and make a list of the services that it provides its users. How valuable are each of these services? Are there services that it could provide, but does not?

2. Consider two or three high-level programming languages with which you are familiar and discuss those features that you think are most valuable to a programmer. Also discuss features that you would most like to see added to the language.

3. How desirable is brevity in a programming language? (Compare Cobol and APL, for example.) Discuss the merits and demerits of brevity and verbosity.

4. What do you believe should be uppermost in the design of a "good" programming language among the following characteristics? How much does your choice depend on the application or the user community? Which desirable features are likely to conflict with each other?

   (a) Ease with which you can grasp the program's algorithm when you read the program.
   (b) Ease with which you can learn the programming language.
   (c) Protection against coding errors, to the degree possible in a language.
   (d) Ability to use any feature supported by the target machine, as needed, to obtain the most efficient execution.
   (e) Convenience of the language for the terminal operator as a typist.
   (f) The number of different operations available in the language.
   (g) Availability of immediate line-by-line syntax checking while preparing the program.
   (h) The number of operations.
   (i) Extensibility of the language—can more control structures be added? Can data structures be extended?

5. Suppose that you are given the assignment of writing a compiler for some language L to be implemented on a machine equipped with a symbolic assembler and a Fortran compiler. Assume that it will be easier to write code in Fortran than in the assembler (not always the case), and that the task of translating L to Fortran will be easier than to assembler (again, not always the case). Determine a compiler implementation strategy, given each of the following objectives:

(a) The compiler may implement only selected features of the language L (the selection is your choice) and may be inefficient, but must be finished as quickly as possible.

(b) The compiler must implement the complete language, may generate inefficient code, but must run as efficiently as possible and require as little memory space as possible. (It will be used for short student programs that are likely to be executed only once.)

(c) The compiler may be as large as you have time and patience to develop it and may be inefficient as a program, but must generate the most efficient code possible for the target machine.

(d) The compiler may generate inefficient code and be inefficient as a program, but must be capable of being transformed into a compiler for another target machine with minimum effort.

CHAPTER **2**

INTRODUCTION TO LANGUAGE THEORY

By being so long in the lowest form [at Harrow] I gained an immense advantage over the cleverer boys . . . I got into my bones the essential structure of the normal British sentence—which is a noble thing.

. . . *Winston Churchill*

This is the sort of English up with which I will not put.

. . . *Winston Churchill*

2.1. Language Elements

The elements of a language are its *alphabet,* its *grammar,* and its *semantics.* The alphabet is a finite set of *tokens* of which sentences in the language are composed. The grammar is a set of structural rules defining the legal contexts of tokens in sentences. The semantics is a set of rules that define the operational effect of any program written in the language when translated and executed on some machine. This and the next four chapters principally deal with grammars and translation apart from semantics.

Sentences in English are constructed from the set of characters consisting of the letters, digits, space, and punctuation marks. These characters are composed into words through the aid of spelling rules and a dictionary, and then words are composed into sentences through the aid of grammatical rules.

A computer program may be constructed similarly from a sequence of characters drawn from the computer's character set. Such a sequence may be composed into tokens (corresponding to English words) and the tokens composed into sentences through a grammar. The principal difference between English and a programming language is that the grammatical and spelling rules for English are complicated and have many exceptions and ambiguities, whereas the corresponding rules for a programming language are concise and highly structured, have few (if any) special cases, and—if well designed—have no ambiguities.

In this chapter, we will develop the notions of alphabets, strings in an alphabet, generative grammar systems, and the problem of *parsing* a sentence. Parsing is the process by which we determine the specific grammar rule applications that yield a given sentence; it corresponds roughly to determining the structure of an English sentence.

2.1.1. Tokens and Alphabets

Polonius: What do you read, my lord?
Hamlet: Words, words, words.

. . . *William Shakespeare*

An *alphabet* is a finite set of *tokens,* fixed at the time of definition of the source language. Every source program consists of some sequence of tokens drawn from the alphabet of the source language.

The alphabet of a programming language could be the set of keyboard characters—each letter, each blank, each digit, and special symbol would be a distinct token. It is possible to define useful programming languages in such an alphabet.

More often, certain easily recognizable sequences of characters are collected together to form the *tokens* of the language. For example, in Pascal, the characters : and = when written together := represent one token that is used for assignments. In Fortran, the character sequence D, O usually represents a special token DO that initiates a loop structure.

The task of assembling a sequence of source characters into tokens comprises that part of a compiler called the *scanner* or *lexical analyzer.* The task may be simple or difficult; the end result in any case is to yield a sequence of tokens for the benefit of the language structural analysis that is to follow.

The Fortran character set, which contains the 26 letters, the ten digits, the special symbols $+ - * / . , ( ) = \$ '$:, blank, the end-of-label, and the end-of-statement, a total of 51 characters, is an example of an alphabet. Every Fortran program therefore can be considered as one long string of characters. For practical reasons, the end of a Fortran label field, an end of a statement, and a blank also should be considered characters and are important as language elements. The end of a Fortran program, or end-of-file, may also be considered a character in the alphabet, bringing the Fortran alphabet to 52 characters.

The set of Fortran special names, identifiers, constants, and special symbols also is an alphabet. Special names such as DO, IF, and READ are separate tokens, distinct from names invented by the programmer. Similarly, a number is considered a token. A name invented by a programmer (an identifier) is considered an element of the alphabet.

The symbol Σ will be used to designate an alphabet. Mathematically, Σ is a set of objects. Lowercase letters near the beginning of the English alphabet (a, b, c, d) usually will represent members of Σ.

2.1.2. Strings

A *string* is a sequence of elements drawn from an alphabet. The set of all strings of length one or more consisting of members of Σ will be designated Σ^+. Thus, if an alphabet Σ consists of the characters #, 4, %, and +, written:

$$\Sigma = \{\#, 4, \%, +\}$$

then each of these strings is a member of Σ^+:

$$\#$$

$$4444\#\#\%+$$

$$+\#\#4$$

$$+++$$

There are, of course, many other possible members.

The length of a string is the number of characters in the string, written:

$$|\text{FORTRAN}| = \text{length of the string ``FORTRAN''} = 7$$

Thus $|4444\#\#\%+|$ is 8, $|\#|$ is 1, and so on. Lowercase letters near the end of the alphabet (w, x, y) will be used to represent strings. A string the length of which is zero is called the *empty string,* written ϵ.

Two strings, w and x, may be connected together to form a single new string, wx. This operation is called *concatenation*. Either of the strings may consist of a single character, multiple characters, or the empty string. Concatenation is an implied operation and as such has no special symbol. The concatenation of an empty string with any other string x results in x; that is:

$$\epsilon x = x$$

$$x\epsilon = x$$

$$x\epsilon y = xy$$

Note that if strings x and y are each members of Σ^+, then the string xy is also a member of Σ^+.

Although the empty string "disappears" when concatenated with any other string, it could be a member of any set of strings. In particular, the set Σ^* is the set Σ^+ together with the empty string, which can be written using the set union operator $\cup$ as:

$$\Sigma^* = \Sigma^+ \cup \{\epsilon\}$$

A source program equivalent to an empty string is in practice a program with no tokens, only an end-of-file mark. A compiler can conclude that the program is an empty string by detecting the end-of-file as the first token.

An empty string is not the same as an empty set, $\varnothing$. A set may consist of only the empty string; such a set is not empty. An empty set contains nothing, not even an empty string. A language may consist of the empty set—it would be rather useless, however. A compiler for an empty language would have to report an error on any source input, including an empty string.

2.2. Generative Grammars and Languages

> *I have laboured to refine our language to grammatical purity,*
> *and to clear it from colloquial barbarisms, licentious idioms,*
> *and irregular combinations.*
>
> *. . . Samuel Johnson*

A *language* is some subset of Σ^*, where Σ is its alphabet; however, this definition is too broad to be of any practical use. If the alphabet consists of the English characters, then Σ^* contains the text of all the books in the world, but also contains whatever happens to be pecked out by a monkey at a typewriter. Σ^* includes meaningful sentences of value to a reader, but also includes random sequences of characters.

A language may be finite or infinite. If a language is infinite, there is no upper bound on the maximum length of a string in the language. If there were such a bound then, because the alphabet is finite, there would be a finite number of arrangements of the tokens in the finite-length strings.

To be useful, a language must exhibit structure. There must be a finite set of rules that governs the manner in which the tokens of Σ may be organized into strings in the language. We call the set of rules that defines a legal class of strings a *grammar*.

For example, telephone numbers in the United States have a certain structure familiar to everyone—an area code, an exchange number, a party number, and an extension; for example:

(212) 555-1212 X643

Some of these components may not appear in a telephone number; if there are no extensions or the area code is understood, they may be omitted. Also some telephone systems permit dialing only the party number. We can represent a telephone number by the structure:

<area code> <exchange> <party> <extension>

Each of these has a structure of its own. The area code is commonly written in parentheses—for example, (212)—so we see that the structure <area code> has the structure:

(<three-digit number>)

and, in turn, the structure <three-digit number> has the structure:

<digit> <digit> <digit>

Finally, each <digit> has one of the forms 0, 1, 2, . . . , 9.

The overall structure of a telephone number can be seen as a set of structures, each of which provides a more detailed description of the number. The "smallest" components are the members of the telephone number alphabet, consisting of the digits, dashes, parentheses, space, and X.

2.2.1. Terminals and Nonterminals

A *terminal* is any member of Σ, and is therefore a synonym for token. A *nonterminal* stands for some set of strings in Σ^*, but is not itself in Σ. Nonterminals are used in a language's structural rules. They stand for a set (possibly infinite or empty) of strings in the terminals. For a given grammar, there will be a finite set of nonterminals; this set usually will be designated N. A *symbol* is a terminal or a nonterminal.

In the telephone number structure example given above, each of the names:

```
<area code>
<exchange>
<party>
<extension>
```

are nonterminals. We could equally well use single characters as nonterminals, and shall do so frequently. For most of the simple example grammars in this text, we will use a capital letter near the beginning of the English alphabet to designate a particular nonterminal (A, B, C). A capital letter near the end of the English alphabet (X, Y, Z) generally will stand for an "arbitrary" nonterminal. Lower-case letters near the end of the alphabet often will stand for a string (possibly empty) of terminals and nonterminals.

For large grammars, we will need more than 26 nonterminals, and will therefore fabricate special nonterminal names. The convention of using $<>$ to designate a nonterminal is used widely to define programming languages. The nonterminals <area code> and <exchange> are examples of this convention.

2.2.2. Production Rules and Grammars

> *'That's not a regular rule: you invented it just now.'*
> *'It's the oldest rule in the book,' said the King.*
> *'Then it ought to be Number One,' said Alice.*
> *. . . Lewis Carroll*

A *production rule*, or *production* for short, has the general form:

$$x \rightarrow y$$

where x and y are strings in the terminal and nonterminal sets of a given grammar. The y may be the empty string, but x cannot be. Productions are used in a special subclass of grammars called *replacement systems*. Essentially, in such a system, we can generate other strings in the language by starting with a string of the form:

$$wxz$$

then applying a production of the form $x \rightarrow y$ to yield a new string:

$$wyz$$

We have effectively replaced x in the string wxz by y, through a given production x → y. The y is called a *simple phrase* of wyz. The replacement step wxz to wyz is called a *derivation step,* and we say that wxz *derives* wyz.

Eventually, given enough such replacements and productions, we could end up with a string of terminal symbols. However, we have not yet specified from where wxz came, nor have we restricted the productions x → y in any way.

If we could start with any string, and then commence with replacement rules, we would have failed to define a language because one possibility is "no replacement"; such a strategy leads to a language consisting of Σ^* again. We therefore need some uniquely specified starting string. We may in fact choose one non-terminal as the starting string, rather than some other string w, without loss of generality, because we can always add a production of the form S → w to a grammar the starting string of which is w. Thus we need an initial nonterminal, from which all strings in the language are derived, called the *goal* nonterminal.

Next we need some precise way of knowing when to stop a sequence of derivations. We choose to stop when we obtain a string that contains no non-terminals; the nonterminals after all are subject to further expansion. This feature implies two other important properties that a grammar should satisfy: (1) the nonterminal and terminal sets are disjoint. If a token is both terminal and non-terminal, it is not clear whether to stop the derivation or not. (2) Every production rule must contain at least one nonterminal in its left member; that is, given a production y → x, then y must contain at least one nonterminal. If both properties are satisfied by the grammar, then no further derivations are possible once we have an all-terminal string.

We conclude that a grammar is a four-tuple (N, Σ, P, S), where Σ is a terminal alphabet; N is a nonterminal alphabet; Σ and N are disjoint; P is a set of productions of the form y → x, where y and x are in (N $\cup$ Σ)* and y contains at least one element in N; and S is a designated goal symbol in N.

Such a grammar is called a *phrase-structured* grammar.

2.2.3. Classes of Grammars

Chomsky [1965] distinguished four general classes of grammars. The most general class, the *unrestricted* grammars, is not phrase-structured, and may follow any conceivable set of rules. The other three classes are phrase-structured: the *context-sensitive, context-free,* and *right-linear* grammars.

The most general phrase-structured class is the *context-sensitive* grammar. In this class, each production has the form:

$$x \rightarrow y$$

where x and y are members of (N $\cup$ Σ)*, x contains at least one member of N, and $|x| \leq |y|$. Note that the last requirement implies that y cannot be empty. An example of a context-sensitive grammar is:

$$G_1 = (\{S, B, C\}, \{a, b, c\}, P, S)$$

where the productions P are:

1. S → aSBC
2. S → abC
3. CB → BC
4. bB → bb
5. bC → bc
6. cC → cc

Let us develop a set of replacements in this grammar. Because S is the designated starting string, we look for a production with S as its left member. Either of the first two will do:

$$S \rightarrow aSBC$$

so that aSBC is a new string. In string aSBC, we can use only another S rule; let us choose the second one:

$$aSBC \rightarrow aabCBC$$

Here, the third or fifth rule may be chosen; let us choose the third:

$$aabCBC \rightarrow aabBCC$$

Continuing, we find the following sequence of replacements:

$$aabbCC$$

$$aabbcC$$

$$aabbcc$$

We end up with all terminals, so this is the end of the possible replacements.

We could reach a string for which no production can apply. For example, in the string aabCBC, if we choose the fifth rule instead of the third, we obtain aabcBC, and we find that no rule can be applied to this string. The consequence of such a failure to obtain a terminal string is simply that we must try other possibilities until we find those that yield terminal strings.

Context-Free Grammars

The next most general class of grammars is the one that we shall be studying in most of this text—the *context-free grammars*. In a context-free grammar, or CFG, each production has the form x → y, where x is a member of N, and y is any string in $(N \cup \Sigma)^*$. Note that y may be the empty string. Hence, any CFG with a rule A → ε cannot be context-sensitive; the latter class does not permit such a rule.

An example of a CFG that we shall be using repeatedly is an arithmetic expression grammar G_0:

$$N = \{E, T, F\}$$
$$\Sigma = \{+, *, (,), a\}$$
$$S = E$$
$$P = \text{the set}$$

1. $E \rightarrow E + T$
2. $E \rightarrow T$
3. $T \rightarrow T * F$
4. $T \rightarrow F$
5. $F \rightarrow (E)$
6. $F \rightarrow a$

Here, the nonterminal set is clearly $\{E, T, F\}$, the terminal set is $\{+, *, (,), a\}$, and the start symbol is E. We may obtain a typical expression by applying the replacement rules, as before:

E   derives $E + T$, using the first rule
$E + T$ derives $T + T$, using the second rule
$T + T$ derives $F + T$, using the fourth rule
$F + T$ derives $a + T$, using the last rule
$a + T$ derives $a + F$, using the fourth rule
$a + F$ derives $a + a$, using the last rule

Hence, the string $a + a$ is in G_0. Many other examples of derived terminal strings in this grammar may be obtained.

When a grammar has several productions with the same left member, we sometimes will use the symbol $|$, which stands for *alternation,* as an abbreviation for two rules. Thus the two rules $E \rightarrow E + T$ and $E \rightarrow T$ may be written:

$$E \rightarrow E + T \,|\, T$$

Right-Linear Grammars

If each production in P has the form $A \rightarrow xB$ or $A \rightarrow x$, where A and B are in N and x is in Σ^*, the grammar is said to be *right-linear.*

The right-linear grammars clearly are a subset of the CFGs. The following grammar G_2 is an example of a right-linear grammar; it defines a set of ternary fixed point numbers, with an optional plus or minus sign:

```
V → N | +N | −N
N → 0 | 1 | 2
N → 0N | 1N | 2N
```

Two other related grammars are the *left-linear* and the *regular* grammar. A left-linear grammar has productions in P of the form $A \rightarrow Bx$ or $A \rightarrow x$, where

A, B, and x have the previously defined meanings. A regular grammar is such that every production in P, with the exception of S → ε (S is the start symbol) is of the form A → aB or A → a, where a is in Σ. Further, if S → ε is in the grammar, then S does not appear on the right of any production.

The following example of a regular grammar defines the fixed point decimal numbers with a decimal point; the d stands for a decimal digit:

```
S → dB | +A | −A | .G
A → dB | .G
B → dB | .H | d
G → dH
H → dH | d
```

Significance of the Grammar Classification

These grammar classifications are to some extent arbitrary. One may define many variations on the basic patterns given. However, these definitions lead to particularly simple classes of sentence recognizing machines or *automata.*

An *automaton,* for our purposes, is some machine with a finite description (but not necessarily containing a finite number of parts) that, given a grammar, can accept some string of terminal symbols and can determine whether the string can be derived in the grammar.

The process of finding a derivation, given a grammar and a terminal string supposedly derivable in the grammar, is called *parsing,* and an automaton capable of parsing is called a *parser.* A parsing automaton is of value in a compiler. A grammar is a concise yet accurate description of some language; it expresses the class of structures permissible in the language. However, so far we see only how to construct legal strings in the language. We need to solve the opposite problem: given some string, how do we determine if it is legal? We also need to go further than that; we must determine the sequence of productions needed to obtain the string. For that we need a parser.

Each of the three phrase-structured grammar classes has a fairly simple yet powerful automaton associated with it:

1. The right-linear grammars can be recognized by a finite-state automaton, which consists merely of a finite set of states and a set of transitions between pairs of states. Each transition is associated with some terminal symbol. We shall define finite-state automata more completely in the next chapter.

2. The CFGs are accepted by a finite-state automaton controlling a push-down stack, with certain simple rules governing the operations. The push-down stack is the only element that can be indefinitely large. However, only a finite group of top stack members are ever referenced in the finite description of this automaton.

3. The CSGs are accepted by a two-way, linear bounded automaton, which is essentially a Turing machine the tape of which is not permitted to grow longer than the input string.

Of these three classes of grammars, only the first two will be dealt with at length in this textbook. It turns out that the class of CFGs is sufficiently powerful to encompass most of the features of nearly every common programming language. Those features not covered by a CFG are not in practice covered by a CSG either, but require special extensions to the recognizing automaton.

2.2.4. Sentential Forms and Language Definition

Recall that in one derivation step, we transform a string:

$$wxz$$

into a string:

$$wyz$$

given a production $x \rightarrow y$ in the grammar. We represent a derivation step by the symbol $\Rightarrow$:

$$wxz \Rightarrow wyz$$

Each of the strings wxz and wyz are called *sentential forms,* provided that we started with the start symbol S of the grammar and obtained wxz through a sequence of derivation steps.

A sequence of one or more derivation steps is indicated by:

$$\Rightarrow^+$$

For example, in grammar G_0, we have:

$$E \Rightarrow E + T \Rightarrow E + T + T \Rightarrow T + T + T$$

hence, we may write:

$$E \Rightarrow^+ T + T + T$$

Here, because E is the start symbol, the string $T + T + T$ is a sentential form in G_0.

A sentential form consisting of only terminals is called a *sentence*. If we have:

$$S \Rightarrow^+ \{some\ sentence\}$$

then we have obtained, or *derived,* a member of the language defined by the grammar. We may put this in set notation as follows; given a grammar $G = (N, \Sigma, P, S)$, then $L(G)$, the language defined by G is:

$$L(G) = \{x \mid x \ \varepsilon \ \Sigma^*, \text{ and } S \Rightarrow^+ x\}$$

The form $\{x \mid C\}$ is read: "the set of all x's such that condition C holds." $L(G)$ is then the set of all strings x such that x is terminal and x can be derived from the start symbol S.

This definition holds for all three language classes (context-sensitive, context-free, and right-linear). Under this definition, $L(G)$ may consist of the null set, or it may consist of one or more terminal strings, possibly including the empty string. For example, consider the grammars G_ϵ and $G_\varnothing$, as follows:

$$G_\epsilon = (\{S\}, \{\epsilon\}, \{S \to \epsilon\}, S)$$

$$G_\varnothing = (\{S\}, \{\epsilon\}, \{\ \}, S)$$

In neither case is the production set empty (it could be, incidentally). However, in the first case, we have a language consisting of one string, the empty string. Such a language might be accepted by a compiler that notices that a source program contains nothing, and then halts (or in practice, goes on to the next job of a job sequence).

In the second case, $G_\varnothing$, there are no productions; hence, S can never derive anything. Nor can it yield the empty string; we need some way for $S \Rightarrow^+ \epsilon$ to do that. We conclude that the language of $G_\varnothing$ is empty ($\varnothing$), and is different from the language of G_ϵ.

Sometimes it is useful to refer to a derivation of ''zero'' steps. This just means ''no step''; the sentential form is left unchanged. We indicate a derivation of zero or more steps by the symbol $\Rightarrow^*$.

2.2.5. Production Trees and Syntax Trees

'But the longer I live on this Crumpetty Tree
The plainer than ever it seems to me
That very few people come this way . . . .'

. . . Edward Lear

Each has his own tree of ancestors,
But at the top of all sits
Probably Arboreal

. . . Robert Louis Stevenson

A tree is useful as an intermediate representation of a program or a portion of a program. It also is useful as a means of representing a derivation of some sentence in a context-free language.

A *tree* is an abstract representation of a certain connectedness among a set of objects. The objects are called *nodes* and the connections among them are called *directed edges*. A tree may be constructed of distinct objects by the following recursive process:

1. One distinguished node is called the *start node*. Let N designate a start node; N is a tree.

2. Given any node N of a tree T with no out-directed edges, we may construct another tree T' from T by adding one or more nodes $N_1, N_2, \ldots, N_n$ (not already in T) to T, and connecting each of these to node N by an edge directed from N to the node. The nodes $N_1, N_2, \ldots, N_n$ are called the

children or *immediate descendants* of N, and N is called the *parent* or *immediate ancestor* of the nodes $N_1, N_2, \ldots, N_n$. The nodes $N_1, \ldots, N_n$ are *siblings* of each other.

Every tree has exactly one node with no in-directed edges; this is called the *root* node. A node with no out-directed edge is called a *leaf* or *terminal* node. Every tree has at least one terminal node that may also be the root. A node with at least one out-directed edge is called an *internal* node. A *path* is any set of nodes $n_1, n_2, \ldots, n_k$ such that one edge connects n_i to n_{i+1}, in that order, for all i such that $1 \leq i < k$.

Each node N of a tree is the root of another tree, sometimes called a *subtree* rooted in N.

The length of some path containing n nodes is $n - 1$. For the sake of generality, we consider one node as a path of length zero.

Given any node N, there is a unique path from the root to that node. If its length is L, then node N is said to be at *level* L in the tree.

There is no path that connects a node to itself. A tree is said to be *acyclic* for this reason; however, there are acyclic graphs that are not trees.

The *height* of a tree is the maximum level in the tree; hence, it is the length of the longest path. This longest path must extend from the root to some leaf node.

We generally will draw our trees upside down, with the root node at the top. Figure 2.1 shows a tree with its parts labeled.

A tree may be embedded in a plane with each node a distinct point and no two edges crossing. The tree definition suggests how this can be done.

A tree embedded in a plane can be ordered in several different ways. The scheme we shall use most often is called a *left-to-right natural order,* illustrated in figure 2.2. We obtain an ordering by imagining the tree surrounded by a directed circle, with the direction counterclockwise, as shown in figure 2.3. Then let the circle collapse around the tree, so that by following its path we contact every edge several times, once on its left, one or more times underneath, and once on its right.

A *preorder* is obtained when a node is assigned a number when *first* touched by the ordering scheme.

A *postorder* is obtained when a node is assigned a number when *last* touched by the ordering scheme.

Any tree can be represented in a linear memory space by a set of nodes, each of which contains two pointers: to its child and to its right sibling. Because either or both of these may not exist, a special pointer—called a *nil* pointer—is needed to indicate this fact. Such a pointer system also imposes an ordering on the children. However, it is difficult to find the parent node of a given tree node N with this system; it is necessary to examine all the nodes in the tree starting with the root until we find that node one of the children of which is N.

To locate a parent node rapidly, we may either add another pointer to each node, pointing to its parent, or set the right sibling pointer of each right-most

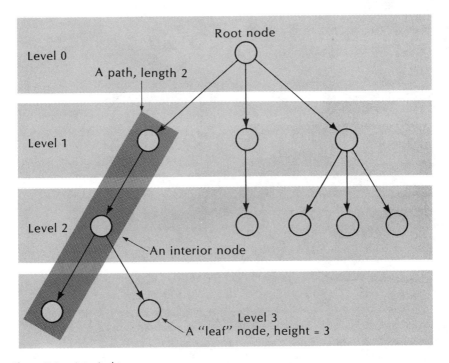

Figure 2.1. A typical tree.

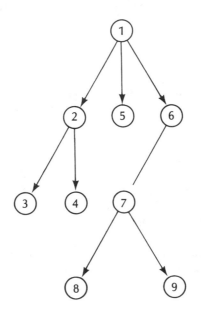

Figure 2.2. Preorder.

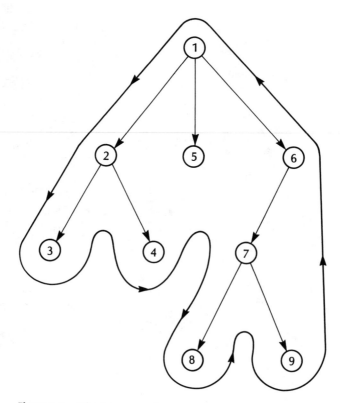

Figure 2.3.   Obtaining preorder.

sibling to point to its parent. The latter kind of tree is shown in figure 2.4. We need only some mark on the right-most sibling to indicate that its right sibling pointer points to the parent, not to its right sibling.

A Pascal data structure for such a tree is:

```
type TREENODE= record
                CHILD, SIBLING: ↑TREENODE;
                PARENT: boolean
              end
```

The symbol ↑ means that CHILD and SIBLING are pointers to a data structure of type TREENODE. If PARENT is TRUE, then SIBLING is the right-most sibling, and it points to its parent.

A tree node is said to be *decorated* when it carries some information in addition to its connectness. We may attach any sort of data to a node; we simply add more record slots to TREENODE in our data structure. For example, a cell may contain some simple data element or a pointer to some other data structure.

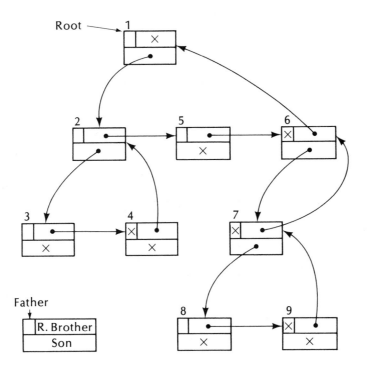

Figure 2.4. A simple pointer representation of the tree of figure 2.2.

Derivation Tree

A *derivation tree* displays the derivation of some sentential form in a grammar. Each node of a derivation is associated with a single terminal or nonterminal. A node associated with a terminal has no children. A node associated with a nonterminal may or may not have a set of children. Let N be a node associated with a nonterminal A, and suppose it has children. Then the children of N are associated with the symbols $x_1, x_2, \ldots, x_n$, where:

$$A \to x_1 , x_2 , \ldots , x_n$$

is a production in G.

Consider grammar G_0, given previously. A typical derivation tree in G_0 is shown in figure 2.5, rooted in the nonterminal element T. Its leaves, read in preorder, comprise the string:

$$a*(E)$$

The string comprising the leaves of some derivation tree, in preorder, is called the *frontier* of the tree. It is easy to show that *the frontier of a derivation tree rooted in some token A is derivable from A in the tree's grammar*.

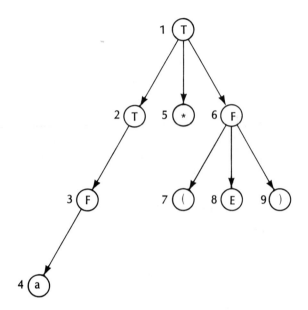

Figure 2.5. A derivation tree in grammar G_0.

Proof

Sir, I have found you an argument; but I am not obliged to find you an understanding.

. . . *Samuel Johnson*

We prove our hypothesis by induction on the height of the tree.

Basis step.   Let the height be 0. We then have $A \Rightarrow^* A$ in a derivation of zero steps, by definition of such a derivation.

Inductive step.   Let the height be h, and consider some tree T of height h + 1. Let N be the root of T. Because $h \geq 0$, N must have at least one child. By the construction process of T, there is a production:

$$A \rightarrow a_1 a_2 \ldots a_n$$

where A is associated with N and a_i is associated with the ith child of N. Now each of the i subtrees has a maximum height h; hence, by the inductive hypothesis, each has a frontier f_i derivable from the token a_i. It should be clear that the frontier of T is the left-to-right concatenation of the frontiers $f_1, f_2, \ldots, f_n$. But also:

$$a_1 a_2 \ldots a_n \Rightarrow^* f_1 f_2 \ldots f_n$$

Hence, the frontier of T is derivable from the root token of T. QED.

The converse also is true. Given some derivation A $\Rightarrow^*$ w in a grammar G, we always can construct a derivation tree rooted in A with frontier w. The proof is left to you.

A picturesque way of looking at a derivation tree is to imagine that we have lots of *tree dominoes,* such as the ones shown in figure 2.6. Each domino represents a production in the given grammar, and each part that carries a nonterminal is keyed so that it will fit only another domino with a matching key. The edges in each domino are made of rubber bands so that we may spread them apart as needed. We can start with any piece and build a tree downward from it. The terminal symbol parts cannot be connected to anything. We assume that we have plenty of copies of each domino, so that we never run out of any one kind of domino.

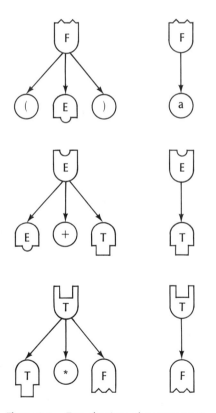

Figure 2.6. *Tree dominoes* for grammar G_0.

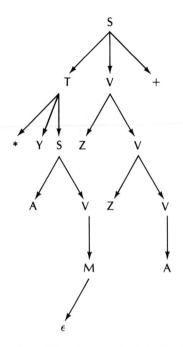

Figure 2.7.   An example derivation tree.

A *complete* derivation tree for a grammar $G = (N, \Sigma, P, S)$ is such that its root node is associated with S and its frontier is a terminal string. The frontier is clearly a sentence in the language $L(G)$. We shall normally assume that a derivation tree is complete unless otherwise stated. A derivation tree may otherwise have a root node other than S, or its frontier may contain a nonterminal. Figure 2.7 shows an incomplete derivation tree; nodes Y, Z, and A are nonterminal.

Production Trees

A *production* tree is a display of all of the productions in some grammar G. It contains two kinds of nodes, a *production* or P node and a *token* or T node. The root is a T node, and every path down from the root contains alternating P and T nodes.

A T node is associated with a terminal or nonterminal token A. It has children if A is nonterminal, and these are all the productions of the form $A \rightarrow w$. The children of a T node are P nodes.

A P node is associated with some production $A \rightarrow w$. Its children are the tokens in w, and these are T nodes.

Figure 2.8 shows a production tree for grammar G_0. T nodes are indicated by circles and P nodes by squares.

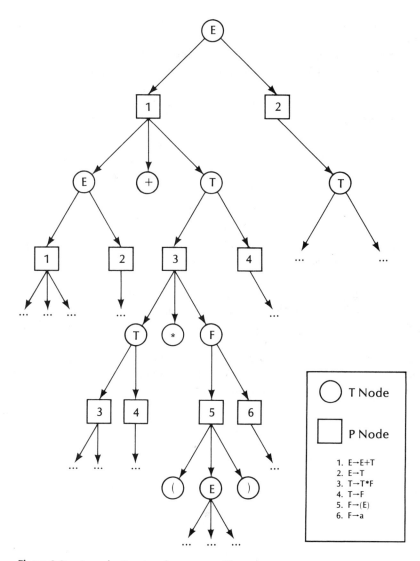

Figure 2.8.   A production tree for grammar G_0.

It should be clear that this defines an infinitely large tree; we can always add more nodes. However, we generally choose to consider a finite production tree in which each production appears exactly once. We build such a tree by starting with the root T node associated with the start symbol. We then add a production to the tree somewhere only if it does not already exist in the tree. The production consists of a set of P nodes and their T-node children. The tree's frontier then consists of T nodes.

An abbreviated representation for a production tree is shown in figure 2.9. Here, the P nodes have become vertical lines with horizontal branches, and the T nodes are simply the tokens of the production right part. This structure lends itself to a simple mechanical printing of a production tree from a set of productions.

A production tree may be transformed into a directed graph, called a *production graph*, sometimes called a *syntax graph*, by adding directed edges as follows:

> Given a nonterminal T node N with no children (it has no children because the productions normally connected to it appear elsewhere in the tree), add a directed edge from N to that T node associated with the same nonterminal symbol that does have a set of children.

Figure 2.10 shows G_0 represented as a syntax graph. We have simply added directed edges from nodes E, T, and F to their defining nodes in the tree of figure 2.9.

A syntax graph is a useful and practical representation of a grammar; it is isomorphic to the grammar and is finite. Cohen and Gotlieb [Cohen, 1970] show how sentences in a language may be generated or parsed by means of simple procedures that interpret a syntax graph.

Context-free languages also are described by syntax graphs, often called "railroad track diagrams." The Jensen and Wirth *Pascal Report* [Wirth, 1974] contains a set of such diagrams in an appendix.

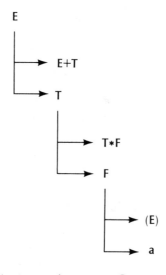

Figure 2.9. A finite production tree for grammar G_0.

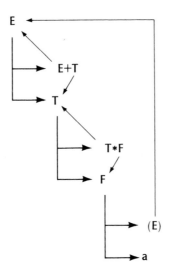

Figure 2.10.   A syntax graph for grammar G_0.

Semantic operations in a compiler often must be performed at just the right point during the sentence analysis. The operation is keyed by a particular production rule, and a syntax graph or tree enables us to determine easily the appropriate production rule for some operation.

2.2.6. Grammar Properties

> *I will not go down to posterity talking bad grammar.*
> *. . . Benjamin Disraeli*

> *Heedless of grammar, they all cried, 'That's him!'*
> *. . . the Reverend R. H. Barnham*

It is possible that a nonterminal X in a grammar G is unable to derive any terminal strings—the following grammar illustrates this situation:

```
G → X
X → X a
X → Y b X
Y → a X c
```

The problem here is that X can derive only strings that contain another X or a Y, and Y derives only strings containing X as well. If we add just one production, for example:

```
Y → z
```

that loop is broken, and all nonterminals can then derive at least one terminal string.

We can easily test for the occurrence of such a problem in a grammar by the following algorithm:

1. Let Q be a set of nonterminals that can derive a terminal string. Let $Q := \varnothing$.

2. Find a production $A \rightarrow w$ such that the right member w is either the empty string or is such that each of its tokens is in $Q \cup \Sigma$. Then add the nonterminal A to set Q.

3. Repeat step 2 until no further progress is made.

At the end of this algorithm, Q will contain all and only the nonterminals that can derive a terminal string. If Q does not contain the goal symbol S, then the language is empty—S itself cannot derive any terminal strings.

We say that a nonterminal that fails to derive any terminal strings is *useless*.

Inaccessible Tokens

Another possible problem with a grammar is that certain terminals or nonterminals may be inaccessible. A token X is said to be *inaccessible* if no sentential form contains X.

The following algorithm determines the set R of *accessible* tokens; the inaccessible set is then just $(N \cup \Sigma) - R$:

1. Let R be the set of accessible tokens. Set $R := \varnothing$ initially. Let L be a set of productions scheduled for examination. Let there be a mark M on each production, and let each production initially be unmarked. Finally, let L contain all the productions $S \rightarrow w$ initially, where S is the goal symbol.

2. If L is empty, halt. Choose an element from L—a production of the form $P \rightarrow w$. Add each element in w to the set R, unless w is empty. If the production is unmarked, mark it.

3. For each token X in w in the production $P \rightarrow w$, add X to R. For every unmarked production Q of the form $X \rightarrow z$, add Q to L. Go to step 2.

These algorithms are useful in debugging large grammars. When an inaccessible token or a useless nonterminal is found, some production probably has been left out by accident.

The QPARSER suite [QPARSER, 1984] contains test programs for grammar debugging.

Nullable Nonterminals

Which nonterminals can derive the empty string? We will need this property in deriving FIRST and FOLLOW sets in chapter 4. The question is easily answered with a simple algorithm, as follows:

1. Let R be the set of nonterminals that can derive ϵ. Let R = $\varnothing$ initially.

2. For every production of the form P $\rightarrow$ ϵ, add P to R.

3. For every production of the form P $\rightarrow$ ω, where every member of ω is in R, add P to R.

4. Repeat step (3) until no further additions can be made to R. R is then the set of nullable nonterminals.

2.2.7. Canonical Derivations

A derivation step requires that two kinds of choices be made; in general: (1) we may have more than one nonterminal symbol in our sentential form, and (2) for each nonterminal symbol, there usually is more than one production that may be used in a replacement.

Let us explore the consequences of the first choice. Consider two derivations of the string 'a * a' in G_0, one in which the *left* nonterminal is always chosen, and the other in which the *right* nonterminal is always chosen:

```
left nonterminal chosen:
   E ⇒ T ⇒ T * F ⇒ F * F ⇒ a * F ⇒ a * a

right nonterminal chosen:
   E ⇒ T ⇒ T * F ⇒ T * a ⇒ F * a ⇒ a * a
```

What is interesting here is that the intermediate sentential forms are different— we get an F * F in the first case, not in the second, and so on. However, the *number* of steps is the same in both cases, and the derivation seems to work correctly in both cases. Is it possible that the order in which the expansion is performed can affect the language? Can we derive some string using left-most rules that cannot be derived using right-most rules?

The answer is *no*. The set of sentences derivable from the goal in any CFG is independent of the order of choice of nonterminal expansions during derivation. We may state this property more formally as follows: given a sentential form xXyYz, where X and Y are in N, that can derive a sentence w through the derivation steps:

$$xXyYz \Rightarrow xryYz \Rightarrow^* w,$$

then there exists a derivation:

$$xXyYz \Rightarrow xXysz \Rightarrow^* w$$

The converse also is true.

Proof.   In the derivation:

$$xXyYz \Rightarrow xryYz \Rightarrow^* w$$

Y must be replaced somewhere. At that point we will have a sentential form:

$$x'r'y'sz'$$

where $Y \Rightarrow s$, $x \Rightarrow^* x'$, $r \Rightarrow^* r'$, $y \Rightarrow^* y'$, and $z \Rightarrow^* z'$. We also know that:

$$x'r'y'sz' \Rightarrow^* w$$

We therefore may reorganize the derivation as follows:

$$xXyYz \Rightarrow xXysz \Rightarrow xrysz \Rightarrow^* x'r'y'sz' \Rightarrow^* w$$

The converse is easily proved in a similar way. QED

This independence of the order of selection of nonterminals is a property of CFGs, but not of CSGs. In a CFG, each nonterminal can be expanded into some terminal string independently of its neighbors, and its expanded string essentially "pushes aside" its neighbors without interfering with their order in any way. Hence it does not matter which of several nonterminals in a sentential form are selected next for a derivation step.

With a CSG, the order of replacement *does* affect the set of derivable strings; a *string,* not just a nonterminal token, is being expanded at each step, and the string may have been formed by two previous replacement steps.

We would like to have a standard derivation order, however, and each of the parsing methods to be introduced later has an inherent derivation order. Whenever we impose some ordering rule for the selection of the next nonterminal to replace in a sentential form, we have a *canonical* derivation. The two most common rules are *left-most* and *right-most*. In a left-most derivation, the left-most nonterminal in each sentential form is selected for the next replacement. In a right-most derivation, the right-most nonterminal is selected.

A top-down parse of some sentence, scanning from left-to-right through the sentence, corresponds to a *left-most* derivation. A bottom-up parse, scanning from left-to-right, corresponds to a *right-most* derivation in reverse order: the parser works from the sentence to the start symbol.

For example, in figure 2.11, we have worked out the partial top-down left-most derivation:

$$E \Rightarrow E + T \Rightarrow T + T \Rightarrow F + T \Rightarrow a + T$$

The remaining parse task is $T \Rightarrow^+ (a * a)$. The next derivation step must invoke the production $T \to F$, to yield:

$$a + T \Rightarrow a + F$$

Note that, at all times, we have a single tree, although one in which some of the leaves are nonterminals.

In figure 2.12, we have worked out the partial bottom-up right-most derivation:

$$E + (F * a) \Rightarrow E + (a * a) \Rightarrow T + (a * a) \Rightarrow F + (a * a) \Rightarrow a + (a * a)$$

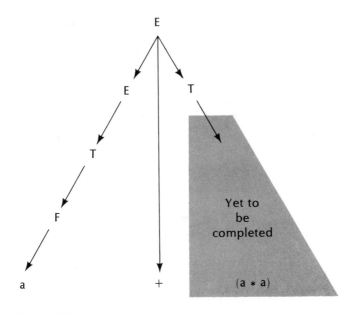

Figure 2.11.   Top-down derivation tree construction.

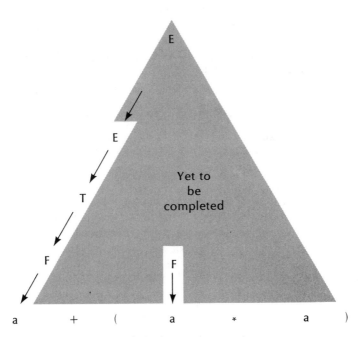

Figure 2.12.   Bottom-up derivation tree construction.

A bottom-up parser has developed this in backward order, starting with a + (a * a) and ending (so far) with E + (F * a). The next parse step should invoke production T → F on the right-most F, so that we will have the derivation step:

$$E + (T * a) \Rightarrow E + (F * a)$$

Note that several trees are under construction simultaneously in a bottom-up parse. One is rooted in E in figure 2.12, and another in F. We shall consider each of the tokens + (* a) as degenerate trees as well. Only when the parsing is complete, with the top-most goal token E attached to a production, will a single derivation tree emerge from the parsing process.

2.2.8. Ambiguity

> *Why care for grammar as long as we are good?*
> *. . . Artemus Ward*

> *We shall never understand one another until we reduce the language to seven words.*
> *. . . Kahlil Gibran*

Suppose that we have a grammar G and a sentence w for which two different derivation *trees* exist. By "different" we mean that the structure or the node labeling is different in some respect. We then say that the grammar is *ambiguous*. If no sentence has more than one derivation tree, we say that the grammar is *unambiguous*.

An ambiguous grammar usually is a poor basis for a programming language. The meaning of a sentence lies mostly in its structure, as determined by the structure of its derivation tree, and not just in the set of symbols that compose it. If there are two different derivation trees for some sentence, then it is possible that two different meanings can be attributed to the sentence.

English is full of ambiguous sentences, because many words can serve in different ways. For example:

Time flies like an arrow

can be interpreted in at least three ways: as an observation on the passage of time, as a command to compare the timing of flies (insects) with the timing of an arrow, or as a statement on the preferences of "time flies," whatever they are. The ambiguity in this sentence is centered on the issue of which is the verb—*Time, flies,* or *like*. Once that is settled, the sentence carries a single meaning.

Similarly, a CFG may be ambiguous. For example, the grammar:

```
E → E + E
E → E * E
E → ( E )
E → a
```

derives exactly the same sentences as G_0, yet is an ambiguous grammar. Figure 2.13 shows two different derivation trees for the sentence:

$$a + a * a$$

Tree (a) indicates that the sentence's meaning is to perform first the multiplication, then the addition. Tree (b) indicates that the sentence's meaning is to perform first the addition, then the multiplication. The results are different: given $a = 3$, the first result is 12 and the second is 18. Convention dictates that the first meaning be selected, but the grammar accepts both.

Let us show that if two different derivation trees for some sentence exist, then there also must be two different canonical derivations for the sentence, and conversely. For example, in figure 2.13, we have the two different left-most derivations:

$$E \Rightarrow E + E \Rightarrow a + E \Rightarrow a + E * E \Rightarrow a + a * E \Rightarrow a + a * a$$

and:

$$E \Rightarrow E * E \Rightarrow E + E * E \Rightarrow a + E * E \Rightarrow a + a * E \Rightarrow a + a * a$$

We also could demonstrate two different right-most derivations.

Grammar: E→E+E
          E→E∗E
          E→(E)
          E→a

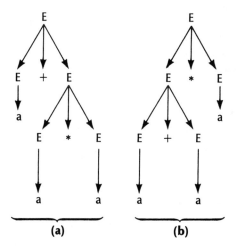

(a)   **(b)**

Figure 2.13.   Two different derivation trees for the sentence a + a∗a, through the ambiguous grammar given.

We offer a left-most derivation proof of this assertion; a right-most proof is similar.

Theorem.   Two or more distinct derivation trees for some sentence w exist if and only if two or more distinct left-most derivations exist for w.

Proof: "If" Part.   We have two distinct left-most derivations. The two agree exactly until some derivation step, in which the left-most nonterminal is replaced by one string in one and another string in the other; for example:

$$S \Rightarrow^{+} uXv \Rightarrow uxv \Rightarrow^{*} w$$

or:

$$S \Rightarrow^{+} uXv \Rightarrow ux'v \Rightarrow^{*} w$$

where x and x′ are different. Now consider the two derivation trees corresponding to these derivations. They obviously may be constructed top-down by following the derivation steps. The two trees are identical until the nonterminal node X is reached; its children are the string x in one tree and x′ in the other. Yet when the construction process is complete, both trees have the frontier w. QED

Proof: "Only If" Part.   Consider two different derivation trees T and T′ with the same frontier w, rooted in S, and with the same grammar. We walk down through both trees (in preorder) starting at their root node, and continue as long as we find agreement, stopping on the first difference.

This tree walk is the same as the top-down construction process corresponding to a left-most derivation. If we are at some node N in T and it agrees with the corresponding node in T′, then we consider the productions rooted in N and N′. If these fail to agree, then we stop on node N. If they agree, then we compare each of the children, in preorder. We start the walk on the root node, and continue until the difference is found.

In the walk, we have also generated two sequences of productions, corresponding to left-most derivations of the trees' frontiers. The sequences will agree until the tree difference is found; then there will be two different derivation steps. For example, for tree T, we have:

$$S \Rightarrow^{*} uXv \Rightarrow uxv \Rightarrow^{*} w$$

and for tree T′, we have:

$$S \Rightarrow^{*} uXv \Rightarrow ux'v \Rightarrow^{*} w$$

where the derivation $S \Rightarrow^{*} uXv$ corresponds to that portion of the tree walk just before the tree difference at node X is detected. QED

A language is said to be *ambiguous* if no unambiguous grammar exists for it. Note that more than one grammar may describe a given language; some of these grammars may be ambiguous and others may not be. However, if one un-ambiguous grammar for a language can be found, then the language is un-ambiguous.

An important assertion in language theory is that there exists no algorithm that can accept an arbitrary CFG and determine that it is either ambiguous or un-ambiguous. However, there exist algorithms that can return one of the results: {unambiguous} or {don't know}. These turn out to be parser constructor algorithms.

2.3. Introduction to Parsing

Egad, I think the interpreter is the hardest to be understood of the two!

. . . Richard Brimsley Sheridan

A *parser* or *parsing automaton* is some system that is capable of constructing the derivation of any sentence in some language L(G) based on a grammar G. We primarily are interested in only parsers for right-linear and CFGs.

A parser also may be viewed as some mechanism for the construction of a derivation tree. As we shall see in chapter 7, a tree is a valuable means of analyzing and optimizing sentences. Let us therefore look at parsing as a tree construction process.

2.3.1. Top-Down and Bottom-Up Parsing

The problem of structural analysis, or parsing, in a compiler may be seen as the problem of constructing a derivation tree, given a grammar and a sentence in the language. The sentence must form the frontier of the tree, and the tree will be rooted in the grammar's start symbol.

This is a nontrivial problem. Let us consider grammar G_0, the productions of which are:

```
E → E + T
E → T
T → T * F
T → F
F → ( E )
F → a
```

Then consider the sentence:

$$(a * (a + a)) + a$$

Several different approaches may be taken. We might begin at the start symbol E and work downward toward the desired frontier. Many guesses usually are needed, and we will find that a wrong guess somewhere in the process will result in an impossible situation. For example, figure 2.14 shows a partially constructed tree that appears reasonable, but in the end cannot possibly be right. Several mistakes were made in its construction. We still have to fit a + a into the inner parentheses, and we have + a left over. We have found a partial tree for a sentence such as (a * (a)), but it will not do for the sentence (a * (a + a)) + a.

If we start at the bottom and work up, we also find ourselves making a number of guesses. It is certainly clear that every token a must be fitted to an F, because

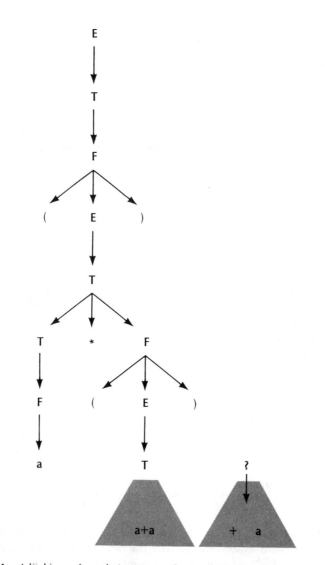

Figure 2.14. A bad guess for a derivation tree for sentence (a*(a+a))+a; top-down construction. The shaded parts cannot be incorporated in the tree.

only one rule exists for that. It is also clear that somehow the left and right parentheses must be fitted into the production F → (E), because only that production contains parentheses. However, it is by no means clear (even with some practice) just how to fit these ideas together into a systematic plan for constructing a derivation tree.

In fact, a number of systematic derivation construction methods have been discovered in recent years. We shall consider four of the most common and powerful of these in chapters 4 and 5. These parsing methods fall into two broad classes—top-down and bottom-up. (A parsing method called *left-corner* is a blend of these two; see Rosenkrantz [1970a] and Demers [1977].)

Each of these methods reduces to the unit operation: "determine a derivation step." Each may scan a sentence from right to left or from left to right. A sentence based in some grammar may be parsed easily from left to right, but with difficulty from right to left. It happens that most common programming languages are parsed easily from left to right and, furthermore, algebraic operations usually are performed in that order, by convention. We therefore will confine our discussion to a left-to-right sentence scan.

Top-Down Parsing Problem

Let us first consider the top-down, left-to-right parsing problem. A typical situation is shown in figure 2.11, for grammar G_0. We have already decided on the productions:

```
E  →  E+T
E  →  T
T  →  F
F  →  a
```

and have accounted for the first two symbols a + of the sentence a + (a * a). The left-most exposed nonterminal in the tree is T; therefore, the parsing decision problem at this point may be stated:

> Which of the productions {T → F, T → T * F} should be connected to the exposed T node, given the partially constructed tree and the remaining input sentence (a * a)?

If we are somehow able to make the correct decision, given the information shown, on each step, then we can repeat this step until the tree is completely constructed. We would like to make each decision correctly by means of an algorithm, so that it never will be necessary to throw away our work and start over again. We also need some assurance, given any grammar, that we can find an algorithm and that it will work correctly for all the sentences in the grammar's language.

There are more considerations. What if it is possible to construct more than one derivation tree for some sentence? How can we be sure that the parsing method will reject sentences that are not in the language? These questions will be resolved when we study the top-down and bottom-up parsers in chapters 4 and 5.

Bottom-Up Parsing Problem

In the bottom-up parsing problem, we work from the given sentence upward toward the start symbol, in a left-to-right manner. We attempt to build trees upward as far as we can before connecting productions to more sentence tokens. A partially constructed tree set for grammar G_0 and the sentence a + (a * a) is shown in figure 2.12. We have decided that the productions:

$$
\begin{aligned}
F &\rightarrow a \\
T &\rightarrow F \\
E &\rightarrow T \\
F &\rightarrow a
\end{aligned}
$$

apply to the parsing process so far, and ask what the next production must be. It appears to be a more difficult decision than that for a top-down parser—there are more possibilities. Should we go on to the next ''a'' token and apply another $F \rightarrow$ a? Or should we extend the F tree through a production such as $T \rightarrow F$? We can limit the choices somewhat by looking at the production right parts that can conceivably apply somewhere in the exposed tree but, in general, this still yields more choices than we can deal with at present.

However, we can still state the bottom-up parsing decision problem as follows:

> Given a partially constructed set of derivation trees for a right-most bottom-up parse, determine the production the right member of which fits the left-most set of roots of the trees, and that adds one more production to the derivation tree set.

When a production, such as $A \rightarrow w$, is chosen, the members of w will exactly match a sequence of tree roots in the set of bottom-up trees. The string w is called the *handle* of the sentential form in which it is embedded. More formally, given the right-most parsing step:

$$S \Rightarrow^* xAz \Rightarrow xwz,$$

the string w is said to be the *handle* of the sentential form xwz.

Neither the top-down nor the bottom-up parsing problem has a trivial or obvious solution. It is significant that these problems were not solved until recently.

2.3.2. Backtracking

> *'It's a poor sort of memory that only works backwards,'* the Queen remarked.
>
> ... *Lewis Carroll*

> *If a tree dies, plant another in its place.*
>
> ... *Linnaeus*

The parsing problem can be seen as one of managing a sequence of choices in such a way as to find a set of choices that leads to a solution. For example, in figure 2.11, we have two choices of the next production to be attached to the T node, T → T * F or T → F. Neither of these contains (, a, or). Although T → T * F contains *, which we will need, it turns out that this choice is a poor one; the derivation tree cannot be finished if T → T * F is used at this point.

One approach to parsing is the general problem-solving method of *back-tracking*. Let us first define the backtracking method in general, then show how it can be applied to top-down parsing.

Backtracking can be applied to any computation with these properties:

1. There exists a starting point and a goal.

2. The goal may be reached by starting at the starting point and following some path consisting of deterministic operations separated by nodes. At each node, some arbitrary choice among a finite set must be made. An operation leading from one node to another can either succeed or fail. We say the computation *blocks* if an operation fails.

3. Depending on the sequence of choices made, the computation will either reach its goal or block on some operation. If the computation blocks, we must back up one node and try another of the set of choices.

4. The computation is said to succeed if some set of choices leads from the starting point to the goal.

A backtracking machine will systematically explore all the choices and continue until either the goal is reached or all the possible choices have been exhausted and lead to blocks. Unfortunately, the computation may continue forever. In every application, we need some proof that the number of operations is bounded. We shall see that certain grammars will cause a backtracking parser to run forever on certain input strings.

There also may be more than one path to the goal. The path first found depends on the order in which the choices associated with the nodes are tried. An ambiguous grammar will yield a backtracking solution with multiple paths to the goal.

Let M be a generalized backtracking machine that contains a read/write tape used as a stack. Each cell of the tape will carry a *state* and a *choice*. Also, M manages the backtracking computation process by providing a systematic means of backing up and restarting when the process blocks.

The *process* will consist of a sequence of computations based on some algorithm, separated by choice points. At each choice point, a record is made on M's tape of the current state of the computation and the particular choice made at that choice point. Each choice set must be finite and ordered in some way so that it always is apparent, given a state and some choice, whether there is another untested choice.

The backtracking system then has these three moves:

1. A *forward* move from some state just recorded, using the particular choice selected by M. This will continue until: the machine blocks (step 2), it reaches its goal (halt), or it reaches another choice point (step 3).

2. A *backtrack* move, initiated by a block. Here, we consult the last-written M cell. If another choice exists in that state, we select it, record it on the tape, set the system to the state recorded in the cell, and do a forward move (step 1). If no more choices exist in that state, we move back one position in the tape. If the tape is empty, we halt (failure to reach goal). If the tape is not empty, we start again on step 2.

3. A *choice* move. Here we have reached a point at which some choice must be made. The tape is advanced one position, and an *initial* choice—the first of the ordered finite set of choices available in this state—is recorded. Go to step 1.

We start the machine in step 3, by assuming that every backtracking process has an initial choice step.

In any machine application, we must show that the process will always halt in a bounded number of moves; otherwise, we do not have an algorithm.

Application to Parsing a CFG

Let us apply our machine to the top-down parsing of a sentence in a CFG. We have an input string $a_1 a_2 \ldots a_n$ of finite length. We also assume that we are building a derivation tree that will be accessible throughout the calculation. The tape will contain references to nodes in this tree.

At any point in the parse, the state of the system is the partial tree constructed so far, which incidentally includes the current position in the input string. We could conceivably just record the entire tree built so far on a tape cell, along with the particular choice of production made for the left-most exposed nonterminal node. However, such a move would be incredibly inefficient. We can accomplish the same result by storing only the two items: the current left-most exposed tree node, and a production choice compatible with that node. The incomplete derivation tree is therefore part of the state of the machine.

Step 1: The Forward Move. On a forward move, we have just chosen a production. We therefore attach it to the tree and examine the situation. Let the production be:

$$A \rightarrow x_1 x_2 \ldots x_n$$

If x_1 is a nonterminal, we have reached another choice point, based on x_1, and therefore go to step 3. Otherwise, x_1 must match the left-most exposed input character. If it fails to match, we block and retreat to the backtrack move step 2.

Each of the tokens $x_2, x_3, \ldots, x_n$ are similarly examined, until we either match all of them or we find the left-most nonterminal.

Suppose all of them match. We then search the partially constructed tree for a left-most exposed node. (This procedure will require an algorithm for moving up to the parent, seeing if it has any exposed right siblings, and so on, the details of which do not concern us here.) If a left-most exposed node exists, and is nonterminal, go to step 3—a choice of production is needed.

If a left-most exposed node exists and is terminal, it must match the left-most exposed input token. On a failure to match, go to step 2 (backtrack). On a match success, repeat step 2.

Finally, suppose that no left-most exposed node exists. Now either the input string is completely attached to the tree or it is not. If it is attached, then we halt and report ''success.'' Otherwise, we block and go to step 2.

Step 2: The Backtrack Move.   On any backtrack move, we must discard a portion of the partially completed tree and try another production at the left-most exposed nonterminal node. We need the two items of information in a tape cell: the left-most exposed nonterminal node and the particular production chosen for it. Given the node, we can delete the subtree hanging from it and determine the input string position. Given the production choice, we can decide if another production choice exists. If it does, take it, record it, and go to step 1. If another choice does not exist, go to step 2 again.

Step 3: The Choice Move.   The choice move is easy. We record the current left-most exposed nonterminal tree node, then select and record a production compatible with that node; it should be the first of an ordered set of compatible productions. (If the exposed node is associated with nonterminal A, then the compatible productions are all those with the form $A \rightarrow w$.)

Example.   A grammar for which the backtracking system will work follows (we shall later demonstrate two deterministic ways to parse sentences derivable in this grammar). This grammar describes decimal numbers (containing a decimal point) with an optional sign. Grammar $G_3 = (\{V, S, R, N\}, \{+, -,$., d, $\perp\}, P, V)$, where P is:

```
1.  V → SR⊥        {⊥ is a stop symbol}
2.  S → +
3.  S → -
4.  S → ε          {ε is the empty string}
5.  R → .dN        {d is a decimal digit}
6.  R → dN.N
7.  N → dN
8.  N → ε
```

Consider the input string:

$$+ .dd \perp$$

A complete trace is shown in figure 2.15. There are no backups required for this

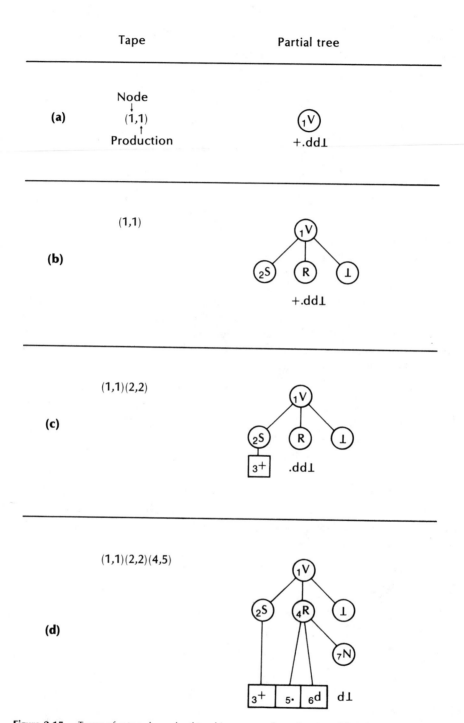

Figure 2.15.   Trace of a top-down backtracking parse of a string "+.dd⊥" in grammar G_3.

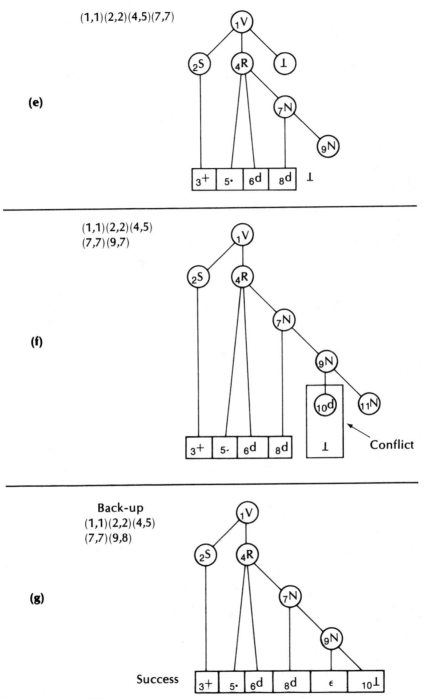

Figure 2.15.   (cont'd.).

string until the state shown in figure 2.15(f) is reached. In trying the first choice (N → dN) for the exposed node 9, we find that d and the next symbol ⊥ fail to match; hence, we must back up. The top cell says node 9 was given production 7 previously. Production 8 (N → ε) is still available, so we try it and find that we can match the remaining exposed node (the token ⊥) and exhaust the input string.

Limitations of Backtracking

This system will succeed if and only if no left-recursive derivation in the basis grammar exists. A left-recursive derivation is such that:

$$A \Rightarrow^+ Aw$$

for some nonterminal A. We shall not prove this; however, we can easily show that a left-recursion will cause a system failure. Consider grammar G_0 and the partial tree of figure 2.11. We have two productions compatible with the left-most exposed node T: T → F and T → T * F. Note that the latter production is left-recursive. If we choose T → T * F, we end up with another tree with the same exposed input string and the left-most exposed node T. The system will again choose T → T * F (assuming this is the first choice), and so on. The tree and the backup tape will continue to grow indefinitely, with no progress in scanning the input string.

We might argue that the trouble lies in choosing T → T * F first. Why not arrange the productions so that left-recursive productions are chosen after the others? This choice seems to work in figure 2.11. We can add T → F to the tree and can continue nicely for awhile. In fact, by placing the left-recursive productions last among the choices, we can parse every string in the language $L(G_0)$.

However, this is not good enough. A parser must also be able to detect and report errors in syntax; that is, it must be able to determine that some strings are not in the language. For example, suppose that in figure 2.11 the left-most exposed input string element is * instead of (. We have a string that obviously is not in the language, and there is therefore no subtree that can be attached to the node T that will match a *. What will the backtracking system do? It will attempt all possibilities. The T → F choice will eventually be found to fail (after many trials and errors); hence, the choice T → T * F will be attempted. This choice, too, must fail because we eventually must get the same exposed input string and exposed nonterminal node as before. The system will run forever. We conclude that with a left-recursive production in the grammar, there are strings for which the system will never halt.

Aho [1972] has shown that the backtracking system will never fail if the grammar is not left-recursive.

Time Bound

Aho [1972, chapter 4] has shown that a parse of a string of length $n \geq 1$ for a non–left-recursive grammar will require no more than c^n operations, where c is some constant, > 1, that is characteristic of the grammar. This is a "best" bound, to the extent that we restrict the grammar in no way other than requiring that it be non–left-recursive.

Indeed, there exist grammars that cause the backtracking system to spend a time proportional to an exponential of the length of the input. For example, consider:

```
S → cSS
S → ε
```

which derives sequences of c's. If $Y(n)$ is the number of partial left parses consistent with string $w = cccc \ldots c$, where $|w| = n$, then $Y(n)$ is certainly greater than 2^n [Aho 1972]. This grammar causes the backtracking parser to construct and discard every possible partial tree before reaching its goal.

The behavior of any backtracking parser encountering a syntax error also is exponential in character. Every possible partial tree consistent with the input string up to the position of the error must result in a block, so the parser constructs and discards all of them. For a reasonably large grammar and strings of practical length, the time spent in such analysis can be enormous.

We conclude that a backtracking parser system is impractical. We shall show that backtracking is unnecessary for a large class of grammars. There also exist more powerful generalized parsing methods (for example, see Earley [1968]), also described in Aho [1972, chapter 4] that not only parse any context-free grammar but do so with a better time bound than any backtracking system.

2.3.3. A Deterministic Top-Down Parser

The backtracking parser of section 2.3.2 is said to be *nondeterministic*. That is, given a choice at some node in the partially constructed tree, it simply makes an arbitrary choice and prepares for the possibility (very likely possibility!) that its choice will be wrong.

Suppose that we have some way of making the correct choice each time. For a top-down parser, we have some information in the exposed input string that could be used to make the correct choice. For example, in figure 2.11, the exposed input string is (a * a), and this should be sufficient to determine that the correct choice of a T production is $T \rightarrow F$. We can then conceive of a large table such that each row is associated with a nonterminal node and each column with some legal input string. The table then will tell us which of several possible productions to choose for the next top-down move.

Unfortunately, such a table would be infinitely large—for interesting grammars, the number of possible unexposed input strings is infinite. For a practical compiler, we need a finite table.

Suppose instead we settle for a table such that every column contains only one input token, the left-most exposed string token, or *next token*. That makes our parsing table finite. Although we are ignoring potentially useful information in the rest of the exposed input string, we cannot use more than a finite amount of it anyway.

We still require that our table (now finite) fix a production choice for every possible situation. This requirement imposes a restriction on the basis grammar. It is possible to build such a table for some grammars and not for others.

Let us again consider grammar G_3, introduced in the previous section. Grammar $G_3 = (\{V, S, R, N\}, \{+, -, ., d, \perp\}, P, V)$, where P is:

```
1.   V → SR⊥      {⊥ is a stop symbol}
2.   S → +
3.   S → -
4.   S → ε        {ε is the empty string}
5.   R → .dN      {d is a decimal digit}
6.   R → dN.N
7.   N → dN
8.   N → ε
```

A top-down, one-symbol parsing table can be constructed for this grammar, by methods described in chapter 4. It is given in figure 2.16. Each row corresponds to a possible exposed left-most nonterminal node in the partially constructed tree. Each column corresponds to the next token. The entries are either a production number (1 through 8) or an X. The X means that there must be a syntax error; there is no way that a derivation based on the exposed nonterminal can match that token. For example, with token "." and nonterminal S, the table says that production 4 (S → ε) is the appropriate one to attach to the tree. Also, if the next token is −, and the exposed nonterminal is R, there must be a syntax error in the source string.

		Next token			
	+	−	.	d	⊥
V	1	1	1	1	X
S	2	3	4	4	X
R	X	X	5	6	X
N	X	X	8	7	8

Left-most Exposed Nonterminal

Figure 2.16. A top-down LL(1) parsing table for grammar G_3.

We can illustrate a parse without drawing a lot of trees. All we need is the frontier of the partially constructed tree and the remainder of the input string. Thus, figure 2.11 has the frontier a + T and the remaining string (a * a).

Given these two strings, we apply the table to the left-most nonterminal in the frontier and the first token of the remaining string, which yields a replacement string w. If the first tokens in w are terminal tokens, they must either match the tokens in the input string or else a syntax error exists. If they match, we drop the matched tokens before applying the table again. Let us trace the process with the string − ddd.dd⊥.

Frontier	Remaining Input	Production
V	− ddd.dd⊥	1
SR⊥	− ddd.dd⊥	3
− R⊥	− ddd.dd⊥	(match, drop −)
R⊥	ddd.dd⊥	6
dN.N⊥	ddd.dd⊥	(match)
N.N⊥	dd.dd⊥	7
dN.N⊥	dd.dd⊥	(match)
N.N⊥	d.dd⊥	7
dN.N⊥	d.dd⊥	(match)
N.N⊥	.dd⊥	8
.N⊥	.dd⊥	(match)
N⊥	dd⊥	7
dN⊥	dd⊥	(match)
N⊥	d⊥	7
dN⊥	d⊥	(match)
N⊥	⊥	8
⊥	⊥	(match and halt)

We stop and report ''success'' when both the tree frontier and the input list are empty. Other possibilities exist on input strings that are not in the language; for these the machine must report ''failure.'' We require that every input string be terminated with the special symbol ⊥, and that this symbol not appear elsewhere in the input.

It can be shown that this parsing process has a time bound that is linear with the length of the input string, obviously a vast improvement over the backtracking approach of the previous section. However, we have paid for this time improvement with a certain restriction in the class of grammars that are amenable to this approach.

This parsing system is called an *LL(1) parser,* and was first described by Rosenkrantz [1970]. It has been used as the basis of several compilers; for example, see Lewis [1968], and Lewi [1979].

LL means *left-to-right, left-most*. The "1" refers to the single input symbol used to resolve the production choice. We could also use 2, 3, . . ., N symbols, yielding an LL(2), LL(3), . . ., LL(N) parser in general.

2.3.4. A Deterministic Bottom-Up Parser

> *No! No! Sentence first—verdict afterwards.*
>
> > . . . *Lewis Carroll*

> *Let's all move one place on.*
>
> > . . . *Lewis Carroll*

The bottom-up parsing problem seems more difficult than the top-down problem. More choices must be made. Not only must we somehow select a production, but we must decide on the portion of the partially completed tree to which it applies. Nevertheless, we often can construct a deterministic nonbacktracking bottom-up parser.

Let us begin with a definition: the *rootline* of a sequence of bottom-up parsing trees (see figure 2.12 for an example) is the left-to-right sequence of their roots. Note that each isolated source token also is considered a tree for the purposes of our discussion.

The rootline always will be a right-most sentential form, provided that the input string is a sentence in the language. For example, in figure 2.12, the rootline is E + (F * a), derivable from S by a right-most derivation.

Now we can introduce the bottom-up parsing machine, called an *LR(1)* parser. *LR* means *left-to-right, right-most*, referring to the equivalent derivation. The "1" refers to the parser's need to examine at most one symbol in the input string past its current parsing point.

The parsing machine is shown in figure 2.17. It consists of a set of states (the circles) connected by transitions. Two kinds of transition appear: a *read* transition and a *lookahead* transition. The lookahead transitions are indicated by braces {. . .}. Note that the transitions are on the tokens in the terminal and nonterminal alphabets of the grammar G_3. There is an initial state, labeled *start* in the figure.

On each *read* transition, we match the current rootline token against one of the tokens shown on the transition arrow, then move to the appropriate rootline token and state. On each *lookahead* transition, we match the current rootline token against one of the tokens shown on the transition arrow, then move to the matching state, but we do *not* move on in the rootline.

The states 9 through 17 in figure 2.17 are *read* or *lookahead* states. For example, if the machine is in state 9, the next legal token in the rootline must be one of {S, +, −, ., d}. If the next token is S, a transition to state 10 is indicated; if +, a transition to state 2 is indicated; and so on.

The states 1 through 8 (marked with a #) are called *apply*, or *reduce*, states. Each one is associated with a production. In an apply state, the associated

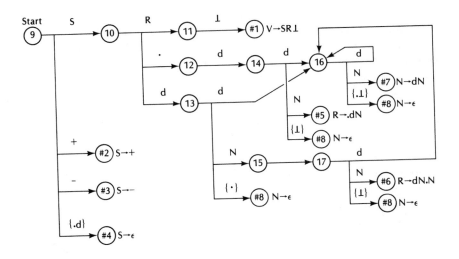

Figure 2.17. A bottom-up parsing machine for grammar G_3.

production can be attached to the right-most exposed tree rootline. When a production is applied, we go back to the start state and also move the rootline pointer to the left-most rootline token.

As in the top-down parsing machine, we do not need to draw trees to illustrate the process; we need only show the rootline string. The initial rootline string is the input sentence. The final, or halt, state is 1, associated with production $V \rightarrow$ SR$\perp$. The rootline will then consist of only the start symbol V, and the derivation tree will be complete. Let us trace this parsing machine with the input string ddd.dd$\perp$

Rootline	State Path	Production
ddd.dd$\perp$	9	4, S $\rightarrow$ ϵ
Sddd.dd$\perp$	9, 10, 13, 16, 16	8, N $\rightarrow$ ϵ
SdddN.dd$\perp$	9, 10, 13, 16, 16	7, N $\rightarrow$ dN
SddN.dd$\perp$	9, 10, 13, 16	7, N $\rightarrow$ dN
SdN.dd$\perp$	9, 10, 13, 15, 17, 16, 16	8, N $\rightarrow$ ϵ
SdN.ddN$\perp$	9, 10, 13, 15, 17, 16, 16	7, N $\rightarrow$ dN
SdN.dN$\perp$	9, 10, 13, 15, 17, 16	7, N $\rightarrow$ dN
SdN.N$\perp$	9, 10, 13, 15, 17	6, R $\rightarrow$ dN.N
SR$\perp$	9, 10, 11	1, V $\rightarrow$ SR$\perp$
V	(halt)	

It should be clear that we have reproduced a right-most derivation of the sentence, in reverse order.

A syntax error is detected in this machine whenever we cannot find a transition from some state that matches the next input symbol. For example, if we reach state 12 and fail to see a d symbol, then there must be a syntax error at that point, and the input string cannot be permissible in the language $L(G_3)$.

We shall discuss bottom-up parsing in more detail in chapters 5 and 6.

2.4. Exercises

In these exercises, formal grammars are given by listing only their productions. In each case, the nonterminals are the capital letters that appear in the productions. The terminals are lowercase letters and other symbols that appear in the productions. The start symbol is the nonterminal on the left side of the first production listed.

1. For each term in the right column, choose a formula from the left column that is an example of the term's meaning:

   $G = (N, \Sigma, P, S)$ production
   $N = \{S\}$ nonterminal alphabet
   $\Sigma = \{+, -\}$ sentential form
   $P = \{S \rightarrow S + S - , S \rightarrow \epsilon\}$ derives in one step
                                    string
   $S \stackrel{*}{\Rightarrow} + - + S + -$ sentence
   $\Rightarrow + - + + -$ empty string
                                    produces
                                    terminal alphabet
                                    grammar
                                    derives in zero or more
                                    steps

2. Classify the following grammars as regular, right-linear, context-free, or context-sensitive. Some grammars may fit more than one category.

S → aB	S → aB	S → aAb	S → aCd
B → Bc	B → bC	aA → aB	aC → B
B → b	C → c	aA → aaA	aC → aaA
C → c	C → ε	B → b	B → b
		A → a	
S → AB	S → AB		
A → a	A → a	S → aA	S → aA
B → bC	B → bC	S → ε	S → ε
B → b	C → c	A → aA	A → bAb
C → c	C → ε	A → aB	A → a
		A → a	
		B → b	

3. Using the grammar:

```
S  → ABSc
S  → Abc
BA → AB
Bb → bb
Ab → ab
Aa → aa ,
```

   derive the strings:

```
abc
aaabbbccc
```

4. Show informally that the strings:

```
aabc
abbc
abcc
```

   are not derivable in the grammar of exercise 3.

5. From Exercises 3 and 4, make a conjecture about the language defined by the grammar and prove your conjecture informally.

6. Design a CSG that generates all nonempty strings of zeros and ones, such that the first half of each string is identical to the last half.

7. Design a CFG that generates the palindromes of zeros and ones. A palindrome is a string that, when reversed from left to right, is the same as the original (for example, 0100101010010).

8. Design a CFG that generates floating-point literals. A floating-point literal consists of an optional sign, zero or more integral digits, a required decimal point, zero or more fractional digits, and an optional exponent. There must be one digit either to the right or the left of the decimal point. An exponent is e, an optional sign, and one or two digits.

9. Show informally that the strings a, ab, ababa, and abababab are permissible in the language of the following grammar, but aba, abab, abababa, and abababab are not.

```
S → A
S → B
A → aCbA
A → ab
B → BCC
B → a
C → ba
```

10. Show informally that the following strings cannot be derived in G_0.

    ```
    a++a
    aa*a
    (a*a)+a)
    ```

11. Show informally that in G_0:

    (a) Any string of the form (. . .(w). . .) can be derived, where the number of opening parentheses equals the number of closing parentheses and w is any string derivable in G_0.
    (b) Any string of the form a * a * a * . . . * a can be derived.
    (c) The pairs * +, + +, * *, and + * never can appear in a sentence.
    (d) The pair aa never can appear in a sentence.

12. Convert the following regular grammar to a left-linear grammar that generates the same language.

    ```
    S → qA
    A → aA
    A → q
    A → qB
    B → qA
    ```

13. Convert the following right-linear grammar to a regular grammar that generates the same language.

    ```
    S → ictA
    A → sfctA
    A → sE
    E → eB
    E → ε
    B → s
    ```

14. Design a grammar that never can derive a terminal string; that is, every sentential form has at least one nonterminal.

15. For each of the following grammars, identify the useless nonterminals. Give a modified grammar with no useless nonterminals but with the same language as the original.

    ```
    S → iEtS      S → AB      N → MdD     E → E + T     C → cDc
    S → iEtSeS    S → E       M → P       E → T         D → Cd
    S → a         A → aE      M → L       T → T * F     E → e
    E → (S)       B → bC      P → +       T → F
                              L → M       T → a
                              D → dD      F → (F)
                              D → d
    ```

16. For each of the following grammars, identify the unreachable nonterminals. Give a modified grammar with no unreachable nonterminals but with the same language as the original.

```
S → iStS        S → aA
S → iStSeS      A → a
S → a           B → bC
E → b           B → b
C → cBD
C → c
D → d

N → d.dD        E → E + T
D → dD          E → T
D → ε           T → T * T
M → P           T → a
M → ε           F → a
P → +           F → (F)
```

17. Design and write your own program to detect useless and inaccessible nonterminals from a grammar and construct an equivalent grammar (that is, one that defines the same language) with the useless and inaccessible nonterminals removed.

18. Using grammar G_0, construct for each of the following sentences: (a) a left-most canonical derivation, (b) a right-most canonical derivation, and (c) a derivation tree.

```
(a + a) * a
a + a * a
a + a + a
a + (a * (a))
(a + a) * (a + a)
```

19. Determine, for the derivation tree of figure 2.18, what terminals, non-terminals, productions, and start symbol must be in the grammar. Can this derivation tree be generated by more than one grammar?

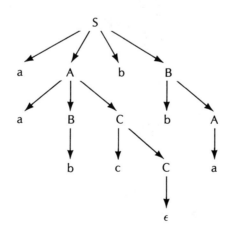

Figure 2.18. Derivation tree for exercise 19.

20. Show that each of the following five grammars is ambiguous.

```
S → iEtS          E → E + E
S → iEtSeS        E → T
S → a             T → T * T
E → b             T → (E)
                  T → a


N → MdD           E → E + E
N → MdD.D         E → E * E
N → D.dD          E → T
M → -             T → (E)
M → ε             T → a
D → dD
D → ε
S → A
S → B
A → aCbA
A → a
B → BCC
B → a
C → ba
```

21. Find five derivation trees for the sentence:

$$a * a + a * a$$

in the following grammar:

```
E → E + E
E → E * E
E → a
```

22. In the grammar of exercise 21, suppose + is emitted whenever E → E + E is used, * is emitted whenever E → E * E is used, and a is emitted whenever E → a is used in a left-most canonical derivation. The result is an expression in Polish prefix notation. Give the emitted codes for the various derivation trees of exercise 21, and discuss their significance.

23. Transform grammar G_3 so that there are no productions with ε on the right, without changing the language generated.

24. Trace the backtracking parser system of section 2.3.2 on the following strings:

```
-d.⊥
ddd⊥
+.dd⊥
d.d⊥
-dd⊥
```

25. Show that the backtracking parser of section 2.3.2 cannot accept these strings:

```
d+⊥
.-d⊥
.d+d⊥
.dd.⊥
-dd+⊥
```

26. Trace the backtracking parser for the ambiguous grammar:

```
S  →  A⊥
A  →  aAaA
A  →  ε
```

    when the input string is:

$$\text{aaaa} \perp$$

    Discuss the factors that determine which of the left-most canonical derivations the parser actually produces.

27. Consider a backtracking parser for the grammar G_0, modified by adding the production:

$$S \rightarrow E\perp$$

    and changing the start symbol to S. Trace its actions on the input string:

$$a + + \perp$$

    far enough to show that it will never halt. Use the left-recursive productions last.

28. Trace the backtracking parser for:

```
S  →  A⊥
A  →  aAaA
A  →  ε
```

    using the strings:

```
aa⊥
aaaa⊥
```

    Discuss the pattern it exhibits of the number of steps required as the string grows longer.

29. Trace the top-down deterministic parser of section 2.3.3 on the strings of exercise 24.

30. Show that the top-down deterministic parser of section 2.3.3 rejects the strings of exercise 25.

31. Trace the bottom-up deterministic parser of section 2.3.4 on the strings of exercise 24.

32. Show that the bottom-up deterministic parser of section 2.3.4 rejects the strings of exercise 25.

33. Write and test a program to implement a deterministic parser for the grammar G_3, using (a) the top-down design of section 2.3.3, and (b) the bottom-up design of section 2.3.4.

34. Write and test a backtracking parser program for the grammar G_3, using the method of section 2.3.2. Instrument your parser with counters of parsing actions and print the results. Compare the performance of the backtracking parser with one of the parsers of exercise 33.

2.5. Bibliographical Notes

Some early papers on grammars and generating systems are found in Chomsky [1956]. A survey paper with additional references is Chomsky [1963]. The notation used for grammars and derivations is from Chomsky [1959]. References for most of the remaining material in this chapter are located in the notes for the subsequent chapters.

CHAPTER 3

FINITE-STATE MACHINES

'Where shall I begin, please, your Majesty?' he asked.
'Begin at the beginning,' the King said, gravely, 'and go on
till you come to the end: then stop.'

... Lewis Carroll

Eppur si muove. But it does move.

... Galileo Galilei

A large digital system cannot be understood through a detailed electrical analysis of all its circuits. There are just too many components and the electrical circuit laws are too difficult to solve. The system as a whole can be understood only by a model that simplifies the system. One such model is the finite-state machine. In this model, a digital system is viewed as one that moves in discrete steps from one *state* to another. Each transition is determined by the state in which it currently is, along with a set of inputs. In the transition, the machine may also output some discrete set of values.

A state in a digital hardware system is defined by some finite set of signal voltages, interpreted in a discrete manner (usually *high* or *low*). A state in a software system might be defined by the set of values of the storage registers, including the current position in the stored program.

The finite-state machine model has many applications. Every digital computer system is conceptually a finite-state machine, albeit one with a vast number of states. Many seemingly difficult language recognition problems yield to a finite-state machine synthesis. Many computer subsystems, such as peripheral device controllers or tape formatters, are first designed as finite-state machines and are then transformed into their logic-circuit equivalents.

We shall examine in detail only one class of finite-state machines—the so-called *incompletely specified* no-output machines. These are particularly useful as language recognizers. We shall see that the class of *finite-state machines* (FSM for short), or *finite-state automata*, is equivalent in recognition power to the class of regular grammars, and also to a special class of language generators called *regular expressions*. Many simple programming languages therefore can be recognized by FSM.

An Example FSM

Before we formally define an FSM, let us examine one that will serve as an example for the formal descriptions to come (figure 3.1). This machine recognizes a language consisting of the signed or unsigned decimal numbers.

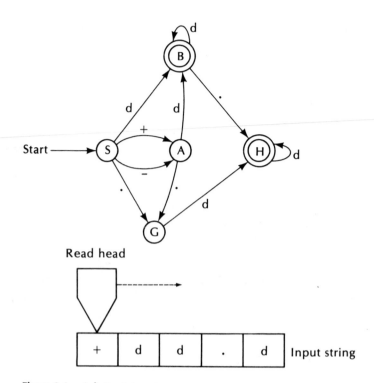

Figure 3.1. A finite-state automaton.

An FSM consists of a set of states, transitions among the states, and an input string scanned by a read head. The read head starts at the left-most string token and moves to the right as the FSM moves from state to state.

The circles containing letters represent states. At any one time, the machine is in exactly one state. The state S is a *start state;* the machine is placed in this state initially. The states B and H are called *halt* or *accepting* states, and are so indicated by the double circles.

The arrows connecting the states represent *state transitions.* Each one is labeled with a member of the alphabet of the language recognized by the machine. For this machine, the alphabet consists of four tokens:

$$\{d, +, -, .\}$$

where d represents one of the decimal digits 0, 1, 2, . . . , 9.

As each token in the input string is scanned, the machine moves from state to state, according to the tokens on the arrows. For example, if the first token is +, then the first transition is from S to A. Then if the next token is a decimal point, "." , the second transition is from A to G.

The FSM continues its transitions until it either finishes the string (scans all the tokens) or encounters a token that has no transition associated with it. If it scans

the string and ends in a halt state (B or H), the string is said to be *accepted*. On
the other hand, if it scans the string but fails to end in a halt state, or if it is unable
to scan the string because of a failure to find a matching transition on some token,
then the machine fails to accept the string, and is said to *block*.

The FSM of figure 3.1 is *incompletely specified;* that is, some states have no
transitions on some tokens. For instance, state A has no transitions on + or −.

The FSM of figure 3.1 is designed to accept only strings in the form of a signed
or unsigned decimal number. For example, it will accept:

```
-15.
75.38
+.002
000001
+34.76
```

but will not accept:

```
-75+
+17-56
3..14
.000.1
```

Now consider the specific string +34.76, which is accepted by the machine
of figure 3.1. The transitions are:

```
S to A on token ``+''
A to B on token ``3'' (a digit d)
B to B on token ``4''
B to H on token ``.''
H to H on token ``7''
H to H on token ``6''
```

H is a halt state, and we have succeeded in scanning the entire string, so the
machine accepts +34.76.

Now consider the string +17−56, which will not be accepted by the machine.
The transitions are:

```
S to A on token +
A to B on token 1
B to B on token 7
```

At this point, the scan must end; there is no transition from state B on token −.
There is only one transition on −, from state S; however, it is of no value now
because the machine is not in state S. State B is a halt state, but the input list also
must be completely scanned, and it has not been. Hence the machine fails to
recognize +17−56; it blocks on the −.

Finally, consider the string +., which will not be accepted. The transitions
are:

```
S to A on token +
A to G on token .
```

The FSM has scanned the entire string, but has ended in state G, which is not a halt state. The machine has failed to recognize the string "+.".

The value of such a machine in a computer system should be obvious—it provides a logically sound way to test input strings for membership in some language; that is, it serves as a *syntax checker*.

An FSM has many more applications. For example, we can associate an output string with each transition; we would then have a simple translator. We can also associate some general operation with each transition; such an FSM could then serve as a basis for a class of algorithms or as a machine controller, and so on.

3.1. Formal Definitions

We now provide a more formal definition of an FSM, one that will be useful in exploring its properties. A *deterministic,finite-state machine*, or DFSM, is a five-tuple $M = (Q, \Sigma, \delta, q_0, F)$, where:

1. Q is a finite set of states.

2. Σ is a finite set of permissible input tokens; that is, it is the alphabet of the machine.

3. δ is a partial function that maps a state and an input token to another state, called the *state transition function*.

4. q_0 is a designated state in Q, called the *initial* or *start state* of the FSM.

5. F is a subset of Q, consisting of at least one final state.

The FSM operates through a sequence of moves. Each move is dictated by the present state and the next input token to be scanned by the machine. The move consists of scanning the next input token and simultaneously transferring from a "current" state to a "next" state (which may be the same as the current state). A move may be made only if the δ function permits it to be made; the current state and the next token must map to another state through the δ function.

For example, consider the FSM of figure 3.1. Its state set $Q = \{S, A, B, G, H\}$, $q_0 = S$, its halt set $F = \{B, H\}$, its alphabet $\Sigma = \{+, -, d, .\}$, and its mapping function is:

```
δ(S, +) = A
δ(S, -) = A
δ(S, .) = G
δ(S, d) = B
δ(A, d) = B
δ(A, .) = G
δ(B, d) = B
δ(B, .) = H
δ(G, d) = H
δ(H, d) = H
```

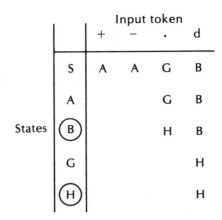

	Input token			
	+	−	.	d
S	A	A	G	B
A			G	B
B			H	B
G				H
H				H

States: S, A, (B), G, (H)

Figure 3.2. Finite-state automaton of figure 3.1 as a table, expressing the transition function δ.

For example, the function δ maps state A and token "." to G. This corresponds to the transition A to G under "." in figure 3.1. The state-transition function does not map all possible states and tokens to states; those state–token pairs that are not mapped are not permitted as machine moves.

Transition Function as a Table

The transition function for an FSM can be expressed as a table. The input tokens are listed along the top and the states along the left side (figure 3.2). The table contains the mapping δ(P, a), where P (a state) defines a row and a (a token) defines a column. A blank entry means that δ is undefined for that state and input. The circled states (B and H) are the halt states.

Configurations

Suppose that an FSM has completed a number of moves in a string. To predict its future behavior, we need know only the remainder of the input string, starting with the next token, and the current state. These two items of information provide a complete description of the FSM at a particular point in a particular application, and are called a *configuration*. A configuration is designated (q, w), where q is a state and w is the string remaining to be scanned.

The configuration (q_0, w), where q_0 is the start state and w is any string to be accepted or rejected by the machine, is called an *initial configuration*. A configuration (q, ε), where ε is the empty string, is called a *final configuration,* provided that q is in F, the set of halt states.

A *move* of the machine (designated ⊢) connects one configuration to another. We have:

$$(q, aw) \vdash (q', w)$$

if and only if a is in Σ, w is in Σ^*, and $q' = \delta(q, a)$, which means that given a machine in state q, with the input string aw (a is the first token and w is the rest of the string), one move results in state q' and string w. The token a has been scanned by the move, leaving the rest of the string w. The move is possible only if the state transition function δ yields a state q' for the current state q and input token a.

A sequence of moves of the machine may be designated $\vdash^*$ or $\vdash^+$. The $+$ means "one or more moves," and the $*$ means "zero or more moves." A zero move results in no change in state and no movement of the read head. The sequence $\vdash^+$ is called the *transitive closure* of $\vdash$, and $\vdash^*$ is called the *reflexive transitive closure* of $\vdash$.

With this notation, we can succinctly define the language L(M) recognized by an FSM M:

$$L(M) = \{w \in \Sigma^* | (q_0, w) \vdash^* (q, \epsilon) \text{ for some q in F}\}$$

which means that the language L(M) is the set of strings w such that the FSM can begin in start state q_0, scan through string w, and end in a halt state when the string is completely scanned.

Machine Equivalence

Two machines, M and M', are said to be *syntactically equivalent* if they recognize the same language; that is, if L(M) = L(M'). The machines need not have the same number of states, nor must the states carry the same state labels. This definition is equivalent to the statement:

> M and M' are equivalent if and only if for every string x, M accepts x if and only if M' accepts x.

If a machine M can be transformed into a machine M' merely by relabeling its states, then M and M' are said to be *isomorphic*.

A fundamental theorem of FSMs is that for every machine M, there exists an equivalent machine M' with a minimal number of states, and that every machine M'' with the same number of states as M', and equivalent to M', must be isomorphic to M'—that is, M' is structurally unique.

We shall expand this notion of equivalence later, and show how an arbitrary machine can be reduced to minimal form.

Nondeterministic Finite-State Machines

> *Lord Ronald . . . flung himself upon his horse and rode madly off in all directions.*
>
> . . . *Stephen Leacock*

An FSM is said to be *deterministic* when no choices are provided in any of its moves. Every move is absolutely determined by the current state and the next token, clearly a desirable machine for any implementation. A nondeterministic FSM is such that some arbitrary choices are permitted in some of its transitions. There are some states and input tokens for which more than one transition may be taken. A number of concepts are easier to express nondeterministically than deterministically. We shall also show that, given a nondeterministic machine, we can always systematically convert it into a deterministic machine that recognizes the same language.

A *nondeterministic FSM*, or *NDFSM*, is defined in exactly the same way as a DFSM, with two exceptions:

1. Some moves may involve a choice. This choice is represented by a state-transition function δ that maps a state–next-token pair into a set of states. The set may consist of a single state, in which case no choice is provided for that particular state–next-token pair. However, in general, some of the state–next-token pairs map to two or more states. We therefore use the notation:

$$\delta(q,\ a) = \{\text{some set of states}\}$$

for a nondeterministic transition function.

2. Some moves may be made without scanning the next token. Such a move is called an *empty move,* and may be included in the state transition function by the notation:

$$\delta(q,\ \epsilon) = \{\text{some set of states}\}$$

There may be one or more possible next states. An empty move may be invoked (if it exists) even when the string has been completely scanned. In this way, it may be possible to reach a halt state through one or more empty moves from a nonhalt state.

We say that an NDFSM *accepts* a string w if there exists some sequence of moves, beginning with the start state and ending in a halt state, that scans the entire string. It is not necessary that each sequence of choices leads to acceptance; one sequence is sufficient.

Figure 3.3 gives an example of an NDFSM. Its transition table is figure 3.4. This machine happens to recognize the same language as does the FSM of figure 3.1; we shall prove this later. Note that it contains a number of empty moves: S to A, A to E, and so on. Also note that, in state A, there are three possible moves on token d. The machine may scan the d and transfer to either B or C, or it may make an empty move to E and then scan d.

Now consider the recognition of the string − 24.57 by the NDFSM of figure 3.3. A correct choice would be the − transition from the start state S to A; the machine might also choose the empty transition to A. However, the empty move results in a block; there is no way to scan − once the machine reaches state A.

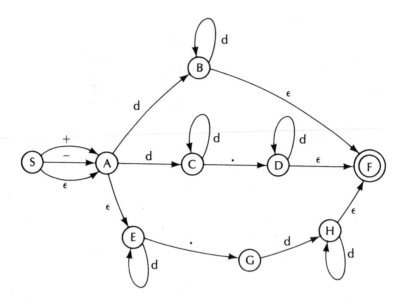

Figure 3.3.   A non-deterministic machine equivalent to the machine in figure 3.1.

When in A, a choice among three possible paths exists: to state B, C, or E. Depending on the next token, any of the three may be possible moves. However, a move along the upper path, through B, means that a decimal point never can be scanned. An examination of the remaining two paths reveals that either one is satisfactory for our example, and results in acceptance of the string −24.57. Thus, the middle path yields the state sequence A, C, C, D, D, D, F. Note again the nondeterminism of the final transition D to F. The machine is in D when the last token (a digit) is read, but may continue to make more empty moves to reach a final state (F).

Although it appears that an NDFSM is more ''loose'' in its recognition capability, this is not really the case. We challenge you to find a string recognized by the FSM of figure 3.3 that is not recognized by the FSM of figure 3.1, or vice versa. The two automata are equivalent.

A Backtracking Machine Model for an NDFSM

An NDFSM can be modeled by a backtracking system of the sort described in section 2.3.2. We do not propose implementing an FSM in this fashion; we merely present the model as another means of viewing an NDFSM.

Recall that a backtracking problem-solving system has three kinds of moves: a *forward* move, a *backtracking* move, and a *choice* move. For an NDFSM, we may make each state transition a choice move, for the sake of generality, whether a state in fact has any choices or not. The backtracking move is invoked on any failure to accept the string. The forward move is simply a transition to the next

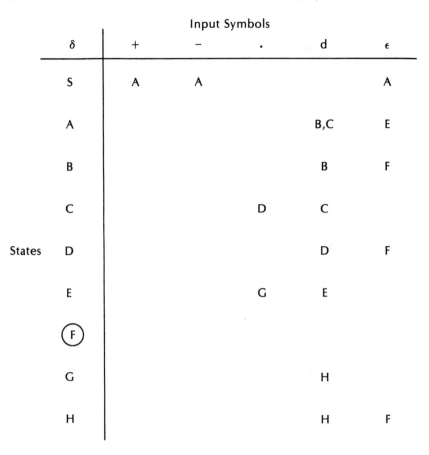

		Input Symbols				
	δ	+	−	•	d	ε
	S	A	A			A
	A				B,C	E
	B				B	F
	C			D	C	
States	D				D	F
	E			G	E	
	(F)					
	G				H	
	H				H	F

Figure 3.4. Tabular form of the non-deterministic finite automaton of figure 3.3.

state, scanning a string character in the process. The input string will be scanned left-to-right by the read head; however, the read head is permitted to move backward in a backtracking move.

The backtracking system tape T will have cells containing the state number, the position of the input token on the input list, and the particular state transition adopted (figure 3.5).

Initially, the tape T is empty and positioned at its left-most end; the machine M is in the start state; and the read head is positioned at the left-most token of the input list.

On leaving any state Q in a forward move, a cell on tape T is written.

If M blocks, the tape T is backed up cell by cell, until a cell is located such that an alternative move is found. The read head of M is then set to the position indicated by the cell, the state of M is set, the alternative move is made, and the cell is replaced by a new cell characteristic of the new move.

This process is repeated until one of two things happens:

1. The tape T is backed up to the first cell, and this cell indicates that no alternative moves exist. In this case, the input string is not in the machine's language.

2. The machine M ultimately reaches a halt state, and the input string has been completely scanned. In this case, the input string has been accepted by M. Tape T contains a record of the moves.

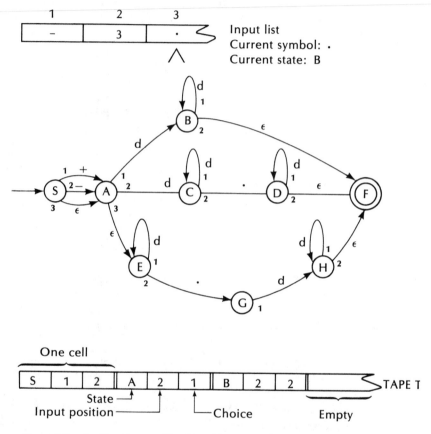

Figure 3.5. Backtracking machine M and its tape T, shown in one configuration. Input string:"−3."

Now consider the NDFSM in figure 3.5, and let the transitions in each state be ordered clockwise from top to bottom. Thus, transition d from A to B is labeled 1, transition d from A to C is labeled 2, and the empty transition from A to E is labeled 3. We also need string positions; let these be 1, 2 and 3, respectively:

```
   -   3   .
   1   2   3
```

Let us trace some of the moves of the system for this string. Initially, T is empty.

The first move from state S must be on the minus transition, 2, (first choice) so the first cell reads (S, 1, 2). The next move involves a digit, 3, in position 2, from state A. We have three possible moves: to state B, to state C, or to state E. We take the first one, creating the cell (A, 2, 1). Tape T now reads (S, 1, 2) (A, 2, 1). The next move, from state B, calls for a decimal point. Although there is no such transition from B, the empty move to F may be taken. This yields the tape (S, 1, 2) (A, 2, 1) (B, 2, 2). Note that the input string position is unchanged. Figure 3.5 shows a snapshot of machine M, its input string, and the tape T at this point in the process.

We now find machine M in state F, with no more possible moves, and the input list incompletely read—which is not an acceptance condition. Hence, we must back up tape T and examine other alternatives. The last cell, (B,2,2), offers no hope, because there are no other moves out of B on the last token ".". The next-to-last cell, (A,2,1), does provide another alternative. The cell indicates that the machine M chose the A to B transition on token 3. We can also move to C on this token; hence, we do so, yielding the modified tape: (S, 1, 2) (A, 2, 2).

We now find the machine M in state C, with token ".". Clearly, the move from C to D (number 2 by the ordering scheme) is legal and yields the tape (S, 1, 2) (A, 2, 2) (C, 3, 2), with machine M in state D. The input list is now fully scanned; however, the empty move to F is legal, yielding acceptance and the final tape T = (S, 1, 2) (A, 2, 2) (C, 3, 2) (D, 3, 2).

As we shall see, it is never necessary to implement an NDFSM with a backtracking tape, because an NDFSM always can be transformed into an equivalent DFSM. A DFSM never needs to back up. If it blocks on a token, there exist no choices that have been made arbitrarily in its previous moves, and the block is therefore sufficient proof that the string is not in the machine's language.

3.2. Transformation of an NDFSM to a DFSM

The transformation of an NDFSM to a DFSM is accomplished by the following steps: (1) detection and removal of empty move cycles, (2) removal of the remaining empty moves, and (3) transformation into a DFSM.

3.2.1. Empty Cycle Detection and Removal

An *empty move cycle* is a sequence of empty transitions that begins with some state A and ends in state A. All the states in such a cycle are clearly equivalent; we can get from any one of them to any other on any input token, without changing the read head position.

An empty move cycle may be eliminated by merging their states. A set of states is, *merged* by giving them all a common name. This has the effect of causing a transition into or out of any one of the empty cycle states to be effectively a transition associated with all of the states. If any one of the merged states is a halt state, the newly named state also must be a halt state.

Example.   Figure 3.6 shows a machine with several empty cycles—ACD, and so on. The ACD empty cycle may be collapsed by merging states A, C, and D. This merger yields figure 3.7, in which the ACED empty cycle has become the cycle AE. Collapsing this one yields the machine of figure 3.8, which contains no empty cycles.

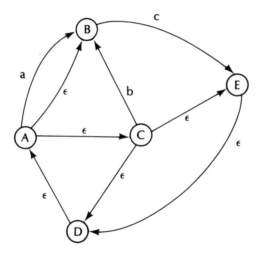

Figure 3.6.   A finite-state automaton with several empty cycles.

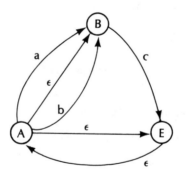

Figure 3.7.   The finite-state automaton of figure 3.6 with the ACD empty cycle removed by merging states A, C, and D.

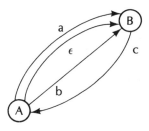

Figure 3.8.   The finite-state automaton of figure 3.7 with all empty cycles removed by merging states.

Empty move cycles are detected and removed by the following algorithm.

Algorithm for Empty Cycle Removal

Let each state carry a mark in the set $\{0,1\}$. Mark 1 indicates that the state has been *considered*. Initially, every state carries mark 0 *(not considered)*.

1. Choose any state p with mark 0. Then construct a tree the nodes of which are states. Its root is p, and the children of any state q are those states for which an empty move from q exists. The construction of any path is terminated on a node with no empty moves, or on a node q' such that q' appears anywhere else in the tree (whether on that path or not). The tree is obviously finite, because it can contain at most as many nodes as there are states.

2. If node p appears twice in the tree, once as the root and again on some node N, then the path from the root to N represents the states on an empty cycle. Merge these states, and return to step 1. (Note that p remains unmarked.)

3. If node p appears exactly once in the tree, as the root, then there are no empty cycles containing p. Mark p (1) and go to step 1.

The number of steps in this algorithm is finite, and it is easy to show that, at its conclusion, the machine M contains no empty cycles.

3.2.2. Removal of Empty Transitions

Once all the empty cycles have been eliminated, the remaining noncyclic empty moves can be removed. Consider some state p in machine M, with empty moves to states $q_1, q_2, q_3, \ldots$ (figure 3.9). This part of machine M is expressed by the transition function:

$$\delta(p, \epsilon) = \{q_1, q_2, \ldots\}$$

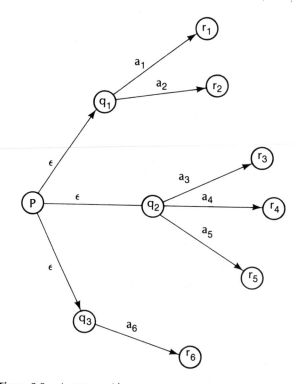

Figure 3.9. A state p with empty moves to states q_1, q_2, ...

Each of the states q_1, q_2, . . . have transitions (in general) to other states r_1, r_2, . . . on tokens a_1, a_2, ... Some of the r states may be q states or the p state, and some of the tokens a_1, a_2, . . . may be empty. However, no transition from p through q to itself can consist of only empty transitions.

Clearly, the empty move from p to q_1 can be eliminated if we add to p's moves the moves:

$$p \text{ to } r_1 \text{ on } a_1 \quad \text{and} \quad p \text{ to } r_2 \text{ on } a_2$$

The idea is that if M can reach r_1 from p on an empty move and then on a_1, then an equivalent move is from p to r_1 on a_1 directly.

Similarly, the empty move from p to q_2 can be eliminated by adding the moves:

$$p \text{ to } r_3 \text{ on } a_3$$

$$p \text{ to } r_4 \text{ on } a_4$$

$$p \text{ to } r_5 \text{ on } a_5$$

One more operation must be performed: if q is a halt state and an empty move from p to q exists, then p must be added to the set of halt states on removing the empty move. We observe that if the input string is completely scanned when M is in state p, then M may move to q on no token and accept the string. If the empty move to q is removed, then this no longer would be possible; hence, p must become a halt state.

The algorithm for this process follows.

Algorithm for Removal of Empty Transitions

Given an empty transition p to q on ϵ—that is, q is a member of $\delta(p, \epsilon)$—set $\delta(p, \epsilon) = \emptyset$, and add r to $\delta(p, a)$, for every a and r such that r is in $\delta(q, a)$. If q is in F, then p must be added to F.

This algorithm may result in one or more new empty transitions from p to some state r, and therefore will have to be repeated. However, it must ultimately end with no empty transitions from p, given that machine M contains no empty cycles. The argument is essentially that n repetitions of this algorithm involve state p, and a sequence of states $r_1, r_2, \ldots$, each of which must be distinct. If the r's are not distinct and different from p, then there must exist an empty cycle, a contradiction.

For example, consider figure 3.3. Although there are no empty cycles, there are five empty moves. Consider the empty move from H to F. There are no moves from F in this machine. However, F is a halt state, so H must become a halt state. Similarly, the empty moves from B to F and from D to F can be removed by making B and D halt states. We end up with a machine with four halt states: B, D, H, and F. Because F no longer can be reached from the start state, state F is called an *inaccessible* state. There is no point in keeping inaccessible states, so machine M looks like figure 3.10 after removing these three empty moves and state F.

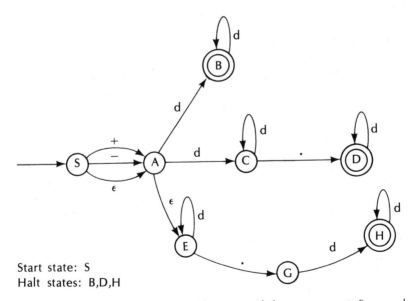

Start state: S
Halt states: B,D,H

Figure 3.10.   The finite-state automaton of figure 3.3 with the empty moves to F removed.

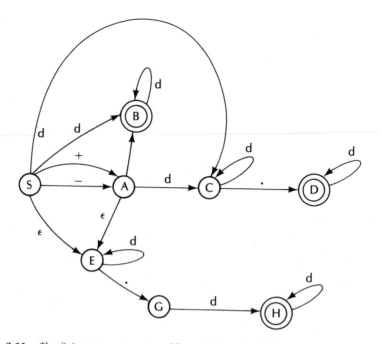

Figure 3.11.   The finite-state automaton of figure 3.10 with the S to A empty moves removed.

Next consider the empty move from S to A in figure 3.10. The rule is that we replace it with three new transitions from S to B, C, and E. Because A is not in the halt set, S is not added to the halt set. The result is the machine of figure 3.11, which still has two empty moves. One of them came from the empty move A to E. (Trust us—the reduction process is not caught in an infinite loop.)

Consider next the empty move from A to E. Its removal means that state A picks up transitions to E on d and to G on ".". Finally, the removal of the empty move from S to E means that state S picks up transitions to E on d and to G on ".". The final machine M′, free of empty moves, is shown in figure 3.12.

Removal of Empty Moves Using a Transition Table

Reducing empty moves can be done more systematically through use of the table representation for the FSM. We first identify every state with an empty move to a halt state. When one is found, it is marked as a halt state. In figure 3.4, states B, D and H have empty moves to F. Hence, they can be circled, yielding figure 3.13. There are no other states that need be marked as halt states; there are no empty moves to B, D, or H.

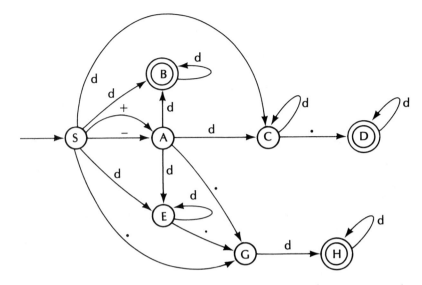

Figure 3.12. The finite-state automaton of figure 3.11 with all empty moves removed.

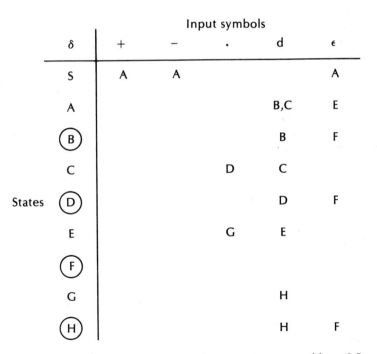

	Input symbols				
δ	+	−	.	d	ε
S	A	A			A
A				B,C	E
B				B	F
C			D	C	
D				D	F
E			G	E	
F					
G				H	
H				H	F

Figure 3.13. Tabular form of the non-deterministic finite-state automaton of figure 3.5, with the halt states marked.

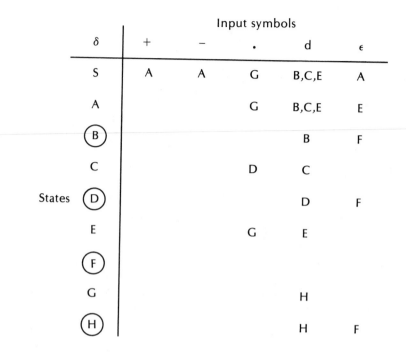

	Input symbols				
δ	+	–	.	d	ϵ
S	A	A	G	B,C,E	A
A			G	B,C,E	E
Ⓑ				B	F
C			D	C	
Ⓓ				D	F
E			G	E	
Ⓕ					
G				H	
Ⓗ				H	F

States

Figure 3.14.   Empty move removal. The ϵ column may be deleted.

Now consider the empty move from state A to state E (figure 3.13). For token +, $\delta(E, +)$ has no members. Hence, $\delta(A, +)$ remains empty. Similarly for token -. For token ".", $\delta(E, .)$ contains state G. Hence, we add state G to $\delta(A, .)$. In the same manner, for token d, state E is added to $\delta(A, d)$. Figure 3.14 shows the resulting A row.

This operation is continued for every state with an outgoing empty transition until no further additions to the table can be made. When this point is reached, all the empty moves may be dropped by crossing out the empty move column. Thus, in figure 3.13, nothing is added to the table by the empty moves from B, D, and H to F, because F is empty anyway. However, the S row is expanded by the A row's states because of the empty transition from S to A. The final table, representing an FSM free of empty moves, is given in figure 3.14.

3.2.3. Transformation from Nondeterministic to Deterministic

The machine of figure 3.12 (or figure 3.14) is still nondeterministic. For example, there are three transitions from state A on a d. Removal of the empty moves has not changed this situation; indeed, it has aggravated it.

The remaining nondeterministic moves of an NDFSM with no empty moves stems from one or more states with several moves on the same token possible.

There are two such states in figure 3.12, S and A. We can resolve the choices in these states by calling each *set* of states a new state; the new state then will be the *merger* of its component states. Thus, we create a new state BCE, which will receive the merger of the transitions from states B, C and E. We are in a sense deferring the choice on token d and state S by introducing a new target state BCE.

The general method is defined in algorithm 3.3, which follows.

Algorithm for Conversion of a NDFSM M into an Equivalent DFSM M′

1. The states of M′ consist of sets of states of M. That is, if A, C, and F are states in M, then {A}, {C}, {F}, {A, C}, {C, F}, {A, F}, {A, C, F} are states in M′. Because it is unusual to think of a set of states as a state, we change our notation slightly by using brackets [] instead of braces {} to represent a state in M′. Then [A,C] is the name of a state in M′, where A and C are states in M.

   Although there are many possible sets of states of M, the maximum number is finite; indeed, if there are n states in M, then the largest possible number of states in M′ is $(2^n - 1)$. This obviously can be a very large number. Fortunately, most of the states in M′ are inaccessible and need never appear in the reduction process.

2. If P is a halt state in M, then every state [. . ., P, . . .] containing P in M′ is a halt state in M′.

3. If S is the start state in M, then [S] is the start state in M′.

4. Let $[P_1, P_2, \ldots, P_n]$ be a state in M′. Then consider all the transition functions:

$$\delta(P_1, a), \delta(P_2, a), \ldots, \delta(P_n, a)$$

   on some token a in M. We then construct a new transition function δ′ in M′ as follows:
   (a) Let $\delta(P_1, a) \cup \delta(P_2, a) \cup \ldots \cup \delta(P_n, a) = \{Q_1, Q_2, \ldots, Q_r\}$. That is, we collect all of the states to which the states $P_1, P_2, \ldots, P_n$ transfer on token a, and call these $Q_1, Q_2, \ldots, Q_r$.
   (b) Then set:

$$\delta'([P_1, P_2, \ldots, P_n], a) = [Q_1, Q_2, \ldots, Q_r].$$

   Note that this is a deterministic transition function; the M′ state $[P_1, P_2, \ldots, P_n]$ on token a transfers to exactly one state $[Q_1, Q_2, \ldots, Q_r]$.

5. Step (4) is repeated for every state in M′ and every transition token a.

This algorithm looks formidable, but is in fact quite easy, particularly when carried out on a state table, as we shall see.

Example: Tabular Reduction of an NDFSM to a DFSM

Consider figure 3.14. Its FSM may be transformed into a DFSM through row
operations similar to those used for removal of the empty moves. The
nondeterminism of figure 3.14 is accounted for by a multiple state-set in the S and
A rows, in the d column. According to the conversion algorithm, we need a new
state [B, C, E] in M', because the set {B, C, E} appears in a transition in M. Let
us therefore add such a state to the table. The transitions from the new state [B,
C, E] are:

- For token +, of NULL, because neither of the states B, C, or E has a
  transition on token +.

- For token −, of NULL.

- For token ".", of a transition to state [D, G], because D is reached from C
  on token "." and G is reached from E on token ".".

- For token d, of a transition to state [B, C, E], because B goes to B on d, C
  goes to C on d, and E goes to E on d.

Thus the new row for state [B, C, E] appears as shown in figure 3.15. Because
the new state [B, C, E] contains a halt state (B) in M, it is marked as a halt state
in M'.

In the process, we have introduced another state, [D, G]. This is a halt state.
Its development in the table leads to the definition of another halt state, [D, H].
The algorithm ends on state [D, H], because every state appearing in the table is
defined as some row in the table. The final DFSM is shown in figure 3.16.

The conversion algorithm generates a machine M' from a machine M, such
that M and M' are equivalent. A proof of this assertion will be given later in the
chapter, after we have defined equivalence more formally.

3.2.4. Accessible States

Some of the states in figure 3.16 cannot be reached from the start state—for
example, state B. We therefore may delete all the inaccessible states from the
DFSM, by using the following algorithm 3.4, which should be self-evident.

3.2.5. Algorithm for Detection of Accessible States in a DFSM

1. Mark the start state S.

2. Given any marked state P, mark every state Q such that a transition from
   P to Q on some input token exists.

3. Repeat step (2) until no more states can be marked.

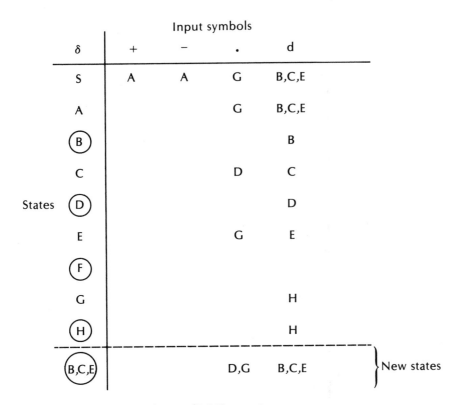

Figure 3.15.   New composite state {B,C,E} created.

On completing this algorithm, every nonmarked state is inaccessible from the start state, and therefore may be discarded.

This algorithm applied to figure 3.16 shows that states B, C, D, E, and F are inaccessible. What happened to them? State F served only one purpose in the machine of figure 3.13—that of providing a halt state. But we have marked several accessible states in figure 3.16 as halt states, and they got that way through empty transitions to F. Hence, F "lives on" in its presence in some other states.

State B also survives in the composite state [B, C, E], as do C and E. State D survives in the composite states [D, G] and [D, H]. Thus, although they are gone, they have left their mark on the FSM.

The DFSM, with its inaccessible states removed, is shown in figure 3.17.

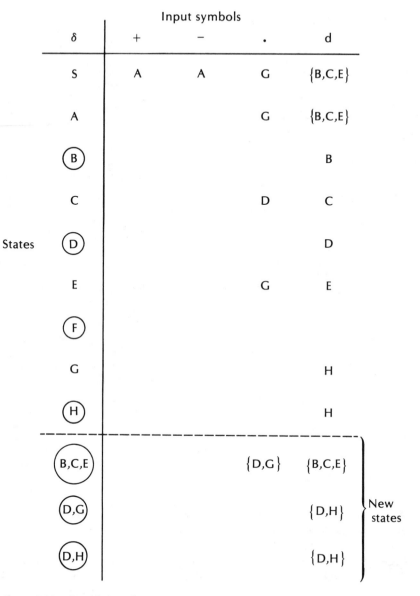

δ	Input symbols			
	+	−	.	d
S	A	A	G	{B,C,E}
A			G	{B,C,E}
Ⓑ				B
C			D	C
Ⓓ				D
E			G	E
Ⓕ				
G				H
Ⓗ				H
B,C,E			{D,G}	{B,C,E}
D,G				{D,H}
D,H				{D,H}

States (label at left). New states (label at right).

Figure 3.16.   Completion of new state creation.

3.3. Machine Equivalence

We have until now used the notion of machine equivalence without developing it. Two machines M and M' are equivalent if they accept the same language—that definition has sufficed thus far. We now develop the concept of equivalence

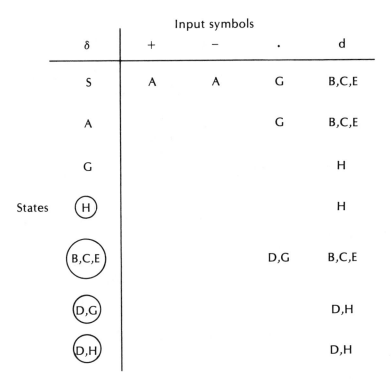

δ	+	−	.	d
S	A	A	G	B,C,E
A			G	B,C,E
G				H
(H)				H
(B,C,E)			D,G	B,C,E
(D,G)				D,H
(D,H)				D,H

Input symbols — δ; States

Figure 3.17. Inaccessible states removed.

more formally, and will arrive at an algorithm for reducing the states in an FSM to the least possible number. The reduction method also will enable us to decide whether two seemingly different FSMs are in fact equivalent. The general notion of language acceptance is not practical; we can seldom try all possible strings on both machines and test their acceptances.

The reduction of a machine to the fewest possible states is of obvious economic value. Among other things, it reduces the task of designing semantic actions for the machine to a minimum.

3.3.1. Definitions

We start by defining the *k-equivalence* between two states P in M and P′ in M′, where k is some integer, $k \geq 0$, and M and M′ may be the same machine.

State P in M and state P′ in M′ are said to be *k-equivalent* if, for every string x of length k or less, machine M in state P accepts x if and only if machine M′ in state P′ accepts x.

If states P and P′ are not k-equivalent, then they are said to be *k-distinguishable;* there is then some string x of length k or less, such that either: (1) machine M in state P accepts x, but machine M′ in state P′ does not, or (2) machine M′ in state P′ accepts x, but machine M in state P does not.

Two states P and P' are said to be *equivalent* if they are k-equivalent for all k.

A machine M is said to be *reduced* if no state in its state set is inaccessible and no two distinct states are equivalent.

A pair of equivalent states P and Q in a machine M may be merged by changing the name Q to P everywhere, without affecting the language recognized by the machine.

Let $P \overset{k}{=} Q$ denote k-equivalence of states P and Q in an FSM M. Obviously $P \overset{k}{=} P$ and, by the symmetry of the definition, if $P \overset{k}{=} Q$, then $Q \overset{k}{=} P$. The k-equivalence is an example of a relation, and any relation that satisfies these two properties is said to be *symmetric* and *reflexive*.

The k-equivalence relation is also *transitive:* If $P \overset{k}{=} Q$ and $Q \overset{k}{=} R$, then $P \overset{k}{=} R$. This is easy to show. Let x be any string of length k or less that is accepted in state P. Then, if $P \overset{k}{=} Q$, it is also accepted in state Q. If $Q \overset{k}{=} R$, it is also accepted by state R. Hence, $P \overset{k}{=} R$.

Any relation that is symmetric, reflexive, and transitive is called an *equivalence relation*. A fundamental property of an equivalence relation, and one that we shall exploit in reducing an FSM to its minimal form, is:

> An equivalence relation R upon a finite set of objects S partitions S into disjoint subsets, such that any two members of any subset are equivalent to each other, and no two members of different subsets are equivalent to each other.

This assertion can be proved by first considering how a set S is divided into subsets by an equivalence relation. Let the members of S be $a_1, a_2, \ldots, a_n$. Then create a sequence of subsets $S_1, S_2, \ldots, S_n$ of S as follows: each subset is initially empty. S_1 is created by placing a_1 into it, then including a copy of every other member of S that is equivalent to a_1.

Note that, by symmetry and transitivity, these must be equivalent to each other. When S_1 is completed, there may or may not be some members of $S-S_1$ left over. Suppose there are some members of $S-S_1$; call these $b_1, b_2, \ldots, b_m$. We then start a new subset S_2 by placing b_1 in it, then adding all the members of S that are equivalent to b_1.

The interesting question is: can there be a state that belongs to both S_1 and S_2? Suppose there is; let it be called Q. Then, by transitivity and reflexivity, Q must be equivalent to a_1—because it is in S_1—and also to b_1—because it is in S_2. But then, by transitivity, a_1 is equivalent to b_1. We are led to a contradiction, because b_1 was specifically one of the states left out of set S_1 when we first collected the states equivalent to a_1. Hence, set S_1 and S_2 must be disjoint. A similar argument applies to sets S_3, S_4, and so on.

Suppose that we have somehow partitioned the state set of an FSM by k-equivalence. What is the nature of the partition induced by (k + 1)-equivalence? The answer is that a (k + 1)-equivalence is a refinement of a k-equivalence. By *refinement*, we mean either that the partition of a (k + 1)-equivalence is exactly the same as that of a k-equivalence or that some of the subsets in the k-equivalence have become further subdivided. The boundaries between the subsets of a partition are not changed by a refinement; rather, additional boundaries are introduced.

Refinement can be illustrated as follows. Suppose we have a set S of states A, B, . . . , J, in a machine M, and they are partitioned such that:

$$S = \{A, D, I\} \{B, C\} \{E, F, G, H\} \{J\}$$

Note that each state appears exactly once and belongs to exactly one subset. A refinement of this partition might be the following state-set:

$$\{A\} \{D, I\} \{B, C\} \{E, F\} \{G, H\} \{J\}$$

When at least one subset of a partition is subdivided in a refinement, the refinement is called *proper*. The preceding example is a proper refinement.

The following partition is *not* a refinement of the partition S:

$$\{A, B, D\} \{I, C\} \{E, J\} \{G, H\} \{F\}$$

Although there are more subsets, states I and C have become members of a common subset, whereas in S they were in disjoint subsets.

Proof. A (k + 1)-equivalence induces a refinement on the partition induced by a k-equivalence. We need show only that a pair of states P and Q that were disjoint in the k-equivalence partition S remain disjoint in the (k + 1)-equivalence partition S′.

Recall that P and Q are disjoint in S because there exists some string x of length k or less that distinguishes these two states. But this string is also of length (k + 1) or less, so P and Q must be disjoint in S′. QED.

3.3.2. Reduction

We are at last in a position to reduce an FSM to its minimal form in a systematic manner. We need only these observations, which should be evident from the preceding discussion:

1. The 0-equivalent partition of the state set of a machine M is {F}, {Q−F}. That is, the 0-equivalent partition consists of the halt states and the nonhalt states. These must be in separate partitions, because the machine is in either an accepting or a rejecting state, depending on which state it is in, for a string of length 0.

2. As a partition is refined by identifying distinguishable states, eventually there must be a (k + 1)-equivalence partition that is exactly the same as the k-equivalence partition. This follows because the state set is finite, and there are therefore a limited number of times a boundary can be introduced into a partition. For this k, the k-equivalent states must be equivalent (with

no string-length restriction), because no further refinement is possible. This partition is (k + 1)-equivalent, (k + 2)-equivalent, and so on. Therefore, each subset of this partition is a set of equivalent states.

3. A partition is refined by noting whether two states in the same subset can be distinguished by some single input token. For example, suppose P and Q belong to the same subset in a k-equivalent partition, and we find (by examining the state transitions) that P goes to P' and Q goes to Q' on some token b. If P' and Q' are in different partitions, then they are distinguishable; consequently P and Q must be distinguishable and belong in different subsets in the (k + 1)-equivalent partition. The two states also may be distinguished if one of them possesses a transition on some token, whereas the other does not. A nonexistent transition on a state P and token b means that the machine cannot scan string b in state P. If state Q has a transition on token b, whereas P does not, then P and Q are distinguishable and belong in different subsets of the partition.

To summarize, we begin with the two-fold partition of halt and nonhalt states. Then we induce refinements on these by looking for single tokens that can distinguish two members of a subset. When no further refinements can be made, the machine has been reduced to minimal form.

Example.   Consider the DFSM the state-transition table of which is given in figure 3.18.

The initial partition, on halt and nonhalt states, is:

$$\{A, B, C, D\} \ \{E, F\}$$

We now attempt to refine this partition by looking for tokens that can distinguish pairs of states within either of the subsets.

Consider the pair (A,B). State B has a transition (to C) on a, but A does not; hence, these states belong in different subsets.

Next consider the pair (A, C). Again, C has a transition on a, but A does not; hence, these belong in different subsets. Note that these conclusions do not prove that B and C belong in different subsets; hence, we must also consider pair (B, C).

States B and C have transitions on each of the three tokens. On token 0, they both transfer to E; on token 1, they both transfer to D. Hence, neither of these tokens serves to distinguish them. On token a, state B goes to C and state C goes to B. Because B and C are in the same partition, token a also fails to distinguish them. We conclude that B and C belong in a common subset in the next partition.

Next consider states A and D, both clearly distinguishable. Also, because D has only one transition (on token 0), it is distinguishable from B and C. Hence, D belongs in its own partition.

Finally, consider states E and F. State E has a transition on 1 not possessed by F; hence, this pair is distinguishable.

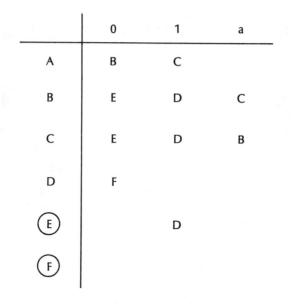

Figure 3.18. A machine to be reduced.

Our 1-equivalent partition therefore looks like this:

$$\{A\} \ \{B, C\} \ \{D\} \ \{E\} \ \{F\}$$

There is only one subset that is a potential candidate for a partition, the $\{B, C\}$ pair. A glance at the table shows that this partition cannot be refined. Hence, these two states must be equivalent. The reduced machine has five states. State C may be renamed B wherever it appears. The reduced machine is shown in figure 3.19.

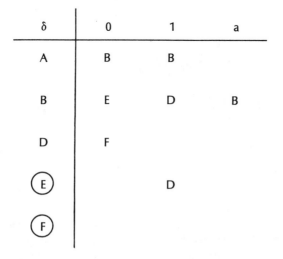

Figure 3.19. Machine of figure 3.18 reduced.

Another Example.   Consider the decimal number machine shown in figure 3.17. Its initial partition is:

$$\{S, A, G\} \ \{H, BCE, DG, DH\}$$

States S, A, and G are clearly distinguishable. Similarly, state BCE belongs in its own partition. However, what about H, DG, and DH? They all transfer to a common subset on token d, whether in this partition or the next one. The final partition is then:

$$\{S\} \ \{A\} \ \{G\} \ \{BCE\} \ \{H, DG, DH\}$$

and the triplet subset cannot be further partitioned. Hence, the final machine has five states, with two halt states, as shown in figure 3.20, which may be compared with figure 3.1; these two machines are clearly isomorphic.

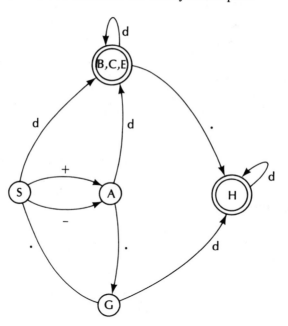

Figure 3.20.   The machine of figure 3.12 made deterministic and reduced.

Summary

Recall that we asserted that the machine of figure 3.1 was equivalent to the NDFSM of figure 3.3. We have now demonstrated that assertion, through the following machine transformation steps. These steps provide a systematic way to construct a program that recognizes an important class of languages.

- Removal of empty move cycles (if any).

- Removal of empty moves.

- Removal of nondeterminism.

- Removal of inaccessible states.

- Reduction by identifying and merging equivalent states.

Because this process may be applied systematically to any FSM, and we have assurance that it always will yield a machine with the minimum number of states, it is possible to determine whether two different-appearing machines are in fact equivalent. We merely reduce each of them by the preceding process, then test them for isomorphism. (We will test isomorphism in an exercise.)

3.3.3. A Systematic Reduction Method

Several systematic tabular methods for machine reduction exist. We describe one, called the *pairs table* method, which can be programmed easily on any computer.

A *pairs table* contains a pair of states or a *null* at the intersection of each row and column. Each column is associated with an input token. Each row is associated with a *feasible state-pair*. The reduction consists of two algorithms, one that builds a pairs table for the nonreduced DFSM and one that marks certain rows. At the conclusion of the second algorithm, each row that is not marked is associated with a pair of equivalent states; each row that is marked is associated with a pair of distinguishable (nonequivalent) states. Furthermore, all the equivalent states appear as unmarked state-pairs in the final table.

A *feasible state-pair* is a pair of states that conceivably could be equivalent upon a cursory examination of the FSM transition table. More precisely, a state-pair (p,q) is a member of the feasible state-pair–set if: (1) $\{p, q\}$ is a subset of either F or Q-F—that is, both are halt states or both are nonhalt states, (2) p $\neq$ q, and (3) for every input token a, $\delta(p, a)$ is $\varnothing$ if and only if $\delta(q, a)$ is $\varnothing$.

By selecting only those state-pairs that satisfy these conditions, we eliminate from further consideration all those pairs of states that are obviously distinguishable; for example, (1) a halt state is distinguishable from a nonhalt state, and (2) a state with a transition on some symbol is distinguishable from another without a transition on that symbol.

For example, consider figure 3.17. The state-pair (S, A) is not a feasible state-pair, because S has a transition to A on token $+$, whereas A does not. The state pair (G, H) is not feasible because H is a halt state, whereas G is not.

Thus the set of feasible state-pairs for the machine of figure 3.17 consists of the set:

$$\{(H, DG), (H, DH), (DG, DH)\}$$

None of the other state-pairs is feasible. This machine is rather trivial under the reduction algorithm, so we will examine a more interesting machine, given in figure 3.21. For this machine, the set of feasible pairs includes all the internal combinations of the sets:

$$\{1, 3\}, \{2, 5, 7\}, \{4\}, \text{ and } \{6\}$$

Thus the feasible pairs are:

$$\{1, 3\}, \{2, 5\}, \{2, 7\}, \{5, 7\}$$

States 4 and 6 do not appear in any feasible pairs, because they are distinguishable from all the other states.

We now describe the pairs table construction. Given a pair (p, q) associated with a row, then the table entry for token a is the pair (p', q'), where $p' = \delta(p, a)$ and $q' = \delta(q, a)$. That is, we simply list the pair of states to which (p, q) transfers on each of the input tokens. Note that by the feasible pair selection process, only those states either possessing or not possessing such transitions are in the pairs table; hence, we will get either a new state-pair or a null entry. Also, the machine is deterministic, which means that $\delta(p, a)$ and $\delta(q, a)$ contain at most one state each.

The resulting pairs table for the machine in figure 3.21 is shown in figure 3.22(a).

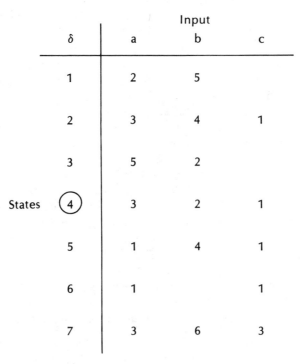

| | δ | Input | | |
		a	b	c
	1	2	5	
	2	3	4	1
	3	5	2	
States	④	3	2	1
	5	1	4	1
	6	1		1
	7	3	6	3

Figure 3.21.   Another machine to be reduced.

(a) Unmarked

		Input		
		a	b	c
	(1,3)	(2,5)	(2,5)	
Feasible	(2,5)	(1,3)	(4,4)	(1,1)
state				
pairs	(2,7)	(3,3)	(4,6)	(1,3)
	(5,7)	(1,3)	(4,6)	(1,3)

(b) Marked

		Input		
		a	b	c
	(1,3)	(2,5)	(2,5)	
Feasible	(2,5)	(1,3)	(4,4)	(1,1)
state	✔ (2,7)	(3,3)	(4,6)	(1,3)
pairs	✔ (5,7)	(1,3)	(4,6)	(1,3)

Figure 3.22.   Pairs table for machine of figure 3.21.

A pair is unordered; for example, the pair (2, 5) is equivalent to the pair (5, 2). To facilitate the recognition of such equivalences, the members of each pair are written in numeric order in figure 3.22. Thus the states (1, 3) actually transfer to (5, 2) on token b; however, the state pair (5, 2) is written (2, 5). By the same reasoning, if a pair (2, 5) appears in the feasible state-pair list, we do not include (5, 2).

The next operation is marking those state-pairs that are distinguishable. The marking rule is: a state-pair in the set of feasible state-pairs is *marked* if there exists a transition to a state-pair (p, q) such that (1) p and q are different and (2) (p, q) is either marked or not among the feasible state-pairs.

This operation is repeated until no more state-pairs can be marked. Thus, in figure 3.22, state-pair (1, 3) transfers to state-pair (2, 5) on both tokens a and b; (2, 5) is in the feasible state-pair set and is unmarked; hence, (1, 3) is not marked.

Consider the pair (2, 5), in the second row, which has transitions to pairs (1, 3), (4, 4), and (1, 1). The transitions to (4, 4) and (1, 1) do not call for marking, nor does the transition to (1, 3), because (4, 4) and (1, 1) are singlet pairs, and (1, 3) is in the table, unmarked.

Pair (2, 7) is marked, however, because there is a transition to pair (4, 6), on token b, and (4, 6) is not in the table. Similarly, pair (5, 7) is marked.

Repeating the operation on pairs (1, 3) and (2, 5), we find that they still are not marked, because (2, 7) and (5, 7) are not among the state-pairs to which they transfer. Hence, we conclude that these two pairs remain unmarked, and are therefore the equivalent state-pairs.

The pairs algorithm therefore indicates that the equivalent state-sets of the machine in figure 3.21 are:

$$\{1, 3\}, \{2, 5\}, \{4\}, \{6\}, \{7\}$$

3.4. Regular Grammars and FSMs

> *Intelligence . . . is the faculty of making artificial objects,*
> *especially tools to make tools.*
>
> *. . . Henri Bergson*

Regular grammars and FSMs have a close correspondence. Given any FSM, a regular grammar the language of which is identical to that of the FSM can be constructed from it; and given any regular grammar, an FSM the language of which is identical to that of the grammar can be constructed from it. We give the constructions for these assertions, with examples.

Construction: FSM from a Regular Grammar.   Recall that a regular grammar $G = (N, \Sigma, P, S)$ has productions in the set P of the form:

```
A → aB       where B ∈ N, and a ∈ Σ
A → b        where b ∈ Σ
```

and such that $S \rightarrow \epsilon$ may be in P.

Given a grammar G, we construct a NDFSM $M = (Q, \Sigma, \delta, q_0, F)$ as follows:

The states of M are associated with the nonterminals of G, except for one additional state q' not in N. The halt state set F is $\{q'\}$. The state q_0 is associated with the start token S in G. Then for every production $A \rightarrow aB$ in G, we add state B to the transition set $\delta(A, a)$. For every production $A \rightarrow b$ in G, we add state q' to the transition set $\delta(A, b)$, where $b \in \Sigma \cup \{\epsilon\}$.

Note that the alphabets of M and G are identical, and that M may be nondeterministic.

For example, consider the simple grammar G_2, with productions:

```
S → + N
S → - N
S → d N
S → d
N → d N
N → d
```

The language of this grammar will be recognized as the signed decimal numbers, where d is a decimal digit.

The machine M will contain the states $\{S, N, F\}$, where F is a new halt state.

Then the transitions of M are defined by the following transition function:

```
δ(S, +) = N
δ(S, -) = N
δ(S, d) = N
δ(S, d) = F
δ(N, d) = N
δ(N, d) = F
```

The moves of M in recognizing a string x mimic the derivation of x in the grammar. For example, consider the string -313, or -ddd as it appears in the grammar. The moves are:

```
S to N on -,
N to N on d,
N to N on d,
N to F on d.
```

The derivation is:

$$S \Rightarrow -N \Rightarrow -dN \Rightarrow -ddN \Rightarrow -ddd$$

We leave a proof that $L(G) = L(M)$ to you.

Construction: FSM to a Regular Grammar. Given an FSM M, a regular grammar G may be constructed from M, such that $L(M) = L(G)$. Let M be deterministic. Let $G = (N, \Sigma, P, S)$, where N, the nonterminals, correspond to the machine states Q; the alphabets of G and M are identical; S corresponds to the start state of the machine; and the productions in P are constructed as follows:

- If $\delta(A, a) = B$, then include production $A \rightarrow aB$ in P.

- If $\delta(A, a) = B$, where B is in the halt set F, then include production $A \rightarrow a$ in P.

- If S is a halt state, include production $S \rightarrow \epsilon$ in P.

The resulting grammar is clearly regular. Again, machine M mimics a derivation in G for some string x. We leave a proof that $L(M) = L(G)$ to you.

3.5. Regular Expressions and FSM

A regular expression is a compact way of representing a regular language. In addition to string elements, a regular expression uses three basic operations: *concatenation, alternation,* and *closure.* We have introduced each of these operations previously, in a less formal manner.

3.5.1. Definitions

Concatenation is an associative, noncommutative binary operation. The token for concatenation is juxtaposition; for example, if E_1 and E_2 are two regular expressions, then E_1E_2 is the concatenation of the two. If E_1 and E_2 denote the sets of strings S_1 and S_2, respectively, then E_1E_2 denotes the set:

$$S = \{uv \mid u \in S_1 \text{ and } v \in S_2\}$$

Another way to express E_1E_2 is: choose any string u in the set denoted by E_1; choose any string v in the set denoted by E_2; then the concatenated string uv is in E_1E_2. Also, any string in E_1E_2 can be divided into a u prefix and a v suffix, where u is in the set denoted by E_1 and v is in the set denoted by E_2.

Alternation is an associative, commutative binary operation, represented by the symbol $|$ or $+$. If E_1 and E_2 are two regular expressions denoting the sets of strings S_1 and S_2, then $E_1 \mid E_2$ is a regular expression denoting $S_1 \cup S_2$, the union of S_1 and S_2. We have introduced alternation previously; it is commonly used in the BNF representation of production rules.

Closure is a unary operation. If E is a regular expression denoting some set of strings S, then $\{E\}$ is a regular expression, called the *closure* of E, and represents the set of all possible strings formed by choosing members of S and concatenating them, together with the empty string ϵ. Thus the closure $\{E\}$ of a regular expression E is a compact way of writing the infinitely large regular expression:

$$\epsilon \mid E \mid EE \mid EEE \mid EEEE \mid \dots$$

Closure also can be defined by the following set expression:

$$\{E\} = \{ xY \mid x \in E \text{ and } Y \in \{E\} \} \cup \{\epsilon\}$$

This definition may appear circular; the closure operation that is being defined appears in its own definition. Let us explore this matter briefly. By the definition, the empty string ϵ is in $\{E\}$, which means that Y can be ϵ within the definition and, by the first half of the union, all those x's in E also are in $\{E\}$. In other words, $\{E\}$ contains $E \mid \epsilon$. Thus, Y may contain anything in $E \mid \epsilon$ and, by the first half of the union, all those xY's such that x is in E are in $\{E\}$; therefore $\{E\}$ contains $EE \mid E \mid \epsilon$, and so on.

Closure can also be represented by the token * following the expression to be closed, thus $E^* = \{E\}$. If E consists of more than one token, it must be enclosed in parentheses when this notation is used.

Recall that we earlier stated that Σ^* represents the set of strings in the alphabet Σ. This statement is clearly consistent with the definition of closure.

Parentheses can be used freely in regular expressions as needed to keep the relative ordering of the operations clear. Closure is represented by a brace structure $\{\}$ and does not require any precedence rule; it operates on the expression contained therein. By convention, concatenation has a higher precedence than alternation; therefore, the regular expression:

$$ab|cde$$

is interpreted:

$$(ab)|(cde)$$

Closure represented by $*$ has a higher precedence than either concatenation or alternation. Thus:

$$a \mid bc^*$$

is interpreted:

$$(a) \mid (b\ (c)^*\ )$$

The elements of a regular expression are the tokens of an alphabet Σ, the empty token ϵ, and the null set $\varnothing$. A null-set regular expression denotes an empty set, containing neither ϵ nor any strings. The regular expression ϵ denotes a string set containing only the empty string.

The symbols for alternation, closure, and so on are called *metasymbols* and cannot be in the alphabet of the regular language. Of course, parentheses appear in many common languages, so that any practical implementation must deal with a potential conflict of metasymbols and the language alphabet. A choice of metasymbols might be provided, or a special quote character might be used to delimit alphabet symbols.

A CFG for Regular Expressions

The language of regular expressions is expressed by the following CFG $G_r = (N, \Sigma, P, R)$, where:

$$N = \{R, C, L\}$$
$$\Sigma = \{+, (,), \{, \}, a, \epsilon\}$$

and the production set P is:

$R \rightarrow R + C$	(alternation)
$R \rightarrow C$	
$C \rightarrow C\ L$	(concatenation)
$C \rightarrow L$	
$L \rightarrow (\ R\ )$	(parenthesizing)
$L \rightarrow \{\ R\ \}$	(closure)
$L \rightarrow a$	(any token in the regular language)
$L \rightarrow \epsilon$	(empty string)

This grammar expresses the precedence of the operations, as well as the structural rules for regular expression formation. In the following discussion, we shall assume that any regular expression can be parsed and a derivation tree created for it.

Examples of Regular Expressions. The regular expression:

$$(+ \mid - \mid \epsilon) \, d\{d\}$$

represents the set of (possibly) signed numbers, where d represents the set of digits. This expression may be interpreted in English as follows:

E consists of a choice of $+$, $-$, or empty (ϵ) followed by a single digit, followed by any number (including zero) of digits.

The regular expression:

$$(+ \mid - \mid \epsilon) \, (d\{d\} \, . \, \{d\} \mid \{d\} \, . \, d\{d\}) \, (\epsilon \mid (E(+ \mid - \mid \epsilon) \, d\{d\}))$$

represents a floating point number. To see this, let us divide the expression into three parts:

```
(+ | - | ε)   (d{d} . {d} | {d} . d{d})   (ε | (E(+ | - | ε) d{d}))
<--------->   <----------------------->   <---------------------->
     I                    II                        III
```

Part I represents an optional sign. Part II is the mantissa. It must contain a decimal point and at least one digit ahead or behind the decimal point. Part III represents an optional exponent, signaled by an E followed by an optional sign and at least one digit.

Note the use of precedence of concatenation over alternation in part II.

3.5.2. Regular Expression Identities

Regular expressions satisfy a number of identities, which may be used to reduce the complexity of a regular expression or to prove that two regular expressions represent the same language. Unfortunately, there seems to be no systematic procedure for transforming regular expressions into standard forms, as there is in ordinary algebra or trigonometry.

Let A, B, and C be regular expressions. Then the following identities hold:

```
 1.  A + B = B + A          (commutivity of alternation)
 2.  {Ø} = ε                (closure of an empty set is the null string)
 3.  A + (B + C) = (A + B) + C   (associativity of alternation)
 4.  A(B C) = (A B)C        (associativity of concatenation)
 5.  A(B + C) = A B + A C   (distributivity of concatenation over
                             alternation)
 6.  A ε = ε A = A          (identity of concatenation)
 7.  Ø E = E Ø = Ø          (zero of concatenation)
 8.  {E} = E + {E}
 9.  {{E}} = {E}
10.  E + Ø = E              (identity of alternation)
```

Most of these follow directly from the corresponding properties of the string sets represented by the regular expression. For example, the $+$ operator corresponds to a set union, which satisfies commutivity and associativity. Similarly, concatenation easily can be shown to be associative.

Identity 2 follows immediately from the definition of closure—regardless of what (if anything) is in a set E, {E} contains ϵ.

Identity 8 follows immediately from the observation that every string in E is also in {E}; hence, the union of these two is exactly {E}.

3.5.3. Correspondence to FSMs

We now demonstrate that, for every regular expression E denoting some language L(E), there exists an FSM M such that $L(M) = L(E)$. The construction of the machine is particularly useful, because it is often more convenient to represent a language as a regular expression than as an FSM. We therefore need a systematic way to construct a recognizer for the language of a regular expression.

The machine we construct will be nondeterministic, in general, but can be reduced to a minimal deterministic machine by the methods of the previous sections.

The basic idea of the transformation is simple. We conceive an FSM that contains a start state S and one halt state F. Somehow, it recognizes a regular expression E, as diagrammed in figure 3.23(a). The square box containing "E" represents a set of states and transitions between states S and F.

Now suppose that E is the empty set $\emptyset$. Because $\emptyset$ is an empty language, which contains neither any string nor ϵ, the only possible machine for $\emptyset$ is the isolated S and F states, figure 3.23(b). This machine refuses to accept any string, including the empty string, because it can never reach the halt state.

Next suppose that E is the empty string ϵ. A recognizing machine for this language, shown in figure 3.23(c), permits one transition—an empty move from S to F. This machine clearly exactly accepts the empty string. A string of length greater than zero is rejected, because there are no other moves from either S or F.

If E is an alphabet token a, the machine of figure 3.23(d) exactly recognizes a string consisting of that token.

Now consider more sophisticated machines. If E is a parenthesized expression, $E = (E')$, a recognizer machine for E is clearly a recognizer for E'.

Consider the concatenation E of two expressions, E1 and E2. A recognizer for E clearly must recognize E1, then E2, in that order. Such a machine is shown in figure 3.23(e).

An alternation expression $E = E_1 \mid E_2$ is recognized exactly by the machine of figure 3.23(f). Recall that the set of strings represented by $E_1 \mid E_2$ is the union of the sets represented by E_1 and E_2. Let machine M_1 recognize E_1 and M_2 recognize E_2. Then consider a string x in E. The string x must be in E_1 or in E_2 (it could

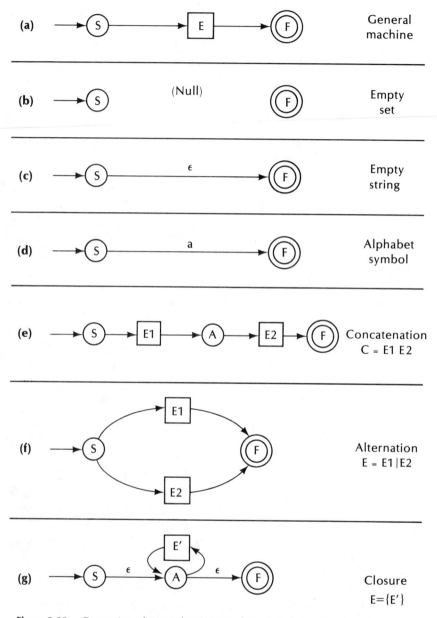

Figure 3.23.   Generation of a non-deterministic finite-state automaton from the components of a regular expression.

belong to both, of course). If it is in E_1, then the upper path of figure 3.23(f) yields a recognition; if it is in E_2, then the lower path yields a recognition. No strings other than those in the union of $L(M_1)$ and $L(M_2)$ are in the composite machine; any string recognized by the composite would have to be recognized in the upper or lower path, therefore by either M_1 or M_2.

Finally, a closure expression $E = \{E'\}$ is recognized exactly by the machine of figure 3.23(g). The empty moves are needed when these machine segments are combined to form a complete recognizer for some regular expression. Machine (g) clearly recognizes the empty string (two empty moves, S to A, A to F), and one or more concatenations of the strings in E'. Thus a string consisting of n members ($n \geq 0$) of the regular expression E' may be recognized by the empty move from S to A, n moves from A to itself through the machine for E', followed by the move from A to F.

Figure 3.23 essentially outlines the rules by which a complete machine for an arbitrary regular expression can be built from its parts. The construction operations are guided effectively by the derivation tree for the regular expression, and can be done bottom-up or top-down. The top-down process will be illustrated as an example. Then a top-down procedure will be given.

Consider the regular expression:

$$E = (+ \mid - \mid \epsilon)d\{d\}$$

which displays all the operations and tokens of regular expressions except the $\emptyset$ set, which should never appear within a regular expression anyway.

A simplified tree for this expression is given in figure 3.24. It is essentially the derivation tree with the single productions and parenthesis nodes removed.

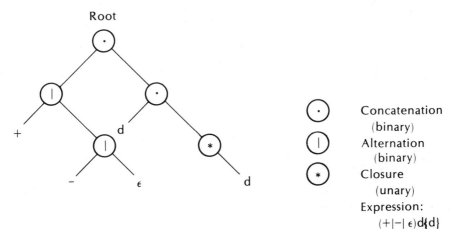

Figure 3.24.   The regular expression "$(+\mid-\mid\epsilon)d\{d\}$" as a tree.

At the root level, E consists of a concatenation of two pieces, which we shall call E_1 and E_2:

$$E = E_1 E_2$$

where $E_1 = (+ \mid - \mid \epsilon)$ and $E_2 = d\{d\}$. Thus the first machine looks like figure 3.25(a). We have introduced a new intermediate state, A.

The transition from S to A is an alternation of $+$ with $(- \mid \epsilon)$, as shown in figure 3.24. The single transition is therefore split into two, one for $+$, the other for $(- \mid \epsilon)$. The latter in turn splits into one for $-$ and one for ϵ. The resulting machine is shown in figure 3.25(b).

Turning to the machine between states A and F, we see that it is another concatenation—of d with $\{d\}$. The machine of figure 3.25(c) is the result, containing another new state, B.

The last machine is between states B and F and is a closure machine: the final NDFSM for the regular expression is shown in figure 3.25(d). As it turns out, neither of the ϵ-moves between states B and F is necessary in this machine; however, there is no harm in keeping them—they will be eliminated and the machine reduced to minimal form by the methods previously described.

We now give a recursive procedure FSM(EXPR, P, Q), which, when given a regular expression EXPR, an initial state $P = S$, and a final state $Q = F$, yields a set of states and a transition function for a machine (nondeterministic in general) the language of which is that of the regular expression. The final machine has one halt state, F.

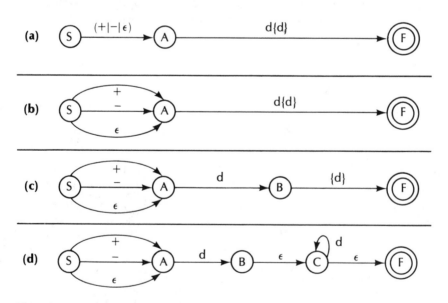

Figure 3.25.   Development of a finite-state automaton from the regular expression "$(+\mid-\mid\epsilon)d\{d\}$".

We use a Pascallike notation for the procedure. The operator = is an equality comparison; operator := means the left side's value is replaced by the value of the right side expression. Lowercase words represent keywords, and uppercase words represent variables and arguments. The ∪ is the set union operation. A comment is enclosed in braces { }. The variable δ represents the tabular representation of the transition function. Thus:

$$\delta(R, A) := \delta(R, A) \cup [Q]$$

means that state Q is added to the set δ(R,A).

```
procedure FSM(EXPR: reg_expr; P, Q: state);
   var A: state;
begin
   if EXPR = ∅ then   {do nothing}
   else
   if EXPR = ε then
   δ(P, ε) := δ(P, ε) ∪ [Q]
   else
   if EXPR = a ε Σ, then
   δ(P, a) := δ(P, a) ∪ [Q]
   else
   if EXPR = (X) then
   FSM(X, P, Q)
   else
   if EXPR = X Y then    {concatenation}
   begin
      A:=newstate;     {make a new state}
      FSM(X, P, A);
      FSM(Y, A, Q);
   end
   else
   if EXPR = X | Y then   {alternation}
   begin
      FSM(X, P, Q);
      FSM(Y, P, Q);
   end
   else
   if EXPR = {X} then    {closure}
   begin
      A:=newstate;
      FSM(ε, P, A);
      FSM(X, A, A);
      FSM(ε, A, Q);
   end;
end;
```

Example.   Let EXPR = (+ | − | ε)d{d}. Then we call FSM(EXPR, S, F). S will be the start state and F the (only) halt state of the final machine for EXPR. The following is a trace of the calls of FSM, the actions taken, and the returns. The periods ". . ." indicate the depth of nesting in the recursive calls.

```
FSM( `(+ | - | ε)d{d}', S, F);
. create a new state: R₁;
. FSM( `(+ | - | ε)', S, R₁);
. . FSM( `+ | - | ε', S, R₁);
. . . FSM( `+', S, R₁);
. . . . δ(S, +) := δ(S, +) ∪ {R₁};
. . . . return;
. . . FSM( `- | ε', S, R₁);
. . . . FSM( `-', S, R₁);
. . . . . δ(S, -) := δ(S, -) ∪ {R₁};
. . . . . return;
. . . . FSM(`ε', S, R₁);
. . . . . δ(S, ε) := δ(S, ε) ∪ {R₁};
. . . . . return;
. . . . return;
. . . return;
. . return;
. FSM(`d{d}', R₁, F);
. . create a new state: R₂;
. . FSM(`d', R₁, R₂);
. . . δ(R₁, d) := δ(R₁, d) ∪ {R₂};
. . . return;
. . FSM(`{d}', R₂, F);
. . . create a new state: R₃;
. . . FSM(`ε', R₂, R₃);
. . . . δ(R₂, ε) := δ(R₂, ε) ∪ {R₃};
. . . . return;
. . . FSM(`d', R₃, R₃);
. . . . δ(R₃, d):=δ(R₃, d) ∪ {R₃};
. . . . return;
. . . FSM(`ε', R₃, F);
. . . . δ(R₃, ε) := δ(R₃, ε) ∪ {F};
. . . . return;
. . . return;
. . return;
. return;
```

The result of this FSM call is the transition function shown graphically in figure 3.25(d).

3.5.4. Regular Expression of a Regular Grammar

A given regular language has many representations in regular expressions, and it is not easy to reduce a regular expression to some minimal form. The method that follows always yields a valid regular expression, but it may be larger than another one that also represents the same language. We know of no systematic reduction process for regular expressions similar to those useful in ordinary algebra.

We first introduce the concept of a *regular expression equation,* which contains regular expressions and variables X[1], X[2], . . . , X[n] that stand for some unknown regular expression. These resemble linear equations and are written in standard form as follows:

$$X[1] = a[1,0] + a[1,1] X[1] + a[1,2] X[2] + \ldots + a[1,n] X[n]$$
$$X[2] = a[2,0] + a[2,1] X[1] + a[2,2] X[2] + \ldots + a[2,n] X[n]$$

$$\vdots$$

$$X[n] = a[n,0] + a[n,1] X[1] + a[n,2] X[2] + \ldots + a[n,n] X[n]$$

Each of the coefficients a[i,j] is a regular expression in general, but contains no variables.

Note that a set of productions in a regular grammar can be represented as a set of regular expression equations. For example, the regular grammar:

```
S → 0A
S → 1B
S → 0
S → 1
A → 0S
A → 1B
A → 1
B → 0A
B → 1S
```

can be written as a set of three regular expression equations in the three unknowns, S, A, and B, as follows:

$$S = (0 + 1) + 0A + 1B \tag{3.1}$$

$$A = 1 + 0S + 1B \tag{3.2}$$

$$B = 1S + 0A \tag{3.3}$$

Thus, the first four productions are equivalent to:

$$S \to 0A \mid 1B \mid 0 \mid 1$$

which may be written, using $+$ for the alternation $\mid$ and $=$ for $\to$, as:

$$S = 0 + 1 + 0A + 1B$$

We then observe that if it is somehow possible to solve a system of equations for the variable S, the solution being a regular expression in the alphabet, we will have a regular expression representing the language of the underlying grammar.

We first need a solution for the equation:

$$S = aS + b \tag{3.4}$$

where a and b are regular expressions in the alphabet and possibly in the other variables. Note that any regular expression equation in any variable S can be written in this form.

A solution for this equation is:

$$S = \{a\}b$$

or:

$$S = a^*b$$

using the alternate notation.

Proof.   Consider the substitution of {a}b for S in equation 3.4:

$$\{a\}b = a\{a\}b + b \qquad (3.5)$$

Factor the right side, yielding:

$$\{a\}b = (a\{a\} + \epsilon)b$$

Now {a} = a{a} + ϵ, because ϵ is in both sides, a is in both sides, and any string in {a}, other than a or ϵ, is in {a} and in a{a}. Hence, equation 3.5 is an identity, and {a}b is a solution of equation 3.4.

We will not show that {a}b is a complete solution of equation 3.4. There are solutions to equation 3.4 that are not in {a}b, if a contains the empty string. Indeed, {a}(b + c) is a solution to equation 3.4, where c represents any set of strings whatsoever, if a contains the empty string. However, it turns out that {a}b, called the *minimal fixed point* of equation 3.4, is sufficient to generate an equivalent regular expression.

Now we can solve a general system of equations for the start token S. We illustrate the method using equations 3.1 through 3.3. The general method should be clear from this example; a more rigorous treatment is given in Aho [1972].

We start with some equation other than the S equation; for example, the B equation, equation 3.3. If this had the form:

$$B = aB + b$$

we would first transform it into the equation:

$$B = \{a\}b$$

which eliminates B from the right side. The right side of (3.3) does not contain B, so this step is unnecessary.

The regular expression obtained for B, which is just equation 3.3, now can be substituted into the other equations. The resulting equations are free of variable B. The result of this substitution in the set of equations 3.1 and 3.2 is:

$$= 1 + (0 + 11)S + 10A \qquad (3.6)$$

$$= (0 + 1) + (0 + 10)A + 11S \qquad (3.7)$$

We have made use of some of the identities in the second step in each case. For example, in the A equation:

$$1 + 0S + 1(1S+0A) = 1 + 0S + 11S + 10A$$

$$= 1 + (0 + 11)S + 10A$$

in equation 3.6.

We next rewrite equation 3.6 in the form A = aA + b:

$$A = 10A + (1 + (0 + 11)S) \qquad (3.8)$$

which has the minimal fixed-point solution:

$$A = \{10\}(1 + (0 + 11)S) \qquad (3.9)$$

Substituting this solution into the remaining S equation yields:

$$S = (0 + 1 + (0 + 10)\{10\}1) + ((0 + 10)\{10\}(0 + 11) + 11)S \qquad (3.10)$$

after some rearrangement and factoring. It has the fixed-point solution:

$$S = \{(0 + 10)\{10\}(0 + 11) + 11\}(0 + 1 + (0 + 10)\{10\}1) \qquad (3.11)$$

which should be a regular expression equivalent to the original regular grammar given previously. As a check, it would be wise to construct a machine from equation 3.11, reduce it, and verify that its regular grammar agrees with the original grammar. It is neither obvious that equation 3.11 reflects our grammar nor clear whether a shorter expression can be found for S. Different expressions result, depending on which variables are eliminated first, and it may pay to do the reduction in different ways to see if a shorter expression can be obtained.

3.6. FSM Representations

A DFSM can be embedded in a computer program in several different ways. We will illustrate two—as a set of tables that are interpreted by a general-purpose program, and as a specially constructed program.

The table approach usually is superior to the program approach for large automata in both memory and in reliability. The table interpreter need be written only once for any machine, and the combined program and machine table often requires less storage space than the equivalent program instructions.

3.6.1. A Sparse Matrix FSM Interpreter

It should be clear that an FSM interpreter will essentially map the pair {state, next-token} into an action and a next state. If we represent the state and the next-token as ordinals, then the problem of one state transition amounts to a two-dimensional array access that yields an action and a state number.

However, most machines will be represented by a sparse array; most of the entries will be syntax errors. A more efficient mapping is achieved through the use of a *sparse matrix* representation, described next.

Figure 3.26 shows the organization of the state tables. The states are numbered 1, 2, . . . , N. An array STATEX then contains indices to a TOKEN array, as indicated by the arrows. For each state, there will be a set of tokens associated

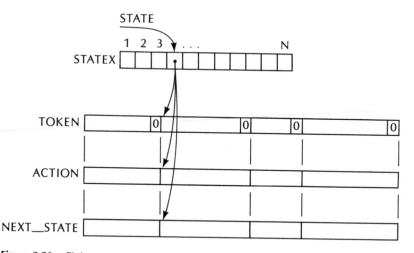

Figure 3.26.   Finite-state automaton state table organization.

with out-going transitions from the state. These are listed in some order, starting with index STATEX[STATE], and ending in the special reserved token 0.

The size of the TOKEN table is equal to the number of states plus the total number of state transitions.

Two other arrays are associated with the TOKEN array—ACTION and NEXT_STATE. Each of these has the same length as TOKEN and is indexed by STATEX[STATE]. The ACTION array carries some semantic action associated with the transition, and the NEXT_STATE array carries the number of the next state.

An ACTION may be a simple integer, or the address of a functional to be executed.

Given a STATE, we obtain a TOKEN array index from STATEX[STATE]. This will point to the first element of a list of possible tokens associated with the state. We then look for one that matches the current token, or a zero. A zero indicates a syntax error, which should be reported.

When a token match is seen, we call an ACTION that depends on a particular state transition, and obtain the next state by a lookup in NEXT_STATE, both of which are indexed by the same index used in TOKEN for the match.

Pascal Interpreter Program

Here is a complete Pascal program that interprets an FSM the data of which have the form of figure 3.26. We have omitted details related to fetching tokens, performing actions, and reporting errors. Note that one action must be *halt*, which will end the FSM state transitions by setting MORE to false.

```
program IFSM;    {FSM interpreter}

  const
    N= 50;  {number of states}
    T= 500;  {number of transitions}
    TOKS= 40;  {number of tokens}
    START= 32;  {start state}

  type
    STYPE= 1..n;
    TTYPE= 1..t;
    TOKTYPE= 1..toks;

  var
    STATE: 1..n;  {current state}
    STATEX: array [1..n] of ttype;
    TOKEN: array [ttype] of toktype;
    ACTION: array [ttype] of integer;
    NEXT_STATE: array [ttype] of stype;
    TX: ttype;
    MORE: boolean;
    TOKEN: toktype;

  procedure ERROR;
  begin
    {complain about an error}
  end;

  procedure NEXT;
  begin
    {fetch the next TOKEN}
  end;

  procedure ACT (ACTVAL: integer);
  begin
    {perform an action based on ACTVAL}
  end;

  procedure INIT;
  begin
    {initialize tables, I/O, etc.}
  end;

begin
  more:=true;
  state:=start;  {initial state}
  while more do
  begin
    next;  {get a token}
    tx:=statex[state];
    while (token[tx]<>0) and
          (token[tx]<>token) do tx:=tx+1;
    if token[tx]=0 then error
    else
      begin
        act(action[tx]);  {semantic action}
        state:=next_state[tx];
      end
  end
end.
```

A note about our style of Pascal source may be in order. We have consistently followed certain stylistic conventions in the QPARSER source and in the fragments in this book. One convention is that variable and procedure names that appear in a *declaration* are in capital letters, whereas *uses* of variables are in lowercase. This facilitates finding the declaration of a variable with an editor. Unfortunately, it also requires a Pascal compiler that is case-insensitive with regard to variable names.

Keywords are in lowercase. BEGIN-END blocks are consistently indented by two spaces, and are usually such that the BEGIN aligns with its matching END on their left-most character.

We occasionally resort to the use of a GOTO statement, as we have in the SKIPBLANKS example given later in this chapter. This may offend the purist (there is always a way of avoiding a GOTO by using a structured form, possible with a Boolean flag to control execution). A common application of a GOTO is as an escape from a WHILE or FOR loop. Note that Pascal provides no structured loop exit mechanism. We have resisted introducing a Boolean variable the sole purpose of which is to control a loop—that would not only decrease program performance, but also decrease readability, in our opinion.

State-Oriented Representation

> *Art thou he that should come, or do we look for another?*
> *. . . Matthew 11:3*

An alternative FSM table format can be organized around the next token instead of the current state. The tables look essentially the same as those in figure 3.26, except that we enter them with a TOKEN, and then search for the current STATE in a list.

Although the table sizes appear to be the same as those in the state-oriented approach, this representation will require different memory size and have a different performance. The choice depends on whether there are more tokens or states, assuming that all tables are packed for minimum value representation.

If there are more states than tokens, then a state organization is better, because the TOKEN array can be more tightly packed than the corresponding state array. There also will be fewer average searches to find a match in a TOKEN array than in a STATE array.

Note that the list of tokens in each TOKEN block can be in any order. The state machine's performance clearly depends on whether a match is found near the end or the beginning of these lists; if possible, the most frequently used transitions should be placed near the beginning.

3.6.2. Program Representation of an FSM

A programmatic representation of an FSM is less abstract than the table approach. However, it is more prone to error and is difficult to modify if the machine changes appreciably.

The following sample program implements the FSM of figure 3.1. The states S, A, B, G, and H are represented by statement labels 0, 1, 2, 3, and 4. Notice how the default in states 2 and 4 is a *halt* action, whereas the default in the other states is an *error* action.

```
program PFSM;
  label 0, 1, 2, 3, 4, 5;
  var TOKEN: integer;

  function IS_DIGIT(CH: char): boolean;
  begin
    is_digit:=(ch>='0') and (ch<='9');
  end;

begin
  init;
  next;  {get first token}

  0:  if is_digit(token) then goto 2
      else
        if (token = '+') or
           (token = '-') then
        goto 1
      else
        if token = '.' then goto 3
        else error;
  1:  if is_digit(token) then goto 2
      else
        if token = '.' then goto 3
      else error;
  2:  if is_digit(token) then goto 2
      else
        if token = '.' then goto 4
      else goto 5;
  3:  if is_digit(token) then goto 4
      else error;
  4:  if is_digit(token) then goto 4
      else goto 5;
  5:  halt;
end.
```

3.6.3. Error Recovery

To err is human, to forgive, divine.

. . . *Alexander Pope*

To err is human, not to, animal.

. . . *Robert Frost*

What should we do when an error is detected? We can tackle this issue now. We will discuss error recovery in conjunction with each of the parser systems developed in later chapters; the problem is similar for all.

When a source string contains a syntax error, it simply is not a member of the grammar's language, and there is no general theory about how a parsing engine can be made to recover. The engine has derailed at a switch; the rest of the input string presumably carries enough information to get it back on a right track, but how? For example, there is no guarantee that the current state is compatible with what the writer of the source string intended—several tokens may have been scanned past an error point.

However, input strings that might contain errors are generated by humans who (presumably) try to write a syntactically correct string, but fail in a few places. Human errors are likely to be highly localized and to appear randomly and infrequently. A reasonable error recovery strategy is to try to patch the input string in the vicinity of the error, and also to place some trust in the validity of the current state.

A simple incremental patch philosophy is to try: (1) inserting a token, or (2) deleting a token, or (3) choosing a state different from the current one. The choice should depend on which strategy or combination of strategies yields a parse through several tokens following the patched region.

An FSM Error-Recovery Strategy

The simplest possible error-recovery strategy is to scan ahead to a token known to represent an end of a clause that always will cause a transition to some known state. For example, the FSM may be designed to parse just one line. On an error, the system could simply reject the rest of the line and reset to the start state for a line.

If the machine's language is not structured in this way, a more sophisticated action is required, as we assume in what follows.

A simple strategy is first to assume that the current state is correct, but that something is wrong with the next token, which we shall call the *error token*. The current state carries several legal tokens that it can parse through; they are in the TOKEN list associated with the STATEX[STATE] index. By inserting one of these, we guarantee that the FSM will scan the insertion.

However, it may again fail on the following error token. The test of whether an insertion has a chance of success depends on whether the following state can scan the error token. We therefore insist that any candidate for token insertion in state S then transfer to a state S' that can accept the error token.

If this condition cannot be met, we have other options. We can try changing the state to one that will accept the error token. Such a state always can be found by scanning the TOKEN list, looking for *any* match. In general, many such matches can be found, corresponding to different states. The test of an effective patch is then whether it yields a state that can accept the token *following* the error token.

Given failure on both counts, we recommend dropping the error token. We can then test whether the current state will accept the next token; failing that, we restart the recovery strategy with a new insertion. Eventually, a patch will be found that has some probability of success of continuation. Note that it is vital that the token *following* an insertion be consumed by the automaton; otherwise, an infinite loop of insertions may result.

The patch may still be incorrect, of course. The consequence will be another error later and still another patch. Given a fairly sparse machine (lots of states, lots of tokens, but relatively few transitions per state), we contend that this simple strategy will be effective. A dense machine will result in many false patches, precipitating long sequences of false errors and poor recovery attempts.

Note that this error-recovery strategy can be implemented easily when state tables are available, and also can be written only once. Error recovery with a programmatic GOTO-style approach is almost hopelessly difficult, because some specific recovery action is required at every ERROR call, and it is difficult to select the correct action. This is another good reason for embedding an FSM representation in tables rather than writing lots of GOTOs.

A clumsy aspect of error recovery is reading ahead on some tokens on a trial basis while seeking a patch. After a patch is found, the "real" machine should be run on the patched source, which usually will require running through tokens previously scanned in error recovery. Source tokens therefore must be kept in a short queue for reuse.

Semantic actions should be suspended while searching for a patch solution; these usually are impossible to undo. Changing the state through an error patch may also have drastic consequences on semantics. It may be necessary to discontinue all semantic actions once an error is detected, but to continue the machine to look for more syntax errors.

3.7. Lexical Analysis

In two words: im-possible.

. . . *Samuel Goldwyn*

I read part of it all the way through.

. . . *Samuel Goldwyn*

A *lexical analyzer* accepts the character sequence of some source form and groups it into tokens for a parser system. We can in theory consider a lexical analyzer as a translator in its own right. Unfortunately, there are many special problems that appear in different languages. We shall discuss Pascal lexical analysis in some detail, and then also discuss some of the lexical problems associated with Fortran and PL/I, each of which poses special problems.

For the most part, the lexical-analyzer system scans its source characters from left to right. There is one lookahead character that can be peeked at to determine a state transition; it usually will be scanned on the next move.

In certain instances, more than one lookahead character is required to determine a state transition. We shall see that one such circumstance exists in Pascal, and that many are found in Fortran.

The lexical analyzer usually must deal with source record boundaries, comments, spaces, encoding of scanned tokens, and compiler directives. In Pascal, a record boundary may occur anywhere between two tokens, and within comments and compiler directives. Any number of spaces may appear between tokens. A comment or compiler directive may appear anywhere. These lexical entities appear *asynchronously* in the source; it is impossible to provide for them in the language's grammar, because any number of them can appear between any pair of tokens.

Some compilers support a macro preprocessor, or even a macro syntax built into the language. The lexical analyzer usually carries the burden of picking up on macro definitions and calls, adding yet another level to its complexity.

3.7.1. Partitioning Lexical Analysis

We first divide a Pascal lexical analyzer into three essentially watertight compartments, each represented by a procedure. The *source compartment* is represented by procedure NEXTCH, and an associated global variable CH. A *delimiter compartment* is represented by a procedure SKIPBLANKS. A *token compartment* is represented by procedure NEXT_TOKEN and a token value TOKEN.

Next Character NEXTCH

NEXTCH deals with the fetching of source records and any macro expansion. It faithfully tracks every space, line ending, and comment, hiding only file access and macro expansion details. Each call to NEXTCH yields the next character of a source. That character will be placed in a variable called CH.

An end-of-file is best indicated by a CH value reserved for that purpose. If CH is normally a printable ASCII character, coded 32 to 126, then a value outside this range might be chosen (for example, three). If an end-of-line or end-of-some-column is significant, a special character can represent that condition. Note that NEXTCH should either reject or apply a special interpretation to nonprintable characters found in the source.

The form of NEXTCH depends considerably on the features provided in the compiler system. An example of one system is found in the QPARSER software.

3.7.2. The Delimiter Compartment—SKIPBLANKS

The procedure SKIPBLANKS will skip over all spaces, comments, and line endings (in a free-form language) associated with the intervals between tokens. After such a call, CH will contain the first character of the next token.

Note that Pascal does not permit a comment, line ending, or space within a token (some older languages do, however!). Thus the token := cannot be written:

```
:   =
```

or:

```
:{here we are splitting something}=
```

The analyzer will then simply call SKIPBLANKS prior to attempting to scan a token. Following the SKIPBLANKS call, CH will be the first character of a token, in preparation for scanning the token. Here is what SKIPBLANKS looks like in QPARSER:

```
procedure SKIPBLANKS;
   label 1;
begin
1:
   while ch=' ' do nextch;
   if ch='{' then
   begin  {open a comment}
     nextch;
     while not(ch in ['}', chr(eofch)] do
       nextch;
     if ch=chr(eofch) then
     error('unclosed comment')
     else
     begin
       nextch;
       goto 1;
     end
   end
end;
```

Note that this procedure contains a trap for a comment that is not closed before the end of a file. It also scans any number of successive comments and spaces, stopping on the first character that is neither a space nor a left brace.

Also note that a space is not always required between two tokens—only between a token-pair that could otherwise be considered a single token. For example:

```
if x then ...
```

could not legally be written:

```
ifx then   ...
```

as that would fool the lexical analyzer into returning the identifier ifx instead of the keyword if followed by x.

Pascal also supports comments that open with (* and close with *). The left parenthesis also is a token, as is *. It is necessary to peek ahead one more character when (is seen to check for *; while scanning for the end of comment, it is necessary to peek ahead for a) when a * is seen. These details add several lines to the procedure.

3.7.3. The Token Compartment—NEXT_TOKEN

> Moth: They have been at a great feast of languages, and stolen
> the scraps.
> Costard: O! they have lived long on the alms-basket of words.
> I marvel thy master hath not eaten thee for a word; for thou
> art not so long by the head as honorificabilitudinitatibus; thou
> art easier swallowed than a flap-dragon.
>
>   . . . William Shakespeare

> I am a Bear of Very Little Brain, and long words Bother me.
>   . . . A. A. Milne

The *token* compartment of a lexical analyzer accepts the time sequence of
characters in CH and proceeds to collect them into tokens. It calls SKIPBLANKS
before trying to scan any token. The Pascal tokens fall into these classes, and they
are typical of most languages:

- Decimal literals—the fixed- and floating-point numbers, such as 155 or 15E-6.

- Identifiers, such as F1 or NEXT_CHAR.

- Keywords, such as IF, WHILE or FOR.

- Strings, such as "I am a long string with spaces"

- Simple special tokens, such as +, -, or *

- Compound special tokens, such as := , .., or <>

Decimal Literals

We have already developed an FSM for decimal number recognition. Let us
add semantic actions to its transitions.

We first assign three variables—or, as we will refer to them, *registers*—
SIGN, P, and N to the machine, and then assign operations on the register
contents to each of the transitions. The result is a machine, as shown in figure
3.27.

SIGN holds either -1 or $+1$. The registers P and N hold floating-point
numbers. We include transitions into the start state and out of the halt states for
completeness.

Initially, SIGN is $+1$, P is 10.0, and N is 0.0. SIGN is changed to -1 only
on the transition S to A on $-$; otherwise it remains $+1$. Each transition on a digit
d (which stands for 0..9) involves the function value(d)—the numeric equivalent
of the character d. Thus, in the S to B transition, value(d) is assigned to N. On
an exit from B or H, the final value of the number is SIGN*N.

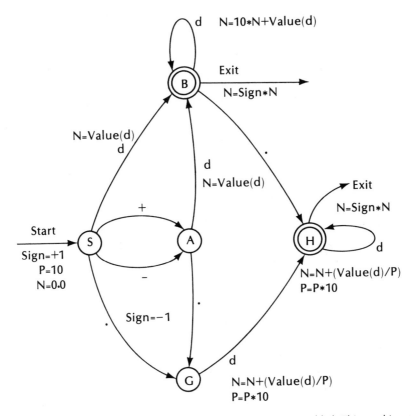

Figure 3.27.   The machine of figure 3.1 with semantic operations added. This machine recognizes a decimal number and converts it to an internal form.

On the transition B to B, the old value of N is multiplied by ten and added to value(d). The digit d precedes any decimal point; hence, each digit causes the place value of those preceding it to be increased by a factor of ten.

On scanning a decimal point, the register P is used; P carries the power of ten corresponding to the place value of the digits following a decimal point. Thus, in the transition G to H, value(d)/P is added to N, and P is increased by a factor of ten.

An exit from halt state B means that no decimal point was scanned; the number is an integer. The exit from halt state H means the number carries a decimal point.

The exits from B and H are taken on any token other than "." or d for B or d for H. A *lookahead* of one token evidently is needed to exit properly.

Pascal Number Literals

The machine of figure 3.27 will not work for Pascal. One problem is the SIGN. It is best not to accept a sign with a numeric literal in the lexical analyzer, because the minus sign will have to appear in the grammar anyway—for example, in a production like E → E − T. If a signed <number> is permitted in a typical expression grammar, then our translator will accept such strings as A − − 15, because − 15 is accepted by the lexical analyzer and the first − is built into the grammar. That is not acceptable under the Pascal syntax rules. In Jensen and Wirth Pascal, a *constant* is a signed number, and may appear in such places as a case label or a range. However, an *unsigned number* is expected in an expression.

Another problem is that the unsigned Pascal numbers are supposed to start with a digit. They do not *have* to work that way, but that is what the definition calls for. Thus, the number .15 is illegal; it must be written 0.15.

Still another problem is that a real number may be followed by an exponent, such as E − 16 or e1. The E is not a reserved word; hence, it and the following exponent value should be picked up by the lexical analyzer. Fortunately, the Pascal syntax does not permit a number to be followed by an identifier—some other token always is placed in between the two. Hence, the E cannot be the first letter of some identifier.

One more special difficulty with Pascal is the use of a period-pair to indicate a subrange; that is:

```
type SR= 15..75;
```

This causes a special problem for the lexical analyzer; because the period following the 15 normally is considered part of the number, our decimal machine will stop in state H after scanning the first period. The second period by itself also is a token in Pascal, but it is illegal in this context. However, the meaning of this portion of the statement clearly must be *integer* 15 followed by the subrange token "..".

Fortunately, the Pascal rules require that the two periods in such a form must belong in the same line and cannot be separated by a space. The number recognizer must therefore "cheat" by peeking at the character following a period as the next character; if it, too, is a period, then the recognizer halts on the integer part without scanning past the first period. In the program that follows, LINE is an array of char representing the source, and LINE[LX + 1] provides a peek at the character following CH, without scanning through CH.

This peek at the next character bypasses NEXTCH. Its use carries a certain penalty. For example, a macro expander cannot then be built into NEXTCH; the "next" character would not necessarily be in LINE[LX + 1], but might be somewhere else. When such a peek is required, it would be better to encapsulate the peekahead into a special function that is more visibly associated with NEXTCH.

Here is a decimal literal recognizer written for Pascal rules. It is found among the QPARSER software. It should be triggered on a digit; it scans through sufficient characters to recognize a full fixed or floating point number. It sets the global variable TOKEN to either int_tokx or real_tokx, corresponding to the token type. It also sets a semantic value NUMVAL or RVAL, to carry the recognized value.

```
{****************}
procedure GET_NUMBER;
  var V1, V2: integer;
      DIGS: int;
      RV: real;

  {..............}
  function GET_INTEGER(var DIGS: int): integer;
    var V: integer;
  begin  {scans a sequence of digits}
    v:=0;
    digs:=0;
    while (ch>='0') and (ch<='9') do
    begin
      v:=10*v + ord(ch) - ord('0');
      digs:=digs+1;
      nextch;
    end;
    get_integer:=v
  end;

  {................}
  procedure GET_EXP;
    var DIGS: int;
        EXPSIGN: boolean;
        EXP: int;
  begin  {collects an exponent part}
    nextch;  {get over e or E}
    expsign:=false;
    if ch in ['+', '-'] then begin
      expsign:=(ch='-');
      nextch;
    end;
    if (ch>='0') and (ch<='9') then begin
      exp:=get_integer(digs);
      if expsign then rv:=rv/pwr10(exp)
      else rv:=rv*pwr10(exp);
    end
    else
      error('missing digit after E');
  end;

  {...............}
  procedure FINISH_IT(SEMTYP: semtype);
  begin  {set TOKEN value and semantics values}
    if semtyp=float then
    token:=real_tokx
    else token:=int_tokx;
    with lsemp↑ do
    begin  {LSEMP is a semantics pointer}
      semt:=semtyp;  {type FIXED or FLOAT}
      if semtyp=float then
      rval:=rv
      else numval:=v1;
    end
  end;
```

```
begin  {Accepts an integer, decimal or real number}
  v1:=get_integer(digs);
  if (ch='.') and
    (line[lx+1]<>'.') then   {NOTE special Pascal problem}
  begin  {real number}
    nextch;
    v2:=get_integer(digs);
    rv:=v1 + (v2 / pwr10(digs));
    if ch in ['e', 'E'] then get_exp;
    finish_it(float);
  end
  else
  if ch in ['e', 'E'] then
  begin  {integer followed by exponent part}
    rv:=v1;
    get_exp;
    finish_it(float);
  end
  else
  finish_it(fixed)
end;
```

3.7.4. Identifiers and Keywords

> *'Zounds! I was never so bethumped with words*
> *Since I first called my brother's father dad.*
> *. . . William Shakespeare*

In Pascal, an *identifier* is a sequence of letters or digits starting with a letter, other than a keyword. The sequence may not be interrupted by a space, comment, or end-of-line. In some Pascals—notably UCSD—the underbar character _ is also legal in an identifier.

An immediate lexical problem is that certain of the Pascal keywords look like identifiers: *WHILE, FOR,* and *IF* all have the syntactic form of an identifier. A Pascal grammar will lump all identifiers into a single class (hence, a single token), whereas the keywords are associated with unique tokens. The lexical analyzer must discriminate between these two classes.

We propose this solution:

1. The analyzer scans each identifierlike object, collecting it into a string.

2. A global symbol table is searched for each such object. The keyword tokens will have a special *attribute* that distinguishes them from user identifiers.

3. Based on that attribute, the lexical analyzer returns either a keyword or an identifier. In the latter case, a pointer to the identifier's symbol table location is provided as semantic information.

Here is a Pascal procedure that fetches identifiers and keywords:

```
procedure GET_SYMBOL;
  var SX: int;
      SYM: symbol;   {a packed array of char}
      STP: symtabp;
begin
  fillchar(sym, maxtoklen, ' ');
  sx:=0;
  while (sx<ident_toklen) and
        (ch in ['a'..'z', 'A'..'Z', '0'..'9', '_'] do
  begin
    sym[sx]:=upshift(ch);
    sx:=sx+1;
    nextch;
  end;
  stp:=makesym(sym, user, 0);
     {look for it in the symbol table}
  with lsemp↑ do
  begin
    if stp↑.symt=reserved then
    begin  {a reserved keyword}
      semt:=other;
      token:=stp↑.tokval;   {token value is
                 carried in the symbol table}
    end
    else
    begin  {a user identifier}
      semt:=ident;
      symp:=stp;
      token:=ident_tokx;
    end
  end
end;
```

Note that we shift all letters to uppercase, following the Pascal convention on user identifiers. Keywords must be uppercase in any event to make them uniquely recognizable. Some implementations permit case differences to affect identifiers, or require that all identifiers and keywords be in uppercase, and so on.

Because the keywords must be in the symbol table, a section of initialization code is required to enter them and their token values.

3.7.5. Literal Strings

A Pascal *string* opens and closes with a single quote mark '. Any printable character is permitted between the quote marks, including blanks or objects that resemble comments. If a quote mark itself must be part of the string, it is written twice; for example:

```
'We can''t find that file'
```

The following procedure, found in QPARSER, collects a string. It will be called by the lexical analyzer when the current character CH is a quote mark.

The characters of the string are written to a large array of char starting at an index position STRTABX, by calling procedure PUTSTRCH. These characters are terminated with a chr(eos). Note that NEXTCH is called to produce the characters; it must faithfully deliver spaces, objects that look like comments, and line endings.

Note that a trap exists for strings that run over the end of a line, as required in Pascal. This is a valuable safety net; otherwise, a missing quote mark would result in a catastrophic error. The WHILE loop will stop on a quote mark, but the following IF test will reenter it if a second quote is seen immediately thereafter.

```
procedure GET_STRING;
  label 1;
begin
  nextch;   {get over the first '}
  1semp↑.semt:=strng;   {token is type string}
  1semp↑.stx:=strtabx; {pointer to string table}
1:
  while not(ch in [chr(eofch), chr(eolch), '''']) do
  begin
    putstrch(ch);
    nextch;
  end;
  if ch='''' then
  begin
    nextch;
    if ch='''' then
    begin
      putstrch(ch);
      nextch;
      goto 1;
    end
  end
  else
    error('string runs over end of line');
  putstrch(chr(eos));
  token:=str_tokx;
end;
```

3.7.6. Special Tokens

We are now ready for the large picture. NEXT_TOKEN is called to scan and produce a token number to the parser, hiding all details of comments, line endings, and so on. It must provide exactly those tokens that appear in the grammar—no more, no less. As we shall see, recognition of the special tokens appears in this procedure explicitly.

NEXT_TOKEN is essentially a SKIPBLANKS followed by a CASE on the next character CH. We show just a few of the Pascal special tokens—the complete set would fill many lines.

```
procedure NEXT_TOKEN;
  label 1;
begin  {Pascal-style lexical analyzer}
  {sets TOKEN to token number}
  1semp↑.semt:=other;  {default semantic case}
1:
```

```
skipblanks;
case ch of
'a'..'z', 'A'..'Z': get_symbol;
'0'..'9': get_number;
'''': get_string;
'*': begin nextch; token:=13; end;
'+': begin nextch; token:=14; end;
':': begin   {could be : or := }
       nextch;
       if ch='=' then
       begin
          nextch;
          token:=16;
       end
       else token:=15;
     end;
  ...  {etc.}
otherwise   {anything else}
  if ch=chr(eofch) then token:=stop_tokx
 else
  begin
    error('illegal character');
    nextch;
    goto 1;  {try again}
  end
 end
end;
```

The *otherwise* clause is an HP Pascal feature; it claims any CH values that fail to match one of the explicit labels. We put EOFCH—the end-of-file character—here because the form chr(eofch) would be syntactically illegal as a case label. Some Pascal implementations do not provide a case default. In that situation, we recommend covering the case with the conditional form:

```
if ch in ['a'..'z', 'A'..'Z', '0'..'9', '''', '*', '+', ':', ... ] then
```

The *else* of this conditional will then effectively catch the *otherwise* clause. The set [. . .] contains all the case labels.

An unrecognized character results in an error message, a skip of the character, and then a retry.

The "hard-wired" numbers associated with the tokens (for example, the 13 associated with token *) are in fact generated by the QPARSER software. We recommend the use of a scalar type or a symbolic constant in a hand-written lexical analyzer.

3.7.7. Fortran Lexical Analysis

The Fortran language requires the most sophisticated and specialized lexical analyzer of all the common languages. Its lexical analyzer is invariably a large and complicated program that is difficult to make work correctly.

Its complexity stems mostly from three general rules: (1) no two Fortran tokens need be delimited by a space, (2) tokens may contain spaces and/or line endings, and (3) there are no reserved keywords.

These rules were built into the language definition years ago, and must be observed by any compiler that is to recognize standard Fortran.

There are also exceptions to the rules. Strings may be written in two different ways, and spaces are permitted within strings. These exceptions create special difficulties; a string form must first be recognized by the lexical analyzer before it can apply the exception!

With the exception of strings, a Fortran line may be normalized first by removing all blanks. Token recognition must then proceed without the aid of delimiters.

Fortran comments are specially marked by a C in column 1, and never appear within a line. Several lines also may be concatenated by another convention involving column 6. Hence, these comments may be removed and whole lines formed before tackling lexical analysis.

> Belinda: Ay, but you know we must return good for evil.
> Lady Brute: That may be a mistake in the translation.
>   . . . Sir John Vanbrugh

Example 1. To get a feel for the difficulty of the problem, consider the following line, written with all blanks removed:

```
DO10I=17E3.GT.X
       ↑
```

The lexical analyzer clearly cannot determine whether this statement begins with the keyword DO or the identifier DO10I until the E is scanned. A DO statement would have to have another digit or a comma at the arrow position. (This example draws on the usual Fortran rule that a DO loop variable must be fixed point. In ANSI Fortran '77, the variable may be real. Thus the lexical analyzer would have to scan to the first "." before determining that the statement is an assignment.)

On the other hand, if one or more blanks were required as delimiters of tokens, but not permitted within a token, the statement would have to read:

```
DO10I = 17E3 .GT. X
```

A DO statement would have to carry a separating blank between the DO and the next token:

```
DO 10I=17,1,25
```

Other blanks are unnecessary; the remaining tokens can be distinguished.

Example 2. Consider the Fortran assignment statement such that the variable assigned to carries an index:

$$X(A + B * (17 - S)) = Y$$

ANS Fortran '77 permits arbitrary expressions as an array index. Thus, an index expression could continue through most of the characters of the statement. Note that the left part of an assignment has the same form as the left part of an arithmetic IF statement or a FORMAT statement:

$$\text{IF}(<\text{expr}>) <\text{number}>,<\text{number}>,<\text{number}>$$
$$\text{FORMAT}(<\text{format specification}>)$$

An IF statement cannot be distinguished from an indexed assignment until the character after the closing right parenthesis is scanned.

A FORMAT can also create difficulties for a lexical analyzer. For example, suppose the strategy is to match left and right parentheses in an attempt to locate the closing right parenthesis of an indexed assignment, ignoring other context. This appears on the surface to be reasonable. Unfortunately, the strategy fails on certain Fortran statements; for example:

$$\text{FORMAT}(5\text{H}223) = , \text{I}5, 4\text{X})$$

Such a scan will continue past the assignment symbol $=$ and falter on the comma. The difficulty, of course, lies in the failure to parse fully an assignment syntax (the 5H223 does not belong as an index).

Lexical Analysis of Fortran Lines

A simple backtracking strategy can deal with the special problems of Fortran and other languages with difficult lexical policies. Essentially, the line is *assumed* to contain a keyword if its opening letters match one. That assumption may fail, but the odds that it will succeed are good. On a failure, the strategy is to back up and act on the alternative assumption—that the line is an assignment starting with an identifier that happens to look like a keyword.

When a line starts with something other than a keyword, it is safe to assume that it is an assignment. A subsequent failure deeper in the line indicates a syntax error, not a false assumption.

A keyword line will have a restricted format that can be parsed by a special procedure. For example, the troublesome FORMAT statement has its own logic and special keyword forms—the main problem is determining that the line in fact is a FORMAT and not an assignment. The other statement forms are similarly fairly easy to analyze once their keyword is fixed.

While trying one of two alternatives, it is important to do nothing that would be hard to unwind later; for example, avoid symbol table entries or code generation.

It may be possible to build an abstract-syntax tree for the statement, with no other immediate action. The initial parsing assumption is that the statement carries a real keyword. When it is apparent that this assumption is wrong, it may be possible to make some minor changes in the tree to reflect the alternative, and continue parsing. This approach requires that the parser be sufficiently general to accept both kinds of statement and that the parse trees for the alternatives not be too different. The symbol table should not be changed until the possibility of a wrong choice has been eliminated.

3.7.8. Delimiter and Reserved Word Policies

There are several distinct language policies regarding the use of blanks and reserved words. They are:

1. No policy; for example, Algol 60. The problem of distinguishing keywords and separating tokens is left to an implementation.

2. Blanks must be inserted as needed as separators, and keywords are re-served. Many implementations follow this policy, for the sake of simplicity of the compiler; for example, Pascal.

3. Blanks must be inserted, and keywords are not reserved; for example, PL/I.

4. Blanks are ignored, as in Fortran, and keywords are reserved; for example, ANS (Fortran subset).

5. Blanks are ignored, and keywords are not reserved; for example, full ANS Fortran.

One of these policies usually applies to a language to be implemented. Policy 1 is really "no policy." With no policy, a program may be untransportable without extensive editing. Modern language specifications do not leave lexical conventions undefined.

Policy 2 is the easiest on the compiler writer. As we have seen, a simple analyzer can distinguish tokens in a deterministic left-to-right scan, and keywords can be distinguished from user identifiers through a table lookup. Unfortunately, policy 2 can be vexing to a compiler user. For example, PL/I contains over 100 keywords. It is unreasonable to expect every user to know every one of these keywords and never to accidentally declare any of them as an identifier.

Policy 3 is somewhat difficult to implement, assuming the language is un-ambiguous under the policy. With inserted blanks, tokens are easily dis-tinguished. However, the compiler may have to scan several tokens into the source string on some assumption regarding an identifier before finding whether the assumption was right or wrong. If wrong, it must backtrack and try an alternative. Keywords rarely are used as identifiers; hence, if the first choice is always "keyword"—when a choice exists—the amount of backtracking re-quired will be small.

Policy 3 is considerably aided by a language policy of predeclared variables, which allows the analyzer to be alert to any keywords that have been declared in its backtracking process. A keyword that has been previously declared as an identifier can be marked as such to alert the analyzer procedures to a potential problem.

Even this procedure breaks down if a variable declaration can begin with a declared identifier. Fortunately, most common programming languages require some keyword in a declaration preceding the declared identifier. Thus, in For-tran, a declaration is triggered by one of the keywords COMMON, DIMEN-SION, REAL, INTEGER, and so on. In PL/I, a declaration is triggered by the keyword DECLARE, or DCL, and the declaration must appear first in a block. In Pascal, a declaration is triggered by one of the keywords CONST, TYPE, VAR, PROCEDURE, or FUNCTION.

However, DCL/DECLARE poses a certain lexical problem in PL/I. Consider the following example, in which an identifier DCL in PL/I is declared in some block:

```
BEGIN
    DCL  DCL FIXED BINARY; /* DCL is declared here */
        ...
    BEGIN
      DCL I FIXED BINARY;  /* <— One problem */
      DCL := I;     /* <— So is this DCL */
      DCL := I-1;   /* This DCL is not a problem */
        ...
    END;
END;
```

When DCL is declared as a variable, it is not clear whether a line beginning with DCL is an assignment or a declaration. The difficulty appears in the two lines marked with an arrow <—.

Once the compiler is in the executable statements of a block, a declaration is no longer permissible, and DCL must stand for the user identifier. Other keywords can be distinguished by the keyword-marking technique discussed, based on the previously declared identifiers.

Policies 4 and 5 are still more difficult. The lexical analyzer must make some decisions based on substrings of statements. Without certain other restrictions in the language, lexical analysis of a policy 5 language may be impossible, and the language may in fact be ambiguous—all this despite the existence of an apparently reasonable and unambiguous high-level grammar for the language. As we have seen, Fortran lexical analysis yields to a limited backtracking strategy due to certain of its properties. One cannot be so sure about an arbitrary policy 5 language.

> *There is a time for many words, and there is also a time for sleep.*
>
> *. . . Homer*

3.8. Some FSM Theorems

> *'Contrariwise,' continued Tweedledee, 'if it was so, it might be; and if it were so, it would be: but as it isn't, it ain't. That's logic.'*
>
> *. . . Lewis Carroll*

In this section, we prove a number of theorems stated earlier in the text.

3.8.1. Equivalence of Empty Cycle States

Let p and q be two states in a machine M such that $p \vdash^+ q$ and $q \vdash^+ p$ on empty moves only. We wish to prove that states p and q are equivalent.

Let x be any string accepted by M starting from state p (p need not be the start state).

Then $p \vdash^+ q$ implies that there exists a sequence of states $p_1, p_2, \ldots, p_n$ ($n \geq 0$) such that:

```
p₁ is in δ(p, ε),
p₂ is in δ(p₁, ε),
    .

    .

    .
pₙ is in δ(pₙ₋₁, ε),   and
q is in δ(pₙ, ε)
```

But then $(p, x) \vdash (p_1, x) \vdash (p_2, x) \vdash \ldots \vdash (p_n, x) \vdash (q,x)$, and therefore x is accepted by M starting from state q.

If we interchange p and q in this argument, we can show that any state x accepted by M in state q is also accepted by M in state p; therefore, states p and q must be equivalent. QED.

3.8.2. Equivalence through Removal of Empty Moves

A simple algorithm for the removal of empty transitions from a machine M to yield a machine M' was given in section 3.2.2. We have already shown that the algorithm terminates (the absence of empty cycles is crucial). It should be clear that no empty moves remain. We need to show equivalence. We do this by proving a somewhat stronger lemma.

Lemma. For all (x in Σ^*, p in Q) ($(p, x) \vdash^* (f, \epsilon)$ in M if and only if $(p', x) \vdash^* (f', \epsilon)$ in M') where f is in F and f' is in F'.

For convenience, we indicate the states in M' with primed letters (for example, p', q') and the states in M with unprimed letters (for example, p, q). Q is the state set in M, and F is the set of halt states in M. The algorithm does not remove or add any states, so every state p in M corresponds to a state p' in M'.

Proof: "Only If" part. Let $(p, x) \vdash^* (f, \epsilon)$ in k moves, $k \geq 0$.

The Basis Step (k = 0). Clearly p = f and is in F. But p' must be in F' by state correspondence.

The Inductive Step (k > 0). Consider the first step in the machine move sequence:

$$(p, ax) \vdash (q, x) \vdash^* (f, \epsilon)$$

where a is in $\Sigma \cup \{(*e\}$. We have several cases to consider. If a is not empty, then q′ is in δ(p′, a) and therefore (p′, ax) ⊢ (q′, x). But then (q′, x) must yield (f, ε) in k − 1 moves or less, by the inductive hypothesis; hence, M′ accepts ax in state p′.

If a is empty, we have (p, x) ⊢ (q, x) ⊢* (f, ε), with q in δ(p, ε). But q′ is not in δ(p′, ε) in M′. We now have two subcases to consider: x empty or not empty.

If x is empty, then (p, ε) ⊢ (q, ε) ⊢* (f, ε). The complete sequence involves only empty moves, with a sequence of states (p, q, q_1, q_2, . . . , f). By the halt state rule in the construction process, each of the states p′, q′, q'_1, q'_2, . . . , f must be halt states. But then (p′, ε) is an accepting configuration for M′.

If x is not empty, there must be some first not-empty move in the move sequence, as follows:

$$(p, ax) \vdash (p_1, ax) \vdash \ldots \vdash (p_n, ax) \vdash (q, x) \vdash^* (f, \epsilon)$$

But by the construction process, we must have:

```
q'      in δ(p'n, a),
p'n-2 in δ(q', a),
        .
        .
        .
p'      in δ(q', a).
```

Hence, (p′, ax) ⊢ (q′, x) ⊢* (f′, ε). (The latter set of moves follows from the inductive hypothesis; there are less than k moves in that sequence.) QED

A proof of the "if" part is similar.

3.8.3. Equivalence of the NDFSM to DFSM Transformation

We show that L(M) is a subset of L(M′), where M′ is derived from M by the NDFSM → DFSM transformation of section 3.2.3.

Proof. Let (p, x) ⊢* (f, ε) in M in k steps. We show that ([. . .p. . .], x) ⊢* ([. . .f. . .], ε) in M′, for every state [. . .p. . .] in M′.

The Basis Step (k = 0). Here p = f and f is in F. But then [. . .p. . .] must be in F′; hence, x is accepted by M.

The Inductive Step (k > 0). Consider the first step:

$$(p, ax) \vdash (q, x) \vdash^* (f, \epsilon)$$

where a is in the alphabet. (Note no empty moves can exist.) But then we have q in δ(p, a) and therefore [. . .q. . .] is in δ([. . .p. . .], a) in M′ for every state of the form [. . .p. . .] in M′. Then:

$$([. . .p. . .], ax) \vdash ([. . .q. . .], x) \vdash^* ([. . .f. . .], \epsilon)$$

QED. The proof that L(M′) is a subset of L(M) is similar.

3.8.4. The Pairs Table Reduction Algorithm

We divide the proof into a lemma and a theorem. The theorem applies to the pairs table on completion of its construction, and the lemma to the completion of the marking process.

Lemma. The feasible state-pairs contain all the equivalent state-pairs of the FSM.

Theorem. The unmarked state-pairs contain all and only the equivalent state-pairs of the FSM.

A proof of the lemma is left as an exercise. A proof of the theorem follows.

Proof: "All" Part. Let (p, q) be an equivalent state-pair in the FSM. Then, by the lemma, it is among the feasible state-pairs in the construction of the pairs table. Now suppose (p, q) becomes marked during the marking phase, and therefore is not among the unmarked set. It became marked because some token caused a transition from it to some marked or absent state-pair, (p', q'). If (p', q') is absent, then states p' and q' must be distinguishable, by the lemma, and therefore (p, q) are distinguishable states. This statement contradicts the assertion of their equivalence. Suppose instead that the state-pair (p', q') is marked. By a repetition of this argument, there must have been a transition from it to some other state-pair that caused it to be marked. The first such marking in this chain had to be caused by a transition to a missing state-pair. Hence, (p', q') is distinguishable, and (p, q) must be distinguishable, which again contradicts the assertion of equivalence.

Proof: "Only" Part. Let (p, q) be an unmarked pair appearing in the pairs table at the end of the process, but p and q are distinguishable in the machine. That they appear in the feasible set is no evidence of equivalence or distinguishability. However, if they are distinguishable, then there is some string $x = a_1 a_2 a_3 \ldots a_n$ such that x is accepted by the machine in state p but not in q, or vice versa. Without loss of generality, assume that q is the nonaccepting state. The failure to accept can be the result of a machine block prior to completing string x, or the result of completing x but terminating in a nonhalt state. Suppose first that the machine blocks. Then the state sequences beginning with p and with q look like this:

$$p \vdash p_2 \vdash p_3 \vdash \ldots \vdash p_n \quad \text{(acceptance)}$$

$$q \vdash q_2 \vdash \ldots \vdash q_m \quad \text{(block)}$$

where $m < n$, and $n = |x|$. Now states p_m and q_m clearly are not in the feasible state-pair set; at least one transition (on the mth token of string x) can occur on p_m, but not on q_m. It follows that (p_{m-1}, q_{m-1}) is either not in the feasible state-pair or has become marked, because there is a transition from the pair (p_{m-1}, q_{m-1}) to (p_m, q_m), and the latter is not in the feasible state-pair–set. Similarly, (p_{m-2}, q_{m-2}) become marked, and so on, and eventually (p, q) become marked.

If the failure to recognize string x in state q is because of a nonhalt state on completing x, then the state sequences beginning with p and with q look like this:

$$p \vdash p_2 \vdash p_3 \vdash \ldots \vdash p_n$$

$$q \vdash q_2 \vdash q_3 \vdash \ldots \vdash q_n$$

Here, p_n is in the halt set, but q_n is not. The pair (p_n, q_n) therefore cannot be in the feasible state-pair–set. Thus (p_{n-1}, q_{n-1}) become marked, and because they are marked and there is a transition step from (p_{n-2}, q_{n-2}) to (p_{n-1}, q_{n-1}), the pair (p_{n-2}, q_{n-2}) become marked, and so on. Eventually (p, q) becomes marked. QED

3.9. Exercises

In these exercises, FSMs are described by giving the transition function only. In each case, the state-set is the set of capital letters that appear. The input alphabet is the set of lowercase letters and other symbols that label the columns of the transition function table. The start state is the state labeling the first row of the table. The halt states are those the names of which are preceded by an asterisk where they appear as row labels.

1. Show that the FSM of figure 3.1 accepts these strings:

   ```
   +1.314
   -.0002
   3.14159
   10000.
   +005
   ```

   but not these:

   ```
   +-14
   .74-
   2+.67
   .001.
   ```

2. Extend the FSM of figure 3.1 to accept decimal numbers with an optional exponent. If present, the exponent consists of E, followed by an optional sign, followed by either one or two digits.

3. Design an FSM that accepts strings of a's and b's, where the number of a's is even and the number of b's is odd. The a's and b's may be interspersed in any order.

4. Design an FSM that accepts strings of a's and b's, interspersed in any order, such that the numbers of a's and of b's are either both odd or both even.

5. Draw a complete trace of the configurations of the machine of figure 3.1 for these strings:

```
d.dd
-.d
+dd.ddd
.d
```

6. Find a sequence of moves of the NDFSM of figure 3.3 that accepts each of the following strings:

```
+13.14
-.002
3.14159
1000.
+056
```

7. Show that the NDFSM of figure 3.3 cannot accept any of these strings:

```
+84-
7.4-
5.+91
.001.
```

8. Trace the backtracking model of the NDFSM of figure 3.3 for these strings:

```
+2.573
-.002
3.14
100.
+05
```

9. Transform the following NDFSM into an equivalent DFSM by removing empty cycles, noncyclic empty moves, and nondeterminism. Also locate and remove inaccessible states.

	a	b	c	ε
A	E,F		B,C	B
B			C	D
*C		E		
*D			C,E	A
E	E,F		C,E	
F			A,E	C

10. Transform the following NDFSM into an equivalent DFSM and remove inaccessible states.

	a	b	c	ε
A			D	
B		F		
C		D	C	G
D	D	F		
E				G
F		H	B	C,E
G		E		A,H
*H	B	D		E

11. Show that if two states are k-distinguishable for $k \geq 0$ then they are $(k + 1)$-distinguishable.

12. Consider all machines of n states each. Give a bound for the largest k such that some pair of states is $(k + 1)$-distinguishable but k-equivalent.

13. Design an algorithm that tests two reduced machines for isomorphism. Program and run your algorithm in your favorite programming language.

14. Show that the two members of each feasible state-pair are 1-equivalent for a FSM in which a halt can be reached from every state.

15. Find the sets of equivalent states for the following DFSM. Construct an equivalent reduced DFSM by merging the equivalent states.

	a	b	c
A	B	E	F
B	C		H
C	A		H
D	F		E
*E	E	F	G
F	D		E
G	B	H	D
*H	H	D	A

16. Make the following NDFSM deterministic. Remove inaccessible states and reduce to a minimum-state DFSM.

	a	b	c	ϵ
S	C	B		A
A	B		C	B
B			B	C
*C			C	

17. From the following DFSM, construct an equivalent regular grammar.

	a	b	c
S	A		
A		B	C
B	A	D	
*C		D	C
*D		B	

18. Show that the regular grammar constructed from an arbitrary DFSM by the method of section 3.4 is equivalent to the DFSM.

19. For each of these regular grammars, (a) construct an equivalent NDFSM, (b) construct an equivalent DFSM, (c) remove inaccessible states, and (d) reduce the DFSM.

```
S → sA | ε                    S → aB | ε
A → aA | aC | bC              B → bC | bD | bE
C → cA | dA | d               C → cB | c
                              E → cB | c
                              D → d
```

20. Show that the NDFSM constructed from an arbitrary regular grammar by the method of section 3.4 is equivalent to the grammar.

21. For each of the following regular expressions, list all strings of four or fewer symbols that are in the language defined by the regular expression.

    ```
    l {d | l}
    {+ | ε}d{d}
    {+ d | ε}{d}
    [a | b}{c | d}
    {ab} | {cd}
    {a}(b | c){d}
    ```

22. Construct an FSM that recognizes the language defined by this regular expression:

    ```
    (+ | - | ε)d{d}
    ```

23. Write a regular expression that defines decimal numbers consisting of an optional sign, one or more digits with a single optional decimal point immediately preceding or following the digits or between two of the digits, and an optional exponent. The exponent consists of E, followed by an optional sign, and one or two digits. Construct an equivalent FSM, make it deterministic, and minimize it.

24. Construct a regular expression that is equivalent to the following regular grammar, using the method of section 3.5.4.

    ```
    S → cC
    S → a
    A → cA
    A → aB
    B → aB
    B → c
    C → aS
    C → aA
    C → bB
    C → cC
    C → a
    ```

25. Design and write a program to read a regular expression, construct an equivalent NDFSM, make it deterministic, minimize it, and emit a program that implements the resulting reduced DFSM. If your generated program is table-driven, emit the necessary table.

3.10. Bibliographical Notes

The earliest work on FSM is in McCullough [1943]. Kleene [1952] and [1956] first introduced the notion of regular expressions. Algorithms for the inter-conversion of state transition functions and regular expressions are found in

McNaughton and Yamada [McNaughton, 1960]. An early review paper is Brzozowski [1962]. The material on equivalence is largely from Huffman [1954], Moore [1956], Mealy [1955], and Aufenkamp and Hohn [Aufenkamp, 1957], as found in Gill [1962]. A regularity test for a CFG is given by Stearns [1967]. The literature on FSMs and their applications to logic circuitry is extensive; some representative texts are Booth [1967], Gill [1962], Harrison [1965], Hartmanis and Stearns [Hartmanis, 1966], Kohavi [1971], Maley and Earle [Maley, 1963], McCluskey [1965a], and McCluskey and Bartee [McCluskey, 1965b]. In addition, Aho and Ullman (Aho [1972a]) and Hopcroft and Ullman [Hopcroft, 1969] contain material on FSMs and their relation to language recognition. Lexical analysis has been discussed by many authors; representative works are Johnson [1968], Conway [1963], DeRemer [1974c], Gries [1971], Feldman [1968].

CHAPTER 4

TOP-DOWN PARSING

Such is our pride, our folly, or our fate, that few, but such as cannot write, translate.

. . . Sir John Denham

A top-down parser conceptually develops a derivation tree for a sentence in the language from the root node down. We have seen previously that the essential problem is that of deciding which of several productions with the same left member applies in the tree next. We always know the next left-member, for it is associated with a tree node known to be a part of the final derivation tree.

We first address ourselves to the general problem of a top-down translator for a context-free language by examining a general nondeterministic parser. Although a nondeterministic machine is impractical in a real compiler, it exhibits many of the properties that must exist in one. Furthermore, any context-free language can be parsed by such a machine and we can easily prove that the machine recognizes exactly the language of the CFG used to construct it.

A deterministic top-down parsing machine unfortunately cannot be constructed for every CFG; there are context-free languages that cannot be recognized by such a machine.

However, those grammars with a deterministic top-down parser are sufficiently powerful to define many common programming languages and therefore to construct useful and efficient compilers.

4.1. Nondeterministic Push-Down Automata

The nondeterministic top-down parser we shall construct is an example of a general class of push-down automata, or PDA. A *push-down* or *stack automaton* contains (1) an *input string* of symbols in the alphabet of the machine, (2) a *read head,* which may examine one symbol in the input list at a time and may move only from left to right, (3) a *finite-state machine,* which serves to control the system's operations, and (4) a *last-in-first-out push-down stack.* See figure 4.1(a).

A *move* in a PDA is governed by the present state, the input symbol under the read head, and the symbol on the top of the push-down stack. In a move, the read head is advanced, the state is changed, and the top stack symbol is replaced by some string (possibly empty).

A PDA scans its input string by a succession of such moves. It may be unable to move at some point, in which case some other set of choices made earlier must be tried. If a set of choices permits the machine to scan the input string and either

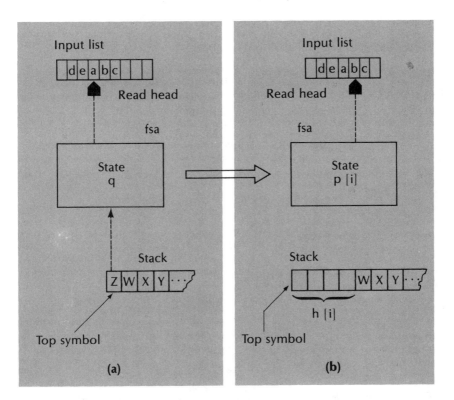

Figure 4.1.   Non-empty move of a push-down automaton. The read head is advanced one token in the input list; the state changes from q to p[i]; token Z on the stack is replaced by a string h[i].

end in a halt state or empty its stack, then the input string is said to be *accepted* by the PDA.

A PDA is therefore a seven-tuple $(K, \Sigma, H, \delta, q_0, Z_0, F)$, where:

- K is a finite set of states.

- Σ is a finite input alphabet; that is, the set of symbols appearing in the input list.

- H is a finite push-down stack alphabet. For generality, we permit symbols used on the push-down stack to be different from those used elsewhere.

- $q_0 \in K$ is the initial state of the machine.

- $Z_0 \in H$ is the initial symbol on the push-down stack.

- $F \subset K$ is a set of final or halt states.

- δ is a transition function, mapping a triple (q, a, Z) to a set of pairs $\{(p_1, h_1), (p_2, h_2), \dots \}$, where q is in the state set K, a is a member of $\Sigma \cup \{\epsilon\}$,

Z is in the push-down stack alphabet H, p_1, p_2, . . . are members of the state set K, and h_1, h_2, . . . are strings in H^*.

A PDA move is governed by its transition function δ, just as in an FSM. However, in a push-down automaton, the move is controlled not only by the next input symbol and the present state but also by the symbol on the top of the push-down stack. Furthermore, the result of a move is not only some new state but also the replacement of the top symbol on the push-down stack by a string of symbols drawn from the stack alphabet H.

Let us explore a typical move in more detail. Consider a member of the transition function:

$$\delta(q, a, Z) = \{(p_1, h_1), (p_2, h_2), . . . , (p_m, h_m)\} \qquad (4.1)$$

In figure 4.1(a), the PDA is shown in a state in which symbol a is under the read head, the controlling FSA is in state q, and the top symbol on the push-down stack is Z. These are the conditions necessary to invoke the move expressed by the transition function member, 4.1. The move is made by choosing one of the pairs in the set $\delta(q, a, Z)$, assuming that at least one pair exists. Suppose we choose the pair (p_i, h_i). Then the next state of the FSA is p_i, the symbol Z on the stack top is replaced by the string h_i, and the read head is advanced to the next symbol in the input list, figure 4.1(b). (Note that the push-down stack is drawn with its top to the left, which is useful in describing a top-down PDA, as we shall see.)

There are two possible variations on 4.1. The symbol a in $\delta(q, a, Z)$ may be the empty string, ϵ. If this is so, then the machine may move without considering the input symbol; it may move on the basis of its state and the top stack symbol alone. The move also is made without moving the read head.

In a second variation, the string h_i in a transition set pair may be empty. Then the stack top symbol Z is effectively popped from the stack, exposing the symbol (if any) beneath it. With this variation, the stack can be reduced and ultimately emptied.

A PDA may halt in either of two ways—by empty stack or by final state. It is said to halt by empty stack and accept the input string if, on the move in which the read head advances just past the end of the input list, the push-down stack is emptied. It is said to halt by final state and accept the input string if, on the move in which the read head advances just past the end of the input list, the FSM enters a member of the final state set F. A given PDA always is defined to halt in one manner or the other. However, it can be shown that for every PDA of one kind, there exists an equivalent PDA of the other kind, so that we may choose whichever is more convenient.

In either case, a nondeterministic PDA (NDPDA) is said to accept a given input string if there exists a sequence of moves that lead from its initial state and stack contents to a halt condition.

The PDA is said to *block* if it fails to accept an input string.

Configurations and Moves

A *configuration* of a PDA is a triple (q, w, h), where q is some state in K, w is the portion of the input list from the read head position to its right end and a member of Σ^*, and h is the contents of the push-down stack and a member of H^*.

A configuration contains all the information needed to predict the future behavior of a PDA. For example, the PDA of figure 4.1(a) can be described by the configuration:

$$(q, abc. . ., ZWXY. . .)$$

The PDA of figure 4.1(b) can be described by the configuration:

$$(p_i, bc. . ., h_iWXY. . .)$$

A move in a PDA can be regarded as a means of transforming one configuration into another one, which provides a more concise way of defining a machine move, as follows.

We say that:

$$(q, ax, Zh') \vdash (p, x, hh')$$

is a possible move if and only if (p, h) is in δ(q, a, Z). (Note that this move definition is consistent with the possibility that a = ϵ, and h = ϵ.)

A sequence of one or more moves is denoted by $\vdash^+$. A sequence of zero or more moves, where a "zero" move is no change in the present configuration, is denoted by $\vdash^*$. With this notation, we can define the language L(M) recognized by a PDA M as:

$$L(M) = \{\ w\ |\ (q_0, w, Z_0) \vdash^* (p, \epsilon, \epsilon)\ \} \qquad (4.2)$$

for some p in K, where machine M halts by empty stack, or as:

$$L(M) = \{\ w\ |\ (q_0, w, Z_0) \vdash^* (p, \epsilon, h),\ p\ in\ F\ \} \qquad (4.3)$$

for some h in H^*, where machine M halts by final state.

The definition in equation 4.2 can be translated to English roughly as follows: the language L(M) of a PDA M consists of all those strings w such that, given a PDA initially in state q_0, with stack contents Z_0 and the read head positioned at the first symbol of w, there exists a sequence of moves that results in the read head completing the input string, an empty stack, and some end state (not necessarily a final state).

The definition in equation 4.3 can be similarly interpreted.

Example.   Consider the two-state machine defined by figure 4.2. The states are P and Q, the input symbols are 0 and 1, and the stack symbols are R, B, and G. This machine recognizes all palindromes in the symbols 0 and 1—that is, the language:

$$\{\ w\ w^R\ |\ w\ \epsilon\ \{0,\ 1\}^*\ \}$$

| | | "From" | | "To" | | | |
Row	State p	Input symbol a	Stack symbol z	State q_1	Stack h_1	State q_2	State h_2
1	P	0	R	P	BR		
2	P	1	R	P	GR		
3	P	0	B	P	BB	Q	ϵ
4	P	0	G	P	BG		
5	P	1	B	P	GB		
6	P	1	G	P	GG	Q	ϵ
7	P	ϵ	R	Q	ϵ		
8	Q	0	B	Q	ϵ		
9	Q	1	G	Q	ϵ		
10	Q	ϵ	R	Q	ϵ		

$$d(p, a, Z) = [(q_1, h_1), (q_2, h_2), \ldots]$$

Figure 4.2. A two-state push-down automaton, recognizing the strings $\{ww^R | w \epsilon (0,1)*\}$, the palindromes in $\{0,1\}*$.

where w^R is the string w, but reversed in order.

This machine is nondeterministic because the moves in rows 3 and 6 contain alternative moves, and also because a move may be made on no input symbol (row 7) and alternatives to this exist.

The starting state is P, and the initial stack contents is R. It halts by empty stack.

Consider the input string 001100, and trace the machine configurations:

```
(P, 001100, R)  ⊢ (P, 01100, BR)   by row 1
           or   ⊢ (Q, 001100, ε)   by row 7 (block)
(P, 01100, BR)  ⊢ (P, 1100, BBR)   by row 3a
           or   ⊢ (Q, 1100, R)     by row 3b
(Q, 1100, R)    ⊢ (Q, 1100, ε)     by row 10 (block)
(P, 1100, BBR)  ⊢ (P, 100, GBBR)   by row 5
(P, 100, GBBR)  ⊢ (P, 00, GGBBR)   by row 6a
           or   ⊢ (Q, 00, BBR)     by row 6b
(P, 00, GGBBR)  ⊢ (P, 0, BGGBBR)   by row 4
(P, 0, BGGBBR)  ⊢ (P, ε, BBGGBBR)  by row 3a (block)
           or   ⊢ (Q, ε, GGBBR)    by row 3b (block)
(Q, 00, BBR)    ⊢ (Q, 0, BR)       by row 8
(Q, 0, BR)      ⊢ (Q, ε, R)        by row 8
(Q, ε, R)       ⊢ (Q, ε, ε)        by row 10 (accept)
```

The trace shows the consequences of running down the various blind alleys that occur; nevertheless, the machine ends in an acceptance of the string.

This PDA does its work essentially by pushing B on the stack for every zero and G for every one found in the first half of the input string. It must decide nondeterministically when the second half of the string begins. If it makes the wrong choice for a turning point, it will either exhaust its stack too soon or exhaust its input string before the stack is empty.

It remains in state P for the first half of the string, and switches to state Q for the second half. While in state Q, the input string elements are effectively matched against the stack symbols; 0 must correspond to a B on the stack, and 1 to a G.

The initial stack symbol R becomes buried in the stack as soon as some symbols in w are matched, and becomes uncovered only as the last symbol in the input string is matched. On uncovering R, the stack also is emptied, permitting a halt. R is never pushed onto the stack; it therefore serves as an end marker for the stack.

If the input string is not a palindrome, the machine is unable to find a sequence of accepting moves. It will fail through an inability to match the stacked B's and G's against the zeros and ones in the second half of the input list in state Q, or it will fail through exhausting the stack before exhausting the input list or vice versa.

Context-Free Languages and PDA

An important theorem connecting PDA and context-free languages is the following:

Theorem 4.1.   For every context-free language L there exists an NDPDA M such that M exactly recognizes L, and conversely.

The practical importance of this theorem in compiler systems lies in the realization that essentially every programming language in existence can be expressed almost exactly by a CFG. Thus, theorem 4.1 implies that a mechanical recognizer for the language must be a PDA.

Of course, every regular grammar is also context-free, by its very form. The converse is not true. There are context-free languages that are not regular. The palindrome language is an example of a nonregular language, yet we have seen that a PDA can recognize it. It may also be possible to transform a grammar that appears to be context-free into a regular grammar. However, such a transformation is not always possible and, when it is not, we must have a recognizer with a push-down stack.

The push-down stack in a compiler may be explicitly coded into the program, or it may be hidden. A recursive-descent compiler is an example of a top-down context-free recognizer in which the PDA push-down stack is in fact a stack of return addresses formed during the procedure calls that constitute the parsing process. Because this return address stacking system is invisible to the user of a modern programming language, the parsing process appears not to involve a stack.

Theorem 4.1 has two faces. The most interesting one from the point of view of compiler construction is that a given context-free language can be recognized by some PDA M. The converse—that, given a PDA M, one can construct an equivalent grammar from it—is also true, but is hardly needed in compiler construction. We shall therefore define the machine construction and prove equivalence to the language of the given grammar.

4.1.1. Algorithm 4.1. CFG to a Nondeterministic PDA

The machine M will be nondeterministic, will have only one state, q, and will have the rules defined as follows:

$\delta(q, \epsilon, A)$ contains (q, w) for every production $A \rightarrow w$ in P.

$\delta(q, a, a)$ contains (q, ϵ) for every a in Σ.

The stack symbols are in $N \cup \Sigma$, and the stack initially contains the start symbol S. Machine M will accept by empty stack.

Example 1.   Consider the simple grammar:

$$S \rightarrow 0S1 \mid c$$

This grammar describes the language $\{0\}c\{1\}$, where the numbers of zeros and ones are equal. The transition function rules are:

```
δ(q, 0, 0) = (q, ε)
δ(q, 1, 1) = (q, ε)
δ(q, c, c) = (q, ε)
δ(q, ε, S) = {(q, 0S1), (q, c)}
```

A trace of the machine moves for the string 00c11 is given next. We omit the state from the configurations because it is always the same.

```
(00c11,    S)   ⊢  (00c11,  0S1)  (O.K.)
            or  ⊢  (00c11,  c)   (N.G.)
(00c11,  0S1) ⊢  (0c11,  S1)
(0c11,   S1)  ⊢  (0c11,  0S11)
            or  ⊢  (0c11,  c1)  (N.G.)
(0c11,  0S11) ⊢  (c11,  S11)
(c11,   S11)  ⊢  (c11,  0S111)  (N.G.)
            or  ⊢  (c11,  c11)
(c11,   c11)  ⊢  (11,  11)
(11,    11)   ⊢  (1,  1)
(1,     1)    ⊢  (ε,  ε)  (acceptance)
```

Example 2.   Empty production rules are acceptable, too:

$$S \rightarrow 0S1 \mid \epsilon$$

The transition function is:

```
δ(q, 0, 0) = (q, ε)
δ(q, 1, 1) = (q, ε)
δ(q, ε, S) = {(q, 0S1), (q, ε)}
```

Then the string 0011 is accepted as follows:

$$(0011, S) \vdash (0011, 0S1) \vdash (011, S1) \vdash (011, 0S11)$$
$$\vdash (11, S11) \vdash (11, 11) \vdash (1, 1) \vdash (\epsilon, \epsilon), \text{ acceptance.}$$

Discussion

By following these examples of machine traces, we can see that the effect of the rule:

$$\delta(q, a, a) = (q, \epsilon) \qquad \text{for all } a \in \Sigma$$

is to *match* input terminal symbols against terminal symbols on the stack top. The move is possible only when the two symbols match, and the result is to move the read head and pop the symbol from the stack. This matching operation ceases only when a nonterminal symbol appears on the stack top. At that point, the other rule applies:

$$\delta(q, \epsilon, A) \qquad \text{contains } (q, w) \text{ for every } A \rightarrow w \text{ in } P$$

The machine must somehow choose among one of several productions with the same left member; the left member is known because it is on the stack top.

Once a choice is made, the nonterminal A is replaced on the stack by the string w, which in general contains both terminals and nonterminals.

Recall that the production rule choice problem also was present in attempting to construct a derivation tree for a sentence from the top down. We have not solved the choice problem, but are examining it from a different point of view.

Proof of Theorem 4.1.   We prove the stronger result expressed by the following lemma.

Lemma 4.1. $(q, wx, Ay) \vdash^* (q, x, y)$ in M if and only if $A \Rightarrow^* w$ in grammar G, where A is in N, wx is in Σ^*, and y is in $(N \cup \Sigma)^*$.

This lemma includes theorem 4.1 as a special case, with $A = S$, and $x = y = \epsilon$.

Proof: "If" Part.   We prove the if part of the lemma by induction on the number of steps in the derivation $A \Rightarrow^* w$. Consider a derivation of one step. Then $A \rightarrow w$ is a production, with w a terminal string. This production implies that there is a transition:

$$\delta(q, \epsilon, A) \text{ contains } (q, w)$$

which yields the machine move:

$$(q, wx, Ay) \vdash (q, wx, wy)$$

Now w is a terminal string. If its length $|w| = n$, then we may invoke n applications of the matching rules, which have the form:

$$\delta(q, a, a) = \{(q, \epsilon)\}$$

for every terminal a in the alphabet. These n applications yield the configuration:

$$(q, x, y)$$

which was to be shown.

Now assume that the derivation $A \Rightarrow^* w$ requires k steps, where $k > 1$, and that lemma 4.1 holds for all $k' < k$. The first step of the derivation has the form:

$$A \Rightarrow X_1 X_2 X_3 \ldots X_n \Rightarrow^* x_1 x_2 x_3 \ldots x_n = w,$$

where:

$$X_1 \Rightarrow^* x_1, X_2 \Rightarrow^* x_2, \ldots$$

and:

$$X_1, \ldots, X_n \text{ are in } N \cup \Sigma$$

Thus the move:

$$(q, wx, Ay) \vdash (q, x_1 x_2 \ldots x_n x, X_1 X_2 \ldots X_n y)$$

exists. Now if X_1 is a terminal symbol, it must be equal to x_1, and the transition $\delta(q, x_1, x_1) = \{(q, \epsilon)\}$ can be made. If X_1 is nonterminal, then by the inductive hypothesis (because $X_1 \Rightarrow^* x_1$ by less than k moves), the moves:

$$(q, x_1 r, X_1 s) \vdash^* (q, r, s)$$

for any strings r and s exist.

Thus, in either case, the following moves exist:

$$(q, x_1 x_2 \ldots x_n x, X_1 X_2 \ldots X_n \ y) \vdash^* (q, x_2 \ldots x_n x, X_2 \ldots X_n y)$$

More repetitions of this process, for $X_2, \ldots, X_n$, eventually yields the configuration (q, x, y), which was to be shown. QED

Proof: "Only If" Part.   Let $(q, wx, Ay) \vdash (q, x, y)$ in k moves; we prove that $A \Rightarrow^* w$ by induction on the number of moves, k.

For $k = 1$, w must be ϵ and $A \to \epsilon$ is in P. (There are no other possibilities with A on the top of the stack, in one machine move.) Thus assume the lemma valid for all moves of length $k' < k$; we prove it valid for k. The first move must have the form:

$$(q, wx, Ay) \vdash (q, wx, X_1 \ldots X_ny)$$

where $A \rightarrow X_1 \ldots X_n$ is in P, and:

$$(q, x_i, X_i) \vdash^* (q, \epsilon, \epsilon)$$

for all $1 \le i \le n$ in k' moves or less, where $w = x_1x_2\ldots x_n$.

Then $X_i \Rightarrow^* x_i$ for all i, by the inductive hypothesis; but putting all this together, we find:

$$A \Rightarrow X_1 \ldots X_n \Rightarrow^* x_1X_2 \ldots X_n \Rightarrow^* x_1 x_2X_3 \ldots X_n \Rightarrow^* \ldots \Rightarrow^* x_1x_2 \ldots x_n = w$$

QED

The Input List, the Stack, and Sentential Forms

An interesting property of the NDPDA defined in algorithm 4.1 is expressed by the following theorem.

Theorem 4.2.   Let (q, y, h) be any configuration of the NDPDA for some grammar G, where the input string is xy, such that:

$$(q, xy, S) \vdash^* (q, y, h)$$

Then xh is a left-most sentential form in G; that is, $S \Rightarrow^* xh$.

The converse is also true: given any sentential form xh in G, such that x is a terminal string, and at most one left-most symbol in h is terminal, then (q, y, h) is a configuration of the NDPDA such that:

$$(q, xy, S) \vdash^* (q, y, h)$$

To visualize the significance of this theorem, consider figure 4.1(a). The string x is "...de", y is "abc...", and the stack string h is "ZWXY...". The theorem says that "...deZWXY..." is a sentential form. In short, the input list to the left of the read head, when concatenated with the stack, is a sentential form.

Proof.   Note that the theorem is trivially true for the initial configuration; the input string prefix x is empty, and S is on the stack. Therefore, assume that the theorem holds for n moves of the NDPDA, $n \ge 0$, and consider the (n + 1)th move. This move either is a *matching* move, or a production rule *replacement* move. If a matching move, the string xh is clearly unchanged, because first symbol in h effectively is moved to the last position in x.

If a replacement move, the string xh before the move is of the form xAz, where h = Az. After the move, the string has the form xwz, where $A \rightarrow w$ is a production. By the inductive hypothesis, xAz is a sentential form; that is:

$$S \Rightarrow^* xAz$$

However, because A → w is a production, xwz also is a sentential form:

$$S \Rightarrow^* xAz \Rightarrow xwz$$

QED

A proof of the converse is similar.

4.2. LL(k) Grammars

The LL(k) grammars are a proper subset of the CFGs. They are the largest such class that permits deterministic left-to-right top-down recognition with a look-ahead of k symbols.

The deterministic top-down parsing problem is represented by figure 2.11, in chapter 2. We have some nonterminal node (T in the figure) and an uncompleted string ((a*a) in the figure).

If the correct production can be deduced from the partially constructed tree and the next k symbols in the unscanned string, for every possible top-down parsing step, then we say that the grammar is LL(k).

It is never obvious whether a given grammar is LL(k); nor can we hope to examine every possible parsing step. We appear to need two algorithms: one to test a grammar for the LL(k) condition and another one to generate a parsing table, similar to figure 2.16, for some grammar. It turns out that only the latter algorithm is needed; the failure to generate a parsing table will be apparent from the algorithm, and this failure will mean that the grammar is not LL(k). If the table generation succeeds, then the grammar is LL(k), and we not only will have a definition of a deterministic parser, but also will know that the grammar is unambiguous.

4.2.1. Definitions

Consideration of lookahead of k symbols is considerably simplified if there always exist at least k symbols to examine. For this reason, we introduce a new terminal symbol ⊥ not already in the grammar, and append k of these symbols to every input string, prior to parsing. Hence, we introduce a new nonterminal S′ and a production:

$$S' \rightarrow S\perp^k$$

where S is the grammar's start symbol, and $\perp^k$ is a string of k symbols ⊥. The symbol S′ becomes the new start symbol.

   1. A production A → x_1 in a CFG G is called an *LL(k) production* if, in G:

$$S' \Rightarrow^* w A y \Rightarrow w x_1 y \Rightarrow^* w z. . .,$$

$$S' \Rightarrow^* w A y' \Rightarrow w x_2 y' \Rightarrow^* w z. . .,$$

$$|z| = k, z \in \Sigma^*, \text{ and } w \in (N \cup \Sigma)^*, \text{ then } x_1 = x_2.$$

2. A nonterminal in a CFG is called an *LL(k) nonterminal* if all its productions
are LL(k) productions.

For example, in the grammar:

$$S \rightarrow Abc \mid aAcb$$

$$A \rightarrow \epsilon \mid b \mid c$$

S is an LL(1) nonterminal, whereas A is an LL(2) nonterminal. The strings
derivable from S are (first production) bc, bbc, cbc, and (second production) acb, abcb, accb. Clearly, the second production is selected
uniquely on the lookahead symbol a, whereas the first is selected on symbols b or c.

For the A productions, we need to consider the sentential forms in which
A is embedded; for example, Abc and aAcb. By the definition, the string
preceding A is different, so we need consider only whether the three A
productions can be distinguished within Abc and within aAcb. In the
former, we have the three lookahead strings bc, bb and cb; these are
distinguishable with k = 2 but not with k = 1. In the latter production, the
lookahead strings are cb, bc, and cc; again, these are distinguishable with
k = 2 but not with k = 1. The A productions are therefore LL(2) but are
not LL(1).

Note that if the lookahead sets were considered without regard to the
particular sentential form prefix w in $S \Rightarrow^* wAy$, then the A nonterminal
would require three lookahead symbols.

It is clear that an LL(k) grammar is also an LL(k + 1) grammar, for
$k \geq 1$.

3. A grammar such that every production is LL(k) is an *LL(k) grammar*.

4.2.2. Two LL(k) Theorems

Theorem 4.3.   Each LL(k) grammar is unambiguous.

Proof.   An ambiguity would lead to contradictions with definitions 1 and 2.

Theorem 4.4.   An LL(k) grammar has no left-recursive nonterminals (nonterminals A such that $A \Rightarrow^+ Aw$ for some w).

Proof.   Suppose that a nonterminal A_0 is left-recursive. Then there is some
sequence of nonterminals $A_0, A_1, \ldots, A_n$ that are all left-recursive, and such
that:

$$A_0 \Rightarrow^+ A_1 x_1 \Rightarrow^+ A_2 x_2 \Rightarrow^+ \ldots \Rightarrow^+ A_n x_n$$

and $A_n = A_0$. Now at least one of these must have another production; otherwise,
all of them would be useless and could be deleted from the grammar. Also, at

least one of the x_i must be incapable of deriving the empty string; if they all could, then we could have a derivation sequence $A_0 \Rightarrow^+ A_0$, and an obvious ambiguity. Thus one of the A_i (call it A from here on) is such that:

$$A \Rightarrow Bx' \Rightarrow^+ Ax$$

where $|x| > 0$, and also $A \rightarrow y$, where y is not Bx'. Then we can construct the derivation sequences:

$$S \Rightarrow^+ rAx^k \ldots \Rightarrow rBx'x^k \ldots \Rightarrow^* rAx^{k+1} \ldots \Rightarrow ryx^{k+1} \ldots \Rightarrow^* rz \ldots$$

$$S \Rightarrow^+ rAx^k \ldots \Rightarrow ryx^k \ldots \Rightarrow^* rz \ldots$$

where $|z| = k$, and they contradict the assumption that the grammar is LL(k). QED

The LL(k) definition states that, given a left-most sentential form wAx, such that w matches the first $|w|$ symbols of the input string, then the next production $A \rightarrow y$ can be inferred from the next k input symbols. It appears that to select the production $A \rightarrow y$ we need a mapping of all strings wAx' to the production set, where $|x'| = k$. The resulting LL(k) parsing table would be impossibly large. The next two theorems show that we do not need such a complete mapping—a mapping of strings Ax' to the production set is sufficient. Before we can introduce these theorems, we need to develop two useful functions: $FIRST_k(w)$ and $FOLLOW_k(w)$.

4.2.3. FIRST and FOLLOW Sets

The domain of $FIRST_k$ is some string w in $(N \cup \Sigma)^*$ and the domain of $FOLLOW_k$ is a nonterminal A in N. The functions are defined as follows:

$$FIRST_k(w) = \{ x \mid w \Rightarrow^* xy \wedge xy \in \Sigma^* \wedge$$

$$(if \ |xy| < k \ then \ y = \epsilon \ else \ |x| = k)\}$$

$$FOLLOW_k(A) = \{ x \mid S \Rightarrow^* uAy \wedge x \in FIRST_k(y)\}$$

where the derivations are left-most. That is, $FIRST_k(w)$ for some string w is the set of all leading terminal strings of length k or less in the strings derivable from w. A string x in $FIRST_k(w)$ is less than k in length only if x is fully derivable from w; that is, $w \Rightarrow^* x$, and $|x| < k$. The empty string is in $FIRST_k(w)$ if $w \Rightarrow^* \epsilon$. Note that w may include or consist of nonterminals.

$FOLLOW_k(A)$ is the set of all derivable terminal strings of length k or less that can follow A in some left-most sentential form. The empty string ϵ will be in $FOLLOW_k(A)$ if A is the last symbol in some sentential form. In particular, ϵ is in $FOLLOW_k(S)$, where S is the start symbol.

With these definitions, the following useful properties can be proved readily. In these, the domain of the $FIRST_k$ set is extended to include a set of strings; that is, $FIRST_k(U \ V)$, where U and V are sets of strings, is the union of all $FIRST_k(u \ v)$, where u is in U and v is in V. Also $FIRST_k(w) = \epsilon$ for $k \leq 0$.

1. $FIRST_k(aw) = \{az \mid z = FIRST_{k-1}(w)\}$ for any string w, where a is in Σ.

2. $FIRST_k(\epsilon) = \{\epsilon\}$.

3. $FIRST_k(x\ y) = FIRST_k(FIRST_k(x)\ FIRST_k(y)) = FIRST_k\ (x\ FIRST_k(y)) = FIRST_k(FIRST_k(x)\ y)$.

4. Given a production $A \rightarrow w$ in G, $FIRST_k(A)$ contains $FIRST_k(w)$.

5. Given a production $A \rightarrow xXy$ in G, $FOLLOW_k(X)$ contains $FIRST_k(y\ FOLLOW_k(A))$. Note that y may be the empty string.

6. $FOLLOW_k(S)$ contains ϵ, where S is the start symbol of G.

Properties 1 and 2 should be obvious from the definitions. Property 3 expresses associativity of the $FIRST_k$ operator and concatenation; however, note that $FIRST_k(x\ y)$ is not identical to $FIRST_k(x)\ FIRST_k(y)$; the former may be of length k at most and the latter may be of length greater than k.

Property 4 follows immediately from the definition.

Example. Consider the following simple grammar G_1. Let us compute $FIRST_k$ and $FOLLOW_k$ for its nonterminals, for $k = 1$:

```
1.  G → E ⊥
2.  E → TE'
3.  E' → + E
4.  E' → ε
5.  T → FT'
6.  T' → *T
7.  T' → ε
8.  F → (E)
9.  F → a
```

- $FIRST_1(F) = \{(, a\}$ from productions 8 and 9

- $FIRST_1(T') = \{*, \epsilon\}$ from productions 6 and 7

- $FIRST_1(T) = FIRST_1(FT') = FIRST_1(F\ FIRST_1(T')) = \{(, a\}$

- $FIRST_1(E') = \{+, \epsilon\}$ from productions 3 and 4

- $FIRST_1(E) = FIRST_1(TE') = \{(, a\}$

- $FIRST_1(G) = FIRST_1(E\bot) = \{(, a\}$

- $FOLLOW_1(E) = \{\bot,)\} \cup FOLLOW_1(E')$ from productions 1, 3, and 8

- $FOLLOW_1(G) = \{\epsilon\}$ using property (6)

- $FOLLOW_1(E') = FOLLOW_1(E)$ from production 2

- $FOLLOW_1(T) = FIRST_1(E'\ FOLLOW_1(E)) \cup FOLLOW_1(T')$ from productions 2 and 6

- $FOLLOW_1(T') = FOLLOW_1(T)$ from production 5

- $FOLLOW_1(F) = FIRST_1(T' FOLLOW_1(T))$ from production 5

By using these relations repeatedly, we obtain the following table of $FOLLOW_1$ sets:

	1	2	3	4	5	6
G	ϵ					
E	$\perp$	$)$				
E'			$\perp$	$)$		
T			$\perp$	$)$	$+$	
T'			$\perp$	$)$	$+$	
F			$\perp$	$)$	$+$	$*$

Columns 1 and 2 are the contents of $FOLLOW_1(G)$ and $FOLLOW_1(E)$ known directly from the productions. The remaining columns are determined by inference from these and the $FOLLOW_1$ and $FIRST_1$ relations given.

FIRST₁ Algorithm

We require a set R[X] associated with each nonterminal X. R[X] ultimately will contain the $FIRST_1$ token strings associated with X. In the following, G is a grammar. The set R[X] is said to be augmented when some token is unioned with R[X] that was not already in R[X]. The *nullable* property was defined in chapter 2: a token is said to be *nullable* if and only if it can derive the empty string in zero or more steps.

```
Set R[X] = ∅ for all nonterminal X in G;
repeat
  For every nonterminal X in G do begin
    For every production X → ω do begin
      Let x₁ x₂ ... xᵣ = ω;
      rx:=1;
      more:=true;
      while more do begin
        if rx>r then begin
          R[X] := R[X] + [ε];
          more:=false
          end
        else if is_terminal(xᵣₓ) then begin
          R[X] := R[X] + [xᵣₓ];
          more:=false
          end
        else begin
          R[X] := R[X] + (R[xᵣₓ] - [ε]);
          if not(nullable(xᵣₓ)) then more:=false
          end;
        rx:=rx+1;
        end {while}
      end {for}
    end; {for}
  until no member of R[X] has been augmented;
```

The core of this algorithm is the WHILE loop that works partially or wholly through the right member ω of a production the left member of which is the nonterminal X. The right member is wholly scanned (by incrementing the index rx) only while each of its tokens (from left to right) is nullable. If the whole right member can be so scanned, then the empty string is added to R[X]. For each nonterminal so seen in the right member, its R set (less the empty string) is used to augment R[X].

QPARSER contains a utility that reports $FIRST_1$ for all nonterminals.

FOLLOW₁ Algorithm

The $FOLLOW_1$ algorithm assumes that we have available the $FIRST_1$ set of every nonterminal. $FOLLOW_1$ will be defined on every terminal and nonterminal symbol in the grammar.

This algorithm is more efficient given a cross-reference table that can locate the position of any token in every production in which it appears in a right member. We need that reference because the follow set of a token T will be the set:

$$FIRST_1(\alpha \ concat \ FOLLOW_1(L)),$$

where α is the portion of a right member following T in some production:

$$L \rightarrow \gamma \ T \ \alpha$$

The algorithm determines whether α is ϵ or derives ϵ from the $FIRST_1$ functions of its components. In either case, the follow set of T will be augmented by $FOLLOW_1(L)$. Otherwise, the follow set of T is augmented by $FIRST_1(\alpha)$. Note that we do not need $FIRST_1$ of a string in the algorithm, only $FIRST_1$ of nonterminals.

One or more passes are required to accumulate the $FOLLOW_1$ sets of all tokens. We stop when a pass fails to augment any of the $FOLLOW_1$ sets. The set F[X] will represent $FOLLOW_1[X]$ on completion of the algorithm.

```
For all tokens X in G do F[X] := [];
Let S be the start token of G;
F[S] := [⊥];
repeat
  for every token X in G do
  if not(X in [ε, ⊥]) then begin
    for (every production Z → ω such that
            X appears in ω) do
    for (every appearance of X in ω) do begin
      let ω = α X b₁ b₂ ... bᵣ;
        {where α ε (N ∪ Σ)*;
          and bᵢ ε N for 1≤i≤r}
      let p := 1;   {p = position in β }
      let more := true;
      while more do begin
        if p ≥ r then begin
          F[X] := F[X] + F[Z];
          more:=false;
        end
```

```
else begin
    F[X] := F[X] + (FIRST₁[bₚ₊₁] - [ε]);
    if nullable(bₚ) then p:=p+1
    else more:=false;
    end {if}
  end {while}
end {for}
end; {if, for}
until (no F[S] has been augmented);
```

QPARSER contains a utility that reports $FOLLOW_1$ for all tokens.

4.2.4 Some Implications of the LL(k) Definition

We now use the FIRST and FOLLOW functions in a set of theorems that will lead to an efficient LL(1) parser.

Theorem 4.5. Let G be a CFG. Then G is LL(k) if and only if, for every distinct pair of productions $A \rightarrow u$ and $A \rightarrow v$, and every left-most sentential form wAx derivable in G, $FIRST_k(ux) \cap FIRST_k(vx) = \varnothing$.

Now suppose that G has no empty productions and that G is LL(1). Then neither u nor v is empty, nor can either of these derive ϵ. Clearly x does not matter, because $FIRST_1(ux) = FIRST_1(u)$ and $FIRST_1(vx) = FIRST_1(u)$. It also means that the particular sentential form in which A appears is no longer important. We then have the weaker condition expressed in theorem 4.5.

Theorem 4.6. Let G be a CFG with no empty productions. Then G is LL(1) if and only if, for every pair of productions $A \rightarrow u$ and $A \rightarrow v$, $FIRST_1(u) \cap FIRST_1(v) = \varnothing$.

Proof. The proof is trivial, given theorem 4.5.

Is there a similar LL(1) condition for grammars with empty productions? Consider theorem 4.5 again. If G contains empty productions, then u or v can be empty, or can derive empty strings. If $u \xrightarrow{*} \epsilon$ is possible, then clearly $FIRST_1(ux)$ includes $FIRST_1(x)$, and $FIRST_1(x)$ need not be a subset of $FIRST_1(u)$. However, note that x follows A in the left-most sentential form wAx of the theorem, and this suggests theorem 4.7.

Theorem 4.7. Let G be a CFG. Then G is LL(1) if and only if, for every pair of productions $A \rightarrow u$ and $A \rightarrow v$, the following condition holds:

$$FIRST_1(u\ FOLLOW_1(A)) \cap FIRST_1(v\ FOLLOW_1(A)) = \varnothing$$

The FIRST-FOLLOW condition is certainly necessary for G to be LL(1). If u can derive ϵ, then $FIRST_1(ux)$ contains $FIRST_1(x)$ and $FIRST_1(x)$ is a subset of $FOLLOW_1(A)$. We must show that the condition is also sufficient—which is perhaps surprising, because $FOLLOW_1(A)$ is related not to any one sentential form, but rather to the entire class of sentential forms containing A. We therefore prove sufficiency—the "if" part of the theorem.

Proof.   Suppose that G is not LL(1). Then there exists a pair of derivations:

$$S' \Rightarrow^* wAx \Rightarrow wux \Rightarrow^* wz$$

and:

$$S' \Rightarrow^* wAx' \Rightarrow wvx' \Rightarrow^* wz'$$

where $u \neq v$, and $FIRST_1(z) = FIRST_1(z')$. Now:

$$ux \Rightarrow^* z$$

$$\text{and } vx \Rightarrow^* z'$$

Now let $z = u'x'$ and $z' = v'x''$ where $u \Rightarrow^* u'$, $x \Rightarrow^* x'$, $v \Rightarrow^* v'$, and $x \Rightarrow^* x''$. Note that $FIRST_1(x')$ is in $FOLLOW_1(A)$, and $FIRST_1(x'')$ also is in $FOLLOW_1(A)$. We now examine three cases, depending on whether u or v, or neither or both, are empty:

Case 1: $u' \neq \epsilon$ and $v' \neq \epsilon$. Then clearly:

$$FIRST_1(z) \subset FIRST_1(u) \subset FIRST_1(u \text{ FOLLOW}(A))$$

and:

$$FIRST_1(z') \subset FIRST_1(v) \subset FIRST_1(v \text{ FOLLOW}(A))$$

Then:

$$FIRST_1(u) \cap FIRST_1(v) \neq \emptyset$$

QED

(We have proven that premise P implies Q by proving that $\sim$Q implies $\sim$P.)
Case 2: $u' = \epsilon$ and $v' \neq \epsilon$.

Here:

$$FIRST_1(z') \subset FIRST_1(v) \subset FIRST_1(v \text{ FOLLOW}(A))$$

and:

$$FIRST_1(z) = FIRST_1(x') \subset FOLLOW_1(A) \subset FIRST_1(u \text{ FOLLOW}(A))$$

Again:

$$FIRST_1(u \text{ FOLLOW}(A)) \cap FIRST_1(v \text{ FOLLOW}(A)) \neq \emptyset$$

Case 3:

$$u' = \epsilon, v' = \epsilon.$$

Here:

$$\text{FIRST}_1(z) = \text{FIRST}_1(x') \subset \text{FOLLOW}_1(A) \subset \text{FIRST}_1(u \text{ FOLLOW}(A))$$

and:

$$\text{FIRST}_1(z') = \text{FIRST}_1(x'') \subset \text{FOLLOW}_1(A) \subset \text{FIRST}_1(v \text{ FOLLOW}(A))$$

QED

Theorem 4.7 suggests the following generalization:

G is LL(k) if and only if for every pair of productions $A \rightarrow u$ and $A \rightarrow v$, $\text{FIRST}_k(u \text{ FOLLOW}_k(A)) \cap \text{FIRST}_k(v \text{ FOLLOW}_k(A)) = \varnothing$.

Unfortunately, this statement is not true for $k > 1$. A grammar satisfying the condition is said to be *strong LL(k)*, and it happens that not all LL(k) grammars are strong LL(k), as the example given earlier shows.

Let G have the productions:

$$S \rightarrow Abc \mid aAcb$$

$$A \rightarrow \epsilon \mid b \mid c$$

Now $\text{FOLLOW}_2(A) = \{bc, cb\}$. Then for $A \rightarrow \epsilon$ we have:

$$\text{FIRST}_2(\epsilon \text{ FOLLOW}_2(A)) = \{bc, cb\}$$

For $A \rightarrow b$ we have:

$$\text{FIRST}_2(b \text{ FOLLOW}_2(A)) = \{bb, bc\}.$$

Hence, this is not strong LL(2), yet it is LL(2), as we have shown previously.

Essentially, the set $\text{FIRST}_k(u \text{ FOLLOW}_k(A))$ for a production $A \rightarrow u$ contains all of the k-symbol lookaheads derivable from Ax in all the left-most sentential forms wAx. However, a top-down decision step in an LL(k) parser is based on a particular left-most sentential form wAx, and the possible k-symbol lookaheads derivable from Ax are a subset of $\text{FIRST}_k(u \text{ FOLLOW}_k(A))$, for a production $A \rightarrow u$.

The case $k > 1$ is different from the case $k = 1$, essentially because a pair of symbols composing a lookahead string can stem from a combination of derivations based on A and on the strings following A, and the combination causes certain grammars to be LL(k) but not strong LL(k).

4.3. Deterministic LL(1) Parser

The PDA given in section 4.1 is nondeterministic for only one reason—when a nonterminal symbol A appears on the top of the stack, then a choice must be made among the set of productions $A \rightarrow w_1 \mid w_2 \mid w_3 \mid \ldots$ in P.

We therefore see that, to make this parser deterministic, we need a table to select one of several productions. Such a table will consider the stack top symbol A and the next k input symbols in the input list; based on this pair, it must uniquely select a production $A \to w_i$.

An *LL(k) selector table* maps a pair (X, u) to a production $X \to w$, where X is a nonterminal symbol (on the stack top), and u is some terminal string of length k. Such a table must yield a many-to-one mapping, because many possible strings u may correspond to a given production, yet a production must be uniquely selected from the pair (X, u). The table size is finite, because there is a finite number of nonterminals and terminal strings of fixed length k.

Theorem 4.7 provides the justification for such a table, and also states that the grammars that can be so parsed are the strong LL(k) grammars.

4.3.1. LL(1) Selector Table

A finite selector table can be constructed for any k. However, its size grows rapidly with k for a typical grammar. It turns out that, in practice, if a grammar is not LL(1), it is likely not to be LL(k) for any k. It is better to transform the grammar in an attempt to find an LL(1) grammar than to attempt to construct a parser with k > 1. We therefore restrict the following discussion to k = 1.

Recall that an LL(0) grammar can contain at most one production $A \to w$ for each nonterminal A, and is therefore useless for any practical purpose; at most one terminal string can be derived in the grammar.

Before we describe the construction of a selector table, let us examine the typical LL(1) selector table in figure 4.3. This table describes a grammar G_2 the

Non-terminal		Input	Production
1	E	a, (	E → TE″
2	E″	+, -	E″ → T′E″
3	E″	), ε	E″ → ε
4	T′	+	T′ → +T
5	T′	-	T′ → -T
6	T	a, (	T → FT″
7	T″	*, /	T″ → F′T″
8	T″	+, -,), ε	T″ → ε
9	F′	*	F′ → *F
10	F′	/	F′ → /F
11	F	a	F → a
12	F	(	F → (E)

Figure 4.3. An LL(1) selector table, for grammar G_2.

language of which is the class of arithmetic expressions with all four operations + − * / and parenthesizing. The productions for the grammar are given in the right column. The language of this grammar is essentially the arithmetic language $L(G_0)$ of chapter 2; however, G_0 is not LL(k) for any k, because it contains left-recursive productions, whereas G_2 is LL(1). Grammar G_0 can be transformed into G_2 by means we will describe later.

4.3.2. LL(1) Parser Algorithm

1. Initially, the parser PDA contains the start symbol S on its stack top.

2. If the stack top contains a terminal symbol a, then the input symbol must be an a, else ERROR. If the two match, then advance the read head and pop the terminal symbol from the stack.

3. If the stack top contains a nonterminal symbol A, then examine the input symbol currently under the read head, and consult the LL(1) selector table (figure 4.3, for example) to determine which production is to be applied. If the selector table indicates production $A \rightarrow w$, then remove A from the stack and push the string w onto the stack.

4. The machine halts by empty stack.

Let us try this machine on the string $a - a - a$. The initial configuration is:

$$[a - a - a, E]$$

because E is the start symbol of the grammar. The selector table row 1 indicates that with E on the stack top and a the next symbol, $E \rightarrow TE''$ should be applied; TE'' replaces E on the stack top, yielding the configuration:

$$[a - a - a, TE'']$$

Next, the selector table indicates that T should be replaced by FT'' on the stack top, yielding:

$$[a - a - a, FT''E'']$$

Then the selector table indicates replacing F by a, yielding:

$$[a - a - a, aT''E'']$$

At this point, the matching rule (2) applies, yielding the configuration:

$$[- a - a, T''E'']$$

The remaining moves are:

$$[- a - a, T''E''] \vdash [- a - a, E'']$$
$$\vdash [- a - a, T'E''] \vdash [- a - a, -TE'']$$

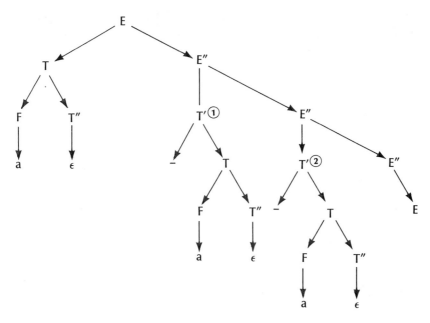

Figure 4.4. Derivation tree for string "a − a − a" in grammar G_2.

$$\vdash [a-a, \text{TE}''] \vdash [a-a, \text{FT}''\text{E}'']$$

$$\vdash [a-a, \text{aT}''\text{E}''] \vdash [-a, \text{T}''\text{E}'']$$

$$\vdash [-a, \text{E}''] \vdash [-a, \text{T}'\text{E}''] \vdash [-a, -\text{TE}''] \vdash [a, \text{TE}'']$$

$$\vdash [a, \text{FT}''\text{E}''] \vdash [a, \text{aT}''\text{E}''] \vdash [\epsilon, \text{T}''\text{E}''] \vdash [\epsilon, \text{E}'']$$

$$\vdash [\epsilon, \epsilon]$$

The derivation tree for this sentence and grammar is shown in figure 4.4. A comparison of the machine moves with this tree reveals that the machine effectively constructs the tree top-down by a left-to-right tree scan. That is, the derivation is:

$$\text{E} \Rightarrow \text{TE}'' \Rightarrow \text{FT}''\text{E}'' \Rightarrow \text{aT}''\text{E}'' \ldots$$

for the first few steps.

Selector Table Construction

Most of our work is done. Given an algorithm for the FIRST and FOLLOW sets, an LL(1) selector table is easy to build.

Let A → w be any production in the grammar, and let the terminal symbol x be in the set $\text{FIRST}_1(w \; \text{FOLLOW}_1(A))$. Then the selector table pair (A, x) maps to production A → w.

If any pair (A,x) maps to two or more different productions, then the grammar cannot be LL(1); we say that we have a conflict.

For example, consider the grammar G_1 (page 153). The selector table for this grammar is free of conflicts:

Pair	Production
E, (	E → TE'
E, a	E → TE'
E', +	E' → +E
E',)	E' → ε
E', ⊥	E' → ε
T, (	T → FT'
T, a	T → FT'
T', *	T' → *T
T', +	T' → ε
T', ⊥	T' → ε
T',)	T' → ε
F, (	F → (E)
F, a	F → a
G, (	G → E⊥
G, a	G → E⊥

On the other hand, the following simple grammar has a selector table containing conflicts; it is therefore not LL(1):

```
S → A⊥
A → B | C
B → aC
C → aa
```

Pair	Production
S, a	S → A ⊥
A, a	A → B
A, a	A → C
B, a	B → aC
C, a	C → aa

The difficulty occurs with the pair of productions A → B and A → C, both of which correspond to the selector pair (A, a). The parser cannot deterministically map (A, a) to a single production; hence, it is not LL(1). Both B and C derive strings beginning with a, hence the PDA cannot decide between the productions A → B and A → C when a is the next input symbol.

4.3.3. LL(1) Grammar Transformations

We now consider a transformation that often is effective on a grammar containing a left-recursion and that (1) will preserve the semantic ordering of binary operations, and (2) will usually succeed in generating an LL(1) grammar.

Given a simple left-recursion of the form:

$$A \rightarrow Ax \mid Ay \mid \dots \mid w \mid z \mid \dots$$

we first *stratify* this production set by introducing two new nonterminals B and C, as follows:

```
A → AB | C
B → x | y | ...
C → w | z | ...
```

Note that B collects the strings past the A in the left-recursive A productions, and that C collects all the other A production right parts. Then the productions $A \rightarrow AB \mid C$ are rewritten:

```
A → CA′
A′ → BA′ | ε
```

where A′ is another new nonterminal.

Here is an example, which yields the production set G_2 displayed in the selector table in figure 4.3, as based on grammar G_0. The basis grammar is:

```
E → E + T | E − T | T
T → T * F | T / F | F
F → a | ( E )
```

which is an obvious extension of G_0.

We first stratify the E productions, introducing the new nonterminals E″ and T′. Write $T' \rightarrow + T \mid - T$, so that the E productions become:

```
E → E T′ | T
```

Then these two productions are rewritten as:

```
E → T E″
E″ → T′ E″ | ε
```

In a similar way, the T productions are rewritten:

```
F′ → * F | / F
T → F T″
T″ → F′ T″ | ε
```

The F productions remain unchanged. We obtain the production set displayed in figure 4.3. You should verify that the resulting grammar is LL(1) by verifying the selection table given in the figure. Figure 4.4 displays a derivation tree for the sentence $a - a - a$, which shows that the two operators are correctly associated.

4.4. An LL(1) Parser in Pascal

LL(1) parser tables can be organized as sparse matrix FSA tables, described in chapter 3. Figure 4.5 shows their organization.

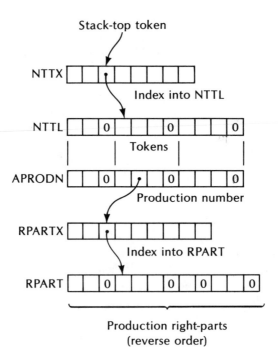

Figure 4.5. LL(1) parser tables.

A parsing step is controlled by a top-of-stack symbol X and the next available token T. If X is a terminal, then T must match X, else an error is reported. If X is a nonterminal, then the tables of figure 4.5 are entered.

The NTTX table carries token index values into the NTTL table. NTTX is entered with the token number of the top-of-stack nonterminal X. NTTX[X] points to the first of a list of possible lookahead tokens associated with X. Each list is terminated with a reserved token—chr(0). A match is sought. If no match is seen, an error occurs; otherwise, an index value I is obtained on the matching item: NTTL[I] = T.

The APRODN table corresponds exactly with NTTL. APRODN[I] yields a production number, which is also an index into the RPARTX table. RPARTX carries an index into RPART, which holds lists of production right parts, arranged in reverse order. Each "right part" in RPART is a token number, either terminal or nonterminal.

A production is *applied* in the LL(1) parser by (1) removing the top stack token (its left member), then (2) pushing its right member onto the stack. The right member is just a list of tokens in RPART, arranged in reverse order to facilitate pushing the elements in the order in which they appear. Each RPART list is terminated by a special token: chr(0).

Here are three procedures that implement an LL(1) parser:

```
{*******************}
procedure APPLY(PNUM: int);
begin  {Called on every production applied}
  write(rfile, 'Applying: ');
  wrprod(pnum);
  writeln(rfile);
end;

{*******************}
procedure PAPPLY(PNUM: int);
  label 99;
  var PX, PPX: int;
begin  {Apply operations}
  px:=rpartx[pnum];  {right part index}
  apply(pnum);
  while rpart[px]<>0 do
  begin  {putting stuff in the three stacks}
    stack[stackx]:=rpart[px];  {replaces current TOS}
    px:=px+1;
    stackx:=stackx+1;
  end;
  stackx:=stackx-1;
end;

{****************}
procedure PARSER;
  var NTTLX: int;
begin  {Carries out a complete parse, until
        stack is empty}
  stack[1]:=goal_tokx;  {Goal initially on stack}
  stackx:=1;
  while stackx>0 do
  begin    {halt on empty stack}
    if stack[stackx]>term_toks then
    begin  {nonterminal on stack top}
      nttlx:=nttx[stack[stackx]];
      if nttl[nttlx]=0 then papply(aprodn[nttlx])
      else
      begin
        next_token;
        while (nttl[nttlx]<>token) and
              (nttl[nttlx]<>0) do nttlx:=nttlx+1;
      end;
      if nttl[nttlx]=0 then
      begin
        error('syntax error 1');
        tokenread;
      end
      else papply(aprodn[nttlx])
    end
    else   {terminal on stack top}
    begin
      next_token;
      if stack[stackx]=token then
      begin
        tokenread;
```

```
      stackx:=stackx-1;
    end
  else  {unable to match the terminal}
    begin
      error('syntax error 2');
      tokenread;
    end
  end
end
end;
```

STACK carries the LL(1) stack, which contains tokens. STACKX is the top-of-stack index. TOKENREAD *prepares* the lexical analyzer to read a token, but the token is not actually *read* until NEXT_TOKEN is called. This "delayed action" causes a token to be fetched from the input source only at the last possible moment. Recall that identifiers are placed in a symbol table by the lexical analyzer, and it is important to do this only as late as possible during parsing.

The APPLY function is called on replacing a top-of-stack nonterminal by its right member. Note that none of the right member elements has been scanned in the input source yet, so this call is made in anticipation of reading them. Semantic operations may be introduced into this function; they are driven by a production number. It is also possible to add semantic actions on matching a terminal token; the action may also depend on the previous production applied by keeping the production number for reference. We merely print the production with procedure WRPROD (not shown).

4.4.1. Errors and Error Recovery

> *I shall try to correct errors when shown to be errors; and I shall adopt new views so fast as they shall appear to be true views . . . .*
>
> . . . *Abraham Lincoln*

We have seen that an LL(1) error may occur through a failure to match a top-of-stack terminal token with the next input token, or through a failure to locate the next token in the FIRST-FOLLOW list associated with a top-of-stack nonterminal. In either case, our simple parser above just dies. The error can be reported, but no graceful patching mechanism is provided. We now discuss a simple recovery scheme; it is similar in concept to that given for FSA error recovery, and—as we shall see—also works effectively for LR(1) parser error recovery.

We will call the offending next token, which causes a parsing failure, the *error token.*

The basic idea is to try inserting a token that is compatible with the stack top, then to test whether the error token can be parsed with the substitution. If we cannot succeed with any compatible token, we then drop the error token and try a parse with the next token. If that fails, we start over with the insertion strategy.

During error recovery, semantic operations are turned off, and a parsing is not permitted to advance past the current error token. When a successful recovery strategy is found, the real parser is launched from where it left off. This is the algorithm:

1. Choose an insertion token compatible with the top-of-stack token. If the TOS token is terminal, that is the choice. Otherwise, it is one of the lookahead tokens found in the NTTL list. Go to 2.

2. Launch the recovery parse; it will scan the insertion token successfully, but may not scan the error token. If successful, stop—a recovery has been found. Otherwise, go to 3.

3. If more choices exist, go to 1. Otherwise, drop the error token and attempt a recovery parse on the next token. If successful, stop. Otherwise, go to 1.

Note that the stack itself is never touched in the recovery process; however, that may be necessary. Indeed, after dropping several next tokens without a success, an improved strategy would also attempt popping the stack.

4.5. Recursive-Descent Parsers

> *Proper words in proper places, make the true definition of a style.*
>
> . . . *Jonathan Swift*

The recursive-descent parsers are closely related to the LL(1) parsers. They are among the most popular of the compiler parsers, perhaps because the parsing and semantic operations appear together as a reasonably lucid and self-explanatory program. The method uses function calls and other programming techniques familiar to most programmers. It is a top-down method, and we shall show that a necessary condition for a recursive-descent compiler to operate correctly is that its source grammar be LL(1).

The most satisfying recursive-descent parsers result from an extended grammar, rather than a simple CFG. Such a grammar may contain closure, alternation, and concatenation operators, similar to those in regular expressions, but both terminals and nonterminals. The extended grammar is closely related to the LL(1) grammars. We shall show how the grammar may be certified as LL(1), and how a parser may be generated.

We first need to develop a theory of extended grammars.

4.5.1. Extended Grammars

An *extended grammar* consists of a set of *extended productions* of the form:

$$A \rightarrow w$$

where w is an *extended structure* (as next defined) and A is a nonterminal; for each nonterminal A, there is exactly one such production in the grammar.

An *extended structure* is a string consisting of terminals, nonterminals, and the metasymbols |, (,), [,], {, and } as follows:

- ϵ (the empty string) is an extended structure.

- If $x \in \Sigma$ (that is, a terminal symbol), then x is an extended structure.

- If $X \in N$ (that is, a nonterminal symbol), then X is an extended structure.

- If S is an extended structure, then each of the following are extended structures:

```
( S ), meaning S itself.
{ S }, closure, meaning zero or more concatenations of S.
[ S ], option, meaning zero or one occurrence of S.
```

- If S_1 and S_2 are extended structures, then each of the following are extended structures:

```
S₁ | S₂, alternation, meaning a choice of S₁ or S₂.
S₁ S₂, concatenation, with the usual meaning.
```

It is clear from these structure rules that the right member w of each extended production $A \rightarrow w$ is a regular expression, except that both terminal and non-terminal symbols are employed in the expression. We also have introduced a new unary operator, *option*.

Example.   Grammar G_0 may be written as an extended grammar as follows. The productions $E \rightarrow T$, $E \rightarrow E + T$, and $E \rightarrow E - T$ define a structure for E that looks like this:

$$E \rightarrow T \{ (+ | -) T \}$$

That is, any expression consists of a *term* followed by any number of $+ term$ or $- term$ elements, including none. Note that E no longer appears in the right part of the extended production. A production left-member may appear in the right member of a production, but not as its left-most element—that would cause the grammar to be non-LL(1).

An equivalent way of expressing these productions is:

$$E \rightarrow T \{ (+ T) | (- T) \}$$

The equivalence is apparent from the distributive law of concatenation over alternation.

Similarly, the productions $T \rightarrow F$, $T \rightarrow T * F$, $T \rightarrow T / F$ define a structure for T that looks like this:

$$T \rightarrow F \{ (* | /) F \}$$

Finally, the productions F → (E) and F → a define the structure:

$$F \rightarrow \textit{lp } E \textit{ rp} \mid a$$

where *lp* and *rp* stand for the terminal symbols "(" and ")", respectively. Because "(" and ")" are metasymbols, we cannot permit these as terminal symbols.

We therefore have an extended grammar G_0':

```
E → T { ( + | - ) T }
T → F { ( * | / ) F }
F → lp E rp | a
```

4.5.2. Extended-Tree Grammars

Rather than introduce metasymbols into a grammar, it will be better to describe an extended grammar as a set of trees. We therefore define an *extended-tree grammar* as a four-tuple (N, Σ, P, S), where:

N is a set of nonterminal symbols,

Σ is a set of terminal symbols, such that N ∩ Σ = ∅,

P is a set of trees such that:

- There is a one-to-one correspondence between P and N. The tree T corresponding to symbol A in N is called *tree*(A); the symbol A corresponding to T is called *symb*(T).

- The leaves of tree T are in N ∪ Σ ∪ {ε}.

- The interior nodes of tree T are in the set {●, |, *, ?}, where ● stands for *concatenation* and has two children, | stands for *alternation* and has two children, * stands for *closure* and has one child, and ? stands for *option,* and has one child.

- S is the goal symbol, and is in N. *Tree*(S) is called the *grammar tree* or *goal tree.*

Example. Figure 4.6 illustrates a grammar tree for the regular expression:

$$a \{ (+ | -) a \}$$

The root node is a concatenation of a and {. . .}; the latter is represented by a closure node, and so forth.

4.5.3. Derivation Tree

Given an extended-tree grammar G, a *derivation tree* T may be constructed from the grammar trees in P as follows:

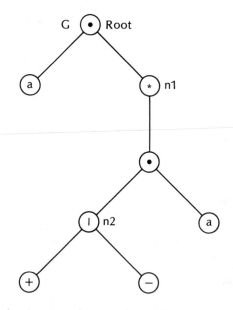

Figure 4.6.   Extended grammar tree for G = a{(+|−)a}.

- The *root node* of T is the root of G's goal tree.

- T is said to be *complete* if every leaf is in the set Σ, the terminal symbols of G. Every node in T corresponds to some node in a tree in P; this correspondence is many-to-one.

- Let H be some leaf of T, not in Σ. Let H' be the corresponding node in P.

- If H is a ● (concatenation) node, let H's children be the children of H'.

- If H is a | (alternation) node, let H have one child, chosen from the two children of H'.

- If H is a * (closure) node, let H have an ϵ child, or have one or more children—each child corresponds to the child of H'.

- If H is a ? (option) node, let H have an ϵ child, or have one child corresponding to the child of H'.

- If H is a nonterminal node associated with the nonterminal A, replace H by *tree*(A).

- If H is a terminal or an ϵ node, it is unchanged.

When the expansion is complete, the leaves of T read in left-to-right natural order compose a *sentence* in the language L(G).

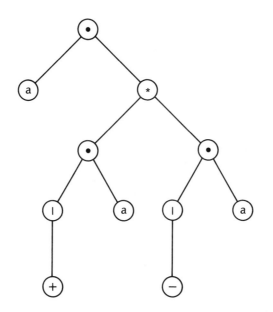

Figure 4.7.   Extended derivation tree for sentence a + a − a in grammar
G = a{ + | −)a}.

Example.   Figure 4.7 illustrates a complete derivation tree based on the grammar tree of figure 4.6. Nodes n1 and n2 of figure 4.6 are the only ones involving some choice. We have chosen to expand the closure node n1 as two sons. In these, the alternation of the left son is expanded into a + node, and the alternation of the right son into a − node.

The leaves of the tree of figure 4.7 yield the string a + a − a.

4.5.4. FIRST and FOLLOW Sets of Extended Grammar Tree Nodes

We can easily extend the concept of a sentence in section 2.2.4 to embrace strings derivable from any node H in a grammar tree T in P. We merely begin construction of a derivation tree at any node, rather than just the goal node. We therefore can define the set S(H), the set of strings derivable from some node H in a tree T in P. We can then define the set of FIRST and FOLLOW symbols associated with each node in P.

FIRST(H) is the set FIRST(S(H)), where FIRST(s) is the set of all left-most symbols in the set of strings s. FIRST(H) may contain ε, if one or more of the strings S(H) contains ε.

FIRST(H) is computed easily. We begin with an empty FIRST set for each node of P, then add members by repetition of the following algorithm:

```
case H of
  ε: add {ε} to FIRST(H);
  terminal x: add {x} to FIRST(H);
  •: add FIRST(FIRST(left(H)) FIRST(right(H))) to FIRST(H);
  ?, *: add {ε} ∪ FIRST(child(H)) to FIRST(H);
  |: add FIRST(left(H)) ∪ FIRST(right(H)) to FIRST(H);
  nonterminal N: add FIRST(tree(N)) to FIRST(H);
end;
```

These operations should be clear from the notion of FIRST and the strings derivable from some node. A terminal or empty node can derive only that terminal or ε. A concatenation node derives strings representing the concatenation of strings of the left and right children; the FIRST of these is clearly only the FIRST of the left child's strings, unless that set contains ε, in which case it includes the FIRST of the right child's strings.

The FIRST of an alternation node is the union of FIRST's of its children. The FIRST of an alternation or closure node is merely the FIRST of its child, together with ε, because such a node can always derive ε.

The FIRST of a nonterminal node is the FIRST of the root node of the grammar tree associated with that nonterminal. This rule also shows that a FIRST set can be associated with a nonterminal symbol in a tree grammar, and that this FIRST is identical to that associated with every node carrying that nonterminal symbol.

The determination of FIRST for a tree grammar can be achieved in a finite number of passes of the trees in P. FIRST always is a synthesized attribute (that is, it is passed from children to their father), except for the nonterminal rule. That rule passes a FIRST set from a root node to one or more leaf nodes in a tree in P; such an action requires passing through each tree so affected by an expansion of the FIRST set in its leaves.

FOLLOW Set

We next define a FOLLOW set on the nodes of P. FOLLOW(N) essentially is the FIRST of the strings that follow the strings derivable from node N. We assume that a stop token ⊥ always is present at the end of every string, but is not part of the grammar. Hence, the FOLLOW set never will be empty—it may, however, contain ⊥.

Let G be the goal node in P, and S(G) be some string derivable from G, such that node N is expanded at some point. Then it is clear that S(G) will have the form:

$$S(G) = \alpha\ S(N)\ \beta$$

by the tree nature of the expansion process. The strings α and β are possibly empty. We then say that FIRST($\beta\ \perp$) is in FOLLOW(N).

FOLLOW(N) consists of all and only those symbols so constructed, for any S(G) and any choice of S(N) that appears in S(G).

FOLLOW(N) is a function of the environment of node N, and not of the strings derivable from N. It follows that two different nodes N1 and N2 associated with the same nonterminal A will have different FOLLOW sets in general.

We can compute FOLLOW for the nodes of P by the following algorithm, which is repeated until no growth in any FOLLOW set occurs:

- Let H be some node in P.

- If H is the root of the goal tree, then add $\perp$ to FOLLOW(H).

- If H is any tree root—including the goal tree—then for every leaf node M associated with *symb*(H) add FOLLOW(M) to FOLLOW(H).

- If H is NOT a tree root then:

```
case H of
terminal, ε, nonterminal: {no action required};
•: begin
    add FIRST(FIRST(right(H)) • FOLLOW(H)) to
        FOLLOW(left(H));
    add FOLLOW(H) to FOLLOW(right(H))
    end;
|: begin
      add FOLLOW(H) to FOLLOW(left(H));
      add FOLLOW(H) to FOLLOW(right(H));
    end;
?: add FOLLOW(H) to FOLLOW(child(H));
*: begin
      add FOLLOW(H) to FOLLOW(child(H));
      add FIRST(FIRST(child(H)) • FOLLOW(H)) to
          FOLLOW(child(H));
    end
end;
```

Discussion

The FOLLOW set computation is fairly obvious from the properties of the extended grammar operations. Consider first the concatenation node •. Let the node be H, and its left and right children be L and R, respectively. Then FOLLOW(R) obviously contains FOLLOW(H), because the strings S(R) compose the right-most subtree under H. However, FOLLOW(L) will contain FOLLOW(H) only if FIRST(R) contains ε—in that case, the right-most subtree may derive ε and the FOLLOW(H) strings will follow the S(L) strings. That is the rationale for the formula:

$$\text{FIRST(FIRST(right(H))} \bullet \text{FOLLOW(H))}$$

found in the • rule.

The alternation rule | also is obvious—the FOLLOW sets of both L and R must contain FOLLOW(H), because only one of them is chosen in an expansion of the grammar tree into a derivation tree.

The closure rule * recognizes that FOLLOW(H) must be in FOLLOW(child(H)), because any one child can be the last one in the expansion. However, one child can follow another child; hence, FIRST(FIRST(child(H))) belongs in FOLLOW(child(H)). We also have considered the possibility of FIRST(child(H)) containing ϵ, and have therefore concatenated FOLLOW(H) to that set. It will turn out that a closure node the child of which can derive ϵ will be unacceptable in a deterministic acceptor. The acceptor will be unable to determine how many iterations to make to accept the closure of ϵ, and therefore must be nondeterministic.

The tree root rules are a reflection of the manner in which a tree in P associated with nonterminal A can replace a leaf associated with A in the expansion of P into a derivation tree. Given that expansion, the FOLLOW set of some root node must contain all the FOLLOW sets of its associated leaf nodes. The converse is not true.

The goal root node contains the stop symbol $\perp$ in its FOLLOW set explicitly, because that symbol is not part of the grammar.

4.5.5. Properties of a Top-Down Recognizer

The following principles constitute an informal description of a top-down acceptor based on the decorated trees in the set P.

The acceptor R is a program containing a set of recursively callable procedures. Each procedure corresponds to one nonterminal in the grammar G. The procedure first called corresponds to the goal nonterminal.

At certain points during the execution of R, a configuration of R can be defined, consisting of:

- A statement about to be executed.

- A node in some tree in P.

- A remaining input string to be scanned.

- A stack of procedure return addresses.

The execution of R can be considered a sequence of moves from one configuration to the next. The initial configuration is:

- About to call the goal procedure.

- Positioned on the goal root node of P.

- The complete input sentence.

- Stack of return addresses is empty.

The final configuration, for a successful recognition of some sentence, is:

- About to execute the statement following the initial goal procedure call. Under our definitions, this will be a MATCH for the stop symbol $\perp$.

- Positioned on the goal root node of P.

- An input sentence consisting of ⊥.

- Stack of return addresses is empty.

R can also *block* through a syntax error in the input sentence. The block will be indicated by calling a procedure ERROR. It will occur through a failure to match an input token against a terminal symbol expected in the program. R is said to *accept* an input sentence if it can execute its program from initial to final configuration without blocking.

We next describe the construction of the recursive-descent program from the FIRST and FOLLOW decorated trees in P.

Recursive-Descent Program Construction

The program consists of a set of procedures, one for each nonterminal in N. The notation "PROGRAM(T)" means "the program constructed from the root of tree T."

Let T be the goal tree of the extended-tree grammar. The main program then reads as follows:

```
program RDPARSER;
  type
    TOKENTYPE: char;
    TOKENSET: set of tokentype;

  var
    TOKEN: tokentype;  {next token}

  procedure ERROR(FFSET: tokenset);
  begin
    {called on a syntax error}
  end;

  procedure NEXT_TOKEN;
  begin
    {called to fetch the next token}
  end;

  procedure ACCEPT;
  begin
    {called upon full acceptance of source sentence}
  end;

  {procedures associated with each tree—see below}

begin
  G;  {G = symb(T) }
  if token='⊥' then accept
  else error(['⊥'])
end.
```

For every tree, we construct the procedure:

```
procedure A;   {A = symb(T) }
  label 1, 99;
begin
  PROGRAM(T);
  goto 1;
99:  {error reporting, recovery}
  error(set_form(FOLLOW(T)));
1:
end;
```

The function set_form($\{s_1, s_2, \ldots s_r\}$) is defined as the Pascal form:

```
[s₁, s₂, ..., sᵣ]
```

It merely produces a Pascal SET from a mathematical set. The function FOLLOW(T) is the follow set associated with node T.

When ERROR is called, it is given the FOLLOW set of the nonterminal A for the purposes of error recovery. We shall discuss error recovery later. With no errors, procedure A merely executes the program statements PROGRAM(T), then branches to the procedure exit. Any error within PROGRAM(T) will cause a branch to label 99, calling the ERROR procedure before exiting.

The following classification defines PROGRAM(T) in terms of its root node N. This can be implemented as a recursive-descent parser generator, which walks top down through the tree T:

- If N corresponds to the empty string ϵ, generate nothing.

- If N corresponds to a terminal token x, generate:

```
if token=x then next_token
else goto 99    {error transfer}
```

- If N corresponds to a nonterminal token X, then generate:

```
X     {call procedure X}
```

- If N corresponds to a concatenation E₁ E₂, then generate:

```
begin
  PROGRAM(E₁);    {left_child(N)}
  PROGRAM(E₂)     {right_child(N)}
end
```

Note that several concatenation nodes may be clustered.

- If N corresponds to the closure { E }, then generate:

```
while token in set_form(FIRST(child(N)) do
begin
  PROGRAM(E)   {child(N)}
end
```

- If N corresponds to the option [E], then generate

```
if token in set_form(FIRST(child(N)) then
begin
  PROGRAM(E)   {child(N)}
end
```

The function set_form has been defined. FIRST(child(N)) is the FIRST set associated with N's child.

- If N corresponds to an alternation of the form ($E_1 \,|\, E_2$) or, more generally, if several nodes can be clustered to yield the form ($E_1 \,|\, E_2 \,|\, \ldots \,|\, E_n$), then generate:

```
case token of
case_form(FIRST(N₁)): PROGRAM(E₁);
case_form(FIRST(N₂)): PROGRAM(E₂);
         . . .
case_form(FIRST(Nₙ)): PROGRAM(Eₙ);
otherwise goto 99;  {error}
end
```

The function case_form($\{s_1, s_2, \ldots s_m\}$) is defined as the Pascal form:

```
s₁, s₂, ... sₘ
```

That is, case_form yields a case label sequence from a set of token values. The nodes N_1, N_2, . . . correspond to the expressions E_1, E_2, ...

Discussion

A PROGRAM(N) in the above construction system will exactly accept the set of strings S(N).

''Acceptance'' implies moving the read head zero or more characters through a string in S(N). If unsuccessful, the read head will not have moved, and an error will be reported.

The construction rules follow this assertion. The rule for a terminal token is obvious. We advance through the token if it matches and otherwise go to 99.

The rule for a nonterminal node X is simply to call procedure X. This executes a program PROGRAM(*tree*(X)). Procedure X will accept any string derivable from X, and is able to return to the environment of node X. The return is through a return address pushed onto the run-time stack when the procedure was called.

The concatenation rule is simple. We invoke the PROGRAM structures associated with each of the concatenation members successively. A failure in any one will result in a branch to label 99 of the covering procedure.

The alternation rule is based on a selection using the Pascal CASE statement. The case labels are FIRST sets associated with each of the alternatives. It is the absence of any pairwise conflicts in these sets that makes the grammar LL(1). Because the Pascal compiler will check its CASE statements for conflicts, it is unnecessary to make an explicit check in the parser generator program.

A failure to match the TOKEN value to any of the case labels must be caught by an OTHERWISE clause.

The closure and option cases simply test TOKEN against a FIRST set associated with the enclosed expression E. Closure is implemented by a WHILE-DO, and option is implemented by an IF-THEN.

We could easily extend our system to an "at-least-once closure"—that is, $(E)^+$—by generating a REPEAT-UNTIL as follows:

```
repeat
  PROGRAM(E)
until not(token in set_form(FIRST(E)))
```

Similarly, the form $(E)^n$ often is useful. It is equivalent to a concatenation of n expressions E. This form should generate a FOR statement, as follows:

```
for i:=1 to n do    {note that i must be declared}
  PROGRAM(E)
```

The Pascal implementation must accept a GOTO out of the scope of the FOR statement; not all do.

Parser Validation

The parser can be validated by ensuring that it always will make the correct decision at every node calling for a choice among one or more alternatives. These are the alternation, option, and closure nodes. The choice must be made on the basis of the next token.

For every alternation node N, where L = left(N) and R = right(N), it should be clear that:

$$\text{FIRST(FIRST(L) FOLLOW(N))} \cap \text{FIRST(FIRST(R) FOLLOW(N))} = \varnothing$$

If this condition is satisfied, then the choice of left or right alternative is determined by the next token. Note that either FIRST(L) or FIRST(R) can contain ϵ, but both cannot. When one contains ϵ, the FOLLOW set of N must be disjoint from the FIRST set of the other.

For every closure and option node, the condition:

$$\text{FIRST(child(N) FOLLOW(N))} \cap \text{FOLLOW(N)} = \varnothing$$

must be satisfied. The choice must be made between acceptance of the node as ϵ or as a string derivable from child(N). Note that ϵ cannot be in FIRST-(child(N)); otherwise, the condition fails. If ϵ were in FIRST(child(N)), then the acceptor would be unable to determine whether to accept N through its empty case or through a nonempty case in which its child derives ϵ. The choice in any case therefore depends on the FIRST set of child(N) being disjoint from the FOLLOW set of N.

As we have noted, the Pascal compiler will verify that no conflicts exist in an alternation node. However, there is no such compiler test for closure and option nodes.

Example.   Consider the grammar G_0':

```
E → T { ( + | - ) T }
T → F { ( * | / ) F }
F → '(' E ')' | a
```

where E is the goal symbol. Because (is a metasymbol, we use quotes to indicate its use as a terminal symbol.

Figure 4.8 shows the extended grammar trees associated with the productions for E, T, and F. They also are decorated with their FIRST and FOLLOW sets.

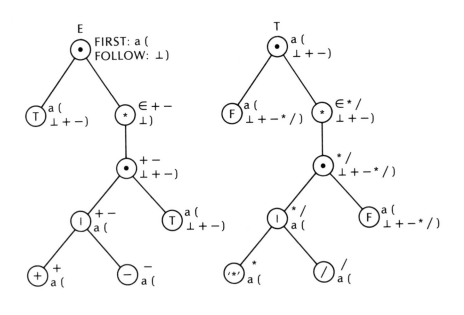

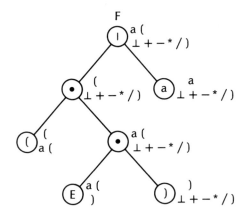

Figure 4.8.   Extended grammar tree for G_0'.

This grammar will generate a valid parser; the validation tests for the closure and alternation nodes are satisfied. For example, consider the closure node in the E tree. Its FOLLOW set is $\{\perp,)\}$, the FIRST set of its child is $\{+, -\}$, and these are disjoint.

Consider also the alternation node in the F tree. The FIRST sets of its children are $\{ (\}$ and $\{ a \}$, clearly disjoint.

The recursive descent parser generated from these trees is:

```
program RDPARSER;
  type
    TOKENTYPE: char;
    TOKENSET: set of tokentype;

  var
    TOKEN: tokentype;   {next token}

  procedure ERROR(FOLSET: tokenset);
  begin
    {called on a syntax error}
  end;

  procedure NEXT_TOKEN;
  begin
    {called to fetch the next token}
  end;

  procedure ACCEPT;
  begin
    {called upon full acceptance of source sentence}
  end;

  procedure E;
  begin
    T;
    while token in ['+', '-'] do
    begin
      begin
        case token of
        '+': if token='+' then next_token
             else goto 99;
        '-': if token='-' then next_token
             else goto 99;
        otherwise goto 99;
        end;
        T
      end
    end;
    goto 1;
99:
    error(['⊥', ')']);
1;
  end;
```

```
procedure T;
begin
  F;
  while token in ['*', '/'] do
  begin
    begin
      case token of
      '*': if token='*' then next_token
          else goto 99;
      '/': if token='/' then next_token
          else goto 99;
      otherwise goto 99;
      end;
      F
    end
  end;
  goto 1;
99:
  error(['⊥', '+', '-', ')']);
1;
end;

procedure F;
begin
  case token of
  '(': begin
          if token='(' then next_token
        else goto 99;
          begin
            E;
            if token=')' then next_token
          else goto 99;
          end
        end;
  'a': if token='a' then next_token
      else goto 99;
  otherwise goto 99;
  end;
  goto 1;
99:
  error(['⊥', '+', '-', '*', '/', ')']);
1;
end;

begin
  E;
  if token='⊥' then accept
 else error(['⊥'])
end.
```

4.5.6. Reductions

Now that we have seen how the complete recursive program appears when fully assembled, we can make one or two program reductions. The form:

```
case token of
'*': if token='*' then next_token
    else goto 99;
'/': if token='/' then next_token
    else goto 99;
otherwise goto 99;
end;
```

can be reduced to:

```
case token of
'*': next_token;
'/': next_token;
otherwise goto 99;
end;
```

because the case operation demands that the value of TOKEN be * or /—the subsequent IF test always will succeed.

Similarly, an IF test on a token inside a WHILE can be eliminated if the WHILE test is on the single token tested by the IF and the IF is the first statement inside the WHILE.

It also is important to identify a cluster of alternations to produce one CASE statement; if this is not done, the cluster yields several nested CASE statements, which is less efficient than a single large one.

Identifying a cluster of alternation nodes is easy. The generation algorithm essentially walks through the tree top down. When an alternation node is seen, the generator should first examine its left and right children for alternation, continuing this recursively until a maximum tree of alternations is found. The leaves are then the children to be considered in constructing the alternation CASE statement.

It is not important to identify a cluster of concatenations. The consequence of generating concatenations in binary fashion is the introduction of additional BEGIN-END pairs. These do not cause the generation of additional compiled code.

4.5.7. Error Recovery

Error recovery in a recursive-descent parser is somewhat more difficult than in a table-driven LL(1) parser, because the stack is not accessible. The parser stack is in fact the trail of return addresses pushed on the Pascal run-time stack by procedure calls. There is no way to experiment with reducing and later restoring that stack.

However, a reasonable error-recovery strategy can be developed. We essentially drop input tokens until one is found that belongs to a token set passed to the ERROR routine. Let us call this set the ETOKEN set. ETOKEN is associated with a nonterminal X the procedure P_X of which detected a syntax error. In a top-down parse, the nonterminal X is supposed to match some string α from the remainder of the input list; when it fails, we can try looking for a character that follows α, which is FOLLOW(X).

Unfortunately, X may be the root of a subtree that never should have been opened by calling P_X. For example, the next token may be EOF, the end-of-file. EOF is not likely to be in the follow set of some interior subtree; hence, it probably is not in FOLLOW(X). The error recovery function would therefore loop forever, failing to find EOF in its token set, and also failing to scan a different token.

One cure is to make ETOKEN the union set of FOLLOW(X) and all non-terminals Y such that procedure P_Y has previously called procedure P_X. This means that:

$$Y \Rightarrow^* \ldots X \ldots$$

is part of the derivation under construction by the parser. We assume that we cannot examine the run-time stack of the parser; hence, this follow set must be accumulated as the parsing proceeds. It can be accumulated by passing it as a value parameter in every procedure call, which is achieved by modifying the parser generation strategy as follows:

- For every tree T, we construct the procedure:

```
procedure A(ESET: tokset);   {A = symb(T) }
  label 1, 99;
begin
  PROGRAM(T);
  goto 1;
99:  {error reporting, recovery}
  error(set_form(ESET+FOLLOW(T)));
1:
end;
```

- If root node N corresponds to a nonterminal token X other than the goal symbol, then generate:

```
X(ESET + set_form(FOLLOW(X)))
```

If X is the goal symbol, then generate:

```
X(set_form(FOLLOW(X)))
```

Of course, passing a set through procedure calls adds considerable overhead to the parser. This can be avoided only by some means of tracing back through the run-time stack, identifying each of the procedures that are active, and forming the union of their follow sets. Their follow sets could be kept in a table indexed by a procedure number, which can be determined by passing the index number as a value parameter instead of a set. That index value then presumably can be found relative to the run-time stack marker. Here is how the parser is generated under this alternative strategy:

- For every tree T, construct the procedure:

```
procedure A(PN: integer);  {A = symb(T) }
  label 1, 99;
begin
  PROGRAM(T);
    goto 1;
99:  {error reporting, recovery}
  error(trace_set);
1:
end;
```

- If root node N corresponds to a nonterminal token X, then generate:

```
X(procedure_index(X))
```

Here, procedure_index(X) is the index of procedure X, which can be assigned when the parser program is generated. The trace_set is a special function that walks back through the run-time stack. For each procedure call, it identifies its procedure number (parameter PN for procedure A), looks up a FOLLOW set from a global table, and unions it with ESET. ESET is empty initially. Function trace_set therefore returns the follow set of the nonterminal associated with the current procedure, unioned with the follow set of all containing nonterminals in the derivation tree created thus far.

That is the basis of our strategy. Once an error set is determined, it is passed to a simple global ERROR function, as follows:

```
procedure ERROR(ESET: tokenset);
begin
  {report the error with a message}
  while not(token in eset) do next_token;
end;
```

Unfortunately, the error recovery can stumble several times on a single syntax error; it will report several spurious errors in addition to the first single one. There is no guarantee that by finding TOKEN in FOLSET we have identified the end of the sentence supposedly being derived by X. We could still be in the middle of it, or we could have been thrown into procedure X by an earlier error. There will be some stumbling in the former case, but there is some hope of recovery in the latter.

In either case, it is conceivable that the ERROR procedure will simply consume all the remaining source. At least the EOF token will appear in every error set, because it is handed down through the procedure calls starting with the first "goal" procedure call. This will prevent an infinite loop after consuming all the remaining tokens.

This strategy should work reasonably well within a sequence of statements ending with END or a semicolon in Pascal. It will have some problems if the error is at the level of a major control structure, such as a procedure or a case statement.

4.5.8. Adding Semantics

Adding semantic actions to our parser is easy. Positions in the procedures correspond to positions in the grammar in a transparent way. We can add semantic actions anywhere within a production—just after its first token has been scanned, somewhere in the middle, or after its last token has been scanned.

However, if the program is generated automatically (and it is easy to see how to write an automatic generator) any semantics added by hand will be lost at the time of a new generation. The generator should provide a mechanism for adding semantic tags or actions directly in the grammar; these will then appear in the appropriate places in the generated programs.

The LILA system, developed by Lewi, DeVlaminck, Huens, and Huybrecht [Lewi, 1979], provides such grammar tools. It can be adapted easily to generate recursive descent programs and semantics in any of several languages.

4.6 Exercises

1. Trace the action of the following NDPDA for the input string abbbbba and determine whether the string is accepted or rejected. You need not explore wrong choices if you can guess right the first time, but be careful not to reject the input falsely because of wrong choices.

```
K = {A,B,C}
Σ = {a,b}
H = {A,B,⊥}
q0 = A
Z0 = ⊥
halts by empty stack
```

Old State	Input	Old Stack	New State	New Stack
A	a	⊥	B	⊥
B	a	⊥	B	A⊥
B	b	⊥	B	B⊥
B	b	⊥	C	⊥
B	a	A	B	AA
B	b	A	B	BA
B	b	A	C	A
B	a	B	B	AB
B	b	B	B	BB
B	b	B	C	B
C	a	A	C	ε
C	b	B	C	ε
C	a	⊥	C	ε

2. Show that the NDFSA of exercise 1 can accept the strings:

```
aba
aabaa
abababa
```

but cannot accept:

```
bab
abba
abaaaba
```

3. Characterize informally the language accepted by the NDFSA of exercise 1.

4. Design an NDPDA that accepts Polish postfix expressions containing operand a and binary operator +. Give all components of the defining seven-tuple and the halting method.

5. Trace the actions of this NDPDA for the given input strings. The NDPA is:

$$K = \{S, T\}$$
$$\Sigma = \{`(`, `)`, a\}$$
$$H = \{A, D\}$$
$$q_0 = S$$
$$z_0 = D$$
$$F = \{T\}$$

$$\delta (S, `)`, A) = (S, AA)$$
$$\delta (S, `)`, D) = (S, AD)$$
$$\delta (S, `)`, A) = (S, \epsilon)$$
$$\delta (S, \epsilon, D) = (T, D)$$
$$\delta (S, a, A) = (S, A)$$
$$\delta (S, a, D) = (S, D)$$

The input strings are:

```
aaa
(()a)a
((a))
a(a(a)a)aa
```

6. Show that the NDPDA of exercise 5 rejects these strings:

```
a((a)
()a)
(((a))
```

7. Describe the language recognized by the NDPDA of exercise 5.

8. Give a general method for constructing a backtracking system for an NDPDA. Can you find a PDA for which your backtracking system fails?

9. Give a complete formal specification for an NDPDA that recognizes the language defined by the following CFG:

```
S → SASC
S → ϵ
A → Aa
A → b
C → DcD
D → d
```

10. For each string, (a) derive the string in the grammar of exercise 9, and (b) give a trace in which the string is recognized by the NDPDA constructed in exercise 9.

```
baaadcd
badcdbdcd
bbadcddcd
```

11. Construct an NDPDA that recognizes the language defined by this grammar:

```
S → M
S → U
M → iEtMeM
M → b
U → iEtS
U → iEtMeU
E → a
```

12. For each nonterminal of the following grammar, compute $FIRST_1$ and $FOLLOW_1$.

```
S → aAd
A → BC
B → b
B → ε
C → c
C → ε
```

13. For each nonterminal of the following grammar, compute $FIRST_1$ and $FOLLOW_1$.

```
A → BCc
A → gDB
B → ε
B → bCDE
C → DaB
C → ca
D → ε
D → dD
E → gAf
E → c
```

14. Prove theorem 4.5.

15. Prove theorem 4.6.

16. Give a CFG that is *not* LL(1), *is* LL(2) and is *not* strong LL(2).

17. Prove the six properties of $FIRST_1$ and $FOLLOW_1$ sets given in section 4.2.3.

18. Design and program an algorithm that uses the six properties of $FIRST_1$ and $FOLLOW_1$ sets to compute $FIRST_1$ and $FOLLOW_1$ for each nonterminal of a CFG.

19. Trace the LL(1) parser of figure 4.3 for these strings:

    ```
    a+a*a
    a*a+a
    (a+a)*a
    a-a+a
    ```

20. Using the grammars of exercises 12 and 13, for each production A → w compute $FIRST_1(w \; FOLLOW_1(A))$. Is the grammar LL(1)?

21. Use the grammar of exercise 11. For each nonterminal of the grammar, compute $FIRST_1$ and $FOLLOW_1$. For each production A → w, compute $FIRST_1(w \; FOLLOW_1(A))$. Is the grammar LL(1)? Construct the LL(1) selector table for a deterministic parser for the grammar.

22. Give an interpretation of the grammar of exercise 11 that shows that it generates traditional nested *if* statements in Pascal style syntax and unambiguously associates *else* clauses to the correct *if* statement.

23. Using the following grammar, construct the LL(1) selector table for a deterministic parser.

    ```
    S → aAbc
    S → BCf
    A → c
    A → ε
    B → Cd
    B → c
    C → df
    C → ε
    ```

24. Finish the LL(1) parser in section 4.4.

25. Modify each of the following grammars so that it is LL(1), without changing the language.

    ```
    S → A⊥
    A → aB
    A → aC
    A → Ad
    A → Ae
    B → bBC
    B → f
    C → c
    ```

    ```
    S → aBDh
    B → Bb
    B → c
    D → EF
    E → g
    E → ε
    F → f
    F → ε
    ```

26. Transform the grammar of exercise 11 into an extended grammar.

27. Redraw the extended grammar of exercise 26 as an extended-tree grammar.

28. Transform the following grammar into an extended grammar and also express it as an extended-tree grammar.

```
S  → lLuET
S  → a
L  → LS
L  → ε
E  → b
T  → dLe
T  → ε
```

29. Compute the $FIRST_1$ and $FOLLOW_1$ sets for each tree node in the extended-tree grammars of exercises 27 and 28.

30. Is your grammar of exercise 27 valid for a recursive-descent parser?

31. Write a recursive-descent parser for the extended-tree grammar of exercise 28. Make the optimizations described in section 4.5.6. Add error recovery to the parsers of exercises 30 and 31, using the techniques described in section 4.5.7.

32. Add semantic processing to the example of a recursive-descent parser developed in section 4.5.5, so that a Polish postfix translation of the input expression is emitted.

4.7. Bibliographical Notes

LL(k) grammars were first defined by Lewis and Stearns [Lewis, 1968]. The theory of LL(k) grammars and their relation to deterministic parsers was developed extensively by Rosenkrantz and Stearns [Rosenkrantz, 1970b]. Other papers on LL(k) grammar theory are Aho [1972a], vol. I, chapters 5 and 8; Kurki-Suonio [1969]; and Griffiths [1974b]. Recursive-descent parsers and compiler systems have been considered by many authors and form the basis of many so-called compiler-writer systems. Representative papers are: Irons [1961]; Metcalfe [1964]; Feldman [1968]; Gries [1971], chapter 4; Aho [1972a], vol. I, chapter 6; Griffiths [1974c]; and Wirth [1976c]. We have followed Lewi, Vlaminck, Hnens, and Huybrecht [1979] in formulating our Pascal-based recursive-descent generator rules. Their two-volume series describes the theory and the generator in great detail.

The notion of using a nonterminal follow set for recursive descent error recovery seems to have originated in Wirth's portable Pascal compiler [1976].

CHAPTER 5

BOTTOM-UP PARSING AND PRECEDENCE PARSERS

Some hold translations not unlike to be
The wrong side of a Turkey tapestry

. . . James Howell

A bottom-up parser reconstructs a right-most derivation in reverse, conceptually starting with a sentence in the language and ending with the goal symbol. We have previously examined bottom-up parsing as a tree-building process. The key to the process is the identification of the handle in any given right-most sentential form and a production that belongs with the handle in that form.

A bottom-up parser always can be constructed for a CFG. It consists, as does the top-down parser, of an input list, a finite control, and a push-down stack. In general, it is nondeterministic, and there may or may not exist a lookahead system through which a deterministic parser can be constructed. There also exist grammars for which no deterministic parser can be constructed.

There are two broad classes of deterministic bottom-up parsers—the so-called *precedence* parsers and the *LR(k)* parsers. Of these two, the LR(k) parsers are considerably more powerful; they accept a much larger class of grammars. The LR(k) grammars also include all the LL(k) grammars, and constitute the largest class of deterministic grammars with left-to-right parsing and a k-symbol lookahead. Consequently, any CFG is more likely to have an LR(k) parser than to have any other.

A bottom-up parser appears to be more complicated than a top-down parser. The parsing theory is somewhat more difficult to follow than for a top-down parser, and the semantic operations are less obvious. We can combat this only by studying a complete compiler system. We shall present not only the bottom-up parsing theory and system, but also a generalized semantics system, with enough rules so that anyone should be able to design a complete compiler from a set of objectives. Bottom-up semantics can be used with any bottom-up parsing method. The parser need only produce an ordered list of production numbers.

5.1. Nondeterministic Bottom-Up Parsing

A bottom-up, nondeterministic parser differs from a top-down, nondeterministic parser in three respects:

190

1. The stack is more conveniently oriented with its top on its right end. The stack then holds some left suffix αw of a sentential form αwβ at any given time. The handle w will appear on the top of the stack just before an apply action, and will be replaced by a nonterminal A in the action, where A → w is a production in the language. The result will be the new stack αA.

2. The PDA is extended by permitting a string of zero or more symbols to be popped from the stack in one operation. Recall that in a top-down PDA, it was never necessary to pop more than one symbol.

3. A NDPDA constructed from a grammar will have two states. Recall that a top-down automaton contained only one state. However, the added state is used only to provide an elegant halt condition.

An *extended PDA* is a seven-tuple $P = (Q, \Sigma, H, \delta, q_0, \perp, F)$, where:

- Q is a set of *states*.

- Σ is a finite *input alphabet* (the tokens of the language).

- H is a finite *stack alphabet*.

- δ is a *finite mapping* from a three-tuple in $Q \times H^* \times (\Sigma \cup \{\epsilon\})$ to the finite subsets of $Q \times H^*$.

- q_0 is a *start state* in Q.

- $\perp$ is an *initial stack symbol*, in H.

- F is a set of *halt states*.

Except for δ, this PDA is exactly like the top-down automaton introduced earlier. In this PDA, the mapping function δ considers the present state (in Q), but it may consider the symbol under the read head, and it may consider a string of zero or more tokens on the top of the stack. In any case, δ is finite; it must be representable as a finite table. Through δ, the state, a top-of-stack string, and the next input token are mapped (in one move) to a new state and the stack top string is replaced by another string.

A *configuration* is written as follows. The stack top is at the right end of the stack:

$$(state, stack, input list)$$

Then a *move* is defined as a transformation of one configuration into another, as follows:

$$(p, zx, bw) \vdash (q, zy, w)$$

where $b \; \epsilon \; \Sigma \cup \{\epsilon\}$, x, y, and z are in H^*, $w \; \epsilon \; \Sigma^*$, and where:

$$\delta(p, x, b) \text{ contains } (q, y)$$

The PDA is *nondeterministic* if some $\delta(p, x, b)$ contains more than one pair, or in other ways; for example, through an empty x or b.

As before, the *language* defined by P, denoted L(P), is the set:

$$\{w \mid (q_0, Z_0, w) \vdash^* (q, x, \epsilon) \text{ for some q in F and x in } H^*\}$$

Note that the stack need not be empty to halt, and that the PDA is defined such that it may make additional moves after its stack is empty.

Equivalence of Extended PDAs and Context-Free Languages

As before, we can define an extended PDA that recognizes the language of any CFG. However, this one reasonably can be said to operate by handle recognition and replacement, making it a bottom-up parser.

Let (N, Σ, P, S) be a CFG G. We construct an extended PDA R such that L(R) = L(G), as follows:

1. R will have two states, q and r.

2. R's input alphabet is Σ.

3. The stack alphabet H consists of $N \cup \Sigma \cup \{\perp\}$.

4. The initial stack symbol is $\perp$.

5. The initial state is q, and the halt set F = $\{r\}$.

6. The mapping δ is defined as follows:

   (a) *Shift rule:* for every terminal symbol b in Σ, $\delta(q, \epsilon, b)$ contains $\{(q, b)\}$. These moves have the effect of shifting terminal symbols from the input source onto the stack top. For example, the configuration (q, x, bw) would go to the configuration (q, xb, w) in such a move.

   (b) *Apply or reduce rule:* for every production A $\rightarrow$ w in P, $\delta(q, w, \epsilon)$ contains (q, A). These moves have the effect of taking a handle w on the stack top and reducing it to a nonterminal symbol A. Thus, a configuration (q, xw, u) would go to (q, xA, u) in such a move. Note that the apply step moves in the opposite direction of a derivation step; in a bottom-up parser we move from the sentence backwards through its derivation to the goal symbol.

   (c) *Halt rule:* $\delta(q, \perp S, \epsilon)$ contains (r, ϵ), where S is the start symbol. This move can occur only once for a given parse and results in a halt. Note that it requires a stack containing only $\perp S$; there is no way for any stack symbols to appear beneath the $\perp$.

Such a parser is sometimes called a *shift-reduce* parser, because most of its moves are based on (6a) or (6b).

Example.   Consider the arithmetic grammar G_0:

```
E → E + T
E → T
T → T * F
T → F
F → (E)
F → a
```

The PDA mapping for this grammar is:

```
δ(q, ε, a) = {(q, a)}           from rule 6(a)
δ(q, ε, +) = {(q, +)}
δ(q, ε, *) = {(q, *)}
δ(q, ε, ``('') = {(q, ``('')}
δ(q, ε, ``)'') = {(q, ``)'')}

δ(q, E + T, ε) = {(q, E)}       from rule 6(b)
δ(q, T, ε) = {(q, E)}
δ(q, T * F, ε) = {(q, T)}
δ(q, F, ε) = {(q, T)}
δ(q, (E), ε) = {(q, F)}
δ(q, a, ε) = {(q, F)}

δ(q, ⊥ E, ε) = {(r, ε)}         from rule 6(c)
```

Although none of the mapping functions contains more than one pair, the PDA is nondeterministic. The first set of five rules may be applied at any time, to shift another input symbol into the stack. Similarly, there may be opportunities to apply more than one of the second group of transitions. For example, with T*F on the stack top, the string T*F may be reduced to T, or F may be reduced to T.

Despite the great number of possible sequences of moves, the PDA recognizes exactly the language L(G). Most of the moves for a given string end in blind alleys.

Consider the string a*a + a. Only the following sequence of moves can reach the halt state:

```
1.   (q, ⊥, a * a + a) ⊢
2.   (q, ⊥ a, * a + a) ⊢
3.   (q, ⊥ F, * a + a) ⊢
4.   (q, ⊥ T, * a + a) ⊢
5.   (q, ⊥ T *, a + a) ⊢
6.   (q, ⊥ T * a, + a) ⊢
7.   (q, ⊥ T * F, + a) ⊢
8.   (q, ⊥ T, + a) ⊢
9.   (q, ⊥ E, + a) ⊢
10.  (q, ⊥ E +, a) ⊢
11.  (q, ⊥ E + a, ε) ⊢
12.  (q, ⊥ E + F, ε) ⊢
13.  (q, ⊥ E + T, ε) ⊢
14.  (q, ⊥ E, ε) ⊢
15.  (r, ε, ε)
```

Now consider the seventh configuration, (q, ⊥T*F, + a). It is possible to apply a shift rule to this, yielding (q, ⊥T*F+, a). However, no rule provides for reducing a stack with $+$ on top, so we must again shift, yielding (q, $\perp T*F+a$, ϵ). At this point, we may reduce a to F, yielding (q, $\perp T*F+F$, ϵ), and then reduce F to T and T to E, yielding (q, $\perp T*F+E$, ϵ). However, we are at the end of the line for this particular sequence of moves. No further reductions or shifts are possible, and we have failed to reach the configuration (q, $\perp E$, ϵ) that permits a halt. There also have been no other possible moves.

We choose this example to illustrate the central point—this PDA recognizes exactly the language defined by the grammar G. A proof follows. We prove a somewhat stronger result, which implies that the PDA language and L(G) are equivalent:

Lemma 5.1. $S \Rightarrow^* xAy \Rightarrow^+ zy$ if and only if (q, $\perp$, zy) $\vdash^*$ (q, $\perp xA$, y), where the derivation is right-most. A is a nonterminal.

Proof: "Only If" Part.   The "only if" part can be proved by induction on the number of steps n in the second sequence of derivations. The lemma states that, given a right-most sentential form xAy, in which A is the right-most nonterminal, and such that xA derives a terminal string z, then the PDA must be able to accept string z through shifts and reduces, and reach a stack that contains xA. The string y is unimportant, except within the inductive assertion of the proof.

Basis Step. For n $= 1$, string x must be empty, and a production A $\rightarrow$ z exists, where z is a terminal string. There clearly exists a sequence of shift moves for the terminal string z, yielding the moves:

$$(q, \perp, zy) \vdash^* (q, \perp z, y)$$

Note that z also may be empty. Then the stack top z may be reduced to A by the PDA construction rules, yielding the result:

$$(q, \perp z, y) \vdash (q, \perp A, y)$$

which was to be proved.

Inductive Step. Now suppose the lemma true for any number of derivation steps less than n and that xAy $\Rightarrow^+$ zy in n steps. The second sequence of derivations begins with:

$$xAy \Rightarrow xwy \Rightarrow^* zy$$

where A $\rightarrow$ w is a production. Clearly, xw $\Rightarrow^*$ z in less than n derivation steps. Now xw may consist solely of terminals, which reduces this to the case n $= 1$. Hence, suppose xw contains at least one nonterminal, B; we also let B be the right-most nonterminal in xw, without loss of generality; then:

$$xw = rBs$$

where s is a terminal string. We now have:

$$S \Rightarrow^* xAy \Rightarrow xwy = rBsy \Rightarrow^* zy = usy,$$

because the terminal z must contain s as a suffix. But by the inductive hypothesis:

$$(q, \perp, zy) = (q, \perp, usy) \vdash^* (q, \perp rB, sy)$$

Then, by some shifting rules:

$$(q, \perp rB, sy) \vdash^* (q, \perp rBs, y)$$

Next, because rBs = xw:

$$(q, \perp xw, y) \vdash (q, \perp xA, y)$$

QED.

A proof of the "if" part is left as an exercise.

Deterministic Bottom-Up Parsing

The PDA constructed from a grammar G described in the previous section is nondeterministic for several reasons:

1. A shift rule always can be applied as long as there exist remaining symbols in the input list.

2. Although a reduction rule can be applied only when the top-of-stack string matches a right part of some production, there may be several different productions the right parts of which match a stack top string. Thus, for a stack top string αw, any production $A \rightarrow w$ might be applied through a reduction rule to yield αA. Note that the length of w is not defined by the PDA.

3. As a special case of point 2, an empty production $A \rightarrow \epsilon$ could be applied at any time, because it requires no stack top match at all. The mapping associated with such a production is $\delta(q, \epsilon, \epsilon)$ contains (q, A); that is, nonterminal A is pushed onto the stack.

There are two commonly used bottom-up, DPDAs—the precedence parsers and the LR(k) parsers. Each of them has a number of variations that may be employed to increase its power or to reduce its size.

5.2. Precedence Parsing

> *Sir, there is no settling the point of precedency between a louse and a flea.*
>
> *. . . Samuel Johnson*

A precedence parser identifies the handle within a right-most sentential form without identifying the production. A *simple precedence parser* associates one of the three relations, $<$, $>$, or $\doteq$, with each pair of adjacent tokens in a sentential form. For a suitable grammar, the handle always becomes delimited between $<$ and $>$, and within it $\doteq$ applies between the pairs. Finally, in the string preceding the handle, $<$ or $\doteq$ appears between pairs, but $>$ does not. The handle therefore can be identified by scanning a sentential form from left to right until $>$ is seen, then from right to left until $<$ is seen.

A typical precedence table is given in figure 5.1, for a simple grammar G_2:

```
E → E - T | T
T → ( E ) | a
```

Every sentence is preceded and followed by a special symbol $\perp$, so that the first and last symbols have a meaningful precedence relation with their neighbors. The table of figure 5.1 contains one entry for which two relations hold: $\{(, E\}$ is in both of the relations $<$ and $\doteq$. This is called a *conflict* and means that the parser is nondeterministic.

For example, in grammar G_2, within the sentential form $\perp ((E - T)) \perp$, the adjacent pairs carry the following precedence symbols:

$$\perp < (< (< \doteq E \doteq - \doteq T >) \ldots$$

	Right						
	$-$	$($	$)$	a	E	T	$\perp$
$-$		$<$		$<$		$=$	
$($		$<$		$<$	$\leq$	$<$	
$)$	$>$		$>$				$>$
a	$>$		$>$				$>$
E	$=$		$=$				$>$
T	$>$		$>$				$>$
$\perp$		$<$		$<$	$<$	$<$	

Left {

G2: E → E - T | T
T → (E) | a

Figure 5.1.   Simple precedence relation table for grammar G_2, shown.

because E − T is the handle of this sentential form. The $\lessdot \doteq$ conflict for $\{(, E\}$ indicates that (E − T could be a handle; however, this fits no production right part and therefore cannot be a handle.

The pairs in the string past the handle are not important; the object is to delimit the handle. Once the handle is reduced by applying a production (in this case, E → E − T), a new sentential form is obtained, and its handle may similarly be found.

Although this appears to be an impossibly weak system, it is sufficiently powerful to parse (with a few special problems) arithmetic expressions in the common programming languages. The precedence idea also is used extensively in programming documentation, and is based on this theory of precedence relations.

A parsing table can be constructed systematically from a basis grammar. If the parsing table is free of conflicts, and no two productions have the same right member, then the grammar is a *simple precedence* grammar, and the precedence parser will work correctly. If conflicts exist, it may be possible to extend the precedence relations to include more than one symbol, or it may be possible to resolve the conflicts by modifying the parsing method slightly. Otherwise, the grammar is either ambiguous or unsuitable as a basis for a precedence parser.

5.2.1. Relations

We need some background development before we can discuss the precedence parsers in more detail.

A *relation* on two sets P and Q is some set of ordered pairs (x, y) such that x is in P and y is in Q. We write:

$$x \; R \; y$$

to indicate that the ordered pair (x, y) is in relation R. We can also write: $y \; \varepsilon \; R(x)$. An example of a relation is equality on pairs of integers; I = J is true if the integer I is the same as J; otherwise, it is false. The members of the integer equality relation are (1, 1), (2, 2), ... Another example of a relation is the set of productions in a grammar G; P is a subset of ordered pairs drawn from the sets N (nonterminals) and $(N \cup \Sigma)^*$. This relation is indicated "→".

A relation R is said to be *transitive* if (A, B) in R and (B, C) in R imply that (A, C) is in R, which may also be written:

$$\text{if } (\forall \; A, B, C) \; (A \; R \; B \text{ and } B \; R \; C) \text{ then } A \; R \; C$$

A relation R is said to be *reflexive* if, for every A in R, (A, A) is in R.

A relation R is said to be *symmetric* if (A, B) in R implies that (B, A) is in R.

A relation may be expressed as a matrix consisting of Boolean zeros and ones. A one indicates that the corresponding row and column variables constitute a pair that is in the relation, and a zero indicates a pair that is not in the relation.

The Boolean matrix for a symmetric relation is diagonally symmetric; an element at (i, j) in the matrix is equal to the element at (j, i). The matrix for a reflexive relation contains all ones along its diagonal.

The *transitive completion* or *closure* of a relation R, denoted R^+, is defined:

1. R^+ contains R.

2. If R^+ contains the pairs (A, B) and (B, C), then R^+ contains (A, C).

It can be seen that the inclusion of one pair through rule (2) may precipitate the inclusion of other pairs. The inclusion process must eventually terminate if R is a finite set.

The *reflexive transitive completion* of a relation R, denoted R^*, is the union of R^+ and every pair (x, x) such that x is in R.

5.2.2. Boolean Matrix Sum and Product

We pointed out that a relation can be expressed as a Boolean matrix. Sum and product operations on two matrices are convenient in constructing precedence tables.

The Boolean sum $P = R \vee S$ of two compatible matrices R and S is defined by:

$$p(i, j) = r(i, j) \vee s(i, j)$$

for all (i, j), where:

$$r(i, j) \ \varepsilon \ R, \ s(i, j) \ \varepsilon \ S, \ \text{and} \ p(i, j) \ \varepsilon \ P.$$

The Boolean product $P = R \wedge S$ of two square Boolean matrices R and S is defined as follows, where r(i, j) is a member of R, s(j, k) is a member of S, p(i, k) is in P, and the rank of the matrices is n:

$$p(i, k) = \bigvee_{j=1}^{n} (r(i, j) \wedge s(j, k))$$

The Boolean product is analogous to the algebraic product of matrices, except that a Boolean matrix contains only zeros and ones. The product matrix element (i, k) is found by multiplying row i of matrix r by column k of matrix s; a bit-by-bit Boolean product is formed, and the resulting bit is the logical OR of these products.

For example, consider the Boolean matrices (a) and (b) in figure 5.2. Their product is given in figure 5.2(c). Thus the first row of (c), 1010, is obtained from the first row of (a), 0010 and the (b) matrix is constructed as follows:

```
1 = 01 ∨ 01 ∨ 11 ∨ 00
0 = 00 ∨ 01 ∨ 10 ∨ 00
1 = 01 ∨ 01 ∨ 11 ∨ 00
0 = 00 ∨ 00 ∨ 10 ∨ 01
```

where 01 stands for $0 \wedge 1$.

$$
\begin{pmatrix} 0 & 0 & 1 & 0 \\ 1 & 1 & 0 & 0 \\ 0 & 1 & 0 & 1 \\ 1 & 0 & 0 & 1 \end{pmatrix} \times \begin{pmatrix} 1 & 0 & 1 & 0 \\ 1 & 1 & 1 & 0 \\ 1 & 0 & 1 & 0 \\ 0 & 0 & 0 & 1 \end{pmatrix} = \begin{pmatrix} 1 & 0 & 1 & 0 \\ 1 & 1 & 1 & 0 \\ 1 & 1 & 1 & 1 \\ 1 & 0 & 1 & 1 \end{pmatrix}
$$

(a)   (b)   (c)

Figure 5.2.   Boolean matrix product illustrated.

Matrix Product and Transitive Completion of a Relation

There is an interesting result: the transitive completion of a relation R can be found by repeatedly replacing R by $R \vee (R \wedge R)$. We will develop a convenient and fast method of constructing precedence tables for a grammar on a digital computer.

This result is a consequence of theorem 5.1.

Theorem 5.1.   Let X and Y be two square Boolean matrices representing the relations R and S, respectively. Then the pair (A, B) is in the product relation X $\wedge$ Y if and only if there exists an element C such that (A, C) is in R and (C, B) is in S.

Proof.   The "if" part carries the postulate that C exists. Then matrix X has a 1 at the intersection of row A and column C, and matrix Y has a 1 at the intersection of row C and column B. Then the product matrix carries a 1 in row A, column B, and (A, B) is therefore in the product relation.

For the "only if" part, suppose the pair (A, B) is in the product matrix X Y. From the matrix product formula, there must be some row k in Y and column k in X such that there is a 1 at column i in Y and row j in X; otherwise the union could not be 1 for i = A and j = B. But this implies that (A, C) is in R and (C, B) is in S, for some C. QED

5.2.3. Warshall's Algorithm

Warshall [1962] found a fast means of computing the transitive completion B^{+} of a relation B. His algorithm is expressed by the following Pascal program, where B is some given square Boolean matrix. Matrix B is tranformed into its transitive completion.

```
type BOOLMAT = array [1..N, 1..N] of boolean;
var I, J, K, N: integer;    {N is the rank of the matrix B}
    B: BOOLMAT;
begin
  for I:=1 until N do
    for J:=1 until N do
      if B[J, I]=TRUE then
        for K:=1 until N do
          B[J, K]:=B[J, K] ∨ B[I, K];
  end;
```

5.2.4. Viable Prefix and Precedence Pairs

A *viable prefix* is some prefix of a right-most sentential form that may include the handle, but no symbols past the handle. Thus, if xhy is a right-most sentential form, such that h is the handle, then a viable prefix of xhy is any string r such that xh = rs, where s may be empty.

An *(m, n) precedence pair*, where m and n are integers zero or greater, is a pair of strings (x, y) such that $|x| = m$, $|y| = n$, xy is a substring of a right-most sentential form, and x lies wholly within a viable prefix. Note that string y may be within a viable prefix, or may lie partially or wholly within the following string. Because we demand that x have exactly the length m and y the length n, we prefix every sentential form with m special symbols $\perp$, and suffix every sentential form with n special symbols.

For example, consider the sentential form ((E − T)) in grammar G_2 (figure 5.1) and let (m, n) = (2, 1). Then we rewrite the form as $\perp \perp$ ((E − T)) $\perp$ so that it is always possible to define a (2,1) precedence pair. Within this form, because E − T is the handle, the viable prefixes and (2, 1) precedence pairs are as follows.

Viable prefixes:

```
ε
(
((
((E
((E -
((E - T
```

(2, 1) precedence pairs:

```
(⊥⊥, ()
(⊥(, ()
(((, E)
((E,  -)
(E-,  T)
(-T,  ))
```

5.2.5. Precedence Relations

An *(m, n) precedence relation* is a relation on the set of (m, n) precedence pairs defined on the right-most sentential forms within a grammar G. The three relations ($<$, $>$, $\doteq$) are defined as follows:

1. A pair (x, y) is in the $>$ relation if and only if $|x| = m$, $|y| = n$, and there exists some sentential form αhβ such that ux = αh and yv = β, and h is the handle. (α and β are assumed to include the necessary prefixes $\perp\perp\perp$... and suffixes ...$\perp\perp\perp$.) That is, (x, y) marks the boundary position between the end of the handle h and the beginning of the following string β. However, x may include h, or h may include x. Note that y is a

terminal string, as are v and β, but not h. The three dots ''. . .'' stand for ''any string including empty.''

2. A pair (x, y) is in the $\doteq$ relation if and only if $|x| = m$, $|y| = n$, and there exists some sentential form αhβ such that ux = αh' and yv = h''β, where the handle h is h'h'' and neither h' nor h'' is empty. That is, (x, y) marks a position within a handle, so that at least one tail symbol of x is in the handle and at least one head symbol of y is in the handle. Note that if the handle length is one or less, no $\doteq$ pair is defined for the handle.

3. A pair (x, y) is in the $\lessdot$ relation if and only if $|x| = m$, $|y| = n$, and there exists some sentential form αhβ such that h is the handle, ux = α, and yv = hβ. That is, the pair (x, y) marks the beginning of the handle, such that the head of y is the head of the handle, and the tail of x is the tail of the string preceding the handle.

4. For every symbol X such that $S \to^* X$. . ., the pair ($\perp$ . . . $\perp$, X) is in $\lessdot$. For every symbol X such that $S \to^*$ . . .X, the pair (X, $\perp$ . . . $\perp$) is in $\gtrdot$. These special relation members are needed to cover the leading and trailing $\perp$ special symbols added to sentences. (S is the goal symbol of grammar G.)

5.2.6. Simple Precedence Grammar

If the grammar is such that no two productions have the same right member, then the grammar is said to be *uniquely invertible*. As we have seen, the precedence relations identify only the handle of a sentential form; they do not specify the production associated with that handle. Hence, a precedence parser can be constructed for a grammar only if the grammar is uniquely invertible.

A grammar is said to be *(m, n) simple precedence* if and only if the relations $\lessdot$, $\gtrdot$, and $\doteq$ are pairwise disjoint, and the grammar is uniquely invertible.

Example. Consider the simple grammar G_2:

```
E → E - T | T
T → ( E ) | a
```

Note that G_2 is uniquely invertible. The (1, 1) precedence relations $\lessdot$, $\gtrdot$, and $\doteq$ are given in figure 5.1. We shall discuss systematic methods of generating such a table later. Let us first consider a short derivation to demonstrate that the precedence relations do in fact enable us to parse deterministically a sentence in $L(G_2)$ bottom-up. Consider the string $(a - a) - a$, which is in the language $L(G_2)$. The first group of relations, based on the table, are:

$$\perp \lessdot (\lessdot a \gtrdot - \ldots$$

(The table indicates that the pairs ($\perp$, ( ) and ((, a) are in the relation $\lessdot$, and that (a, −) is in >.) The handle is clearly ''a'', which can be reduced only to T. The reduction yields a new sentential form:

$$\perp < (< T > - \ldots$$

which indicates that T is to be reduced to E, yielding:

$$\perp < (< E \doteq - < a >) \ldots$$

The table contains a (<, ≐) conflict for the pair {(, E}. We shall deal with this matter next. For now, we select the correct choice by a nondeterministic oracle. Note that although a ≐ has appeared, the handle is a, delimited by < ... >, which indicates a reduction of a to T, yielding:

$$\perp < (< E \doteq - \doteq T >) \ldots$$

The handle here is E − T, which reduces to E. The next few steps are:

```
⊥ < ( ≐ E ≐ ) > - ... ⊥
⊥ < T > - ... ⊥
⊥ < E ≐ - < a > ⊥
⊥ < E ≐ - ≐ T > ⊥
⊥ < E > ⊥
```

This terminal sentential form consists of the goal symbol bracketed by the special delimiter symbols ⊥ . . . ⊥.

Now let us examine the precedence table itself in the light of these definitions of a (1, 1) precedence relation. Each of the three relations may be determined (in theory at least) by examining all the possible right-most sentential forms. Unfortunately, there usually are an infinite number of them, so this is hardly practical. Nevertheless, here are some derivations that bring out some of the table entries:

- ⊥E⊥ ⇒ ⊥T⊥, therefore {⊥, T} is in < and {T, ⊥} is in >.
- ⊥E⊥ ⇒ ⊥E−T⊥, therefore {⊥, E} is in <, {E, −} is in ≐, and {−, T} is in ≐.
- ⊥T⊥ ⇒ ⊥(E)⊥, therefore {⊥, (} is in <, {(, E} and {E,)} are in ≐, and {), ⊥} is in >.
- ⊥T⊥ ⇒ ⊥a⊥, therefore {⊥, a} is in <, and {a, ⊥} in >.
- ⊥E − T⊥ ⇒ ⊥E−a⊥, therefore {−, a} is in <.

Blank Entries

What about the blank entries in a precedence table? They apparently mean that the associated pair cannot appear in a sentential form and that therefore any symbol-pair showing up in a parse that maps to a blank entry must be the result of a syntax error. But how can we prove that a given entry is truly blank? We can be quite ingenious in finding sentential forms to fill in various table values, but we can never be quite sure that we have found them all. We therefore need a more systematic approach to precedence table generation than simply looking at various sentential forms. We take up this matter in section 5.2.7.

Three Theorems on Precedence Relations

Theorem 5.2.   No grammar containing an empty production can be a precedence grammar.

Proof.   Suppose a grammar G contains an empty rule, $A \to \epsilon$. Then some derivation:

$$S \to^* xuAvy \to xuvy \to^* \ldots$$

exists, where u and v are terminal or nonterminal symbols (not strings). The handle of the form xuvy is an empty string between u and v. By the precedence relation definitions, therefore, $u \lessdot v$ and $u \gtrdot v$, which creates a precedence conflict.   QED

Theorem 5.3.   Given any right-most sentential form xhy, where h is the handle, in a simple precedence grammar G, then either $\lessdot$ or $\doteq$ holds between every pair within x.

Proof.   Let $xhy = ruvs$, where u and v are some (m, n) precedence pair, and ru is contained in x. Thus (u, v) marks a boundary between symbols in x, or between x and the handle.

Consider the partial derivation tree T for the sentential form ruvs, and the nodes N_u and N_v. N_u is associated with the right-most symbol in u, and N_v with the left-most symbol in v. Then consider the upward paths in T from N_u and N_v; these must intersect in some node N_B associated with nonterminal B.

Suppose first that N_B is not the parent of N_u. There is then a subtree rooted in a child of N_B with a height of at least one. It therefore contains the handle, contradicting the premise that the handle of ruvs is in vs. Therefore N_B is the parent of N_u.

If N_B also is the parent of N_v, the pair (u, v) is in $\doteq$. If N_B is not a parent of N_v, it is nevertheless an ancestor. We then have a right-most derivation of the form:

$$S \Rightarrow^* \ldots B \ldots \Rightarrow \ldots uV \ldots \Rightarrow^* \ldots uV' \ldots \Rightarrow \ldots uv \ldots$$

and by the precedence definitions, we see that (u, v) is in $\lessdot$. QED

Theorem 5.3 implies that a sentential form may be scanned from left to right through the string that precedes the handle. If the grammar is simple precedence, then only $\lessdot$ or $\doteq$ applies between the pairs of this prefix string, and the scan may continue until the handle is found; it is delimited by $\gtrdot$ on its right end. Note that the fundamental precedence rule 3 does not specify precedence relations between the pairs in the string preceding the handle, and it might have turned out that some of these could be in $\gtrdot$ or in no precedence relation. Either case would be fatal to the prefix-scanning operation. We now have assurance that the prefix scanning will work properly.

Theorem 5.4. Let $\perp^m w \perp^n$ be accepted by an (m, n) precedence parser. Then w is a right-most sentential form in G.

Proof. This theorem assures us that an (m, n) precedence parser accepts only strings in L(G). It should be obvious from the previous discussion that a string in L(G) is accepted by a (m, n) precedence parser, because the (m, n) precedence relations are set up in such a way as always to recognize the handle.

We prove this by induction on the number of steps in the reduction process. For zero steps, we must have $\perp^m S \perp^n$, where S is the start symbol, obviously a sentential form. Therefore assume the theorem true for all steps less than some k.

Let $\perp^m w \perp^n$ be accepted in k steps, and consider the first step in which the parser identifies the string h within w such that:

$$\perp^m x \lessdot y_1 \doteq y_2 \doteq \ldots \doteq y_1 \gtrdot z \perp^n$$

where $h = y_1 y_2 \ldots y_r$. Here, x and/or z may be empty, and r may be equal to one. In any case, the parser must see the relation $\gtrdot$ somewhere prior to or at the terminating $\perp^n$. Then, working backward through w from this point, marked by the end string z, it looks for the first $\lessdot$, marked by the prefix x. In between, the relation $\doteq$ must apply. If $\lessdot$ and then $\gtrdot$ are not found in that order, the string w is not accepted by the parser.

Now the string y so found must also be the right-hand part of some production $A \rightarrow y$ for acceptance; the nonterminal A also is unique because the grammar is uniquely invertible. The $\doteq$ relation applies among the members of some production right part, and the parser permits a reduction only if y matches a production right part. Hence, the parser produces the new string $\perp^m x A z \perp^n$, which it accepts and which, by the inductive hypothesis, is a right-most sentential form; therefore:

$$S \rightarrow^* x A z$$

but $A \rightarrow y$, hence $S \rightarrow^+ xyz = w$, which shows that w is a right-most sentential form.   QED

Theorem 5.4 also can be stated: if a sentence w is not in L(G), then it is not accepted by the precedence parser. This error-detection ability is obviously important; we expect a parser to detect syntax errors as well as to analyze correct sentences. How are errors detected? The parser may encounter a precedence pair with an empty entry in its table; that is, a pair (x, y) not in any of the three relations. It also is conceivable that it may isolate a string between $<$ and $>$ within some sentence that fails to match a production right member. We now give a simple example of a precedence grammar and a sentence that can be rejected only by a failure to match a delimited string to a production right part:

```
S → A | B
A → a b c
B → b c d
```

It is easy to show that the (1, 1) precedence table is as follows:

	a	b	c	d	A	B	S	⊥
a		≐						
b			≐					
c				≐			>	
d							>	
A							>	
B							>	
S							>	
⊥	<	<			<	<	<	

so that there are no conflicts; the grammar is (1, 1) simple precedence. However, consider the string abcd. The parser reaches this configuration:

$$\perp\ <\ a\ \doteq\ b\ \doteq\ c\ \doteq\ d\ >\ \perp$$

which indicates that abcd is the handle, but it fails to match any of the production right parts. Furthermore, the string abc probably should have been reduced to A, yet the parser continued past it and failed to detect an error until the $\perp$ was seen. (It is easy to construct grammars similar to this one in which the parser continues an arbitrary number of symbols past an error point.)

Summary

Consider a precedence parser for a grammar G, with a table free of conflicts. Then:

1. Given a sentential form in the language L(G), the parser will accept the sentential form, reconstructing a right-most, bottom-up parse.

2. Given some sentence not in L(G), the parser must ultimately fail to accept the sentence; however, it may fail either (a) by finding a symbol pair not in any of the relations $<$, $\doteq$, or $>$, or (b) by failing to match the left-most string delimited by $<\ \ldots\ >$ with the right part of any production.

It is the possibility of failing through case 2(b) that makes a precedence parser less desirable than an LR(k) parser, because it implies that a precedence parser may continue far past a reasonable error point before discovering an error. Nevertheless, much of this ''weakness'' depends on how one regards a sentence in error. A program with a syntax error should be rejected; no compiler that attempts to ''read'' the programmer's mind should be fully trusted. The important question is not whether an error is detected early or late; it is whether the parser can somehow patch over the error and continue parsing in a reasonable manner, so that there is a fairly good chance of detecting other syntax errors. The patching-over process is one form of error recovery.

5.2.7. Wirth–Weber Relations

The definition of a precedence relation given in section 5.2.5 is not particularly useful as a means of obtaining the relations, because it is expressed in terms of the (usually) infinite set of sentential forms rather than the finite set of productions. We may restate the relations in an equivalent, but more useful form, called the *Wirth–Weber (1, 1) precedence relations:*

1. The relation $>$ always is defined on a pair (X, a), where a is a terminal symbol, because the symbol immediately to the right of any handle must be terminal. We say that $X > a$, or (X, a) is in $>$ if and only if, for some production $A \rightarrow xBYy$ in P, $B \Rightarrow^+ \ldots X$ and $Y \Rightarrow^* a \ldots$ x and y are in $(\Sigma \cup N)^*$.

2. A pair of symbols (X, Y) is in $\doteq$ if and only if there exists a production $A \rightarrow \ldots XY \ldots$ in P. Note that X and Y may be terminal or nonterminal symbols.

3. A pair of symbols (X, Y) is in $<$ if and only if there exists a production $A \rightarrow xXBy$ in P such that $B \Rightarrow^+ Y \ldots$.

Equivalence Proof. We now show that the Wirth–Weber relations are equivalent to the $(1, 1)$ precedence relations given in section 5.2.5.

Consider the $\doteq$ relation first. Because a handle always is the right member of some production rule, it follows that the $(1, 1)$ precedence relation $\doteq$ is equivalent to the Wirth–Weber $\doteq$ relation.

Next consider the $<$ relation, and let (X, Y) be in $<$ by the Wirth–Weber rules; then there exists a right-most derivation:

$$S \Rightarrow^* uAv \Rightarrow uxXByv \Rightarrow^+ uxXYwyv$$

Here $B \Rightarrow^+ Yw$, and Yw is the handle of uxXYwyv. u, v, x, and y are in $(\Sigma \cup N)^*$. Then, by the $(1, 1)$ precedence relation (3), (X, Y) must be in $<$.

Now suppose that (X, Y) is in $<$ by the $(1, 1)$ precedence relations. Then there exists a sentential form xhs such that h is the handle, X is the tail symbol of x, and Y the head symbol of h. Now this form has a derivation tree in which X and Y are leaf symbols (they may be nonterminal symbols). The upward paths from X and Y must intersect in some nonterminal symbol A, and A is associated with some production $A \rightarrow w$. Now X must be in w; that is, A is X's parent.

Otherwise, X is derived from a nonterminal in w, and a handle would have to exist in x, contradicting the assumption that h is the handle in xhs. Now Y cannot be in w, because the handle must be derived from Y. . . in the A production, not simply be a right part of it. These considerations, put together, imply the Wirth–Weber relation 3—namely, that X must be in a production A → xXBy, and B $\Rightarrow^+$ Y. . . .

Finally, consider the $>$ relation. Given the Wirth–Weber relation 1, production A → xBYy such that B $\Rightarrow^+$ . . .X and Y $\Rightarrow^*$ a. . ., then the string . . .X derived from B is a handle at some point in a derivation, and is followed by the terminal symbol a. Therefore (X, a) is in the (1, 1) precedence relation. Then suppose that the sentential form xhs exists, where h is the handle, and let a be the first symbol in s and X the last symbol in h. Consider the derivation tree for this sentential form and paths up the tree from the leaf nodes X and a. These paths must converge first on some nonterminal node A, associated with a production A → xBYy, where the X path goes through B and the a path goes through (or is) Y. By arguments similar to those given for the $<$ relation, B must derive . . .X in at least one step; otherwise, . . .X = h is not a handle. However, Y may be a or may derive a. . ., which implies the Wirth–Weber relation $>$. QED

Constructing the Wirth–Weber Relations

The Wirth–Weber relations are valuable in constructing a precedence table because they focus on the productions and not on sentential forms. However, we also need some relations that yield derived first and last symbols. We express them as relations in order to develop the simple precedence relations as matrix products.

LAST$^+$

$$(A \ LAST^+ \ X) \ \text{if and only if} \ (A \Rightarrow^+ \ . . .X)$$

This relation defines the set of trailing symbols, terminal and nonterminal, derivable from A in one or more steps.

FIRST$^+$

$$(A \ FIRST^+ \ X) \ \text{if and only if} \ (A \Rightarrow^+ \ X. . .)$$

This relation defines the set of leading symbols, terminal or nonterminal, derivable from A in one or more steps.

FIRST*

$$(A \ FIRST^* \ X) \ \text{if and only if} \ (A \Rightarrow^* \ X. . .)$$

This relation defines the set of leading symbols, terminal or nonterminal, derivable from A in zero or more steps.

TFIRST*

$$(A \text{ TFIRST}^* x) \text{ if and only if } (A \Rightarrow^* x \ldots \text{ and } x \ \varepsilon \ \Sigma)$$

Symbol x is a member of the set of leading *terminal* symbols that can be derived from A, including A itself, if A is terminal.

TRANSPOSE

TRANSPOSE(M) is the transpose of matrix M: an element in row i and column j is moved to row j, column i, for all i and j.

Now the Wirth–Weber relations may be defined concisely in terms of the products of certain relations as follows:

- The $\doteq$ relation is found by inspection of the production set:

$$X \doteq Y \text{ if and only if there exists a production } P \rightarrow uXYv$$

- The relation $<$ is equivalent to:

$$\{ (R, S) \mid (\exists \ A, B)(A \rightarrow ..RB.. \text{ and } B \Rightarrow^+ S \ldots) \},$$

which is equivalent to:

$$\{(R, S) \mid (\exists \ B)(R \doteq B) \text{ and } (B \text{ FIRST}^+ S)\}$$

Therefore, $<$ is equivalent to $(\doteq)(\text{FIRST}^+)$, viewed as a Boolean matrix product of $(\doteq)$ and (FIRST^+).

- The relation $>$ is:

```
{(R, a) | (∃ A, B, C)
(A → ...BC... ∧ B ⇒* ...R ∧ C ⇒* a.. ∧ a ε Σ)}
```

Now $A \rightarrow ..BC..$ is equivalent to $B \doteq C$, $B \Rightarrow^+ \ldots R$ is equivalent to B LAST$^+$ R, and $C \Rightarrow^* a \ldots$ to C TFIRST* a. Therefore:

$$R > a \text{ is } (R \ (\text{TRANSPOSE}(\text{LAST}^+))B) \wedge (B \doteq C) \wedge (C \text{ TFIRST}^* a)$$

hence:

$$> \text{ is equivalent to } (\text{TRANSPOSE}(\text{LAST}^+))(\doteq)(\text{TFIRST}^*)$$

viewed as a product of Boolean matrices.

The special symbol $\perp$ placed at the beginning and end of a sentence requires attention. The correct treatment is:

1. Define a new nonterminal, G, and a new production:

$$G \rightarrow \perp S \perp$$

where S is the grammar start symbol. Make G the new start symbol.

2. Include $(\perp, S)$ and $(S, \perp)$ in the $\doteq$ relation.

3. Include $\perp$ in FIRST(G) and $\perp$ in LAST(G).

When the $\lessdot$ and $\gtrdot$ relations are developed by matrix products, a conflict between $\gtrdot$ and $\doteq$ will be found in $(S, \perp)$. This conflict is spurious, and one about which the parser never will be concerned. Delete the $\doteq$ part of it. Also, a conflict between $\lessdot$ and $\doteq$ will be found in $(\perp, S)$; delete the $\doteq$ part. Any other conflicts are real and must be dealt with. These two arise because we placed $(S, \perp)$ and $(\perp, S)$ in $\doteq$, as we need to do to develop $\lessdot$ and $\gtrdot$ for the other symbols and $\perp$. However, S derives other strings, which means that $(\perp, S)$ will show up in $\lessdot$ and $(S, \perp)$ will show up in $\gtrdot$. The parser must halt when the sentential form $\perp S \perp$ is found.

Example.   Figure 5.3 gives an example for a simple grammar, $G_2{'}$, containing a binary $-$ and parenthesizing. The productions of the basis grammar $G_2{'}$ are $\{G \to \perp E \perp; E \to E - T \mid T; T \to (E) \mid a \}$.

Figure 5.3(a) shows the $\doteq$ relation, easily found by inspection of the production set. The pairs $\{E, \perp\}$ and $\{\perp, E\}$ are in the relation because of the first production, $\{E, -\}$ and $\{-, T\}$ are in it because of the second production, and $\{(, E\}$ and $\{E,)\}$ are in it because of the fourth production.

Figure 5.3(b) gives the FIRST relation, easily found from the productions by inspection. Thus $\{G, \perp\}$ is in FIRST because of the first production; hence, G FIRST $\perp$ is true, and so on.

The transitive completion of FIRST is given in figure 5.3(c).

The reflexive transitive completion FIRST* of FIRST is given in figure 5.3(d). It is simply matrix (c) with the diagonal filled in with ones.

The relation TFIRST*, which is all the members of FIRST* such that the second member of each pair is terminal, is given in figure 5.3(e).

Figure 5.3(f) gives the LAST relation. Thus $\{T,)\}$ is in LAST because of the production $T \to (E)$, etc.

The transitive completion of LAST is given in figure 5.3(g), and the transpose of LAST$^+$ is given in figure 5.3(h). This transpose is needed to form the $\gtrdot$ relation, which is the product of three matrices, figure 5.3(k).

The $\lessdot$ relation is developed in figure 5.3(i) as the product of the $\doteq$ relation and the FIRST$^+$ relation.

Finally, the complete precedence table, which is a summary the of tables in figure 5.3(a), (i), and (k), is given in figure 5.3(l). Except for the goal symbol row and column, it agrees with figure 5.1. We do not need to include a row and column for the goal symbol because the precedence parser halts on the stack contents $\perp G \perp$.

The $(\lessdot, \doteq)$ conflict in $\{\perp, E\}$ and the $(\gtrdot, \doteq)$ conflict in $\{E, \perp\}$ should be replaced by $\lessdot$ and $\gtrdot$, respectively, removing the spurious $\doteq$ relation membership for these two pairs.

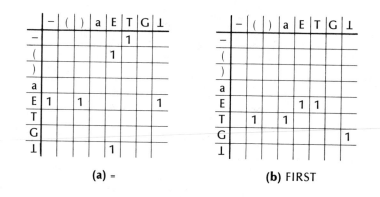

(a) =

	−	(	)	a	E	T	G	⊥
−					1			
(				1				
)								
a								
E	1		1					1
T								
G								
⊥				1				

(b) FIRST

	−	(	)	a	E	T	G	⊥
−								
(								
)								
a								
E						1	1	
T		1		1				
G								1
⊥								

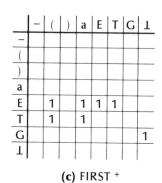

(c) FIRST +

	−	(	)	a	E	T	G	⊥
−								
(								
)								
a								
E		1		1	1	1		
T		1		1				
G								1
⊥								

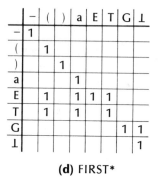

(d) FIRST*

	−	(	)	a	E	T	G	⊥
−	1							
(		1						
)			1					
a				1				
E		1		1	1	1		
T		1		1		1		
G							1	1
⊥								1

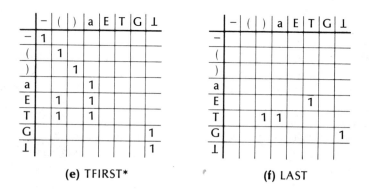

(e) TFIRST*

	−	(	)	a	E	T	G	⊥
−	1							
(		1						
)			1					
a				1				
E		1		1				
T		1		1				
G								1
⊥								1

(f) LAST

	−	(	)	a	E	T	G	⊥
−								
(								
)								
a								
E						1		
T				1	1			
G								1
⊥								

Figure 5.3. Development of the precedence table for grammar G_2, using Boolean matrix operations.

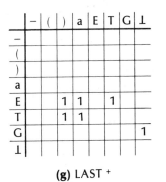

(g) LAST⁺

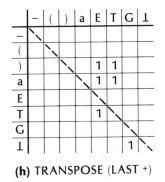

(h) TRANSPOSE (LAST⁺)

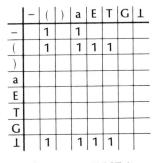

(i) < ≡ (=) (FIRST⁺)

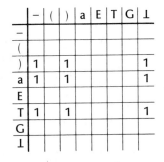

(j) TRANSPOSE (LAST⁺)) (=)))

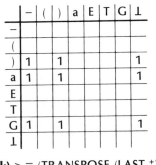

(k) > ≡ (TRANSPOSE (LAST⁺)) (=) (TFIRST*)

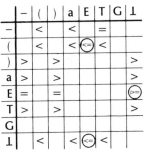

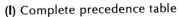

(l) Complete precedence table

Figure 5.3. (cont'd.)

5.2.8. Other Precedence Parsers

A grammar is a *simple precedence* grammar if it is uniquely invertible and its simple precedence table contains no conflicts. As we have seen, even the simple grammar G_2' exhibits a conflict. As a grammar grows in complexity, more conflicts are likely to appear, and they may increase in severity.

The conflicts found in G_2' are between $<$ and $\doteq$. When such conflicts only are found, they create a certain problem in locating the left-most end of a handle, but do not affect the identification of the right-most end. It is often possible to fix the handle unambiguously by some simple rule, such as "match the longest possible production right-hand member" when a conflict is seen. When it is possible to so identify a handle despite a $(<, \doteq)$ conflict, we say that the grammar is a *weak precedence* grammar.

A conflict with $>$ is much more serious; it means that the precedence table cannot deterministically locate the end of the handle. However, it may be possible to transform the grammar to remove the conflict or to consider a larger (m, n) in the precedence table.

An (m, n) larger than (1, 1) is impractical if the entire precedence table must be based on such strings. The size of an (m, n) table grows rapidly with m and n because it must consider a large number of possible combinations of m characters and n characters.

McKeeman, Horning, and Wortman [McKeeman, 1970] proposed a secondary precedence table that applies only when the primary (1, 1) table contains a conflict in relation $>$. The secondary table is a (2, 1) table, which they find is sufficient to resolve most of the conflicts remaining in common programming grammars. Because the (2, 1) table need consider only the class of strings associated with the (1, 1) precedence pair found at the conflict, it usually is small. We shall not further consider the interesting question of deriving a secondary table, as the matter is thoroughly discussed in their text. Such a parser is called a *mixed-strategy precedence* or *MSP parser*.

An *operator precedence* parser is constructed by considering precedence relations among terminal symbols only. The word "operator" arose through the consideration of grammars in which most of the terminals were in fact algebraic operators; operator precedence works nicely for them. Many compilers use operator precedence for arithmetic expressions and recursive descent for the other structures.

The construction of an operator precedence parser table is exactly like that for a simple precedence table, except that the nonterminals are ignored within the productions when looking for pairs of symbols. Grammar G_0 (page 24) is a classic example of an operator precedence grammar. Its operator precedence relations are given in the following table:

	(	a	*	+	)	⊥
)			>	>	>	>
a			>	>	>	>
*	<	<	>	>	>	>
+	<	<	<	>	>	>
(	<	<	<	<	≐	
⊥	<	<	<	<		

For example, (≐) is obtained from the production $F \rightarrow$ (E), by ignoring E. The relation member a $>$ + is obtained from the production $E \rightarrow E + T$, and LAST(E) contains a. The precedence relations are generated essentially as before, except that the FIRST* and LAST* relations are redefined as follows:

- X FIRST* a if and only if X $\Rightarrow^*$ xay and x is empty or consists of only nonterminals.

- X LAST* a if and only if X $\Rightarrow^*$ xay and y is empty or consists of only nonterminals.

That is, we examine the sentential forms derivable from X, and ignore leading (in the case of FIRST*) or trailing (in the case of LAST*) nonterminals, picking out only the terminal symbols.

It is remarkable that algebraic expressions can be reduced to such a simple set of rules as conveyed by an operator precedence table. Such a table in fact conveys the popular notion of the *strength* or *hierarchy* of operators in a programming language. Precedence is a useful way of explaining to a neophyte programmer the ordering relations among various operators. For example, a programming manual may say that ''* has higher precedence than + .'' This means that a * production will be reduced prior to a + production, causing a multiply to be emitted first, whether * precedes or follows + .

Consider two operators with equal precedence, say + and − . The *equal precedence* means (in program terms) that the left-most of two operators are applied first, regardless of which it is. In parsing terms, the left-most production is reduced first.

In terms of productions, two operators, @ and #, have *equal precedence* if they are part of productions associated with the same left member:

```
E → E @ T
E → E # T
E → T
```

On the other hand, an operator @ has *higher precedence* than # if it is derivable from a production containing #; for example,

```
E → E # T
E → T
    . . .
T ⇒* . . . @ . . .
```

This production set is such that the T production containing @ will be reduced prior to the E → E # T production.

In this way, it is possible to design a grammar that contains any desired precedence or ordering relationship among its operators and other functions.

5.3 Exercises

1. Design an extended NDPDA that does bottom-up shift-reduce parsing for this grammar:

```
S → iEtS
S → iEtSeS
S → a
E → b
```

2. Trace the parsing PDA of exercise 1 for the following input strings. Is there more than one possible trace?

```
ibtibtaea
ibtibtaeaea
```

3. Show that the PDA of exercise 1 cannot accept these strings:

```
ibtaeaea
ibea
```

4. Give a general rule for transforming an extended NDPDA into an equivalent nonextended NDPDA such that, for any input string, every configuration the nonextended machine obtains is also a configuration of the extended machine for that same input string.

5. Prove the "if" part of lemma 5.1.

6. Find the handle in each of the following sentential forms, using the precedence table of figure 5.1:

```
⊥ E - (E) ⊥
⊥ E - (T - a) ⊥
⊥ a ⊥
⊥ T - a ⊥
```

7. Show that each string in exercise 6 is a sentential form by (a) giving a right-most derivation, and (b) repeatedly reducing the handle until ⊥E⊥ is obtained. Resolve the precedence conflict on "(, E" by choosing the longest handle. Compare (a) and (b).

8. What happens when you parse each of the following strings using the precedence relations of figure 5.1? Can these strings exist in a shift-reduce PDA?

```
⊥ E - T - a ⊥
⊥ a - (E) ⊥
```

9. Consider a monogamous society that forbids divorce. Determine whether each of the following relations between A and B is reflexive, transitive, and/or symmetric.

   (a) A is the parent of B.
   (b) A is a descendent of B.
   (c) A is a sibling of B.
   (d) A is a sister of B.
   (e) A is an uncle of B.
   (f) A is the same age as B.
   (g) A is the opposite sex of B.
   (h) (A is the father of B) or (A is the son of B).
   (i) A is married if B is married.

10. Design and write a program that reads in a relation, expressed as a list of pairs, and determine whether it is reflexive, transitive, and/or symmetric.

11. Design and write a program that reads in a relation, expressed as a list of pairs, and compute its transitive completion, using Warshall's algorithm.

12. Find derivations in G_2 that produce the precedence pairs that were not justified in the text in section 5.2.6.

13. Design and write a program that implements a precedence parser. Read the grammar and precedence table as input. Emit the sequence of production numbers used in reductions. Design efficient internal data structures.

14. Derive figure 5.1 directly, using the Wirth–Weber precedence relations.

15. Use the matrix multiplication technique of section 5.2.7 to compute the precedence table for each of the following grammars. Are the grammars (1,1) simple precedence?

```
S → 1LuE
S → 1LuET
S → a
E → b
L → S
T → dLe

S → M
S → U
M → iEtMeM
M → a
U → iEtS
U → iEtMeU
E → b
```

16. Design and write a program that reads a grammar, and compute the precedence table using the matrix multiplication technique of section 5.2.7.

17. Verify the operator precedence table given for grammar G_0.

18. Trace an operator precedence parser for G_0 for the following input strings:

```
(a+a)*(a+a)
a+a+a
a+a*(a)
a+(a+(a))
```

19. Design and write an operator precedence parser program. Read the grammar and precedence table as input. Emit the sequence of production numbers used in reductions. Design efficient internal data structures.

20. Sometimes it is possible to define a function f(t) for each token t such that:

```
f(a) < f(b) if a < b
f(a) = f(b) if a ≐ b
f(a) > f(b) if a > b
```

Of what value would such a function be in implementing a precedence parser? Design an algorithm that accepts a precedence table and computes such a function or determines that none exists.

5.4. Bibliographical Notes

The idea of using adjacent operators to control a recognizer was introduced intuitively by Perlis [1956]. It eventually became apparent that operator precedence was closely related to the language structure as expressed by its CFG. Paul [1962] essentially solved a class of recognition problems in his thesis; however, his work did not become known in the United States for several years. Floyd's [1963] paper on operator precedence thus was the first rigorous treatment of the problem of generating a parser mechanically given a CFG. Wirth and Weber [Wirth, 1966] generalized Floyd's ideas into simple and weak precedence.

> 'What is the use of a book,' thought Alice, 'without pictures or conversations?'
>
> . . . Lewis Carroll

CHAPTER 6

BOTTOM-UP LR(K) PARSERS

6.1. LR(k) Grammars and Parsers

> *The translator of Homer should above all be penetrated by a*
> *sense of four qualities of his author—that he is eminently*
> *rapid; that he is eminently plain and direct both in the evo-*
> *lution of his thought and in the expression of it, that is, both*
> *in his syntax and in his words; that he is eminently plain and*
> *direct in the substance of his thoughts, that is, in his matter*
> *and ideas; and, finally, that he is eminently noble.*
>
> *. . . Matthew Arnold*

The LR(k) parsers constitute a family of bottom-up parsers that come as close to ideal left-to-right parsers as is theoretically possible. An LR(k) parser not only identifies a handle but also the production associated with the handle, with no additional decisions required of the rest of the compiler. Furthermore, it takes as much information as it possibly can from the portion of the program preceding and including the handle (the *viable prefix*). The only limitation is that it can examine at most k tokens in the input list past the handle.

An LR(k) parser for a grammar always can be constructed if any deterministic bottom-up parser for the grammar, limited to a k-symbol lookahead, can be constructed. This means that the largest class of grammars is covered by an LR(k) parser. Furthermore, an LR(k) parser covers a set of grammars that is a direct superset of the grammars covered by a top-down LL(k) parser.

6.1.1. LR(k) Grammars

Let G be some grammar with goal symbol S; consider a right-most derivation of a terminal string w in the grammar:

$$S \Rightarrow w_1 \Rightarrow w_2 \Rightarrow \ldots \Rightarrow w$$

Now consider a typical step in the derivation:

$$uAv \Rightarrow uxv$$

where $A \rightarrow x$ is the production used in this step, uxv is one of the w_i or w itself, and u and v are in $(N \cup \Sigma)^*$.

We say that G is LR(k) if, for every such derivation and derivation step, the production $A \rightarrow x$ can be inferred by scanning ux and (at most) the first k symbols of v. Note that because A is the right-most nonterminal in uAv, v must be a terminal string.

Given that G is LR(k), we have several useful properties that make possible the development of a deterministic bottom-up parser:

1. The parser will know when to cease scanning a given sentential form uxv; it can detect the boundary between x and v.

2. The parser will be able to identify the handle x.

3. The parser will be able to select uniquely the production A → x that corresponds to the handle and to this sentential form. It happens that a grammar can be LR(k) and yet have several productions A → x, B → x, and so on, with the same right member.

4. The parser will know when to halt.

As a totally impractical means of constructing a parser for an LR(k) grammar, we might somehow construct a large table that can map every string of the form uxv', where v' is a k-symbol head of v, to a production A → x. Unfortunately, for most grammars, the table would have to be of infinite size, because the strings u can be indefinitely long. (However, the strings xv' make up a finite set.) We need a finite table for a practical compiler.

Knuth [1965] has shown that the set of all viable prefixes of right-most sentential forms can be recognized by a finite-state machine. This FSM can be used as the control machine in an LR(k) parser.

We first define an LR(1) parser. The "1" means that at most one token past the viable prefix will have to be examined to make any parsing decision. For most grammars, this token, called a *lookahead token,* is needed only for certain parsing decisions.

There are several different ways of constructing an LR(1) parser (or LR(k) in general), but every such parser operates the same way. The different construction means are classified as SLR(k), SLALR(k), LALR(k), and LR(k). The difference in the parser (if any) appears in the number of states and the size of a set of lookahead tokens when a k-symbol lookahead is required.

Each of the construction methods can be generalized to a k-symbol lookahead, although we shall develop only the case k = 1 in depth. LR(0) languages do exist, although in general LR(0) is too weak to be of practical value.

6.1.2. An LR(1) Parser

An LR(1) parser consists of an input list, a stack, and a finite control, essentially as required of any parser for a CFG. The finite control in an LR(1) parser typically has a fairly large number of states. In a rough sense, the states keep track of vital information in the viable prefix.

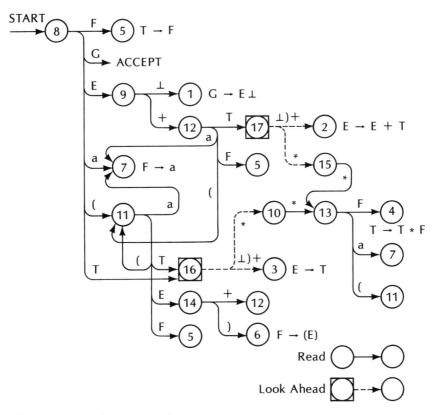

Figure 6.1.   Complete LR parser for grammar G_0.

Figure 6.1 shows an example finite-state control for grammar G_0, given in section 2.2.3. Notice that this machine contains transitions on both terminal symbols (a, +, *, (,), ⊥) and nonterminal symbols (E, T, F, G). The parsing principle is quite simple—the finite control recognizes the viable prefix of any right-most sentential form and falls into a state that uniquely identifies a production exactly when the handle is fully scanned.

Three kinds of state exist in the machine of figure 6.1: *read states, lookahead states,* and *apply states.* In a read state, the parser must accept the next token in the input list, shift it to its stack, then move to some new state associated with the token. The read states in figure 6.1 are 8, 9, 10, 11, 12, 13, and 14. A read transition is sometimes called a *shift,* because its effect is to shift a terminal token from the input list to the stack.

In a lookahead state, the machine "looks at" the next token, in order to make a state transition, but does not shift it into the stack. The lookahead states in figure 6.1 are 16 and 17.

In an apply state, a production is indicated the right member of which will be on top of the stack (it is the handle) and should be replaced by the left member of the production. At this point, the sentential form has been scanned just past its handle and the state is associated with a production. An *apply* operation is sometimes called a *reduce* operation.

The stack will contain the handle and the string preceding the handle on falling into an apply state. Upon the reduction, the stack followed by the remaining input string comprises the next sentential form subject to a reduction. Therefore, conceptually, we construct a new input list consisting of the stack followed by the remainder of the old input list, and start over again. The apply states in figure 6.1 are numbered 1 through 7 and correspond to the production numbers.

In one cycle of the system, a right-most sentential form xwy is transformed into another one, xAy, such that:

$$S \rightarrow^* xAy \rightarrow xwy \text{ (right-most)}$$

Example. Let us trace the machine of figure 6.1 with a sentence, $a + (a * a) \perp$. (A $\perp$ is added to every sentential form to provide a uniform lookahead and halt symbol.) The start state is number 8, and it indicates a transition on a to state 7, an apply state. The machine configuration at this point is:

```
        stack:   a
rest of input list:   +(a*a)⊥
```

State 7 indicates a reduction with the production $F \rightarrow a$; hence, the new machine configuration is:

```
        stack:   F
rest of input list:   +(a*a)⊥
```

These two strings together constitute the next-to-last sentential form in a right-most derivation of $a + (a * a) \perp$; that is:

$$G \rightarrow^* F + (a * a) \perp \rightarrow a + (a * a) \perp$$

One cycle of the machine's operation is now complete. In the next cycle, we have the sentential form $F + (a * a) \perp$, and we start over in state 8. This time, the indicated transition on F is to state 5, another apply state, which then yields the sentential form:

$$T + (a * a) \perp$$

on reduction. Then, starting over with this in state 8, we are first led to the lookahead state 16 on symbol T. In this state, we must transfer to state 3, because + is a legal symbol along that transition path. The + is not shifted into the stack, however, which means that the apply state 3 operates on T and yields the next sentential form:

$$E + (a * a) \perp$$

When we start over again, the machine indicates a move on E to state 9, then on + to state 12, then on (to state 11, and finally on a to state 7. State 7 indicates that the handle is a and is to be reduced to F. The resulting sentential form is:

$$E + (F * a) \perp$$

Figure 6.2 summarizes the complete parsing process on the string $a + (a{*}a)\perp$. (We have numbered the variables "a" to distinguish them; the machine makes no distinctions.) It can be seen from the "apply" column in figure 6.2, which gives the indicated productions to be applied in each cycle, that the machine reconstructs a right-most parse of the sentence, in reverse order, but of course does so through a left-to-right scan.

The parsing process ends on a move from the start state 8 to halt, which occurs on the goal symbol G.

The parser also rejects every invalid sentence—that is, every sentence not in the language $L(G_0)$. Furthermore, it does so on the first illegal symbol. Error detection occurs in a lookahead or a read state, because these must accept or reject the next input symbol from the input list.

When the parser is in some read or lookahead state, it can accept only a certain subset of the language's alphabet. For example, if in state 11, the parser may accept only one of the terminal tokens $\{a, (,)\}$ next in the input list. (The nonterminal tokens do not count for error detection.) Failure to see one of these must be a syntax error and may be immediately reported as such.

String parse = $a_1 + (a_2 * a_3) \perp$

States	Apply	Stack	Input
8, 7	$F \rightarrow a_1$	F	$+ (a_2 * a_3)\perp$
8, 5	$T \rightarrow F$	T	$+ (a_2 * a_3)\perp$
8, 16, 3	$E \rightarrow T$	E	$+ (a_2 * a_3)\perp$
8, 9, 12, 11, 7	$F \rightarrow a_2$	E + (F	$* a_3)\perp$
8, 9, 12, 11, 5	$T \rightarrow F$	E + (T	$* a_3)\perp$
8, 9, 12, 11, 16, 10, 13, 7	$F \rightarrow a_3$	E + (T * F	$)\perp$
8, 9, 12, 11, 16, 10, 13, 4	$T \rightarrow T * F$	E + (T	$)\perp$
8, 9, 12, 11, 16, 3	$E \rightarrow T$	E + (E	$)\perp$
8, 9, 12, 11, 14, 6	$F \rightarrow (E)$	E + F	$\perp$
8, 9, 12, 5	$T \rightarrow F$	E + T	$\perp$
8, 9, 12, 17, 2	$E \rightarrow E + T$	E	$\perp$
8, 9, 1	$G \rightarrow E \perp$	G	
8, HALT		HALT	

Figure 6.2.   Trace of LR parser of figure 6.1 for input $a + (a{*}a)\perp$.

The problem of dealing with an error will be discussed at greater depth later in this chapter. We now discuss a number of reductions on the parser operations and table sizes.

Adding a Stack

We first discuss a reduction in the number of machine operations executed, achieved by adding a push-down stack. The stack will contain state numbers, which correspond to the symbols in a viable prefix of a sentential form.

Note first from figure 6.1 that every state S has associated with it exactly one incoming symbol—the symbol on which a transition is made to the state S. For example, state 5 is associated with the *in-symbol* F, state 11 with (, and so on. This property is true for every LR parser, as we shall see when defining the construction process. (It is not true in general for an arbitrary FSM.)

We can therefore replace the symbols in the viable prefix of some sentential form by the states with which they are associated. However, note that a given symbol may be the in-symbol of more than one state; for example, E is an in-symbol for states 9 and 14. The list of states is effectively the states passed through during the scan of the sentential form. For example, consider the sentential form $E + ((a))$, in which the handle is a. On scanning a, the stack will contain states 8, 9, 12, 11, 11, and 7.

The right parentheses are not associated with states; they are not yet part of a viable prefix. On reducing the handle, a, to F, because this is indicated by state 7, we have the stack 8, 9, 12, 11, 11, 5, which corresponds to the sentential form $E + ((F))$. We may view the correspondence of stack states and the viable prefix symbols at this point as follows:

$$_8E\ _9 +\ _{12}(\ _{11}(\ _{11}F\ _5)\ )$$

Note that the state number (11) just preceding the handle (F) has not changed; it cannot, because it is associated with a symbol in the viable prefix preceding the handle. We do not need to rescan the entire sentential form on each reduction; it is necessary only to pick up at the state just preceding the handle. The states associated with the handle are popped, a new nonterminal is pushed, and a transition that depends on the state just below the new nonterminal is made.

6.1.3. Eliminating Nonterminal Transitions

The apply operation suggests another reduction. One nonterminal token is pushed in an apply, then the next state is determined by the (former) top-of-stack state and this nonterminal. We therefore can construct a table that maps a production number and the top-of-stack state (found after popping the number of states required by the apply) into a next state. With such a table and operation, we no longer need any of the nonterminal transitions from read states.

LR(1) Parser Tables

An efficient implementation of an LR(1) parser consists of an interpreter and the tables shown in figure 6.3. These are organized as sparse matrix FSM tables, similar to those described in chapter 3.

The STATEX table is entered with the current state number STATE. The states are ordered—the reduce states first, then the read states, then the lookahead states. Table STATEX contains an index into other tables. For the read and lookahead states, the next table is a TOKNUM table, containing lists of terminal tokens that are associated with transitions from the current state.

Each list in TOKNUM is terminated with a special character—chr(0). The parser must find a match in a TOKNUM list with the current TOKEN; each list starts at the index STATEX[STATE].

In the read section, reaching chr(0) implies that a syntax error has been detected. That could also be the case in the lookahead section, except that,

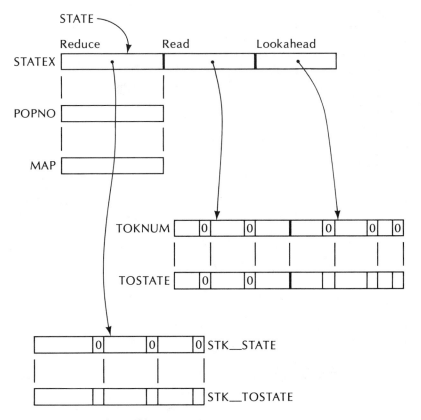

Figure 6.3.   LR machine table organization.

because the read head does not move, the error will be detected later. We therefore associate the chr(0) case with a "leftover" set of lookahead tokens.

When a match is found between TOKNUM and the current TOKEN, the TOSTATE table carries the next state number, ending one cycle of the parser. The read head is advanced one token and the current state is pushed onto the stack if in a read state.

If in a lookahead state, the next state is found from TOSTATE. Nothing is pushed on the stack and the read head is not advanced.

Now consider a reduce action. The STATEX table carries an index into a table of states STK_STATE. STATEX also is directly associated with two other tables, MAP and POPNO. MAP carries a tag associated with the production— usually different from the production number. POPNO carries the length of the handle, which will be the number of tokens in the right part of the production.

The reduce action involves five steps: (1) call an APPLY semantics action, if needed, (2) remove POPNO-1 states from the stack top—recall that the "current state" is not on the stack top, (3) find a match of the newly exposed stack top state with the list in STK_STATE, (4) use the index of the match to obtain the next state from STK_TOSTATE, and (5) push the current state onto the stack.

This reduce action is satisfactory for all but an empty production, which requires a slightly different approach: (1) call an APPLY semantics action as before, (2) remove no states from the stack top, (3) push the STK_STATE entry onto the stack, and (4) obtain the next state from STK_TOSTATE.

Each list in STK_STATE is terminated with a zero; this in fact stands for "all other" states—a failure to find the state in the list results in choosing that one.

Constructing Tables from the Machine

Consider the machine in figure 6.1. Each state has a set of terminal out-symbols associated with it; for example, state 11 has the out-terminals (and a. The list of out-terminals for the state will become a list in TOKNUM, pointed to by a STATE entry in STATEX. The TOSTATE entry corresponding to a TOK-NUM entry is just the state to which the transition occurs.

Thus for STATE = 11, TOKNUM will carry the list {(, a, chr(0)}, and TOSTATE will carry the state list {11, 7, chr(0)}.

The lookahead lists in TOKNUM and TOSTATE are similar. However, we consider the "most popular" next state in order to reduce the length of each list. For example, lookahead state 16 has transitions to state 3 and to 10. The 16 to 3 transition carries three lookahead symbols, whereas the 16 to 10 transition carries only one. We therefore add {*, chr(0)} to TOKNUM, and {10, 3} to TOSTATE.

We have seen that POPNO is just the length of a production's right member. A production is uniquely associated with each reduce state number.

Computing the STK_STATE list for a reduce state is somewhat complicated.

It is necessary to find each of the states with a path to R that spells the right member of the production P associated with R. We call such a state Q. We then find the transition from Q on the out-symbol X to some state S, where X is the left member of P. For example, consider state 2 and its production $E \rightarrow E + T$ in figure 6.1. One traceback is to state 11; another is to 8. There are no others; there is only one T transition to 17 (from 12), two + transitions to 12 (from 9 and 14), and one E transition each to 9 and 14.

Lookahead transitions do not count in the traceback, because the read head does not move.

We then write the starting states Q into STK_STATE as a list terminated with zero. These will be the exposed states just after a production right member has been popped from the stack.

The corresponding STK_TOSTATE is S. Thus, we follow the E transition from state 8 to 9, and from state 11 to 14, because E is the left member of production $E \rightarrow E + T$. We see that for this machine, STATEX[2] will point to the list {8, 11, 0} in STK_STATE and the list {9, 14, 0} in STK_TOSTATE.

In fact, we economize on table size slightly by permitting the zero entry to stand for "anything else." We have total assurance that our machine will be correctly constructed, so the last entry of a list can be eliminated. However, there will be a state, not zero, in the last position of STK_TOSTATE. Hence, our lists can be reduced to {8, 0} and {9, 14}.

We may in fact eliminate several list members, because it often happens that several different STK_STATE states transfer to the same STK_TOSTATE. We therefore choose the most popular STK_TOSTATE, and arrange that it be the last entry.

An empty production requires a slightly different approach, owing to the way in which we have constructed the parser. The "current state" never is on the top of the stack, but in a separate variable CSTATE. We normally pop the stack of (POPNO − 1) elements, but this fails for an empty production. The parser instead uses the single STK_STATE entry to push on the stack, and the STK_TOSTATE entry as the next state. No list search is required.

The STK_STATE is found as described by backtracing to the immediately preceding state, which will be a lookahead state. One of the transitions from this state must be on the nonterminal left member of the production. That transition will go to the state that belongs in STK_STATE; this will be a read state. Finally, there will be a transition out of it on the nonterminal left member to another state; it goes in STK_TOSTATE.

For example, figure 6.6 (section 6.4.3) illustrates a complete LR machine with an empty production $T \rightarrow \epsilon$ in reduce state 9. The traceback goes to state 1, from which we find a lookahead transition to state 8 on the nonterminal T. State 8 therefore belongs in STK_STATE, and STATEX[9] must therefore point to it, for this machine. State 8 moves to state 2 on nonterminal T; hence, state 2 belongs in STK_TOSTATE.

Production MAP Numbers

In QPARSER, a production may be tagged with a symbolic name; for example:

E → E + T #add

The sharp sign indicates that a name tag follows immediately. The QPARSER generator then assigns a unique small integer—for example, 25—to the tag, and writes a CONST declaration into the generated program of the form:

```
const
  ADD= 25;
```

It also generates an entry in the MAP table containing a 25, associated with the reduce state associated with the production. Finally, the production tags are used for semantic operations. This application is described more fully in chapter 7.

MAP is necessary because the generated LR machine usually will have several reduce states associated with the same production. MAP also returns zero (not associated with any production) for untagged productions. The parser notices a zero value and suppresses a call to APPLY.

LR Parser Table Interpreter

The following is an interpreter for the tables in figure 6.3. It is found in file LR1SKEL of QPARSER:

```
procedure PARSER;
  var CSTATE, RX: int;
      TSEM: semrec;  •

  {..............}
  procedure PUSHREAD(CSTATE: int; var SEM: semrec);
  begin
    stackx:=stackx+1;
    if stackx>stacksize then
      abort('stack overflow');
    semstack[stackx]:=sem;
    stack[stackx]:=cstate;
  end;

begin  {Carries out a complete LR parse, until
         the halt state is seen — same as empty stack}
  cstate:=start_state;  {cstate is the 'current' state}
  stackx:=-1;
  tsem.semt:=other;
  pushread(stk_state_1, tsem);
  while cstate<>0 do
  begin
    if cstate < readstate then
    begin  {a reduce state}
      tsem.semt:=other;  {default}
      if map[cstate]<>0 then
        apply(map[cstate], popno[cstate], tsem);
          {the semantics action}
```

```
      if popno[cstate]=0 then
      begin  {empty production}
        pushread(stk_state[statex[cstate]], tsem);
        cstate:=stk_tostate[statex[cstate]];
      end
      else
      begin  {non-empty production}
        stackx:=stackx - popno[cstate] + 1;
          {semantics is preserved on a unit production
                A —> w, where |w| = 1, unless something is
                in TSEM.  Note that if w is
                nonterminal, the production may be bypassed}
        if (popno[cstate]>1) or
          (tsem.semt<>other) then
          semstack[stackx]:=tsem;
        rx:=statex[cstate];   {compute the GOTO state}
        cstate:=stack[stackx];
        while (stk_state[rx]<>cstate) and
              (stk_state[rx]<>0) do rx:=rx+1;
        cstate:=stk_tostate[rx];
      end
    end
    else
    if cstate < lookstate then
    begin  {a read state}
      next_token;  {need next token now}
      rx:=statex[cstate];
      while (toknum[rx]<>0) and
            (toknum[rx]<>token) do rx:=rx+1;
      if toknum[rx]=0 then
      begin
        error('syntax error');
        cstate:=error_recovery(stack, stackx, cstate);
      end
      else
      begin
        pushread(cstate, lsemp↑);
        cstate:=tostate[rx];
        tokenread;  {token has been scanned}
      end
    end
    else
    begin  {lookahead state}
      next_token;  {need another token now}
      rx:=statex[cstate];
      while (toknum[rx]<>0) and
            (toknum[rx]<>token) do rx:=rx+1;
      cstate:=tostate[rx];
    end
  end
end;
```

Discussion

Some of the lines in PARSER support a semantic system that will be discussed in more detail in chapter 7. The variables semstack, lsemp, tsem, and so on are used for that purpose.

Otherwise, PARSER is essentially a WHILE loop containing three cases corresponding to the current state CSTATE. The reduce state is the most complicated, and depends on whether an empty production is being reduced. There also is a mechanism for carrying over semantic information into the next parser step under certain conditions.

Aside from the semantic processing, PARSER works from the tables described in figure 6.3 and by the algorithm described previously.

6.2. LR(0) Parser Construction

It is more of a job to interpret the interpretations than to interpret the things, and there are more books about books than about any other subject; we do nothing but write glosses about each other.

. . . Montaigne

We shall now describe a construction algorithm for an LR(0) machine. It will become the basis for the SLR(0) and SLALR(0) parsers. The construction of an LR(k) machine will be described in section 6.5.

In the LR(0) construction, each machine state is associated with a set of *items,* where an item is a production carrying a position marker. The rules for constructing the item-set corresponding to some state, and for starting new states, are reasonably simple and lend themselves to a machine implementation. The resulting parser machine also is in minimal form when the process is complete.

Recall that a viable prefix is a prefix of some right-most sentential form that includes no symbols past the handle of the form. We will emphasize a viable prefix for one reason: the LR parser FSM recognizes viable prefixes, and a viable prefix is connected with a sentential form. A viable prefix therefore serves as a kind of conceptual link between derivations (which involve sentential forms) and the LR parsing automaton.

Now consider an arbitrary state P in the complete LR machine, and the set (usually infinite) of viable prefixes associated with that state P. A viable prefix w is associated with state P if and only if the machine accepts w on falling into state P. It should be clear that a given viable prefix can be associated with only one state, because we demand that the machine be deterministic. (We have not yet shown that it is finite.)

We say that two viable prefixes belong to the same LR equivalence class if they are associated with the same state.

The association of viable prefixes with states is an interesting notion, but is not useful because each state may have an infinite number of viable prefixes associated with it. For example, all of the following viable prefixes in grammar G_0 are associated with state 12:

```
E +
( E +
( ( E +
T * ( E +
T * ( ( E +
( E + ( E +
```

It is easy to find many more. We need only trace through all the paths starting at state 8 and ending at state 12. The loop on (in state 11 can be traversed any number of times, yielding another left parenthesis each time, as can the loop through 12-11-14. We obviously need to find some finite set that can be associated with each state.

Such a finite set is a set of items. An *item* is a marked production enclosed in brackets; for example,

$$[A \rightarrow x \, . \, y]$$

is an item if $A \rightarrow xy$ is a production in G. Here, either x or y or both may be empty.

An item $[A \rightarrow x \, . \, y]$ is said to be *valid* for some viable prefix ux if and only if there exists some right-most derivation:

$$S \Rightarrow^* uAv \Rightarrow uxyv$$

Note that xy is the handle of the sentential form uxyv, and that v is a terminal string. The mark "." in an item valid for some viable prefix indicates that this point in the production marks the end of the viable prefix.

There are in general many items valid for a given viable prefix, although there can be only a finite number of items altogether, because they consist of a finite number of mark positions in a finite number of productions.

Now consider some state P in the finite-state control for an LR parser. State P is associated with some set of viable prefixes, and therefore with some finite set of items valid for those viable prefixes. We propose to identify and distinguish the states in the finite control of the parser by constructing the set of valid items associated with each of the states.

For example, consider the machine of figure 6.1, and state 12. We previously presented a list of some viable prefixes associated with state 12. We now construct a set of valid items associated with state 12.

Because state 12 is entered on scanning +, the item $[E \rightarrow E + .T]$ must be associated with state 12. Although this is the only possible item in which the mark can follow +, as required by the in-symbol of state 12, this is not the only item associated with state 12. The following also are associated with state 12:

```
[T → .F]
[T → .T * F]
[F → .(E)]
[F → .a]
```

To show this association, note that the viable prefix:

$$E+$$

is part of a sentential form:

$$E + T$$

with the derivation:

$$E \Rightarrow E + T \Rightarrow E + F$$

and therefore the item $[T \rightarrow .F]$ is valid for the viable prefix $E+$. (From the definition given earlier, in this instance we have $S = E$, $u = E+$, $x = \epsilon$, $y = F$, $v = \epsilon$.)

Similarly, the derivation:

$$E \Rightarrow E + T \Rightarrow E + T*F$$

shows that the item $[T \rightarrow .T*F]$ is valid for the viable prefix $E+$.

6.2.1. Item-Set Construction

We now see how a finite set of items and a (possibly) infinite set of viable prefixes may be associated with each state in the LR control automaton. We next need to develop rules for building the item-sets and, from them, the states and transitions of the LR automaton. The following rules do just that. We shall also show that they are correct and will make each aspect of them manifest.

The three construction rules for an LR(0) control automaton are called the *start*, the *completion*, and the *read* operations:

1. *The start operation.* Let S be the goal symbol of the grammar. For every production $S \rightarrow w$, add item $[S \rightarrow .w]$ to the start state. This operation is needed to start the construction process. The other two operations assume that some states and items associated with the states already exist. The start state may eventually have several items in it.

2. *The completion operation.* If $[A \rightarrow x . Xy]$ is an item in some state P, then every item of the form $[X \rightarrow .z]$ must be included in state P. Note that X must be a nonterminal symbol. This rule must be repeated until no more new items can be added to the state.

3. *The read operation.* Let X be a terminal or nonterminal symbol in an item $[A \rightarrow x . Xy]$ associated with some state P. Then $[A \rightarrow xX . y]$ is associated with a state Q (possibly the same as P), and a transition:

$$P \text{ to } Q \text{ on symbol } X$$

exists.

We call this a read operation because it becomes a READ action in the final parser if X is a terminal symbol. When X is a nonterminal symbol, we have seen that a transition on X becomes part of the APPLY action, following the replacement of the handle on the stack top by that nonterminal symbol.

6.2.2. Parser Construction

These three operations are all that are needed to generate a finite control for an LR(0) parser, such as the one in figure 6.1, except for lookahead states. We shall see why lookahead states are necessary and how they are constructed shortly. For now, let us summarize the construction of the finite-state system as implied by these three operations.

1. Give the start state a number, and use the start operation to put one item into it. Then use the completion operation repeatedly, if necessary, to get more items into this state. In completing a state, we look for a nonterminal symbol X that follows the mark ".", and then add items of the form [X → .w] to the state, where X → w is a production. Eventually, this completion operation has to end.

2. We now have one state, consisting of a set of items. It will not be any different in principle from any other state constructed by this process, so we consider a general state.

3. Use the read operation to start one or more new states, based on the present state. The idea is to look for items of the form [A → x . Xy]—that is, items in which some token X follows the mark—then build a new state from the item [A → xX . y]—that is, the mark "moved past" the symbol X. This new state incidentally also must contain all the other items from the old state in which this symbol X follows the mark. For example, if the old state contains the two items:

```
[E → E + .T]
[E → .T]
```

(among others), then the new state must contain (at least) the items:

```
[E → E + T.]
[E → T.]
```

Let the old state be P and the new state be Q. Then we know that the FSM in the LR parser will have the transition P to Q on X. This explains why we carry over into state Q all the items in which X follows the mark.

The "new" state may be exactly like some other state previously constructed. We can tell whether two states are equivalent by examining the list of items associated with them. If the two lists are identical, when completed, then the two states must be equivalent. In this way, the state-building process must eventually terminate, because there can be only a finite number of distinguishable sets of items. Eventually, we have to construct a state that is identical to some state constructed previously.

It is not necessary to compare all the items in two states to judge their equivalence. We need compare only the *kernel* items; those items that are initially placed in a state through the read or start operation. Usually, they have some symbol preceding the mark, but they may not have one if empty productions exist in the grammar.

4. Complete the new state started in step 3 by applying the completion operation repeatedly.

5. Repeat steps 3 and 4 until no more new states are obtained.

Example.   Let us apply the construction to grammar G_0; the yield should be the FSM in figure 6.1. We shall assign the first set of states to completed items for the seven productions of the grammar. An LR parser generator is likely to produce states in some other order.

There is no reason to number the states in any particular way, except that we already have introduced the finite control for the parser (figure 6.1) and it is less confusing to adopt the state numbers used there.

The LR parser generator provided with QPARSER will print all the item-sets in a form similar to the following. We recommend examining one of its dumps on your favorite grammar.

The productions of G_0 are:

```
1.   G → E ⊥
2.   E → E + T
3.   E → T
4.   T → T * F
5.   T → F
6.   F → ( E )
7.   F → a
```

The production numbers 1 to 7 will be apply state numbers. We assign the next number, 8, to the start state, which initially contains the item $[G \rightarrow .E \perp]$. This item must be completed by adding to state 8 all the items associated with the E productions: $[E \rightarrow .E + T]$, $[E \rightarrow .T]$. The second of these in turn leads to a further completion operation, bringing the items $[T \rightarrow .T * F]$ and $[T \rightarrow .F]$ into state 8. Finally, the last item calls for a completion with the items $[F \rightarrow .(E)]$ and $[F \rightarrow . a]$. This operation yields the set of items in state 8, as follows:

```
8.   [G → .E ⊥]
     [E → .E + T]
     [E → .T]
     [T → .T * F]
     [T → .F]
     [F → .(E)]
     [F → .a]
```

We now apply the read operation to these items. The first two items, with E following the mark, yield a new state, 9, and a transition (8 to 9 on E). The next two items yield state 10, and a transition (8 to 10 on T). The next item ($[T \rightarrow .F]$) yields state 5 and a transition (8 to 5 on F). Finally, the last two items yield states 11 and 7, with transitions on (and a, respectively. Each of these states must be worked on by the completion and read rules, yielding new states, and so on. Let us therefore continue with state 9.

State 9 arises from the two items [G → .E ⊥] and [E → .E + T]. The read operation requires moving the mark past the E symbol; hence, state 9 is initialized with the kernel set:

```
9.   [G → E. ⊥]
     [E → E. + T]
```

This set is complete; there is no nonterminal symbol following a mark in either item. The read operation applied to this set yields state 1 (for the first item), with the transition (9 to 1 on ⊥), and state 12 (for the second item), with the transition (9 to 12 on +).

State 1 therefore stems from the first item in 9 and looks like this:

```
1.   [G → E ⊥.]
```

No completion or read operations are possible. This kind of item, with the mark at the end of the production, is called a *completed* item and normally is associated with a reduction or apply state.

Another apply state obtained from state 8 is state 7:

```
7.   [F → a.]
```

We now show the complete state set when the completion and read operations are carried out to the bitter end. We have added the state transitions to the right of the production, in the form (transition symbol, next state):

8. [G → .E⊥]   (E, 9)
   [E → .E + T]   (E, 9)
   [E → .T]   (T, 10)
   [T → .T * F]   (T, 10)
   [T → .F]   (F, 5)
   [F → .(E)]   ((, 11)
   [F → .a]   (a, 7)

9. [G → E.⊥]   (⊥, 1)
   [E → E. + T]   (+, 12)

10. [E → T.]
    [T → T. * F]   (*, 13)

11. [F → (.E)]   (E, 14)
    [E → .E + T]   (E, 14)
    [E → .T]   (T, 10)
    [T → .T * F]   (T, 10)
    [T → .F]   (F, 5)
    [F → .(E)]   ((, 11)
    [F → .a]   (a, 7)

12. [E → E + .T]   (T, 15)
     [T → .T * F]   (T, 15)
     [T → .F]   (F, 5)
     [F → .(E)]   ((, 11)
     [F → .a]   (a, 7)

13. [T → T * .F]   (F, 4)
     [F → .(E)]   ((, 11)
     [F → .a]   (a, 7)

14. [F → (E.)]   ( ), 6)
     [E → E. + T]   (+, 12)

15. [E → E + T.]
     [T → T. * F]   (*, 13)

The first seven states correspond to the set of completed productions:

```
1.  [G → E⊥.]
2.  [E → E+T.]
3.  [E → T.]
4.  [T → T*F.]
5.  [T → F.]
6.  [F → (E).]
7.  [F → a.]
```

We now have enough of the finite state controller for a comparison with figure 6.1. Only the state transitions and an indication of the parse states need survive.

Unfortunately, we have a problem with this grammar. Although we would like to assign state 2 to the item [E → E + T.], we see that it in fact appears with another item in state 15. Similarly, the item [E → T.] should occur only in state 3, but appears in state 10 with another noncompleted item, [T → T. * F]. What are we to make of this situation?

Consider state 10, which contains the item [E → T.] and the item [T → T. * F]. When the finite control reaches this state on some sentential form, there may be two possible moves. The completed item [E → T.] essentially says that the parser should reduce the T on the stack top to E. On the other hand, the item [T → T. * F] essentially says, "Do not reduce the stack top; shift token * (if seen) into the stack." For example, the sentential form T * a leads to just such an indecision—called a *shift-reduce* conflict. We cannot have it both ways, and we do not want the parser to be nondeterministic, so something must be done to make a deterministic decision at this point.

Parser Generators

Several parser-generator programs are available for various computers. QPARSER is described elsewhere in this book. YACC [YACC, 1978] is a popular system available to Unix users. YACC stands for *Yet Another Compiler-Compiler*. Both QPARSER and YACC produce state-machine tables for an LR parser. Both resolve inadequate states by the LALR approach, described later.

A parser generator should do more than generate parser tables. QPARSER produces a complete Pascal or C program based on the grammar. It uses several macro expansion techniques to generate the tables inline as constant arrays, and to generate a lexical analyzer. In YACC, fragments of C program are added to the grammar rule set, and become part of a complete translator. A lexical analyzer, LEX, also on Unix, is a popular tool that produces an FSM lexical scanner.

Both QPARSER and YACC can be made to produce LR[0] item-sets in a readable form. Given such software tools, there is no reason to try to generate LR parser tables by hand, other than to grasp the principles.

6.2.3. Inadequate States

State 10 is called an *inadequate* or *inconsistent* state. In general, an inadequate state is any state containing both a completed item (of the form [A → w .]) and any other item. Such a state represents a conflict in a parsing decision, in the same way that a conflict in an operator precedence table represents a potential difficulty in parsing some string. The conflict arises from the grammar. There are grammars for which no LR conflict arises, and others that produce one or more conflicts.

There is no easy way to determine in advance of an item-set construction whether a given grammar will create a conflict. We must simply forge ahead and construct the state-sets, and discover the conflicts as they arise.

An inadequate state often can be resolved by one of several methods, as described in section 6.4.

If the LR states contain no inadequate states, the grammar is said to be LR(0). We are then also sure that the grammar is unambiguous. We shall not prove this result, but it should be apparent from the deterministic character of the parsing machine that results from the state-set construction. Of course, we have not yet shown that the parsing machine accepts exactly those sentential forms in the source grammar. We shall prove this assertion next.

6.3. Construction Correctness Proof

A proof of correctness of the parser system as defined will establish that the LR(0) FSM constructed from a grammar G (hereafter simply called "the machine") recognizes exactly the class of viable prefixes of right-most sentential forms in G. The proof is in two parts. We first show that the items within any state are exactly consistent with the class of viable prefixes for that state. Then we can show that the machine recognizes viable prefixes exactly.

The machine may or may not contain inadequate states. The proofs essentially deal with only read and apply states, and even these are not distinguished as such.

We merely consider a machine that can accept a right-most sentential form up to, but not past, its handle—that is, a viable prefix.

We need a few definitions first.

Recall that an item $[A \rightarrow x . y]$ is said to be *valid* for some viable prefix ux if and only if there exists some right-most derivation:

$$S \Rightarrow^* uAv \Rightarrow uxyv$$

A string w is said to be *associated with* or *valid for* some state P in the machine if and only if the machine falls into state P on scanning w.

An item is said to be *valid* for some state P in the machine if and only if it is valid for some viable prefix w associated with state P.

Now we may state and prove the first part of the construction correctness theorem.

Lemma 6.1. Every state P contains all and only the items valid for P.

Proof: "Only the" Part. Let $[A \rightarrow x . y]$ be in P through the construction process, and assume that it was placed in P through $k + 1$ steps of the process. We assume the lemma true for $k' \leq k$ steps.

If $x = \epsilon$, and $P \neq S$, then this item got into P through a completion operation through some other item, $[B \rightarrow w.Az]$, also in P. By the inductive hypothesis, this item is valid for P; hence, there must be a viable prefix u and a derivation:

$$S \Rightarrow^* uBv \Rightarrow uwAzv \Rightarrow uwyzv$$

Therefore, $[A \rightarrow .y]$ also is valid for P, because viable prefix uw is.

If $x = \epsilon$ and $P = S$, then k may be 1, so that we have item $[S \rightarrow . y]$, which is valid for the start state. For $k > 1$ and $P = S$, we have item $[A \rightarrow . y]$, which is valid for the start state by an argument similar to that in the preceding paragraph.

For nonempty x, the item $[A \rightarrow x . y]$ has the form $[A \rightarrow rX . y]$, where $|X| = 1$. It can be only in state P, because an item $[A \rightarrow r . Xy]$ exists in some other state R, with a transition (R to P on X). Now $[A \rightarrow r . Xy]$ is valid for some viable prefix ur, valid for R, by the inductive hypothesis, through a derivation:

$$S \Rightarrow^* uAz \Rightarrow urXyz$$

But this also shows that $[A \rightarrow rX.y]$ is valid for the viable prefix urX. Finally, if ur is valid for state R, and a transition (R to P on X) exists, then urX is valid for P. Therefore $[A \rightarrow rX . y]$ is valid for P. QED

Proof: "All the" Part. Consider any viable prefix w valid for state P. We use induction on the length of w.

For $|w| = 0$, P must be the start state S_0. (There are no empty moves from S_0 to any other state.) But S_0 contains all items $[S_0 \rightarrow . u]$ that are valid for the empty viable prefix.

Now let $|w| = k + 1$, and assume the lemma true for all strings w of length k or less. String w has the form:

$$w = xX$$

where $|X| = 1$ and X is in $(N \cup \Sigma)$. With w valid for P, we have the derivation:

$$S \Rightarrow^* wy = xXy$$

Consider the step in which X was introduced through a production:

$$S \Rightarrow^* rAz \Rightarrow rsXtz \Rightarrow^* rsXy$$

where $rs = x$, $tz \Rightarrow^* y$, and $A \rightarrow sXt$. This derivation shows that $[A \rightarrow sX . t]$ is valid for $w = xX = rsX$, hence for P. Is this item in P? Note that $[A \rightarrow s . Xt]$ is valid for viable prefix x; because xX is valid for P, there must be a state R for which x is valid, with a transition (R to P on X). However, the inductive hypothesis implies $[A \rightarrow s. Xt]$ must be in R; therefore, by the construction, $[A \rightarrow sX . t]$ is in P. We have shown that every state contains all the items valid for it. QED

6.3.1. The Main Theorem

We now turn to the principal theorem.

Theorem 6.1.   The machine M (constructed as described) recognizes exactly the class of viable prefixes of grammar G.

An immediate consequence of this theorem is that M will serve as a (possibly) nondeterministic bottom-up parser for sentences in G. It will be deterministic if there are no inadequate states; the handle of any sentential form will be identified by falling into an apply state containing a single completed item $[A \rightarrow w.]$. If there are inadequate states, then each of these represents a nondeterminism that must be resolved by lookahead methods to be developed later.

Proof: (M recognizes every viable prefix in G).   First, let w be some viable prefix in G; then we have:

$$S \Rightarrow^* wv \text{ (right-most)}$$

Let v be terminal, without loss of generality. We prove by induction on the number of derivation steps that M recognizes w.

For zero steps, the start state clearly recognizes the class of empty viable prefixes. Therefore, consider a $(k + 1)$-step derivation:

$$S \Rightarrow^* uAv' \Rightarrow uxv'$$

where A is such that w is some prefix of ux. If w is a prefix of u, then, by the inductive hypothesis, M recognizes u and therefore w. Hence, let w be a prefix of ux but not u. Let $x = X_1X_2 \ldots X_n y$, where each of the X_i is of length 1, such that:

$$w = u \, X_1 \, X_2 \ldots X_m$$

and $m \leq n$. We then have:

$$S \Rightarrow^* uAv' \Rightarrow u \, X_1 \, X_2 \ldots X_n \, y \, v'$$

Now u is accepted by M by falling into some state P_0 for which u is valid, by induction. The derivation shows that $[A \rightarrow . X_1 \, X_2 \ldots X_n \, y]$ is valid for u and, by lemma 6.1, must be in P_0. Then, by the construction process, there must be a sequence of states $P_1, P_2, \ldots, P_n$ associated with items and viable prefixes as follows:

P_1 with $[A \rightarrow X_1.X_2X_3 \ldots X_n \, y]$ and uX_1.
P_2 with $[A \rightarrow X_1X_2.X_3 \ldots X_n y]$ and uX_1X_2.

P_n with $[A \rightarrow X_1X_2X_3 \ldots X_n . y]$ and $uX_1X_2 \ldots X_n$.

But this construction also shows that M accepts $uX_1X_2 \ldots X_m = w$. QED

Proof: (M Recognizes Only Viable Prefixes in G).   Let w be a string accepted by M. By induction on $|w|$: for $|w| = 0$, M accepts w in the start state, and the empty string is a viable prefix in every grammar.

For $|w| = k + 1$, consider the next-to-last move of M, from some state R to P on some symbol X:

$$w = rX$$

By induction, r is a viable prefix valid for R. Also, because of the transition (R to P on X) and lemma 6.1, every item valid for R is in R. There therefore must be an item of the form $[A \rightarrow x . Xy]$ in R such that a derivation:

$$S \Rightarrow^* uAz \Rightarrow uxXyz$$

exists, with $ux = r$. But this derivation also shows that $uxX = w$ is a viable prefix and therefore valid for state P. QED

6.3.2. Finiteness of Machine States

We have not required that the number of states in M be finite in these proofs— only that they be countable (induction requires the countable property). The proofs establish a correspondence among the states, the set of items constructed for them, and the (usually infinite) set of viable prefixes in the grammar. However, the state-set must be finite, because there are a finite number of possible ways of constructing item-sets. We therefore also have indirectly shown that the set of viable prefixes in some grammar are recognized by an FSM.

6.4. Resolution of Inadequate States

We now return to the problem of the inadequate states that can arise in the construction of an LR parsing machine. We can deal with these in several ways, as follows:

1. Lookahead sets for each inadequate state can be found by computing the FOLLOW$_k$ sets for the nonterminal left member of one of the production in the inadequate state. When this is done, and we have no conflict remaining, we have an *SLR(k)* resolution.

2. The LR(0) machine itself can be used to infer lookahead sets for the inadequate states. A common algorithm used for the purpose is given later. Essentially, we may infer k-token lookaheads by backtracking the LR(0) machine from an inadequate state. We call such a resolution an *SLALR(0)* machine.

3. A full LR(k) construction can be compromised in the interest of reducing the number of states and state-set size by merging certain states. The result, if successful, is identification of the lookahead set for every inadequate state, as well as generation of the LR machine. This technique yields a so-called *LALR(k)* parser. We shall not discuss LALR(k) construction— details may be found in DeRemer [1982].

4. Discard the LR(0) construction and attempt the construction of an LR(k) machine, first for k = 1, then for k = 2, and so on. We shall define the construction of an LR(k) machine later. We note here only that the size of each state set and the number of states increase exponentially with k, so that the construction is practical for only a small k or a small grammar.

These resolution approaches are ranked in increasing strength. Thus, there are grammars that yield to an LALR treatment, but not an SLALR, and so on. Nevertheless, even the SLR(0) resolution approach is sufficiently powerful to be useful for practical grammars; it is also the easiest to implement.

We defer the LR(k) resolution (for arbitrary k) until section 6.5, as it requires considerable development.

SLR stands for "simple LR," and was first reported by DeRemer [1971]. *LALR* stands for "lookahead LR," and was described in Aho and Johnson [1974].

6.4.1. Splitting an Inadequate State

An inadequate state first must be changed into a lookahead state, and some new states introduced. The inadequate state will be *split* in this operation.

Let the inadequate state be P; it is then associated with one or more reductions (for example, productions P_1 and P_2, figure 6.4(a)) and with zero or more read transitions (for example, states S_1 and S_2, figure 6.4(a)). P is clearly a mixed state—it has at least two reduce items and/or a reduce item and a read item.

We first convert P into a lookahead state—figure 6.4(b).

We then add a new read state N, with transitions to S_1 and S_2 on symbols A_1 and A_2—figure 6.4(b)—if there are any read transitions from P. N collects all the read transitions. The lookahead set associated with the transition P ⊢ N is $\{A_1, A_2\}$.

One new state is introduced for each reduction associated with P—for example, R_1 and R_2 in figure 6.4(b). The edges from P to these states carry lookahead sets that we shall determine next—for example, L_1 and L_2 in figure 6.4(b). These states are clearly pure *reduce* states.

These new states yield a modified machine with a pure lookahead state (P), a new pure read state (N), and new pure reduce states (R_1 and R_2).

A new state may be equivalent to some other state in the machine. Two reduce states are equivalent if they are associated with the same production. Two read

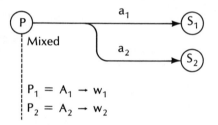

(a) Before

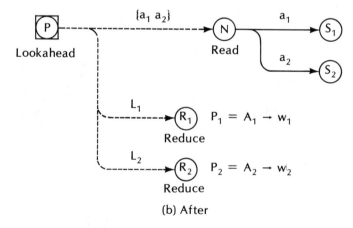

(b) After

Figure 6.4. Inadequate state splitting.

states are equivalent if they have the same out-transitions to equivalent states.

Given a splitting, we say that a *reduce-reduce* conflict occurs in state P when two lookahead transitions from P carry a common lookahead token. A *shift-reduce* conflict exists when a lookahead transition carries a token in common with the read state transition.

6.4.2. SLR(k) Resolution

State P is inadequate if it contains a completed item $[A \rightarrow w .]$ and some other item of any kind. The presence of $[A \rightarrow w .]$ in a state P means that there is some set of derivations of the form:

$$S \Rightarrow^* xAy \Rightarrow xwy$$

such that the LR(0) machine accepts xw by falling into state P. Clearly, the set $L = FIRST_1(y\ FOLLOW_1(S))$ is the desired lookahead set for this item in P. That is, L can be used to decide whether to apply $A \rightarrow w$. However, L is clearly a subset of $FOLLOW_1(A)$. The latter set is easy to determine, and if the use of $FOLLOW_1$ is sufficient to resolve every inadequate state (it often is), then we have an SLR(1) resolution. A resolution of inadequate states in an LR(0) machine using $FOLLOW_k$ would be an SLR(k) resolution.

For example, consider the machine of figure 6.1, with the items developed as described previously. State 10 is inadequate; it contains the two items:

```
[E → T.]
[T → T.*F]
```

The set FOLLOW(E) is $\{), +, \perp\}$, as is easily shown from the grammar. (See chapter 4 for a complete discussion.) This set does not contain symbol *; hence, state 10 may be resolved by a one-symbol lookahead. It is shown in figure 6.1 as a new state, 16, with two lookahead transitions to states 10 and 3.

Similarly, state 15, which contains the items:

```
[E → E+T.]
[T → T.*F]
```

also may be resolved with the same FOLLOW(E) set. It is shown in figure 6.1 as a new state, 17, with lookahead transitions to states 2 and 15.

Thus, in figure 6.4(b), the lookahead set L_1 is $FOLLOW(A_1)$, and L_2 is $FOLLOW(A_2)$. If the three sets $\{A_1, A_2\}$, L_1, and L_2 are mutually disjoint, then we have resolved inadequate state P.

The use of the FOLLOW function may or may not resolve an inadequate state. If it fails, the grammar may still be SLALR(0). Essentially, the FOLLOW function yields all the symbols that can follow some nonterminal A in a sentential form. It makes no distinctions based on the particular inadequate state in which we are interested. The FOLLOW function therefore tends to yield a larger set of lookahead symbols than can actually exist for that nonterminal in that state.

6.4.3. SLALR(0) Resolution

The inadequate states may be resolved by computing a set of lookaheads associated with transitions in the LR(0) machine, using the machine transitions themselves. Although weaker than a merged-state LR(k) parser, it is more powerful than an SLR(k) resolution. As usual, we consider only k = 1, and assume that the state-splitting represented by figure 6.4(b) has been made for every inadequate state.

1. The lookahead sets associated with every transition from a lookahead state to a reduce state are empty initially. These are L_1 and L_2 in figure 6.4(b).

2. Let the reduce states introduced by state-splitting be called the *new* states— for example, states R_1 and R_2 in figure 6.4(b).

3. Consider the production A → w associated with a *new* state R. Let L_R be the lookahead set associated with the in-edge of R. Identify every state W such that a path from W to R that spells the right part w exists; then identify the state X such that a transition from W to X on symbol A exists. Let X_R denote the set of all such states X associated with state R.

4. Add all the tokens associated with out-transitions from the states X in set X_R to the lookahead set L_R.

5. Repeat steps 3 and 4 for every *new* state.

6. Repeat step 5 until no change in any lookahead set occurs.

Example. The following grammar generates an LR(0) machine with four inadequate states:

```
1.   S → E ⊥
2.   E → E ; T
3.   E → T
4.   T → T a
5.   T → ε
```

The LR machine for this grammar is shown in figure 6.5. It contains four inadequate states, 1, 2, 5, and 6, each with a shift-reduce conflict.

After splitting the inadequate states, the machine appears as in figure 6.6. We need to compute the lookahead sets L_9, L_{11}, L_{13}, and L_{15}. Consider L_{13} first. The production associated with state 13 is E → E ; T. Its right member can be spelled out in only one way, starting at state 8 and proceeding through 4, 5, 10, 6 and 13. The E transition from state 8 is to 4, and the lookahead set associated with 4 is $\{\perp \, ;\}$; hence, this is L_{13}'s value.

L_9 is determined from the production T → ε, the right member of which is "spelled" from state 1. However, the T transition from state 1 goes to state 2 (through state 8), the lookahead sets of which are L_{15} and $\{a\}$. The set L_{15} is easily found to be $\{\perp \, ;\}$; hence, L_9 is $\{\perp \, ; \, a\}$.

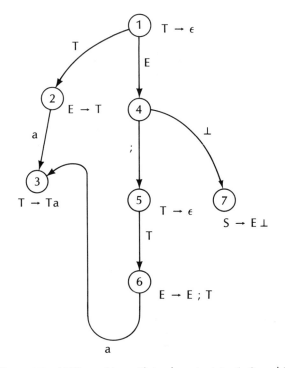

Figure 6.5. LR(0) machine with inadequate states 1, 2, and 5.

We find that this grammar is SLALR(0). The test is whether the lookahead sets and the terminal read sets from each state are pairwise disjoint, and they clearly are for this machine. (It happens that this grammar is also SLR(0).)

LALR Resolution

DeRemer and Penello have reported a resolution algorithm that is stronger than the SLALR we have described [DeRemer, 1982]. It is much too complicated to review here. The complications arise from nullable nonterminals, and possible sequences of them in right parts of productions. Read their paper for details.

6.4.4. Adding Disambiguating Rules

Aho [1975] pointed out that an ambiguous grammar can be used to generate a deterministic LR parser, given enough disambiguating rules. A *disambiguating rule* essentially provides a way for the language designer to eliminate the conflicts in an inadequate state that cannot be eliminated by one of the lookahead methods we have described.

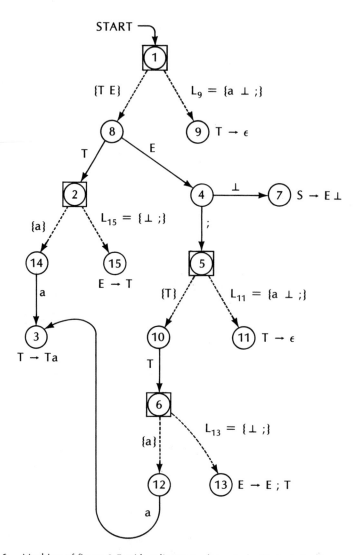

Figure 6.6.   Machine of figure 6.5 with split states, decorated with lookahead sets.

To be useful, disambiguating rules should be stated in terms of the grammar and its tokens, not in terms of particular states that the parser generator develops. The parser states depend on details scattered throughout a grammar, and can change radically when a minor change in the productions is made.

The simplest disambiguating rules are the following; they are used in YACC and in QPARSER:

1. In a shift-reduce conflict, the default is to do the shift. This essentially gives heavier weight to longer productions.

2. In a reduce-reduce conflict, the default is to reduce by the grammar rule that appears *earlier* in the source list of grammar rules.

These rules are sufficient to resolve all inadequate states that cannot be otherwise resolved. However, the resolution may not be what was intended; hence, all such resolutions must be reported in detail by a parser generator.

For example, the Pascal grammar carries the productions:

```
stmt → IF boolean THEN stmt
stmt → IF boolean THEN stmt ELSE stmt
stmt → other
```

These are ambiguous, because the sentence:

```
IF b1 THEN IF b2 THEN s1 ELSE s2
```

can be interpreted as either

IF b1 THEN begin IF b2 THEN s1 ELSE s2 end

or:

IF b1 THEN begin IF b2 THEN s1 end ELSE s2

A special Pascal semantic rule is that the former interpretation must apply—an ELSE is to be bound to its immediately preceding THEN.

This ambiguity will show up in an inadequate state that will carry the items:

```
[stmt → IF boolean THEN stmt . ]
[stmt → IF boolean THEN stmt . ELSE stmt ]
```

which will exhibit a shift-reduce conflict on the token ELSE. By favoring a shift over a reduce, we obtain the correct Pascal interpretation of this ambiguity.

The YACC parser generator provides additional disambiguating rules in the form of precedence rules. For example, we can add the statement:

```
%%left '+' '-'
```

to a YACC grammar. Then an ambiguity centered on the productions:

```
expr → expr + expr
expr → expr - expr
```

will be resolved such that a sequence of + and - operators will be reduced left to right. When two such statements are listed, for example:

```
%%left '+' '-'
%%left '*' '/'
```

the operators * and / are considered to have *higher* precedence than the preceding ones, + and − . Thus conflicts involving * and / will be favored over shifts or reductions involving + and − .

YACC precedence rules are different from the precedence rules described in chapter 5 in that the latter are inferred from the grammar itself, whereas the former provide additional information needed to disambiguate a grammar.

Other special forms in YACC provide exceptions to these to allow additional control over inadequate state resolution.

6.5. LR(k) Parsers

We now describe a general means of constructing an LR(k) parser.

An *LR(k) item* is a marked production and a terminal string w in Σ^*. The length |w| is at most k, and w is called a *lookahead string*. We denote such an item by:

```
[A → x.y, w]
```

The marked production A→ x . y is called the *core* of the item. Several items with the same core may be combined through the notation:

```
[A → x.y, {u₁, u₂, ..., uₙ}]
```

which stands for the set of items:

```
[A → x . y, u₁]
[A → x . y, u₂]
    ...
[A → x . y, uₙ]
```

A state in the LR(k) parser will consist of a set of such items. Consider an item of the form [A → x . y, u] in some state S. When the parser is in state S, for a certain input string, x will be on the stack top and $FIRST_k(yu)$ is the next k input tokens. (S also can be associated with many other stack tops and input strings—but each of these also will be related to an item in S.)

Suppose y is empty in the item [A → x . y, u]. A reduce action therefore is indicated and string u is a k-symbol lookahead that can be used to decide whether that reduce is to be made or some alternative action taken—a shift or another reduce, perhaps.

If y is not empty, then u represents one of the possible legal k-symbol heads of the strings that can follow xy in a sentential form associated with an application of A → xy.

We can summarize this discussion by stating that S will contain an item of the form [A → x . y, u] if and only if the parser, in state S, can exhibit a stack top string x, some prefix w of the remaining input string eventually will reduce to y (that is, y derives w), and, on that reduction, u is the k-symbol head of the remaining input string.

We see that by carrying a lookahead string in the items when the parser state set is constructed, we will automatically have the necessary lookahead strings available. A k-symbol lookahead will be used on both read and reduce actions, for the sake of generality. This lookahead always will appear in an item-set as the lookahead string. It can be shown that an LR(k) constructor accepts the broadest class of grammars, larger than that accepted by the SLR(k) or SLALR(k) constructors described earlier.

The LR(k) item-set construction proceeds in three steps:

1. *Initial state construction:*

   (a) For every production S $\rightarrow$ w, add [S $\rightarrow$ .w, ϵ] to the initial state. S is the grammar's goal symbol.

   (b) If [A $\rightarrow$ .Bx, w] is in the initial state, and B $\rightarrow$ y is a production, then add all the items of the form [B $\rightarrow$ .y, z] to the initial state, where z is in the set $FIRST_k$(xw). Of course, this is added to the set only if it is not already there. We repeat this step until no more items can be added to the initial state.

2. *Starting a new state:* Let [A $\rightarrow$ r . Xy, w] be an item in some state P, where X is a terminal or nonterminal token. We locate every item in state P such that X follows the mark ".", then start a new state Q with these items, but with the mark moved past X. Thus, item [A $\rightarrow$ r . Xy, w] will become item [A $\rightarrow$ rX . y, w] in state Q. The set of items so used to start state Q is called the *kernel set* of Q.

   The kernel set of Q may be identical to the kernel set of some other state Q' already constructed. If so, states Q and Q' are equivalent and may be merged. By merging such states, we guarantee that the construction process will terminate in a finite number of steps.

   A transition from P to Q on X therefore will be part of the LR(k) parser.

3. *Completing a new state:* For every item of the form [A $\rightarrow$ x . By, w] in a state Q, and for every production B $\rightarrow$ z, add to Q all the items of the form [B $\rightarrow$. z, u], where u is in the set FIRSTk(yw). This step is repeated until no more items can be added to Q.

After step 1 is finished, steps 2 and 3 are repeated alternately, in that order, until no more new states can be constructed or completed.

As before, some states will carry completed items of the form [A $\rightarrow$ x ., w]. For them, a reduction is indicated in that state, with the production A $\rightarrow$ x. Now in general there will be several items in that state of the form [A $\rightarrow$ x ., . . .]. We therefore have a set of lookahead strings W such that the reduction is permitted only if the next k (or less) tokens in the input list are among the set W. The lookaheads also may be used to resolve one of several possible reductions or to resolve a conflict between a reduction and one or more read operations.

It can be shown that the grammar is LR(k) if and only if the following condition is met by the state set constructed as described: for every state P containing an item of the form [A → x ., w], there exists no other item of the form [B → y . z, w] in P.

Example. Let us construct the LR(1) item sets for grammar G_0, as follows:

```
1. E → E + T
2. E → T
3. T → T * F
4. T → F
5. F → (E)
6. F → a
```

We need the $FIRST_1$ sets for the nonterminals, as follows:

nonterminal v	$FIRST_1(v)$
E	(a
T	(a
F	(a

The initial state 0 contains the items [E → . E + T, ε] and [E → . T, ε], through construction rule 1(a). The completion rule on item [E → . E + T, ε] implies that each of the following items must be included in state 0:

```
[E → .E + T, +], from FIRST₁(+ T)
[E → .T, +], from production E → T
[T → .T * F, +], from production T → T * F
[T → .F, +], from production T → F
[T → .T * F, *], from item [T → .T * F, +] and FIRST₁(* F +)
```

Six items eventually appear in state 0. This state and the remaining states in the complete LR(1) state set follow. The kernel items are marked ">".

State	Item	Lookaheads	Go to state
0	>E → .E + T	ε +	1
	>E → .T	ε +	2
	T → .T * F	ε + *	2
	T → .F	ε + *	3
	F → .(E)	ε + *	5
	F → .a	ε + *	4
1	>E → E. + T	ε +	6
2	>E → T.	ε +	reduce (2)
	>T → T. * F	ε + *	7
3	>T → F.	ε + *	reduce (4)
4	>F → a.	ε + *	reduce (6)

5	$> F \rightarrow (.E)$	ϵ + *	8
	$E \rightarrow .E + T$	) +	8
	$E \rightarrow .T$	) +	9
	$T \rightarrow .T * F$	) + *	9
	$T \rightarrow .F$	) + *	10
	$F \rightarrow .(E)$	) + *	12
	$F \rightarrow .a$	) + *	11
6	$> E \rightarrow E + .T$	ϵ +	13
	$T \rightarrow .T * F$	ϵ + *	13
	$T \rightarrow .F$	ϵ + *	3
	$F \rightarrow .(E)$	ϵ + *	5
	$F \rightarrow .a$	ϵ + *	4
7	$> T \rightarrow T * .F$	ϵ + *	14
	$F \rightarrow .(E)$	ϵ + *	5
	$F \rightarrow .a$	ϵ + *	4
8	$> F \rightarrow (E.)$	ϵ + *	15
	$> E \rightarrow E. + T$	) +	16
9	$> E \rightarrow T.$	) +	reduce (2)
	$> T \rightarrow T. * F$	) + *	17
10	$> T \rightarrow F.$	) + *	reduce (4)
11	$> F \rightarrow a.$	) + *	reduce (6)
12	$> F \rightarrow (.E)$	) + *	18
	$E \rightarrow .E + T$	) +	18
	$E \rightarrow .T$	) +	9
	$T \rightarrow .T * F$	) + *	9
	$T \rightarrow .F$	) + *	10
	$F \rightarrow .(E)$	) + *	12
	$F \rightarrow .a$	) + *	11
13	$> E \rightarrow E + T.$	ϵ +	reduce (1)
	$> T \rightarrow T. * F$	ϵ + *	7
14	$> T \rightarrow T * F.$	ϵ + *	reduce (3)
15	$> F \rightarrow (E).$	ϵ + *	reduce (5)
16	$> E \rightarrow E + .T$	) +	19
	$T \rightarrow .T * F$	) + *	19
	$T \rightarrow .F$	) + *	10
	$F \rightarrow .(E)$	) + *	12
	$F \rightarrow .a$	) + *	11

17	$> T \rightarrow T * .F$	) + *	20
	$F \rightarrow .(E)$	) + *	12
	$F \rightarrow .a$	) + *	11
18	$> F \rightarrow (E.)$	) + *	21
	$> E \rightarrow E. + T$	) +	16
19	$> E \rightarrow E + T.$	) +	reduce (1)
	$> T \rightarrow T. * F$	) + *	17
20	$> T \rightarrow T * F.$	) + *	reduce (3)
21	$> F \rightarrow (E).$	) + *	reduce (5)

6.6. Some LR Table Minimizations

A number of minimizations have been proposed. We mention a few that are easy to implement in a parser generator.

6.6.1. Eliminating Single Productions

One minimization that is easy to introduce is *elimination of single productions*. A single production has the form A → B, where both A and B are nonterminal. Such productions appear many times in an expression grammar, but serve no useful semantic purpose. We would like to arrange the LR machine so that on the reduction chain A → B → w, the reduction of w to A will occur in one rather than two parse steps, thus eliminating the single production step.

In fact, the elimination is simply a matter of adjusting the appropriate entries in the STK_TOSTATE table in figure 6.3. Recall that this was constructed by tracing backward through the LR machine. Consider state 5 in the machine of figure 6.1, associated with the single production T → F, clearly a candidate for elimination.

The backtrace from state 5 leads to states 8, 11, and 12. Each of these accepts an F and transfer to 5. On the reduction of T → F, we then follow T from one of these to the next state; for example, 8 to 16, 11 to 16, or 12 to 17. We may clearly eliminate state 5—and the reduction T → F—by redirecting the F transition from state 8 to state 16, the F transition from state 11 to 14, and the F transition from state 12 to 17.

The production E → T cannot be so eliminated. There is a lookahead transition from 16 on * to 10, which must be preserved.

6.6.2. Removing Inaccessible States

When one or more single productions are removed, there will be some inaccessible states. These are easily identified and removed from the machine. Each state carries a mark that may be clear or set. A list R carries states that have been found to be accessible, remaining for consideration.

1. Clear the mark on all states. Clear a list R.

2. Push the start state onto R.

3. If R is empty, halt. All unmarked states are inaccessible.

4. Pop the top state S from list R. Mark state S. For every state Q such that there is a transition from S to Q, push Q onto R. Go to 3.

6.6.3. Combining Lists

Another minimization involves looking for a list already in TOKNUM before adding another one. The TOSTATE list entries must also match, but if a match exists, several items in these lists can be eliminated.

The same consideration applies to the STK_STATE and STK_TOSTATE lists.

6.6.4. Ambiguous Grammars

When one uses a highly ambiguous grammar with some disambiguating rules, the number of states tends to be smaller than if one wrote an equivalent unambiguous grammar. This effect was first noted by Aho [1975], and is particularly apparent in arithmetic expression grammars. By writing an expression in the form:

```
E → E + E
E → E - E
E → E * E
    ... etc.
E → P
P → ( E )
P → var
```

and then adding precedence disambiguating rules, the number of parser states is smaller than for a grammar in which all precedence is carried in an unambiguous form. Disambiguating rules have been discussed earlier.

6.7. Error Recovery in an LR Parser

A book may be very amusing with numerous errors, or it may be very dull without a single absurdity.

. . . Oliver Goldsmith

Man errs as long as he strives.

. . . Goethe

We have seen that an LR parser will detect a syntax error in a read state—the next input token fails to match a transition token associated with the current state. As usual, the error must be reported. We then have a number of action choices:

- Insertion of a terminal token.

- Insertion of a nonterminal token.

- Popping the stack.

- Skipping an input token.

In each case, it is important to test the consequences of an error recovery approach by attempting a parse within the situation.

6.7.1. Nonterminal Insertion

We first demonstrate that we need not bother with insertion of a nonterminal token, provided that the grammar has a suitable form. Nonterminal insertion requires some messy semantic operations in general, because nonterminals usually are associated with some semantic structures.

We insist that the grammar be such that for every nonterminal A, there is at least one production of the form A $\rightarrow$ c, where c is terminal. Then consider a sentential form:

$$wSxy$$

where x is a terminal, and wS is the viable prefix at a point where the *read* operation has failed on the token x. We call x an *error token* in general.

Now if insertion of the nonterminal A causes the parse to be successful—that is, the sentential form should read:

$$wSAy$$

then we claim that the insertion of x will achieve the same end, because the subsequent reduction will involve A $\rightarrow$ x. Note that "insertion of nonterminal A" is in fact equivalent to pushing A onto the stack; this in turn will be valid only if the resulting viable prefix can be associated with a path in the LR parser's machine.

We therefore reject nonterminal insertion; the same patch can be achieved by inserting the appropriate terminal symbol, given a production A $\rightarrow$ x for every nonterminal A. For this reason, special error productions should be added to a grammar if necessary to provide full terminal insertion capability on error recovery.

6.7.2. A Simple Error-Recovery Strategy

This error-recovery strategy does not require a lookahead of more than one token in the input string. LR1SKEL of the QPARSER suite contains this algorithm. Better recovery schemes have been proposed, but they all require an unlimited number of lookaheads. We will examine some of these later.

1. *Initialization.* On encountering a syntax error, the stack will consist of the states:

$$S_n, S_{n-1}, \ldots, S_1, S_0$$

where S_0 is the stack top state. Let X be the error token, and let S_0 be a read state. We will operate within an environment in which trial parses may be undertaken with no associated semantic actions. A copy of the stack must be made for the sake of stack restoration. Set variable j: $= 0$; j will mark the current stack top. In the following steps, the operation *restore the stack* will result in the stack:

$$S_n, S_{n-1}, \ldots, S_{j+1}, S_j$$

This is the original stack, less the top j states.

2. *Terminal insertion.* For every terminal T that is accepted by state S_j, insert T before X in the input string and attempt to parse the input string through token X—but no further! If a T exists such that the parse is successful, we have found a patch. Otherwise, restore the stack and repeat step 2 until no more options exist.

3. *Dropping a state.* If j $=$ n, go to step 4. Otherwise, set j: $= j + 1$. Attempt to parse through X with the new stack top. If successful, we have a patch. Otherwise, restore the stack and go to step 2.

4. *Bottom of stack.* Here, j $=$ n. Set j $= 0$. Restore the stack. Reject X, read the next token, then go to step 2.

On a successful completion of this algorithm, the real stack must be cut back to level j, and the parsing restarted. A terminal insertion usually involves no semantic action, unless the terminal stands for a class of tokens, such as <identifier> or <real>. In that case, an inserted terminal must be accompanied by some semantic value appropriate for the terminal.

Discussion

We have found that the recovery with this simple strategy may not be very effective. There are several problems. There is a tendency to remove more states from the stack than is necessary. Spurious error reports often are the result of removing too many states from the stack.

Often, an inserted token is an unfortunate choice. For example, we found that a relatively common syntax error caused the token CASE to be inserted under this algorithm. The CASE statement is highly structured, and the insertion of CASE is rarely needed; hence, many subsequent spurious errors are generated.

The information in the input list past the error token X is not used. This information could be used to more effectively select j or an insertion token or to force more input scanning.

6.7.3. Variations on the Strategy

Certain variations on this strategy easily can be implemented to correct some of the deficiencies. Of these, we have studied error recovery based on the first two problems. A discussion of the strategy's effectiveness is given in section 6.7.7.

1. Report a syntax or semantic error only if no error has been reported on the last m tokens, where m is some small number. That is, if an error is seen on a token a_0 in the string $a_0a_1. . .a_k. . .$, then report an error found at token a_k only if $k > m$. Note that only error reports are affected, not the recovery. However, the apparent effectiveness of recovery is increased exponentially as m increases.

   To see why, suppose that the probability of an erroneous recovery with a single error token is P; then the probability of an erroneous recovery after successfully scanning m successive tokens is P^m. Thus for $P = 0.2$ and $m = 3$, $P^m = 0.008$.

2. Assign costs to tokens and to state removal. Then, instead of just choosing the first workable insertion state strategy, explore them all and choose one with least cost. A limited state removal is useful, but removing too many may be a sign of a runaway recovery. The state removal cost therefore should rise sharply with the number of states removed. The cost also should go up as the number of states left on the stack approaches zero.

   The costs assigned to tokens can be judged by the degree of syntactic structure associated with each one. In Pascal, for example, an insertion of such tokens as arithmetic operators, commas, right parentheses, and right brackets should be low, because these often are left out inadvertently. However, the cost of insertion of a CASE or PROCEDURE token should be fairly high, because these require some elaborate structure that must be in place in the remaining input string.

   In general, a cost will be low for a token that appears at the end of some structure, and high for a token that appears at the beginning of some structure.

3. The tokens that may be inserted can be limited to a subset of the grammar's alphabet. In addition, a limit can be placed on the degree to which the stack

can be reduced by dropping states. We have found the following guidelines to be effective:

(a) Select a set of tokens that should *not* be inserted. These should be terminal tokens and each one, if it were to be inserted, should demand some subsequent structured form that is unlikely to be present in the source. Candidates for the "do not insert" list are such keywords as PROCEDURE, IF, CASE, WHILE, VAR, to use Pascal as an example.

(b) Select a set of states S' such that if S' = S_j, then j will not be decremented. State S' can best be chosen by selecting a set of tokens T' such that the states S' are accessed by the members of T'. The members of T' should be those terminals and nonterminals that represent the heads of major structures in the language. Such tokens as PROCEDURE, CASE, BEGIN, are reasonable candidates for this list.

Once these two lists have been chosen, the error-recovery strategy is modified by permitting an insertion only of tokens not in the list (a) and not reducing the stack below a state in the set S', list (b).

There is a hazard in limiting insertion candidates and that is the risk of disabling recovery on certain classes of errors. We can offer no guidelines on this strategy.

6.7.4. Scanner Feedback

An LR(1) parser often will require the lexical scanning of one token past a handle. The error-recovery strategy in the previous section is designed to make use of this next token and the stack contents to devise a patch.

As an improvement, we can read several tokens past the error token in an attempt to arrive at a more effective patch. As we shall see, the use of a "forward move" requires that the lexical analyzer scan an arbitrary number of tokens past the error point.

However, in some languages, the lexical analysis may depend in some fashion on parsing decisions. We saw in chapter 3 that, in Fortran and PL/1, reserved words also may be used as user identifiers under certain circumstances. For that to be possible, the lexical analyzer must be able to infer from a symbol table whether an identifier is a keyword, and that decision will depend on previously parsed declarations or statements. We say that *feedback* exists from the parser to the lexical analyzer.

If feedback exists, then the scanning of tokens past the error token is not reliable. There will be no apply operations resulting from such a scan to guide the scanning, and the token codes supplied by the scanner are likely to be incorrect.

Given a feedback-free scanner, it is relatively easy to scan several tokens in the input string past the error token. These tokens may then be used either to construct a patch that is compatible with these tokens or to discard more input tokens until a patch can be devised.

6.7.5. Forward Move

Given that the objective of error recovery is to continue parsing with a minimum of subsequent spurious error reports and a maximum of checking of the subsequent input text, it is clear that the input text past the error point is of considerable importance to an effective error-recovery strategy.

The notion of a *forward move* was devised by Graham and Rhodes [Graham, 1975], who studied error recovery in an operator precedence parser. A forward move essentially is an attempt to reduce, through parsing actions, a portion of the text following the error token before selecting a recovery strategy. Those reductions are made that would have to be made in any case. A forward move reduces the number of trials needed for a feasible error-recovery solution and increases the forward context information needed for an effective recovery.

With operator or simple precedence, a forward move is relatively simple. The error token followed by the remaining input list is assumed to be some string to be parsed, with the usual start token included as a prefix. Reductions are then made as usual, halting when another error is found. Recall that an error is detected through either a token-pair that is not in the precedence table or a handle that fails to match any production right member. The forward move may also continue to the end of the input list.

Pennello [1978] describes a forward move algorithm suitable for use with an LR(1) parser. In his scheme, an LR parse is begun just past the error token (it could also just as well begin with the error token), with a special parser called an *error parser*. Each state of the error parser represents a set of states of the LR(1) parser. The initial state consists of all those read states that can accept the first input token of the remaining input list. The error parse continues through read, lookahead, and apply actions, just as in an LR(1) parser, except that every action must agree (in a sense to be described more precisely next) and any apply action must be such that there are sufficient states on the stack to support the action.

Let Q' represent a set of states in the error parser and T some token to be read next. Then a transition in the error parser on (Q', T) is permitted only if each of the states q' in Q' either (1) have no move on T or (2) if they show a move agree in action. That is, if any of the Q' states call for a READ action, then every state must either call for READ or for ERROR. (An ERROR simply means that some state will be dropped from the state-set on the move.) If any of the Q' states call for an APPLY, then every state must call for either an APPLY on the same production or an ERROR. If any of the Q' states are ACCEPT, the forward move halts. Finally, if an APPLY move is indicated, and there are insufficient states in the forward move stack to support the apply action, the forward move halts.

A special stack is used for the forward move, initially containing only the state-set accepting the first token. Given a READ action, a set of states representing the successor states of the members of Q' on token T is pushed on this stack. Given an APPLY action such that sufficient states exist on the stack to support the action, those states are popped and replaced by the indicated apply set.

The action of the forward move essentially performs a number of reductions of the input following the error token. It condenses the information in the input list and can be used to devise a patch. It is possible that the forward move may continue to the end of the program and perform a large number of reductions. It may also halt within one or two tokens, because of another syntax error or for some other reason.

Consider a right-most derivation:

$$S \rightarrow^* vAy \rightarrow vwxy$$

where $A \rightarrow wx$ is a production. vw is some viable prefix of the sentential form vwxy. We say that z is a *viable fragment* of the viable prefix if z is a suffix of vw. Further, we say that U is a *derived viable fragment* of the sentence suffix zy if (1) U derives z, and (2) during a parse of any sentence ending in zy, at some point the parser must reduce z to the viable fragment U.

Pennello [1978] shows that his forward move yields a viable fragment U that represents the largest possible subsequent input string. Let that string be z. Then $U \rightarrow^+ z$ is a derivation that must be made eventually by any parse. An experimental evaluation of his scheme is given in section 6.7.7.

6.7.6. Forward Move and Parse Reversal

Mickunas and Modry [Mickunas, 1978] propose reversing the parse in some cases to achieve an effective patch. This involves much more than just dropping states—it must be possible to reconstruct the parse steps in reverse and obtain some previous parser configuration. A parse reversal can be achieved only by maintaining a complete history of the parse, or by keeping on hand the tokenized input string along with input string positions in the stack. This information must be kept for any parse, and represents a cost of compiling error-free as well as erroneous source text. Parse reversal also carries significant semantic implications—the semantic actions also should be reversed if the intention is to continue semantic actions through an error recovery.

However, if a parse reversal is possible, their approach apparently yields a good repair of a number of otherwise difficult syntax errors.

Their algorithm consists of two phases—a *condensation phase* and a *correction phase*. The condensation phase essentially is a forward move. A set of states S that can shift on the error token is determined, and a parse is made of the remaining input string, using one of the states in S as a start state. A forward move terminates in one of two ways: (1) an attempt is made to reduce over the error point, or (2) another error occurs. In case 2, the parse configuration is called a *holding candidate*, and is held for possible use when other strategies fail. In case 1, the configuration is called a *correction candidate*.

At least one correction candidate always will be found—it may be the error configuration itself. If several are found, they are examined independently.

The *correction phase* is a systematic recovery strategy that incorporates the following operations:

- Inserting a terminal token.

- Reversing the parse. The parse is backed up to some former configuration.

- Dropping a state representing a terminal token from the stack. If no terminal token is on the stack top, then the parse must be reversed until one is. When a state is dropped, the set of possible insertion tokens changes.

- Assigning a cost to each insertion and each stack deletion, and accumulating a total cost for some strategy path.

- Abandoning a strategy path when its cost exceeds a preset limit and launching an alternative path.

- If all else fails, selecting a holding candidate and invoking recursively the entire condensation-correction strategy on it. Recall that a holding candidate is generated when a second parsing error is encountered during a forward move.

There usually are many different paths to follow, depending on the results of the condensation phase and on the number of insertions that are found to be compatible with some stack and the condensation states. A path is followed until either a successful repair is found or the net cost exceeds a preset threshold. All the paths are followed, and a repair with least cost is selected.

The correction phase will never drop the error token. If it succeeds in finding a path involving one or more of the operations listed, it reports success, and an effective recovery patch is found. If it fails, then the error token must be dropped and new condensation and correction phases must be launched.

Mickunas and Modry implemented this error-recovery scheme on a small grammar containing about 40 productions and 356 states. A number of examples of recovery from seemingly intractable error states are given in their paper [Mickunas, 1978].

6.7.7. Error-Recovery Experiments

We performed an experiment with our simple error-recovery system by running 75 erroneous programs through a parser. Each program contained exactly one error, but a different one in each case. The performance of the recovery system was judged by the number of error complaints, or *symptoms,* made while parsing the program. Ideally, just one error symptom should be reported but, due to inadequate recovery, several were often reported.

The experiment was performed four different ways, depending on whether semantic errors were considered and whether error suppression was used.

The performance of our error-recovery strategy is summarized by the bar charts of figure 6.7. Each chart shows the fraction P (ordinate) of programs that exhibited n error reports (abscissa), with n = 1, 2, 3, 4, 5, and greater than 5. Charts (a) and (b) illustrate an error recovery in which every error is reported, and charts (c) and (d) illustrate error recovery with variation 2 (error report suppressed if within three tokens of a previous error symptom). Charts (a) and (c) are for syntax errors only, and charts (b) and (d) are for syntax and semantic errors. Every semantic error was reported, whether near a previous one or not. If nearby semantic errors were suppressed, we would expect some improvement in graph (d).

Graph (c) shows that the simple strategy was quite effective if only syntax errors were considered. Over 80% of the recoveries were optimal (one error

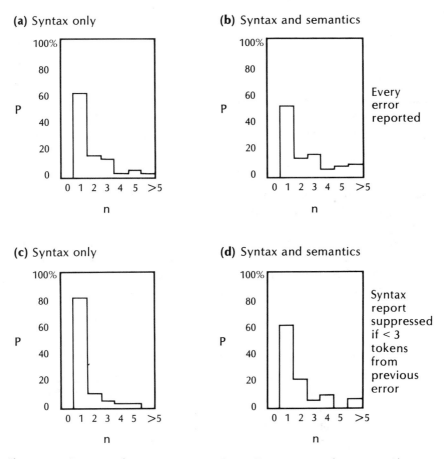

Figure 6.7.   Summary of error recovery experiment. P = percentage of programs with n error reports.

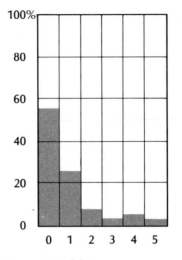

Figure 6.8.   Distribution of tokens rejected during error recovery.

symptom reported), and none of the recoveries reported more than five symp-toms. If the semantic errors were also considered, the recovery was only 60% effective—graph (d)—and about 6% of the recoveries generated more than five symptoms.

Few input tokens were dropped in the average recovery, as indicated by the distributions in figure 6.8. No tokens were rejected in about 57% of the cases, and one token was dropped in 27% of the cases. In no case were more than five tokens dropped. Thus, 84% of the recoveries were effected by dropping one or no tokens.

These results may be somewhat misleading, because the program was small. The recovery sometimes is very bad in a large program. For example, an error in a long list of repeated constants or expressions sometimes causes a cyclic recovery failure in which a large number of spurious errors are reported or a large number of tokens are dropped.

Results of Pennello's Forward-Move Recovery Strategy

Pennello [1978] reports a similar experiment on 70 Pascal programs. Each of these programs is different, but each contained just one syntax error. They were student programs, with student errors. His results are summarized in figure 6.9. Graph (a) represents Pennello's classification of recovery—"excellent," "good," "poor," and "unrepaired." The "excellent" and "good" categories are in fact optimal recoveries—in every case the recovery generated just one error report. The "poor" category generated two reports for a single error. In the

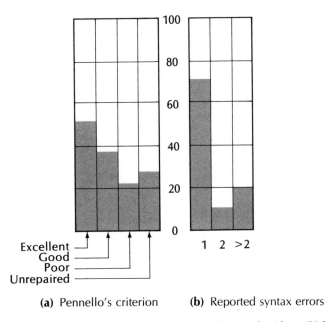

(a) Pennello's criterion   (b) Reported syntax errors

Figure 6.9. Error recovery based on Pennello's forward move algorithm—70 Pascal programs studied.

"unrepaired" category no repair was selected, but the remainder of the program was parsed through the forward-move machine rather than the parser. These rob the system of upper-level parsing, and destroy the detection of subsequent errors.

Pennello's system is between 60% and 90% effective, depending on how one regards the "unrepaired" errors. However, these results are for syntax errors only. He does not state how many of the "good" error recoveries generated spurious semantic error messages.

6.8. Exercises

1. Trace the machine of figure 6.1 for these input strings:

```
a + a * a
a * a + a
(a + a) * a
a + a + a
```

2. Show that the machine of figure 6.1 rejects these input strings:

```
a ++ a
+a * a
a ↑ a)
```

3. For the following grammar, compute the LR(0) item sets. Give the transition function of the corresponding FSM, identify read and apply states, and give the production to be used in each apply state.

```
S → A S
S → c
A → a A
A → b
```

4. For each of the following grammars, compute the LR(0) item sets. Construct the corresponding FSM. Is the grammar LR(0)? If not, use the SLR technique to construct a deterministic FSM. Identify its read, lookahead, and apply states and give the production to be used in each apply state.

```
(an unambiguous nested if statement grammar)
S → M
S → U
M → iMeM
M → a
U → iS
U → iMeU

(a regular expression grammar)
E → E + T
E → T
T → TF
T → F
F → F*
F → (E)
F → a
F → ∅
```

5. For the following grammar, compute the LR(0) item sets. Construct the corresponding FSM. Is the grammar LR(0)? If not, use the SLR technique to construct a deterministic FSM. Is the grammar SLR(1)? If not, use the SLALR technique to construct a deterministic FSM. Is the grammar SLALR(1)? Identify its read, lookahead, and apply states and give the production to be used in each apply state.

```
E → E + F
E → F
F → (E)
F → a(E)
F → a
```

6. For each of the following ambiguous grammars, construct the LR(0) item sets. Use the SLR technique to construct an FSM. Use disambiguating rules to resolve any remaining nondeterminacy. Choose rules that correspond to traditional interpretations of common programming languages. Identify the read, lookahead, and apply states of the resulting FSM and give the production to be used in each apply state.

```
(an expression grammar)
E → E + E
E → E * E
E → (E)
E → a

(a nested IF statement grammar)
S → iS
S → iSeS
S → a
```

7. For each grammar, construct the LR(1) item sets. Construct the corresponding FSM. Is the grammar LR(1)? Identify the read, lookahead, and apply states and give the production to be used in each apply state.

```
S → a A a
S → b A b
S → a B b
S → b B a
A → c
B → c

S → aSb
S → A
A → bA
A → b
```

8. For the following grammar, construct the LR(1) item sets and the corresponding FSM. Is the grammar LR(1)? Construct the LR(0) item sets from the LR(1) item sets by discarding the lookaheads and eliminating any duplicate item sets that result. Use the SLALR technique to construct an FSM. Compare this to the LR(1) FSM. Is the grammar SLALR(1)? Use the SLR technique to construct an FSM and compare it to the SLALR FSM. Is the grammar SLR(1)? Finally, construct an LR(0) FSM and compare it to the SLR FSM. Is the grammar LR(0)?

```
(a Polish postfix expression grammar)
E → EE +
E → EE *
E → a
```

6.9. Bibliographical Notes

The LR(k) parsing system generally is attributed to Knuth [1965], in which both the item-set construction and the augmented grammar construction are presented, with arguments for their correctness. He also proves that the LR(k) grammars are the largest class that can be parsed deterministically left to right with a k-symbol lookahead. Despite the significance of these results, little additional work on LR parsers was done until recently.

The SLR(k) resolution is from DeRemer [1969, 1971]. The SLALR(k) resolution was first reported by LaLonde [1971a]. The LALR(k) system was first proposed by Anderson, Eve, and Horning [Anderson, 1973]; it and the SLR(k) system seem to be the LR systems of choice for the known LR parser generators.

The optimizations of canonical LR(k) tables are from Aho [1972].

YACC is a popular LR parser generator that works well with programs written in C. It is available on most systems that support the Unix operating system. See the paper by Johnson [1978] for details.

Leinius [1970] described the first error-recovery technique reported for an LR parser. James [1972] describes an implementation of Leinius's method, with some recovery statistics.

In a top-down compiler, the predictive nature of the compiler can be used to insert one or more tokens. Irons [1963] describes such a system.

Levy [1975] and LaFrance [1971] proposed a nondeterministic recovery system that carries out a set of parses, one for each of a set of possibilities. Unfortunately, if this algorithm is carried out for more than a few steps, the resulting computation becomes unreasonably large; as we have seen, such a strategy has exponential complexity.

A minimal error-correcting algorithm is given by Aho and Peterson [Aho, 1972c], described earlier.

McGruther [1972] describes a syntax error-recovery and correction system that requires the grammar to be both LR and RL. (An RL grammar is such that sentences can be parsed in reverse by an LR parser.) On detecting an error, an RL parser is applied to the remaining string in reverse.

Graham and Rhodes [Graham, 1975] describe a recovery method for precedence parsers that consists of a forward move followed by a correction step. The forward move performs a sequence of reductions on the input list following the error token; they call this the *condensation phase*. Pennello [1978] describes a similar condensation step for an LR parser. Both authors give strategies for the correction step.

Feyock and Lazarus [1976] describe a bottom-up system similar to the bounded-range strategy described above. They propose only insertion, deletion, replacement, or interchange of terminal symbols as correction strings.

Mickunas and Modry [Mickunas, 1978] describe an LR(1) recovery system with a forward move and error region patching. Their approach is described in section 6.7.6.

> *This is not the end. It is not even the beginning of the end. But it is, perhaps, the end of the beginning.*
>
> ... *Winston Churchill*

CHAPTER 7

SYNTAX-DIRECTED TRANSLATION

We are conceptually at the midpoint of our subject. We have developed mechanisms for recognizing the structure of sentences written in the source programming language. The end result of this process of lexical analysis and parsing is a sequence of productions that constitute a bottom-up or top-down parse of the input. We also may view the end result (so far) as a derivation tree.

We have seen how a source string can be subdivided and analyzed according to an underlying CFG and transformed into a structure (a derivation tree), in terms of which the underlying meaning of an input sentence can be defined.

We must now develop tools for the construction of the translation or object sentence. The output of any compiler can be viewed as a sentence in some object or target language, whether the object be another high-level programming language, a symbolic assembly language, or sequences of binary machine instructions.

The general task of accepting the tree structure created by a parser and generating from it the object sentence (or code) is called the *synthesis* phase of a compiler. The synthesis phase can be conceptually subdivided into a number of reasonably distinct subtasks, as described in chapter 1, namely: collection and distribution of attributes of the data objects found in the abstract-syntax tree, optimization on the tree, allocation of data-object space, and code generation.

7.1. General Principles

A *syntax-directed translation scheme,* or *SDTS,* specifies a source language, a target language, and rules for the translation of any string in the source language into a target string. The rules of an SDTS are production rules, extended to include translation forms. No mechanism for the translation of source to target is implied by the SDTS definitions, although we shall see that the translation can be achieved easily.

As a conceptual model, the SDTS provides a good framework for understanding some of the underlying principles of translation. An implementation of an SDTS is a *string translator,* but of a limited kind. The SDTS model does not contain provisions for collecting and distributing attributes, and without attributes a translator is of little practical use. Nevertheless, certain ordering properties stem from the SDTS model, and these are of considerable value in planning an attribute system for a complete compiler.

We shall first define the SDTS model and explore some of its properties. A general implementation will be presented. The chapter ends with the development of a general-purpose translator system that can serve as the framework of a practical bottom-up compiler.

7.1.1. Definitions

A *syntax-directed translation scheme* is a five-tuple consisting of

1. A finite *input alphabet* Σ, comprising the symbols of the source language.

2. A finite set N of *nonterminal symbols* used in a CFG to define the input language.

3. A finite *output alphabet* Δ, containing symbols that will appear in the *translation* or *output string*.

4. A finite set of *rules* R of the form A $\rightarrow$ w, y, to be defined later.

5. A *start symbol* S in N with the same meaning and use as in the definition of a CFG.

A rule in R of the form:

$$A \rightarrow w, y$$

is such that w consists of a string of terminals and nonterminals, just as in a CFG, and y is a string of symbols from N and Δ. The symbol A is in N. Furthermore, there must be a one-to-one association of nonterminals in w with the nonterminals in y. The string w is called the *source element* and the string y is called the *translation element* of this rule.

The four-tuple (N, Σ, P, S), where P is a set of rules of the form A $\rightarrow$ w, and A $\rightarrow$ w, y is a rule in R, is called the *underlying source grammar* of T. That is, we obtain the underlying source grammar by stripping the translation element from the rules and discarding the output alphabet.

There is also an *underlying target grammar*, obtained by removing the source element from each production and discarding the input alphabet.

For example, consider the SDTS S_1 = ({a, b, c, +, $-$, [,]}, {E, T, A}, {ADD, SUB, NEG, x, y, z}, R, E), where R consists of the set of translation rules:

```
1.    E → E + T,  T E ADD
2.    E → E - T,  E T SUB
3.    E → - T,    T NEG
4.    E → T,      T
5.    T → [ E ],  E
6.    T → A,      A
7.    A → a,      x
8.    A → b,      y
9.    A → c,      z
```

The underlying source grammar of S_1 is:

```
E → E + T | E - T | - T | T
T → [ E ] | A
A → a | b | c
```

A *translation form* is a pair of strings (u, v), such that u is a sentential form of the underlying grammar of an SDTS and v is a *translation* consisting of elements drawn from N and Σ.

A translation form is defined as follows:

1. (S, S) is a translation form, and the two S's are said to be *associated*. Also, S is the start symbol of the SDTS.

2. If (a A b, a' A b') is a translation form, and the two A's are associated; further, if A → g, g' is a rule in R, then (a g b, a' g' b') also is a translation form. The association of nonterminals in g to those in g' must be carried into the translation form exactly as it is in the rule.

The notation:

$$(a \ A \ b, \ a' \ A \ b') \Rightarrow (a \ g \ b, \ a' \ g' \ b')$$

expresses the transformation of one translation form into another.

We see that the first part of the translation form is exactly a sentential form of the underlying CFG; the second part is an associated translation, a sentential form of the underlying target grammar.

The *translation* defined by an SDTS T is the set of pairs:

$$\{(x, y) \mid (S, S) \Rightarrow^* (x, y), x \ \varepsilon \ \Sigma^*, \text{ and } y \ \varepsilon \ \Delta^*\}$$

which is clearly analogous to the definition of a language in a CFG given in chapter 2.

Example.   Consider the input string:

$$- \ [a \ + \ c] \ - \ b$$

that is derivable in the underlying grammar of S_1 as follows:

$$E \rightarrow E \ - \ T \rightarrow \ - \ T \ - \ T \rightarrow \ - \ [E] \ - \ T \rightarrow \ - \ [E \ + \ T] \ - \ T$$
$$\rightarrow \ - \ [T \ + \ T] \ - \ T \rightarrow \ - \ [A \ + \ T] \ - \ T \rightarrow \ - \ [a \ + \ T] \ - \ T$$
$$\rightarrow + \ - \ [a \ + \ c] \ - \ b$$

The derivation tree for this string is shown in figure 7.1(a).

The translation for this string is given next. We have introduced subscripts on certain nonterminals in the translation forms as needed to indicate the association between the input and output nonterminals. Thus two T's appear in the second translation form; they are distinguished by the subscripts 1 and 2.

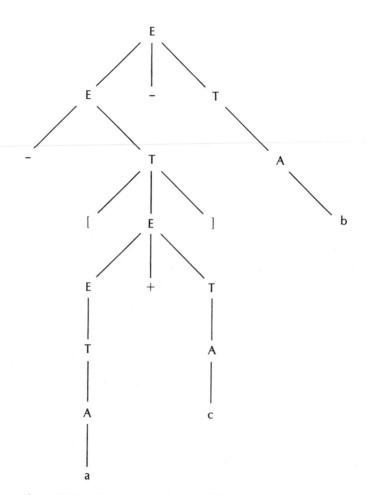

Figure 7.1(a). Derivation tree for $-[a+b]-b$.

$$(E, E) \rightarrow (E - T, E\ T\ SUB)$$
$$\rightarrow (- T_1 - T_2, T_1\ NEG\ T_2\ SUB)$$
$$\rightarrow (- [E] - T, E\ NEG\ T\ SUB)$$
$$\rightarrow (- [E + T_1] - T_2, T_1\ E\ ADD\ NEG\ T_2\ SUB)$$
$$\rightarrow^+ (- [A + T_1] - T_2, T_1\ A\ ADD\ NEG\ T_2\ SUB)$$
$$\rightarrow (- [a + T_1] - T_2, T_1\ x\ ADD\ NEG\ T_2\ SUB)$$
$$\rightarrow^+ (- [a + c] - T, z\ x\ ADD\ NEG\ T\ SUB)$$
$$\rightarrow^+ (- [a + c] - b, z\ x\ ADD\ NEG\ y\ SUB)$$

The translation of $-[a + c] - b$ in the SDTS T is therefore:

$$z\ x\ ADD\ NEG\ y\ SUB$$

We evidently have a translator for some simple arithmetic expressions to a postfix notation, with the twist that pairs of addition operands are interchanged in the output string.

We have introduced some lexical operations in this grammar, through the last three translation rules (A → a, x | b, y | c, z) in order to clarify the translation process. Of course, a set of identifiers will appear as one terminal symbol in a practical compiler and be distinguished by the lexical analyzer.

7.1.2. Tree Transformations

A tree interpretation of the syntax-directed translation process is shown in figure 7.1. Part (a) of this figure shows the derivation tree for the string $-[a+c]-b$ in the underlying grammar of T. The translation can be viewed as a transformation of this tree into another tree, the transformation consisting of (1) removing the terminal nodes, (2) permuting the children of each interior node according to the appropriate translation rule, and (3) adding terminal nodes that correspond to the translation terminal set Δ.

Thus, figure 7.1.(b) shows the derivation tree in (a) with the terminal nodes removed. In this step, it is possible that two different productions can appear to be the same. For example, the productions:

$$E \rightarrow - T \text{ and}$$
$$E \rightarrow T$$

look the same in the tree after the terminal nodes are removed. We therefore label each node with a production number.

In figure 7.1(c), the children of each node have been permuted according to the translation rules and the terminal output symbols have been added. Note that the children of each interior node now are exactly a translation element of some translation rule. For example, the children of node ₁E were originally:

$$E + T$$

The translation rule is:

$$E \rightarrow E + T, T E \text{ ADD}$$

Hence, the children of this node become:

$$T E \text{ ADD}$$

T and E stand for a pair of subtrees that move with the permutation; this movement causes the string z to appear first in the translation although its corresponding source symbol c appears second in the source string.

The completed translation tree (figure 7.1(c)) now may be scanned in left-to-right natural order to yield the translation string

$$z \text{ x ADD NEG y SUB}$$

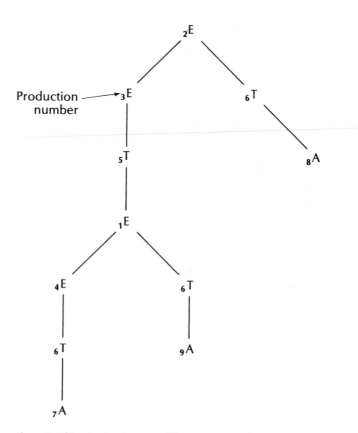

Figure 7.1(b).   Derivation tree of figure 7.1(a) with terminal nodes removed.

It is clear that the resulting translation string is independent of the order in which the translation is performed. Thus, a bottom-up (right-most) or top-down (left-most) translation will yield the same translation string.

7.2. Simple SDTSs and Top-Down Transducers

A SDTS is said to be *simple* if the order of the nonterminals in the translation part of each rule is the same as the order of the nonterminals in the source part. For example, a rule:

$$S \rightarrow S_1 + S_2, \; S_2 \; S_1 \; ADD$$

in a SDTS T causes T to be nonsimple.

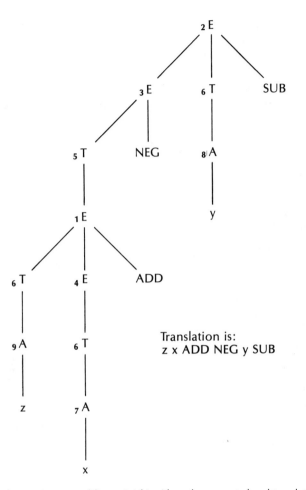

Figure 7.1(c).   Derivation tree of figure 7.1(b) with nodes permuted and translation elements added, according to translation scheme.

A simple SDTS is such that no permutation of the derivation tree nodes is required for the translation. We have only removal of the source string terminals and insertion of the translation string terminals.

The significance of a simple SDTS for a top-down parser is expressed in the following theorem.

Theorem 7.1.   If $T = (N, \Sigma, \Delta, R, S)$ is a simple SDTS the underlying grammar of which is LL(k), then there exists a top-down deterministic pushdown transducer that accepts any string in the input language of T and yields the corresponding output string.

A *push-down transducer* (PDT) is analogous to the push-down automaton of chapter 4, except that it is permitted to emit a string of finite length (the translated output) on each move. We define a PDT P as follows:

A *configuration* of P is a four-tuple (q, x, y, z), where q is a state in its finite control, x is the remaining input list yet to be scanned, y is a stack, and z is an output string emitted up to this point. Then, in one move, we have:

$$(q, ax, Yy', z) \vdash (r, x, gy', zz')$$

where there exists a machine rule:

$$\delta(q, a, Y) \text{ contains } (r, g, z')$$

That is, given state q, with input symbol a, and stack top symbol Y, the machine is permitted to move to state r; in this move, the input symbol a is discarded, Y on the stack top is replaced by g, and the string z' is emitted as output.

Then we say that w is an *output* for x if $(q_0, x, Z_0, \epsilon) \vdash^* (q, \epsilon, u, w)$ for some state q and stack string u. State q_0 is the initial state and Z_0 is the initial stack contents; ϵ is the empty string. We say that P *halts by empty stack* if $u = \epsilon$ is a halting condition; alternatively, P *halts by final state* if q is a member of a defined set of halt states F, a subset of the machine's state set. These definitions are analogous to those of the PDA's defined in chapters 4 and 5.

We say that the PDT P is deterministic when both of the following conditions are met:

1. For all states q, strings a, and stacks Z, $\delta(q, a, Z)$ contains at most one element.

2. If $\delta(q, \epsilon, Z)$ is not null, then no symbol a exists such that $\delta(q, a, Z)$ is not null. That is, there must be no conflict between an empty and a nonempty move for some state and stack.

We may now describe the construction of a PDT P, given an SDTS T, where the underlying source grammar of T is LL(1), such that P: (1) accepts every string in the underlying grammar of T, and (2) emits exactly the translation in T of every such string. The general case of LL(k), $k > 1$, is discussed in Lewis [1968].

Recall, from chapter 4, that the top-down LL(1) recognizer has two kinds of move:

1. An *apply* move, in which a nonterminal A on the stack top is replaced by a string w, where $A \rightarrow w$ is some production rule. This operation is made deterministic through a selection table based on the stack top nonterminal A and the next input symbol.

2. A *matching* move, in which a terminal symbol a on the stack top is matched against the next input symbol. In a matching move, the stack top symbol is removed and the read head is advanced one symbol. A failure to match must be a syntax error.

Now a PDT operates as follows:

1. In an apply move, with a nonterminal A on the stack top, we know that a production $A \rightarrow w$ is involved, from the deterministic selector table. Let the translation rule in R be:

$$A \rightarrow w, z$$

where:

$$w = a_0 \ B_1 \ a_1 \ B_2 \ a_2 \ \ldots \ B_k \ a_k$$

and:

$$z = b_0 \ B_1 \ b_1 \ B_2 \ b_2 \ \ldots \ B_k \ b_k$$

The B_i are nonterminals, the a_i are input alphabet strings (or are empty), the b_i are output alphabet strings (or are empty), and $k \geq 0$. Note that this translation rule is *simple*.

We assume that the input and output alphabet symbols are distinguishable. Then A is replaced on the stack top by the composite string:

$$b_0 \ a_0 \ B_1 \ b_1 \ a_1 \ B_2 \ \ldots \ B_k \ b_k \ a_k$$

with b_0 on the stack top.

2. If the symbol on the stack top is a member of the output alphabet, then it is removed and emitted as output.

3. If the symbol on the stack top is a member of the input alphabet, then it is matched against the input string (syntax error otherwise), it is removed from the stack, and the read head is advanced one position.

Example.   Consider the simple SDTS:

```
        *
S → 1 S 2 S , x S y S z
S → 0 , w
```

Note that we do not need to subscript the S's, because the SDTS is simple. The underlying grammar is obviously LL(1). Using an example input string, we shall define the push-down transducer:

1. On stack top S, if the input symbol is:

   (a) 1 then pop S and push x1Sy2Sz

   (b) 0 then pop S and push w0

2. On stack top in $\{x, y, z, w\}$, emit the stack top as output.

3. On stack top in $\{0, 1, 2\}$, match against the next input symbol.

A machine trace for sentence 1102020 follows:

Operation	Remaining Input	Output	Stack
Initially	1102020		S
1a	1102020		x1Sy2Sz
2	1102020	x	1Sy2Sz
3	102020		Sy2Sz
1a	102020		x1Sy2Szy2Sz
2	102020	x	1Sy2Szy2Sz
3	02020		Sy2Szy2Sz
1b	02020		w0y2Szy2Sz
2	02020	w	0y2Szy2Sz
3	2020		y2Szy2Sz
2	2020	y	2Szy2Sz
3	020		Szy2Sz
1b	020		w0zy2Sz
2	020	w	0zy2Sz
3	20		zy2Sz
2	20	zy	2Sz
3	0		Sz
1b	0		w0z
2	0	w	0z
3	ϵ		z
2	ϵ	z	ϵ

The output string is therefore xxwywzywz. Note that the transducer accepts by empty stack.

If we did not have an LL(1) selector table, we would have a nondeterministic PDA. We have seen in chapter 4 that a PDA that accepts any CFG can be constructed. We need only extend the notion of nondeterminism to a transducer, and this is easily done. Let *acceptance* of an input string mean that some set of choices based on stack top symbols eventually leads to an empty stack and input list. Then the emitted output is a translation.

If the underlying grammar is ambiguous, then no deterministic PDT exists, although a nondeterministic PDT does exist; there may then exist more than one translation for one or more input strings.

If the underlying grammar is LL(1), then it is unambiguous, and there is exactly one translation for every acceptable input string.

The determinism of an LL(1) transducer means that the output can be immediately printed or punched on each move; it need not be saved on some erasable tape until the entire parse is complete. Output also can be generated as soon as a production is identified; the translator need not suspend output until the entire right part of the production is completely associated with the input list. Of course, it obtains this predictive ability through the one-symbol lookahead—the next symbol in the input list must be an infallible guide to the production rule about to come up, or else the grammar is not LL(1).

Among other things, determinism means that an entry in a symbol table could be made at the beginning, in the middle, or at the end of a production. Although we technically are discussing string-to-string translators, certain output string elements can in fact carry other kinds of operations, such as: "enter the preceding identifier in a symbol table" or "turn off the compiler listing flag." Such actions may be difficult or impossible to undo and also must be performed at the right time in the compilation. Such timing questions can be resolved for a LL(1) push-down transducer through a study of the production tree structure and the position of the action in some production.

7.3. Simple Postfix SDTSs and Bottom-Up Transducers

A SDTS is said to be *simple postfix* if it is simple and, in addition, every translation rule has the form:

$$A \rightarrow a_0\ B_1\ a_1\ B_2\ a_2\ \ldots\ B_k\ a_k\ ,\ B_1\ B_2\ \ldots\ B_k\ w$$

That is, no translation terminals may appear in the translation element except as the right-most string w. The significance of a simple postfix SDTS is expressed in the following theorem.

Theorem 7.2.   For every simple postfix SDTS the underlying grammar of which is LR(k), there exists a deterministic LR(k) PDT that (1) accepts every sentence derivable in the underlying grammar and (2) emits as output the translation of that sentence.

Recall from chapter 6 that the LR(k) parser has three actions, selected by a current state and a next symbol, as follows:

1. *Read action:* the next input symbol must be among the terminal symbols associated with this state; if so, then advance the read head, push the next state S', and go to state S'.

2. *Apply action:* the stack top contains a set of states associated with the handle of some production i. The production number is specified by this state. Pop the states corresponding to the handle, push a state S' determined from the exposed stack top state and the GOTO table, then go to state S'.

3. *Accept action:* a goal-symbol production has just been reduced, and the stack contains one state corresponding to the goal symbol. Halt, with an indication that the input string is accepted. (We assume that the goal symbol never appears in the right-hand part of any production.)

These operations are directed by a finite-state control, with one or more states, that is permitted to examine as many as k symbols in the input in determining its action.

This machine can be easily transformed into a postfix transducer, by adding the following operation to the apply rule:

> Emit the terminal portion of the translation element associated
> with rule i.

We leave machine traces and a proof of theorem 7.2 to the exercises. Theorem 7.2 has an important converse, which is theorem 7.3.

Theorem 7.3. There are unambiguous simple SDTSs with an underlying LR(k) grammar that cannot be translated by any deterministic push-down automaton. (Note that this theorem has no LL(k) counterpart.)

This theorem emphasizes the importance of the postfix condition. For example, consider the SDTS T with the rules:

```
S → Sa, xS
S → Sb, yS
S → ε, ε
```

These rules are simple, but not postfix. It is easy to show that the underlying grammar is LR(1); however, no deterministic PDT can be devised that will translate its input language. Intuitively, it is necessary to emit an x or a y before the transducer can determine which of the three productions applies. Let us go through an example.

Consider the string ba, which translates to xy (figure 7.2). A trace of the LR(1) machine apply states looks like this:

Stack	Input List	Production
ε	ba	S → ε
Sb	a	S → Sb
Sa	ε	S → Sa

To emit the required string xy, the machine must somehow predict that production S → Sa will eventually appear. What it in fact reports as apply states are the other two productions first.

A top-down automaton could conceivably emit an x first, based on its start state and the first k input symbols. The top-down derivation of ba begins with S → Sa; and x therefore could be emitted. However, this grammar is not LL(k) for any k; it contains left-recursive productions. This means that, for whatever k we choose, there is a string in the source language that will require a lookahead of at least k + 1 to determine the next production in a top-down manner. We conclude that no deterministic transducer exists for this SDTS; the information that it needs to emit a translation can be arbitrarily far ahead in the input string.

1. $S \rightarrow Sa, xS$
2. $S \rightarrow Sb, yS$
3. $S \rightarrow \epsilon, \epsilon$

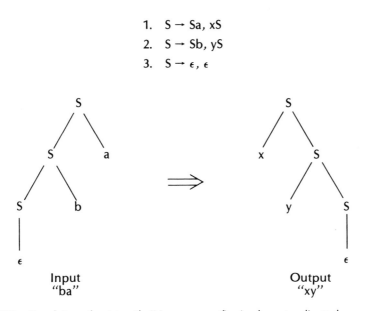

Figure 7.2. Translation of a string "ba" in a non-postfix simple syntax-directed translation scheme.

It would appear that a simple postfix SDTS is more restrictive than a simple nonpostfix SDTS, and that a top-down SDTS is therefore somehow more powerful than a bottom-up SDTS. Such is not the case; this view overlooks the possibility of modifying the grammar to achieve the effect, if not the substance, of a simple nonpostfix SDTS.

Suppose that we want a translation output y within a translation element:

$$A \rightarrow X\,Z, X\,y\,Z$$

where the rule $A \rightarrow XZ, XZ$ is simple postfix and Z is nonempty. We may then consider the pair of productions:

```
A → X Y' Z, X Y' Z
Y' → ε, y
```

Note that both productions are simple postfix. If the underlying source grammar is still LR(k) with this change, then a bottom-up deterministic transducer will generate the desired translation.

Another way to transform the productions is as follows:

```
A → X' Z, X' Z
X' → X, X y
```

Here, we have assigned the string X to a new production, permitting the postfix translation Xy; the A production then becomes postfix as well.

The restriction to *simple* in both the bottom-up and top-down transducers is easily removed by a system based on the SDTS transducers, as we shall see in section 7.4. Essentially, we can simply generate derivation trees (or, better, abstract-syntax trees) and then rearrange the nodes internally as needed to achieve the necessary nonsimple translation. Such a scheme is limited in practice by the amount of random access storage space available for the trees; however, most modern computer systems are free of such limitations.

Postfix Translations

Arithmetic Expressions.   Consider grammar G_0 augmented with these postfix translation elements:

```
E → E + T , E T ADD
E → T , T
T → T * F, T F MPY
T → F, F
F → A, A LOAD
F → ( E ) , E
A → A a , a
A → a , a
```

This SDTS is clearly simple postfix. A translation of the expression:

$$aa * (aaa + a)$$

is easily shown to be:

$$aa \text{ LOAD } aaa \text{ LOAD } a \text{ LOAD ADD MPY}$$

and is exactly that required by a postfix stack machine. The LOAD operation operates on the preceding identifier. If we wish LOAD to operate on the following identifier instead, we can modify one of the F productions. Instead of production F → A, A LOAD, we introduce the two productions:

```
F → L A, L A
L → ε, LOAD
```

The LOAD will then precede its identifier. The grammar is still LR(1); the reduce operation for the empty production L → ε can be inferred from a one-symbol lookahead of the following identifier.

The translation of aa * (aaa + a) will then be:

$$\text{LOAD } aa \text{ LOAD } aaa \text{ LOAD } a \text{ ADD MPY}$$

IF-THEN-ELSE Control Statement.   As another example, consider the common control statement:

$$S → \text{if } E \text{ then } S \text{ else } S$$

where E is an expression and S is a statement. In this form, a simple postfix

translator will generate evaluation code for E, then evaluate the two statements
S. Only when both of these are complete is it known that an if-then-else control
statement is being parsed. But such a statement requires the emission of a
conditional branch instruction between the E and the first S, and an unconditional
branch instruction between the two S's. How can this be done?

One solution is to partition this production into three productions:

```
S → T else S
T → I then S
I → if E
```

The three together are equivalent to the original production. However, by so
separating the three productions, we may generate a simple postfix translation as
follows:

```
S → T else S,        T S ; LOC L1 ;
T → I then S,        I S ; UJP L2 ; LOC L2 ;
I → if E,            E ; FJP L1 ;
```

Here, UJP L2 means "jump unconditionally to the statement labeled L2," and
FJP L1 means "jump to L1 if the stack top expression is false; otherwise
continue. Delete the stack top in any case." Also, LOC L1 labels the following
instruction for the benefit of the branch instructions.

Then the statement:

$$\text{if a then S1 else S2}$$

translates to:

```
LOAD a;
FJP L1;
S1;
UJP L2;
LOC L1;
S2;
LOC L2;
```

Given the same if-then-else structure, we can achieve the same output by
introducing productions for the "then" and "else" keywords; for example:

```
S → if E H S L S ,    E H S L S ; LOC L2 ;
H → then ,            ; FJP L1 ;
L → else ,            ; UJP L2 ; LOC L1 ;
```

The effect of the added productions is to bring out some translation strings at the
desired point in the parsing of the whole statement.

Finally, empty productions can be used:

```
S -> if E then H S else L S,   E H S L S ; LOC L2 ;
H → ε,                         ; FJP L1 ;
L → ε,                         ; UJP L2 ; LOC L1 ;
```

These three translation schemes are equivalent and are LR(1), assuming that the
remainder of the grammar is reasonable.

Function Call   Consider a function call, with the underlying source grammar:

```
F → A ( L )
L → L ; E
L → E
A → A a
A → a
```

The call parameter list L consists of parameters E separated by semicolons. (The usual separator is a comma, but we are using a comma as a metasymbol.)

For discussion purposes, we would like the procedure call to appear at the end of the code for the procedure parameters; this is how procedures are called on many (but not all) machines. However, the procedure name appears first in the syntax. We therefore need a nonsimple transducer if the call and the call name are to appear after the actual parameter coding.

However, a postfix call may be acceptable on certain machines, and is easily generated by the simple postfix grammar:

```
F → A ( L ) ,     A L ; CALL
L → L ; E ,       L E
L → E ,           E
A → A a ,         A a
A → a ,           a
```

Then the function call:

$$aa(a; aaa + aaaa)$$

will translate to:

$$aa; \text{LOAD } a; \text{LOAD } aaa; \text{LOAD } aaaa; \text{ADD}; \text{CALL}$$

and the CALL operates on the first identifier, aa.

We need a more general translation scheme to move the function name after the CALL.

7.4. A General Transducer

A simple SDTS can be implemented by a push-down stack automaton, augmented with a translation string emitter, as we have shown in the preceding two sections. A nonsimple SDTS is implemented easily by constructing a rearranged tree for the translation string as part of the parsing stack operations. When the parse is complete, the translation tree can be scanned in natural order to yield the translation string. Of course, the resulting machine is no longer a PDA.

The system presented in the following algorithm assumes that the underlying source grammar is LR(k). However, the extension to any underlying source grammar or to other parsers is trivial.

Let M be a translation machine that carries two stacks, one the usual LR(k) viable prefix stack (the *parse stack*) and the other a stack of translation subtrees (the *translation stack*). During the parsing process, each translation subtree will correspond to a nonterminal in the parse stack, and will represent a translation tree valid for that nonterminal and the derivations that previously stemmed from it. The translation stack will carry the roots of translation trees. Each nonterminal in the parse stack corresponds to a root in the translation stack.

Machine M has the actions read, apply, and accept as follows. (The error action in an LR parser is of no special interest just yet.)

1. *Read action:* The next input symbol is shifted into the parse stack. The translation stack is unaffected. A terminal in the parse stack need not have a corresponding translation stack element.

2. *Apply action:* Suppose we have the translation rule:

$$N \rightarrow a_0 \, A_1 \, a_1 \, A_2 \, \ldots \, A_m \, a_m, \, w_0 \, B_1 \, w_1 \, B_2 \, \ldots \, B_m \, w_m$$

Remove from the parse stack the string $a_0 \, A_1 \, \ldots \, A_m \, a_m$ but not the associated subtrees (yet). The translation stack is associated with trees rooted in the A_i. Remove these trees from the translation stack and permute them according to the translation rule; they now correspond to the B_i. Create a new tree root N' and new tree leaves for the translation elements w_i and arrange these two sets of trees as the children of the new node N'. Now push N' into the translation stack.

At the end of the APPLY step we have a new subtree rooted in N'. The children of N' consist of leaves and subtrees, corresponding to the elements of the translation part of the rule—that is, to $w_0 \, B_1 \, w_1 \, \ldots \, B_m \, w_m$. The B_i have been obtained from the translation stack and the w_i have been newly created.

3. *Accept action:* The tree associated with start symbol S in the parse stack is the translation tree. It may be scanned in left-to-right natural order to yield the translation string.

This translator is illustrated in figure 7.3 for the nonsimple SDTS:

```
1. S → aSA , 0AS
2. S → b , 1
3. A → bAS , 1SA
4. A → a , 0
```

and the input string abbab. The underlying grammar is SLR(1). Only the apply steps are shown. For example, just before the first apply action, the stack contains ab and the input is bab. Rule 2, when applied, causes b on the stack top to be replaced by S, linked to a son 1. String ba then is shifted into the stack in preparation for the next apply action.

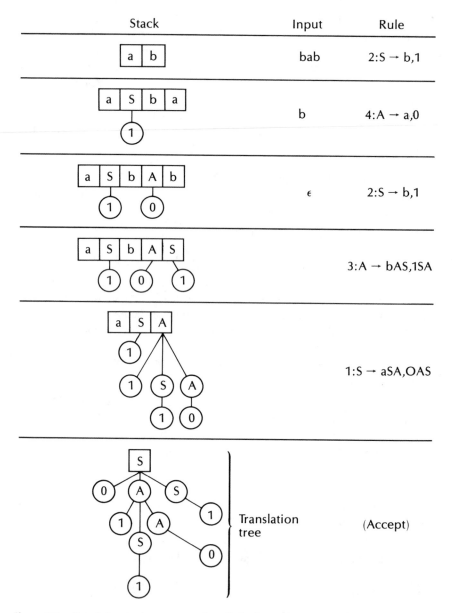

Stack	Input	Rule

Figure 7.3.   Translation by tree construction. Only the apply steps are shown.

Just before the last apply step, the parse stack contains aSA and the translation rule is:

$$S \rightarrow aSA \ , \ 0AS$$

A new leaf is created for the 0 of the translation element, and the A and S trees are interchanged. The stack top trees are replaced by a tree representing the translation subtree corresponding to S; in this case, the complete translation tree. This tree can be scanned from left to right to yield the translation string 01101.

7.5. String Transducers and Their Limitations

We have seen how an SDTS transducer can be applied as a string-to-string translator. Such a translator has certain practical applications, especially if extended by incorporating symbol-table functions and some simple arithmetic. Some compilers are essentially string translators, from a high-level source language to symbolic assembly language for a machine. The advantage of writing such a compiler is its low cost. The translator can be written as an SDTS and interpreted by a simple general-purpose system.

We have also seen that an SDTS transducer can be used to construct a translation tree directly (section 7.4). We can modify that algorithm and generate an abbreviated tree, called an *abstract-syntax tree;* this notion will be expanded in section 7.6.

Finally, rather than simply emit a string, certain string tokens or all the tokens can be interpreted as synthesis actions.

7.5.1. String Translators

Let us assume that a general SDTS transducer is available, such as that described in section 7.4. What sorts of translations can be achieved and what are the transducer's limitations?

Let us examine some of the translation needs that cannot be satisfied by a pure string translator.

Data Types

Data variables usually are typed; for example:

var INT1: integer; REAL1: real;

The effect of such statements is to associate one or more attributes with the identifiers INT1 and REAL1, as well as allocate space for them. A variable reference, such as:

REAL1 := INT1 + 1;

usually requires knowledge of the variable types to generate correct code. Thus knowing that INT1 is type "integer" and REAL1 is type "real," a compiler might generate the assembly code:

```
LOAD I INT1        {fetch integer INT1 to top of stack}
LOAD =1            {push a 1 into stack}
ADD I              {integer ADD}
FLT                {convert to REAL}
STOR R REAL1       {store real in location REAL1}
```

for a stack machine. The choice of each instruction in this sequence depends on the types of the two variables.

Typing is achieved through a token table mechanism and, without some extensions to a string translator, we cannot hope to generate suitable translation sequences that consider variable typing.

However, typing can be bypassed in one of these ways:

1. The language may have only one type (for example, ''real'') so that every operation is determined by only the algebra and not the variables.

2. The machine representation of a data item may contain a data type descriptor along with the data item. Then all the necessary conversions and the choice of the appropriate operation become a machine function and not a compiler function. For example, a single generic add instruction might be interpreted by the machine as a real add, an integer add, and so on, depending on the operand descriptor.

3. The translation may be to a high-level language that supports the features of the simpler language. The syntax may be different, but if the object language can support all the features of the source language, then a straightforward string translation is feasible.

However, variable typing occurs in most programming languages, and usually must be dealt with.

Array Dimensions

Consider an array declared as follows:

$$\text{array } X[0 .. 25, 0 .. 35] : \text{real};$$

A reference to this array of the form X[I, J] may require knowledge of one or the other dimensions, depending on the storage conventions for multidimensioned arrays in the target machine system. For example, the array may be stored in rows in one long linear array. An offset N of the form:

$$N := 36 * I + J;$$

must then be computed for the reference X[I, J]; the 36 is the second dimension plus one (because of zero basing). Again, a simple string translator cannot supply the 36 without some help.

Nevertheless, there are ways:

1. Given an array declaration, a string translator can create a constant declaration, by making up new names based on the old ones; for example:

    ```
    source:   array X[0 .. 25, 0 .. 35] of real;

    object:   array X[(25 - 0 + 1) * (35 - 0 + 1)] of real;

              const # X0 = 35 - 0 + 1;
    ```

    Then the new name #X0 can be used in a variable reference of the form X(J, I) in place of the needed dimensional factor 36:

    $$N := \# X0 * I + J;$$

    However, this approach to array indexing supposes that the object language translator can support a class of manufactured names and constant expression structures, which is seldom the case.

2. An array might be supported by a *dope vector* at run-time that is associated with the array elements and contains the array dimensions. Then an array reference can be handled by a call to some general purpose procedure that accepts the indices I and J and a reference to the dope vector.

3. A multidimensioned array could be accessed through a transfer vector system. Consider a reference to X[I, J] again, and let there be a vector of 36 pointers (corresponding to the 36 possible J values). Each of the 36 pointers points to an I vector; for example, one slice of the array. Then a fetch of X[I, J] could be coded without knowing the J dimension: indirect through V(J), then indexed by I. For some machine architectures, this kind of array access may be considerably more efficient than one based on a calculation of a linear array index.

Despite these solutions to array indexing, there is really no practical alternative to a symbol table system.

Branches and Procedure Calls

A string translator can organize branches and procedure calls only symbolically; without arithmetic or a token table, it cannot fix any program addresses. Furthermore, a string translator cannot ascertain whether a given branch label or procedure name has appeared more than once, so an error of this kind cannot be reported until the object translation occurs.

Parameter Passing

The parameters of a procedure usually are of several different kinds (reference, value, name, and so on). Thus, the generated code for the actual parameters depends on the declarations of the formal parameters. This dependency is another area of deficiency of a simple string translator—it must somehow generate object strings for actual parameters that are acceptable regardless of the declarations of the corresponding formal parameters, which may be impossible to do.

Some languages, such as Fortran, have only one passing mechanism—reference. In that case, a string translator can generate acceptable code.

In any case, an error in the number of actual parameters cannot be detected until the object is translated.

If a function call and an array reference appear syntactically the same, the object language of a string translator must be indifferent to the two. Thus in the Fortran statement:

$$Y = X(I, J)$$

the X(I, J) could be an array reference or a function call. The two cases are distinguished through a prior declaration of X as an array or a function. A symbol table is necessary to associate such an attribute with each identifier.

Certain languages, such as Lisp, support tagged values. All the operands are generic and carry different interpretations depending on the tags associated with the values at run-time. Function calls in Lisp also have a generic form; hence, a Lisp string translator is feasible.

7.6. Abstract-Syntax Tree Construction

An *abstract-syntax tree* or AST is a condensed tree representation of some language structure. It contains only that information needed for the remaining transformations or reductions of the structure. Any language structure (for example, expressions, control statements, input or output statements, and declarations) potentially can be represented as an AST.

An AST can serve as an intermediate structure in a partitionable compiler. The compiler system that generates it might be one distinct piece of software, and the system that interprets it and generates code from it might be another distinct piece. By so partitioning the compiler software for different languages, a given code generation piece might be used with different AST generation pieces. Of course, the code generation piece must accept any AST that any of the AST generators can construct, which will increase its complexity.

Conversely, several different code-generation modules can be used with a common AST to produce code for multiple machines.

We shall see that code generation and certain optimizations are facilitated by an AST representation.

Consider grammar G_0:

```
E → E + T
E → T
T → T * F
T → F
F → ( E )
F → a
```

The derivation tree for even simple expressions is large. For example, the expression a*(a + a) has the derivation tree shown in figure 7.4. This tree has seven leaf nodes and 11 interior nodes, yet the expression itself contains only two operators and three operands. Why the complexity?

Most of the complexity arises from the form of the grammar. Every derivation step is reflected in a tree node, yet many of the derivation steps merely provide a suitable precedence for the operators + and * and cause operations inside parentheses to be performed before those outside.

We can reduce the derivation tree to an AST by first removing all the tree links associated with the single productions; that is, E → T, T → F, and F → a. They serve a purpose in the derivation process, but have no useful role in the final structure.

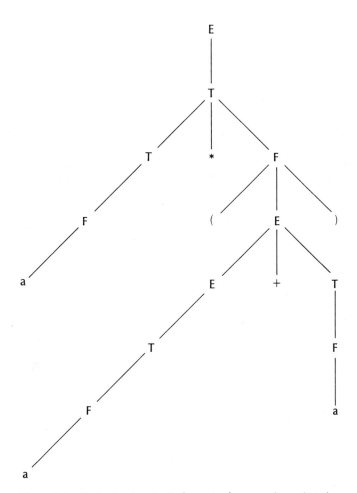

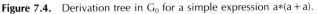
Figure 7.4. Derivation tree in G_0 for a simple expression a*(a + a).

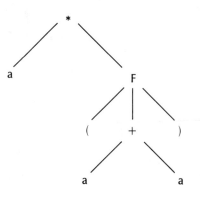

Figure 7.5. Derivation tree of figure 7.4 reduced by collapsing single productions and operator productions.

Next, consider the E node with a + node. We bring the + node up, replacing the E, forming a binary operator node. Similarly, any * node can be brought up into its parent. We clearly no longer have a derivation tree, but so far have not lost any structural information either. At this point, our reduced tree looks like figure 7.5. It still says that the addition must be done first, then the multiplication. What about the parentheses? If we collapse the parenthesis production F → (E) will the operator ordering established by the parentheses be lost? The answer is no—the a node inside the parentheses came from a sequence of derivation steps that have already provided for the precedence of the + operator inside the parentheses over the * outside. We arrive at the AST in figure 7.6.

This tree is also the abstract-syntax tree for the expressions:

```
a * ((a) + a)
a * (a + (a))
(a * (a + a))
```

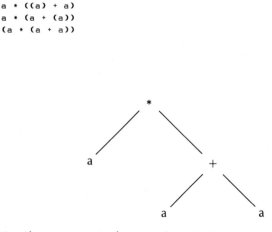

Figure 7.6. Abstract-syntax tree for expressions a*(a+a).

as should be obvious. Each of these is mathematically equivalent, suggesting that an abstract-syntax tree for an expression is a canonical form for an equivalence class of expressions. However, an AST is not a canonical form; it does not take into account commutativity or associativity of the operators. For example, the following expressions, although mathematically equivalent, yield different ASTs:

```
a * b + c,
c + b * a,
c + a * b, etc.
```

Note that computer arithmetic is noncommutative in general—real arithmetic is subject to round-off differences and integer arithmetic to differences in overflow conditions.

We can easily generate an AST directly by some simple changes in the SDTS implementation. Instead of generating a complete translation tree, we simply generate an AST by pointer mechanisms similar to those in section 7.4. A grammar and the corresponding tree translation elements are illustrated in figure 7.7.

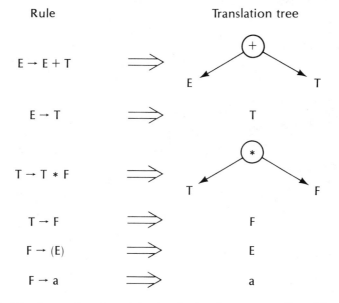

Rule   Translation tree

$E \rightarrow E + T$

$E \rightarrow T$

$T \rightarrow T * F$

$T \rightarrow F$

$F \rightarrow (E)$

$F \rightarrow a$

Figure 7.7.   Direct generation of an abstract-syntax tree from grammer G_0 and its parser.

Bottom-Up AST Construction

For a bottom-up parser, the rules in figure 7.7 can be understood as follows. Consider the E → E + T rule. When E + T appears as the handle on the top of the parser stack, there will be two subtrees connected to the E and the T elements. (Nothing is connected to the + .) The translation rule says: create a new node, labeled + , and give it two sons—the E and T subtrees. We now have a new tree rooted in the + node; attach it to the E that replaces E and T on the stack.

The translation rule E → T is applied as follows: when T is the handle, it is attached to some subtree; attach this subtree to the E that replaces T in the stack.

Finally, the translation rule F → (E) calls for attaching the E subtree to the element F on the stack, and the rule F → a calls for attaching the terminal token a as a tree consisting of one node to the element F in the stack.

When the accept state is reached, we will have the AST attached to the start token on the stack top.

AST Extensions

The general form of an AST is a tree the interior nodes of which are operators and the leaves of which are simple variables or constants. The operators may be of any variety—unary, binary, or n-ary. For example, an array reference can be represented by the AST shown in figure 7.8, where X is a multidimensional variable, and e_1, e_2, . . . , e_n represent expression ASTs for the indices; the reference in source form would look like this:

$$X(e_1, e_2, . . . , e_n)$$

A procedure call AST would have the same form, except that the operator would be different, of course, and a different class of actual parameters might be permitted by the language.

An AST can represent control structures and declarations as well. For example, a CASE statement can be modeled as an AST, as shown in figure 7.9. The nodes labeled "case statement" can all be the children of the CASE node, or can form a parent–child chain as shown, the last one with a nil right-most child.

General Properties of an AST

Considerable freedom in the definition of an AST exists. However, an AST should satisfy several properties:

1. Each interior node must carry a tag that defines its structure uniquely. We recommend a Pascal variant case record structure.

2. Every operator should carry some information and not just be a "place holder." The test is whether it can be removed from the AST without losing information in some way.

3. A subset of the AST nodes should be associated with each nonterminal.

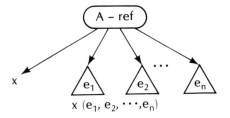

Figure 7.8. An array reference or procedure call AST.

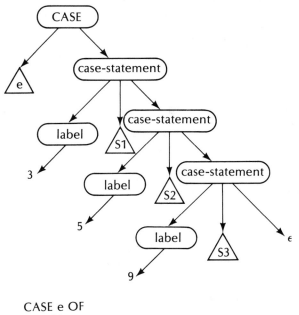

```
CASE e OF
    3: S1;
    5: S2;
    9: S3
END;
```

Figure 7.9. A CASE statement AST.

The association of AST nodes with nonterminals arises through the discussion of section 7.4, in which the root of an AST appears in a semantics stack associated with some symbol. Terminal symbols are associated with an empty subset, because they stand for themselves.

The semantic operations required in the compiler will be implied largely by the AST node subset associated with the nonterminals on the stack. We shall see just how vital this association is in the discussion that follows.

7.7. Pascal Structures for LR(1) Synthesis

The source code for a complete translator is part of the complete QPARSER system. We shall discuss the general code synthesis principles used in that system but, for additional details, we urge you to study its source code.

We shall be drawing on a set of productions that describe a subset of Pascal in the discussion of this section. That production set is as follows:

```
Goal -> Program
Program -> ProgHead ProgParms ; Pblk Pblock .
     \ This production is supposed to look like PBEND below

ProgHead -> PROGRAM <identifier> #pdecl
ProgParms -> <empty>   \ could be filled in with parameters

Pblock -> LBList TYPList VRList PList Pbegin StmtList END #pblock
Pbegin -> BEGIN #pbegin

Block -> BEGIN StmtList END

LBList -> LABEL LabList ;
       -> <empty>
LabList -> LabList , <integer> #label1
        -> <integer> #label2

VRList -> Var VList ;
       -> <empty>
Var -> VAR #varst
VList -> VList ; VarItem
      -> VarItem
VarItem -> IdentList : Type #vitem
IdentList -> IdentList , <identifier> #idl1
          -> <identifier> #idl2

TYPList -> TYPE TList ;
        -> <empty>
TList -> TList ; TypItem
      -> TypItem
TypItem -> <identifier> = Type #typeid

Type -> SimpType
     -> ARRAY [ Sint .. Sint ] OF Type #arraytype
     -> RECORD FieldList END #rectype
```

```
SimpType -> <identifier> #simptype
      \ REAL, BOOLEAN, INTEGER or another type name

FieldList -> IdentList : Type  #fitem
          -> IdentList : Type ; FieldList #fitemf
          -> CASE SimpType OF CaseList  #casefield
                  \SimpType = BOOLEAN or INTEGER

CaseList -> CaseItem ; CaseList  #caselist
         -> CaseItem
CaseItem -> ConstList : ( FieldList ) #caseitem

PList -> PList PFDecl
      -> <empty>
PFDecl -> ProcDecl
       -> FuncDecl
ProcDecl -> ProcHead Parms ; FORWARD ; #pfend
         -> ProcHead Parms ; Pblk Pblock ; #pbend
ProcHead -> PROCEDURE <identifier> #pdecl
FuncDecl -> FuncHead Parms : <identifier> ; FORWARD ; #ffend
         -> FuncHead Parms : <identifier> ; Fblk Pblock ; #fbend
FuncHead -> FUNCTION <identifier> #fdecl
Parms -> <empty>
      -> ( ParmList ) #parmsl
ParmList -> ParmList ; Parm #parml
         -> Parm
Parm -> VAR IdentList : SimpType #fparmv
     -> IdentList : SimpType #fparm
Pblk -> <empty> #pblk
Fblk -> <empty> #fblk

StmtList -> StmtList ; Stmt
         -> Stmt
Stmt -> IF Boolean Then Stmt #ifth
     -> IF Boolean Then Stmt Else Stmt #ifthelse
     -> WHILE Boolean Do Stmt #whiledo
     -> Repeat StmtList UNTIL Boolean #runtil
     -> FOR VarHead := Boolean TO Boolean Fup Stmt #forst
     -> FOR VarHead := Boolean DOWNTO Boolean Fdown Stmt #dforst
     -> Variable := Boolean #assign
     -> ProcCall #prcall
     -> GOTO <integer> #gotolab
     -> Label : Stmt
     -> Block
     -> ReadWrite ( IOList ) #readwrl
     -> <empty>
Then -> THEN #thent
Else -> ELSE #elset
Fup -> DO #fup
Fdown -> DO #fdown
Do -> DO #dot
Repeat -> REPEAT #rept
Label -> <integer> #lstmt
ReadWrite -> READ #rwread
          -> WRITE #rwwrite

IOList -> IOList , IOItem #boollist1
       -> IOItem #boollist2
```

```
IOItem -> Boolean
       -> <string>

ProcCall -> <identifier> ( BoolList ) #proccall
BoolList -> BoolList , Boolean #boollist1
         -> Boolean #boollist2

Boolean -> BoolTerm
        -> Boolean OR BoolTerm #orop
BoolTerm -> BoolUnary
         -> BoolTerm AND BoolUnary #andop
BoolUnary -> BoolPri
          -> NOT BoolPri #notop
BoolPri -> Expr
        -> Expr Relop Expr #relop

Relop -> <    #less
      -> >    #gtr
      -> <=   #leq
      -> >=   #geq
      -> =    #eq
      -> <>   #neq

Expr -> Expr + Term #add
     -> Expr - Term #sub
     -> Term
Term -> Term * Unary  #mpy
     -> Term / Unary #quot
     -> Term MOD Unary #modulo
     -> Term DIV Unary #divide
     -> Unary
Unary -> Primary
      -> - Primary #neg
Primary -> ( Boolean ) #parexp
        -> ProcCall
        -> Variable #pvar
        -> Constant

Variable -> VarHead VarExtension #varid
VarHead -> <identifier>
VarExtension -> VarExtension VarExt #varextl
             -> <empty>
VarExt -> [ BoolList ] #varexta \ array index
       -> . <identifier> #varextr \ record access
Constant -> <real>
         -> <integer>
         -> TRUE #ctrue
         -> FALSE #cfalse
ConstList -> ConstList , Constant  \ but no REALs
          -> Constant
Sint -> <integer>
     -> - <integer> #cneg
```

We shall not describe all the semantic operations implied by this grammar; we shall consider only enough of them to illustrate the principles of semantics operations with a bottom-up LR parser.

7.7.1. The State and Semantics Stacks

QPARSER is based on an LR(1) parser in which two stacks are maintained in parallel. Both are represented as Pascal arrays. One of them, STACK, carries the LR(1) parser state numbers as described in chapter 6. The other, SEMSTACK, carries an array of pointers, each to a structure of type SEMREC. The top-of-stack index is STACKX.

Recall that, in the apply operation, a production A → w is being reduced, and the stack top carries the members of the production's right part w. We intend that each of the members of w will also be associated with some semantic information in SEMSTACK; that is, each nonterminal in w will be the root of an AST associated with some subset of all the possible nodes of the AST.

Suppose that w = $a_1a_2a_3$. We then have SEMSTACK[STACKX] carry semantic information associated with a_3, SEMSTACK[STACKX − 1] carry semantic information associated with a_2, and SEMSTACK[STACKX − 2] carry semantic information associated with a_1. There also will be information deeper in the stack, at STACKX − 3, and so on. This section will be devoted to a discussion of using that information effectively.

The SEMSTACK Structures

Here are simplified declarations of the STACK and SEMSTACK structures used in QPARSER:

```
type
    SEMRECP= ↑ semrec;
    SEMREC = record
                VTYPE: vtypes;  {arithmetic type}
                case SEMT: semtype of
                    {other: ; }  {the default case}
                    ident: (SYMP: symtabp);
                    fixed, bool: (NUMVAL: integer);
                    float: (RVAL: real);
                    strng: (STX: int);

                    add_node, sub_node, mpy_node, div_node,
                    quot_node, mod_node, and_node, or_node,
                    eq_node, geq_node, gtr_node, leq_node,
                    les_node, neq_node:
                        (SNL, SNR: semrecp);
                    neg_node, not_node: (UNARYP: semrecp);
                    ...  {there are more}
            end;

var STACK: array [0..stacksize] of int;
    SEMSTACK: array [0..stacksize] of semrecp;
    STACKX: int;
    TSEMP: semrecp;
```

Note that SEMSTACK is an array of pointers to structures, rather than an array of structures. The structures themselves may be allocated as needed, or allocated initially only once. SEMT is the AST tag. It identifies the nature of an AST.

Thus, the tags ADD_NODE, SUB_NODE, and so on, each designate a binary operation; the operands are SNL and SNR, each of which points to another AST. Tags NEG_NODE and NOT_NODE are unary operator nodes; their operand is the AST pointed to by UNARYP. The tag IDENT corresponds to an identifier; its value SYMP is a pointer to a symbol table entry that carries more information about the identifier. The tags FIXED and BOOLEAN refer to a literal integer NUMVAL. Tag FLOAT refers to a literal floating point number RVAL. Tag STRNG carries an index into a string table; each string is terminated with a null character.

The empty or default tag is SEMT = OTHER. Each terminal and certain nonterminals will be tagged as OTHER. SEMSTACK may also be NIL.

The field VTYPE identifies an arithmetic type, where this is appropriate.

The variable STACKX marks the current top-of-stack in both STACK and SEMSTACK. Variable TSEMP is used to return a semantics value from an APPLY operation.

Parser States

An LR(1) parser has four states: READ, APPLY, LOOKAHEAD, and AC-CEPT. Because the LOOKAHEAD and ACCEPT states have no effect on code generation or SEMSTACK information, we shall not consider them further.

The READ operation accepts the next token from the source stream. In QPARSER, a terminal token may either stand for itself or represent a class of tokens. The tokens +, *, :=, and so on, stand for themselves. The token <identifier> represents an arbitrary Pascal identifier, <integer> represents an integer, and <real> represents a real number. QPARSER also supports a quoted string <string>. Although these class tokens are in fact nonterminals, they are picked up as special terminal tokens in QPARSER's lexical analyzer for the sake of performance.

The READ operation also pushes a state on the STATE stack, by incrementing STACKX and copying the state into STATE[STACKX]. It will also modify the structure SEMSTACK[STACKX] ↑ as follows: (1) if the token is a simple one, the structure is set to NIL or marked OTHER; (2) if the token is an <identifier>, SEMT is set to IDENT, a symbol table entry is made, and a pointer to the symbol table is placed in SYMP; and (3) if the token is an <integer> or <real>, SEMT is set to FIXED or FLOAT, and the value is placed in the structure in the slot NUMVAL or RVAL, respectively.

READ therefore will prepare the semantics stack by setting the SEMSTACK entry appropriately to correspond to the current STATE entry. See the PARSER procedure of file LR1SKEL in QPARSER. It is therefore automatic and can be essentially ignored in the code generation actions.

The APPLY Operation

All the semantic operations of interest to a compiler designer start with the parser's apply operation. The parser will call a procedure APPLY, which must in general be written by a compiler designer. APPLY is declared as follows:

```
procedure APPLY(PFLAG, RPLEN: int; var TSEMP: semrecp);
```

PFLAG is a small integer that denotes which production is being applied. RPLEN is the number of tokens in the right part of the production—it usually is not needed and could be dropped from the parser system.

TSEMP points to a semantic structure that some action in the APPLY procedure may choose to fill in. If nothing is done with TSEMP, it will remain NIL or carry the default OTHER tag, meaning that it is empty.

There also is a special case that deals with untagged single productions; that is, $X \rightarrow Y$, where $|Y| = 1$. Note that Y may be a terminal or a nonterminal. In this and only this case, the semantic structure of the single right member is copied into the left member by the parser.

The APPLY procedure will be called by the parser just before the stack reduction and pushing of the left member state. If some action is to be taken on the information in SEMSTACK, this is the time to do it. Note also that all the SEMSTACK information corresponding to the production's right member will go away after APPLY returns. Information written into the temporary structure TSEMP will be pushed onto SEMSTACK, corresponding to the production's left member.

APPLY Operation Illustrated

Figure 7.10 illustrates the state of SEMSTACK just before the APPLY actions, for the production:

$$\text{Stmt} \rightarrow \text{<identifier>} := \text{Expr}$$

TSEMP will be set to NIL or its default value OTHER. The top three elements of SEMSTACK will carry information corresponding to the right member.

SEMSTACK[STACKX] (index 12 in figure 7.10), will carry some expression tree corresponding to Expr. This has been constructed through previous APPLY calls in which productions of the form:

$$\text{Expr} \rightarrow \dots$$

have been applied.

SEMSTACK[STACKX − 1] (index 11) will be NIL or carry the OTHER attribute, because the := token needs no special semantic structure.

SEMSTACK[STACKX − 2] (index 10) will carry an IDENT structure (see the SEMREC declaration in section 7.7.1), which contains a pointer to a symbol table entry containing information about the <identifier>.

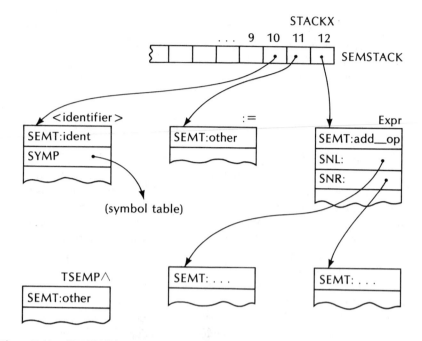

Figure 7.10. SEMSTACK operations on applying production stmt→⟨identifier⟩: = Expr (before APPLY action).

All three of these will vanish on returning from APPLY, and will be replaced by TSEMP (figure 7.11). If any SEMSTACK information must be carried in the stack for future reference, it must be folded into the TSEMP structure.

For the assignment statement, machine instructions may be generated for the evaluation of the Expr, then an instruction to store the result in an address associated with the <identifier>:

```
{evaluate Expr}
STOR I <address>
```

There is no need to keep track of anything in the stack; hence, TSEMP can be set to NIL or remain tagged as OTHER. Its contents will be copied into SEMSTACK[10] in figure 7.11, and STACKX will be decremented by two.

Form of the APPLY Procedure

The APPLY procedure will be essentially a large CASE statement, the labels of which correspond to the productions. In QPARSER, productions may be tagged symbolically; for example:

$$Expr \rightarrow Expr - Term \; \# \; sub$$
$$Term \rightarrow Term * Primary \; \# \; mpy$$

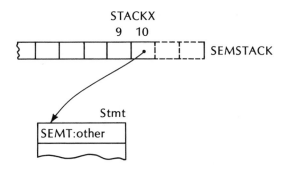

Figure 7.11. SEMSTACK configuration just after APPLY operations on production
stmt→⟨identifier⟩:= Expr.

so that the APPLY procedure looks like this:

```
procedure APPLY(PFLAG, RPLEN: int; var TSEMP: semrecp);
begin
   case pflag of
   ...    {other production tags}
      SUB: begin   {Expr -> Expr - Term}
              ...  {semantics for this production}
          end;
      ...
      MPY: begin   {Term -> Term * Primary}
              ...  {semantics for this production}
          end;
   ...
   end
end;
```

The tags SUB and MPY will have been declared as constants:

```
const
   SUB= 15;      {for example}
   ...
   MPY= 23;
```

Thus, on each APPLY call, there will be an immediate transfer to a code
fragment associated with a unique production.

7.7.2. Code Generation on the Fly

The easiest code generation action is simply to use the information in SEMSTACK to generate some code, modify the symbol table, or whatever, and then let the SEMSTACK information disappear.

We have seen how stack machine code can be generated on the fly without bothering with an AST. That strategy works well for a simple postfix translator, but must be extended for commercial computers.

For example, the production:

$$\text{Term} \rightarrow \text{Term} * \text{Primary}$$

can be used to generate the code:

```
MPY
```

for a stack machine, assuming that only one type of Term and Primary must be dealt with. Note that code will have been issued previously to evaluate the Term and—later—the Primary, when this production is applied. The Term value will therefore be at TOS − 1 in the run-time stack and the Primary value will be at TOS.

The production:

$$\text{Primary} \rightarrow <\text{identifier}>$$

where Primary is an instance of an Expr, can be used to generate a LOAD instruction. The <identifier> will be associated with the IDENT structure, and it in turn points to a symbol table entry. The symbol table presumably will carry the address of the <identifier> and other information; hence, the instruction:

$$\text{LOAD } address$$

can be emitted on such a production.

The productions:

$$\text{Primary} \rightarrow <\text{integer}>$$
$$\text{Primary} \rightarrow <\text{real}>$$

can be used similarly to emit the instruction:

```
LOAD = number value
```

This instruction would be generated by the line:

```
writeln(codefile, 'LOAD =', semstack[stackx]↑.numval:1)
```

for the <integer> case and the line:

```
writeln(codefile, 'LOAD =', semstack[stackx]↑.rval:15);
```

for the <real> case.

Type Conversion

Unfortunately, we usually must deal with two or more arithmetic types (such as integers, integer subranges, reals, or long reals), any of which can be part of an arithmetic operation in almost any combination. The choice of operand will then depend on the types associated with Expr and Term in the production:

$$\text{Expr} \rightarrow \text{Expr} * \text{Term}.$$

Thus, if Expr is type REAL and Term is type INTEGER, we must issue a conversion instruction that converts the TOS value—associated with Term—from an INTEGER to a REAL:

```
FLT
MPY R
```

We have also qualified the multiplication as a type REAL multiplication.

Should Expr be type INTEGER and Term be type REAL, we need an instruction that converts the value in TOS − 1 from INTEGER to REAL. UCSD Pascal provides such an instruction. Often, a REAL takes more space than an INTEGER on the run-time stack, so the integer in TOS must be moved to make room for the conversion:

```
FLO
MPY R
```

Here FLO moves the integer in TOS, then converts the INTEGER in TOS − 1 in place to a REAL.

As soon as types appear in arithmetic, it is important that type information be carried in the SEMSTACK corresponding to the Expr and the Term. We have included arithmetic typing in the SEMREC structure, in variable VTYPE. VTYPE is an enumerated type:

```
type
    VTYPE= (unk_type, bool_type, int_type, real_type, str_type);
```

The unk_type refers to an unknown type. The others refer to type BOOLEAN, INTEGER, REAL, and STRING. More primitive types are easy to add. In fact, in QPARSER, VTYPES carries several more categories and also is used to distinguish symbol table attribute classes.

Number type conversion also is handled more efficiently if the conversion can be introduced at just the right time. Thus, the FLT operation should be applied to the Expr just when the Expr is in TOS in the run-time stack, not after the whole production has been parsed. That is facilitated in our bottom-up parser if we first construct an AST for arithmetic expressions.

We therefore have no choice but to deal with the issue of attaching semantic information of our own into SEMSTACK.

7.7.3. Building SEMSTACK Structures

The parser system developed in QPARSER embodies two forms of semantic stack management, which we shall call the value and the pointer philosophies. We have glossed over the differences previously, but must now discuss the two possible approaches in more detail.

In the *value philosophy,* the semantic stack values are allocated from the heap before any parsing, but never again. The stacks themselves are fixed-dimension arrays. Hence, in the absence of any APPLY actions that call NEW, heap space is not further allocated by semantic actions.

In the *pointer philosophy,* the semantic stack carries pointers that are initialized to NIL. Whenever a nonterminal token requires a data object to be attached to a semantic stack element, space for the object is allocated from the heap. In QPARSER, the lexical analyzer allocates space for numbers, identifiers, and strings, as we have seen. Objects associated with other nonterminals are the responsibility of the user in writing APPLY actions. Note that the parser unbinds these objects on completing an APPLY action, except for the TSEMP pointer. Reclaiming the unbound heap space may be troublesome. This problem is discussed later.

The value philosophy appears to work best in simple translators such as assemblers, in which tree-structured data rooted in the semantics stack are not required. Its primary advantage is that heap reclamation need not be considered. The pointer philosophy is recommended for any translator that generates trees rooted in the stack. Both philosophies are illustrated in QPARSER.

The pointer TSEMP passed as a parameter in the APPLY call will be used to build SEMSTACK structures. TSEMP will point to a structure that should be modified directly in a semantics action. Under the value philosophy, it always will be non-NIL, but will be tagged OTHER by default. Under the pointer philosophy, TSEMP always will be NIL; hence, heap space must be allocated to attach information to SEMSTACK.

The parser's action just after APPLY returns will be to reduce the stack index STACKX by the length of the right part, then push a new state on the stack. At the same time, the structure TSEMP↑ will be *copied* to SEMSTACK[STACKX] (under value philosophy) or the pointer TSEMP copied to SEMSTACK[STACKX] (under pointer philosophy), where STACKX is the new top-of-stack pointer.

Copying a structure in Pascal, fortunately, is a generic operation; the statement:

```
semstack[stackx]↑:=tsemp↑;
```

is part of standard Pascal, and usually is implemented efficiently through byte move operations. This makes the value philosophy viable for simple translators.

We must therefore design the SEMREC structure such that all possible semantic structures are represented, preferably with unique SEMT tags. Also, because a SEMREC structure will be associated with the left member of a production in the APPLY operation, it is important to establish the relationship between the nonterminals of the grammar and their associated members of SEMREC.

Arithmetic AST

Each of the binary and unary arithmetic operations has a separate SEMT tag. The structure for a binary operation is a left and a right SEMRECP pointer (see the SEMREC record structure in section 7.7.1). However, any of the tags:

```
add_node, sub_node, mpy_node, ...
```

may be associated with any of the nonterminals Expr, Term, and so on, in general.

The production:

$$\text{Term} \rightarrow \text{Term} * \text{Primary}$$

is typical of the productions that define binary operations. There usually are many binary operations in a language, so we define a procedure GEN_BINNODE to handle them all. The APPLY case for the preceding production will be simply this:

```
MPY: begin {Term -> Term * Primary}
   gen_binnode(mpy_node);
  end;
```

Here is procedure GEN_BINNODE, as found in QPARSER, written under the pointer philosophy. We have added some comments that refer to the preceding MPY production, but it supports all the binary arithmetic operators:

```
procedure GEN_BINNODE(NTAG: semtype);
begin
  new(tsemp);
  with tsemp↑ do
  begin
    semt:=ntag;   {TSEMP↑ is marked with the tag}
    vtype:=set_bintype(ntag, semstack[stackx-2]↑.vtype,
                              semstack[stackx]↑.vtype);
    snl:=semstack[stackx-2];  {grab the Term}
    snr:=semstack[stackx];    {grab the Primary}
  end
end;
```

Note that one new TSEMP structure is allocated, and the semstack structures corresponding to the Term and the Primary are attached to it. At the end of GEN_BINNODE, TSEMP will carry the root of an AST; the root has the tag NTAG, and its left and right subtrees represent the operands of the operator NTAG. The function SET_BINTYPE determines the resulting type VTYPE, based on the types of the two children nodes. GEN_BINNODE happens to be in the scope of the APPLY procedure; hence, TSEMP is lexically accessible to it.

Leaf Nodes of the Arithmetic AST

The leaf nodes of an arithmetic AST will be numeric constants or variables. We saw that these will be a SEMREC structure with the tags IDENT, FIXED, or FLOAT. We therefore consider these part of the expression class. An identifier variable will show up through a production such as:

$$\text{Var} \rightarrow \text{<identifier>}$$

In fact, we need not do anything in APPLY for this production. The parser follows the rule that if the production has a single token in its right member, then the semantic form associated with that member will be passed to its left member. In short, the Var will carry the <identifier> data structure.

However, the <identifier> may not be of the right class for an expression. It could be a procedure name, or it could be undeclared. To report such errors, we must add a tag to the production and write an APPLY case:

```
VARID: begin {Var -> <identifier>}
    if not(semstack[stackx]↑.symp↑.symt in
            [variable, func] then
    begin  {there is an error}
      error('undeclared or invalid identifier');
      with tsemp↑ do
      begin  {we set up something valid to avoid future trouble}
        semt:=ident;
        vtype:=int_type;
        symp:=makesym(errsym, variable, plevel);
            {this creates a new error symbol of type
                VARIABLE}
        with symp↑ do
        begin
          saddr:=0;  {stack address}
          vtype:=int_type;
        end
      end
    end
  end;
```

Note that we do not have to do anything about TSEMP ↑ if there is no error—the parser will just copy the <identifier> structure into the Var position on the stack. If the <identifier> is of the wrong type, a new one is created in the symbol table of type integer, with a phony stack address. This action yields a valid AST leaf node in spite of the error.

Literal Leaf Nodes

A literal constant also may be an AST leaf node. It will appear through productions of the form:

```
Primary → Constant
Constant → <real>
Constant → <integer>
Constant → TRUE   #ctrue
Constant → FALSE  #cfalse
```

Of these, only the TRUE and FALSE productions need to be handled in APPLY. For the others, the parser will automatically pass the semantic information up through their left members; a <real> will be passed through Constant, and the Constant will be passed to Primary, and thence be fitted into the AST as a leaf node.

The TRUE production is handled as follows:

```
CTRUE: begin   {Constant -> TRUE}
    new(tsemp);
    with tsemp↑ do
    begin
      semt:=bool;
      vtype:=bool_type;
      numval:=1;
    end
  end;
```

We have chosen to represent a Boolean value as a number: one will stand for TRUE and zero for FALSE—see the SEMREC structure in section 7.7.0. However, a Boolean type is not the same as an integer type; hence, it carries the special tag BOOL.

The FALSE production is handled the same way, except that NUMVAL will be set to zero.

Constant Folding

We have seen how constants may be used as leaf nodes of an AST. Suppose that a constant's parent node is a unary operation, or that a binary node carries two constant children. We would like to carry out the constant arithmetic in the compiler and then replace the operand node by a constant node.

Constant folding is a bottom-up process on the AST. We are building the tree bottom-up, too, by the way the LR1 parser operates. Hence, we may fold constant arithmetic as the tree is constructed, rather than when walking through the tree later.

We illustrate the process for the binary case. The folding operation belongs in the procedure GEN_BINNODE, which we discussed previously. We extend this procedure as follows:

```
procedure GEN_BINNODE(NTAG: semtype);
begin
  new(tsemp);
  with tsemp↑ do
  begin
    semt:=ntag;
    snl:=semstack[stackx-2];
    snr:=semstack[stackx];
    vtype:=set_bintype(ntag, snl↑.vtype, snr↑.vtype);
    if (is_const(snl↑.semt)) and
       (is_const(snr↑.semt)) and
       (ntag in arithtypes+booltypes) then
    cbin_arith(ntag, vtype, snl, snr, tsemp);
  end
end;
```

We have merely added a new function CBIN_ARITH, which will carry out the constant arithmetic based on the operation (NTAG), the two children nodes (SNL and SNR), force a conversion to the type VTYPE, and place the result in TSEMP↑. This function is lengthy because it must deal with all the possible constant type mixtures and operands in the language. However, its purpose is simple: it must perform the constant arithmetic precisely as the emitted instructions would have done it at run-time.

That purpose may not be achieved easily. Our compiler may be a *cross-compiler*, which means that it executes on one computer but generates instructions for another. The compiler must then carry out arithmetic in the manner in which the target machine would do it. For example, if the target machine supports only 16-bit integers, then 16-bit overflow is possible in constant folding, and must be emulated safely by the cross-compiler. Constant arithmetic overflow must appear as a compiler error, not a compiler failure.

The Pascal subrange type with bounds checking enabled is useful for this purpose. However, suitable traps also must be able to catch errors. The QPARSER system does not support constant folding range checking, because there is no standard for Pascal trap handling.

The IS_CONST function determines whether a child is a constant suitable for folding. The third test of the IF:

```
(ntag in arithtypes + booltypes)
```

establishes that the binary operator is in the class of operators subject to constant folding—in this case, the arithmetic and Boolean types.

7.7.4. Target Code Generation from an Arithmetic AST

The operations described in the preceding section will construct an AST rooted in the semantics stack without generating any target code. Target code generation typically will be triggered on one of the following productions:

```
Stmt → Var := Boolean #assign
Stmt → IF Boolean Then Stmt #ifth
Stmt → WHILE Boolean Do Stmt #whiledo
ProcCall → <identifier> ( BoolList ) #proccall
```

In the first three, the Boolean will be an arithmetic AST. In the fourth production, the BoolList will be the root of a *list* of ASTs. We shall discuss list construction later.

For now, consider the first production. No code has been generated on parsing the Var and Boolean parts. In fact, the Var will stand for an <identifier>. We wish to generate the following code sequence—for a stack machine, of course:

```
{code to yield the Boolean's value in TOS}
{possibly a type conversion instruction}
STOR  <the Var address>
```

Something similar will happen in the other three productions. The IF production will have to evaluate its Boolean and convert it—if necessary—to a TRUE or FALSE. This Boolean value then will be tested by a conditional branch instruction—see section 7.3 for details.

It is clear that we need a procedure EVAL with two parameters: SP, a pointer to an AST root, and TOTYPE, a type to which the resulting tree evaluation is to be converted. We will always know to which type the result must be converted when EVAL is called. If EVAL is *instructed* to perform the necessary conversion, an explicit type conversion instruction often is unnecessary. For example, if the AST is a constant node, then EVAL may simply convert the constant to type TOTYPE and emit a LOAD instruction.

Procedure EVAL

Here is procedure EVAL essentially as found in QPARSER. Note that it is recursive. When we need the evaluation of the children of a node, we simply call EVAL on each of the children.

```
{ * * * * * * * * * * * * * * * * * * }
procedure EVAL ((SP: semrecp; TOTYPE: vtypes)) ;
  var LN, RN: semrecp;
begin  {Master AST evaluator}
  with sp↑ do
  begin
    case semt of
      add_node, sub_node, mpy_node, div_node: {and more}
        bin_arith(semt, utype(snl↑.vtype, snr↑.vtype), snl, snr);
      and_node, or_node:
        bin_logic(semt, snl, snr);
      neg_node:
        begin
          eval(unaryp, vtype);
          genstring('NEG ');
          wrtype(vtype);
          genline('');
        end;
      ident:
        begin
          genstring('LOAD ');
          wrtype(vtype);
          wraddr(symp);
          genline('');
        end;
      fixed, bool, float:
        begin
          convert(sp, totype);
          genstring('LOAD =');
          if gencode=0 then
          begin
            if semt=float then
            writeln(tgfile, rval:20)
            else writeln(tgfile, numval:1);
```

```
            end
          end;
      funcall: proc_call(fsymp, faparms);
      otherwise error('eval screwup');
    end;
    conv_type(vtype, totype);
  end
end;
```

EVAL is essentially a CASE statement based on the node's tag. Binary operations are handled by procedure BIN_ARITH (for arithmetic) and BIN_LOGIC
(for Boolean functions). BIN_ARITH is given later.

An identifier will be associated with some variable, resulting in generation of
a LOAD instruction. Procedure WRTYPE adds a type (R or I in PSGSEM), and
WRADDR generates the variables' address. GENLINE('') generates a line feed.

A constant node yields a constant LOAD. We first convert the constant to the
required type TOTYPE; the conversion also will cause VTYPE for the node to
become the same as TOTYPE.

A function call is more complicated to handle. The AST node will be a linked
list of expression trees. Each tree will be evaluated to the type required by the
associated formal parameter of the function. These will be left behind on the
run-time stack and accessed within the function's code. Function-calling mechanisms will be discussed in greater detail in chapter 9.

Strings are not supported by this EVAL; hence, an error message will appear
if the expression node has that type.

After code is emitted for the AST evaluation, a type conversion instruction
may be emitted. We established the type of each node during the bottom-up
construction of the AST; this type is carried in the variable VTYPE.
CONV_TYPE then emits the appropriate conversion—possibly none—for type
VTYPE to TOTYPE.

Here is procedure BIN_ARITH:

```
procedure BIN_ARITH(ST: semtype; RT: vtypes; SL, SR: semrecp);
begin  {evaluates left and right members of a
        binary arithmetic node, then the operation}
  eval(sl, rt);    {left operand evaluation, to type RT}
  eval(sr, rt);    {right operand evaluation, to type RT}
  case st of
    add_node: gen_inst( 'ADD ');
    sub_node: gen_inst( 'SUB ');
    mpy_node: gen_inst( 'MPY ');
    div_node, quot_node: gen_inst( 'DIV ');
    mod_node: begin
                 if rt<>int_type then
                 error('MOD supported for integers only')
                 else
                 genstring('CXP MOD');
              end;
    eq_node: gen_inst( 'EQU ');
    neq_node: gen_neq(rt);
    leq_node: gen_leq(rt);
```

```
    les_node: gen_inst( 'LES ');
    gtr_node: gen_inst( 'GTR ');
    geq_node: gen_geq(rt);
  end;
  genline('');
end;
```

Note that this just calls EVAL on the left child then on the right child of the AST root node. EVAL calls BIN_ARITH, and BIN_ARITH then calls EVAL on the node's children.

BIN_ARITH then generates one or more instructions appropriate for the node's tag. Most of the operations are supported directly by instructions; however, a few are not. The MOD operation is supported by a system procedure call; hence, the code

```
 CXP  MOD
```

will be generated. MOD also is not supported for reals, so an error will result from that (the error should in fact be reported during tree building, not during evaluation).

The not-equal operation has no machine instruction, so we call GEN_NEQ, which in turn yields the pair of instructions:

```
 EQU
 NOT
```

Similarly, there is no less-than-or-equal-to instruction in our machine, so GEN_LEQ produces:

```
 GTR
 NOT
```

7.7.5. Building Semantic Lists

We have seen how a tree can be easily built and rooted in the semantics stack. Let us now examine list building. The principle is the same: we must allocate new SEMREC structures from the heap, copying what we need from SEMSTACK and linking them together. We will use the following productions for an example:

$$\text{BoolList} \rightarrow \text{BoolList , Boolean \#boollist1}$$
$$\text{BoolList} \rightarrow \text{Boolean \#boollist2}$$

The Boolean will be an expression tree, but that is not important. A BoolList clearly will be a sequence of expressions separated by commas in the source; for example:

```
 75.3, A*(9-B), FCN(C, D, 15*E)
```

qualifies as a BoolList.

A BoolList will be supported in SEMREC by the tag BLIST_NODE:

```
SEMREC= record
          VTYPE: vtypes;
          case SEMT: semtype of
             ...  {all the other cases}
             blist_node: (BLNEXT,
                             BLRECP: semrecp);
       end;
```

We will use BLNEXT to form a linked list of expressions, each of which is pointed to by BLRECP. We also intend that the BLNEXT chain be in the same order as the expressions appear in the source; that is, the left-most Boolean will be the first item in the chain. It happens that there always will be at least one member in the chain as a result of the form of the productions.

The two BoolList productions are supported by the following APPLY actions:

```
BOOLLIST1: begin {BoolList -> BoolList , Boolean}
    tsemp:=semstack[stackx-2];  {grab the BoolList record}
    t1semp:=tsemp;
    while t1semp↑.blnext<>nil do
       t1semp:=t1semp↑.blnext;  {find the end of the chain}
    new(t1semp↑.blnext);  {tack on a new one}
    with t1semp↑.blnext↑ do
    begin
       vtype:=unk_type;
       blnext:=nil;  {no next one}
       blrecp:=semstack[stackx];  {grab the Boolean record}
    end
  end;
BOOLLIST2: begin {BoolList -> Boolean}
    new(tsemp);
    with tsemp↑ do
    begin
       semt:=blist_node;
       blnext:=nil;  {no next one}
       new(blrecp);
       blrecp:=semstack[stackx];  {grab the Boolean}
    end
  end;
```

The BOOLLIST2 case simply allocates a new SEMREC structure pointed to by TSEMP. The Boolean structure is caught by it through the pointer BLRECP. BLNEXT will be NIL because there is no "next" one.

In the BOOLLIST1 case, we must first walk through the chain of BLNEXT pointers to the last element, which is marked by BLNEXT = NIL. The BoolList part of the production will be some chain of members, whereas the Boolean element is a single member, formed as described in the preceding paragraph and obviously belonging at the end of the chain.

The temporary structure pointer T1SEMP is used to walk through the chain; TSEMP cannot be used for this purpose.

7.7.6. Predecessors

Before we can proceed any further, we need to discuss a useful way of accessing information deeper in the stack than that associated with the current production. For example, we shall be looking at the production:

Then → THEN # thent

which is invoked as part of the productions:

IF Boolean Then Stmt # ifth
IF Boolean Then Stmt Else Stmt # ifthelse

When the thent production is applied, the stack top will contain the token THEN, but below this token will be information associated with the Boolean, and—below it—the token IF. We can then access the information associated with Boolean on the thent production through:

```
semstack[stackx-1]
```

The theory of predecessors is simple. Each symbol X in the grammar is associated with a *predecessor set* S = *pred*(X), defined as follows:

1. For each appearance of X in the right member of any production P such that there exists a preceding symbol W in the right member of P—that is, the right member of P has the form . . .WX. . .—W is a member of S.

2. If X is the left-most symbol of the right member of a production P, of the form A → X. . ., then *pred*(A) is in S.

3. No other symbols are in S.

It can then be shown that if X appears in the stack of an LR1 parser at index I_x, then one of the members of *pred*(X) will appear at index $I_x - 1$.

The predecessor set for any grammar symbol is found easily by inspection of the grammar. The parser generator in QPARSER also will produce a table of predecessors for each terminal and nonterminal token.

7.7.7. Branches and Labels

Two sorts of branches appear in Pascal, explicit and implicit. An *explicit branch* occurs through a GOTO statement; the label is a literal positive integer, and must have been declared previously in a LABEL statement. An *implicit branch* occurs through one of the Pascal control structures.

We will assume that the target machine branch instructions will be one of the following. Most commercial machines have a much richer set of branch instructions, but these are sufficient for most of the Pascal implicit and explicit control structures:

```
UJP   label        {unconditional branch}
FJP   label        {false branch}
```

Here label may be a symbol or a number. The *target* of a branch—label—will be some other instruction. We associate the label with some instruction by writing:

```
LOC   label
```

just before the instruction.

These simple conventions will suffice to illustrate code generation for branches. We will assume that our branch and LOC instructions will be processed later by an assembler, which will produce machine-level instructions with instruction addresses.

Pseudo Labels

For an explicit branch, the label may be the user-chosen label itself. However, that can lead to scoping problems. Most assemblers do not support nested variable and label scopes in that way that Pascal does; hence, the use of, say, "2" for a label in more than one procedure may cause a scoping error during assembly.

It is better to consider the Pascal branch label as a symbol in the same way that variable names are symbols. It should be entered in the symbol table and associated with an assembler branch label. It will be placed in the symbol table by the LABEL declaration, and accessed later when a GOTO or a label: appears on a statement.

We will therefore want to create any number of distinct artificial labels, or *pseudo labels*. In the QPARSER PSG system, these will have the form DLABEL_01, DLABEL_02, and so on. A procedure GEN_LABEL will write an instruction followed by a pseudo label, the value of which is determined by the integer variable LX:

```
procedure GEN_LABEL(INST: string8; LX: int);
begin
  if gencode=0 then writeln(tgfile, inst, ' DLABEL_', lx:1);
end;
```

7.7.8. GOTOs and GOTO Labels

The GOTO statement is supported by several productions. The first of these declares labels to be used in a GOTO. (Such a label declaration is required in Pascal, but certain other languages, such as Fortran, do not support label declarations.)

```
LBList → LABEL LabList ;
LBList → ε
LabList → LabList , <integer> #label1
LabList → <integer> #label2
```

Here is the supporting action for label1 and label2:

```
LABEL1, LABEL2: begin {LabList -> LabList , <integer>}
                      {OR: LabList -> <integer>}
    t1symp:=sym_label(semstack[stackx]↑.numval);
    with t1symp↑ do
    begin
      if symt=stlabel then error('previously declared');
      symt:=stlabel;
      decld:=false;
      refd:=false;
      labval:=dumlabx;
      dumlabx:=dumlabx+1;
    end
  end;
```

The function SYM_LABEL enters the label value <integer> in the symbol table and associates a dummy label LABVAL with it. A multiple declaration of a label value (in a LABEL statement) is detected by the test symt = stlabel, which means that the label has been entered previously as a statement label.

DECLD will be FALSE until the label is used to label a statement; then it will become TRUE. It is used to detect the use of the same label on different statements. The REFD flag will be FALSE until some GOTO is seen; then it is set to TRUE. REFD and DECLD will be checked at the end of a procedure to make sure that every statement label is both declared and used somewhere in the procedure.

Statement Labeling

The productions:

$$\text{Stmt} \rightarrow \text{Label : Stmt}$$
$$\text{Label} \rightarrow \text{<integer> \#lstmt}$$

support a GOTO label associated with a statement. The semantic action for the lstmt production is:

```
LSTMT: begin {Label -> <integer> #lstmt}
    t1symp:=sym_label(semstack[stackx]↑.numval);
    with t1symp↑ do
    begin
      if symt<>stlabel then
      begin
        error('undeclared label');
        symt:=stlabel;
        refd:=false;
        labval:=dumlabx;
        dumlabx:=dumlabx+1;
      end
      else
        if decld then error('previously declared');
        decld:=true;
        gen_label('LOC ', labval);
      end
    end;
```

As in the LABEL productions, the numeric label value is converted into a symbol table entry by function SYM_LABEL. There are tests to ensure that the label has been declared and that it has not previously marked a statement. DECLD is set to TRUE, and a single pseudo instruction LOC <labval> is emitted. LABVAL is a number in the symbol table associated with the label.

The GOTO Statement

The GOTO statement is defined by the production:

$$\text{Stmt} \rightarrow \text{GOTO} \ <\text{integer}> \ \#\text{gotolab}$$

and the semantics:

```
GOTOLAB: begin {Stmt -> GOTO Label}  {Label is an integer}
    t1symp:=sym_label(semstack[stackx]↑.numval);
    with t1symp↑ do
    begin
      if symt<>stlabel then
      begin
        error('undeclared label');
        symt:=stlabel;
        decld:=false;
        labval:=dumlabx;
        dumlabx:=dumlabx+1;
      end;
      refd:=true;
      gen_label('UJP ', labval);
    end;
  end;
```

This program fragment generates an unconditional jump (UJP), after performing a declaration test. We do not care whether DECLD is true or false; a GOTO may precede or follow its target. REFD is set TRUE to indicate that at least one GOTO has appeared using this label.

7.7.9. IF-THEN-ELSE Control Structure

Let us now describe code generation for implicit control structures. We begin with the simple IF-THEN-ELSE—other control structures are essentially variations on this one. IF-THEN-ELSE is supported by the following productions:

```
Stmt → IF Boolean Then Stmt #ifth
Stmt → IF Boolean Then Stmt Else Stmt #ifthelse
Then → THEN #thent
Else → ELSE #elset
```

We saw in section 7.3 that it is important to catch the Then just after parsing the Boolean. We will use the Then semantic structure to hold two label numbers, LABEL1 and LABEL2. We also need to catch the Else between the two statements in the second production.

We need an extension to the SEMREC structure to support this and other control structures, as follows:

```
SEMREC= record
           VTYPE: vtypes;
           case SEMT: semtype of
              ...    {the others}
              jp_node: (LABEL1, LABEL2: int);
        end;
```

We first examine the Then action, because it occurs before all the others:

```
THENT: begin {Then -> THEN}
    new(tsemp);
    with tsemp↑ do
    begin
      semt:=jp_node;
      label1:=dumlabx;
      label2:=dumlabx+1;
      dumlabx:=dumlabx+2;
      if semstack[stackx-1]↑.semt<>bool then
      begin  {the general case}
        eval(semstack[stackx-1], bool_type);
        gen_label('FJP', label1);
      end
      else  {an IF with a constant boolean}
      if semstack[stackx-1]↑.numval=0 then
      gencode:=gencode+1;  {false —> skip THEN part}
    end
  end;
```

We create two label numbers, LABEL1 and LABEL2, attaching them to the TSEMP record. The reference:

```
semstack[stackx-1]↑.semt
```

refers to the Boolean that precedes Then in the stack. We peek at that expression to optimize the IF statement for the case of a constant Boolean. If Boolean is constant, there is no reason to emit evaluation code for it followed by a conditional branch instruction—we can simply emit the code for the THEN or the ELSE case, suppressing the other code.

Code will be suppressed if the global parameter GENCODE is greater than zero. GENCODE will be increased by one to inhibit code, and decreased to enable generation. Note that control structures may be nested to any level; hence, if the code is suppressed at an outer level, it must remain suppressed at all included levels; it becomes fully enabled only after GENCODE returns to zero.

In the preceding code, we inhibit generation if the Boolean is a constant 0—FALSE. We shall see that code generation will be enabled at the end of the THEN Stmt for the sake of any following ELSE Stmt.

If the Boolean is not constant, it must be evaluated; the EVAL call achieves this. The FJP instruction will then cause a branch around the THEN Stmt if the Boolean evaluation yields FALSE.

Reasons for Using Constant Optimization

You may wonder why we bother optimizing an IF-THEN for a constant Boolean. Why was such a statement written in the first place? Because Pascal programs often are generated automatically by other programs, perhaps a macro generator. These are considerably easier to write if the Pascal compiler is sufficiently clever at detecting optimizations.

Also, many programmers like to write into their source extensive debugging or verification code that will be run while the program is under development. Removal of that source can be time-consuming and error-prone. However, it can be left in if it is covered by an IF-THEN with a constant Boolean. When the constant is set TRUE, the compiler will generate the testing code; otherwise, it will omit it.

The IFTH Production

The APPLY action for the IFTH production is:

```
IFTH: begin {Stmt -> IF Boolean Then Stmt}
    if semstack[stackx-2]↑.semt<>bool then
    gen_label('LOC', semstack[stackx-1]↑.label1)
    else
    if semstack[stackx-2]↑.numval=0 then
    gencode:=gencode-1;   {was a FALSE Boolean}
    end;
```

In the general case, we emit a LOC with the label LABEL1. The label's value was associated previously with Then. This will be the target of the FJP instruction emitted by the Then production. Note that all code for the Stmt has been emitted when this production is applied; hence, the LOC will refer to whatever follows the IF-THEN statement.

If the Boolean is a constant, and is FALSE, we enable code generation by decrementing GENCODE. Note that this is the dual of the operation performed by the Then production.

The ELSET Production

We mentioned that we need to catch the Else appearing between the two Stmt's in an IF-THEN-ELSE, in order to insert a branch and a LOC. Here is the APPLY action for the ELSET production:

```
ELSET: begin {Else -> ELSE}
    if semstack[stackx-3]↑.semt<>bool then
    with semstack[stackx-2]↑ do
    begin
      gen_label('UJP', label2);
      gen_label('LOC', label1);
    end
    else
    if semstack[stackx-3]↑.numval=0 then
    gencode:=gencode-1    {was a FALSE boolean}
    else gencode:=gencode+1   {a TRUE boolean}
    end;
```

The reference semstack[stackx-3] is to the Boolean that will appear at this position when this production is called. Although we are referring to something that is two stack positions below the stack stop object ELSE, it is easy to show from the grammar's predecessor tables that this reference is safe.

As usual, we see whether the Boolean is a constant. If so, it must be TRUE or FALSE. If TRUE, we have evaluated the THEN part and wish to suppress the ELSE part by incrementing GENCODE. If FALSE, we have suppressed the THEN part and wish to enable the ELSE part by decrementing GENCODE.

In the general case, the Boolean has been evaluated previously and an FJP instruction emitted. We need only emit a UJP to skip over the ELSE statement, followed by a LOC for the sake of the FJP instruction. Note that we can pick up the correct label numbers LABEL1 and LABEL2 from the reference to semstack[stackx-2], because these were attached earlier to the semantic information associated with Then.

The IFTHELSE Production

The action for the full IF-THEN-ELSE statement form is:

```
IFTHELSE: begin {Stmt -> IF Boolean Then Stmt Else Stmt}
    if semstack[stackx-4]↑.semt<>bool then
    gen_label('LOC', semstack[stackx-3]↑.label2)
    else
    if semstack[stackx-4]↑.numval=1 then
    gencode:=gencode-1;   {was a TRUE Boolean}
    end;
```

As usual, the label values are associated with Then, and we need to inspect the Boolean semantic information to decide if it is constant. A TRUE Boolean requires that we enable code generation; recall that it was inhibited in the Else production in this case.

In the general case, we need only generate a LOC referring to whatever instructions follow the IF-THEN-ELSE statement.

Partial Evaluation

Certain Pascal compilers support *partial evaluation* of the Boolean that appears in the IF-THEN, WHILE-DO, REPEAT-UNTIL, and other places. This may be contrasted to *full evaluation* by considering the Boolean expression:

$$x \text{ AND } y$$

Under full evaluation rules, both x and y are evaluated, then the expression's result is determined by applying the AND operation to the two results.

Under partial evaluation rules, x is evaluated. If it is FALSE, the result is assumed to be FALSE without evaluating y; otherwise y, too, is evaluated and its result is the expression's result. Partial evaluation also requires an assumption that evaluation proceed from left to right.

Partial evaluation is easily supported by writing the semantic operations for the AND as though it were equivalent to IF x THEN y. Thus the machine instructions would have the form:

```
{evaluate x}
FJP  L1
{evaluate y}
LOC  L1
```

7.8. Compiler Storage Management

As we discussed under QPARSER's value philosophy, space for SEMSTACK objects and TSEMP are allocated only once, obviating the need to reclaim unbound objects. However, under the pointer philosophy, heap space will be allocated to support identifiers, numbers, and other user-defined semantic objects. Storage reclamation is then an issue.

Symbols and attributes are added to a symbol table during compilation. (This will be discussed further in chapter 8.) The appearance of a uniquely different <identifier> in the compiler's source file will cause allocation of heap space for the symbol table; hence, the space required will grow with the length of the source.

If strings are used in QPARSER, each string is written to a large byte array, and its index is incremented. No attempt is made to locate previously used strings; hence, this index eventually will exceed the array's bound.

The best approach to heap space management depends on the nature of the system that supports the compiler. Some modern machines support a large address space and sufficient virtual memory to meet any heap space demand. In such a case, you can simply let the heap allocation continue to the end of the source, without regard to its limit.

More often, heap space is limited. A small microcomputer is not likely to support large address spaces and virtual memory; it may have a quite severe limit on available heap space. Reclamation of unused memory is therefore critically important to compile long programs.

7.8.1. A DISPOSE Strategy

ISO Pascal recognizes only DISPOSE as a means of reclaiming memory. This function requires a pointer to some structure; the structure will then be released from the heap and the pointer set to NIL.

Unfortunately, a DISPOSE of a structure S containing a pointer P to a subsidiary structure S' does nothing about S'. Thus, if S is the root of a tree, dispose(S) does not release the entire tree, only its root node S. Indeed, it should not be so implemented. Some of the members of the tree may be associated with pointers that have not been disposed, and must therefore be retained. The Pascal language is sufficiently powerful to create all manner of graphs through pointers and heap structures, and a system to disentangle the graphs for a safe DISPOSE would be difficult to design.

However, for our compiler, a DISPOSE philosophy can be used to reclaim space. It must be invoked whenever an AST rooted in the semantics stack has seen its last use. The AST dispose must walk through the tree, disposing of each leaf node before disposing of its parent. Fortunately, such a procedure need be written just once, because all ASTs are based on a single record structure, SEMREC.

Symbol table space may be reclaimed just before leaving the scope of a procedure. The problem here is to dispose and unlink each symbol belonging in the inner scope without removing symbols belonging to the covering scope. QPARSER provides a simple means of achieving that through a LEVEL number associated with each symbol. The LEVEL must be assigned by the compiler designer; it should increase as one moves into a nested scope.

Using LEVEL, it is then possible to remove all the symbols associated with an inner scope, leaving those at the outer scope.

The scoping rules are more complicated than this in Pascal, unfortunately. Consider a procedure P the name of which is at scoping level N. Its formal parameters belong in scope N + 1, and are candidates for removal through DISPOSE. Certainly, the formal parameter names should not be in the symbol table outside the scope of P. However, a call of P will require a list of the formal parameter types, and these normally are part of the symbol table attributes associated with the formal parameters. That call can be outside the declaration scope of the formal parameters.

We must therefore keep formal parameter symbol table entries, yet unlink them from the symbol access mechanism when the end of their lexical scope has been reached.

Of course, the local variables associated with a procedure can be both disposed and removed from the symbol table at the end of the procedure's scope, because no later reference to them is possible.

The string table index clearly can be reset at the end of a procedure's scope. It might also be reset just after the string has been written to target code, provided that the code synthesis discipline follows a strict first-in-last-out philosophy on literal strings.

7.8.2. Mark-Release Strategy

Some Pascal implementations support MARK and RELEASE. This simple mechanism has the virtue of speed, and is safe if employed correctly.

We recommend carrying a mark pointer with each procedure head in the semantics stack. This pointer marks the dividing line between the procedure's formal parameters and its local parameters. At the end of the procedure, the symbol table must be trimmed back by adjusting its pointers—then RELEASE can be called.

Some care must be taken when identifying the dividing line. Note especially that a symbol's structure is allocated when the lexical analyzer scans the symbol, not when it appears on the stack in an APPLY call. Also, a lookahead action may scan a symbol, causing an apply action on a production that does *not* contain the symbol.

Finally, note the discussion in the preceding section regarding the need to retain the semantic information associated with formal parameters; the formal parameter names themselves, however, can be discarded.

7.8.3. Direct Management

Many compilers have been written without the benefit of any built-in memory allocation and management schemes. We also can choose not to allocate space dynamically from the heap, or to do so only selectively.

Note first that in practice only two structures require management—a symbol table structure and a semantic stack structure. Each of their members can be considered to be of fixed length; hence, a pool of each can be allocated only once as an array.

We may then essentially write a mark-release manager for each of the two pools. The advantage is that disposition can take place in the two pools independently of each other, at different times, without interference. Mark-release works well for the symbol table, semantic stack items, and even the stacks themselves in our bottom-up compiler, provided that the pools can be managed independently.

Unfortunately, each pool must be given a fixed size when the compiler is compiled; there are then two or more arbitrary fixed limits, rather than a single limit, on program complexity and size.

7.9. Exercises

1. Using this SDTS:

```
S → D < E, E > D
D → E, E
E → E + T, E + T
E → T, T
T → (E), (E)
T → a, a
```

construct a complete derivation of translation forms, the derivation tree in the source grammar, and the derivation tree in the target grammar for each of the following input strings. Is the SDTS simple?

```
a < a
a + a < a
(a) < a + ( a )
```

2. Using this SDTS:

```
E → E + T, add(E, T)
E → E - T, sub(E, T)
E → T, T
T → ( E ), E
T → a, a
```

construct a complete derivation of translation forms, the derivation tree in the source grammar, and the derivation tree in the target grammar for each of the following input strings. Is the SDTS simple?

```
a + a - ( a )
a - a - a
a + ( a - a )
```

3. Prove that if an SDTS has an unambiguous underlying source grammar, then, for every input string, there exists exactly one translation string, and it is independent of the order in which rules are applied to translation forms.

4. Design an SDTS that converts arithmetic expressions containing $\{+, -, /, *, (,), a\}$ to Polish prefix notation, with parentheses removed. Be sure to preserve the usual precedence and associativity of arithmetic operators.

5. Design an SDTS that converts expressions with mixed integer and real operands to Polish postfix. Use $\{+, (,), a, b\}$ as the source alphabet. a is an integer operand and b is a real operand. Make the target alphabet contain a and b, binary operators int+ and real+ for integer and real addition, and the unary operator float for conversion from integer to real. Make addition left-associative, as usual.

6. Give a general method for inverting an SDTS. That is, for any SDTS S, give a method for constructing its inverse S^{-1}, such that if (x, y) is a translation defined by S, then (y, x) is a translation defined by S^{-1}. Discuss the uniqueness of the translations and their inverses.

7. For each of the following SDTSs, prove that there either does or does not exist an equivalent, simple SDTS. "Equivalent" means the set of translations (x, y) is the same.

```
S → AB, BA        S → AB, BA
A → Aa, Aa        A → Aa, Aa
A → ε, b          A → ε, b
B → Cc, cC        B → Bc, cB
B → ε, ε          B → ε, ε
C → ,d, d
```

8. Give a complete, formal description for an LL(1) PDT that is equivalent to the following SDTS:

```
E → E + T,   (E; T)+
E → E - T,   (E; T)-
E → T,   T
T → (E),   E
T → a,   a
```

9. Trace the LL(1) PDT of exercise 8 for these input strings:

```
a + (a)
a - a - (a + a)
(a - a)
```

10. Convert this SDTS to an equivalent, simple postfix SDTS:

```
E → E or T,   E infor T or
E → T,   T
T → T and F,   T infand F and
T → F,   F
F → (E),   E
F → a,   a
```

11. Prove theorem 7.2 by showing that the PDT constructed by the method given in the text satisfies the theorem.

12. Design a simple postfix SDTS for translating the Pascal REPEAT and WHILE statements into the jump instructions of section 7.7.7.

13. Design abstract syntax trees for the Pascal IF and WHILE statements, and give relevant productions and apply rules to construct them. Be sure to handle begin and end, used to bracket then clauses, else clauses, and loop bodies.

7.10. Bibliographical Notes

The notion of an SDTS was first formalized by Lewis and Stearns [Lewis, 1968]. The top-down and bottom-up transducers are adapted from Aho and Ullman [Aho, 1972a], chapter 3. A general discussion of tree generation and tree transformations can be found in DeRemer [1974a].

A great deal of literature exists on automatic translator writing systems. An old, but comprehensive, review is presented in Feldman and Gries [Feldman, 1968]. A more recent survey is given by Griffiths [1974c]. Specific syntax-directed translators are described in Koster [1974], Brooker and Morris [Brooker, 1963], and Metcalfe [1964].

CHAPTER 8

DECLARATIONS, TYPES, AND SYMBOL MANAGEMENT

Every common programming language permits a programmer to invent names for various entities that the compiler or run-time system is to manipulate. Properties may be assigned to the programmer's names through special language forms called *declarations*. These properties then can be used to define classes of operations for the named entities, or to create new declarations.

For example, an addition operator + can be used for a variety of different kinds of addition—real, vector, fixed point—by assigning a type to its operands through declarations. In this way, a few operators can be used for a large number of related mathematical operations, increasing the power and clarity of the language. Abstract structural forms, such as array, pointer, or record types, also may be declared and accessed by names.

This chapter deals with the static association of user-defined names with attributes. By *static,* we mean those associations that the compiler must keep track of, as opposed to those that must exist when the compiled program is executed. There are several aspects to static name association:

- Names appear in the source program more or less at random. Their association with a set of attributes requires some means of locating a particular name in a table efficiently.

- In many languages, names can vary greatly in length. The maximum length allowed may be much larger than the average length programmers use, or there may be no maximum length at all.

- Several languages provide static scoping of user names through blocks. A name will be useful only within its block. The same name may appear in different blocks, but will represent different entities.

- A compiler may operate through one or several passes through the source or through an abstract-syntax tree (AST) generated on the first pass. In general, the attributes of the user names are needed in all the passes.

- If the source code is free of errors, the names are no longer needed once their attributes have been established and linked to the AST. However, the compiler must be prepared to deal with source errors, and error messages often are enhanced by including appropriate names.

- A name is associated with an *attribute,* which may take a number of forms, ranging from a simple address to a complicated structure.

8.1. Symbols—Declarations and Uses

Different kinds of symbols appear in most source languages. There are symbols such as $+$, $*$, (,) that carry at most one or two specific, fixed meanings in the language. There are strings of characters that represent constants, such as quoted strings and numbers, called *literals*. There are strings that resemble user-defined identifiers, but in fact are reserved keywords—examples are the keywords IF, WHILE, and FOR in Pascal. Finally, there is a class of user-defined names, called *identifiers*, that carry no inherent meaning, but rather are assigned an attribute through one or more declarations in the source program.

An *identifier* typically is a string starting with a letter and containing only letters and digits. It may have a bounded length (one to seven characters in Fortran, for example) or be unbounded. The strings in the source that comprise identifiers usually are distinguished by a lexical analyzer. As we have seen in chapter 3, the lexical task of distinguishing identifiers from reserved words in certain languages is not always easy.

An identifier can be associated with any of a number of entities in a programming language; for example:

- As a reference to some data area. The area may contain a primitive datum or a structure of primitive data.

- As a reference to a named constant.

- As a reference to a type.

- As a reference to a statement location in a program; that is, as a *statement label*. We shall use the term *label* in this sense hereafter.

- As a procedure name.

- As a macro name.

- As a procedure or macro parameter.

- As a file, or a program, or a device connected to an input–output port of the computer.

8.1.1. Symbol Attributes

The set of meanings associated with an identifier is called its *attribute*. An important attribute is the class to which the name belongs. In addition, here are the attributes usually associated with each of the entities named:

- The object is a primitive datum, its location and one of a finite set of primitive types it belongs. If it represents a structured type, its base location and a pointer to an abstract representation of the structure.

- The object is a constant, the constant's value and a pointer to an abstract representation of the constant's type structure.

- The object is a type, a pointer to an abstract representation of the type's structure.

- The object is a label, the address of the instruction the label to which is attached, and/or the addresses of branches to the label.

- The object is a procedure, the location of the procedure; the number, names, and types of its parameters; whether it is user- or system-defined, whether it can be called legally by a user, and so on. For a function, its return value type and location also are required.

- The object is a file, the characteristics of the file—record size, whether fixed or variable length, whether sequential, random access, file buffer location, and so on.

The compiler data structure that associates identifiers with their attributes is called a *symbol table*. A statement the principal purpose of which is to assign attributes to some identifier is called a *declaration*. An identifier is said to be *declared* when it has appeared in a declaration. An identifier is said to be *referenced* or *used* in a statement in which it appears, but in which no attributes are added to the identifier's attribute set.

Sometimes, an appearance of an identifier is both a declaration and a use. For example, the Fortran statement:

$$SAM = I + 1$$

in which I appears for the first time in the source program is both a declaration and a use of I. Under the Fortran rules, identifiers beginning with I, J, K, L, M, or N are assumed to be simple integer variables, unless there is a preceding declaration to the contrary—all others are assumed to be simple real variables.

In general, a declaration causes no object code to be emitted, except possibly to allocate space for data. A reference usually is associated with some generated object code. A macro name reference results in the generation of an expansion source string and may not be associated with any object code generation.

An identifier that appears only in declarations and is never referenced is useless—it need never appear at all. An identifier that appears in two or more conflicting declarations in the same static scope is said to be *multiply declared*. An identifier that appears in a reference but never in a declaration is said to be *undeclared*.

All the declarations of some identifier usually must precede any reference of the identifier. There is no particular implementation reason for this language policy, as compilers can be designed to deal with declarations and references in any order. However, it is good programming style to group the declarations together in a section of the source program that precedes all the executable statements that refer to them. When declarations *must* precede references, the compiler can generate completed object code in one pass, except for forward branches.

8.2. String Storage

The names declared in a typical program vary in length, sometimes over a wide range. Using highly mnemonic identifiers is a good programming practice, so most modern languages allow relatively long identifiers. Some have no maximum length at all. The result is that although a compiler must be prepared to handle maximum length strings, the average length will be much less. This creates a problem in space allocation for the identifier strings.

Fixed Allocation

The simplest technique is always to allocate enough space for the maximum length identifier. This allows a symbol table to be a simple array with fixed-sized elements. It also allows string comparisons during table searching to be done using relatively efficient whole-string comparison operations. Of course, it is possible only if the language being compiled has a maximum length for its identifiers.

The *Pascal Report* [Wirth, 1974] allows identifiers to be of unbounded length, but says that only the first ten characters are significant. This rule also allows a compiler to use fixed allocation, because only the first ten characters need be stored in the symbol table entry. Unfortunately, it creates opportunities for the programmer to create inadvertently pairs of identifiers that appear to be different but really are not. A declaration error on the second one will be the result. (Other Pascal implementations support different significant lengths, ranging from eight to unbounded.)

The problem with this technique is that it is likely to waste a large amount of space in the unused parts of the strings. If the maximum length is considerably greater that the average length of identifiers, this will amount to the majority of the space allocated. On the other hand, if the maximum length is short, say ten or less, the waste is not unreasonable, and other string storage techniques will provide little improvement.

Separate String Space

An alternative is to create a separate array of characters, called the *string space,* just to hold the strings themselves. The strings are concatenated in the string space, in the order they are first stored, with no wasted space between. The symbol table entries themselves then will contain pointers into the string space.

Each table entry will require a subscript into the string space, showing where the first character of the identifier is found, and a separate field giving the length

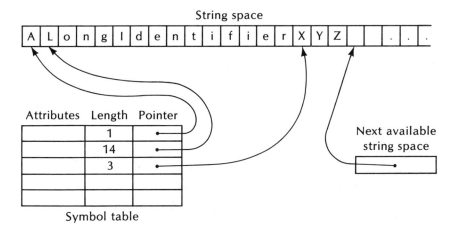

Figure 8.1. Identifiers stored in a string space.

of the identifier. (Instead of a length, a unique terminator character at the end of each identifier string may be used.) This pair is of fixed size and thus can be part of an array of fixed-sized elements. We can think of this latter array as the symbol table, with the string space as an adjunct to it. Figure 8.1 shows an example of these data structures, where the names "A", "LongIdentifier," and "XYZ" are stored.

This technique obviously eliminates the wasted space inherent in fixed sized string allocation. On the other hand, there is a space penalty in the storage of the string space pointer and length for every identifier. These fields have no counterparts in the fixed-string technique. Thus one would expect a net space saving only if the amount of wasted space in the fixed-string technique is greater than the sizes of these added fields. On a modern machine with eight-bit bytes, these fields are likely to require a total of three bytes at a bare minimum, and probably four bytes, because 2^{16} characters is probably too small for a string space.

The string space technique probably will slow down symbol table search somewhat, because a loop doing character-by-character comparison will be required each time two strings are compared. However, this is slowed down by a constant factor; that is, it does not increase with the number of identifiers. Thus, it is less important than some of the factors discussed in section 8.4.

Finally, the string space technique requires the compiler writer to decide in advance, for all programs, how to divide the available space among the symbol table, the string space, and other tables. The relative requirements for space in these tables will vary from source program to source program. Thus, it is likely that, for some source programs, the compiler will overflow one of the tables while others have unneeded space.

Linked List of String Fragments

A third technique is to represent each string as a linked list of nodes, each of which contains a fixed-length fragment of the total string. The first fragment might be contained directly within the symbol table entry. If an identifier is longer than the fragment length, an additional node is allocated and linked to the first. If the identifier is longer than two fragments, another node is allocated and linked to the second, and so on. Figure 8.2 shows an example of this data structure, with fragments of length eight. The identifiers stored are the same as those in figure 8.1.

This technique also eliminates some of the wasted space of fixed-size–string allocation. It is not as space-efficient as the string-space technique, because the last fragment of each identifier's list usually will be only partly filled. This waste is comparable to that of a fixed-string symbol table the maximum length of which equals the fragment length. However, the list-of-fragments technique needs no maximum length at all. Its space overhead also is higher than the string-space technique, because each fragment requires a pointer. There will be more of these than there are string-space pointer/length pairs, and they may also be bigger, because they must be true pointers.

String comparison also is more difficult. A loop is required to go through the fragments when comparing two strings, unless the supporting machine allows a fast string comparison of the right kind. This is again a slowdown by a constant factor.

The main advantage of this technique is that the space for strings is allocated dynamically as needed. Thus the same pool of storage can be shared by string fragments and other data structure needed by the compiler. This relieves the compiler writer of the burden of trying to anticipate how the available space should be divided among the various data structures. If the operating system under which the compiler is running has a sufficiently flexible space management mechanism, it may even allow the compiler to run without any advance estimate of the total amount of space required.

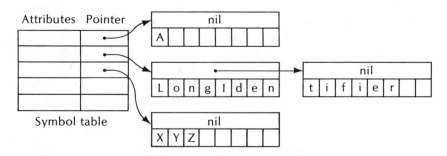

Figure 8.2. Identifiers stored in a fragment list.

8.3. Scope of Identifiers

Every identifier possesses a region of validity within the source program, called its *static scope* of definition. An identifier is *available* within its scope and *unavailable* outside its scope. A reference to some object through its identifier is valid only if the reference lies within the identifier's scope.

The Fortran language has a simple scope rule—the scope of any identifier is an entire program or procedure, and one procedure cannot be nested within another procedure. The scope of a Basic identifier is a whole file unit, which may include a number of subroutines.

Lisp and certain other interpretative languages provide *dynamic* scoping. In these, declarations occur during execution, and a variable's scope includes all the instructions executed to the end of the region designated as the variable's scope. A new declaration of a variable always is permitted; it will temporarily override the existing one until the end of its scope is reached.

Static and Dynamic Scoping

The difference between a statically scoped and a dynamically scoped language can be understood from the following example, using Pascal as the language of expression:

```
program DIFF;

   procedure INNERLEVEL;
   begin
     s:=25;
   end;

   procedure TOPLEVEL;
     var S: integer;
   begin
     s:=15;
     innerlevel;
     writeln(s);
   end;

begin
  toplevel;
end.
```

Under static scoping rules, the statement:

$$s := 25;$$

appearing in procedure INNERLEVEL is illegal. A Pascal compiler would complain that s has not been declared.

Under dynamic scoping rules, the *execution* of TOPLEVEL causes s to be declared, and then set to the value 15. When INNERLEVEL is called, the variable s is considered to be that declared earlier in TOPLEVEL; it is then set to 25 without complaint. Upon return, the WRITELN in TOPLEVEL prints a 25. When returning from TOPLEVEL, the scope of s is terminated. It would be an error (for example) to attempt to access s in the outer block program. Note that the identity of the s referred to in TOPLEVEL could actually vary dynamically if TOPLEVEL also were called by some other procedure with its own local s.

Clearly, static scoping rules are the norm for programs intended for compilation; dynamic rules seem to suit interpreters better. The compiler "sees" the sequence of source lines as printed, not as executed, whereas the interpreter "sees" statements in order of execution, rather than as printed.

However, a compiler can be designed to support dynamic scoping rules, and an interpreter can be made to operate under static rules—the design just requires extra attention to the run-time structures.

Block-Structured Static Scoping

In a block-structured statically scoped language, the scope of an identifier is that of the block in which it is declared. The scope rules can be expressed as follows.

1. A *block* in Pascal is a sequence of source with the structure:

   HEAD DECLS BLOCKS STMTS TAIL

   where HEAD usually is a keyword (procedure or function in Pascal, '{' in C), DECLS are declarations the scope of which is between HEAD and TAIL, BLOCKS is a sequence of blocks, STMTS are executable statements, and TAIL usually is the keyword end.

2. Two blocks A and B must be disjoint, or one must be contained in the other. If block A is contained in B, A must be in the BLOCKS of B. Block A is then said to be *nested* in block B, and block B is said to *cover* block A.

3. An identifier declared in DECLS in a block A is available throughout block A, with the exception noted in rule 4. It is not available outside block A.

4. An identifier X may be declared in a block A and also in a block B nested in A. The same identifier X then represents two different objects, X_A and X_B. Object X_B is said to *shadow* object X_A. Thus, within block B, X refers to X_B, not to X_A. Within block A, X refers to X_A except within block B. The objects X_A and X_B may have dissimilar attributes—one could be a procedure name and the other a statement label, for example.

5. The same identifier X may be declared in two disjoint blocks A and B. Within block A, X refers to an object X_A, whereas within block B, it refers to an object X_B. The two objects X_A and X_B may have dissimilar attributes.

These scope rules are of considerable value to programmers. A new block of source code may be simply inserted into an existing program. If new temporary variables are needed in the new block, they may be declared within the block without any concern that one of their names may have been used already in a covering or disjoint block. Because the new locals shadow all existing names declared external to the block, the external data objects are protected from a careless reference.

However, most languages permit a reference to a variable X the declaration of which is in a covering block. That is, some block A carries the declaration of X, but a reference to X may legally appear in a block B nested within A. This is called a *global reference*.

Some experimental languages forbid global references for certain names without a special declaration in block B permitting them. Although the special declaration forces the programmer to write more statements, it provides an additional safeguard that prevents inadvertent references to externally declared variables. It also advertises clearly that some external references exist within block B. Finally, it helps in the application of formal verification techniques, because the complete set of referenced variables can be determined from the procedure heading. Block B cannot then be moved or copied somewhere else in the source without something being done about its external references.

8.3.1. Block-Structured Symbol Tables

The scope rules of block-structured languages require a more complicated form of symbol table than a simple list of associations between names and attributes. In this section, we present three methods for organizing tables that properly reflect these rules.

We assume that some solution to the string storage problem has been chosen. Thus, a string can be represented by a field of fixed size—the string itself, pointers into a string space, or the root of a fragment list. We also assume that some table-search algorithm has been chosen, which is capable of finding or inserting a name in a simple table of name–attribute associations. Search algorithms are discussed in section 8.4.

A Stack of Symbol Tables

One technique is to keep multiple symbol tables, one for each *active block*—that is, each block inside which the compiler is currently. Each table is a list of names and their associated attributes, for those names declared local to the table's associated block. The tables are organized into a stack. Whenever a new block is entered, a new, empty table is pushed onto this stack. This table will contain all names declared local to this new block.

When a declaration is compiled, the top table on the stack is searched for the name. If it is already present, the declaration is a duplicate. If not, the name is inserted. In either case, only the top table is involved, because it contains exactly the names declared local to the current block. Note that static scoping means that block entry occurs when translating a procedure *declaration,* not a procedure call.

When a reference to a name is translated, each of the tables must be searched, starting with the top table on the stack. This will locate correctly the innermost declaration of the referenced name, if it is declared in two or more active blocks.

Whenever the block is exited, its table is popped and the table's contents are discarded. Figure 8.3 shows an example of this data structure, for the Pascal program shown here:

```
program P
   var X,Y,H:boolean;
   procedure B1;
      var X,Z:char;
      procedure B2;
         var X,Y,W:integer;
         ...
         end {of B2}
      ...
      end {of B1}
   ...
   end {of P}
```

Figure 8.3 shows the state of the tables when the compiler is inside B2. Note that the name of a procedure is declared local to the *containing* block.

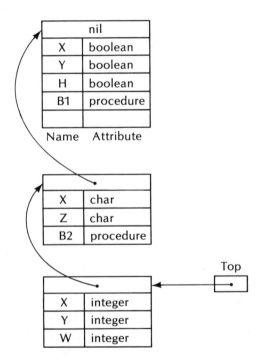

Figure 8.3. Block-structured symbol table using a linked stack of tables.

This technique is simple to understand and implement. It has the minor disadvantage that it will store multiple copies of an identifier that is declared at multiple static nesting levels. On the other hand, the space occupied by identifier strings can be reclaimed on scope exit, because they obey a stack discipline.

Multiple symbol tables have a serious limitation. As we shall see in section 8.4.5, the most efficient method of searching a table is based on some kind of hashing. However, this requires an advance estimate of how much table space will be required for each scope. Because scopes typically vary dramatically in the number of locally declared names, this can be difficult to do, except by consistently allocating liberally sized tables. This wastes a large amount of space in much the same way that allocating a maximum length string for every identifier wastes space. Other search strategies are compatible with this technique.

A Symbol Table of Stacks

Another technique uses only one symbol table; each of its entries is a stack of attribute values. The entry need contain only one copy of the identifier string itself. The stack contains one entry with attributes of each of the shadowed declarations of the name. The stack entries are, top to bottom, for the innermost to outermost of these. Note that if an identifier is not declared in the current block, then the top set of attributes may be for a declaration in some outer block. Each set of identifier attributes also must carry the scope level of the declaration they represent.

A single variable also is required to keep track of the level of nesting of the current block. Scope levels are numbered from zero for the outermost, increasing as more deeply nested blocks are entered. Figure 8.4 gives an example of this data structure, for the same Pascal program as that of Figure 8.3.

When entering a new block, the only action is to increment the scope level number of the current block. The table and stacks are not altered.

When translating a declaration, the table is searched for the declared name. If the name already has an entry in the table and the top element has the same scope level as the current block, then this is a duplicate declaration. Otherwise, if the name is not in the table at all, it is inserted. A new set of attributes, derived from the declaration, are then pushed onto the stack at the name's entry in the table, with the current scope level.

When translating a reference, the table is searched for the referenced name. If the name is absent, the name is undeclared in all active blocks. Otherwise, the top set of attributes are the relevant ones.

When exiting a block, a scan of the entire table is required. Each stack the top attribute set of which represents a declaration at the scope level being exited must be popped. This deletes the record of all declarations local to this block.

A special problem occurs when a name is not declared in the outermost block but is declared in an inner block. When the inner block is exited, the stack at the name's table entry will become empty. We must remove the name from the table altogether, because it is now not declared in any active block. However, none of

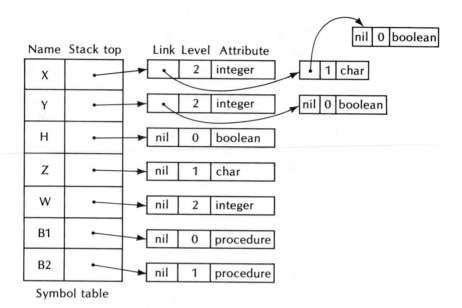

Symbol table

Figure 8.4. Block-structured symbol table using a table of linked stacks.

the common table-search methods caters to efficient removal of table entries. Thus, it is better to define a table entry that is present and contains a name but has an empty stack of attribute sets to be equivalent to the case in which the name is not in the table at all. The translations of declarations and references have to be altered to observe this rule.

Because there are many stacks, which usually but not always are shallow, it is best to save space by linking the stacks. An interesting consequence of the scope rules of block-structured languages is that the attribute sets of all the individual stacks collectively also obey a stack discipline. Thus, space for the nodes of these linked stacks can be allocated from a single stack of such nodes.

The principal advantage of this technique is that only one symbol table is used. Static allocation of the table is feasible, and thus any table search method can be chosen. Furthermore, multiple copies of shadowed identifier strings are not kept.

This technique is efficient for block entry, declarations, and references. Block exit is inefficient, however—each block exit requires time proportional to the number of names in the table, and the number of block exit operations is equal to the number of blocks in the program. This can be improved by a variation of the technique.

An Update Stack

In the update stack variation, we keep a single symbol table, the entries of which can be thought of abstractly as stacks, but we change the data structure. Each table entry contains space for exactly one set of attributes. This always contains the attributes of the innermost declaration of the table entry's name.

Attribute sets for redeclared names are moved to a single area, which is shared by all names. Because redeclarations of all names collectively obey a stack discipline, this area is a single global stack called the *update stack*.

Suppose a name is redeclared. We will call the former attributes of the name its *old meaning* and the attributes introduced by the redeclaration the *new meaning*. When the redeclaration is encountered, the old meaning will be in the table entry for the name. It will be pushed onto the update stack; then the table entry can be changed to contain the new meaning.

The old meaning will not be needed until this block is exited, when it must be copied back into the table entry. All the old meanings to be reinstated into table entries are together in a group at the top of the update stack. We need to know how many of the top update stack entries are to be reinstated. This can be accomplished by marking the update stack each time a block is entered. At block exit time, we know that all entries above the top mark have been pushed during translation of this block.

If we add to the update stack entry a pointer or subscript to the table entry from which it was removed, we have, in the top part of the update stack, a compact list of the table entries that must be returned to a former state. This allows us to avoid a scan of the table to find these table entries.

The update stack marks can be implemented by keeping another stack of subscripts into the update stack. This is called the *update display*. It will have one entry for each active block and will point to the last (if any) of the old meanings of names that were declared in its corresponding block. Note that the top pointer on the update display is the stack pointer for the update stack. It must be incremented or decremented whenever the update stack is pushed or popped. Figure 8.5 shows an example of this structure, for the Pascal program of figure 8.3.

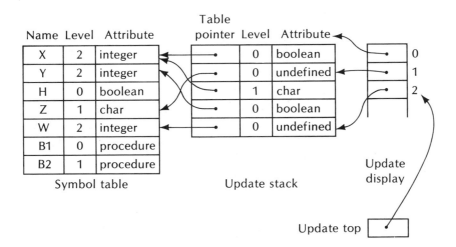

Figure 8.5. Block-structured symbol table using an update stack.

As before, it is possible to have a name declared in an inner block that is not declared at all in the outer blocks. When leaving the inner block, we have to change the table entry back so that this name is again undeclared. This requires that *undeclared* be a special value of a set of attributes. *Undeclared* meanings then can be pushed onto the update stack when the name is declared for the first time in the inner block.

An exception occurs when translating declarations local to the outermost block. Because we never leave this block except at the end of the entire compilation, there is no need to push *undeclared* old meanings when translating global declarations.

When entering a new block, the current level is incremented. The top pointer on the update display is duplicated to serve as a new stack marker. This effectively pushes a new, empty group of update stack entries.

When translating a declaration, the table is searched for the declared name. If it is present and its current meaning is for the current scope level, then this is a duplicate declaration. Otherwise, if necessary, the name is added to the table. Then the current meaning is pushed onto the update stack, along with a pointer to this table entry. This latter step is unnecessary if the current level is zero. Finally, a new set of attributes is constructed from the declaration and inserted into the table entry with the current scope level.

When translating a reference, the table is searched using the referenced name. If the name is absent or the table entry is *undefined*, this is a reference to an undeclared variable. Otherwise, the attributes in the table entry are used to translate the reference.

When exiting a block, update stack entries are popped and reinstated until the top two pointers on the update display are equal. Each update entry points to a table entry, and the attributes in the update entry are copied into this table entry, overwriting the attributes that were there. Finally, the update display is popped once and the current scope level is decremented. The current level can be the update display top pointer too.

This technique has the advantages of the simpler table-of-stacks technique but, additionally, it is more efficient in handling block exit.

8.3.2. Statement Labels

In many languages (for example, Algol 60, PL/I, and C, but *not* Pascal), a label is considered declared when it appears attached to a statement. There is no label X declaration as in Pascal to indicate that label X's scope must be in the scope of the label declaration.

For example, the following is a legal block in Algol 60:

```
begin
   goto LBL;      {use of LBL}
   I:=I+15;
 LBL: I:=I+1;      {labeled statement—becomes LBL's declaration}
 end;
```

The usual scope rules apply to labels: the scope of a label is the innermost block that contains the labeled statement. Thus, in this program segment, LBL's scope is the fragment within the begin-end pair.

To handle Algol labels, we assign one of the following three attributes to each statement label:

D: declared only (no reference)
R: referenced at least once, but undeclared
DR: declared, and referenced at least once

We say that a label is *declared* when it has appeared as attached to some statement. State D applies to a declared label, but one that has not yet appeared in a GOTO. State R applies to a label that has appeared in a GOTO, but not as a statement label. State DR applies to a label that has appeared both ways.

The compiler then can detect a multiple declaration of a label—when a declaration is seen, state D or DR indicates that it has been previously declared, which is an error.

At the end of a block, the compiler can detect either of the following conditions, which deserve to be reported as a warning:

- R: a GOTO, but no declaration within the block (*error*).

- D: a declaration, but no use within the block (*warning*).

State R would be a *warning,* because a GOTO within a block that branches to a label in a covering block is legal. Hence, the target of the GOTO may appear later in the source, in a covering block. In Pascal, state R would be an *error,* because the label declaration specifies the block in which a labeled statement must appear.

We can then implement the label states as follows, for these scope rules:

- *Block entry:* As usual.

- *Block exit:* Scan the current stack scope for the label attributes, noting the errors and warnings as before. However, there is a complication with an R attribute, as noted. The next section deals with the complication.

- *Statement label:* If the label is not in the symbol table, then enter it with attribute D. If it is in the symbol table, it must be a label. Then, if its state is DR or D, we have a multiply declared label—an error. If R, this appearance is legal, and the attribute must be changed to DR.

- *Reference:* Here, the label appears in a GOTO. If the label is not in the symbol table, then enter it with attribute R. If it is in the symbol table, it must be a label. Any of the three states is legal; however, attribute D is changed to DR, whereas attributes R and DR are unchanged.

Filling In Forward Branch Addresses

When a label is changed from state R to DR, all previously translated GOTO's to it must be altered to point to this spot in the program. These are called *forward branches,* because they cause execution to jump forward in the program listing. At the time each is translated, the target address is not known and so must be left unfilled. The operation of filling in one of these addresses later is often called a *backpatch* or *fixup.*

If this pass is generating machine code, this will be accomplished by putting the actual address of the instruction about to be generated into the already generated GOTO instructions. Otherwise, a pointer to the AST node about to be generated is required, and it will have to be put into all AST nodes for the GOTO's. In either case, the pointer value required is now known for the first time.

We must also have a way of finding the GOTO's to be filled in. The classical method is to put them all on a linked list and put the root of the list in an attribute field of the symbol table entry for a label in state R. Because the target address fields of the branches contain no values, they can be used to hold the link pointers for this list.

More problems arise if the machine does not have sufficient memory to hold all its code. A great advantage of branches the scopes of which are restricted to a single procedure is that only sufficient space for one procedure's code is needed. What can be done otherwise? We can defer all branch-location and procedure-call fixups to link time. A table of fixup locations then will be emitted, which the linker can pick up and use to fix references. This assumes that the linker is a sufficiently small program that all the code can be held in memory.

Internal Labels

If we are constructing links between AST nodes for branch addresses, the whole process will have to be repeated in much the same way for forward branches when machine code finally is generated. To avoid this duplication, it is sometimes convenient instead simply to replace the source-program labels by a compiler-generated series of internal labels.

These can be just a series of integers, with a new value generated each time an internal label is needed. The AST node for a GOTO will then contain one of these internal labels. A label in the source program will be translated into a special AST node the operation of which means "define label"; the node also contains an internal label.

All the compiler is doing now is translating source-program labels into internal labels. However, the internal labels have the important property that they are globally unique. That is, no block-structured symbol table mechanism is required to associate references with declarations. Also, because the internal labels are numbered compactly, it is possible to construct a table of them in a later pass, which can be accessed directly using the label itself as a subscript to the table. This avoids the problems associated with table search techniques.

This technique also may help if optimization is to be done, because it is often necessary to determine whether a statement is the target of a branch. The explicit "define label" nodes convey this information to the optimizer conveniently.

A Complication with Algol Statement Labels

Under the Algol scope rules, a GOTO in one block can refer to a statement label anywhere within a covering block, so a transfer from within some nesting level can occur to outside the block.

Thus, consider the following program fragment:

```
{1}  begin  {start of block B1}
{2}    begin  {start of block B2}
{3}      goto L1;
              .
              .
{4}    end;    {end of block B2}
{5}  L1: ...
{6}  end;      {end of block B1}
```

When the compiler encounters statement 3, which contains the first appearance of the statement label L1, L1 must go into the symbol table. In the absence (so far) of any other information, it is placed in the block B2 scope. At the end of block B2 (statement 4), the declaration of L1 has not yet appeared. Under Algol scope rules, the label need not be in block B2—it can be in some covering block. This causes a problem for the compiler on reaching statement 4. An extension to the block exit mechanism is needed to deal with this situation.

We need some means of moving the L1 attribute from the block B2 scope into the block B1 scope. This may have to be repeated at the end of block B1, if the label L1 has not yet been declared, until the end of the program is reached, if necessary. Only then can the compiler conclude that label L1 is undeclared. In this way, label L1 is "handed down" through the covering blocks until its declaring block is found, or until the end of the program is reached.

When the stack-of-symbol-tables technique is used, moving entries for R state labels is relatively easy. The entries do not need to be deleted from the inner block's table, because it is about to be discarded anyway. It is necessary only to insert a copy of the entry into the next outer block's table, using the usual insertion algorithm for the table-search method in use.

When one of the table-of-stacks strategies is used, moving a label entry is even easier. All that is required is to decrement the scope level number associated with the top set of attributes on the stack by one.

A further complication arises because of the possibility that a label may be declared in an outer block *before* the inner block. Consider this example:

```
{1}  begin  {start of block B1}
{2}  L1: ...
{3}    begin  {start of block B2}
{4}      goto L1;
              .
              .
```

```
{5}    end;    {end of block B2}
{6}  end;     {end of block B1}
```

Here, when the GOTO in line 4 is translated, L1 is already declared in B1. However, we do not know at this time whether there also will be a declaration of L1 later inside B2. If so, then it will be the target of the GOTO; otherwise, the L1 of line 2 is the target.

To translate such cases, the rules for handling references and declarations of labels must be modified slightly so that only the innermost scope is ever considered. In this way, line 4 in the example will create a new label in the symbol table for B2, with state R.

The rule for moving labels in state R out one scope at block exit time also must be altered. It is possible that the label entry to be moved out is for a name already present in the outer scope. We can handle this by treating each leftover label in state R at the end of B2 exactly as if it were a reference local to B1.

8.4. Name Search Algorithms

We now consider the problem of locating efficiently a literal string representing a symbol in a symbol table. Efficiency of symbol searching is important to the performance of a compiler because a typical source program contains large numbers of symbols appearing in essentially random order.

We mentioned that a *name table* provides an association between a set of identifiers, or names, and some attributes. The *access* system for a name table should provide some or all of the following functions:

1. *Declaration:* given a name and a scope, complain if the name already appears in the table within the scope. Then add the name to the table, whether already there or not, with its attributes.

2. *Use:* given a name, locate it with its attributes. Complain if not found. The name located should be the appropriate one for the scope, although several entries with the same name may exist.

3. *Entry:* on entering a scope, mark the table such that all subsequent new entries are known to belong to the new scope.

4. *Exit:* on exiting from a scope, remove all name–attribute pairs belonging to that scope from the table.

We shall discuss four access methods—*linear, binary, tree,* and *hash*—and evaluate their merit with respect to the four functions listed. Of these, the hash method is the most efficient, but does not yield a sorted name list. The tree method is easy to write in Pascal, and has the advantage of yielding a sorted list of identifiers, but is often less efficient.

Efficiency

Efficiency is important to compiler performance because so much of a typical source file consists of names. Each name must be located in the name table by a search process. The name table will grow as more names appear in declarations. Memory allocation and retrieval also may be a consideration, especially for small machines and a block-structured language.

The total declaration time t_D for a program usually will be different from the total reference time t_R for the following reasons:

1. The current scope is being built when translating declarations, whereas it is essentially complete when translating references. (The truth of this assertion depends on the language. We are assuming Pascal declaration rules for this discussion.)

2. If the source program is free of declaration errors, an identifier will not be in the table for a declaration search, but will be in the table for a reference search.

3. A reference search may span the entire table, whereas a declaration search spans only the current scope. The difference in search-time also is influenced by the usage patterns of identifiers. The most heavily used identifiers usually are locals, and the next most heavily used identifiers are globals (block level zero).

4. A given identifier is declared once, but may be referenced several times in its block.

To make reasonably meaningful comparisons among the name-access methods, we will develop "decl" and "ref" average times separately and make reasonable assumptions about the remaining factors. In section 8.4.5, we compare the net access times of the four methods and show there that the hash access method is superior to the others in access time.

8.4.1. Linear Access

The linear-access method, the simplest of the four access methods, is illustrated in figure 8.6. The program is the same as used in the example figures before. When translating a declaration, a new name is added to the name table. The names are unordered, so a search requires a comparison with each of the names in some region of the pointer table.

A variation of the stack-of-tables technique is used here to account for the block structure. The entries of each table are physically contiguous. Furthermore, only the top table can be growing. This means that all the logically separate tables for the various active blocks can share the same array of table entries. This array works like a stack.

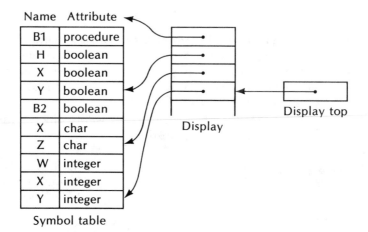

Symbol table

Figure 8.6. Linear access, block-structured symbol table.

The *display* is a stack of pointers that mark the beginning of each block's table. The top pointer of the display is the stack pointer for the symbol table. This mark also could be carried in other ways; for example, by a dedicated bit in each entry of the symbol table.

When translating a declaration, we must make a search through just the present scope. If the scope contains n names, then the search time is:

$$kn$$

where k is some unit comparison time. On each declaration, another name is added to the end of the innermost table, increasing n. If N' names are declared, then the net declaration time for one block is:

$$t_D = \sum_{i=1}^{N'} ki = kN'(N' - 1)/2$$

When translating a reference, the search must proceed through the tables for all blocks. A simple search loop from top to bottom that ignores the boundaries between the logically separate symbol tables will work.

The net reference time per block depends on the total number of active identifiers N in the table and on the usage pattern. Assume that references are distributed uniformly among the covering blocks and the current block. We know only that $N \geq N'$ and that each referenced identifier will be in the table (very nearly—barring programs with a large number of undeclared identifiers). The average access time per identifier will be:

$$kN/2$$

because we need scan only halfway through the table to find a given identifier (some will be near the top, some near the bottom of the identifier stack).

We also need the average number of references per declaration, b; then, given N' identifiers in the block, we have bN' references total, for a net reference time per block of:

$$t_R = kbNN'/2$$

Block entry consists of duplicating the top pointer of the display, thus pushing a new, empty table onto the symbol table stack. Block exit requires popping all entries for the current block off the symbol table, and one pointer off the display. Actually, the latter step will accomplish the former as a side-effect. The block entry and block exit times are both small and independent of the number of identifiers.

If a sorted symbol table listing is required at the end of a block, the sort may be applied to the current scope of the pointer stack. Many sort algorithms require $n(\log_2 n)$ operations to sort n items; hence, the sort requires a net time of:

$$kN'(\log_2 N')$$

8.4.2. Binary Access

A binary search requires that the identifiers in a single table be sorted. The search for an identifier always looks at the middle of some contiguous region of the table. The identifier being sought must be in this region if it is present at all. Initially, the region is the entire table. A comparison with the center identifier in the region then indicates which of the two region halves should be considered for the next region. This process is repeated on each half until only one identifier is left—which may or may not match the searched-for identifier. The process can terminate earlier if the middle entry of some larger region happens to be the one we want.

If N identifiers exist in the table, then $(\log_2 N)$ comparisons are needed to locate an identifier, or determine that it does not exist in the table.

Again, the stack-of-symbol-tables technique is used, with the tables all sharing a single array, as they do in a linear search. Block entry and block exit are handled as before and require only constant time. Figure 8.7 shows this form of table for the Pascal program of figure 8.3.

A *declaration* requires a search of the top scope's table only, followed by a sorted insertion. The insertion requires moving half the table down, on the average, to make room for the new entry. Its location is clear from the search result. The move operation per item inserted is:

$$a + k'n/2$$

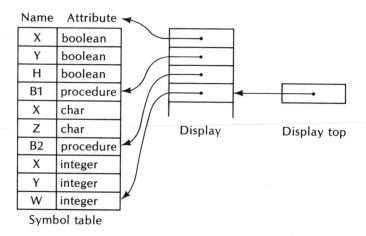

Symbol table

Figure 8.7.   Binary access, block-structured symbol table.

where a is some move overhead time and k' is the time per unit move. Many computers have a fast move instruction that can carry out this operation, so that a and k' will be fairly small numbers.

The net time for a set of N declarations is then:

$$\sum_{n=1}^{N} (a + k'n/2) = aN + k'N(N - 1)/4$$

which must be added to the search and comparison times for the declarations, given by:

$$\text{Search time} = k(\sum_{n=1}^{N} (\log_2(n) + 1)) \sim kN(\log_2(N) + 1)$$

On a reference, we must perform a binary search of each table, starting with the innermost table. The depth of nesting eventually does not continue to increase with the length of the program being compiled. The net reference time therefore is approximately:

$$t_R \sim kN'(\log_2(N'))/2$$

Although the reference time is proportional to the unit comparison time k, it increases much more slowly with N' than for the linear-search method and will be smaller, unless blocks are typically small and global references infrequent.

A sorted symbol table report for a single scope is easy to generate, because all the symbols are in order.

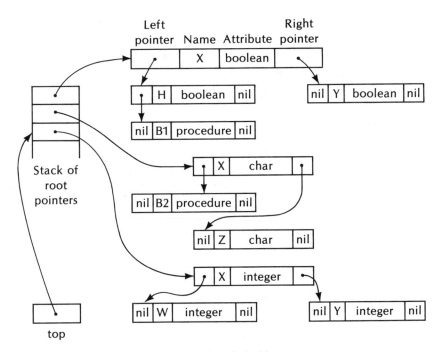

Figure 8.8.   Tree access, block-structured symbol table.

8.4.3. Tree Access

Figure 8.8 illustrates the tree-access method for the Pascal program of figure 8.3. When translating a declaration, a new tree node is created, consisting of a *left* and a *right* pointer pair, along with an identifier string element. The left and right pointers constitute a binary tree description. Each node has no children, a left child, a right child, or both a right and a left child; *nil* indicates no child. The tree is built so that, in the collating sequence, all identifiers in the entire left subtree are less than the identifier in the root and all the identifiers in the entire right subtree are greater. This allows a search step to reject half of the unexplored part of the tree in one comparison, much as a binary search rejects half of its unsearched region in each step.

In placing a new identifier in the tree, we search the tree exactly as if looking for an identifier that is already present. If the name is absent, the search terminates at some nil pointer. We create a new node and make it the new child at this nil pointer. We put the new identifier and nil left and right pointers into the new node. This preserves the subtree ordering property described.

Notice that the order in which identifiers are inserted affects the shape of the tree; most important, the degree of *balance* is influenced. When left and right subtrees contain almost the same number (within one) of nodes, the tree is

balanced. If the identifiers happen to be inserted in alphabetical order, the resulting tree will have all left pointers nil and searching will degenerate to linear
search of a linked list, where the right pointers are the links. Fortunately, most
programs introduce identifiers in sufficiently random fashion that the resulting
trees are only mildly unbalanced. These are sometimes called *unbalanced binary
trees*.

For example, consider a new identifier K. Then K $<$ X so we move left and
compare K with H. Now K $>$ H, and H has no right child, so K goes into H's
right child position. The new K entry has empty left and right children.

The following Pascal function TENTRY implements a tree symbol table entry
function—the symbol SYM is either found in the tree or added to it. In either
case, a pointer to the new tree node is returned. The root of the tree is carried by
a global pointer TREE, which is initially nil. When TENTRY is called with the
nil pointer, the pointer is set to a new symbol table entry. A new entry also is
generated on a nil LEFT or RIGHT pointer.

```
type SYMTREEP= ↑symtree;
     SYMTREE= record
                   LEFT, RIGHT: symtreep;
                   SYMB: symbol;
                   {other attributes}
              end;
var TREE: symtreep;    {set to NIL initially}

function NEWENTRY(SYM: symbol): symtreep;
  var NE: symtreep;
begin  {allocate a new entry, return a pointer to it}
  new(ne);
  newentry:=ne;
  with ne↑ do
  begin
    left:=nil;
    right:=nil;
    symb:=sym;
  end
end;

function TENTRY(var ROOT: symtreep; SYM: symbol): symtreep;
begin  {either find or link a new entry in symbol table}
  if root=nil then
  begin
    root:=newentry(sym);
    tentry:=root;
  end
  else
   with root↑ do
   begin
     if sym=symb then tentry:=root
     else
     if sym<symb then tentry:=tentry(left, sym)
     else
     tentry:=tentry(right, sym)
   end
end;
```

The average declaration time is $k(\log_2 N)$ plus a small, fixed time to add the tree node fields. We do not have to move a list of entries as we did with the binary method, so we appear to have a time reduction. In the binary search, the searching always is balanced.

The average use time is $k(\log_2 N)/2$; an identifier will be found halfway down the tree on the average.

As the trees become more unbalanced, insertion and search perform more like linear search. Algorithms that preserve perfect balance exist for insertion into severely unbalanced trees. These algorithms can be used to ensure good search performance. The asymptotic performance of the algorithms is no worse than the unbalanced insert, but the constant is larger. For compiler symbol tables, keeping the trees perfectly balanced is of doubtful worth; they are usually nearly balanced anyway.

The stack-of-tables technique is highly appropriate for tree searching. Each table is represented by just a root pointer to the root of a tree; the stack of tables is just a stack of pointers. Block entry consists of pushing a nil pointer onto this stack. Block exit consists of popping a pointer and discarding the tree to which it points. It may be necessary to reclaim the discarded tree nodes; the obvious method requires a walk through them all. It also is possible to maintain a free "list" as a tree, but this in general requires free tree insertion and deletion operations, which take $k(\log_2 N)$ time. Also, the lifetimes of all tree nodes is first-in-first-out, so wholesale contiguous deallocation is possible, if tree nodes do not share space with other kinds of objects with other lifetimes.

Binary tree tables have the advantage that space is allocated dynamically as new declarations are translated. They also make it easy to save the entries for one scope outside the entire symbol table data structure. This is needed for records in Pascal and other similar language structures. Section 8.8.1 discusses this requirement.

An important disadvantage of binary tree tables is that a large amount of extra space is consumed by the left and right pointers. Every identifier requires two of these. Furthermore, a brief analysis of the numbers of nodes and pointers will show that, in every binary tree, almost exactly half of the pointers must be nil.

An inorder tree walk yields a sorted list for a single scope.

8.4.4. Hash Access

The hash-access method is illustrated in figure 8.9. A *hash function* is defined on the class of identifiers; this function maps every identifier into an integer between one and h, where h is a fixed hash table size. Thus, in figure 8.9, X maps to three, Y and H map to four, and Z and W map to one. It is not essential that the hash function map every identifier to a distinct integer (indeed, this is impossible if the number of identifiers is greater than h), but it should provide a reasonably random and uniform mapping. We call the hash function value for some identifier its *hash code*.

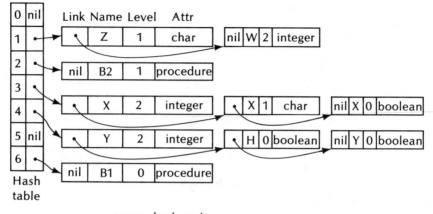

Figure 8.9. Hash access, block-structured symbol table.

The scheme we present is an example of the table-of-stacks technique for handling nested scopes. Given the hash code of an identifier, we enter the hash table directly, using the hash code as an index. Because several identifiers can have the same hash code, they all must be accessible from this hash table entry. When this occurs, it is called a *collision*. The method of finding the right identifier among those that collide is called the *secondary-search* method. We shall choose to collect all colliding identifiers in a linear linked list, rooted at the hash table entry. The secondary-search method is then a linear search of this list.

When inserting a new identifier, we add its new list node at the head of its hash entry's list. A single list, rooted at a particular hash table entry, may thus contain several identifiers with the same hash code. It may also contain several nodes for the same identifier, if it is declared in several active blocks. This list is in fact the combination of the stack and the secondary search list for collisions at this hash table entry.

Note that a declaration search need go down a list only until the present scope is terminated. A reference search must follow a list to its end, if necessary, because an identifier may be in any scope.

The declaration time for a name is kN/h. On the average, each hash list contains N/h names from the current scope, and we must search one of them completely to establish that the name is missing.

The use time is kN'/(2h), because on the average we hit the identifier halfway down a list. Note that these times are essentially linear search times, reduced by a factor of h, the number of hash buckets.

Some overhead is incurred in computing the hash function, but it can be kept small by using a simple hash algorithm.

The block entry time is negligible. The block exit time is appreciable. We must search down all lists of the hash table entries, and delete nodes for the scope level being left. However, because the names are encountered last-in-first-out, only the present scope name list entries are scanned. Those deeper in the lists can be ignored.

The block exit time can be greatly improved by using the update stack technique; the linked lists will contain only one entry for each identifier. There still may be several nodes for different identifiers that collide here. If the identifier is declared in several active scopes, only the current meaning will be in its list node. The others will be on the update stack. The update stack entries will have to point to list nodes, where they are to be reinstated on the appropriate block exit.

The names are not sorted in this scheme, so a sort algorithm must be applied to the table to list the symbols alphabetically. If this is to be done for each block exited, the entries or pointers to them will have to be copied somewhere else and sorted there, because the entries for all scopes are together in the hash table. The hash table could be conveniently sorted once at the end of compilation for a single composite list, but by then the attributes of many identifiers would be gone.

Bounded Table Hash Access

Sometimes we can guarantee that the number of symbols entered is less than or equal to h. If so, we do not need the secondary lists; we can simply apply a *rehash* algorithm repeatedly until we find an empty cell in the hash table. Morris [1968] has shown that this algorithm is superior in performance to a hash-list method.

The rehash method is useful for tables with a fixed number of entries; for example, a table of reserved words for a compiler or a table of assembler mnemonics. However, it is usually unnecessary to maintain two distinct name tables—the reserved names can be accessed by the same algorithm as used for the user identifiers. Their reserved status can be inferred from their position in the table or recorded in an attribute field.

An optimal strategy for such a symbol table, from Morris [1968], is expressed by the following Pascal program:

```
var C, R: integer;
    IDENT: array [1..n] of char;  {identifier}
    .HASHTAB: array [0..h] of integer;  {hash table}
```

```
function RAND: integer;
begin
    r:=(r*5) mod (h*4);   {h is hash table size}
    rand:=r div 4;
end;

{the hash access algorithm starts here}
function FIND_IDENT: boolean;
    var MORE: boolean;
begin
    c:=hashit(ident);    {returns a hash code}
    r:=c;
    more:=true;
    find_ident:=false;

    while more and (hashtab(c)<>nil) do
    begin
      if nametab[hashtab[c]]=ident then
      begin
        more:=false;
        find_ident:=true;
      end
      else
        c:=(c + rand) mod (h);   {try another hash code}
    end
end;
```

The average number of probes required to locate an item known to be in the table is the same as the number of probes required to enter the item, because the same path of probing is followed in both cases. Morris shows that the average number of probes is approximately:

$$E \sim - (1/\alpha) \log (1 - \alpha)$$

where $\alpha = N/h$ is called the *load factor*. N is the size of the table and h is the number of hash buckets. Some sample values of E are given in the following table:

Load Factor α	E
0.1	1.05
0.5	1.39
0.75	1.83
0.90	2.56

Deletion of entries made using this scheme is a troublesome process. One cannot simply mark an entry as empty in order to delete it, because other entries may have collided at that place and they would become unreachable.

Hash Functions

We now consider the problem of a suitable hash function. We need a simple algorithm that will map a class of commonly used identifiers as uniformly as possible into an interval 0..h-1, where the hash table contains h buckets.

Knuth [1973] has shown that an effective hash function on some key K is simply a modulo h division or multiplication. The key K must be some integer, possibly formed from a few characters in the identifier by concatenation. Then:

$$h(K) = K \bmod M,$$

where M should be a prime number, yields a reasonably random hash code. Values of M that divide $r^k + a$, or $r^k - a$, where k and a are small numbers and r is the radix of the alphabetic character set (usually 64, 256, or 100, depending on the machine), should be avoided.

Suppose we have 32-bit integer arithmetic. Then we can form a hash code from an identifier string by the following algorithm:

```
const LEN= 16;
      HASHSIZE= 177;   {or whatever}
type IDTYPE= packed array [0..len] of char;

function HASHIT(var STR: idtype): integer;
  var K, H: integer;
begin
  k:=0;
  h:=0;
  while k<=len-3 do begin
    h:=h + 65536*ord(str[k+2]) + 256*ord(str[k+1]) +
           ord(str[k]);
    k:=k+3;
    end;
  hashit:=k mod hashsize;
  end;
```

The following table shows the results of an experiment with a program containing 623 identifiers and a hash table with 81 buckets:

Chain Length L	Number of Chains with Length L
0	0
0/4	9
5/9	54
10/14	17
15/19	1
>19	0

The chain lengths are quite uniform. The dominant chain length is close to the expected average, 7.7, and there are no unused chains or chains of unusually large size.

8.4.5. Comparison of Access Methods

The four access methods described can be compared through their required space or time. In comparing space, we note that all four require the same identifier, scope, and pointer space. We therefore compare the space required in addition to this:

- Linear: zero

- Binary: zero

- Tree: 2 * N, where N = number of table symbols

- Hash: h + N

A comparison of access times is somewhat more difficult. We have previously developed formulas for entry, exit, declaration, and reference (use) times. These formulas are summarized in the next table.

Summary of Access Times

	Entry	Exit	Declaration	Use
Linear	10	10	$25 * N' * (N' - 1)$	$25 * N^2$
Binary	10	$16 * N$	$25 * N' * (\log(N') - 1)$	$25 * N * \log(N)$ $+ 5 * N$ $+ k' * N * (N - 1)/2$
Tree	10	$8 * N$	$35 * N' * (\log(N') - 1)$	$35 * N * \log(N)$
Hash	10	$8 * N'$	$25 * N' * (N' - 1)/h$	$25 * N^2/h$

Each of the table entries represents some net access time, in arbitrary units, for a typical program block. N is the number of identifier declarations in the block, and N' the number of identifier references. Parameter h is the number of hash buckets. The remaining factors all have been estimated on the basis of our experience. For example, the use time for tree access is similar to that for a binary sort, except that the factor (35) is larger because of tree imbalance. The binary sort exit time is larger than a tree exit time on account of the pointer table compression required.

We next fold these time estimates into the following set of frequencies, given by McKeeman [1974b]. These are based on measurements of a number of XPL (block-structured) programs.

f1, entry	f2, exit	f3, decl	f4, use
10	10	100	700

We then may compute an average unit access time, through the following averaging formula:

Time = (f1 * entry + f2 * exit + f3 * decl + f4 * use)/(f1 + f2 + f3 + f4)

We assume that N' = N/5; that is, for every identifier declared in the current scope, there are four others in covering scopes in the symbol table. (This number may be too large for an average program, but it does not greatly affect our conclusions.) We also assume that the number of hash buckets h is 100.

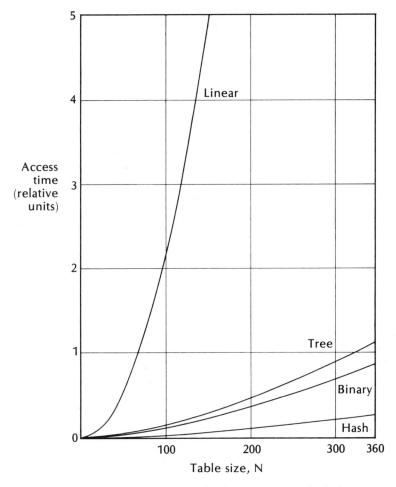

Figure 8.10.   Comparative access times for the four access methods: linear, tree, binary, and hash, as a function of table size.

   The graph in figure 8.10 shows the net time as a function of N in the range one through 360. Nearly all the hash buckets must be full at N = 360, yet the hash method remains superior to the others far beyond this N. In fact, the hash and binary methods have about the same time at N = 1200: binary is 288, hash is 279. At N = 1200, the average hash chain is 12 symbols long, requiring about 12 comparisons. However, 1200 is approximately 2^{10}, so the binary method also requires about 11 comparisons.
   For N > 1200, the binary method is the most efficient; however, the efficiency of the hash method increases with the number of hash buckets h, so that a larger h might be justified for such a large string table.

The tree method is consistently poorer than the binary method; note that it also requires more storage. The linear access is orders of magnitude more costly in time than any of the other three. At only 100 symbols, linear access requires 100 times the search time as hash access. (This factor of 100 is the number of hash buckets.)

Summary of Access Methods

The most efficient access method, by time comparison, is the hash access method. It requires a function that maps an identifier into a finite range of integers 1 to $h - 1$ in a uniform manner. The hash code resulting from the mapping is then used to isolate the identifier to one of h separate linear chains of identifiers. The desired identifier is found by a linear search along that chain. Although the binary and tree search methods result in a sorted table, convenient for a symbol table listing, this apparent advantage is outweighed by the larger overhead in declaration and reference times.

8.5. Symbol Tables in Multipass Compilers

When a compiler is designed with multiple passes, it usually is necessary for many or all of the passes to have access to the symbol table. Obviously, symbol table searching can become complicated when string storage, block structure, and searching are all handled. The data structures require significant space and the algorithms can be time-consuming. We would like to avoid repeating all this in each pass.

Fortunately, this is quite easy. The first pass will have to implement all the mechanisms we have discussed, because it has only source program names to use in locating symbol table entries. However, we can easily design the intermediate form of the source program so that names are replaced by some form of pointers to symbol table entries. The later passes can use these to locate immediately the right set of attributes, with no searching at all.

This also means that all parts of the symbol table that were necessary for searching no longer will be needed. All that remains is a collection of independent entries that contain attributes but show no structural relationships to one another.

The pointers can be true pointers to attribute objects created during the first pass and remaining in memory from pass to pass. They also can be subscripts to an array of attribute entries, again remaining in memory. Alternatively, the attribute entries can be maintained on a random access file and brought in only when needed. In this case, the pointers would be file addresses.

Instead of putting pointers to attribute entries in the intermediate form of the source program, we could just place copies of some attribute values directly into the intermediate form, in place of references to source program names. This is called *distributing* the attributes. This will work for all cases in which it is not necessary in a later pass to use the attribute entry to communicate newly generated information from one occurrence of an identifier to another.

It is not necessary to insert a complete set of attributes in place of every reference. Instead, only those attributes that will be needed at this point by later passes need be distributed. The exact set required can vary with the kind of reference and from pass to pass.

This technique tends to create considerably larger intermediate forms of the program. However, it also avoids random access to the attribute entries. If memory is limited, it may be considerably more efficient to process a large intermediate form sequentially than a smaller intermediate form randomly. (Here we must count the attribute entries themselves as part of the intermediate form.)

It may be possible to divide responsibility for the symbol table processing steps we have discussed among two or more passes. A reasonable division is to have the pass that does lexical scanning handle string storage and name searching, whereas some later pass takes care of nested scopes. We shall assume a design in which the first pass does only lexical scanning; the second does only parsing. No symbol table is needed. The third pass takes care of nested scopes.

In this technique, the scanner treats all occurrences of the same identifier as equivalent, even though they may belong to different blocks. The identifiers are simply replaced by a compactly numbered series of integer values. We will call each such integer value a *spelling index*. The same identifier always is replaced by the same spelling index, whenever it occurs.

This requires a method of string storage and a single symbol table. No distinction is made between declarations and references. In fact, not until parsing has been done is such a distinction even possible. When an identifier is scanned, the table is searched. If the name is absent, it is inserted with a newly generated spelling index. This spelling index also is inserted into the intermediate form of the program, in place of the identifier. If the name already is present in the table, then the spelling index from the table entry is used. Only a single table is required, so an efficient hash search can be used.

The parser will simply forward spelling indexes with identifiers. In the third pass, a spelling index can be used simply as a subscript to a table. This avoids searching altogether. To exploit this saving, it is necessary to have a single table in the second pass. One of the table-of-stacks techniques can be used, with indexing replacing the search operations on the table.

When a small number such as a spelling index is used to select a table entry, all entries are automatically present in the table, whether or not their indexes have been used. Thus, it is necessary to initialize all table entries to some special ''undefined'' or ''absent'' value and to check for this value when accessing the table.

The third pass, which does the block-structured symbol table manipulation, could in turn translate spelling indexes into yet another compactly numbered series of integers, with the property that each is globally unique. These can then be used again in subsequent passes as subscripts to a table of attribute entries.

8.6. The QPARSER Symbol Table System

The QPARSER symbol table system uses hashing. The hash chain is carried in the symbol table record declaration, as well as a level number. The LEVEL of a name is its nesting depth, starting with zero for a global and increasing with depth.

The symbol table record declaration is as follows:

```
const
  HASHSIZE= 67;    {hash table size — prime number!}
  HLIMIT= 66;      {limit in hash table}


type
  SYMBOL= packed array [1..maxtoklen] of char;
  SYMTYPE= (reserved, user, symerror, variable,
               proc, func, stlabel);
  SYMTABP= ↑symtabtype;
  SYMTABTYPE= record    {structure for <identifier>s and
                          keywords}
                  NEXT: symtabp;  {along hash chain}
                  LEVEL: int;
                  SYM: symbol;
                  case SYMT: symtype of
                    reserved: (TOKVAL: tokrange);
                    variable: (SADDR: int;
                               VTYPE: vtypes);
                    {other attributes}
              end;
  var
    SYMTAB: array [0..hlimit] of symtabp;
```

The hash table is SYMTAB, an array of pointers to SYMTABTYPE record structures. Each SYMTABTYPE carries a NEXT pointer to the next SYM-TABTYPE in a hash chain—see figure 8.9.

A new entry is allocated from the heap, then added to the table by attaching it to the head of the hash chain. These will belong to the most local scope; hence, they are to be first removed on a scope exit. There is no separate scope table, but the scope of an entry is designated by its LEVEL number. On a scope exit, we simply walk down through each chain until LEVEL is less than the current level; that entry then becomes the new chain head.

There are several different kinds of name in Pascal, requiring a few different tags and symbol table attributes. The tag *reserved* is used for all the reserved words: IF, THEN, WHILE, and so on. These are picked up by the lexical analyzer, which assumes that an ordinary identifier is being scanned. It then calls MAKESYM (discussed later) either to fetch or to place the name in the symbol table. The analyzer will detect whether the name is a reserved word and, if it is, will return its token number from the table attribute TOKVAL.

The default attribute is USER, which means that the name has not been declared anywhere. Other attributes stem from needs in the language. A variable is anything declared in a VAR. A proc is a procedure, a func is a function, and a stlabel is a statement label used in a GOTO somewhere.

The QPARSER Hash Function

The hashing function is as follows:

```
function HASHIT(FSYM: symbol): int;
begin
  hashit:=(128*(ord(fsym[1])+ord(fsym[3])) +
          ord(fsym[2])+ord(fsym[4])) mod hashsize;
end;
```

Because FSYM is a packed array of char, its individual characters can be accessed. We use the ORD function to convert each character to a number, then combine the numbers and form the hash code by a modulo hashsize. This will be a suitable index into SYMTAB.

Access Functions

Three access functions are provided, as follows:

```
function FINDSYM(FSYM: symbol): symtabp;
  label 99;
  var SP: symtabp;
begin  {Finds a symbol, returning NIL if not there}
    {Use this for variable references, calling error if
       it returns NIL}
  sp:=symtab[hashit(fsym)];
  while sp<>nil do
  with sp↑ do
  begin  {walk down the hash chain}
    if sym=fsym then
    begin
      findsym:=sp;
      goto 99;
    end;
    sp:=next;
  end;
  findsym:=nil;
99:
end;
```

FINDSYM merely looks for a name in SYMTAB, and returns NIL if it is not there. This is useful in a variable reference, because we do not always want to create a new entry if we cannot find the name. If an entry is found, FINDSYM returns a pointer to the SYMTABTYPE record structure. Note that Pascal supports a comparison of two packed arrays of char of the same type:

```
function MAKESYM(FSYM: symbol; SYT: symtype; LEV: int): symtabp;
   label 99;
   var SP: symtabp;
       HX: int;
begin  {this returns a symbol entry if there;
          makes a new one if not}
     {Useful for FORTRAN-style variable declaration — declare
        name on first appearance, whether in a declaration or not}
   hx:=hashit(fsym);
   sp:=symtab[hx];
   while sp<>nil do
   with sp↑ do
   begin
     if sym=fsym then
     begin
       makesym:=sp;
       goto 99;
     end;
     sp:=next;
   end;
   new(sp);  {need a new one if here}
   with sp↑ do
   begin  {put at the head of the hash list}
     sym:=fsym;
     symt:=syt;
     next:=symtab[hx];
     symtab[hx]:=sp;
     level:=lev;
   end;
   makesym:=sp;
99:
end;
```

MAKESYM is similar to FINDSYM, except that it will create an entry for the symbol if one cannot be found. It will never return NIL. SYT is the symbol's tag: variable, proc, and so on. LEV is the LEVEL for the symbol. In QPARSER, the lexical analyzer will call MAKESYM automatically on every identifier, so that a pointer to some symbol table structure is returned as an identifier.

```
function FORCESYM(FSYM: symbol; SYT: symtype; LEV: int): symtabp;
   var SP: symtabp;
       HX: int;
begin  {this forces a new symbol entry}
     {Use this for declarations when you intend to
        cover a previous declaration with the same name}
   hx:=hashit(fsym);
   new(sp);
   with sp↑ do
   begin  {put at the head of the hash list}
     sym:=fsym;
     symt:=syt;
     next:=symtab[hx];
     symtab[hx]:=sp;
```

```
    level:=lev;
  end;
  forcesym:=sp;
end;
```

FORCESYM always will create a new entry, whether or not one is already there. The new entry will be at the head of its hash chain, covering up a similar name deeper in the chain.

Pascal Declarations

A Pascal name is declared by first calling MAKESYM. If this function made a new name, it will carry the tag user, and it is therefore safe to set its attributes. Note that MAKESYM is called automatically by the lexical analyzer in any case.

If MAKESYM found an existing name, it will be a conflict with the attempted declaration or it will not, depending on the implementation rules. Under Pascal rules, the new declaration should override a previous one if the previous one is at a lower level. Hence, we complain if the existing name is at the same level, and call FORCESYM if at a different level. Note that FORCESYM will create a new entry without searching for an existing one.

Pascal References

A variable reference is easy. The lexical analyzer calls MAKESYM; hence, the symbol table structure is available in the semantics stack under the ident tag. However, because Pascal variables must be predeclared, it is important to check the identifier's tag: user means it has not been declared.

Pascal Scope Exit

The following procedure, CLEARSYM, is called on a scope exit. It walks through each hash chain until it finds a LEVEL that is less than the CLEVEL passed to the procedure. That object is then made the head of its hash chain by adjusting SYMTAB. Note that each object is disposed when it is found to be rejected.

The reserved words also are carried in the symbol table, at level -1. These are protected from accidental removal by a special clause in CLEARSYM.

```
procedure CLEARSYM(CLEVEL: int);
  label 1;
  var HX: int;
      SP, SPTEMP: symtabp;
begin  {Sets the symbol table pointers to not see everything
         at level >= CLEVEL.  Prepares for a RELEASE}
  if clevel<0 then clevel:=0;
     {Don't clear the reserved words—just in case}
  for hx:=0 to hlimit do
  begin
    sp:=symtab[hx];
```

```
    while sp<>nil do
    with sp↑ do
    begin
      if level<clevel then goto 1;
      sptemp:=sp;
      sp:=next;
      dispose(sptemp);
    end;
  1:
    symtab[hx]:=sp;
  end
end;
```

8.7. Data Objects and Their Static Representation

A *data object* is some entity associated with a name that comes into existence when the program that contains it is executed. It is carried by some memory field for the duration of its life, and it is operated on by various program instructions. A given object may carry a variety of different values during execution and may reside in physically different sections of memory at different times. Its key property is continuity; its value is preserved between accesses and is changed only through some assignment statement in the program. Its life may or may not end when the program control passes out of its identifier's scope. Some data objects are created initially and survive for the life of the program, whereas others survive only while program control remains in the static scope of its identifier.

A data object has an external and an internal structure. Externally, its structure is defined by its language declaration—for example, REAL or BYTE ARRAY. Internally, it is some field of binary information in memory, possibly scattered about in the available memory space.

To a compiler, a data object is an entry in a symbol table. It possesses a set of attributes, and they may include a prescription of its location in memory during execution. The location may even change within the object's scope—for example, the object may be assigned to one register initially, then shifted to another register later, and so on.

The operations on a data object implied by the source language are partially determined by its attributes and result in a certain sequence of emitted code that, when executed, affects the memory cells assigned to the data object.

The treatment of the data object associated with an identifier depends on the attributes assigned to the object through its declaration. In most computer systems, the internal form of each data object is some set of bytes that by itself provides no clue as to its purpose. It is the task of the compiler to associate meaning with every data object and to guarantee that the specifications of the program with respect to the data object are faithfully reflected in the sequence of machine code being generated.

8.7.1. Primitive Objects

A *primitive data object* is an object that is normally treated as a unit by the operations of the language. It usually cannot be subdivided by any operation, and its internal structure is undefined in many modern language definitions. The structure chosen for its representation for a particular target machine should, of course, reflect those structures that are processed most efficiently by the machine's instruction set. For example, if the machine supports a particular representation for a floating-point number in its hardware, it would be foolish to adopt a different representation in designing a compiler for that machine.

Each data object is internally encoded in some manner that depends on the object machine system and the programming language system. For example, the 16-bit binary number:

$$1110010100000010 \text{ or (octal) } 162402$$

can be interpreted in any of the following ways on an HP3000 computer:

1. As the memory reference instruction STB Q + 2, I (store a byte on the top of stack into a location marked by an indirect address located two words relative to the Q register).

2. As the "integer" −6910 (decimal form).

3. As the "logical" 58626 (decimal form).

4. As an indirect address, pointing to a location 6910 words offset from the contents of the program register, "PB".

5. As the pair of bytes (eight-bit data objects) 345 (octal) and 2. These bytes may be interpreted as the ASCII characters c and STX; for example, lower-case letter c and the special character STX.

One of these interpretations is selected during execution by an operation on the data. Thus the STB interpretation holds when that word is fetched into the instruction register and executed.

If the word is fetched and loaded in a data register, and then an "integer add" operation is executed, it is effectively interpreted as an "integer." If the operation is a "logical multiply," then it is interpreted as a "logical," and so forth.

Every computer has a set of definitions of the primitive data objects on which its instruction set is designed to operate. Matching the computer operations and data objects to those required by a source language is sometimes troublesome. For the sake of efficiency, as many of the machine operations as possible should be used for the compiled instructions; if a difference in specification exists, then the language operation must be simulated by a procedure call or a sequence of machine operations.

For most common languages, the common machine operations and language operations are arithmetic in character, making a match possible. However, different machines use different word lengths and representations, which affect the maximum range of numeric values. Some idea of the variety of number representation may be gained from the following examples.

1. On the IBM 1620, numbers are represented as a string of characters, representing decimal digits. Special marks are included for the representation of floating-point numbers, signs, and the end of a number, because numbers may be of different lengths.

2. On the IBM 360, numbers may be represented in a variety of forms. There is a set of binary integer forms, 16 and 32 bits in length, short and long binary floating-point numbers, and two decimal numbers (packed and unpacked). A small positive integer may be represented as a byte.

3. On the CDC 6000 series, only floating-point numbers 60 bits long are handled by the instruction set. The format is interesting, as there are representations for "infinity" and for "undefined." Integer multiply and divide is done with the floating-point hardware. The number format is one's complement, rather than the usual two's complement.

The representation of characters as an internal code is similarly nonstandard among the computer manufacturers. IBM has used EBCDIC, many smaller manufacturers use ASCII, and CDC uses its own kind of six-bit character code, called *display code,* for character representation. Even within one manufacturer and one standard code, some variations are found; for example, ASCII has different versions to reflect differences in foreign languages.

Printers, terminals, and other character-oriented devices also exhibit coding variations, even within a single manufacturer's product line.

Source Language Primitives

Now consider the source language. What are its specifications with regard to its primitive data objects? Let us consider some examples of source specifications.

1. ANS FORTRAN [Campbell, 1976] says this of the integer type and real type:

   An integer datum is always an exact representation of an integer value. It may assume a positive, negative, or zero value. It may assume only an integral value. An integer datum has one noncharacter storage unit in a storage sequence.

A real datum is a processor approximation to the value of a real number. It may assume a positive, negative, or zero value. A real datum has one noncharacter storage unit in a storage sequence.

Of characters, the Fortran standard [Campbell, 1976] states that "a character datum is a string of characters" and "a character datum has one character storage unit in a storage sequence for each character in the string." The internal form of a character is left unspecified. The standard only addresses the issue of connectedness of a set of characters that constitutes a string.

2. In Algol 60 [Naur, 1963], three primitive objects (integer, real, Boolean) are provided. Little is said about them except that integers and reals may be positive or negative numbers, and that Booleans may assume only the values TRUE and FALSE.

3. ISO Pascal [Pascal, 1983] recognizes four primitive objects: integer, real, char, and Boolean. The report says of integer that "The values shall be a subset of the whole numbers . . ." (section 6.4.2.2). Of real, the report says "The values shall be an implementation-defined subset of the real numbers . . . ."

We see that the structure of the primitive data objects is not specified in any of these languages, each of which is intended to be implemented on a variety of computers. The languages are also such that the internal details of primitive objects are not essential to an algorithm and should not be. If nothing in a program depends on the implementation details, then the program can be transported to several quite different computer systems. A modern language definition therefore is written to be as *machine-independent* as possible.

However, a program may yield different results on different systems, especially if it makes use of real numbers and the representation form of reals is different on the machines.

Also, a program that depends on the integer type may fail from a bounds violation on one machine and not on another through differences in supported maximum number range. ISO Pascal provides some functions to check the range of the generic integer type, but we suspect that few Pascal programs make use of them.

Compiler Implications

A compiler is implemented on some machine—its *host* machine—and has a particular *object* machine for which its target translation is directed. It usually is desirable that the compiler be as nearly machine-independent as the language, although it cannot be entirely so.

The characteristics of primitive data objects enter a compiler in several ways: (1) some choice of host data type must be made to handle conversion of literal constants from source to target form, (2) some section of the compiler must deal with conversion (if any) from host form of literal constant to the target form, and (3) if the compiler is to perform constant arithmetic, it must do so exactly as its target machine would do so, despite possible differences in arithmetic operations between host and target.

These tasks should be relegated to a few low-level procedures that can be easily modified as needed for the sake of portability. The bulk of the compiler algorithm should be indifferent to the internal representation details demanded by any one host machine.

Subrange Operations

Pascal permits integer subrange declarations such as:

```
var SR: 15..30;
```

which enables the compiler to reduce the memory space allocated for the variable—the range 15..30 can be carried in four bits. Access of the four-bit field usually will become more complicated, affecting run-time performance. With range checking enabled, the compiler easily can add instructions to check that the result of an arithmetic computation is in range before storing its value in a subrange.

In PL/I, the user may specify a base (decimal or binary), a scale (number of places by which a decimal point is assumed shifted), a precision (number of significant digits), and a mode (type). All of these ranges may be specified in a declaration, and the compiler is expected to select a target machine data object that meets or exceeds the source specification, and to perform whatever special operations are necessary to make the machine data object operations conform to the source specifications. A structured object may be required to support a large number of decimal places.

Fortran provides no number range specification. Also, standard Fortran permits quite general equivalences of one data object to another; for example:

```
DOUBLE D
REAL R
EQUIVALENCE (D, R)
```

With these, the data space associated with the double D and the real R are shared. A determined (or naive) programmer can access the internal structure of a REAL (very machine-dependent) in an otherwise high-level program. Similar equivalences are found in most languages—Pascal supports a variant case declaration similar to the Fortran equivalence.

8.8. Types

A *type* is an attribute possessed by every value and variable in a language. Some older languages (for example, Fortran) provide implicit default typing of a variable (for example, based on the first few characters of the variable's name). PL/I is similar to Fortran in this respect. Other languages, such as Pascal and Cobol, require an explicit type declaration for each declared memory object. Newer languages, most notably Pascal and Ada, permit declarations of types in their own right, as abstract entities apart from any run-time memory space that they might ultimately represent. Type declarations are now widely recognized as a valuable tool in structured programming. We now review the concept of types, drawing on ISO Pascal [Pascal, 1983] for specific definitions and examples.

ISO Pascal recognizes the following types:

- *Simple types:* an ordered set associated with a subset of the ordinals.

- *Structured types:* a composite set of simple types and other structured types.

The class of simple types is further classified as:

- *Integer type:* a dense subrange of the ordinal integers.

- *Real type:* a dense subrange of the real numbers.

- *Boolean type:* two values, true and false.

- *Char type:* a set of implementation-defined characters, some possibly without graphic representations.

- *Enumerated type:* an ordered set of values denoted by a finite set of identifiers.

- *Subrange type:* a dense subset of *integer type*.

The class of structured types is further classified as:

- *Array type:* a mapping from an integer subrange (an *index*) to a member of the set of array type.

- *Record type:* a mapping from a record tag name to a member of the set of record type.

- *Variant type:* a mapping similar to a record type, except that memory space may be shared among its substructures.

- *Pointer type:* a mapping from a pointer to a primitive or structured type.

- *Set type:* a mapping to a powerset from the base type of the set type.

- *File type:* a sequence of elements carried in an external mass storage device.

The elements of a structured type may be a primitive type or another structured type.

Operations on Typed Objects

Although ISO Pascal provides a rich and general mechanism for declaring arbitrary structures, the set of built-in operations provided for structures—as opposed to operations on primitive types—is quite limited.

The most primitive operation is *access*—identifying some sub-structure, which may be a primitive type. Access is specified in Pascal through a *compound name;* for example:

```
sam.mike[15]↑.fred
```

Here, sam refers to the root, or base node of a structured object. sam will have a record structure, such that the name mike specifies one of its record slots. The object sam.mike must then be an array structure; the [15] refers to a slot in the array. The uparrow ↑ designates a pointer indirection; the object pointed to is another record with a slot tagged fred.

The Pascal operations on its primitive objects include arithmetic, Boolean, comparison, and set operations. The built-in operations on structured objects are relatively few and are constrained in most Pascal implementations. Thus, all Pascals permit assignment between two structured objects of the same type. All Pascals support a limited form of string movement and comparison between a packed array of character and literal strings. Some Pascals have elaborate string operations, where a string is a special object consisting of an ordered sequence of characters of variable, but finite, length.

Many Pascal implementations permit arbitrary structured objects to be passed to and returned from functions. With this capability, it is easy for a programmer to define any number of special operations on structured objects by writing functions that carry out the operations.

Type Constraints and Conversion

Given a variety of types, and the rule that every object is associated with some type, it is natural to investigate how the built-in operations of the language are to deal with their operand types, and whether the built-in operators can be extended through user-written declarations. It is also natural to consider how an object of one type can be *converted* by some function into an object of another type.

Pascal contains sufficient built-in conversions among its primitive objects to get from one primitive type to another. Thus chr converts an ordinal number into a type char, and ord performs the opposite. ord can also be used to obtain the ordinal value associated with an enumerated type, but there is no reverse conversion. An integer or subrange will be converted to real as needed, implicitly.

The reverse conversion (real to integer) must be achieved explicity through the trunc or round operation.

There are no built-in conversions for structures, but a function can be designed to accomplish whatever is required.

Strong Typing

Pascal is a *strongly typed* language with only one implicit type conversion—from integer to real. By strongly typed, we mean that the compiler considers all the following circumstances illegal:

- An assignment of an object B to a variable A, unless the type of B is identical to that of A.

- A binary operation between objects A and B, unless the types of A and B are compatible with the operation.

- A correspondence of a procedure (or function) actual parameter with its formal parameter, unless both are of the same type.

One pairing is missing from this list—between a file and a read or write operation. We know of no Pascal implementation that tags each file with its type in order to protect a user from an invalid file type operation. Indeed, that is impossible for a compiler to check because the file does not exist during compilation. A run-time check is similarly difficult because the file cannot be tagged with type information that fails to survive compilation.

An implication of these rules is that any mixed-type pairing must be corrected by a type conversion.

Some languages support type *coercion,* which causes the compiler to regard an object of one type to be equivalent to one of another type. Coercions are used freely in C programs as a way of accessing primitive data elements at a primitive level without inducing compiler-generated type conversion code. Note that a coercion involves no code generation, only a change of viewpoint during compilation.

Type Equivalence

An issue in Pascal until the ISO Pascal standard appeared is just when two types are considered to be "equivalent."

The nub of this controversy centered around whether two types T1 and T2 are equivalent if their internal *structures* are equivalent, or whether they refer to the same structure through a *declaration*. Thus, T1 and T2 might have the declarations:

```
T1= array [5..9] of real;
T2= array [5..9] of real;
```

Are T1 and T2 equivalent? Under the structure rule, they are; under the declaration rule, they are not.

ISO Pascal holds to the declaration rule; for T1 and T2 to be equivalent, the declarations should read:

```
T1= array [5..9] of real;
T2= T1;
```

The significance of this to a Pascal compiler lies in whether the compiler can simply compare the pointers to a type declaration structure, or must perform a detailed comparison of their structures; ISO Pascal permits the former.

8.8.1. Implementing Structured Types

The implementation of structured types in a compiler has several facets:

- How type information as derived from their declarations may be carried internally in the compiler.

- How the declaration productions and parser semantic stack yield the internal data structures.

- How instructions to access a compound object may be generated.

We shall consider each of these issues, drawing on a portion of the QPARSER system for examples.

Structured Type Declarations

A structured type declaration is a tree the root of which is a type or var identifier carried in the compiler's symbol table. In Pascal, we need to represent user-defined record and array structures, primitive types, and variables of any one of these types.

The following symbol table structure is used in QPARSER for that purpose:

```
type
   VTYPES= (reserved, unk_type, str_type, bool_type,
            int_type, real_type, user, symerr,
            variable, user_type, array_type, rec_type,
            proc, func, stlabel);
   SYMTABP= ↑symtabtype;
   SEMRECP= ↑semrec;
   SYMTABTYPE= record    {structure for <identifier>s and
                                      keywords}
               NEXT: symtabp;  {along hash chain}
               LEVEL: int;     {lexical level}
               SYM: symbol;    {the symbol}
               case SYMT: vtypes of  {symbol type}
                  reserved: (TOKVAL: tokrange);  {token number}
                  variable: (SADDR: int;  {base address}
                             VTYPEP: symtabp);  {its type}
```

```
user_type: (UTYPEP: symtabp);   {its type}
bool_type, int_type, real_type,
  array_type, rec_type:
    (SIZE: int;
     SUB_TYPE: symtabp;
     case vtypes of
         rec_type: (PAR_RECP,   {parent type}
                    NEXT_RECP: symtabp);
         array_type: (LDIM, UDIM: int));
  {more for functions, procedures and labels}
end;
```

The variable tag is used for an identifier declared in a var declaration; it is associated with a base address in run-time memory (SADDR) and a pointer to a type structure (VTYPEP).

The user_type tag is used for an identifier declared in a type declaration. It is associated only with a type structure (UTYPEP).

Three primitive types are supported: BOOL_TYPE, INT_TYPE, and REAL_TYPE. These have a SIZE equal to the number of data words required to support them—one for Boolean and integer, two for real. SUB_TYPE is nil, and there is no variant case.

The ARRAY_TYPE tag supports an array declaration with a single dimension. An array has a SUB_TYPE, which is its element's type. It also has an upper and lower dimension UDIM and LDIM, which are fixed integers. Its SIZE is the total number of data words required to support the array.

The REC_TYPE tag supports record and variant case structures. Here, the SYM field carries the record tag symbol, which will be linked into the symbol table, but in a slightly unusual fashion, as we shall explain shortly. The PAR_RECP points to its parent record tag, the first one encountered in a record structure. The NEXT_RECP links all the tags of a record into a single, ordered linear list. The NEXT_RECP pointer is required only during construction of the symbol table structure.

We hasten to point out that this SYMTABTYPE does not support enumerated types, subranges, file types, pointer types, and set types—it supports only the primitive types, array type, and record type. However, the latter are the interesting ones. Extensions to support full Pascal can be made easily.

Examples.   Consider the following array declaration:

```
type AR= array [5..15] of real;
```

It will be supported in the symbol table under identifier AR as a user_type; the associated UTYPEP will point to the following structure (-> is a pointer indirection):

```
SYMT user_type
SYM 'AR'
UTYPEP -> SYMT array_type
            SYM nil   {array itself has no name}
```

```
LDIM 5
UDIM 15
SUB_TYPE -> SYMT real_type   {predefined primitive REAL}
            SYM 'REAL'
PAR_RECP -> self
NEXT_RECP nil
```

Next, consider the following record declaration:

```
type REC= record
          A, B: integer;
          C: real;
      end;
```

This will expand into four symbol table entries, one for the symbol REC and one each for the tags A, B, and C. REC will be associated with a user_type entry pointing to a rec_type entry with the following structure (-> designates a pointer):

```
SYMT user_type
SYM 'REC'
UTYPEP -> SYMT rec_type
          SYM 'A'
          SUB_TYPE -> SYMT int_type   {predefined INTEGER type}
                      SYM 'INTEGER'
          PAR_RECP -> entry for 'A'
          NEXT_RECP -> SYMT rec_type
                       SYM 'B'
                       SUB_TYPE -> SYMT int_type
                                   SYM 'INTEGER'
                       PAR_RECP -> entry for 'A'
                       NEXT_RECP -> SYMT rec_type
                                    SYM 'C'
                                    SUB_TYPE -> SYMT real_type
                                                SYM 'REAL'
                                    PAR_RECP -> entry for 'A'
                                    NEXT_RECP nil
```

Although the record tag entries are linked together by the NEXT_RECP field, we shall see that these links are not needed to generate access code for a compound name. The named record components of the name can be found efficiently through the symbol table lookup mechanism.

Size of a Type

The SYMTABTYPE structure contains one other entry, SIZE, associated with some of its tags. This is the number of target machine words (or bits, if packed structures are to be supported) that this structure requires in memory, measured from its root to the farthest leaf of the structure.

This single measure is sufficient to allocate memory space to a var of a given type; we simply assign the root variable's address to the "next available" address, then add its type structure's size to that address. (That is, assuming that addresses increase; in some implementations, the addresses decrease).

The size of a primitive object is just its representation size. For example, a Boolean and an integer usually fit in a single word—their size is one. A real may be two, three or four words in size—its size is two in QPARSER.

The size of an array_type is just the product of its subelement's size and the number of objects in the array; that is:

```
(udim-ldim+1)*atype↑.size
```

The size of a rec_type depends on whether its NEXT tagged object is part of a RECORD field or is the first object of a new variant CASE. Assume for the moment that there is no such thing as a variant case. Then the size of a rec_type is just the sum of its subelement's size and the size of the NEXT object. (The size of the latter is zero if NEXT = nil.)

In dealing with a variant case, we wish the memory space allocated to the variants to be shared. Because the compiler will not know which of the cases are to be invoked at run-time, it must allow sufficient space for the longest variant; the SIZE assigned to the each variant CASE group therefore is the maximum of all the variant case group sizes.

Thus, given the declaration:

```
type VC= record case integer of
        1: (A, B: real);
        2: (C: integer);
        3: (D: array [0..5] of integer);
      end;
```

the largest variant will be case 3, of size six words, assuming that a real occupies two words and an integer one. We then must assign a SIZE of six to each of A, C and D, because these are the first subelements of each variant case field. The SIZE of B will be four, because it is two words closer to the end of the structure than A. We want to generate the following structure for this declaration—we have left out some details for clarity:

```
SYMT user_type
SYM 'VC'
UTYPEP -> SYMT rec_type   {entry 'A'}
             SYM 'A'
             SIZE 6
             SUB_TYPE -> SYMT real_type
                         SIZE 2
             PAR_RECP -> entry 'A'
             NEXT_RECP -> entry 'B'

SYMT rec_type   {entry 'B'}
SYM 'B'
SIZE 4
SUB_TYPE -> SYMT real_type
            SIZE 2
PAR_RECP -> entry 'A'
NEXT_RECP -> entry 'C'
```

```
SYMT rec_type  {entry 'C'}
SYM 'C'
SIZE 6
SUB_TYPE -> SYMT int_type
                SIZE 1
PAR_RECP -> entry 'A'
NEXT_RECP -> entry 'D'

SYMT rec_type  {entry 'D'}
SYM 'D'
SIZE 6
SUB_TYPE -> SYMT array_type
                SYM nil
                SIZE 6
                SUB_TYPE -> SYMT int_type
                                SIZE 1
                LDIM 0
                UDIM 5
PAR_RECP -> entry 'A'
NEXT_RECP nil
```

Limited Scope of RECORD Tags

Consider the record declaration

```
var VC: record
            I, J: integer;
            case integer of
                1: (A, B: real);
                2: (C: integer);
                3: (D: array [0..5] of integer);
            end;
```

The names I, J, A, B, C, D are the *record tags* of the record field list. One of these will appear in a compound name, so they must be pairwise disjoint. Furthermore, Pascal requires that the scope of these names be limited to: (1) their record declaration, (2) a position within a compound name, when prefixed with a declared variable name, or (3) within the scope of a *with* clause.

Thus the scope of the record tags I, J, and so on, is merely the lexical scope of the VC declaration. Outside the scope of the VC declaration, these tag names are considered to be unbound.

However, in a compound name such as:

```
vc.a
```

the record tag a must be accessible. Two strategies for dealing with this peculiar scoping problem are possible within our SYMTABTYPE structure. We shall describe a simple but inefficient strategy first, then a more subtle but efficient strategy.

Record Tag Access—A Simple Strategy

The simplest possible strategy is first to *unlink* all the record tag symbol table entries from access as symbols. This means that given an identifier a, the symbol table fetching mechanism will be unable to locate an entry a in the symbol table. However, the table entries are kept alive in the heap, and can be located through the next_recp links from some parent *var* or *type*.

All the record tags associated with a user type or a variable will be located by a linear search through the next_recp links. Hence, given the compound name vc.a, we locate vc in the symbol table as usual—vc is a user type, not a record tag. We then step through the next_recp links until we find an entry the symbol sym of which matches the identifier a. If a match cannot be found, the compound name vc.a is considered illegal.

This process can be repeated for a longer compound name. Once a match is found, it is repeated using the sub_type.

This strategy is inefficient because it requires a linked list search and string comparison. We have assumed that an efficient mechanism is already in place for locating an identifier string in the symbol table. In fact, it will have been invoked already on each identifier. Why not keep record tags in place in the symbol table, and use the existing search mechanism?

Record Tag Access—An Efficient Approach

We can choose to keep all record tags linked into the symbol table. First assume that all names are unique—there is only one tag with a given name, and no other variable has that name. We then have an immediate reference to each tag as it appears in a compound name, thanks to the free symbol table search made on each identifier. Thus, in the compound name vc.a, we will know the symbol table entry for both vc and a without a linked list search.

The same holds for a compound name of any length.

Unfortunately, we must consider multiple uses of the same name. For any given record tag name, there can be other uses of the name in other records. There also may be a *type* or *var* the name of which is the same as a record tag.

The rule must be that a *type* or *var* name must *shadow* any record tag name— that is, the tag name must be deeper in the symbol table name stack, so that the *type*/*var* name will be seen first.

Whether one record tag shadows another is not important. However, it is important to verify that a tag entry is the appropriate one to use when tracing a compound name.

The efficient approach requires the following operations during the declaration phase of a record, and also during access of a compound name.

Tag Declaration.   Let I be a record tag identifier. The symbol table fetch mechanism will return an attribute A the SYM of which is I. There are three cases:

1. A is undeclared—this is the first appearance of I in the source. Then A simply can be made into a rec_type entry.

2. A is declared as something other than a rec_type. We need to create a new symbol table item A' whose SYMT = rec_type. It must then be entered *below* A in the table, so that A will shadow A'.

3. A is declared as a record tag. Here, the question is whether A is part of the current record (a multiple-use error) or whether it is part of some other previously declared record (no error). It happens that we can use the par_recp to decide which is the case. If par_recp is NIL, then A is part of the current record; otherwise it is part of some other record. In either case, we create a new symbol table item A' whose SYMT = rec_type; it may be entered above A so that it shadows A.

In any case, we set par_recp to NIL, and arrange for next_recp to link all the tag fields together in order. The size field can be computed bottom-up. The par_recp will be set later.

Var or Type Declaration.   On completing the declaration of all the record components, we finish the variable/type declaration by setting utypep or vtypep to the first of the record components, which we shall call F. We then walk through the next_recp chain, setting each of the par_recp pointers to their parent—the entry F. In this way, par_recp will be NIL during declaration of a record's tags, then it will be non-NIL.

Compound Name Recognition.   We can now consider the parsing of a compound name; for example, vc.a.b. The name vc should appear immediately through the free symbol table search. It will be linked to a type specification through vtypep or utypep, which we shall call F.

The name a also will be associated with a symbol table entry; however, it may be the wrong one, owing to the shadowing phenomenon. We can tell by its symt and its par_recp fields—the symt must be rec_typep, and its par_recp must point to F. If the a entry does not meet these criteria, then we must fetch deeper entries in the symbol table until we find one the sym of which matches a and that does meet these criteria. Note that with no name shadowing, we will have an immediate hit; we need to continue the name searching only if shadowing exists.

The next component b in the compound name vc.a.b is identified in a similar way. The only difference is that the sub_type pointer of the entry for a now points to a parent that must agree with the par_recp of symbol b.

Address Computation

We may consider a compound name as simply a means of specifying the address of some primitive data object. In Pascal, the name begins with a var name, which will be associated with an address SADDR as a symbol table attribute.

Each component of the compound name then contributes some offset to this address. A rec_type component a contributes an address offset that is equal to a SIZE difference size1 − size2, where size1 is the SIZE of the *parent* of component a, and size2 is the SIZE of a. Note that the parent of a is specified by the par_recp pointer, and that it is the first of the sequence of records of which a is one component. We have associated a memory address with a's parent; hence, this size difference is the desired offset to a.

Note that we need not be concerned about whether a is part of a record structure or a variant case structure. The size's of these components have been computed in such a way as to take that into consideration.

An array_type component contributes an offset that in general must be computed by run-time code. Suppose the array reference is [e], where e is some expression. Then the offset is:

```
(e - ldim)*atype↑.size
```

8.8.2. More About Compound Names

A compound name is specified in the PSG grammar by the productions

```
Variable -> VarHead VarExtension #varid
VarHead -> <identifier>
VarExtension -> VarExtension VarExt #varextl
             -> <empty>
VarExt -> [ BoolList ] #varexta   array index
       -> . <identifier> #varextr  record access
```

Thus a Variable always carries a VarHead, which must be a type variable in the symbol table. The compound name's VarExtension may be empty, in which case the variable's SADDR is the desired address. In a VarExtension, we may have a sequence of array or record address extensions. For an array index, the BoolList is an arithmetic expression in general.

Code Generation for Compound Names

There are a number of ways in which access instructions can be generated using these productions. We shall illustrate the construction of a semantics structure for the name. This structure usually will be part of a larger expression tree subject to evaluation after a complete expression has been scanned.

We carry record and array access information by two extensions to the SEMREC type, as follows:

```
SEMREC= record    {semantic stack structure}
          VTYPE: vtypes;   {type — where appropriate}
          case SEMT: semtype of
            { ... other fields }
            aryext, recext:
```

```
(ARNEXT: semrecp;   {next component}
 case semtype of
   aryext: (AX: semrecp);   {array index}
   recext: (RSYM: symtabp)   {record symbol}
 );
end;
```

Here, each VarExt is carried by a new SEMREC. Its SEMT is either aryext or recext. The components of the compound name are linked together through the ARNEXT pointer. When ARNEXT is NIL, the end of the compound name has been reached.

For an array component, the index expression is carried by AX. For a record component, the tag symbol table entry is carried in RSYM. Recall our discussion about dealing with shadowing: we assume that any possible shadowing can be dealt with before the semantics entry RSYM is made.

Eventually, procedure EVAL is called on the variable part of the compound name. What EVAL should do for optimal code generation is first decide if the address of a compound object can be computed at compile-time. This would be the case if there are no aryext components or if each of them refers to a compile-time constant. In this special case, a LOAD or STOR instruction can be emitted with a known address.

In the general case, one or more aryext expressions AX refer to a nonconstant index. In this case, an address must be computed by run-time instructions. We start by LOADing the address of the variable, then adding some offset that prepares the address for a run-time array index calculation. The index calculation looks like this:

```
(evaluate index)   {must be evaluated at run-time}
SUB =ldim
MPY =(array element size)
ADD I
```

The MPY in this may be omitted if the element size is one. Similarly, the SUB may be omitted if the ldim is zero. The ADD yields the address of the indexed array element, in preparation for the next part of the compound name.

Matrix Pointers

The array access outlined in the previous section assumes that the array occupies a sequence of contiguous words such that simple arithmetic operations yield an element's address. Each index requires at least one multiplication and one addition. On some machines, multiplication is much more expensive in time than addition. For these, the following method using arrays of pointers is more efficient.

For example, consider a two-dimensional array:

```
var X: array [0..m, 0..n] of integer;
```

We construct a vector V of size m + 1, containing pointers. Each pointer is directed to a different row (second dimension) of the two-dimensional array. Then the access of an element Z[i, j] is a matter of fetching V(i), which points to an array slice, then indexing into this slice through index j. On certain machines, this combined operation can be very fast—we need only a set of index registers and a special operation that steps the machine through the pointer arrays to the final data array element.

The fetching of Z[i, j] might appear as follows in stack machine code:

```
LOAD @Z        ; load address of Z
(eval i)       ; index i
ADD   I        ; new address
LOAD I         ; load from TOS address
(eval j)       ; index j
ADD   I        ; new address
LOAD I         ; load from TOS address
```

This clearly eliminates the MPY's seen earlier. Even these instructions can be reduced by combining the two instructions:

```
ADD   I
LOAD I
```

into a single instruction, which will reduce program size and presumably run faster.

8.8.3. The Pascal WITH Form

Pascal compound names can be abbreviated through a structured means of supplying partial names—the WITH statement. The general form of a WITH block is:

```
with <name-list> do
begin
   ...
end;
```

where:

```
<name-list> ::= <name-list> , <composite-name>
            ::= <composite-name>
```

The composite names in the <name-list> may contain indexing, pointer dereferencing and record component access. Some of the indices may be expressions, requiring run-time evaluation. Each composite name is a portion of a full name, either a full prefix or some middle section.

Pascal WITH blocks also may be nested, and an inner one may particularize a variable name heading started by an outer one. For example, given the declarations:

```
type NAMEPART = array [1..20] of char;
     NAME = array [1..3] of namepart;
     VITA = record
               NAME: name;
               SALARY: integer;
            end;
     OFFICER = record
                 TITLE: (pres, vp, secy, treas);
                 VITAE: vita
               end;
     COMPANY = record
                 NAME: name;
                 OFFICERS: array [1..100] of officer;
                 PERSONNEL: array [1..1000] of vita;
               end;
var CONSWIDGET: company;
    X: integer;
```

the following WITH clauses are legal:

```
with CONSWIDGET do
begin
   . . .
   {default prefix CONSWIDGET}
   with OFFICERS[X+3] do
   begin
      . . .
      {default prefix CONSWIDGET and
                 CONSWIDGET.OFFICERS[X+3] }
      with VITAE do
      begin
         . . .
      end
   end
end
```

Implementing WITH

Implementing a WITH is fairly easy, given our symbol table organization and the earlier discussion regarding address computations for compound names. Essentially, a WITH defines some incomplete address at run-time; the remainder of this address's offset is determined by the remainder of a compound name.

At the compiler level, a with forces one or more record tag names to be exposed as valid symbols. For example, the variable CONSWIDGET in the preceding example is a record with the tags NAME, OFFICERS, and PERSON-NEL. We first push three new entries into the symbol table associated with these three tags. Each entry will be of type variable. Its address saddr will be the address of a newly allocated pointer associated with the with. The entry will be marked for indirection (not supported by the SYMTABTYPE structure given). The entry's vtypep field will point to the sub_type of each of the three tags.

The goal in these operations is to yield a symbol table entry for each tag that will make it appear as though the tag is in fact a var the memory address of which is the word W. Word W is considered a pointer to the rest of the structure, which will appear when the rest (or more) of the compound name appears within the body of the with. Thus, no change is needed in the access mechanism for compound names.

Also, because a with can be nested in another with, the successive withs will add additional prefixes to compound names by the same algorithm.

Here are the required actions in more detail. All of these actions occur on entering a with compound name; nothing special is then needed for any variable reference, whether partial or complete:

- Allocate a word W from the run-time stack top for use as an indirect address. This will carry the address of the with prefix of a set of compound names. Let this prefix be denoted by P.

- Compute the contents (an address) of W by walking through the prefix P and generating the appropriate address code. Note that the contents of W will have to be computed by run-time code if the prefix P carries a computed array index. At the end of the prefix P, we also will have a compile-time reference to some symtabp record R.

- Create a new symbol table entry for each of the tag names associated with R as type variable. They will be associated with the address of W and an offset, as explained previously.

The remaining task is to unwind these new symbol table entries at the lexical end of the with body. An easy way to arrange for their unwinding is to assign a new lexical level to each with, then remove all symbols at that level or lower. The with pointers also should be deallocated by code generated at the lexical end of the with.

8.8.4. PL/I Structures

An aggregate declaration form similar to the Pascal record is supported by PL/I, illustrated next. Unlike Pascal, PL/I does not support an abstract type declaration. Every structure must be explicitly written out in full detail. Here is an example:

```
DCL 1 PAYROLL(75),
      2 NAME,
        3 LAST CHARACTER(12),
        3 FIRST CHARACTER(8),
        3 MIDDLE CHARACTER(1),
      2 PAY_NO CHARACTER(5),
      2 HRS,
        3 REGULAR FIXED DECIMAL(2),
        3 OVTIM FIXED DECIMAL(2),
      2 RATE,
        3 STRATE FIXED DECIMAL(3,2),
        3 OVRTIM FIXED DECIMAL(3,2);
```

This structure defines a payroll file for a firm with 75 employees. We have a static tree structure with the leaves: LAST, FIRST, MIDDLE, PAY_NO, REGULAR, OVTIM, STRATE, and OVRTIM. The remaining names are internal nodes. Each of the leaves is an elementary data object or an array. Each of the interior nodes can be an array and, if it is, it means that its subtree is replicated in memory by as many elements as specified in the array dimension.

The integer prefixes define the *level number;* the syntax does not otherwise fix the tree level numbers.

A PL/I data element is accessed through a composite name; for example:

$$PAYROLL(15).HRS.OVTIM$$

or:

$$PAYROLL(P).NAME.LAST(X)$$

The latter name designates character X of the last name of employee P.

A set of data objects also may be accessed through the name of some internal node in the structure. For example, PAYROLL(2).NAME stands for the set of three data objects LAST, FIRST, and MIDDLE of the second employee.

The name:

$$NAME.HRS$$

is illegal; the two parts NAME and HRS are drawn from the same level.

PL/I Name Abbreviation

PL/I permits abbreviating a structure element name by omitting any of its components, provided that the specified data object is unambiguously designated. Abbreviation poses an interesting and nontrivial problem of symbol table access, and creates a need of detecting ambiguous name references, which we shall deal with shortly. Array indices also may be moved to the right, but may not be reordered or omitted. Because of index movement, every array reference must carry an index. For example:

$$PAYROLL.NAME.LAST(P)(X)$$

and:

$$LAST(P)(X)$$

are legal representations for the name PAYROLL(P).NAME.LAST(X), provided that PAYROLL.NAME can be inferred unambiguously as a prefix for LAST.

The remaining features in the PL/I PAYROLL structure are attributes of the leaf node data object:

- CHARACTER(12) is an array of 12 characters.

- DECIMAL(2) is a decimal number with two significant places; for example, any number in the range zero to 99.

- DECIMAL(3, 2) is a decimal number with a decimal pointer three digits ahead of and two behind the decimal point; for example, 345.67.

A picture of part of this structure as it might appear in memory at run-time is given in figure 8.11. Only one of the 75 PAYROLL subtrees (the one for index 5) is broken out and displayed completed. For example:

PAYROLL(5).HRS.REGULAR

has the value 40 according to this structure.

PL/I Name Scanner

A PL/I structure name may be completely or partially specified. Any partial specification (consisting of only some of the names along a path from a root to the data object leaf) is legal if a unique data object is thereby specified.

A name in PL/I, whether partial or full, is considered ambiguous only if, as a full name, it refers to two or more data objects. (Note that a "data object" may be a set of primitive objects in a structure.) If some name N can refer to two different objects, as a full name for one object A and as a partial name for another object B, then it is assumed to refer to object A; that is, a full name overrides any possible partial names.

It is also possible that the structures of a PL/I program are such that some data objects cannot be accessed unambiguously. If no reference to one of these data

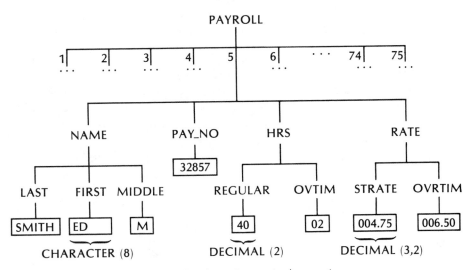

Figure 8.11.   A PL/I structure displayed as it is organized at run-time.

objects exists in the program, then the structures are acceptable, despite their inherent ambiguity. We see that any structure is permissible per se; however, each of the name references must be examined for possible ambiguities.

A clever solution to this name abbreviation problem was proposed by Gates and Poplawski [Gates, 1973]. It is an interesting application of finite-state automaton methods; read the paper for details.

8.9. Exercises

1. Write a program to read source programs written in your favorite language and collect statistics on identifier lengths. Include a length/frequency table, the average, and the maximum length. Use the results to estimate wasted space/space overhead for each of the three string-storage methods. Make and document suitable assumptions about array sizes. Use a sample of input programs in the language of your choice. You can use a simple lexical scan to find identifiers.

2. Write the data structure declarations and manipulation procedures for a block-structured symbol table, using a single table and update stack. Write procedures for block entry, block exit, identifier declaration, and identifier reference. Assume that a separately implemented string-search method will locate the correct table element and supply its subscript to your procedures.

3. Implement two or more of the identifier-access methods. Gather statistics on numbers of declarations and references. Time the methods and compare their speeds to each other and to the statistics. Use a sample of input programs in the language of your choice. For simplicity, assume there is only one scope. You can use a simple lexical scan to find identifiers and a simple partial parsing to distinguish declarations from references.

4. Determine what are the type compatibility rules for your favorite dialect of Pascal. Some types allow structure compatibility, whereas others require name compatibility. With luck, you can get this information from a language reference manual. If the rules are documented inadequately, you will have to resort to reading the compiler's code (if source listings are available) or to performing experiments with the compiler.

8.10. Bibliographical Notes

The use of symbol tables in computer systems appears to have ample precedent. Access methods, with detailed examples, are given by McKeeman [1974b]. Knuth [1968], vol. 1, chapter 2, contains a treatment of symbol table tree structures suitable for PL/I or Cobol names. Knuth [1973] discusses searching and hashing at length.

A formal symbol table and attribute system of considerable power and generality, called *property grammars,* is defined by Stearns and Lewis [Stearns, 1969]. A good review of property grammars, with examples, is given in Aho [1972a], vol. 2, chapter 10; Aho also develops statistical formulas for the evaluation of the efficiency of the hash table-search method.

CHAPTER 9

RUN-TIME MACHINE STRUCTURES

Saying is one thing, and doing is another.

. . . Montaigne

9.1. Introduction

The target machine of a compiler often is some particular manufacturer's product, such as a Motorola 68000, an HP 3000, or an IBM 360. A target machine's specification must define its memory resources—registers and random-access memory—and the set of operations provided for those resources. There often are special instructions that access peripheral devices. Other machines—microprocessors especially—access peripherals by reading or writing special memory locations. Some architectures support multiple registers of equal status; in others, multiple registers with unique functions are provided. Still other architectures are based on a stack; others operate with three-address instructions directly in memory.

Attempting to generalize code generation is seemingly impossible.

But it need not be so. A language may be implemented on a *fictitious machine*, which is relatively simple in concept, yet which supports all the requirements of the language. The advantage of this approach is that we can thereby uncover principles of language implementation that must be supported on whatever real target machine is chosen. The differences in architectures then can be reduced to a few major considerations: (1) are there multiple registers with arithmetic and addressing capability? (2) what are the addressing conventions? and (3) what are the special instructions that might improve the performance of certain language features?

The popular PCODE implementation of Pascal, which is available on several microcomputers, is an example of the fictitious machine approach to compilation. PCODE was devised by Wirth [1976] as a means of separating most of the Pascal compilation issues from a particular form of hardware that must support the language. His PCODE definition was subsequently modified by Bowles [1978] at the University of California, San Diego, who wrote the popular UCSD Pascal system for small computers. (UCSD is a trademark of the Regents of the University of California.)

Bowles defined a relatively small set of instructions and an encoding for them that resulted in highly compact object code and considerable portability of his UCSD Pascal system. His system can be ported to any computer by writing an emulator, called the *P-machine*, for the PCODE instructions. Once the P-machine and a few primitive I/O procedures are written and debugged for some host machine, the whole UCSD Pascal system can be made to run on the host computer with little human effort.

We will define a set of instructions called *SPC*, for *simple pcode,* that accomplishes the same end as the UCSD PCODE. SPC is considerably smaller than UCSD PCODE, although it can be expanded easily. Despite its simplicity, SPC deals effectively with most of the fundamental issues of a language such as Pascal, namely,

- Recursive procedure calls.

- Pascal control structures.

- Real and integer types.

- Procedure lexical nesting.

- Functionals.

- Arbitrary expressions and assignment statements.

- Arrays and record structures.

- Unstructured exits.

We have omitted several classes of PCODE instruction, because we believe that they add little to the fundamental concepts of run-time structures; these are:

- String operations.

- Powerset operations.

- Heap management operations.

- I/O formatting operations.

- Optimizing operations.

Instructions to support all of these are easily added and have little effect on the run-time system about to be described. Optimizations on our instruction set are discussed near the end of the chapter.

Instruction traps are essential in any useful computer system, and have an influence on the design of the abstract machine. We shall discuss these and some solutions toward the end of the chapter. A *trap* is a mechanism for dealing with arithmetic underflow or overflow; for example, a division by zero.

Full QPARSER contains an assembler and simulator for this instruction set, written in Pascal. Full source is provided for these tools to permit experimentation and extensions. We recommend examining the simulator in conjunction with the material in this chapter. We shall refer to this assembler and simulator occasionally in the text as the *SPC assembler and simulator.*

9.2. Run-Time Support Issues

We shall focus on the run-time issues posed by Pascal. Other languages pose additional problems for the design of a run-time support system; we shall discuss some of these later in the chapter.

The most interesting—and the most difficult to grasp—Pascal issues are those connected with calling a procedure or function, and with accessing a variable.

A procedure call requires that fresh memory space be allocated for the information passed to the procedure—its *actual parameters*—and for the local variables of the procedure. This space must not have been assigned previously to other variables. Another requirement is that the procedure's return address be noted somewhere, because it is possible for the procedure to be called from different locations.

Because a Pascal procedure may call itself, it also is important that fresh memory space for its actual parameters and local variables be provided on every call. This may require any number of different memory spaces—in general, one is needed for each active call. In a language that does not support a self-call, or *recursion,* a single space can be allocated once for these variables by the compiler.

When the procedure is completed, an EXIT instruction is executed, which causes control to return to the instruction following its call instruction. At that time, the memory space allocated for actual and local variables may be released and later used for other purposes.

A vital part of our run-time model is providing an efficient and simple mechanism for managing memory under these conditions; we shall see that a simple stack is sufficient for this purpose.

Accessing a Pascal variable is complicated by the need to support recursion and to access variables outside the scope of the currently active procedure; for example, outer block variables.

Pascal pointers, record structures, and arrays pose some additional problems for the compiler writer but, as we shall see, they require little in the way of instructions to support them adequately.

The Pascal control structures (the FOR loop, WHILE-DO, and GOTOs) are mostly a matter of managing two simple branch instructions.

A few of the ideas for our fictitious SPC machine are derived from the UCSD system, but the machine owes its fundamental control concepts to an abstract machine designed by Randell and Russell [Randell, 1964] to support Algol 60.

9.3. The SPC Machine Organization

Our SPC machine has two linear sequential memories, one for *instructions* and one for *data*. These share a single stack in the UCSD Pascal implementation. We choose to separate them for the sake of a simple emulator; the first is organized by bytes and the second by double-byte words.

The machine instruction memory can be organized in any convenient manner to suit an implementation or a simulator. It is read-only; the SPC machine is not permitted to alter its instructions. It is sufficiently large to support any program. Finally, it is accessed by a *program counter* p, which will point to the next instruction to be executed by the machine. (The program counter is variable PC in the simulator.)

The instructions may be fixed length or variable length; one or the other may be better for a particular implementation. Our SPC simulator uses a variable-length byte (eight bits) organization. Many of its instructions are single bytes. Other instructions are two and three bytes long. The first byte of every instruction is called its *operation code*, or *op-code*, and fits in a seven-bit field. That leaves one bit, which is used in the emulator to mark the instruction for a debugging breakpoint.

The SPC machine's data memory is organized as a linear array of *words*. The word length is arbitrary but, for the sake of clarity, we shall assume that each word is two bytes (16 bits). Our machine will support two kinds of data: 16-bit integers and 32-bit real numbers. These correspond to the *integer* and *real* primitive types of many Pascal compilers. A real datum therefore requires two words for its representation. These conventions are followed in the SPC simulator programs.

This data memory will be organized as a stack. As such, two pointers always will be maintained: s, which points to the top-most word in the stack, and m, which points to a special group of words in the stack called a *stack marker*. The stack marker carries the return address of the procedure and certain other information that we shall discuss later. (s is variable TOS in the simulator, and m is SMARKER.)

Every datum and structure will be allocated by moving the s pointer to a higher value; this makes one or more words available. Whenever a procedure or function is called, s is moved higher to provide space for its actual parameters, a stack marker, and its local variables. When the procedure is finished, s is moved lower to release the now-unneeded space.

A stack-oriented data space is sufficient to support everything in a Pascal program except multiple processes and the NEW function. Each of a set of multiple processes requires an independent stack in general, and some means of referring to a foreign stack from within the environment of another stack.

The NEW function requires a *heap* and a *heap manager*. The heap manager is responsible for allocating a block of memory space somewhere (*not* from the data stack), then maintaining it until told that it can be released. In Pascal, the function new(pntr) allocates a block of space and causes the pointer pntr to point to it. The function dispose(pntr) releases that block, setting the pntr to NIL.

9.4. Stack Contents Notation

The contents of cell **j** in the data memory will be denoted by **C(j)**. (STACK[j] in the SPC simulator.) The notation:

$$C(j) \leftarrow x$$

means "store the value x in location j." Because data may be in one- or two-word units, depending on whether an integer or real is referenced, C(j) will be understood as referring to either a single or a double word depending on the type. When C(j) refers to a double word, j will refer to the lesser of the two word addresses in data memory.

The contents of cell i in program memory is denoted PM(i). Because program memory is read-only, only operations of the form:

$$x \leftarrow PM(i)$$

are legal. In fact, the function PM(i) will be required in only the master execution procedure, described later. In our abstract machine discussion, each instruction will be assumed to occupy one cell in program memory; in the SPC simulator, the instructions occupy different numbers of cells.

If $i < 0$ or $i > n$, then PM(i) = *halt*. The master execution program may access PM(n + 1), but no instruction outside the range $0 \le i \le n$ ever should be executed in a valid program.

The program memory is fixed at compile-time, in principle at least. An implementation may defer some operations on the program memory to just prior to execution of the program. However, no alterations in program memory are permitted during execution. This machine model is therefore less general than the general Von Neumann machine. It supports any language in which some program is compiled, loaded, and executed in separate discrete steps. It does not support such languages as Lisp, in which code may be generated at run-time.

The machine has special registers for the variables i, s, m, and l. i is the instruction pointer, s is the stack-top pointer, m points to the stack marker, and l is a *lexical level*. We shall discuss m and l in greater detail later.

9.4.1. Instruction Execution

The overall operation of the SPC machine is described by the master execution program that follows. Initially, data memory is empty, $m = s = -1, l = 0$, and $i = 0$. The program memory is loaded with instructions, and then execution of the instructions begins at location zero. The program will expand and contract the data memory stack and will stop when the stack is empty.

Execution is initiated by building a "fake" stack marker on the stack; an exit through this stack marker determines that the program has completed. There is no HALT instruction.

```
procedure EXECUTE;
{SPC machine master execution program}
  var INS: integer;
begin
  LOAD(program);
  s:=-1;
  m:=-1;
  i:=0;
  INS:=PM(i);    {first instruction}
  INIT;          {build initial stack marker}
  while stack <> empty do
  begin
    i:=i+1;
    EXECUTE(INS);    {execute the instruction}
        {Note: Execution of INS may change i}
    INS:=PM(i)       {fetch the next instruction}
  end
end;
```

The description of the individual instructions and their rationale constitute the rest of this chapter.

The SPC machine could be implemented in a number of different ways, viz:

1. Build a machine according to the specification of these notes, perhaps through a combination of hard-wired logic and microprogramming.

2. Write an interpreter for the instructions. This interpreter might be an assembly language program implemented on a microprocessor.

3. Write a program to translate SPC into machine code for some machine.

4. Write a set of macros that generate machine code in assembly language.

The SPC simulator system includes a symbolic assembler for SPC instructions; it generates a condensed set of instructions that can be loaded and executed by the simulator. We shall use this assembler's mnemonics in what follows and will illustrate the concepts with several programs written in these mnemonics. The instructions themselves will be defined in a more abstract fashion, or through an English description and examples.

9.5. Constants and Arithmetic Expressions

An expression such as:

$$15 + (75 - 35) * 86$$

can be evaluated easily by a stack machine, as we saw in chapter 7. A bottom-up or top-down compiler can simply emit stack load instructions and appropriate stack operations on each operator, as they are encountered in the parsing process. We are thus led to the following SPC load and arithmetic instructions:

```
LOAD = <integer>        ... push an integer
       s ← s + 1
       C(s) ← <integer>
```

Note that the LOAD first increments the stack top pointer s, then writes the integer into that top location. s always will point to the top-most item in the stack.

In the simulator, the LOAD op-code requires one byte, and the integer value appears in the following two bytes.

```
LOAD = <real>           ... push a real
       s ← s + 2
       C(s - 1) ← <real>   ... double word
```

Here, two words are pushed onto the stack. We assume that a real number can be carried in a double word in this chapter. (In QPARSER, three words are required on the IBM PC computer, and four on an HP series 200 computer. These variations are accommodated easily by changing a global constant.)

The SPC assembler distinguishes an integer from a real number by the form of the number—thus, -1576 is an integer, whereas 55.76 and $16E-5$ are reals.

```
ADD I          ... integer addition
      C(s - 1) ← C(s - 1) + C(s)
      s ← s - 1

ADD R          ... real addition
      C(s - 3) ← C(s - 3) + C(s - 1)
          ... these refer to double words
      s ← s - 2
```

Addition and the other binary operations—SUB, MPY, DIV—assume that two numbers are in the top of the stack. The operation is performed on these values and the result replaces both the values. The instruction depends on whether an integer or real operation is wanted; hence it carries a flag I or R. Thus, ADD I expects an integer in TOS and in TOS $-$ 1, adds them, removes them, and pushes the result on the stack.

In what follows, we shall define only the integer operations. The real operations are similar to the ADD operations described, and involve multiple words.

```
SUB I          ... integer subtraction
      C(s - 1) ← C(s - 1) - C(s)
      s ← s - 1
```

Note that the convention here is that the integer at TOS is subtracted *from* the integer at TOS-1. This convention stems from the way in which an arithmetic expression parser is arranged most easily—in evaluating the expression A $-$ B, A is pushed, then B, then the SUB instruction is executed.

```
MPY I          ... integer multiplication
      C(s - 1) ← C(s - 1) * C(s)
      s ← s - 1

DIV I          ... integer division
      C(s - 1) ← C(s - 1) / C(s)
      s ← s - 1
```

For example, the following instruction sequence computes the expression 15 + (75 − 35) * 86, leaving its result on the stack top. The notation follows that used in the SPC symbolic assembler; for example, a semicolon opens a comment, which extends to the end of the line.

```
LOAD =15
LOAD =75
LOAD =35
SUB  I          ; 75 - 35
LOAD =86
MPY· I
ADD  I
```

Any of the binary instructions will fail when the result is out of the range of representation of the number form. In the SPC simulator, this range is −32768 to 32767 for integers, and undefined for reals (real representation depends on the supporting computer system and its Pascal compiler). Such a failure in our abstract model is undefined; in the SPC simulator, there will be a Pascal system trap or a range error.

9.6. Variables

A variable is accessed by a double address, which consists of a *relative lexical level* r, and a *marker-relative address* a. Two numbers are needed to locate a variable, for reasons that we shall discuss more fully later. Essentially, the lexical level determines whether the variable is among the local variables of this procedure or some covering procedure, or even global. Within that lexical level, the marker-relative address defines the variable's word address relative to a certain place in the stack.

The relative lexical level is a nonnegative integer, whereas the marker-relative address may be positive or negative.

The combination of these two is called a *textual address,* and usually will appear in form [r, a]. We shall extend our notation slightly: C(r, a) will refer to the contents of the stack value at the textual address [r, a]. A function STKADDR(R, A) will be defined to return the absolute stack address from a textual address [r, a].

We shall assume for now that r = 0. Then the data memory location of a reference [0, a] will be C(m + a); that is, the reference will be to a words relative to the location m of the stack marker. When a is negative, the reference will be to a parameter passed to the currently active procedure; when positive, it will be to a local variable.

Such addresses are used in another variation of the LOAD and STOR instructions, as follow. These copy variable values from some location in the stack to or from the stack top:

```
LOAD I B j      ... copy and push integer at [B, j]
      s ← s + 1
      C(s) ← C(B, j)

LOAD R B j      ... copy and push real at [B, j]

STOR I B j      ... stack top integer to [B, j], pop stack
      C(r, a) ← C(s)
      s ← s - 1


STOR R B j      ... stack top real to [B, j], pop stack
```

The LOAD instructions make a space at the top of the stack, then copy a value found somewhere else in the stack to this space; it is illegal to copy this value onto itself.

The STOR instructions copy the stack top value to some other location in the stack, then remove it. We shall see that although this is sufficient to support Pascal, a nonremoving STOR instruction often is useful as an optimization.

If the resulting stack location exceeds s or is less than zero, an error is declared.

The meaning of a reference to an address [r, a] when r is greater than zero will be explained later.

For example, the following program fragment implements the assignment statement $X := B - C$, where X has the address [0, 5], B has the address [0, −4], and C has the address [0, 7]. All are integers:

```
LOAD I 0 -4    ;  B
LOAD I 0 7     ;  C
SUB   I
STOR I 0 5     ;  X
```

9.7. More Operations

The following instructions provide more arithmetic and logical capability:

```
NEG I           ... negation
     C(s) ← -C(s)

NEG R           ... real negation
     C(s - 1) ← -C(s - 1)
```

These are *unary* operations; the value in the top of the stack is replaced by its arithmetic negation.

```
EQU I           ... integer equal
     C(s - 1) ← if C(s - 1)=C(s) then TRUE
                                 else FALSE
     s ← s - 1

EQU R           ... real equal
```

EQU compares the top two stack values as numbers and replaces them by a single Boolean value. A Boolean value is represented by an integer one for TRUE and zero for FALSE in the simulator.

```
LES I               ... integer less than
        C(s - 1) ← if C(s - 1) < C(s) then TRUE
                                      else FALSE
        s ← s - 1

LES R               ... real less than

GTR I               ... integer greater than
        C(s - 1) ← if C(s - 1) > C(s) then TRUE
                                      else FALSE
        s ← s - 1

GTR R               ... real greater than
```

Boolean values also may be subjected to logical operations. In the simulator, any nonzero value is considered TRUE and a zero value is considered FALSE, although a compiler always will generate a one or a zero for these.

```
AND                 ... logical AND
        C(s - 1) ← if C(s - 1)=TRUE and C(s)=TRUE
                      then TRUE else FALSE
        s ← s - 1

OR                  ... logical OR
        C(s - 1) ← if C(s - 1)=TRUE or C(s)=TRUE
                      then TRUE else FALSE
        s ← s - 1

NOT                 ... boolean complement
          (defined only for C(s)=TRUE or FALSE)
        C(s) ← if C(s)=TRUE then FALSE
                            else TRUE
```

The AND operation compares the top two stack values as Boolean variables and replaces them with a TRUE or FALSE, according to the usual meaning of logical AND.

9.8. Addresses and Address Calculations

A datum in the stack also can be referred to by a single word regarded as its address. In QPARSER, this word is just the index of a word in a word array that represents the stack.

We have two ways of referring to a variable—by its textual address and by its absolute stack address. The textual address always will be the means of referring to a variable in a source program, whereas the absolute address is useful in computing the location of a variable within a data structure.

We need some supporting instructions for absolute addresses, as follows:

```
LOAD @ B j          ... generate an absolute address
      s ← s + 1
      C(s) ← STKADDR(B, j)

LOAD I              ... load integer through a TOS address
      C(s) ← C(C(s))

LOAD R              ... load real through TOS address

STOR I              ... store integer through a TOS address
      C(C(s - 1)) ← C(s)
      s ← s - 2

STOR R              ... store real through TOS address
```

Note that LOAD I expects an absolute address in TOS; it then replaces that address by a copy of the stack value referred to by the address. STOR I expects a value in TOS and an address in TOS $-$ 1; it writes a copy of the value in the stack to the given address.

These new instructions are sufficient to support structure and indexed array references. For example, suppose that the compiler has allocated an array of integers at the textual address [0, 20], and we wish to access the Ith integer, where I is an integer at the textual address [0, 18]. The following program fragment achieves that:

```
LOAD @ 0 20        ; base address
LOAD I 0 18        ; index offset
ADD   I
LOAD I             ; load through TOS value
```

A structure reference often is just a reference through a base address offset by some constant value—the compiler can figure out the offset from the structure's declaration. For example, given the Pascal var declaration:

```
var
  ONE_REC: record
             SSNUM,
             ADDR,
             LOC: integer;
           end;
```

assume that ONE_REC has the textual address [0, 15]. The textual address of SSNUM will be [0, 15], of ADDR will be [0, 16], and of LOC will be [0, 17].

A combination of record and array structures can be organized as a sequence of address calculations. For example, consider the following declarations:

```
type
  RECT= record
          WIDTH,
          LENGTH: integer;
        end;
var
  RA: array [0..15] of rect;
  K: integer;
```

Assume that RA's base address is [0, 8]. RA contains $16 \times 2 = 32$ integers; hence, K's address will be [0, 40]. If we wish the value of RA[K].LENGTH, the following program fragment computes that:

```
LOAD @ 0 8        ; RA base address
LOAD I 0 40       ; value of K
LOAD =2           ; each RECT is 2 words
MPY  I
ADD  I            ; now have base address of RA[K]
LOAD =1           ; LENGTH is offset by 1
LOAD I            ; load through the computed address
```

Notice how the SPC instructions fall into place in the same order as the Pascal compound variable reference components.

9.9. Stack Space Allocation

Two instructions are provided for allocating data memory space in the stack, as follows:

```
INCS   v          ... allocate v words
   s ← s + v

INCS              ... allocate C(s) words
   C(s + C(s)) ← s
   s ← s + C(s)
```

INCS V just allocates V words by moving the stack pointer higher. To be useful, the compiler must be capable of knowing the textual base address of the allocated space. This is only possible if space has been allocated *only* by the use of this instruction.

This static form of INCS will be used to allocate space for the local variables of a Pascal procedure.

INCS (without the V) expects an integer in TOS, and allocates a number of words equal to its value. This value is dynamic—that is, it is known only during execution of the program. The repeated use of INCS in a code sequence will make it impossible for the compiler to know the base address of any such block of memory. We therefore require that INCS place the base address of its allocated space in TOS; the address can be stored subsequently in a known single-word textual address location.

Note that the *number* of words must first appear in TOS; the space is allocated and then the *base address* of the allocated space is pushed onto the stack. The original number is in the first word of the allocated space.

The dynamic form of INCS provides us with a mechanism of allocating space that depends dynamically on the result of some run-time calculation. Pascal has no provision for such space, but certain other languages do. With INCS, it is easy to extend Pascal by adding declarations for local arrays or structures the dimensions of which are variables or expressions.

INCS does *not* provide support for the Pascal NEW function. Because INCS allocates stack space, this space will disappear on exiting the procedure containing INCS. NEW must allocate space that will remain indefinitely, even though the space was allocated during the execution of some procedure. A separate heap space is required for NEW.

The static form of INCS also can be used to deallocate space; it is an error to use the dynamic form for this. As we shall see, it is generally unnecessary to use either instruction in this way; when a procedure exits, the stack space is reclaimed regardless of which INCS instructions were executed during its activation.

9.10. Branch Instructions

Almost every programming language contains several means of controlling the path of execution of the instructions. We have seen that a simple sequential execution of an instruction followed by its successor is built into the machine. However, we need more than that.

Most high-level languages provide several common *control structures*. Pascal supports six, as follows:

```
goto <label>
if <boolean> then <statement> else <statement>
while <boolean> do <statement>
repeat <statement-list> until <boolean>
for <var> := <expr1> to/downto <expr2> do <statement>
case <expr> of <case-statements>
```

Variations on these can be found in nearly all programming languages.

From the point of view of our abstract machine, we need only two branch instructions, as follows, to support the first five of these. The CASE control structure requires additional special instructions, and will be discussed later.

```
UJP   L                ... unconditional jump
    p ← L

FJP   L                ... conditional 'false' jump
    p ← if C(s) then p + 3
               else L
    s ← s - 1
```

The UJP forces the next instruction to be drawn from location L in the program memory. There is no effect on the stack.

The FJP forces the next instruction to be drawn from location L only if the TOS value is FALSE; that is, it is an integer zero. Otherwise, the instruction following the FJP is next (this is at location p + 3 in the SPC simulator). In either case, the TOS value is dropped from the stack.

The SPC assembler expects L to be a *symbolic location;* that is, a name or a number referring to some location in the program. The symbolic location is associated with a real location through the *pseudo instruction* LOC, defined as follows:

```
LOC  L              ... associates label L with next instruction
    (no operation)
```

LOC has no effect on the stack or the program; it merely indicates that the name or number L is to be associated with the following instruction.

A name is useful as a label in some languages, whereas a number is used in others, such as Pascal. We shall see that the compiler must create unique labels in order to support the non-GOTO control structures, and a numeric label is easy to generate.

9.10.1. Pascal Control Structures

We shall now show that these two instructions are sufficient to support the Pascal control structures (other than the CASE). The GOTO control structure maps directly to a UJP, and its target label to a LOC.

IF-THEN-ELSE

The IF-THEN-ELSE structure:

```
IF <boolean> THEN <then-clause>
             ELSE <else-clause>
```

maps to the following program fragment:

```
<boolean>        ; evaluate boolean, result left in TOS
FJP L1           ; if FALSE, go to L1
<then-clause>
UJP L2           ; branch around the ELSE clause
LOC L1
<else-clause>
LOC L2
```

Here, the Boolean expression is evaluated first by some sequence of instructions—however long. The result will be a zero or a one in TOS. The FJP instruction then either branches to L1 or the <then-clause>, popping the Boolean value from the stack before continuing. At the end of the <then-clause>, an unconditional jump to L2 skips the <else-clause>.

Note that the labels L1 and L2 do not appear in the Pascal source; hence, they must be generated by the compiler. A reasonable strategy is simply to assign successive integers to all labels, including GOTO labels, using symbol table lookup to associate the Pascal GOTO labels to the newly generated ones.

When the <else-clause> is absent, the following fragment is sufficient:

```
<boolean>
FJP L1
<then-clause>
LOC L1
```

WHILE-DO

The WHILE-DO structure:

```
WHILE <boolean> DO <statement>
```

maps easily to an SPC program fragment, as follows:

```
LOC L1
<boolean>          ; evaluate boolean test expression
FJP L2             ; test for quitting
<statement>
UJP L1             ; return for another test
LOC L2
```

The REPEAT-UNTIL structure is a minor variation of the WHILE-DO structure.

FOR Loop

The FOR structure:

```
for <var> := <expr1> to/downto <expr2> do <statement>
```

is somewhat more complicated. In addition to the loop variable <var>, we need
a temporary location for the endpoint value <expr2>. Pascal rules requires that
<expr2> be evaluated just once before entering the loop; however, the end
comparison must be made on each iteration.

We shall just allocate one stack-top word for the <expr2> value. However,
we need a way to perform repeated comparisons against it without losing the
original value. That requires a new instruction, as follows:

```
DUP I              ... duplicate stack top
    s ← s + 1
    C[s] ← C[s - 1]
```

For the sake of completeness, DUP R also is supported by the SPC assembler and
simulator; however, it is not needed for anything described in this chapter.

Take the TO case first; the DOWNTO case requires a slightly different instruction sequence:

```
<expr1>            ; calculate initial value
STOR I 0 V         ; loop variable
<expr2>            ; calculate endpoint value
                   ;   it will be in TOS
LOC L1             ; mark loop entry location
DUP I              ; starting the endpoint test
LOAD I 0 V
LES I
NOT
FJP L2             ; get out if V ≥ E2
<statement>        ; execute the FOR statement
LOAD I 0 V         ; prepare to increment V
```

```
LOAD = 1
ADD  I
STOR I 0 V
UJP  L1          ; then go back
LOC  L2          ; mark exit location
INCS -1          ; get rid of endpoint value
```

CASE Statement

An implementation of the Pascal CASE statement is considerably more complicated than that of the other control structures. Although CASE could be implemented as a sequence of comparisons of the CASE variable against each of the CASE label values, most compilers implement it by generating a *branch table* that is indexed by the CASE label.

Note that, in Pascal, the labels of a CASE statement belong to an enumerated set of the same type as the CASE variable expression. They usually will be represented by small integers. The labels cannot be expressions evaluated at execution-time. These properties make it possible for the compiler to construct a CASE branch table.

The compiled code must:

- Evaluate the CASE variable.

- Check for bounds violations.

- Access a table (in code) of branch locations, by indexing.

- Branch to that location.

In addition, each CASE statement must end in a UJP to a LOC at the end of the CASE statement.

We find that we need more instructions to support the CASE, because we have no mechanism for computing a code address and branching through it. Here is one:

```
CJP   T                ... case jump
   let L:=PM(T);       ... least value
   let U:=PM(T+1);     ... greatest value
   let D:=PM(T+2);     ... self-relative default address
   let A:=C(s)-L+T+3; ... location in table
   if (C(s) < L) or (C(s) > U) then
      p ← D + T + 2    ... take the default
   else begin
      p ← PM(A)+A;     ... table address
      end;
   s ← s - 1
```

The CJP instruction refers to a table of locations in code. The table begins in location T. Its first three entries are the least value, the greatest value, and a self-relative default address.

Following these, at positions T + 3, T + 4, . . . , T + N, are self-relative locations of the CASE statements for the CASE labels L, L + 1, L + 2, . . . , L + N.

The table can be indexed by the integer value in TOS when suitably offset.

To construct this table, we need a symbolic means of putting a code address into code:

```
ADR  L1              ... address in code
    PM(p) = address(L1);
    p = p+1;
```

We will also need a symbolic means of putting an integer *constant* into code:

```
CON <integer>        ... integer appears in code
    PM(p) = <integer> value;
    p:=p+1;
```

The case table could be positioned just after the CJP instruction, except that this is awkward to manage in a one-pass compiler. The table's size depends on the range between the least and the greatest of the case statement labels, which will not be known until the end of the CASE statement has been parsed. In the meantime, the program material from the CASE statements should have been written to code. It therefore is easiest to place the case table after the last case statement. Because it is accessed through a symbolic location, it can be anywhere in code space.

Example.   Suppose our CASE statement is the following:

```
case <var> of
2: <expr1>;
1: <expr2>;
3: <expr3>;
end;
```

The compiler should then generate the following program fragment:

```
<var>            ; evaluate case variable
CJP  T1          ; case jump referring to table T1

LOC  V1          ; here come the case statements
<expr1>
UJP  L2

LOC  V2          ; in the order of appearance
<expr2>          ; in the program
UJP  L2

LOC  V3
<expr3>
UJP  L2

LOC  T1          ; here is the case branch table
CON  1           ; least case label
```

```
CON 3          ; greatest
ADR L2         ; default location
ADR V2         ; note the reordering
ADR V1
ADR V3
LOC L2
```

Each ADR field of the branch table must appear in the table in a position that corresponds to the *value* of the CASE statement label, rather than its lexical position in the source. For example, if the labels are three, two, and five, then the table would appear as follows:

```
ADR V2         ; 2
ADR V1         ; 3
ADR L2         ; branch out on 4
ADR V3         ; 5
```

This example brings up another point about the CASE: ISO Pascal does not require that the labels form a dense set between the least and greatest. Hence, missing label positions are best just filled in with the address of the exit location L2.

ISO Pascal as well as Jensen and Wirth Pascal provide no ''otherwise'' form, and insist that the result of entering a CASE statement with a value that cannot be matched to a CASE label is *undefined*. Other Pascals provide an otherwise clause that catches all out-of-range CASE label values.

When an otherwise appears, we need only fill in the unspecified locations with the location of the otherwise clause. Without an otherwise, an invalid CASE value should initiate a trap.

One more extension is needed to cover CASE numbers that exceed the greatest label or are less than the least. This test should result in either accessing the CASE table or just branching to the otherwise CASE or L2. We have incorporated this test in the instruction.

9.11. Input-Output

Pascal and other languages support a rich variety of ways of reading formatted textual material from a file or a terminal keyboard, and for writing text to files, printers, or terminal screens. These are implemented in most Pascal compilers by special primitive I/O functions. I/O often passes through several levels of procedure calls.

At the level nearest the language, compound WRITE and READ statements are decomposed by the compiler into simple unit operations. The types of the objects are noted by the compiler in order to generate the appropriate function. For example:

```
writeln(myfile, V:5, RL:10:3, I2);
```

will be decomposed into three function calls—an integer WRITEI for V, a real

WRITER for RL, and an integer WRITEI for I2. The values V, RL and I2 usually are expected to be in TOS, and the primitive WRITE function will remove this value. The WRITEI and WRITER functions will expect other parameters as well; for example, the file number associated with MYFILE, and formatting numbers. Thus, the preceding writeln might look like this in SPC code (however, some of these functions are *not* provided in the simulator):

```
LOAD I myfile        ; myfile reference
LOAD =5
LOAD I v             ; get V
CXP  WRITEI          ; write an integer
LOAD I myfile
LOAD =10
LOAD =3
LOAD R rl            ; get RL
CXP  WRITER          ; write a real
LOAD I myfile
LOAD =10             ; default format
LOAD I i2
CXP  WRITEI          ; write an integer
LOAD I myfile
CXP  WRITELN         ; line return
```

Different functions are required for writing text (character streams) and for writing records. A text stream must be generated from the internal representation of a number and concatenated onto a line under construction. When the last operation of a WRITELN is coded, the line is sent to a still lower-level file writing function.

At the lowest level, a block of bytes—whether a record or formatted text—must be copied to a disc, tape, printer, or whatever. This operation is performed by a *device-specific function*. Within a multiuser operating system, this function often must coordinate several unrelated read/write operations on a single storage volume. It usually must accumulate material in a buffer until a printer or storage device is available.

A READ statement usually is supported by writing an address in TOS; the first-level read function then writes a value into the indicated stack location.

9.11.1. SPC I/O Operations

The SPC simulator supports I/O through a special *system call* instruction CXP. Only four system functions are provided for the sake of simplicity:

```
CXP  PRINTI      ... print integer
     Print C(s)

CXP  PRINTR      ... print real
     Print C(s - 1), C(s)
```

Note that the stack top value is *not* removed by these instructions, as might be expected. We chose to implement these instructions in this way so that they could be freely added anywhere in a sequence of assembly code for debugging purposes. The compiler must be careful to follow a PRINTI call with INCS -1, and a PRINTR call with INCS -2, however.

There also are neither file designator nor formatting parameters.

```
CXP  READI      ... read integer
       s ← s + 1;
       C(s) ← integer from reader

CXP  READR      ... read real
```

Each of the READ functions obtains a value from an input source and pushes it onto the stack.

The SPC simulator asks for an input and an output file before starting the simulation; these control the destination of the PRINT functions and the source of the READ functions. The file also can be the keyboard of the simulating computer.

Messages

A useful SPC instruction is the MSG instruction, which expects to be followed by a Pascal-style string; for example:

```
MSG 'Should be 100'
```

MSG sends the string to the default output device—usually the terminal. This is strictly a debugging aid; SPC does not support strings and string variables. MSG has no effect on the machine or its stack, but it does take up space in code.

9.12. Procedure Calls and Local Variable Space

We have not yet discussed allocation of variables to the memory. The easiest plan is to allocate variables to stack addresses 0, 1, 2, . . ., N.

This simple plan effectively gives us a Fortran machine; in Fortran, each variable can be given a fixed, permanent location in memory. This also applies to variables that only appear within some function, because only one instance of a Fortran function can be active at any one time—Fortran functions cannot be called recursively.

However, in Pascal and most other modern languages, any function or procedure can be called recursively. With recursion, this simple variable allocation scheme will not work. For example, consider the following factorial function:

```
function FACT(N: integer): integer;
begin
  if n=1 then fact:=1
  else
  fact:= fact(n-1) * n;   {R}
end;
```

When FACT is called with N = 3, it calls itself with N = 2, then N = 1. Only with N = 1 does the function return without calling itself again. After it returns, it multiplies its return value of 1 by N, which is 2 (see the line marked R above). The 2 needs to have been saved somewhere while the function was working on the 1 case. Under a Fortran allocation scheme, the 2 would have been overwritten by the 1 and lost forever. Similarly, the 3 would have been overwritten earlier by the 2.

Function Activation

Each call is considered to be an *activation* of a procedure. Because the call is suspended in order to make another call, a trail in memory must be kept of the previous values of the variable N, and also of the procedure's return location. The procedure's code does not have to be copied because it is inalterable; when we want to activate a procedure, we can simply transfer control to its entry point. However, a procedure can be called from different places, so each activation requires a unique memory word to hold a return location.

A local variable (such as N in FACT) may require any number of distinct memory locations, one for each possible procedure activation. The compiler cannot determine how many activations may be required, so these must be provided dynamically.

An activation occurs as a result of a procedure call, and in no other way. The activation will disappear when the procedure exits, and its local variable values also can disappear. Furthermore, if a procedure P1 is called, then, while P1 is active, another procedure P2 is called, then P2 must exit *before* P1 is permitted to exit. Procedure calling does not *have* to work that way, but it does in Pascal and other languages. Thus, procedure activations are properly nested during execution.

Call nesting makes it possible to allocate space on the stack top for any local variable, the return address, and other activation information (there is more). Each call allocates more such space, and each exit removes the stack space associated with its procedure activation.

9.12.1. Mechanism of a Procedure Call

We can now identify some of the operations involved in calling a procedure, through the instruction:

```
CLP n          ... call local procedure N
```

The call operation starts with evaluation of the procedure's actual parameters, before CLP is executed: each actual parameter is evaluated; its value is left on the stack. Then CLP is executed, with the following actions:

- A *stack marker* is pushed on the stack. This will contain a return address and certain other information.

- The special marker register m is set to the value of TOS, which will be the top word in the stack marker.

- Program control is passed to the first instruction of the procedure.

The first instruction of the procedure usually is an INCS N, which allocates more stack space for local variables.

The procedure's instructions most likely will include LOAD and STOR references to local variables. These are accessed through a textual address that refers to a location relative to the marker register's contents C(m).

9.12.2. Mechanism of a Procedure EXIT

Eventually, an EXIT instruction is executed:

```
EXIT  n          ... exit from a procedure, popping
                     n words below the stack marker
```

What this must do is first pick up the return address carried in the top-most stack marker. All the space above the stack marker, and a certain amount of space below it, can be discarded by changing the TOS pointer s to some smaller value. The marker register m also must be changed to some smaller value—it must point to a previously written stack marker, the one belonging to the procedure that called the current one.

How much space can be discarded? Where is the previous stack marker?

The answer to the first question can be determined by the Pascal compiler. It knows how many actual parameters are required for each procedure and exactly how many words were required to hold them. The discarded stack space therefore is a known number of words below the stack marker. This number therefore can be included as part of the EXIT instruction.

Note that this will not work if procedure calls are permitted to have a variable number of actual parameters, or if an actual parameter can have a varying length, as is the case in Ada, C, and Lisp.

The second question also can be answered by the compiler under strict Pascal space allocation rules. (Do you see how?) However, we have chosen to include the location of the previous stack marker in a new stack marker when a procedure is called. The EXIT instruction can then simply look in that stack marker slot and set m to the value found therein. Having a previous stack marker reference also facilitates debugging and unstructured procedure exits.

9.12.3. Stack Marker Definition

We can now define the stack marker. It consists of four words, as follows:

- m − 3: number of the currently active procedure.

- m − 2: back pointer to stack marker for previous lexical level.

- m − 1: back pointer to stack marker for previous procedure.

- m: return location

Of these four words, the currently active procedure number is needed only for program debugging. The SPC simulator associates the name of each procedure with a number so that procedure tracing can be reported by procedure name. This also is useful in a debug break state to report the current procedure name, and to report the currently activated, but suspended, procedures.

The second word, at m − 2, is required to locate variables that are not in the current procedure's lexical scope. The sequence of these back pointers is called the *static chain,* or *lexical chain.* Let the top-most stack marker refer to the currently active procedure P; then the prior marker in the static chain refers to the procedure lexically enclosing P. A static pointer may skip over several stack markers. More about this later.

The third word, at m − 1, points to the previous stack marker in the stack. It is used in the EXIT instruction to reset m on returning from a procedure. The sequence of these back pointers is called the *dynamic chain,* and links each of the stack markers down into the stack to the first one.

The fourth word, at m, contains the return location in code space; it too is used by the EXIT instruction.

Example.   Consider the following Pascal program:

```
program SIMPLE;
  var I1, I2: integer;

  {..............}
  procedure A (FA1: integer);
    var IA1, IA2: integer;
  begin
    write(fa1);
    write(i2);              { <— }
  end;

  {..............}
  procedure B (FB1: integer);
    var IB1: integer;
  begin
    if fb1>0 then
    begin
      b(fb1-1);
      a(fb1);
    end
    else a(fb1);            { <— }
    write(i1);
  end;
```

```
begin
  i1:=27;
  i2:=3;
  b(i2);                    { <— }
end.
```

The arrows { <— } define a particular state during execution of the program. Procedure B has been called with FB1 = 3, then again with FB1 = 2, again with FB1 = 1, and finally with FB1 = 0. When FB1 = 0, procedure A is called with this value.

We clearly have six procedure activations at this point. The first activation is the program itself, the next four are for procedure B, and the last one is for procedure A. Each activation has its own stack marker and space for local and formal variables. The stack configuration at this moment is shown in figure 9.1, with the stack markers labeled SM1 to SM6.

The bottom-most stack marker SM1 is created when the program is started. Its static and dynamic links are zero, which means there are no deeper stack markers. The program's variables I1 and I2 are allocated as shown just above this stack marker. After the two assignment statements:

```
i1:=27;
i2:=3;
```

these slots contain 27 and three, respectively.

Next, procedure B is called via b(i2) in the main program. Space for I2 is allocated and filled with the value three; this location will be referred to as FB1 when inside procedure B. On calling B, the stack marker SM2 is created. Its static link points back to SM1, because the global variables I1 and I2 are in the lexically covering procedure—the main program. Procedure B will refer to variable I2 (for example) by the textual address [1, 2]—the one refers to the marker one removed by static link from the current one, and the two refers to a word offset of two relative to the marker.

The dynamic link in SM2 points to SM1; this link always points to the immediately preceding stack marker.

When B is called for the second time, SM3 is created. Its dynamic link points to SM2, whereas its static link points to SM1. Note that no matter how many times B is recursively called, its immediately enclosing lexical scope always is the main program.

Each B call generates another stack marker. Eventually, A is called and SM6 is created. The static link again points to SM1, because the global variables are one lexical level removed from A, as they are for B.

After the A call is completed, the procedures successively reach their EXIT instructions. On the A exit, the stack TOS is moved down to point to IB1 just below SM6. This EXIT instruction carries a one, because A is known to have one word of formal parameters, the FA1. Hence, TOS is moved one word below the word just below SM6. The stack marker position register m also is moved down

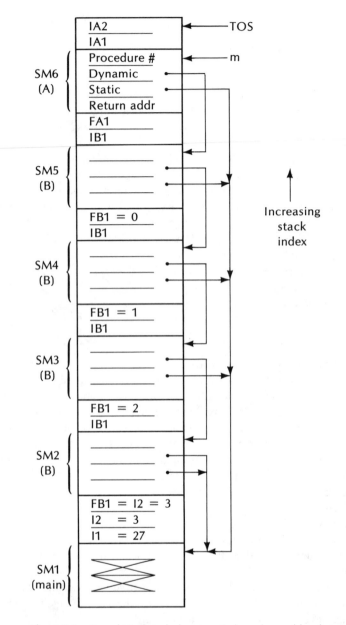

Figure 9.1.   Snapshot of stack showing stack marker and local variables.

to point to SM5. We see that this environment is precisely the one that prevailed while procedure B was active. The only difference is that some words have been written above TOS; these words will be left behind as garbage and probably overwritten in some later arithmetic calculation or a procedure call.

Eventually, procedure B will exit through an EXIT 1. Each exit discards some more stack top words and restores a previous procedure environment. Eventually, the first activation of B is terminated, leaving just the main program stack marker SM1 and its two global variables. When the main program completes, the system will notice from the zero dynamic link in SM1 that there are no remaining procedures—the program will halt.

9.12.4. Procedure Call and Exit

A stack marker is created upon a procedure call. There are various ways of organizing procedure calls; we shall discuss one that is employed in the UCSD Pascal system and in the SPC simulator.

A procedure call will occur when the CLP instruction is executed. CLP carries a unique procedure number, assigned by the compiler:

```
CLP n           ... call procedure N
    {generate a stack marker, saving procedure
     number, static link, dynamic link, return
     address.  Transfer control to procedure}
```

The number N is in the range of zero to 255 in the SPC simulator for convenience. (The range can be extended easily.) The number is treated as an index into a *procedure table*, which contains the following information:

- PLOC: the code entry point.

- PROCLEVEL: the absolute procedure lexical level.

- PTRACE: a procedure trace bit.

The trace bit PTRACE is set if the procedure is to be traced and cleared otherwise; it is useful for debugging.

The PROCLEVEL is needed to set the static link in the stack marker. It does this as follows. The current lexical level is carried in a special machine register l. Its value is compared with PROCLEVEL. If they are the same, then the static link in the existing stack marker is copied into the new one—the two procedures are at the same lexical level. Another possibility is that PROCLEVEL is one greater than l; this happens when the new procedure is nested inside the old one. In this case, the new static link points to the previous stack marker; a new link in the static chain is formed. The remaining case is PROCLEVEL less than l. Here we have the new procedure at a lower lexical level than the old one; it can be at any number of levels lower. We must then step down through the static links by an amount equal to the difference and copy that link into the new stack marker.

The dynamic link is filled easily; it is just a copy of m, which points to the previous dynamic link.

The return address is the location in code just past the procedure call instruction.

On an EXIT, all the preceding steps are unwound. The stack is reduced, removing all local variables, the stack marker, and the formal parameters. Control is returned to the previous procedure, as noted from the stack marker.

9.12.5. Locating Variables

We can now explain in detail how textual addresses work. Recall that a textual address is a number pair; for example, [2, 15]. The "2" requires stepping down through the static chain by two links; this yields a stack marker. We then access word 15 relative to the location of that marker. A textual address [0, n] refers to the nth word relative to the current stack marker. Here is a function that computes and returns an absolute stack address, given a textual address [B, j]:

```
function STKADDR(B, J: integer): integer;
   var STLINK: integer;
begin
   stlink:=m;     {current stack marker}
   while (b>0) and (stlink>0) do
   begin  {walk down the static links}
      stlink:=stack[stlink-2];
      b:=b-1;
   end;
   if stlink<=0 then error('stack underflow');
   stkaddr:=stlink+j;
end;
```

The test for stlink = 0 in the WHILE loop and the IF statement is not really needed; it adds robustness to the static link search. A zero or negative stlink indicates that something is very wrong.

The compiler can generate textual addresses for any variable by keeping track of the lexical level of a procedure being compiled, and also noting the lexical level of a referenced variable—the difference is just the first member of the textual address. The second member is the variable's relative location, and depends on only the declarations for its associated procedure.

9.13. Dynamic Arrays

A *dynamic array* is an indexed array structure the upper and lower limits of which are determined at run-time. ISO Pascal provides no declaration mechanism for a dynamic array; however, a number of languages do. We therefore introduce a simple extension that will not be found in any Pascal implementation—a VAR with indeterminate array limits, and an ALLOCATE statement that fixes the limits and allocates stack space for the array.

An example of a program fragment with these new features follows:

```
var I, J: integer;
    P: array [0..*] of integer;   {NOT ISO standard!}
```

```
begin
  readln(i);    {get a dimension from outside}
  begin
    allocate(p, i);   {set the array limits}
    for j:=0 to i do
      p[j]:=j*j;
  end
end
```

Note that this kind of array can be allocated from the stack top, despite the variable dimension. The compiler will lose track of the location of the stack top, but that is OK provided it has allocated a pointer near the stack marker in a position it *does* know.

ALLOCATE can be used any number of times on the same array by simply allocating new space from the stack. However, our simple implementation will *not* copy old values into the new space—the old values are lost. This semantics mechanism is simple to implement, but wasteful of stack space. It will also leave behind garbage space on the stack unless we do something more clever about reusing such space, but the garbage will be collected anyway on an exit.

A more powerful form of ALLOCATE would; (1) copy any existing values into the newly allocated space, and (2) attempt to reclaim space left behind.

Dope Vectors

What, if anything, is allocated by the VAR for a dynamic array? We shall see that we must allocate a *dope vector,* a structure that carries a pointer to the array and information about its array limits. The dope vector has a size known to the compiler; hence, it can be allocated on the stack under the usual Pascal rules. Figure 9.2 shows a dope vector (lower box) and an array value space (upper box).

Arrays can be implemented in at least two ways. The first of these, *indexed* arrays, conserves memory space at the expense of element access time. The second, *matrix pointer* arrays, requires more memory space but provides a rapid access means. Both methods use the same allocation and access formats and the same dope vector format. The only difference is in the implementation of MAS.

9.13.1. Array Instructions

Array allocation and access can be implemented through two new instructions, MAS and AVA, as follows:

```
MAS B j R    Allocate space, adjust dope vector
AVA B j R    Compute an address label
```

MAS expects a dope vector of rank R to be located at [B, j]. The vector contains an element size S, but not the rank. MAS also expects lower and upper dimensions of the array to be pushed on the stack, in order from left to right. After these are placed, S is pushed. (S is the number of words required for each array element.) For example, given the array declaration:

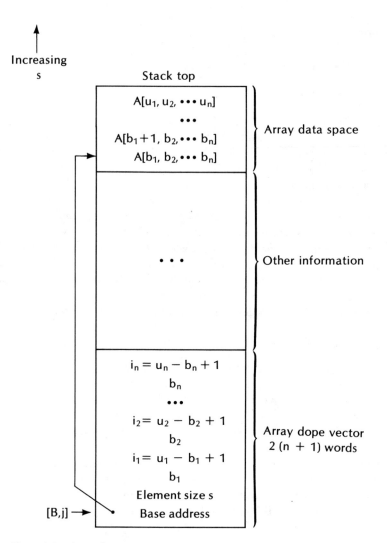

Increasing
s

Figure 9.2.   Array dope vector.

```
var A: array [2..*, -5..10] of integer;
```

and the allocation:

```
allocate(a, n)
```

the ALLOCATE results in the following SPC code:

```
LOAD =2
LOAD I n          ; n's textual address needed here
LOAD =-5
LOAD =10
MAS  B j 2        ; A' textual address is [B, j]
```

Note that the compiler knows the constant dimensions; the ALLOCATE function supplies variable dimensions. All dimensions must be pushed on the stack, however. MAS adjusts the dope vector as indicated in figure 9.2, then allocates sufficient space from the stack to accommodate an array consisting of S-word elements each.

When MAS is executed, the dope vector is adjusted to reflect the new array dimensions and element size, space is allocated at the top of the stack, and the array base address is set.

In general, the dope vector and the allocated array space will be separated by an unknown number of words. Only the dope vector textual address is known to the compiler.

Array space and the dope vector created for the array declaration:

```
var A: array [b₁..u₁, b₂..u₂, ..., bₙ..uₙ] of integer;
```

by MAS are shown in figure 9.2. For dimension i, b_i is the least value that a subscript may take and u_i is the greatest value that subscript i may take. These may be expressions in general, containing variables previously declared and defined. The dope vector's size is $2 \times n + 2$ words, and is independent of the array dimensions and its element size.

An array's data space is allocated somewhere higher in the stack than its dope vector. The array elements start with:

$$A[b_1, b_2, \ldots, b_n], A[b_1 + 1, b_2, \ldots, b_n] \ldots$$

and end with:

$$A[u_1, u_2, \ldots, u_n]$$

Note that the left-most index is the most rapidly varying one. We shall see that this arrangement leads to an efficient implementation for AVA.

AVA

AVA will calculate the address of an array element, given its subscripts arranged in order on the stack. The stack arrangement is similar to that for MAS, except that single index subscripts are written rather than a lower–upper dimension pair. Thus, in accessing an array A[a, b, c], the SPC code will be:

```
LOAD I a
LOAD I b
LOAD I c
AVA  B j 3        ; A's textual address is [B, j]
```

AVA also may check that the given subscripts lie within the dimensioned range of the array. This is clearly the instruction required to access an array element for reading or writing.

Example.   Consider the program fragment:

```
var N: integer;
    A: array [1..*] of integer;
    B: array [3..6, *..*] of real;
    K: integer;
begin
    read(n, k);   {dimension is variable}
    allocate(a, n);
    allocate(b, n+1, n*n-1);
    a[k]:=15;      {typical array references}
    b[k, k+1]:=25.3;
    ...
end
```

This program translates to the following SPC fragment. The TA of variable N is [0, 1], of A is [0, 2], of B is [0, 6], and of K is [0, 12].

```
    INCS 12              ; space for everything

    CXP   READI          ; read(n)
    STOR I 0 1
    CXP   READI          ; read(k)
    STOR I 0 12
    LOAD = 1             ; allocate(a, n)—A's lower bound
    LOAD I 0 1           ; A's upper bound—N
    LOAD = 1             ; A's element size—integer
    MAS 0 2 1            ; dope vector at [0, 2] with rank 1

                         ; allocate(b, n + 1, n * n - 1)
    LOAD = 3             ; first lower bound of B
    LOAD = 6             ; first upper bound of B
    LOAD I 0 1
    LOAD = 1
    ADD I                ; B's second lower bound
    LOAD I 0 1
    LOAD I 0 1
    MPY I
    LOAD = 1
    SUB I                ; B's second upper bound
    LOAD = 2             ; B's element size—real
    MAS 0 6 2            ; B's dope vector address and rank

    LOAD I 0 12          ; fetch K
    AVA 0 2 1            ; computes A[K] address
                         ;   dope vector at [0, 2], rank 1
    LOAD = 15            ; thing to put into a[k]
    STOR I               ; store through TOS address

    LOAD I 0 12          ; fetch K — first index
    LOAD I 0 12
    LOAD =1
```

```
ADD I                ; K + 1—second index
AVA 0 6 2            ; computes B[K, K + 1] address
LOAD = 25.3          ; thing to put into b[k, k + 1]
STOR R               ; store through TOS address
```

Implementing MAS

The MAS procedure is implemented as follows. It expects a dope vector textual address [B, J], and the array rank N. Other information is drawn from the stack.

```
procedure MAS(B, J, N: integer);
   {[B, j] = TA of dope vector,
    N = array rank}
   var X: integer;

   function BUILDV(DV: integer): integer;
     var T, I, S, X: integer;
   begin   {make array space}
     s:=stack[tos];   {element size}
     stack[dv+1]:=s;
     x:=1;
     t:=tos-2*n;
     stack[dv]:=t;   {adjusted base address}
     dv:=dv+2;

     for i:=0 to n-1 do
     begin   {fill dope vector}
       stack[dv]:=stack[t];   {lower bound, b₁}
       dv:=dv+1;
       stack[dv]:=stack[t+1]-stack[t]+1;   {i₁}
       x:=x*stack[dv];   {accumulated elements}
       t:=t+2;
       dv:=dv+1;
     end;
     buildv:=x;   {returns number of elements}
   end;

begin
   x:=buildv(stkaddr(b, j));   {construct dope vector}
   tos:=tos-2*n-1+s*x;   {adjust stack TOS}
   pc:=pc+4;   {adjust program counter}
end
```

MAS executes at run-time. However, it cannot use the data stack of the user program. If MAS is called as a user procedure, a stack marker will be established, yielding a new stack top address TOS. The array will be allocated using this new TOS, after the temporary variables of MAS have been allocated. Unfortunately, on returning, all the allocated space will disappear.

Implementing AVA

Now consider the location of an array element:

$$A[i_1, i_2, i_3, \ldots, i_n)$$

This array element is stored in the stack location:

$$(\text{base location}) + i_1 - b_1 + l_1 * (i_2 - b_2 + l_2 * (i_3 - b_3 + \ldots + l_{n-1} *$$
$$(i_n - b_n) \ldots))$$

The AVA instruction expects the following list on the stack: $i_1, i_2, \ldots, i_n$. The necessary code sequence to access the array elements is therefore:

```
{evaluate i₁}
{evaluate i₂}
     .
     .
     .
{evaluate iₙ}
AVA B j n
{array element address is
   left on the stack}
```

The following procedure defines AVA. This, like MAS, cannot operate on the user stack.

```
procedure AVA(B, J, N: integer);
   var T, U, I, S: integer;
begin    {compute array element address
            from stack information}
   t:=stkaddr(b, j);  {dope vector address}
   t:=t+2*n+1;  {address of iₙ}
   u:=0;   {u = word offset for 1-word
                   element size}
   for i:=n downto 1 do
   begin
      u:=u*stack[t] + stack[tos] - stack[t-1];
      t:=t - 2;
      tos:=tos - 1;  {pop the stack}
   end;
   tos:=tos+1;
   stack[tos]:=u*stack[t] + stack[t-1];
         {final element address}
   pc:=pc+4;
end
```

In AVA, I is used as a counter to step down through the dope vector, T is an address into the dope vector, and U is an element offset variable that becomes the offset from the base address of the array at the end of the for loop. There are several arithmetic operations in each pass of the loop, including a multiplication. We shall next discuss an alternative approach to array access that eliminates all these operations at the expense of some memory space.

9.13.2. Array Access With Matrix Pointers

By indirections find directions out.

. . . William Shakespeare

Given an array of rank n, we may organize the array access by allocating *pointer vectors* in the stack, as well as allocating space for the array elements. The determination of an array element address is much faster with pointer vectors than through the preceding index calculations of AVA if the rank is two or more. If the rank is one, the two methods are essentially the same.

Let us begin with access. We construct a dope vector exactly as before at the textual address [B, j]. However, the base address and allocation are handled by procedure MMAS, which follows. Element access then is performed by an inline code sequence like this:

```
LOAD @ B J          ; base address
{evaluate i₁}
ADD I               ; end of one index

LOAD I              ; starting second index—fetch
                    ; address from indexed pointers
{evaluate i₂}
ADD I               ; end of the second index
    ...             ; etc.
                    ; element address left on stack
```

The simplicity of this scheme speaks for itself. Instead of building a list of indices, then calling AVA, the simple instructions LOAD and ADD are used to determine the address. LOAD I replaces the stack top address with a new address. By adding an index to this address, we are left with either the element address or the address of the next pointer.

A conceptual diagram of this access scheme is given in figure 9.3. Only one dope vector element, the base address [B, j], is needed. The dope vector is similar to that in figure 9.2, except that its elements are not really used in accessing an element unless array bounds checking is required.

The base address of the dope vector points to a fictitious memory location, b_1 words below a vector of l_1 pointers. Note that the first index i_1 must be at least b_1, and is added to the base address during access. After the first ADD, we therefore have the address of one of the l_1 pointers. LOAD I fetches its contents, and this is the address of another fictitious memory location, b_2 words below a vector of l_2 words. At the end of the access sequence, we have the address of an element. The last pointer vector must take into consideration the size of an element. We shall assume in the following example that the element size is one.

Example. A specific stack configuration for the declaration:

```
var X: array [2:4, 3:4] of integer;
```

is shown in figure 9.4. X's textual address [B, j] is 11. The dope vector is in locations 11/16, the first (and only) matrix pointer vector is in locations 22/24, and the data elements are in locations 25/30. The configuration is exactly as MMAS, given next, would generate.

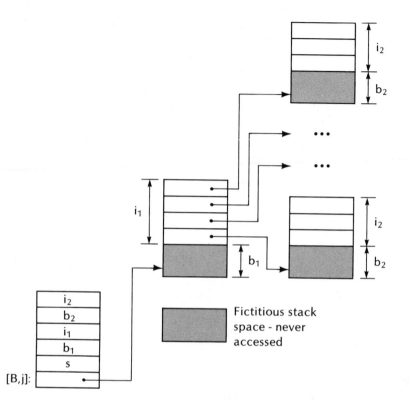

Figure 9.3.   Stack configuration for array [3:4, 3:4] of integer.

Consider accessing X[3, 4], which is located at address 28. The code sequence would be:

```
LOAD B j            ; stack[tos] = 20
LOAD =3
ADD I               ; stack[tos] = 23
LOAD I              ; stack[tos] = 24
LOAD =4
ADD I               ; stack[tos] = 28
```

Matrix Pointer MAS—MMAS

Now let us define procedure MMAS. This sets the base address for an array, allocates space for it, and sets the pointer vectors appropriately for our matrix pointer array scheme.

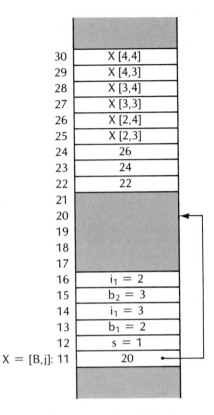

Figure 9.4. Actual stack configuration for array [2:4, 3:4] of integer.

```
procedure MMAS(B, J, N: integer);
   var DV, S, X: integer;
   {make matrix array space.
         [B, j]: dope vector
                  transfer address,
         N: array rank}

   function BUILDV(DV: integer): integer;
     var T, I, S, X: integer;
   begin
     {exactly as above in MAS}
   end;

   function SETP(DVA, N, TOS: integer): integer;
     var I, MP: integer;
   begin {set pointers}
     if n>0 then
```

```
begin  {want a pointer vector}
  mp:=tos+1;  {index of first pointer}
  tos:=tos+stack[dva+1];
          {allocate space for pointers}
  for i:=1 to stack[dva+1] do
  begin
    stack[mp]:=tos+1-stack[dva+2];
    tos:=setp(dva+2, n-1, tos);
    mp:=mp+1;
  end;
  setp:=tos;
 end
else
  setp:=tos+s*stack[dva+1];
end;  {of procedure SETP}


begin
  dv:=stkaddr(b, j);  {dope vector location}
  s:=stack[tos];      {element size}
  x:=buildv(dv, s);   {build dope vector}
  tos:=tos-2*n-1; {clear stack}
  stack[dv]:=tos+1-stack[dv+2];
  tos:=setp(dv+2, n-1, tos);
      {construct the matrix array space}
  pc:=pc+4;    {adjust program counter}
end
```

Function BUILDV constructs a dope vector of the same form as in MAS. Its base address will be different, however.

Function SETP is the key to understanding MMAS. It is called with an index into the dope vector, pointing to b_N, where N refers to the dimension—but counting down rather than up. The value TOS passed is the current stack top, considering whatever has been allocated for matrix pointers, and so on. SETP will return a new adjusted TOS value, based on what it has required.

If $N > 0$ in a SETP call, it is necessary to build a vector of pointers, for example I_1 in figure 9.3. We accordingly set MP to point to the bottom of this vector; it will be incremented as we fill the vector. TOS is then increased by i_n—the number of words we need for the vector.

The FOR loop then fills each of the vector slots with a fictitious lower address value, based on stack[dva + 2]. For example, in filling the I_1 vector, we need the offset b_2 (figure 9.3). After that address is computed, we call SETP recursively at the next lower N level. This call also adjusts TOS correctly for the next pass of the loop. MP is advanced by one to deal with the next pointer slot.

At the end of the FOR loop, the current TOS value is returned by SETP.

When $N = 0$, we have reached a situation in which the space to be allocated is array value space, rather than a pointer vector. That space is simply the element size S times the last dimension stack[dva + 1].

MMAS will result in sets of data space and pointer vectors intermixed in the stack in some fashion. It obviously is essential that array indices lie within their declared bounds; otherwise, data values will be treated as pointers, or pointers will be overwritten with data. Array access should be embellished with array bounds tests for safety's sake.

9.14. More General Dynamic Arrays

The most general and powerful dynamic array mechanisms are found in interpretive systems, which include APL, Snobol, and Lisp. A fundamental principle in these languages is that storage space for variables and structures will be provided on demand whenever needed, and that no structure size need be bound at compile time. Storage life is not bound to function life as in Pascal. Storage space will be reclaimed as needed by a general-purpose garbage collector (GC). An array may even be expanded on demand by functions that allocate a new array and copy old elements into the new array.

Lisp also makes it possible to allocate an object within a procedure, then bind the object to something that survives the procedure's exit. As we have seen, our stack allocation scheme cannot be used that way.

General garbage collection is convenient for the programmer, but can be costly in memory and execution time. Storage management is a bookkeeping function that may not be required if the computer algorithm is suitably organized.

For one thing, each array's location and bounds must be known globally by the GC—the GC after all should be concerned with neither the algorithmic purpose of any of the data space nor how it is linked together; but it must be able to move objects around in order to compact them. That requires at least one indirection per object in general; there will be a location known to the compiler of a dope vector that points to the object. The GC can be informed about all the dope vectors, which must not be moved—they can be on a run-time stack. The GC is then free to move the objects themselves and adjust the pointers in the dope vectors.

Stack objects need not be garbage collected, however; only those stack objects need be that are pointers to objects or to dope vectors of objects. For the GC to tell these apart, objects and pointers should be *tagged*. That is how Lisp works— all Lisp objects are tagged, making it easy for the GC to do its work. Tagging also facilitates debugging and program tracing.

In the absence of tagging, a GC could operate from a symbol table organized by procedures. It knows about the stack markers, and can use the symbol table to understand how the stack data objects are organized—which are pointers, and so on. The symbol table must have fast access, or be brought into memory when needed for GC; but then the space might as well be used for tagging.

We know of no Pascal system that has a general-purpose GC.

9.14.1. The Pascal Heap

The Pascal heap system is a reasonably good compromise for many programs. Most implementations support a single heap. An object K of compiler-known size may be allocated at will from the heap and bound to a pointer P through the NEW function. NEW simply maintains a separate stack, and allocates space from the current top of this stack. The object K is thenceforth accessed through P, which may be locally or globally bound. If P is locally bound, it is lost on a procedure exit. Its object K is therefore unbound. Its heap space sometimes can be reclaimed, and sometimes cannot be, as we shall see.

Two space reclamation methods are commonly implemented in Pascal. The simplest—the one most often implemented on small computers—is the mark-release system. A *mark pointer* M must be declared—usually of type ↑ INTEGER. At some point during execution, M is set or *marked* by the statement MARK(m). This sets M to the current heap stack top. Later, the statement RELEASE(m) resets the heap stack top to the saved value of M.

Mark-release is extremely dangerous to use. The danger lies in releasing heap space that may still be in use by some part of the program. Global knowledge of the program's execution is required for safety. The consequence of releasing heap space that later must be accessed by some other program section will be an obscure bug—the released space is likely to have been stepped on by some new heap allocation.

Because of its danger, ISO Pascal does not support a mark-release heap strategy. This standard requires support of the DISPOSE function instead. Mark-release is supported in UCSD Pascal.

DISPOSE carries one parameter: a pointer bound to an object to be released. It essentially informs a GC that the object's space may be reclaimed, then binds the pointer to NIL. That sounds good; unfortunately, dispose also is dangerous, because more than one pointer may be directed at the object. Disposing the first pointer, then using the second pointer will cause a run-time error. Like the corresponding release error, this dispose error will eventually result in a pointer access error of an obscure nature that is difficult to identify.

DISPOSE implementation can take two forms—objects can be either moved to reclaim space or not. If not, the dispose system will simply try to coalesce space from disposed objects. If two adjacent objects O1 and O2 are disposed, then their combined space becomes available for a larger object.

If objects can be moved, then, when the coalescing strategy fails, some or all of the objects are moved to make space for some large object.

In either case, the NEW function is more complicated. Rather than just allocate space from the top of a stack, it must be ready to look for a sufficiently large space. If clever, it will find and allocate a space that is minimally large enough, rather than just the first space large enough. Finally, if it cannot find a large enough space, it must call a compacter to release space. Objects are moved around until a large enough hole exists.

The ISO standard does not specify any of these strategies; the Pascal implementor can choose to work hard on the problem or to do little about it.

More material on heap allocation issues may be found in Standish [1980].

Other DISPOSE Problems

We discussed how multiple pointers to a disposed object can crash a program. DISPOSE poses another problem for the programmer—a structure built from pointer structures may be complicated to dispose completely. For example, a tree can be declared as follows:

```
type
   SYMTREEP= ↑tree;
   SYMTREE=  record
                LEFT, RIGHT: treep;
                {other stuff in the tree node}
             end;
var
   T: symtreep;
```

The tree then can be built by calling NEW whenever a new node is required, then linking it to the LEFT and RIGHT pointers as needed. LEFT and RIGHT are initially set to NIL.

To dispose of a tree, the programmer must write a procedure that can walk down through the tree, disposing of leaves first, then nodes. DISPOSE must be called on each leaf node, but it cannot be called until everything that the object points to has been disposed.

Directed graphs are particularly vicious to dispose. Leaf nodes must first be disposed, so it is necessary to identify every node pointing to the leaf, dispose the node once, and then set its pointers to NIL. Such a forward-backward walk essentially forces the programmer to include back pointers in DAG data structures.

In fact, many Pascal programs that use the heap are set up to run to completion without any space reclamation. Nothing is done about objects that become unbound through loss of their pointers. In such programs, the heap may be exhausted on a sufficiently large problem.

Pascal programs that must run continuously—for real-time operation control, for example—cannot afford to sacrifice heap space or leave any heap object unreclaimed, nor can large programs that require a large number of *new* calls with consequent unbinding of allocated objects.

Pascal could be implemented with tagged objects, but it normally is not for the sake of space efficiency. We saw how the run-time stack of the SPC carries no tags. The compiler knows certain things; other things must be inferred from stack marker information.

That makes garbage collection impossible in Pascal—the GC must have complete information about the nature of every object in the data spaces of the stack.

The GC can locate the stack markers easily enough, but how can it determine just what the data space between markers means? All these objects either must be tagged, as in Lisp, or else the GC must have access to a complete online symbol table, from which it can obtain complete information about the data objects.

9.14.2. Implementing NEW/DISPOSE

Storage management is a complicated issue, and is not particularly germane to compiler construction, except that any compiler implementor (except one fortunate enough to be using Lisp!) must confront the problem. An excellent review of storage management may be found in Knuth's *Fundamental Algorithms* [1968], chapter 2. We review here the general principles.

The space available for a heap usually must be shared with the stack. On a small computer, the stack is allowed to grow in one direction while the heap grows in the other direction. Program and system space are allocated at the bottom or top to keep them out of the way.

Some slack space between the two must be provided because the stack goes up and down rapidly as the program executes. Also, a trap-handler program may require some user stack space and, if it is not available due to a heap–stack conflict, there will be trouble.

Every instruction that extends the stack or the heap should check for an overlap and force a trap if one exists. The older versions of UCSD Pascal were careless about this, but most commercially supported versions now trap on the first occurrence of a stack–heap overlap.

Allocation of Heap Space

The available heap space will consist of regions that are occupied by data blocks and other regions that are available, interspersed in some manner. The available regions will have appeared as a result of previous DISPOSE calls.

Available regions need to be identified. A simple way to do this is to require that every block have at least two words. The first word will point to the next available region and the second word will carry the size of the current region. Figure 9.5 shows such a heap organization.

When NEW is called, say with a space request of L, it walks through the heap links starting with the register AVAIL. It may simply choose the first one whose length exceeds L, or it may walk through them all, choosing the one with minimum length $> L$. It may also fail to find any sufficiently long. One requirement is that any leftover space must be either zero or at least two words in length.

If NEW finds a suitable space, it rearranges the links to occupy that space but to preserve the structure of figure 9.5. One possibility is that the space is exactly right (this can happen frequently). The links simply point around that space. If the space is larger than required, a simple strategy is to allocate the NEW space beyond the size value, then adjust the size—this requires no changes in the links.

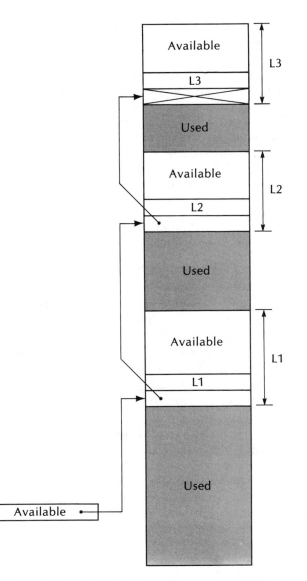

Figure 9.5.   Heap structure organized to support DISPOSE.

If NEW cannot find a suitable space, it tries to extend the end of the heap space, to make more room at the top. This happens a lot during initial heap allocation but, eventually, the heap space length is restricted by the system. If this approach fails due to a stack conflict or for some other reason, the program dies.

It is at this point that a compactor could extend the program's life—but compacting in Pascal requires still more mechanisms and is not feasible in general.

Let us now discuss DISPOSE. This function carries a pointer, and the compiler can supply a length. The block must be among the used areas, or there has been a system error. DISPOSE must walk down the AVAIL chain and notice at what point its new block appears. The chain is then adjusted by adding a new available space with its own length. One more thing must be done—adjacent available spaces must be coalesced. The adjacent space may be above or below the newly released space, or both.

By coalescing space, we offer the user the hope that a diligent application of DISPOSE will keep his or her heap swept clean with lots of space available for use. But that will not always work; it is possible just to fragment the space with lots of little separated holes that will eventually cause a NEW to fail.

9.14.3. Summary

These problems with dynamic storage allocation are not unique to Pascal. Ada and C support essentially the same scheme—an allocation without general garbage collection. Both support a NEW-DISPOSE mechanism.

In C and in some Pascal extensions, storage can be allocated simply as a number of bytes to allocate. Such a mechanism makes possible the allocation of variable-length arrays or triangular arrays, for example, which are impossible in standard Pascal.

In Ada, dynamic allocation can be controlled somewhat by requiring that the space be released on exiting from the scope of the variable's declaration. This makes dynamic storage feasible through the scheme described previously. However, the reference manual does not require an implementation to release space.

Mainsail does provide dynamic storage management of its objects but, within an object, all data carry fixed dimensions. Fortran supports no dynamic storage.

There are a number of papers on storage management. Many of these refer to mass storage management problems (disks), but the problems are essentially the same in memory management.

9.15. Functionals

A *functional* is a procedure or function the definition of which is treated as an item of data. ISO Pascal does not support functionals; however, many Pascal implementations do. We shall use a functional declaration system that appears in Hewlett-Packard (HP) Pascal for their series 200 to illustrate the concepts.

In HP standard Pascal, a functional may be declared as follows:

```
type
   FUNCT1= procedure (A, B: integer; C: real);

var
   F1: funct1;
```

The type declaration is just like a procedure declaration except that the name is left out. The var simply says that some data space will be reserved for the functional data item. (Function-style functionals are not supported in HP Pascal, a curious omission.)

Eventually, some procedure declarations will appear; for example:

```
procedure SAM (A, B: integer; C: real);
begin
   ...
end;

procedure ED (A, B: integer; C: real);
begin
   ...
end;

procedure FRANK (A, B: integer; C: real);
begin
   ...
end;
```

Note that these all have the same formal parameters as in FUNCT1, making them type-compatible with FUNCT1.

Given these, we can then assign F1 to either SAM, ED or FRANK:

```
f1:=ed;    {for example}
```

Now, functional F1 is called through a special calling function, as follows:

```
call(f1, 5, 10, 25.17);
```

Note that the functional name appears first; its current value (SAM, ED, or FRANK) is picked up at run-time. The parameters follow, and must correspond to the parameters of the functional. The procedure call otherwise occurs exactly as if the call were:

```
ed(5, 10, 25.17);
```

The possibility of a semantic disaster exists in calling functionals. The functional must either contain no free variable references or be called within the same static environment in which it was called. (A *free variable* is some variable used in a procedure the declaration of which lies outside the function.)

Implementing Functionals

Functionals are easy to implement. Two new SPC instructions are sufficient:

```
LDP   p        ... push a functional reference

CFP            ... call functional reference in TOS
```

A *functional reference* in SPC is just a procedure number—one word. The LDP instruction expects a procedure name and pushes its number on the stack. That number can thereupon be treated as data. When CFP is executed, it expects a procedure number in TOS. It pops TOS, then calls the procedure just as CLP would. Procedure parameters must be in place below TOS.

Reasons for Using Functionals

A full discussion of the reasons for using functionals is beyond the scope of this text. A good reference is the book *Functional Programming,* by Henderson [1980]. Essentially, functions are a mathematician's view of the world, and functionals are a close reflection of that view.

Numerous practical applications can be found in all fields of computer science. For example, a generic *sort* procedure could be written that accepts not just some linear data structure to be sorted, but a functional that performs a pairwise comparison. Or, consider a procedure that can walk through a symbol table and then apply a functional to particular (or every) item found in the table. Such applications provide a separate encapsulation of a control function from an application function.

Functionals are used extensively in Lisp; in fact, the easiest way to write a Lisp interpreter is by first constructing a general purpose functional executor. The popular language Forth also is based on functional definition and execution.

9.16. Optimizations

We have fully defined a simple stack-oriented language that is sufficiently powerful to implement most of the features of the more common block-structured languages, such as Pascal, C, Fortran, Algol, and PL/I. Our language, however, is sadly lacking in a number of optimizations that could make a significant difference in the performance of a computer based on it.

We shall briefly discuss some broad classes of optimizations that can be used to extend our machine.

9.16.1. More Instructions

The easiest optimizations to make in SPC are those that recognize that certain instruction combinations occur frequently, and can therefore be replaced by single instructions. Whether this in fact results in a performance improvement depends on whether the implementing machine is inherently faster than the instructions themselves. If it is not, then little is gained.

However, UCSD Pascal is implemented on most small machines by writing assembly code in the base microcomputer for each instruction. The so-called P-machine is in fact a tightly coded interpreter for PCODE instructions. Another common way of implementing a PCODE set is by writing microcode to implement each high-level instruction. Given either of these implementation strategies, there is indeed good reason to extend the instruction set with composite instructions.

Some useful composites are the following:

- Increment a variable's value by a small number (for example, one). The form $I := I + 1$ appears frequently in programs.

- Include a STOR instruction that preserves the stack top. Often, it is possible to use this result next or later.

- Introduce an instruction that performs a multiplication followed by a constant offset as one operation. This is useful for structure address computation.

- Improve string operations by using special instructions. A string format must be defined but, once it is, concatenation, deletion, and matching are useful functions.

- Include math functions (trig, exponential, and so on) as instructions.

- Make matrix operations be instructions on machines designed to support matrix operations efficiently.

9.16.2. Instruction Packing

Because most machines have limited memory, a concerted effort to reduce the need for memory usually is worthwhile. Not much can be done about data memory, except to try to reclaim space as efficiently as possible under the circumstances, and to provide mechanisms for the programmer to enable him or her to reduce the data memory load.

However, instruction packing is fruitful. Much of the success of the UCSD Pascal system is owed to Ken Bowles' [1978] work in identifying an efficient instruction set and packing for PCODE. Here are some of the tricks used in that system; the instructions are defined in the UCSD manuals.

- Instructions are variable length, in byte units. The first byte defines the operation. Subsequent bytes, if any, extend the instruction.

- Small constants, from zero to 127, may be LOADed with a single instruction byte. This leaves only 127 more instructions, but the frequency of occurrence of small constant LOADs makes it worthwhile.

- Global variables can be directly accessed by special instructions. In SPC, globals are accessed by walking down the static chain. The most commonly referenced variables on the average are locals, followed by globals, then intermediates. The inefficiency of static chain walking therefore can be tolerated if locals and globals can be accessed rapidly.

- Local words with a small offset (zero to 15) can be accessed with a one-byte instruction. Most procedures have less than 16 local words, so this helps.

- Multiple words can be loaded and stored with a single instruction. This implements structure movement efficiently—note that Pascal permits structure assignments, which call for multiple-element movement of data.

- String operations are supported by a few instructions. UCSD Pascal contains numerous useful built-in string functions.

- A word pointer in TOS can be indexed by X words and loaded by one instruction. X is less than 7. This improves the efficiency of record variable access.

- Let stack[tos] be an integer index, stack[tos-1] be an array base word pointer, and B (part of the instruction) be the size of an array element. Then a single instruction pushes a word pointer to the indexed element on the stack.

- The common trig functions sin, cos, atan, exp, ln, log, as well as square root, square, and power of 10 are instructions.

- The set operations are implemented by special instructions.

- Tree search is implemented on some Pascals—it looks for an eight-byte packed array of char in a binary tree, adding it if not there.

- Local and global procedure calls are supported separately.

9.16.3. Multiple Registers

The highest-performance machines are not pure stack machines of the SPC type, but are hybrid systems that combine some simple stacking operations with a number of general-purpose registers. How many registers and what operations they support varies widely, from several thousand in a Cray or Symbolics 3600 architecture, to less than ten in some microprocessors. However, there are demonstrable advantages to having multiple registers, especially when supported by an optimizing compiler.

Registers carry several architectural advantages:

- Register access generally is much faster than random-access memory (RAM) access. With LSI design, registers and operational units are part of the same chip and have direct high-speed bus paths between them. RAM requires sending an address off the chip and waiting for the memory system to respond.

- The average instruction size can be reduced, because fewer bits are needed to refer to a register than a memory address in an operator instruction. However, note that more bits are needed for this than for a stack operator.

- Most arithmetic expressions require temporary storage, which can be allocated to registers rather than to a stack or RAM. The calculation of a· structure address, which occurs frequently in Pascal, is a good example of· an expression with many intermediates.

- Addressing conventions can be embellished by including a register as an offset or indirection or both.

- Instructions can be reduced by using a register as a memory address reference.

- Passing procedure parameters in registers pays off for languages in which procedure calls play an important role, such as Lisp and Pascal.

Efficient register allocation is a difficult topic, and will be partially treated in chapter 10. We note here that the introduction of registers does not really invalidate the concepts of the SPC machine, although its operations may be conducted between registers rather than on the stack top.

Thus, the LOAD and STOR instructions will still carry a textual address, but may also refer to a register. The arithmetic operations in general will refer to two or three registers. In the IBM/360, binary operands may be in two registers, or in a memory and a register. There are no memory–memory operations. The result appears in a register.

When a procedure is called, it may be useful to assign its parameters to successive registers, transferring them to memory locations only when the registers must be used for something else. The result of a function call may be left in a register. This treatment of formal parameters—and of local variables as well—may result in small procedures executing almost entirely in register operations.

9.17. Traps and Unstructured Exits

Trap handling is a vital component of any computer system used for any purpose other than experimentation or research. A *trap* is said to occur when a condition that occurs during a computation, if allowed to continue, will yield an invalid result. The completeness of trap handling and the quality of its recovery differentiates a superior computer system from one that is merely adequate.

Traps can occur in several ways. Here are some common ones:

- Arithmetic overflow or underflow.

- Arithmetic conversion error.

- Array or string bounds violation.

- Unknown procedure number.

- Branch to invalid location.

- Invalid CASE label.

- Invalid I/O operation.

- End of file.

- System I/O operation—peripheral not responding or timing out.

- Invalid instruction.

Programmers cannot possibly write statements in their code to protect themselves against any occurrence of these error conditions—nor should they have to. For example, arithmetic overflow or conversion trouble can occur within any assignment statement or expression; trap statements do not belong in these.

Unfortunately, when a trap occurs, it is not always clear what can be done to recover from the problem. I/O difficulties usually can be corrected or compensated within a program, if the system permits catching a problem. Sometimes arithmetic errors can be compensated if the code designer thinks that there is good reason to do so.

9.17.1. PL/I Trap Handling

PL/I provides an ON <condition> mechanism for trap recovery. The ON statement carries a trap condition and some statement to execute. It is dynamic. When a trap occurs, the statement is executed. There are provisions for getting a snapshot or calling a system trap handler. The system requires specifying the trap conditions (it is easy to miss one) and making sure the trap condition is enabled (it may not be). No automatic exit is provided, although the statement can force a return from a procedure.

9.17.2. HP Pascal Trap Handling

HP Pascal provides an attractive mechanism for trap recovery. It works like this:

- Assuming that a trap may be expected in some section of code, a TRY-RECOVER section is written that encapsulates that section.

- The main body is in the TRY part.

- At the end of the section, a new code section is added enclosed by RECOVER BEGIN . . . END. This will be executed on something that traps out of the TRY section.

- The function ESCAPE(code) may be called to force an escape from within the TRY region, or anywhere else. The code is a number that can be checked in a RECOVER region; it is bound to a global variable ESCAPECODE.

- A trap condition will be passed down dynamically through several procedures until one is found with a RECOVER section; that section is then executed. In the absence of any RECOVER sections, the trap is passed out to the Pascal system and results in program termination.

TRY-RECOVERs can be nested. The nesting is *dynamic,* according to the calling sequence at run-time, not statically scoped like nonlocal GOTOs, which can reach only labels declared in containing scopes. On a trap occurring within a TRY, the immediately following RECOVER is executed.

Here is a simple example of a TRY-RECOVER program fragment in HP Pascal. It implements a terminal emulator. Any number of things can go wrong, or the user can hit a special interrupt key to abort the emulation. In such a circumstance, the loop in the TRY section is interrupted, and the RECOVER code is executed:

```
try
  setup;
  while true do
  begin  {endless loop except for an aborting condition}
    if not(unitbusy(modem)) then
        {the modem has received a character}
    begin
      read(modem, ch);  {read it}
      write(ch);  {write it to the computer screen}
    end
   else
    if not(unitbusy(kbdunit)) then
    begin  {the computer keyboard has a character ready}
      ch:=getterm;  {read it}
      if ch=escape_char then escape(101);  {user escape}
      putmod(ch);  {write to the modem}
    end
  end;

recover
  begin
    if escapecode=ioescapecode then
    writeln('IO error')  {something unusual}
    else
    if escapecode=101 then
    writeln('Terminated by user')
    else
    escape(escapecode)    {system escape}
  end
```

With this mechanism, programmers have considerable ability to control wayward operations. If they know that one approach may lead to a problem, they may schedule several to be tried one after another, or even repeat the same one with different options. (A GOTO from a RECOVER section to a TRY section in the same procedure is legal.)

The ESCAPE function also provides a programmed escape hatch. It forces a trap, finding the nearest accessible RECOVER section.

9.17.3. Unstructured Exits

Part of the trap-handling problem is dealing with an unstructured exit from a procedure to some previously called, active procedure. UCSD Pascal supports such an exit; for example,

```
exit(fred);
```

where FRED is some procedure somewhere down the dynamic chain.

The support is easy, given a stack marker containing a procedure number. Every procedure is associated with a unique number N, so the system need only walk down the dynamic links until a marker containing N is found. Then an exit instruction is executed on the *higher* stack marker, to force a return to FRED. We leave it to you to design an instruction to support this operation.

Support for the HP trap system requires that the code for every procedure carry two entry addresses (a TRY address and a RECOVER address) whether or not a RECOVER section is actually present. Then an ESCAPE or trap condition forces a branch to the RECOVER address of the procedure.

Once in a RECOVER section, an ESCAPE is executed by walking down the dynamic link one place and branching to the RECOVER section there.

If there is no explicit RECOVER section, the code is simply another ESCAPE. The RECOVER sections, whether empty or not, are therefore executed one after another while walking down the stack. Eventually, a nontrivial RECOVER is executed; it may be the system trap handler. No additions to the stack maker are required, and there is no effect on performance.

9.17.4. System Issues in Trap Handling

The other side of trap handling is detecting a trap condition. Detection of a trap condition may start in the processor hardware. Some microprocessors can be set up to force a transfer to an interrupt location on arithmetic or other internal trap conditions. Others require an explicit test of a status byte after each arithmetic operation.

An interrupt is essentially a procedure call. A return location and register status is pushed on a stack, then a special section of code is entered—the trap handler.

A trap handler usually has no idea what is going on to cause the trap; it knows only the trap condition itself, passed as a parameter. Under the HP recovery strategy, it need only set an escape code value, then pass control to the RECOVER section of the currently active procedure.

Within the UCSD environment, the trap handler may set an IORESULT flag (for an I/O trap condition) or just return to the base-level Pascal system. No programmer recovery mechanism is provided other than explicitly testing IORESULT just after a problem is expected to occur.

9.18. Summary of SPC Instructions

Stack Load and Store Operations

```
LOAD = <integer>        ... push an integer

LOAD = <real>           ... push a real

LOAD I B j              ... copy and push integer at [B, j]

LOAD R B j              ... copy and push real at [B, j]

LOAD @ B j              ... generate an absolute address

LOAD I                  ... load integer through a TOS address

LOAD R                  ... load real through TOS address

STOR I B j              ... stack top integer to [B, j], pop stack

STOR R B j              ... stack top real to [B, j], pop stack

STOR I                  ... store integer through a TOS address

STOR R                  ... store real through TOS address

DUP I                   ... duplicate stack top integer

DUP R                   ... duplicate stack top real
```

Binary and Unary Operations

```
ADD I         ... integer addition

ADD R         ... real addition

SUB I         ... integer subtraction

SUB R         ... real subtraction

MPY I         ... integer multiplication

MPY R         ... real multiplication

DIV I         ... integer division
```

```
DIV R             ... real division

NEG I             ... negation

NEG R             ... real negation

EQU I             ... integer equal

EQU R             ... real equal

LES I             ... integer less than

LES R             ... real less than

GTR I             ... integer greater than

GTR R             ... real greater than

AND               ... logical AND

OR                ... logical OR

NOT               ... boolean complement
```

Branch and Addressing Operations

```
UJP  L            ... unconditional jump

FJP  L            ... conditional 'false' jump

LOC  L            ... associates label L with next instruction

CJP  T            ... case jump

ADR  L1           ... address in code

CON <integer>     ... integer appears in code
```

Space Allocation

```
INCS  v           ... allocate v words

INCS              ... allocate C(s) words

MAS B j R         ... allocate space, adjust dope vector

AVA B j R         ... compute an address label
```

Function Call and Exit

```
CLP <procedure>   ... call user procedure

EXIT n            ... exit, pop n words

LDP  p            ... push a functional reference
```

```
CFP                     ... call functional reference in TOS

CXP  PRINTI             ... print integer

CXP  PRINTR             ... print real

CXP  READI              ... read integer

CXP  READR              ... read real

MSG  <string>           ... print message
```

9.19. Exercises

1. Translate each of the following Pascal statements into appropriate SPC code. Make and state appropriate assumptions about the types and textual addresses of the variables used.

```
A := B + C
A := BA [ I ] + C
AA [ I ] := B + C
if X < Y then Z := 0
while I < 10 do I := I + 1
for I := 1 to 10 do AA [ I ] := 0
case R.F of 0: R.F := 6 ; 1: R.F := 9 end
```

2. For the following program, give a translation into SPC. Assume that the global stack mark already will have been pushed before your SPC code begins execution. Also give the contents of the relevant procedure table entries. Draw the stack as it will exist when execution reaches the point labeled with the comment { here } in the program. Use SPC code line numbers for code addresses and arrows for pointer values.

```
program P0
; var X : integer
; procedure P1
  ; begin
      P2
    end { P1 }
; procedure P2
  ; begin
      X := 1
    end { P2 } { here }
; begin
    P1
  end { P0 }
  .
```

3. Draw the stack of the SPC machine when the instruction on line 7 of the SPC code is about to be executed. Use SPC code line numbers for code addresses and arrows for pointer values. An original Pascal program from which this code might be generated is given for your information.

```
program P
; var A , B : integer
; procedure P1 ( var Y : integer )
   ; var C : integer
   ; begin { P1 }
       C := 1
       ; Y := C
     end { P1 }
; procedure P2 ( X : integer )
   ; var D : integer
   ; begin { P2 }
       D := X
       ; P1 ( D )
     end { P2 }
; begin { P }
     A := 1
     ; B := 2
     ; P2 ( B )
   end { P0 }
.
```

```
 1       UJP   P
 2 P1  INCS  1
 3       LOAD  1
 4       STOR  I 0 0
 5       LOAD  I 0 -5
 6       LOAD  I 0 0
 7       STOR  I
 8       EXIT  1
 9 P2  INCS  1
10       LOAD  I 0 -5
11       STOR  I 0 0
12       LOAD  I 0 0
13       CLP   P1T
14       EXIT  1
15 P   INCS  2
16       LOAD  1
17       STOR  I 0 0
18       LOAD  2
19       STOR  I 0 1
20       LOAD  I 0 1
21       CLP   P2T
22       EXIT  0
```

Procedure table entries:

```
P1T: address = P1 = 2
     proc level = 1
     ptrace = false

P2T: address = P2 = 9
     proc level = 1
     ptrace = false
```

4. Write, in Pascal, run-time support procedures NEW and DISPOSE for
   Pascal. Use the allocation scheme of section 9.14.2. Treat the heap as a
   large array. The heap elements are sometimes pointers, sometimes lengths,

and sometimes parts of an object of arbitrary type, so you will have to circumvent Pascal's usual type compatibility rules. Describe each place where you must do this and explain why. Assume you have a compiler that will allow these breaches of type rules when needed.

9.20. Bibliographical Notes

Much of the material in this chapter is adapted from Randell and Russell [Randell, 1964], who first defined a set of instructions for implementation of Algol 60. Ingerman [1961] gives an algorithm for the rearrangement of an OWN array that is redimensioned in place. Sattley [1961] discusses space allocation and dope vectors for Algol 60 local variables and arrays.

Bauer [1968] describes an Algol 60 implementation in some detail. Berkeley [1964] describes Lisp implementation, of interest for the automatic allocation of list elements and garbage collection of dead elements. Griffiths [1974a] and Hill [1974] contain a comprehensive review of run-time storage management, with special attention to the management of Algol 68 data structures.

Lee [1967] discusses some special addressing problems that arise in Fortran compilers; in particular, he examines allocation considering equivalences. Mc-Keeman [1970] contains complete source for the XPL compiler, a derivative of Algol 60 designed for compiler and systems programming.

Concurrent garbage collection was first proposed by Steele [1975], and was later refined by Dijkstra [1976a] and Gries [1977].

For more information on the UCSD instructions and stack arrangements, refer to any UCSD Pascal manual.

Wirth [1971a] describes a Pascal implementation on a CDC 6000 system. His implementation could be adapted to any computer system, however. Wirth [1976c] also gives a complete compiler for a small language, written in Pascal.

CHAPTER 10

OPTIMIZATION

The term *optimization* in a compiler is applied to any technique designed to yield more efficient object code than would be obtained by a simple, straight-forward code generator. An optimization may replace a simple coding algorithm by a more sophisticated one, or it may be an operation on some compiler data structure that transforms the structure into an equivalent but more efficient one.

The goals of optimization are the reduction of execution time and the improvement in memory usage. These two objectives often (unfortunately) conflict. For example, execution time may be reduced to some extent by adding more instructions. Thus, a procedure call might be replaced by its code, thereby saving the execution time required to call a procedure. However, the code usually requires more space than the call instruction. Ideally, a compiler user should be able to specify whether he or she wishes a minimum number of instructions or a minimum execution time; however, this is seldom feasible. Usually, some compromise is possible, and often a reduction in amount of code results in a reduction of execution time as well.

Optimization is desirable because a simple code generator may fail to exploit fully the algebraic properties of the source language, or the full potential of the target machine's instruction set. For example, a direct translation of a statement such as:

$$A := 1 + B + 6$$

would emit two additions. An optimization that exploits associativity of addition would rearrange the expression to $1 + 6 + B$. This in turn would be reduced to the expression $7 + B$. The result would be translated into one addition. Also, a statement of the form:

$$I := I + 1$$

is common in source programs. A general translation on a stack machine would yield the code:

```
LOAD   I;
LOAD   =1;
ADD;
STOR   I;
```

Many machines have "increment memory" instructions, so the statement $I := I + 1$ could be translated into:

```
INCM   I;
```

An optimization can be classified as *machine-dependent* or *machine-independent*. Machine-dependent optimizations stem from special machine properties that can be exploited to reduce the amount of code or execution time. Machine-independent optimizations depend on only the arithmetic properties of the operations in the language and not on peculiarities of the target machine. Some common machine-independent optimizations are:

- Constant arithmetic subsumption or folding; that is, operations on constant expressions performed by the compiler rather than emitted as code.

- Identification and removal of identity or null operations; for example, adding zero, multiplying by one.

- Rearrangement of expression trees, exploiting commutativity, associativity, or distributivity of certain operators, with the objective of reducing the number of operations.

- Identification of common subexpressions, for possible one-time evaluation.

- Moving two or more identical computations to a place in the program where the computation can be done once and the result used in all of the original places (often called *hoisting*).

- Elimination of useless or unreachable code.

- Movement of code from inside to outside a loop, possibly changing its form to preserve the program semantics (sometimes called *frequency reduction*).

We shall not attempt to develop or even classify all the possible optimizations. Nor will we present a systematic approach to optimization. We will discuss some of the most commonly used optimizations in sufficient detail for them to be useful in most compilers. Beyond that, you must refer to the voluminous literature on the subject.

10.1. Machine-Dependent Optimizations

The nature of a machine-dependent optimization is heavily influenced by the target machine and the source language. A machine-dependent optimization may be applied to the AST by identifying special subtrees that happen to fit a machine feature, or it may be applied to an object code sequence. Still other optimizations deal with register and memory allocation and arrange that data appear in the appropriate registers in a reasonably optimal manner.

Some examples of machine-dependent optimizations are

1. *Register allocation*. In a typical computer, the most efficiently accessed memory is the most scarce resource (for example, one or a few arithmetic

registers, or the top-of-stack registers); the least efficiently accessed memory is the most plentiful (for example, solid-state memory, disk, drum, or tape). Most operations can be performed on only data in registers, and the consequent movement of data between registers and mass memory is a bookkeeping maneuver that contributes nothing directly to the computation. Hence, the allocation of the scarce resources to achieve high efficiency in program execution is an important optimization.

2. *Special machine features.* Some common machine features (or *idioms,* a term first applied by Hall [1974]) that potentially can be exploited include: immediate instructions (a value is part of the instruction), incrementation (a memory location can be incremented by some constant), use of indexing or indirection, and vector operations.

3. *Data intermixed with instructions.* On many machines, data can be accessed more efficiently if they are intermixed with the instruction sequence. Some optimal arrangement of instructions and data therefore exists.

10.2. Machine-Independent Optimizations

Machine-independent optimizations are based on the mathematical properties of a sequence of source statements. An optimization essentially amounts to analyzing the overall purpose of the statement sequence, then finding an equivalent sequence that will translate to the least amount of code.

Thus, constant arithmetic always can be done by the compiler, rather than by emitting instructions to perform the arithmetic during execution. Arithmetic properties of the operations also can be exploited in the search for minimal code; their use might uncover some additional constant arithmetic, or some common subexpressions.

Whether an arithmetic property may be exploited depends on the specification of the language. If the language clearly specifies that all operations be performed from left to right in exactly the sequence dictated by the form of the expression, then arithmetic optimization is limited. On the other hand, many modern languages specify that the operations may be performed in any order consistent with the arithmetic meaning of the expression.

Of the several arithmetic properties of the real numbers, the identity and null properties always can be exploited to reduce emitted code. Commutativity and associativity are useful in subsuming constants, identifying common subexpressions, and optimizing register allocation. Distributivity is potentially useful in constant subsumption and subexpression recognition, but is difficult to exploit in a general way. The language may prohibit the use of distributivity for optimization—it may require that a parenthesized expression be performed first and not under any circumstances be distributed among outer operations.

Computer arithmetic technically fails to satisfy any of the three properties of commutativity, associativity, and distributivity, as the following three examples indicate:

Failure of Commutativity

Consider the statement:

$$I := I + F(A)$$

where F(A) is a function call that happens to change the value of I as a side effect. (I must be in a domain that is accessible to the function F.) On a stack machine, in the order shown, the emitted code might be:

```
LOAD I;    {current value}
LOAD A;    {the parameter for the function call}
CALL F;
ADD;       {the change in I does not affect the copy
              previously written on the stack}
STOR I;
```

In commuted order, we would have instead:

```
LOAD A;
CALL F;
LOAD I;    {the new value}
ADD;
STOR I;    {a different result}
```

This side effect of the function call stems from an undesirable property of functions in several common languages; their ability to access and modify variables within them in arithmetic expressions. For this reason, certain modern languages restrict functions to assign to those variables local to the function call. Then this side effect could not exist; the compiler would be able to determine from the replacement statement alone whether the function could affect any other variables.

Failure of Associativity

Consider the following statements implemented on a machine with integer arithmetic in the range -32768 through 32767 (16-bit twos complement integers):

```
I := 30000;
J := 20000;
K := 21000;
I := I-J+K;
```

If the last statement is executed in left-to-right order, the result 31000 is obtained without overflow. However, if the statement were instead:

$$I := I + K - J$$

then the addition would overflow before the subtraction was performed.

Here, if the language specification permits associativity for the sake of optimization, the programmer is at fault for not considering the possibility of overflow.

Failure of Distributivity

Consider the following example:

```
I := 15;
J := 4000;
K := 3000;
I := I * (J - K);
```

The last statement, if performed in the order indicated by the parenthesizing, will yield 15000 without overflow. However, the distributive equivalent

$$I := I * J - I * K$$

will overflow twice.

Other sources of failure of computer arithmetic to satisfy mathematical properties stem from (1) integer division, in which the fractional part is truncated to yield the largest integer less than the quotient, and (2) floating-point subtraction, in which the two numbers are very nearly alike; the result is likely to have lost all significance.

Despite these difficulties, algebraic optimization often is provided by a compiler for those languages that permit it. Where optimization is provided, the programmer must be alert to the potential failure of a coded algorithm; the optimizing compiler may generate a somewhat different algorithm than was coded.

10.3. Code Improvement over a Sequence of Statements

The generation of optimal code for a single expression is hardly worthwhile in an average program. Knuth [1971], in a study of a large sample of FORTRAN programs, found that of all the assignment statements in his sample, 68% were a simple replacement of the form A = B, with no arithmetic operators, and 13% were of the form A = A op B, with the first operand on the right the same as the replacement variable. Hence, only 19% had a more complex structure, most of which apparently involved few operators. Of the variables, 58% were not indexed, 30.5% had a single index, 9.5% had two and only 1% had three (the maximum number under the Fortran in use at Stanford and Lockheed, the sources of the test programs).

An optimization for expression trees only probably will have little effect on the efficiency of a typical program. Usually, few statements have an expression tree large enough for an optimization algorithm to yield an improvement. Of course, these expressions might reside in a frequently executed section of the program, magnifying their importance to the program's performance.

The prospect of eliminating common subexpressions and register assignment over a sequence of assignment statements, called a *block,* is more promising.

Knuth [1971] also studied the improvement that would result from different levels of optimization. At the lowest level, blocks were considered for constant subsumption, rearrangement, and redundancy elimination. A reasonable register allocation strategy was employed. At a second level, the flow of control among blocks was considered to achieve global constant subsumption and rearrangement and some frequency reduction. Improvements were found at each level, the second yielding somewhat greater relative improvement (40% increase and 170% increase over the raw nonoptimized code, respectively). A further improvement could be made by exploiting idioms for the IBM/360 system, other than its basic multiregister organization.

Code can be improved in a sequence of statements in several ways: a larger field of expressions can be made available for identifying common sub-expressions; register allocation (for a multiregister machine, at least) can be improved; and loop-invariant expressions can be moved outside a loop.

None of these is possible without the development of methods for determining the status of all the program variables at any one point. For example, the value of a variable may be undefined at certain locations in the program, then defined later—a given definition will hold through some sequence of statements, then be replaced by another definition. A variable may become *dead* after some reference; that is, it may no longer be used after the reference. The status of the variables obviously influences register allocation and the identification of common subexpressions and loop invariants.

We see that development is needed along three lines. We need: (1) a more general optimization plan for a block, which can identify common sub-expressions and allocate registers efficiently, (2) an analysis of program control flow and its effect on the status of each variable, and (3) the exploitation of variable status in intrablock as well as interblock optimization.

10.3.1. Blocks

A block consists of a sequence of assignment statements $S_1, S_2, \ldots, S_b$ that are executed in that order, such that control can pass only into the first statement, from any one statement to its successor, and out of the last statement. No program branch may enter the block except to its first statement.

Each statement is a simple assignment of the form:

$$C \leftarrow \theta\ B_1, B_2, \ldots, B_n$$

where θ is an n-ary operator, $B_1, B_2, \ldots, B_n$ are its operands, and C receives the single scalar result of the operation. C is said to be *defined* by the statement, and the B_i are said to be *referenced* or *used.*

This schema is sufficiently general to cover many common program statements. A simple replacement statement of the form:

$$X := A + B * C$$

can be subdivided into a sequence of simple assignments by introducing a temporary variable T:

$$T \leftarrow *, B, C$$

$$X \leftarrow +, A, T$$

A function call returns a single value; however, if some of its parameters are called by reference or by name, then the possibility exists that they have been defined. Such parameters may be marked *defined* by the null operation DEF:

$$B \leftarrow DEF$$

indicates that B has been defined in some previous statement, such as a function call:

$$R \leftarrow FN, P_1, P_2, \ldots B, \ldots, P_r$$

An indexed replacement, for example:

$$B[X] := E$$

involves an assignment for X and then for B; however, because the compiler cannot determine which of the vector of B variables has been defined, it can only assume that any one of them has been. An array variable therefore is referenced or defined as a unit; the optimization algorithms usually cannot distinguish the members of the vector.

A vector move statement is similarly treated. Thus, in PL/I, if A and B are compatible structures, the statement:

$$A = B$$

represents an assignment to A of each of the components of B, and the optimization algorithms must deal with structures A and B as units.

10.3.2. Variables and Their Domains

A *variable* is some value created at run-time by a definition that is preserved until another definition or the end of the program is reached. A variable is associated with some name, but a given name may represent several different variables.

Thus, in the following statements, one variable associated with X is marked by the arrows (↑):

```
X  := X + Y;
↑

A  := X + 5;
      ↑

X  := X - Y;
      ↑
```

Note that the first reference and the last definition of X are not part of this variable; they are part of another variable, one that happens to carry the same name in these statements.

The *domain* of a variable is the set of all statements in the program that includes the definition statement, every reference statement, and every statement S such that a control path may pass from the definition through S to some statement containing a variable reference. The variable is said to be *live* at some statement if the statement is within its domain.

If the domain of a variable extends through the end of a block B, the variable is called an *output* variable of B. If the domain includes any statement passed through before reaching the beginning of the block, the variable is an *input* variable of B. All other variables are *local* or *temporary* variables; their domains are contained within the block.

The input variables of a block can be identified—they have some reference prior to a definition. Unfortunately, the output and local variables cannot be distinguished from an examination of the block alone; it is necessary to examine the control paths that lead from the block. Certain local variables can be identified: (1) the declared local variables, for a source language that permits variables to be declared at the head of any block, and (2) temporaries introduced through the reduction of arithmetic expressions to simple assignment statements.

10.3.3. Equivalent and Normal Blocks

Two blocks are said to be *equivalent* if they carry the same sets of input and output variables, and if, for every set of values of input variables, the resulting output variable values are the same on execution of the block statements. One of the blocks always can be transformed into the other through a sequence of four equivalence transformations, as Aho [1974b] has shown. The four transformations are:

1. Removal of useless statements and variables.

2. Identification of two computations producing the same value (common subexpressions).

3. Renaming of variables; for example, temporary variables.

4. Interchange of two adjacent statements, under conditions that ensure preservation of equivalence.

A *normal* block is such that every variable carries a unique name. Any block can be transformed into an equivalent normal block by renaming certain of the temporary or input variables. For example, consider the block:

```
X := A + B;
Y := A - B;
X := X * Y;      {second use of variable name X}
Y := Y * X';     {second use of variable name Y}
```

The names X and Y are associated with more than one variable each in this block; we therefore introduce new names X' and Y', to yield the following equivalent normal block:

```
X := A + B;
Y := A - B;
X' := X * Y;      {beginning of second variable X'}
Y' := Y * X';     {beginning of second variable Y'}
```

An input variable X must be renamed if a definition of X appears in the block. An input variable that also is an output variable need not be renamed. We adopt the convention that output variables never will be renamed. Only normal blocks will be considered in the following sections.

10.3.4. Representation of a Block as a Directed Acyclic Graph

A normal block may be represented as a directed acyclic graph, or DAG, in much the same way that an expression can be represented as a tree. A DAG consists of a number of nodes connected by directed edges, such that there are no cycles (or loops). The directed edges point from the node representing the definition of a variable to the nodes representing the variables referenced in that definition. A DAG has one or more root nodes, with no in-directed edges, and one or more leaves, with no out-directed edges. A node with at least one out-directed edge is an *internal* node. (The root nodes may be internal nodes.) We will be interested only in DAGs for which every root is not a leaf.

Each node of a block DAG is associated with a variable. In addition, each internal node is associated with an operation.

A DAG is constructed from a normal block as follows:

1. The statements $S_1, S_2, \ldots, S_b$ of a block are considered in that order. Each statement in general adds nodes and edges to the block DAG.

2. Given a statement:

$$C \leftarrow \theta B_1, B_2, \ldots, B_n$$

we add a new leaf node for every variable B_i not already in the DAG. A new node N_C for variable C and operation θ is added to the DAG. Then edges from node N_C to each node $B_1, B_2, \ldots, B_n$ are added. For example, consider the block:

```
T ← +, A, B
C ← *, T, A
A ← /, C, A
F ← +, E, E
B ← /, T, D
```

where {A, B, D, E} are input variables and {A, B, F} are output variables. A and B are redefined in the block, so we must rename the corresponding input variables. The equivalent normal block is:

```
T ← +, A', B'
C ← *, T, A'
A ← /, C, A'
F ← +, E, E
B ← /, T, D
```

This block has the DAG shown in figure 10.1.

10.3.5. Value of a DAG

The *value of a DAG* is a set of values associated with the DAG's nodes. These values are determined by the values associated with the input variables and a DAG evaluation rule. Each node of a DAG is associated with a value, computed by the *DAG Evaluation Rule:* if the node is a leaf, it must be an input variable; its value is therefore the value of that variable. If the node is internal, its value is the result of its operator applied to its children's values.

An input node's value cannot be determined until each of its children's values are determined. Each node represents a unique variable because of block normality. Evaluation of some node results in fixing the value of its associated variable; however, no other node evaluation can affect that variable's value.

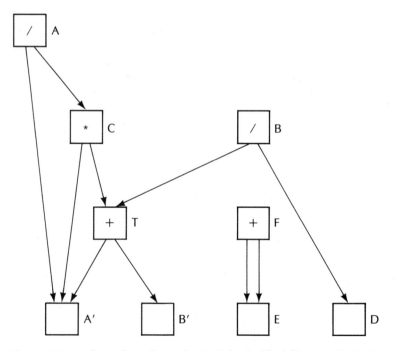

Figure 10.1. A directed acyclic graph (DAG) for the block {T ← A' + B',C ← T*A',A ← C/A',F ← E + E,B ← T/D}.

Hence, every evaluation is uniquely determined, regardless of the order in which evaluation occurs. The DAG value also is the value returned by the block.

We therefore are free to explore DAG evaluations without regard to the order in which the evaluations take place. Evaluation is subject only to the constraint that a node can be evaluated only if all its children have been previously evaluated.

Furthermore, all of the internal nonoutput nodes represent temporary variables. These may be assigned to registers and never be allocated a temporary memory location, for the sake of efficiency, even though the source program may have assigned a name to the variable.

10.3.6. Common Subexpression Identification

During construction of a DAG, the appearance of two subexpressions, such that the second one need not be recomputed, is detected easily. We are interested in a pair of assignment statements:

$$S_i: \quad C \leftarrow \theta B_1, B_2, \ldots, B_n$$
$$S_k: \quad C' \leftarrow \theta B_1, B_2, \ldots, B_n$$

such that none of the B_m $(1 \leq m \leq n)$ are defined in any statement S_j where $i < j \leq k$. That is, statement S_k will return the same value to C' as statement S_i returned to C, because none of the referenced variables have been redefined in the interim.

Block normality guarantees that none of the B_i are redefined; if one were, we would have a reference of that variable prior to its definition and its name could not appear in both S_i and S_k. The mere existence of the pair of statements $\{S_i, S_k\}$ is sufficient to guarantee that C' will receive the same value as C. In terms of the DAG being constructed, when statement S_k is under consideration, each of the nodes $B_1, B_2, \ldots, B_n$ already will be in the DAG, and a one-level tree with a root associated with operator θ and variable C will exist. We need only look for this situation, and add variable C' to the node that contains C. We see that a node can carry more than one variable.

10.3.7. DAG Reduction

All of the temporary variables may be eliminated from the DAG, once built, which will incidentally also remove any redundant operations. A node may still carry more than one output variable. If it does, we have a situation in which a single variable is represented by more than one name. A common name can be assigned to these variables.

Finally, any root node that does not contain an output variable name may be eliminated. Such a node represents a definition of a temporary variable that is never referenced.

Example.   Consider the block:

```
V ← A * B
T ← A + C
C ← B * D
X ← V + C
Z ← T - C
C ← V + C
```

with the input set {A,B,C,D} and output set {C,V,Z}. An equivalent normal block is:

```
V  ← A * B
T  ← A + C"
C' ← B * D
X  ← V + C'
Z  ← T - C'
C  ← V + C'
```

with the input set {A, B, C", D} and the output set {C, V, Z}.

The evaluation of V + C' is redundant; the redundancy is detected during the DAG construction. The final DAG is shown in figure 10.2. We also see that X is useless; it appears in a root node, but is a temporary variable; it is associated with node n_4. The local variables T and C' are associated with nodes n_2 and n_3, respectively.

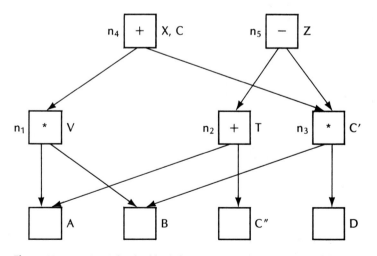

Figure 10.2.   A DAG for the block {V ← A∗B, T ← A+C", C' ← B∗D, X ← V+C', Z ← T−C', C ← V+C'}.

10.3.8. DAG Evaluation

Let us assume binary operations only in the following discussion, for the sake of simplicity. (This restriction is not hard to remove.) Also let us assume that a multiregister machine is to be used for evaluation of a DAG. Such a machine will have LOAD and STOR operations between a memory location and a register, and binary operations between two registers or between a register and memory, the result going to a register.

We would like an algorithm that, given any DAG, will generate optimal code. Unfortunately, such an optimization is a large combinatorial problem—the computational complexity of any optimal algorithm increases exponentially with the number of nodes (see Aho [1977]). Even simpler target machines (for example, machines with one register or with an unlimited number of registers) have no optimal algorithm of less than exponential complexity.

However, there are several heuristic algorithms for single- and multiregister machines; these algorithms are reviewed in Aho [1977]. Let us examine one of them in some detail, suggested by Waite [1974b], called the *top-down greedy* (TDG) algorithm.

The TDG algorithm builds a list L of internal nodes. This list, when used in reverse, yields a reasonably good node evaluation sequence for a multiregister machine containing NR registers.

```
program TDG;

    procedure TDGP(N, K: integer);
        {N is a DAG node, K is the number of
            available registers}
    begin
      if (K <= 1) and (N is an internal node
            all of whose parents
            are on the list L) then
      begin
        Add (N) to list L;
        TDGP(LEFTCHILD(N),K-1)
        TDGP(RIGHTCHILD(N),K);
        end
      end;

begin   {TDG main program}
    while (not all internal nodes are
            on the list L) do begin
      (select an internal node N, all of
                whose parents are on L);
      TDGP(N, NR);
      end
    end.
```

The TDG algorithm begins by selecting some root node of the DAG (no parents). Then TDGP will place it on the list L. TDGP will then pursue the left branches of its current node, adding them to the list until some node is found that has a parent not on the list, or until no more registers are available. It then pursues the right branches in the same way.

The selection of a node could be influenced by some additional tests. Given a set of possible nodes (that is, none are on the list and all have no ancestors), choose a node n the left descendant n' of which is such that n is the only ancestor of n' not on the list. If there is more than one such n, look at the left descendants of n', and so on. This strategy yields a sequence of DAG nodes that tend to be linked together; the number of temporary memory references thereby is minimized to the extent possible under such a simple approach.

Example.   Consider a machine with NR = 2 (two registers) and the DAG of figure 10.3, with input variables A, B, C, D and output variables X and Y. TDG yields the list:

$$7, 5, 6, 3, 4, 1, 2$$

We then use this list in reverse, with a reasonable register allocation scheme (one is described later), to obtain the following code sequence. The following table indicates the node or variable currently in one of the two registers {R1, R2}.

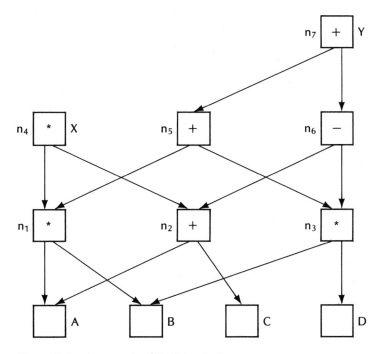

Figure 10.3.   An example of DAG (see text).

| | contents of | |
	R1	R2
R1 ← A	A	
R2 ← R1 + C		n_2
R1 ← R1 * B	n_1	
T1 ← R1 {temporary}		
R1 ← R1 * R2	n_4	
X ← R1		
R1 ← B	B	
R1 ← R1 * D	n_3	
R2 ← R2 − R1		n_6
T6 ← R2 {temporary}		
R2 ← T1		n_1
R1 ← R2 + R1	n_5	
R1 ← R1 + T6	n_7	
Y ← R1		

10.3.9. Register Assignment and Code Generation

Suppose that we are given an ordering of the internal nodes such as that provided by the reverse of the list generated by TDG. We may then assign registers and emit code by a heuristic algorithm similar to the following.

A list of assignments of registers to nodes is maintained. A register R is assigned to a node N if, at that point in the code sequence, node N's value is carried by register R. Initially, no register is assigned to any node. A register is said to be *available* if it is not assigned to a node. We also assign a level number to each node in the DAG; initially, this will be the number of parents of the node. As operations are coded, the level numbers will be reduced to zero.

Then the following procedure EMITNODE is executed for each node N on the node list generated by TDG or some other algorithm:

```
procedure EMITNODE(N: dag_node);
    {N is a DAG node, all of whose
        children have been evaluated}
    var R, R1: integer;
begin
  if (leftchild(n) value is held in register R) then
  begin
    if level(leftchild(n))=1 then
    begin {a level of 1 means that after this use, the
            left child's register will be available}
      emitop(op(n), r, value(rightchild(n)), r);
        {the right child may or may not be in a register;
            either instruction form may be emitted}
      assign(r, n)    {assign R to node N}
    end
    else
      begin {left child will be needed after this operation}
        r1 := allocate;  {get a register; it could be R}
```

```
                emitop(op(n), r, rightchild(n), r1);
                assign(r1, n)
              end;
            {begin some cleanup for node N}
            if (N carries an output variable X) then
                emitstor(x, register(n));  {emit a store
                      to X from the register assigned to N}
            decrlevel(n)  {adjust levels and release registers}
          end
        else
          begin {left child is not in a register}
            r := allocate;  {allocate a register}
            emitload(value(leftchild(n)), r);
                {load leftchild in register R}
            assign(r, leftchild(n));
            emitnode(n);  {try again; left child is now in
                a register}
          end
      end;
procedure DECRLEVEL(N: integer);
   var NLC, NRC: integer;  {temporary node numbers}
begin
   {this decrements the level numbers of the
    children of node N.  If the level of N or any of
    its children is then 0, the corresponding registers
    are released}

   nlc:=leftchild(n);
   nrc:=rightchild(n);
   level(nlc):=level(nlc)-1;
   level(nrc):=level(nrc)-1;
   if level(nlc)=0 then release_node(nlc);
      {if a register or temporary is not assigned to node N,
          release_node(n) does nothing; otherwise it makes
          the register or temporary assigned to N available}
   if level(nrc)=0 then release_node(nrc);
   if level(n)=0 then release_node(n)
end;


function ALLOCATE: integer;
   var R, T: integer;
begin  {allocates a register, returning its number}
   if (any register R is available) then allocate:=R
   else
   begin
      t:=allocatetemp;  {allocate temporary memory cell}
      if (any register R is assigned to a node N such
          that N is not a left descendant of any of
          its ancestors) then
        emitstor(r, t)  {save R in cell T}
      else
      begin  {no reasonable basis for choice}
         Choose any register R assigned to a node N;
         emitstor(r, t)  {save R in cell T}
      end;
      assign(t, n);  {temporary T assigned to node N}
      allocate:=R;
   end
end
```

These procedures exploit several possible situations. If a register is needed and one is available, then it is used. If a register is needed and none are available, then we look for one assigned to a node that is only a right descendant of its ancestors; such a node later can be accessed directly through its temporary memory cell and need not be allocated a register. Barring these possibilities, there is probably no good basis for a register choice.

The register allocator is responsible for saving the present contents of an assigned register; that value will be needed later, because the register cannot be assigned to a node at the end of an EMITNODE call if the level of the node has fallen to zero.

10.4. Data-Flow Analysis

In considering optimization of blocks, we need information regarding the definition and use of data items that cannot be found by an examination of the block alone. For example, we cannot distinguish output and temporary data items; we need to know whether any reference to some data item will lie in a control path leading from the block, uninterrupted by another definition. In short, we cannot determine the domain of the block variables by information in the block alone.

If we had a complete data-flow analysis of a program, we could provide, in addition to block optimization, some useful tests and other optimizations as follows:

1. A sneak path, along which a reference to some data item is not preceded by a definition, can be detected. The programmer should be made aware of such paths, although the logic of the program may be such that the path never can be followed completely to the reference point.

2. Redundant or useless code can be detected. A redundant assignment statement is one that is followed eventually by an identical one. A useless assignment is one for which no subsequent reference exists.

3. Redundant or useless variables often can be detected. A redundant variable is one for which another variable always carries the same value. A useless variable is one for which only definitions and no references exist. A redundant variable can be detected only under certain circumstances; in general, it is not possible to determine from a static analysis of a program whether two variables carry identical values.

4. Register allocations can be carried from one block into others, or through a block, if it appears that some code savings might result.

5. Loop invariant variables often can be identified.

Data-flow analysis is based on a *control flow graph*. Given a program, its flow graph G consists of a connected, directed graph (not necessarily acyclic) having a single entry node n_0. Graph G consists of a set of nodes $N = \{n_1, n_2, \ldots, n_m\}$, representing blocks of instructions, and a set of edges E, connecting pairs of nodes, that represent the branching paths between blocks.

Each block has one entry and one exit point and consists of the largest sequence of program steps that can be so formed. A block might also consist of the instructions of a set of blocks connected together so as to contain only one entry and one exit point; we call such a block an *extended block*.

The detailed nature of a branch decision is ignored in data-flow analysis, as are the details of the calculations within a block. The only information of interest is (1) the possible branches, (2) the definitions of data items, and (3) the uses of data items. It is entirely possible that the branching decisions in a program are such that some paths never can be followed during execution; however, for our purposes, we must assume that any directed path can be followed during execution.

10.4.1. Definitions

A *definition* of a data item R is some statement that assigns a value to R, replacing a previous assignment. A *use* of R is some statement that requires the current value of R in a computation.

A *locally available definition* of a data item R in a block B_i is the last definition of R appearing in that block. We denote the set of available definitions for block B_i by DB_i.

Any definition of an item R is said to *kill* all definitions of R that can reach the block containing the definition. Any definition of a data item R that can reach a block is *preserved* by the block if R is not defined in the block. The set of all definitions in the program that are preserved in block B_i will be denoted PB_i.

A definition d in a block B_1 is said to *reach* block B_2 if both of these conditions hold:

1. Definition d is locally available from B_1,

2. Definition d is preserved on some directed path P from B_1 to B_2 (but not necessarily on all paths.) Path P may be null.

The notion of reaching is essentially that the value of a data item X assigned in block B_1 can somehow get through to B_2, without an intervening redefinition of X. The set of definitions that reach a block B_i will be denoted R_i.

A definition in a block B is said to be *available* at block B' if it is locally available in B and can reach B'. We denote the set of available definitions at a block B_i by A_i.

A *locally exposed use* of a data item X in a block B is a use of X in B that is not preceded in the block by a definition of X. A variable with a locally exposed use in block B is an input variable of B.

A use of a data item X is *upwards exposed* in block B if it either is locally exposed in B, or if there exists a path through B and to some other block B' that does not contain a definition of X, and such that X is locally exposed in B'. Here, the notion is that some use of X in block B' can be the terminus of some path running through a number of blocks, including a block B; that use is then upwards exposed at B. The set of upwards exposed uses of a block B_i will be expressed as a set U_i. Note that this set contains uses that appear in block B and elsewhere in the program.

A definition d is *active* or *live* at block B_i if d reaches B_i (that is, $d \in R_i$) and there is an upwards exposed use at B_i of the data item defined by d. The set of live definitions at block B_i will be denoted L_i, and is called the block's *live set*. Clearly:

$$L_i = R_i \cap U_i$$

The set intersection of R_i and U_i corresponds to the two requirements that there be an upwards exposed use and that definition d reach block B_i.

Examples.   Consider the following block:

```
K := 3;      {1}
J := 3 * K;  {2}
N := J - 2;  {3}
J := 3 * N;  {4}
N := J + 6;  {5}
```

The *locally available* definitions out of this block are those for J, K, and N, lines 1, 4, and 5. The definitions in lines 2 and 3 are *killed* by the subsequent lines 4 and 5.

There are no locally exposed uses for this block; these uses would be input variables, and there are none. If the first statement were:

```
K := J + N;
```

instead, then these uses of J and N would be *locally exposed*.

Now consider the following block:

```
K := 17;     {1}
J := M + 3;  {2}
K := J - M;  {3}
```

A definition of M preceding this block is *preserved* by the block; there are no definitions of M in it. If the program contains definitions for variables {A, B, J, K, M}, then this block also preserves any definitions for A and B, but not for J and K.

Consider figure 10.4. A definition d (the assignment statement K := 17) appears in block B_1. There are no subsequent definitions of data item K in blocks B_1 or B_2. We then say that definition d *reaches* block B_3; whether it is killed in block B_3 is immaterial. There also may be other paths from B_1 to B_3 along which

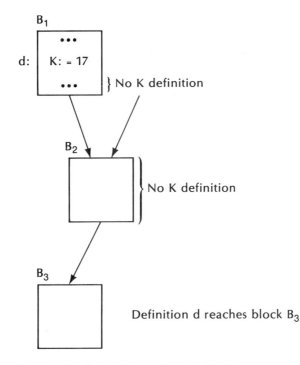

Figure 10.4. *Reach* of a definition d to block B$_3$.

definition d is killed; we need only one along which the definition is preserved for d to reach B$_3$. Block B$_1$ also may be the same as block B$_3$; we then have a loop through which a definition in block B$_1$ can reach its own block.

The definition d in block B$_1$ in figure 10.4 is *locally available* in B$_1$ and is *available* in blocks B$_2$ and B$_3$.

Consider figure 10.5. A *use* u of K appears in block B$_3$, through the statement M := K + 3. If no definition of K appears prior to u in block B$_3$ or anywhere in blocks B$_1$ and B$_2$, then use u is *upwards exposed* in all three of these blocks.

Next, consider figure 10.6. We have a definition d of data item K in block B$_1$, with no subsequent definition in B$_1$, B$_2$, B$_3$, or B$_4$. A use of K appears in B$_4$. We then say that d is *live* in blocks B$_2$, B$_3$, and B$_4$. d has clearly *reached* each of these blocks, and an *upwards exposed use* of K exists in each of them. Again, the existence of other paths or of definitions in other blocks not shown in figure 10.6 is immaterial.

Finally, consider figure 10.7. We have several blocks containing three definitions and two uses of a variable X. All the control flow paths are shown. We denote a definition of a data item X in a block i by X$_i$. Sets R$_j$ and L$_j$ for a block j consist of definitions. Set U$_j$ for block j consists of the one data item X or is empty.

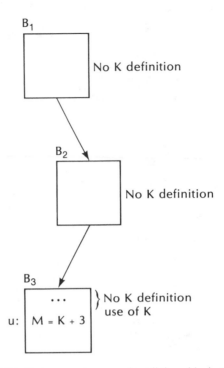

Figure 10.5.   *Use* u *of K in B$_3$ is* upwards exposed *in all three blocks B$_1$, B$_2$, B$_3$.*

For example, consider block 3. Only the definition X_2 can reach this block; the definitions in blocks 6 and 7 cannot. Hence, R_3 consists of X_2. Set U_3 contains X, because a use of X appears in block 3 not preceded by a definition. Finally, definition X_2 is *live* in block 3; none of the other definitions are.

A complete table of reaches, upwards exposed uses, and live definitions for the graph of figure 10.7 follows.

Block i	Reach R_i	Upwards Exposed U_i	Live Definitions L_i
1	$\varnothing$	$\varnothing$	$\varnothing$
2	X_2	$\varnothing$	$\varnothing$
3	X_2	X	X_2
4	X_2	X	X_2
5	X_2	X	X_2
6	X_2	$\varnothing$	$\varnothing$
7	X_2, X_6	$\varnothing$	$\varnothing$

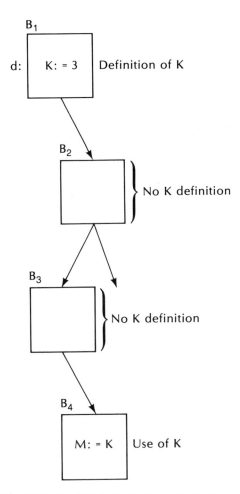

Figure 10.6. *Definition* of K in block B_1 is *live* in blocks B_2, B_3, B_4.

10.4.2. The Basic Data-Flow Analysis Method

It should be apparent that the determination of the various sets defined here can be made by first determining the local sets PB and DB for each block, then exploring all the paths that lead into or out of each of the blocks and the implications of PB and DB on these paths. Unfortunately, path exploration in a directed graph often is a difficult computational problem—the number of operations tends to increase exponentially with the number of nodes in the graph. It turns out that data-flow analysis computation is not hard, provided that a graph-reduction technique called *interval ordering* is used. Interval ordering reduces the computation of flow analysis to one requiring O(n log n) operations, where n is the number of nodes.

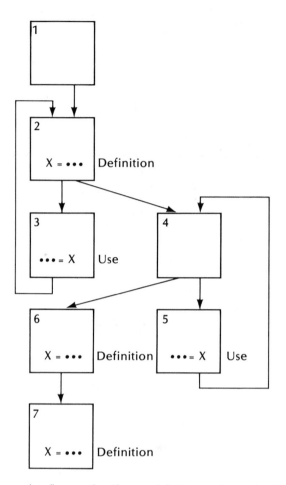

Figure 10.7.   A complete flow graph with some definitions and uses of variable X.

Let us first examine the basic method. It should be apparent that the set of definitions that reach a block B_i is the union of the definitions available from the nodes that are the immediate predecessors (the parents) of B_i. That is:

$$R_i = \cup A_p$$

where the A_p are the available definitions of the blocks B_p that are the parents of block B_i.

Now the set of available definitions A_i for block B_i consists of all those locally available definitions DB_i, together with all those definitions in the program that reach B_i (namely R_i) and that are preserved in B_i. That is:

$$A_i = (R_i \cap PB_i) \cup DB_i$$

These two set equations are sufficient to determine the sets A_i and R_i for all the blocks B_i through a simple algorithm called the *basic reach algorithm:*

Basic Reach Algorithm

The inputs are the PB_i and DB_i for each block B_i in the control flow graph. The outputs are R_i and A_i for each block B_i.

1. Initialize all of the A_i and R_i to the null set.

2. Apply the following two formulas to the nodes of the graph until there is no change in any R_i or A_i:

$$R_i = \cup A_p$$
$$A_i = (R_i \cap PB_i) \cup DB_i.$$

   where the A_p are the available definitions of the blocks B_p that are the parents of block B_i.

Kildall [1973] has shown that the information in A_i and R_i does stabilize. However, the rate at which the sets stabilize depends critically on the order in which the nodes of the graph are examined; the process can be time consuming if the node ordering is not chosen carefully.

Note that, to be useful, we must consider a program at least as large as a typical procedure, and build definition and preservation sets for all its definitions and uses. We cannot restrict our interest arbitrarily to some subset of the program. It therefore is important to develop an efficient method of determining these sets.

10.4.3. Intervals

Given a node h, an *interval I(h)* is the maximal, single entry subgraph in which h is the only entry node and in which all closed paths contain h. The unique interval node h is called the *interval head* or *header node*. An interval consists of an ordered list of nodes; the ordering is determined by the following algorithm, and is important in an improved reach algorithm.

Interval Algorithm

1. Let H be a set of header nodes. Initially, let it contain node n_0, the unique entry node of the flow graph.

2. For every node h ∈ H, fix the interval list I(h) as follows:
   (a) Put h in I(h) as the first element.
   (b) Add to I(h) any node all of whose immediate predecessors are already in I(h).
   (c) Repeat step 2(b) until no more nodes can be added to I(h).

3. Add to H all nodes in G that are not already in H and that are not in I(h), but that have immediate predecessors in I(h). A node is added to H the first time any, but not all, of its parents become members of an interval.

4. Select the next unprocessed node in H and repeat steps 2 and 3. If no more unprocessed nodes exist in H, terminate the procedure.

The result is a list of intervals I(h₁), I(h₂), . . . , I(hₙ) that represents a partition of the nodes of the flow graph.

Example. Figure 10.8 illustrates the partitioning of a graph into intervals. Interval I(1) consists of only one node 1, because its successor, node 2, has more than node 1 as a parent; there is a path from node 7 to node 2 as well as from node 1, and node 7 is not in I(1). Interval I(2) is begun with node 2, and again consists of only that node. (Node 3 can be reached from node 6.) Interval I(3) is begun with node 3, then nodes 4 and 5 can be added, then node 6. Node 7 cannot be added, because a path from node 2, not in I(3), exists. Finally, interval I(7) consists of nodes 7 and 8.

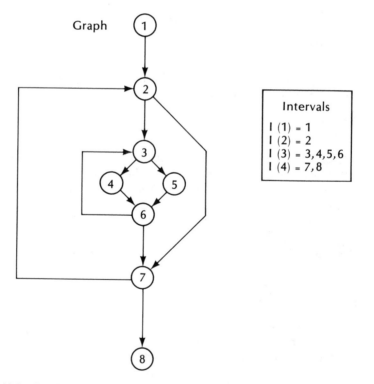

Figure 10.8. Partitioning a graph into intervals.

Higher-Order Intervals

The intervals just determined from the original flow graph G^1 can be expressed as another graph G^2. We construct G^2 from the intervals of G^1 by merging the nodes within each interval, and discarding all edges connecting two nodes in the same interval. We thus obtain a *second-order interval* graph. This, too, can be reduced by interval partitioning to obtain a third-order, fourth-order, or nth-order interval graph.

Eventually, a graph G^i is obtained by interval analysis of a graph G^{i-1} that contains the same number of nodes as G^i. If G^i contains one node, we say that G^i is *reducible;* otherwise G^i is *irreducible.*

An example of an irreducible graph is given in figure 10.9; I(1) consists of one alone, I(2) consists of two alone, and so on.

It is interesting that programs that consist of only structured control statements (IF-THEN-ELSE, WHILE-DO, FOR, sequential statements) are reducible. Irreducible graphs stem from programs with GOTO statements.

An irreducible graph can be *split* by replicating one or more nodes. For example, if nodes 3 and 4 are duplicated in figure 10.9, we obtain a reducible graph, figure 10.10. Splitting is merely an analysis technique; we are not suggesting that the program code must be duplicated. It also turns out that even if a control flow graph is irreducible, the analysis that yields sets R and A nevertheless terminates and computes the sets correctly. It just takes more time than does a reducible graph with a comparable number of nodes.

The details of the reach algorithm based on intervals can be found in Allen and Cocke's paper [Allen, 1976]. The general reach algorithm has two phases. In the first phase, two items of information are collected by working through the interval

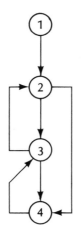

Figure 10.9. An irreducible graph.

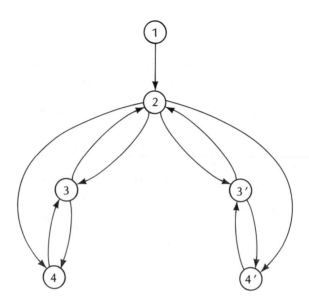

Figure 10.10.   Splitting states 3 and 4 in the graph of figure 10.9.

graphs in the order G^1, G^2, . . ., G_n (the order in which they were constructed) as follows:

1. The definitions defined in the interval and locally available from it; they will become a DB set for the node representing the interval in the next higher-order graph.

2. The definitions preserved by the interval; they will become the PB sets for the next higher-order graph.

   In the second phase, the graphs are worked through in the opposite order of construction; the set of definitions reaching each node is thereby generated.

   The essential property of an interval that reduces the length of the analysis is that control that reaches any node within the interval must have passed through the interval header. We say that the header *dominates* the nodes of the interval for this reason. Furthermore, an interval I' that is the successor of an interval I is such that control must pass from some node in I into the header of I'. By considering the interval sets in their generation order, we can minimize the number of path combinations to be considered.

   It is interesting that Knuth [1971], in his empirical examination of a number of Fortran programs, found that over 90% of their control flow graphs were reducible, which implies that a control flow analysis based on intervals generally will be quite efficient. An analysis of programs written in a more structured language, such as Ada or Pascal, undoubtedly would yield an even higher percentage of reducible control flow graphs.

Use and Live Information

Given the upwards exposed use U_i and the definitions R_i that reach a block B_i in a program, the live set can be determined readily.

However, this set contains only the data items that are live on entry into a block. It usually is more desirable to know those items that are live on each of the exit edges from a block. For example, register allocation requires live information on exit from a block, rather than on entrance. Rather than retain both entrance and exit information, it is better to retain live information for edges and construct the entry live data item sets as needed; the latter is the union of the former over the entering edges.

We need the set of definitions A_e available on each edge. Then, for a given edge e, incident into node i:

$$L_e = A_e \cap U_i$$

The algorithm for generating the U_i sets for the graph nodes by the use of the interval sets requires two phases, the first in interval-generation order and the second in opposite order. The first phase can be a part of the reach algorithm. The second phase, however, works backward through the nodes in each interval.

The upwards exposed uses from each interval is found in the first phase as follows:

1. Prior to processing each interval h, a set U_h is created and initialized to the upwards exposed uses in that interval.

2. For each node i in the interval (i = 2, 3, . . . , N), U_h is updated with the locally exposed uses UB_i in i that can be preserved along some path from h to i, which is done by forming the set:

$$(\cup P_p) \cap UB_i$$

where the union is over the sets P_p; P_p is the set of data items preserved on input edge p to node i. Its computation is part of the basic reach algorithm.

The complete algorithms and a procedure in PL/I can be found in Allen [1976].

The Interval-Based Reach Algorithm

Inputs

1. The ordered set of graphs $(G^1, G^2, . . . , G^n)$ determined by interval analysis.

2. The intervals in each graph with their nodes given in interval process order.

3. The definitions *defined* and *preserved* on each edge in the first-order graph. These are expressed in the DB and PB sets.

Outputs

1. A set R of the definitions that reach each node.

2. A set A of the definitions available on each edge.

Phase I

1. For each graph G^g in the order G^1, G^2, . . . , G^{n-1}, perform steps 2 and 3.

2. If the current graph is not G^1, then initialize the PB and DB sets for the edges of the graph. PB and DB are initialized by first identifying the edge in G^{g-1} to which each edge in G^g corresponds (these will be interval exit edges). Then, using the information generated during step 3 for G^{g-1}, for each edge i in G^g with corresponding exit edge x from interval with head h in G^{g-1}, set:
   (a) $PB_i := P_x$
   (b) $DB_i := (R_h \cap P_x) \cup D_x$

3. For each exit edge of each interval in G^g, determine P—the definitions preserved on some path through the interval to the exit—and D—the definitions in the interval that may be available on the exit. These definitions are determined by finding P and D for each edge in the interval as follows:
   (a) For each exit edge i of the header node:

$$P_i := PB_i$$
$$D_i := DB_i$$

   (b) For each exit edge i of each node j (j = 2, 3, . . . , N) in interval order:

$$P_i := (\cup P_p) \cap PB_i$$
$$D_i := ((\cup D_p) \cap PB_i) \cup DB_i$$

   where the union over P_p and D_p is for all p input edges to node j.

While processing an interval, determine the set of definitions R_h that can reach the interval head h from inside the interval by:

$$R_h := \cup D_l$$

for all interval edges l that enter h. If there are none, set R_h to $\emptyset$.

Between phases I and II, the R vector for the single node in the nth-order derived graph is initiated: $R_1 = \emptyset$ or whatever set of definitions is known to reach the program from outside.

Phase II

1. For each graph G^g in the order G^{n-1}, . . . , G^2, G^1, perform the following steps 2 and 3.

2. For each node i in G^{g+1}, form $R_h := R_h \cup R_i$, where h is the head of the interval in G^g that i represents in G^{g+1}.

3. For each interval, process the nodes in interval order determining the definitions reaching each node and available on each node exit edge as follows:
   (a) For each exit edge i of the header node h:

$$A_i := (R_h \cap PB_i) \cup DB_i$$

   (b) For each node j (j = 2, 3, . . . , N) in interval order, first form:

$$R_j := \cup A_p$$

   for all input edges p to j; then, for each exit edge i of j, form:

$$A_i := (R_j \cap PB_i) \cup DB_i$$

10.4.4. Applications of Data-Flow Information

We are now in a position to outline a number of useful optimizations based on the information developed in a data-flow analysis.

Useless Definitions

A definition d is *useless* if the value assigned to the data variable X in d never is required subsequently by any reference. The definition d can be removed with no effect on the program. Let d reside in a block B_i. d is useless if:

1. Definition d is live on the B_i block exit; that is, d is in L_i.

2. No upwards exposed use of d exists on exit from B_i.

Let U' be the union of the sets L_e for each edge e leaving block B_i. If d is not in U', then d is useless. Set U' is a *useful* set of definitions.

Uninitialized Variable Use

If a use u is upwards exposed in the "start" block B_0, then a path from the program origin to u exists that does not contain a definition of the use data variable. A test for potentially uninitialized variables in a program is that $U_0 = \emptyset$. We say *potentially*, because data-flow analysis does not consider the logic of program branching, and it may happen that the path to the uninitialized variable use cannot be followed during program execution.

Basic Block Input and Output Variables

An input variable X of a block B is such that a use u of X appears in B, and u is upwards exposed in B. As we discussed earlier, we do not need a data-flow analysis to identify input variables of a basic block.

An output variable X of a basic block B must appear in B (use or definition) and is live on exit from B. The *live* set, of course, derives from data-flow analysis.

Loop Code Movement

Suppose that a loop is identified as indicated in figure 10.11. B1 and B2 are some collections of code with single entries and exits; they are not necessarily basic blocks. B3 is a basic block containing a statement S of interest. T is a test for loop exit, and contains only uses. Statement S has the form:

$$X \leftarrow \theta\ Y_1, Y_2, \ldots, Y_r$$

where θ is an r-ary operation, the X receives the result, and the Y_i are the operands.

It is sometimes possible to move S from B3 into block B1 without affecting the program. If this can be done, we will have one execution of S in the optimized program for every n executions in the original program, where n is the number of loop iterations. Let us develop necessary and sufficient conditions for such a code movement.

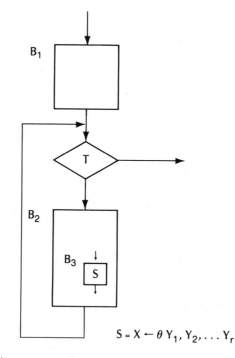

$$S = X \leftarrow \theta\ Y_1, Y_2, \ldots Y_r$$

Figure 10.11.   Code movement of a statement S from block B_2 to block B_1.

S can be moved to the bottom of B1 only if no reachable definitions of any of the Y_i or X exist in B2, other than in S. Because block B2 is not necessarily basic, we need the results of a data-flow analysis.

All of the uses u_i $(1 \le i \le r)$ corresponding to the operands Y_i in S must be in the upwards exposed use set U_2 of block B2. They also must be live at the block B2 exit. These conditions guarantee that no loop path can change any of the Y variables.

The definition of X in statement S must be live at block entry B2 (therefore also at exit of B2) and at block entry B3. This requirement precludes any other definitions of X in B2 (except in S and unreachable definitions); such a definition would kill the S definition either at block B2 exit or at block B3 entry.

10.5. Exercises

1. Construct a DAG for the block:

   ```
   X := A * (B + C);
   Y := (B + C)/A;
   X := X - A;
   B := X/Y;
   Y := A + B + C;
   ```

   X and Y are the output variables; A, B, and C are input variables.

2. Show that a TDG list for the DAG of figure 10.2 is:

   $$5, 2, 4, 1, 3$$

   Develop a code sequence for this list for NR = 2. Can you find a shorter sequence for some other list?

3. Let the reverse of a TDG list be $n_1, n_2, \ldots, n_r$, and let the nodes be evaluated in that order. Show that when any node N is to be evaluated, all of its children (if any) have been evaluated previously.

4. Generate a code sequence for the DAGs of figures 10.2 and 10.3 using TDG and EMITNODE.

5. Show that EMITNODE emits correct code for a DAG, given a node list with the evaluation order property that a node is selected for evaluation only if each of its children has been evaluated.

6. Discuss extensions to TDG and EMITNODE for n-ary operators; for example, a function call or a MAX operator. Can an n-ary operator be transformed into a sequence of binary operators?

7. Devise data structures for a block, a DAG, and whatever else is needed to implement a code-generation system. Write Pascal procedures that emit code for a given block, expressed as a sequence of binary assignment operations.

8. Where are arbitrary choices possible in ALLOCATE and TDG? Suppose, as an optimizing strategy, that these choices are made through a back-tracking, nondeterministic machine. We can then generate all possible equivalent code sequences and choose the shortest one. Show that such a system must halt in finite time. Is this computationally feasible? How would the number of operations vary with the size of the DAG? (A measure of the size of a DAG might be the number of nodes.)

9. Consider the graph of figure 10.12, which consists of 7 blocks. There are definitions of a data item X in blocks 5 and 7, and uses in blocks 2 and 4. Determine the sets R_i, U_i, and L_i for each block i, $1 \le i \le 7$.

10. A Basic program carries a line number on each statement. If such a program contains a computed GOTO statement of the form GO N, where N has been evaluated previously and must evaluate to a line number during program execution, is it possible to construct a data-flow graph for the program? What form would it have? Similarly, consider a Fortran program with a computed GOTO, but such that only some of the statements carry line numbers.

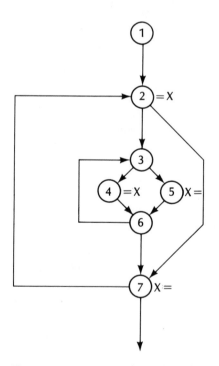

Figure 10.12.   An example graph—see exercise 1.

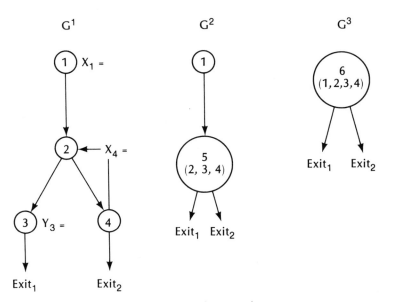

Figure 10.13.   A graph and its higher order intervals.

11. Consider the graph G^1 and its higher-order interval graphs, shown in figure 10.13. There are two variables, X and Y, and three definitions, X_1, X_4, and Y_3.
(a) Show that figure 10.14 expresses DB and PB for the graphs.
(b) Show that figure 10.15 expresses the reach and availability sets R and A after the second phase of the reach algorithm.

	Edge	DB	PB
G^1	1-2	X_1	$X_4\ X_3$
	2-3	0	$X_1\ X_4\ Y_3$
	2-4	0	$X_1\ X_4\ Y_3$
	$3\text{-}e_1$	Y_3	$X_1\ X_4$
	4-2	X_4	$X_1\ Y_3$
	$4\text{-}e_2$	X_4	$X_1\ Y_3$
G^2	1-5	X_1	$X_4\ Y_3$
	$5\text{-}e_1$	$X_4\ Y_3$	$X_1\ X_4$
	$5\text{-}e_2$	X_4	Y_3
G^3	$6\text{-}e_1$	$X_1\ X_4\ Y_3$	$\emptyset$
	$6\text{-}e_2$	$X_1\ X_4$	Y_3

Figure 10.14.   DB and PB for the graph of figure 10.13.

	Node	Reach	Edge	Available
G^3	6	∅	6-e_1	X_1 X_4 Y_3
			6-e_2	X_4
G^2	1	∅	1-5	X_1
	5	X_1	5-e_1	X_1 X_4 Y_3
			5-e_2	X_4
G^1	1	∅	1-2	X_1
	2	X_1 X_4	2-3	X_1 X_4
	3	X_1 X_1	2-4	X_1 X_4
	4	X_1 X_4	3-e_1	X_1 X_4 Y_3
			4-2	X_1 X_4
			4-e_2	X_1 X_4

Figure 10.15.   REACH and AVAILABILITY sets for the graph of figure 10.13.

12. Consider the following program, which is an attempt at a portion of a merge-sort program:

```
program BADSORT;
  var N: integer;

  procedure MSORT;
    var I, K, P: integer;
        UP: boolean;
  begin
    up := true;
    p := 1;
    repeat
      if up then begin
        i := 1;
        k := N+1;
      end
      else begin
        n := k+1;
        i := n-1;
      end;
      up := not up;
      n := i+1;
    until p=n;
  end;

begin
  n := 10;
  msort;
end.
```

Show that its data-flow graph has the form shown in figure 10.16. Fill in the boxes in figure 10.16 with uses and definitions of the variables.

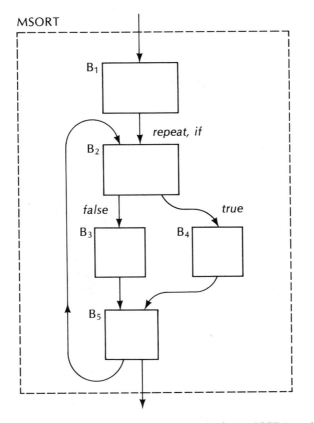

MSORT

repeat, if

false   *true*

Figure 10.16.   Data flow outline for procedure MSORT (exercise 12).

Determine the upwards-exposed variable set at the entry of block B_1. What does this set reveal about the validity of the MSORT procedure? (NOTE: assume that the local variables of MSORT are uninitialized upon entering the main body of the procedure.)

10.6. Bibliographical Notes

Nakata [1967] and Meyers [1965] developed the optimal algorithm for the generation of code from an expression tree; their algorithm yields the minimum number of registers for commutative operators only. Sethi and Ullman [Sethi, 1970] restated their algorithm, and showed that it is optimal for noncommutative and nonassociative operators as well as for commutative and associative-commutative operators.

The notion of collecting complicated nodes to the left of simple nodes for a machine with noncommutative instructions that operate between a register and memory can be traced to an early paper by Floyd [1961].

The discussion of blocks, block statements, and renaming is principally drawn from Aho [1972b]. A presentation similar to ours can be found in Aho and Ullman [Aho, 1972], chapter 11.

The data-flow analysis material is from Allen and Cocke's paper [Allen, 1976].

Beatty [1974] describes an algorithm that assigns registers in a highly optimal fashion; he considers both the local domain of a block and its global environment.

Chaitin [1982] has shown that register allocation can be treated as a graph coloring problem. Although the problem of determining whether a graph is n-colorable is NP-complete, his experimental evidence indicates that it is a practical technique.

Bruno and Sethi [Bruno, 1976] and Aho, Johnson, and Ullman [Aho, 1977b] show that the problem of code optimization for a general class of single- and multiregister machines, given a DAG with common subexpression subsumption, is NP-complete; that is, it has a computational complexity that is exponential in the size of the DAG. The significance of this result is that optimal solutions can be demonstrated only for rather small DAGs.

Cocke and Kennedy [Cocke, 1977] have given a simple algorithm that performs reduction of operator strength by moving certain statements out of a FOR loop. A general discussion of loop strength reduction, identification of induction variables, and so on, is given in Aho and Ullman [Aho, 1972a], chapter 11.

Recent efforts in optimization theory have led to new unified transformations for flow graphs. These transformations attempt to reduce the cost of optimization by combining conventional transformations into one unified transformation. An overview can be found in Dhamdhere and Keith's paper [Dhamdhere, 1983].

Ramanath and Solomon [Ramanath, 1982] have developed a linear algorithm for generating a linear sequence of instructions from a flow graph. Their criterion is minimization of the number of unconditional jumps. They give a linear-time algorithm for the optimal translation.

BIBLIOGRAPHY

Abbreviations:

ACM: Association for Computing Machinery
CACM: Communications of the Association for Computing Machinery
IEEE: Institute for Electrical and Electronic Engineers
IRE: Institute for Radio Engineers
JACM: Journal of the Association for Computing Machinery
SIAM: Society of Industrial and Applied Mathematics

Abrahams [1974], P. W., "Some Remarks on Lookup of Structured Variables," *CACM* **17**(4) 209/210. Comment on Gates [1973], on lookup of structured Cobol or PL/I variables, pointing out an error in Gates' approach. Alternative methods also are presented that solve the general problem without undue inefficiency.

Aho [1969a], A. V., J. D. Ullman, "Properties of Syntax Directed Translations," *J. Computer and System Sciences* **3**(3) 319/334.

Aho [1969b], A. V., J. D. Ullman, "Syntax Directed Translations and the Pushdown Assembler," *J. Computer and System Sciences* **3**(1) 37/56. The push-down assembler (PA) is a multitape stack machine. Given a syntax-directed translator (SDT) with at most k variables on the right part of any one production, then the push-down assembler requires k + 1 stacks. One stack contains parsing states, and the other k contain strings arising from the syntax-directed transduction. Hierarchy of translators is introduced, and he shows that the class of PAs is exactly the class of STDs. Rules for constructing the finite control for a given set of productions are presented.

Aho [1971], A. V., J. D. Ullman, "Translations on a Context Free Grammar," *Inf. and Control* **19**(5) 439/475. Syntax-directed translation, context-free grammars, parse trees, generalized syntax-directed translators, bounds on translation, length relationships, tree automata, and conclusions.

Aho [1972], A. V., J. D. Ullman, *The Theory of Parsing, Translation, and Compiling,* 2 vols, Englewood Cliffs, NJ: Prentice-Hall. Extensive theoretical framework for languages, grammars, parsers, optimization. Vol I: Math preliminaries, introduction to compiling, elements of language theory, theory of translations, general parsing methods, one-pass no backtrack parsing, limited backtrack parsing algorithms. Vol II: techniques for parser optimization, theory of deterministic parsers, translation and code generation, bookkeeping, code optimization. All with formal definitions and many proofs.

Aho [1972b], A. V., J. D. Ullman, "Optimization of Straight Line Programs," *SIAM J. Comput.* **1**(1) 1/19. Provides a set of transformations on a sequence of statements into equivalent sequences, then shows that optimization of a straight line sequence under "reasonable" cost criteria always can be accomplished by applying a sequence of these transformations in a prescribed order. (Much of this material also is in Aho [1972].)

Aho [1972c], A. V., T. G. Peterson, "A Minimum Distance Error-Correcting Parser for Context-Free Languages," *SIAM J. Comput.* **1**(4) 305/312. A grammar G for some context-free language is transformed into a grammar G' that accepts every sentence in the alphabet of G, by the addition of error productions. A sentence containing one or more errors can be parsed through an Earley parser (Earley, 1970), and the minimum number of error productions that generates a parse is selected. The method operates in $O(n^3)$ steps at worst, where n is the number of tokens in the input sentence.

Aho [1974], A. V., S. C. Johnson, "LR Parsing," *Computing Surveys* **6**(2) 99/124. Grammars, derivation trees, parsers, parser action and goto tables, parser construction, parsing ambiguous grammars, parser optimization, and error recovery. Very readable, with many examples and illustrations.

Aho [1974], A. V., J. E. Hopcroft, J. D. Ullman, "The Design and Analysis of Computer Algorithms," Reading, MA: Addison-Wesley.

Aho [1975], A. V., S. C. Johnson, J. D. Ullman, "Deterministic Parsing of Ambiguous Grammars," *CACM* **18**(8) 441/452. Generating an LR parser for an ambiguous expression grammar, then fixing the table to reflect some desired associativity rules for the operators. Results in considerably smaller table than is otherwise the case.

Aho [1976a], A. V., S. C. Johnson, "Optimal Code Generation for Expression Trees," *JACM* **23**(3) 488/501. Algorithms for code generation from expression trees, with theorems.

Aho [1977a], A. V., S. C. Johnson, J. D. Ullman, "Code Generation for Machines with Multiregister Operations," *Fourth ACM Symposium on Principles of Programming Languages,* 21/28. Some conclusions regarding register allocation with single- and double-length results with even assignment for doubles, and the problem of optimal allocation.

Aho [1977b], A. V., S. C. Johnson, J. D. Ullman, "Code Generation for Expressions with Common Subexpressions," *JACM* **24**(1) 146/160. Shows that the problem of generating optimal code for expressions containing common subexpressions is computationally difficult, even for simple expressions and simple machines. Some heuristics are given.

Alexander [1975], W. G., "Static and Dynamic Characteristics of XPL Programs," *Computer* **8**(11) 41/46. Statistics on 19 XPL programs—distributions of statements by type, parser reductions, operators in expressions, numeric constants, instruction usage (360 target), and branch distances.

Allen [1976], F. E., J. Cocke, "A Program Data Flow Analysis," *CACM* **19**(3) 137/147. Static analysis methods leading to global data-flow analysis. Algorithms given that can determine all the definitions that can reach any node of the control flow graph, and all the live definitions.

ANSI Pascal [1983], *American National Standard Pascal Computer Programming Language,* IEEE standard 770X3.97-1983. A derivation of the ISO standard for Pascal. Defines terminology, syntax, and semantics of ANSI Pascal.

Anderson [1973], T., J. Eve, J. J. Horning, "Efficient LR(1) Parsers," *Acta Informatica* **2**(1) 12/39.

Aufenkamp [1957], D. D., F. E. Hohn, "Analysis of Sequential Machines," *IRE Trans.* Vol EC-6, 276/285.

Backus [1957], J. W., *et al.,* "The FORTRAN Automatic Coding System," *Proc. Western Joint Computer Conference,* vol 11, 188/198. The original definition of the FORTRAN language and the first automatic translator of FORTRAN to IBM704 machine code. (Reprinted in Rosen [1967].)

Bauer [1968], H., S. Becker, S. L. Graham, "ALGOL W Implementation," CS98, Stanford, CA: Computer Science Department, Stanford University. ALGOL W, designed by Wirth, is a simplified Algol-60 language. Describes an IBM 360 implementation. Rich in detail.

Bauer [1974], F. L., "Historical Remarks on Compiler Construction," in *Lecture Notes in Computer Science,* Goos, G., J. Hartmanis (eds), New York: Springer-Verlag, 603/621. Classification of compiler methods and brief historical review of original work and development.

Beatty [1974], J. C., "Register Assignment Algorithm for Generation of Highly Optimized Object Code," *IBM J. Res. Develop.* (1) 20/39. An algorithm that permits a high level of optimization at both local and global levels. Finds appreciable improvement over a conventional production compiler. No attempt to assess either implementation labor costs or expected improvements.

Berkeley [1964], E. C., D. G. Bobrow (eds), *The Programming Language LISP: Its Operation and Applications,* Cambridge, MA: MIT Press. A collection of papers on LISP, including the programming system, styles of programming, applications, implementation, and many examples of programs. Among the applications: techniques for automatically discovering interesting relations in data; automation of inductive inference on sequences; machine checking of mathematical proofs; an interpreter for string transformations; and a language for an incremental compiler.

Berry [1983], D. M., "A New Methodology for Generating Test Cases for a Programming Language Compiler," *SigPlan Notices* **18**(2) 46/56. Proposes a new methodology for testing compilers based on the frequency of use of statement types.

Bertsch [1977], E., "The Storage Requirement in Precedence Parsing," *CACM* **20**(3) 192/194. Short paper on the compression of precedence tables.

Bochmann [1976], G. V., "Semantic Evaluation from Left to Right," *CACM* **19**(2) 55/62. Describes attribute grammars and their use for the definition of programming languages and compilers. Emphasis on attribute conditions that can be fully evaluated in a single pass over the abstract-syntax tree.

Bowles [1978], K., "UCSD Pascal System," San Diego, CA: Softech. A popular implementation of Pascal for microcomputers.

Booth [1967], T. L., *Sequential Machines and Automata Theory*, New York: Wiley. A general text on finite-state automata. Complete theoretical development, many examples, applications, practical methods, and exercises.

Breuer [1969], M. A., "Generation of Optimal Code for Expressions via Factorization," *CACM* **12**(6) 333/340. A complete but complicated algorithm for finding all factors of a set of expressions to be compiled, then sequencing the operations to minimize the time they need be in memory, then assigning temporary storage cells. Global optimal results are not necessarily obtained.

Brooker [1963], R. A., D. Morris, "The Compiler-Compiler," *Ann. Review in Auto. Programming* vol 3, Elmsford, NY: Pergamon 229/275. The first compiler-writing system using a compressed notation and recursive descent technique.

Bruno [1976], J., R. Sethi, "Code Generation for a One-Register Machine," *JACM* **23**(3) 502/510. Shows that generating optimal code for a one-register machine is hard; it is in same class as the traveling salesperson problem.

Brzozowski [1962], J. A., "A Survey of Regular Expressions and Their Applications," *IRE Trans. on Electronic Computers* **11**(3) 324/335. One of the early papers on finite-state automata. An exposition of ideas developed by earlier authors. Collects notions of regular expressions, and finite-state automata and their transformation.

Campbell [1976], L., *et al.*, "Draft Proposed ANS FORTRAN," *Sigplan Notices* **11**(3). Modern draft definition of standard Fortran, with syntax graphs, conventions, and semantic specifications.

Chaitin [1982], G. J., "Register Allocation and Spilling via Graph-Coloring," *ACM Sigplan Notices,* **17**(6) 98/105.

Chomsky [1956], N., "Three Models for the Description of Language," *IEEE Trans. on Information Theory* **2**(3) 113/124. One of the three models is the phrase-structured grammar.

Chomsky [1959], N., "On Certain Formal Properties of Grammars," *Inf. and Control* **2**(2) 137/167.

Chomsky [1963], N., "Formal Properties of Grammars," in Luce, R. D. (ed). *Handbook of Mathematical Psychology,* vol 2, New York: Wiley, 323/418. A survey paper on formal grammars, with a set of references.

Chow [1983], F. C., M. Ganapathi, "Intermediate Languages in Compiler Construction: A Bibliography," *SigPlan Notices* **18**(11) 21/23. Short, nonannotated bibliography on intermediate languages. (See also the bibliography by Ottenstein[1984].)

Chow [1984], F., J. Hennessy, "Register Allocation by Priority-Based Coloring," *SigPlan Notices* **19**(6) 222/232. Presents a heuristic, linear-time approach to allocating registers.

Cocke [1977], J., K. Kennedy, "An Algorithm for Reduction of Operator Strength," *CACM* **20**(11) 850/856. A simple algorithm that uses an indexed temporary table to perform reduction of operator strength in strongly connected program-flow regions. The strength of a multiply in a loop can be reduced to an addition if one of the factors is constant.

Cohen [1970], D. J., C. C. Gotlieb, "A List Structure Form of Grammars for Syntactic Analysis," *Computing Surveys* **2**(1) 65/82. Syntax graph, graph reductions, compilation from graphs, recursive/nonrecursive compilers, and bottom-up parsing with reversed graph.

Conway [1963], M. E., "Design of a Separable Transition-Diagram Compiler," *CACM* **6**(7) 396/408 A COBOL compiler design. Accepts a COBOL subset, operates in small memory, requires two working tapes plus a compiler tape. Uses coroutines as modules.

DeMorgan [1977], R. M., I. D. Hill, B. A. Wichman, "A Supplement to the ALGOL 60 Revised Report," *Sigplan Notices* **12**(1) 52/66. More cleanup on the Algol report.

DeRemer [1969], F. L., "Practical Translators for LR(k) Languages," Ph.D. thesis, Cambridge, MA: MIT. Reviews and classifies LR(k) languages and parsers. Introduces SLR grammar (see DeRemer [1971].)

DeRemer [1971], F. L., "Simple LR(k) Grammars," *CACM* **14**(7) 453/460. First paper on SLR(k) grammars. These are generated by an LR(0) construction process, then FOLLOW(k) sets are used to resolve inconsistent states.

DeRemer [1974a], F. L., "Transformational Grammars," in *Lecture Notes in Computer Science,* Goos, G., J. Hartmanis (eds), New York: Springer-Verlag, 121/145. A case for language processing as a sequence of tree transformations. Lexical and syntactical processing, standardization, flattening, subtree transformational grammars, extension to regular expressions, and example of PL/I declaration defactoring.

DeRemer [1974b], F. L., "Review of Formalisms and Notation," in *Lecture Notes in Computer Science,* Goos, G., J. Hartmanis (eds), New York: Springer-Verlag, 37/56. Concise review of formalisms. Rewriting systems, grammars, Chomsky hierarchy, phrase structures, tree derivation, regular grammars and regular expressions, parsing, parsing strategies, ambiguity, transduction grammars, string-to-tree grammars, and self-describing grammars.

DeRemer [1974c], F. L., "Lexical Analysis," in *Lecture Notes in Computer Science,* Goos, G., J. Hartmanis (eds), New York: Springer-Verlag, 109/120. Lexical terms—scanning, screening, characters, tokens, reserved symbols, regularity. Scanner generation via LR construction, hand-written scanner, error recovery, advisability of including conversion routines.

DeRemer [1982], F. L., T. Pennello, "Efficient Computation of LALR(1) Look-Ahead Sets," *ACM Trans. on Prog. Langs. and Systems* **4**(4) 615/649. Develops relations that capture the essential LALR look-ahead resolution problem. Efficient programs for computation of the relations, given an LR(0) machine.

Demers [1975], A. J., "Elimination of Single Productions and Merging Nonterminal Symbols of LR(1) Grammars," *Computer Languages* **1**(2) 105/119. Formal treatment of single production removal and merging to optimize LR(1) parser tables, with proofs.

Demers [1977], A., "Generalized Left Corner Parsing," *Fourth ACM Symposium on Principles of Programming Languages,* 170/182. LC parsing is a combination of LL and LR. Develops a parsing machine and demonstrates some minimal properties of the system that facilitate semantic operations through an "announce point" within each production; the announce point is established by the system as near to the left end of the production formula as possible.

Despeyroux [1983], J, "An Algebraic Specification of a Pascal Compiler," *SigPlan Notices* **18**(12) 34/48. Uses a formal specification method, algebraic specification, to specify Pascal, low-level P-code, and a compiler from Pascal to P-code.

Dhamdhere [1983], D. M., J. S. Keith, "Characterization of Program Loops in Code Optimization," *Comput. Lang.* **18**(2) 69/76. Studies the representations of loops in flow graphs. Proposes an approach suitable for generalized optimization techniques.

Dijkstra [1976], E., *A Discipline of Programming,* Englewood Cliffs, NJ: Prentice-Hall. Explores the thesis that a program should derive from a mathematical statement of a problem in a natural way, thereby automatically resulting in a correct program. Introduces a simple but powerful language suited to the task. Semiformal treatment with many interesting examples.

Dijkstra [1976a], E. W., "On-the-Fly Garbage Collection: An Exercise in Cooperation," in *Lecture Notes in Computer Science* 46, New York: Springer-Verlag. Notes for the 1975 NATO Summer School on Language Hierarchies and Interfaces.

Donovan [1972], J.J., "Systems Programming," New York: McGraw-Hill. An introduction to machine structure, machine language, assembly language, assemblers, macros, loaders, programming languages, compilers, and operating systems. IBM 360 conventions used extensively. The author was associated with project MAC at MIT.

Earley [1970], J., "An Efficient Context-Free Parsing Algorithm," *CACM* **13**(2) 94/102. The general parser—capable of parsing any sentence in any CFG algorithmically. It runs in linear time for a large class of grammars, is bounded by n ↑ 2 for unambiguous grammars, and n ↑ 3 otherwise. Shows that it is superior to the top-down and bottom-up algorithms of Griffiths and Petrick by empirical studies.

Evans [1964], A., Jr., "An ALGOL 60 Compiler," *Ann. Review in Auto. Programming,* vol 4, Elmsford, NY: Pergamon 87/124.

Feldman [1966], J. A., "A Formal Semantics for Computer Languages and Application In a Compiler-Compiler," *CACM* **9**(1) 3/9. A system that accepts a production language (Floyd) and a special semantics language keyed to the production language, and yields a compiler. Has symbol table operations and a set of mnemonics to identify kind of expression/statement under consideration.

Feldman [1968], J., D. Gries, "Translator Writing Systems," *CACM* **11**(2) 77/113. Review paper on compiler-writing systems. Syntax, syntax trees, grammar, operator precedence, precedence, transition matrices, production language, bounded-context grammars, DPDA, LR(k), and Tixier's recursive functions of regular expressions. Semantics: TMG (top-down one-pass c writer), META, COGENT, ETC. Compiler compilers: FSL, TGS, CC (Brooker–Morris). Meta-assemblers and extendable compilers: META-PLAN, PLASMA, XPOP, ALGOL C. Large bibliography.

Feyock [1976], S., P. Lazarus, "Syntax-Directed Correction of Syntax Errors," *Software—Practice and Experience* **6**(2) 207/219. An error-correction method related to XPL bottom-up system. Examples, graph of compiler speed vs. error density.

Fischer [1977], C. N., D. R. Milton, S. B. Quiring, "An Efficient Insertion-Only Error-Corrector for LL(1) Parsers," *Fourth ACM Symposium on Principles of Programming Languages,* 97/103. Defines a class of insert-correctable LL(1) languages as those for which any error can be corrected by insertion of a suitable terminal string. System will so test a grammar and generate a set of tables that provide optimal string insertion for the correction of syntax errors. Examples.

Floyd [1961], R., "An Algorithm for Coding Efficient Arithmetic Operations," *CACM* **4**(1) 42/51 Specialized method for dealing with arithmetic expression groups to reduce code for single-register machine.

Floyd [1963], R. W., "Syntactic Analysis and Operator Precedence," *JACM* **10**(3) 316/333. Landmark paper on operator precedence. Has an Algol 60 precedence matrix, theory of operator precedence.

Floyd [1964], R. W., "Bounded Context Syntactic Analysis," *CACM* **7**(2) 62/67. A bottom-up parsing method based on context analysis of production right-parts.

Forman [1982], I. R., "Global Data Flow Analysis by Decomposition into Primes," *6th Int. Conf. on Soft. Eng.* 82, 386/392. Discusses prime program decomposition. It applies this technique to global data-flow analysis, in particular to the live variables problem.

Gates [1973], G. W., D. A. Poplawski, "A Simple Technique for Structured Variable Lookup," *CACM* **16**(9) 561/565. A method for the lookup of structured Cobol or PL/I variables. Also checks legality of Cobol identifiers.

Gill [1962], A., *Introduction to the Theory of Finite State Machines*, New York: McGraw-Hill. Early text on finite-state automata. Discusses classes of automata, equivalence, reduction, and reduction algorithms. Semiformal treatment. (No treatment of regular expressions or regular grammars.)

Ginsburg [1962], S., *An Introduction to Mathematical Machine Theory*, Reading, MA: Addison-Wesley.

Ginsburg [1966a], S., *The Mathematical Theory of Context-Free Languages*, New York: McGraw-Hill. First general text on formal context-free language theory. Many general theorems, most original to the author.

Ginsburg [1966b], S., S. Greibach, "Deterministic Context-free Languages," *Inf. and Control* **9**(6) 620/648.

Glanville [1977], R.S., S.L.Graham, "A New Method for Compiler Code Generation," *Fifth Annual ACM Symposium on Principles of Programming Languages, 1978*, 231/240. A construction algorithm for generating machine instructions from a prefix translation of a suitable abstract-syntax tree, based on a table representation of the target machine. Conditions for correctness and normal termination of the algorithm are given.

Graham [1975], S. L., S. P. Rhodes, "Practical Syntactic Error Recovery," *CACM* **18**(11) 639/650. Error recovery for precedence parsers. Experimental results from several different grammars.

Gries [1971], D., *Compiler Construction for Digital Computers*, New York: Wiley. Compiler construction textbook. Emphasis on practical methods for Algol control structures and expressions. Reviews grammars and languages, scanner, top-down recognizers, simple precedence, other bottom-up recognizers, production language, run-time storage organization, symbol table organization, internal forms of the source, semantic routines introduction, semantics for Algol constructs, storage allocation, error recovery, interpreters, code generation, code optimization, macros, and translator-writing systems.

Gries [1977], D., "An Exercise in Proving Parallel Programs Correct," *CACM* **20**(12) 921/930. A parallel program correctness proof method, and its application to an on-the-fly garbage collector. (See also Dijkstra [1976]; Steele [1975].)

Griffiths [1974a], M., "Run-Time Storage Management," in *Lecture Notes in Computer Science*, Goos, G., J. Hartmanis, (eds), New York: Springer-

Verlag, 195/221. Classical storage allocation and access. Static allocation, dynamic allocation, block linkage, display, stack compaction, parameter linking, labels/goto, aggregates, lists, garbage collection, storage collapse, and parallel processes.

Griffiths [1974b], M., "LL(1) Grammars and Analyzers," in *Lecture Notes in Computer Science,* Goos, G., J. Hartmanis, (eds), New York: Springer-Verlag, 57/84. Predictive analysis, LL(1) conditions, decision algorithm, recursive-descent construction, grammar transformation, semantic insertion, LL(k) grammars, and practical results.

Griffiths [1974c], M., "Introduction to Compiler Compilers," in *Lecture Notes in Computer Science,* Goos, G., J. Hartmanis, (eds), New York: Springer-Verlag, 356/365. Brief review of compiler-writing systems and current research.

Hall [1974], A. D., private communication, reported in Waite [1974b].

Hansche [1982], B., S. Hudson, B. Huey, "Selected Bibliography of Compiler Optimization Topics," *SigPlan Notices* **17**(8) 74/83. Fairly extensive bibliography on optimization topics, including sections on data-flow analysis, code generation and register allocation, and evaluation of expressions.

Hanson [1983], D. R., "Simple Code Optimization," *Software Pract. and Exp.* **13**(8) 745/763. Discusses three types of optimization techniques: expression rearrangement, instruction selection, and resource allocation.

Harrison [1965], M. A. *Introduction to Switching and Automata Theory,* New York: McGraw-Hill.

Harrison [1977], W., "A New Strategy for Code Generation: The General Purpose Optimizing Compiler," *Fourth ACM Symposium on Principles of Programming Languages,* 29/37. Uses global flow analysis and an intermediate language of simple primitives to achieve general optimization, regardless of source-language form.

Hartmanis [1966], J., R. E. Stearns, *Algebraic Structure of Sequential Machines,* Englewood Cliffs, NJ: Prentice-Hall.

Hill [1974], U., "Special Run-Time Organization Techniques for Algol 68," in *Lecture Notes in Computer Science,* Goos, G., J. Hartmanis, (eds), New York: Springer-Verlag, 222/252. Data storage and management required for Algol 68. Static and dynamic storage, heaps, generative and interpretative handling, special data objects, slicing, rowing, scope checking, scope of procedures, generation of local objects, blocks and procedure calls, actual parameters, and garbage collection.

Hoare [1969], C. A. R., "An Axiomatic Basis for Computer Programming," *CACM* **12**(10) 576/581. Definition and development of the Hoare axiomatic program correctness proof method. For example, A1 {S} A2; A1 and A2 are assertions regarding the state of a program system, and S is some executable statement. Proof problem is to show that A1 implies A2, given execution of S.

Hoare [1973], C. A. R., N. Wirth, "An Axiomatic Definition of the Programming Language PASCAL," *Acta Informatica* **2** 335/355. Brief review of Hoare axiomatic approach. Has PASCAL statements expressed in axiomatic form. PASCAL syntax graphs.

Hopcroft [1969], J. E., J. D. Ullman, *Formal Languages and Their Relation to Automata,* Reading, MA: Addison-Wesley. Text on formal language and automata theory. Largely superceded by Aho [1972].

Horning [1974a], J. J., "What the Compiler Should Tell the User," in *Lecture Notes in Computer Science,* Goos, G., J. Hartmanis, (eds), New York: Springer-Verlag, 525/548. Normal output, reaction to errors, syntactic errors, other errors, and error diagnosis.

Horning [1974b], J. J., "Structuring Compiler Development," in *Lecture Notes in Computer Science,* Goos, G., J. Hartmanis, (eds), New York: Springer-Verlag, 498/513. Goals of compiler development—correctness, availability, generality, adaptability, helpfulness, and efficiency. Tradeoffs and processes in development: specification, design, implementation, validation, evaluation, and maintenance. Management tools: project organization, information distribution and validation, and programmer motivation. Technical tools: compiler compilers, standard designs, off-the-shelf components, structured programs, and appropriate languages.

Horning [1974c], J. J., "LR Grammars and Analysers," in *Lecture Notes in Computer Science,* Goos, G., J. Hartmanis, (eds), New York: Springer-Verlag, 85/108. Intuitive description, definitions of terms, interpreting LR tables, constructing LR tables, representing LR tables, reduction for efficiency, properties of LR grammars and analyzers, some grammar modifications to obtain LR, grammar/language inclusions.

Huffman [1954], D. A., "The Synthesis of Sequential Switching Circuits," *J. Franklin Inst.* **257**(3) 161/190; 275/303.

Ingerman [1961], P. Z., "Dynamic Declarations," *CACM* **4**(42) 59/60. Algorithm for mapping an OWN array in which dimensions have been changed. The nontrivial multidimension dynamic array problem is dealt with.

Irons [1961], E. T., "A Syntax Directed Compiler for ALGOL 60," *CACM* **4**(42) 51/55.

Irons [1963], E. T., "An Error-Correcting Parse Algorithm," *CACM* **6**(11) 669/673. A top-down error-correcting parsing system.

Iverson [1962], K., *A Programming Language,* New York: Wiley. Original book on APL. Defines the language and gives many examples of its applications to broad areas of computing, such as mapping and permutations, ordered trees, graph traversal, microprogramming, matrices, searching, sorting, and the logical calculus.

James [1972], L. R., *A Syntax Directed Error Recovery Method,* Technical Report CSRG-13, Toronto, Canada: University of Toronto. Table-driven error recovery embedded in an LALR(1) parser. Method drops stack states and input symbols, searches for an insertion or compatible state. Uses a two-symbol lookahead limit, then five-symbol lookahead in dire cases. Limits stack cutback through a fixed limit.

Johnson [1968], W. L., *et al.*, "Generation of Efficient Lexical Processors Using Finite State Automatic Techniques," *CACM* **11**(12) 805/813. Description of the AED RWORD system that accepts regular expressions and generates a finite-state automaton to recognize the expression's language. Has "escape hatches" to provide for unusual lexical constructs. Used in several different compilers as a lexical analyzer.

Kernighan [1978], B. W., D. M. Ritchie, "The C Programming Language," Englewood Cliffs, NJ: Prentice-Hall.

Kildall [1973], G. A. , "A Unified Approach to Global Program Optimization," *ACM Symposium on Principles of Programming Languages,* Boston, MA, 194/206.

Kleene [1952], S. C., *Introduction to Metamathematics,* New York: Van Nostrand Reinhold.

Kleene [1956], S. C., "Representation of Events in Nerve Nets," in *Automaton Studies,* Shannon, C., J. McCarthy, (eds), Princeton, NJ: Princeton University Press.

Knuth [1965], D. E., "On the Translation of Languages from Left to Right," *Inf. and Control* **8**(6) 607/639. Original paper on LR(k) languages. Shows that LR(k) languages are equivalent to the deterministic k-symbol lookahead languages, gives two parser construction methods, and proves that the viable prefix set is a regular language.

Knuth [1968], D. E., *Fundamental Algorithms*, vol 1 of *The Art of Computer Programming,* Reading, MA: Addison-Wesley.

Knuth [1971], D. E., "An Empirical Study of FORTRAN Programs," *Software—Practice and Experience* **1**(2) 105/133.

Knuth [1973], D. E., "Sorting and Searching," vol 3 of *The Art of Computer Programming,* Reading, MA: Addison-Wesley.

Kohavi [1971], Z., "Switching and Finite Automata Theory," New York: McGraw-Hill.

Korenjak [1969], A. J., "A Practical Method for Constructing LR(k) Processors," *CACM* **12**(11) 613/623. Large grammar is partitioned into several smaller parts, each of which is parsed independently; the mechanism of parser intercommunication and reporting is developed.

Koster [1974], C. H. A., "Using the CDL Compiler-compiler," in *Lecture Notes in Computer Science,* Goos, G., J. Hartmanis, (eds), New York: Springer-Verlag, 366/426. Detailed review of the CDL compiler writer. Includes a top-down system with symbol table manager system, macros.

Kurki-Suonio [1969], R. "Notes on Top-Down Languages," *BIT* **9** 225/238. Short paper on the properties of LL(k) languages and grammars.

LaBlanc [1984], R. J., *et al.,* "Simple Separate Compilation Mechanism for Block-Structured Languages," *IEEE Trans. Soft. Eng.* SE-10 (3) 221/227. Presents a simple technique for introducing separate compilation features into compilers while retaining the checking capabilites of compiling the whole program.

LaFrance [1971], J. E., "Syntax Directed Error Recovery for Compilers," Ph.D. thesis, Computer Sci. Dept. ILLIAC IV Doc. 249, Urbana, IL: University of Illinois.

LaLonde [1971a], W. R., E. S. Lee, J. J. Horning, "An LALR(k) Parser Generator," Proc. IFIP Congress 71, TA-3, Netherlands: North Holland, 153/157. (See LaLonde [1971b].)

LaLonde [1971b], W. R., "An Efficient LALR Parser Generator," Tech. Rpt. CSRG-2, Toronto, Canada: University of Toronto. Review of LR machines, introduction of LALR(1) parsing algorithm that finds lookahead sets for inconsistent states based on LR(0) machine and state tracing. DeRemer, however, has shown that LaLonde's system actually accepts a subset of the LALR(1) languages.

Lampson [1977], B. W., *et al.,* "Report on the Programming Language Euclid," *Sigplan Notices* **12**(2) 1/79. Euclid draws heavily on Pascal for its structure and many of its features. The intention is to express programs that are to be verified by formal methods.

Ledgard [1975], H. F., M. Marcotty, "A Genealogy of Control Structures," *CACM* **18**(11) 629/639. Review and classification of known control structures. Discussion of equivalence, reducibility, and hierarchy. Examples, four general conclusions.

Lee [1967], J. A. N., *Anatomy of a Compiler,* New York: Van Nostrand Reinhold.

Leinius [1970], R. "Error Detection and Recovery for Syntax Directed Compiler Systems," Ph.D. thesis, Madison: University of Wisconsin. Mostly simple precedence error-recovery treatment. One chapter on LR(k) systems. Uses EULER as model language. Method requires additional states in the LR(k) parser, created heuristically.

Lewi [1979], J., *et al., A Programming Methodology in Compiler Construction,* 2 parts, Netherlands: North-Holland. Background theory and detailed discussion of the LILA compiler-writer system. Based on recursive-descent construction.

Levy [1975], J. P., "Automatic Correction of Syntax-Errors and Programming Languages," *Acta Informatica* **4** 271/292. Formal models of error correction. Notion of error, global error correction, local error correction, detailed error correction method for one language construct, problems, and practical error correction.

Lewis [1968], P. M., R. E. Stearns, "Syntax-Directed Transduction," *JACM* **15**(3) 465/488. Transduction grammars, relation to LR and LL grammars, and machines.

Lewis [1971], P. M., D. J. Rosenkrantz, "An ALGOL Compiler Designed Using Automata Theory," *Proc. Polytechnic Inst. Brooklyn Symposium on Computers and Automata*, 75/87.

Loveman [1977], D. B., "Program Improvement by Source-to-Source Trans-formation," *JACM* **24**(1) 121/145. User-provided assertions in an Algol program are shown to be valuable in optimization.

Maley [1963], G. A., J. Earle, *The Logic Design of Transistor Digital Comput-ers*, Englewood Cliffs, NJ: Prentice-Hall.

Marcotty [1976], M., H. F. Ledgard, G. V. Bochman, "A Sampler of Formal Definitions," *Computing Surveys* **8**(2) 191/276. Presentation of four well-known formal definition techniques: w-grammars, production systems with an axiomatic approach to semantics, the Vienna definition language, and attribute grammars. Each technique is described tutorially and examples are given; then each is applied to define the same small programming language.

Maurer [1975], W. D., T. G. Lewis, "Hash Table Methods," *Computing Sur-veys* **7**(1) 5/19. Hashing functions, collision, bucket overflow, and alterna-tives to hashing. Limited analysis of efficiency.

McCarthy [1960], J., "Recursive Functions of Symbolic Expressions and Their Computation by Machine," *CACM* **4**(4) 184/195. Original paper on the mathematical basis of LISP. Five primitive recursive functions are shown to form the basis of a complete programming language. Interpretation of struc-tures as directed graphs.

McCarthy [1962], J., *et al.*, *LISP 1.5 Programmers Manual*, Cambridge, MA: MIT Press. A programmer's manual for LISP. Some examples, but best used as a reference document.

McCluskey [1965a], E. J., *Introduction to the Theory of Switching Circuits*, New York: McGraw-Hill.

McCluskey [1965b], E. J., T. C. Bartee, *A Survey of Switching Circuit Theory*, New York: McGraw-Hill.

McCullough [1943], W. S., E. Pitts, "A Logical Calculus of the Ideas Immanent in Nervous Activity," *Bull. of Math. Biophysics* **5** 115/133. Original paper on finite-state automata and their relation to regular expressions.

McKeeman [1970], W. M., J. J. Horning, D. B. Wortman, *A Compiler Gener-ator*, Englewood Cliffs, NJ: Prentice-Hall. Text on compiler construction. Introduction to formalism, LR(k), and precedence parsing. Emphasis on MSP (mixed strategy precedence) method. Contains complete compiler-generator programs in XPL, and a definition of XPL as a language.

McKeeman [1974a], W. M., "Compiler Construction," in *Lecture Notes in Computer Science*, Goos, G., J. Hartmanis, (eds), New York: Springer-

Verlag, 1/36. Broad, informal review of compiler components. Definitions, source/target language, implementation language, recursive-descent compilers, modularization, specification, lexical feedback, vertical/horizontal fragmentation, and transformations.

McKeeman [1974b], W. M., "Symbol Table Access," in *Lecture Notes in Computer Science,* Goos, G., J. Hartmanis, (eds), New York: Springer-Verlag, 253/301. Review of linear, sorted, tree, and hash symbol table access methods. Block structured symbol tables. Contains complete XPL programs and sample traces. Hash functions, secondary stores, evaluation of access methods.

McKeeman [1974c], W. M., "Programming Language Design," in *Lecture Notes in Computer Science,* Goos, G., J. Hartmanis, (eds), New York: Springer-Verlag, 514/524. Who should or should not design languages? Design principles, models for languages (street language, the Algol family).

McNaughton [1960], R., H. Yamada, "Regular Expressions and State Graphs for Automata," *IRE Trans. on Elect. Computers* **9**(1) 39/47. Reprinted in Moore, *Sequential Machines: Selected Papers,* Reading, MA: Addison-Wesley, (1964). First paper giving algorithms for interconverting state graphs, regular expressions. Deals with all possible regular expressions— union, intersection, complement, closure, and concatenation. Theorems and proofs given.

Mealy [1955], G. H., "Method for Synthesizing Sequential Circuits," *Bell System Tech. J.* **34**(5) 1045/1079.

Metcalfe [1964], H. H., "A Parameterized Compiler Based on Mechanical Linguistics," *Annual Revs. in Auto. Programming,* vol 4, Elmsford, NY: Pergamon Press, 125/165. Descriptive paper on some recursive-descent programming techniques, with special mechanisms for semantic operations. Well suited to a top-down string translator. Informal. Brief discussion of the validation problem of verifying LL(1), but no solution.

Meyers [1965], W. J., "Optimization of Computer Code," unpublished memorandum, Schenectady, NY: G. E. Research Center.

Mickunas [1976], M. D., R. L. Lancaster, V. B. Schneider, "Transforming LR(k) Grammars to LR(1), SLR(1), and (1,1) Bounded Right-Context Grammars," *JACM* **23**(3) 511/533. Grammar transformation results and algorithms.

Mickunas [1978], M. D., J. A. Modry, "Automatic Error Recovery for LR Parsers," *CACM* **21**(6) 459/465. A scheme for detecting and recovering from syntax errors based on LR parsing. Uses a forward move and a state-stack backup to achieve an error recovery that is both simple and powerful.

Minsky [1967], M., *Computation: Finite and Infinite Machines,* Englewood Cliffs, NJ: Prentice-Hall. Textbook on finite-state automata. Many unusual and interesting examples and side issues.

Morgan [1970], H. L., "Spelling Correction in System Programs," *CACM* **13**(2) 90/94. Spelling-correction algorithm and its applications.

Moore [1956], E. F., "Gedanken-Experiments on Sequential Machines," in *Automata Studies,* Shannon, C. E., J. McCarthy (eds), Princeton, NJ: Princeton University Press, 129/153.

Morris [1968], R., "Scatter Storage Techniques," *CACM* **11**(1) 38/43.

Nakata [1967], I., "On Compiling Algorithms for Arithmetic Expressions," *CACM* **10**(8) 492/494.

Naur [1963], P. (ed), "Revised Report on the Algorithmic Language ALGOL 60," *CACM* **6**(1) 1/17. The original Algol 60 definition.

Ottenstein [1984], K.J., "Intermediate Program Representations in Compiler Construction: A Supp Bib," *SigPlan Notices* **19**(7) 25/27. Contains additions to the Chow [1983] and Ganapathi bibliography on intermediate representations.

Pager [1977], D., "A Practical General Method for Constructing LR(k) Parsers," *Acta Informatica* **7**(3) 249/268.

Paul [1962], M., "A General Processor for Certain Formal Languages," *Proc. Symp. Symbolic Languages in Data Processing,* New York: Gordon and Breach, 65/74.

Pennello [1978], T. J., F. DeRemer, "A Forward Move Algorithm for LR Error Recovery," *Fifth Annual ACM Symposium on Principles of Programming Languages,* 241/254. A "forward move" is useful in syntax error recovery. In a forward move, the text past an error token is partially reduced in an attempt to develop information useful in patching over the error. Pennello and DeRemer develop this for an LR parser.

Perlis [1956], A. J., *et al.,* "Internal Translator (IT): A Compiler for the 650," Lincoln Laboratory, Div. 6, document 6D-327.

Pittman [1985], T.J., "Practical Code Optimization by Transformational Attribute Grammars Applied to Low-Level Intermediate Code Trees," Ph.D. thesis, Santa Cruz, CA: University of California. Presents a unified approach to code optimization based on attribute grammars. Includes a survey and classification of current approaches.

Poole [1974], P. C., "Portable and Adaptable Compilers," in *Lecture Notes in Computer Science,* Goos, G., J. Hartmanis, (eds), New York: Springer-Verlag, 427/497. Survey of issues of transporting languages and compilers. Problems with current compilers, standards. Survey of techniques: high-level language coding, bootstrapping, language–machine interface, abstract machine modeling, Janus. Case studies: AED, LSD, BCPL, Pascal, and IBM Fortran G.

Purdom [1974], P., "The Size of LALR(1) Parsers," *BIT* **14** 326/337. Statistical results enabling prediction of size of LALR parser tables from some simple grammar measures, based on a large set of grammars.

Qparser [1984], *The Qparser User Manual*, San Jose, CA: QCAD Systems. Description of the Qparser translator writing system and listings of several related Pascal programs.

Ramanath [1982], M.V.S., M. Solomon, "Optimal Code from Flow Graphs," *Comput Lang.* **7** 41/52. Shows how to generate a linear sequencing of statements from a flow graph to minimize the number of jumps.

Randell [1964], B., L. J. Russell, *ALGOL 60 Implementation*, New York: Academic Press. Contains a detailed machine model for Algol 60 implementation. Review of nested block structure, procedure calls, parameter passing, branching, and control structures.

Rosen [1967], S. (ed), *Programming Systems and Languages*, New York: McGraw-Hill. An early collection of papers on languages, compilers, and macros.

Rosen [1973], B. K., "Tree-Manipulating Systems and the Church–Rosser Theorems," *JACM* **20**(1) 160/187. Considers subtree replacement systems (RPSs) and develops sufficient conditions for the Church–Rosser property (which says that the result of a set of subtree replacements under some replacement-system RPS is independent of the order of the replacement). This property does not hold for all tree RPSs. Applications to recursive definitions, the lambda calculus, and McCarthy's recursive calculus are discussed.

Rosenkrantz [1970a], D. J., P. M. Lewis, "Deterministic Left-Corner Parsing," *IEEE 11th Annual Symposium on Switching and Automata Theory*, 139/152. The original left-corner paper. (See also Demers [1977].)

Rosenkrantz [1970b], D. J., R. E. Stearns, "Properties of Deterministic Top-Down Grammars," *Inf. and Control* **17**(3) 226/256. Test for LL(k) and strong LL(k), e-rules, canonical push-down automata, LL(k) hierarchy, equivalence decidability, and properties. Definitions.

Saib [1983], S., R. Fritz, *The Ada Programming Language: A Tutorial*, New York: IEEE Computer Society Press. A collection of papers on Ada's development history. Examples, implementation issues, and so on.

Sammet [1969], J. E., *Programming Languages: History and Fundamentals*, Englewood Cliffs, NJ: Prentice-Hall. Catalog of and brief introduction to the reported programming languages known at that time.

Sammet [1976], J. E., "Roster of Programming Languages for 1974–5," *CACM* **19**(12) 655/669. A sorted list of 167 languages, each with a brief description of availability, implementation, and so on. (See also Sammet [1969].)

Sattley [1961], K., "Allocation of Storage for Arrays in ALGOL 60," *CACM* **4**(42) 60/65. General problem of dynamically allocating array space for Algol 60.

Sethi [1970], R., J. D. Ullman, "The Generation of Optimal Code for Arithmetic Expressions," *JACM* **17**(4) 715/728. A machine with $N \geq 1$ general-purpose registers, arithmetic instructions that may operate between register/ register or register/memory (for example, IBM 360), and arithmetic expressions is assumed. No optimization for common subexpressions. Then two optimal register assignment algorithms are given: one in which no algebraic properties are assumed and another in which certain operators are commutative or both commutative and associative. These algorithms are shown to require a minimal number of storage references in the evaluation and a minimal number of instructions.

Shamir [1971], E., "Some Inherently Ambiguous Context-Free Languages," *Inf. and Control* **18**(4) 355/363. Introduces a class of inherently ambiguous context-free languages.

Sigplan [1973], "Proceedings of a Symposium on High-Level-Language Computer Architecture," *Sigplan Notices* **8**(11). Nineteen papers on this subject.

Sigplan [1974], "Proceedings of a Symposium on Very High Level Languages," *Sigplan Notices* **9**(4). Fifteen papers on high-level languages.

Sigplan [1975a], "Programming Language Design," *Sigplan Notices* **10**(7). Nine short papers on language design. Structured control, data types and program correctness, extensibility, structured languages, abstract data types, exception handling cognitive psychology and programming language design.

Sigplan [1975b], "1975 International Conference on Reliable Software," *Sigplan Notices* **10**(6). Sixty-three papers in this area; three are related to languages and their influence on reliable software.

Sigplan [1976], "Interface Meeting on Programming Systems in the Small Processor Environment," *Sigplan Notices* **11**(4). Twenty-four papers; four are related to programming languages for small processors.

Soisalon-Soininen [1977], E., "Elimination of Single Productions from LR Parsers in Conjunction with the Use of Default Reductions," *Fourth ACM Symposium on Principles of Programming Languages,* 183/193. Review of LR construction. Development of method for elimination of single production transitions, with concomitant reduction of table size.

Stearns [1967], R. E., "A Regularity Test for Pushdown Machines," *Inf. and Control* **11**(3) 323/340. An algorithm for determining whether a given context-free grammar is regular.

Stearns [1969], R. E., P. M. Lewis, "Property Grammars and Table Machines," *Inf. and Control* **14**(6) 524/549. Formal definition of an attribute system for CFGs; attributes are effectively attached to derivation tree nodes and used to control bindings and legal derivations.

Steele [1975], G.L., Jr., "Multiprocessing Compactifying Garbage Collection," *CACM* **18**(9) 495/508. On-the-fly garbage collector. (See also Dijkstra [1976] and Gries [1977].)

Tanenbaum [1983], A. S., *et al.*, "A Practical Tool Kit for Making Portable

Compilers,'' *CACM* **26**(9) 654/662. Introduces the Amsterdam Compiler Kit (ACK), an integrated set of programs designed to simplify the production of portable compilers. ACK is based on the UNCOL approach of using a common intermediate language.

Tanenbaum [1976], A. S., ''A Tutorial on ALGOL 68,'' *Computing Surveys* **8**(2) 155/190. Very readable introduction to Algol 68. Many examples and good discussion.

Van Wijngaarden [1969], A. (ed), ''Report on the Algorithmic Language ALGOL 68,'' *Numerische Mathematik* **14**(2) 79/218. Definition of Algol 68.

Waite [1974a], W. M., ''Assembly and Linkage,'' in *Lecture Notes in Computer Science*, Goos, G., J. Hartmanis, (eds), New York: Springer-Verlag, 333/355. Model for assembly. Object and statement procedures, cross-referencing, backchaining, storage constraints, two-pass assembly, the RESERVE expression problem, and partial assembly and linkage.

Waite [1974b], W. M., ''Optimization,'' in *Lecture Notes in Computer Science*, Goos, G., J. Hartmanis, (eds), New York: Springer-Verlag, 549/602. Classification of techniques: transformations, regions, and efficacy. Local optimization: expression rearrangement, redundant code elimination, and basic blocks. Global optimization: redundancy and rearrangement, frequency and strength reduction, and global analysis.

Waite [1974c], W. M., ''Relationship of Languages to Machines,'' in *Lecture Notes in Computer Science*, Goos, G., J. Hartmanis, (eds), New York: Springer-Verlag, 170/194. Considerations in selecting a suitable interface between a language and a target machine. Data objects: encodings, interpretations, primitive/derived modes, mode conversion, and formation rules. Register structure, data access, aggregates, procedures, and procedure calls.

Waite [1974d], W. M., ''Semantic Analysis,'' in *Lecture Notes in Computer Science*, Goos, G., J. Hartmanis, (eds), New York: Springer-Verlag, 157/169. Discussion of what to do after abstract-syntax tree is formed. Optimizing transformations, attribute propagation, and flattening through traversals. Postfix versus prefix. Operator identification and coercion, and semantic ambiguity.

Waite [1974e], W. M., ''Code Generation,'' in *Lecture Notes in Computer Science*, Goos, G., J. Hartmanis, (eds), New York: Springer-Verlag, 302/332. A model of code generation, based on Wilcox [1971]. Contains a transducer and simulator. Handles common subexpression optimization.

Warshall [1962], S., ''A Theorem on Boolean Matrices,'' *JACM* **9**(1) 11/12. A fast algorithm for computing the transitive closuré of a relation, with proof. (Also proven in a different way in Aho [1972].)

Whitney [1969a], G., ''An Extended BNF for Specifying the Syntax of Declarations,'' *AFIPS Spring JCC*, 801/812. Formal symbol table functions and grammar extensions, suitable for top-down compiler system for block-structured grammar. Example language (MAL).

Whitney [1969b], G., "The Generation and Recognition Properties of Table Languages," in *Information Processing 68*, Netherlands: North-Holland, 388/394. Formal paper on his table language generators, a table automaton, and five closure properties.

Wirth [1966], N., H. Weber, "EULER: A Generalization of ALGOL, and its Formal Definition," (part 1) *CACM* **9**(1) 13/25; (part 2) *CACM* **9**(2) 89/99. Part 1: elementary notation for algorithms, phrase structured grammar, simple precedence, precedence matrix, and higher-order precedence. Part 2: EULER language: precedence matrix and functions, language definition, productions, interpretation of operators, and examples.

Wirth [1971], N., "The Programming Language PASCAL," *Acta Informatica* **1**(1) 35/63. First published definition of PASCAL. Semiformal.

Wirth [1971a], N. "The Design of a PASCAL Compiler," *Software—Practice and Experience* **1**(4) 309/333. A description of the design of a PASCAL compiler for the CDC 6000 series, including symbol table structure details, organization of the project, various statistical results on instruction usage, and nesting levels. Most of the article is applicable to a PASCAL implementation on any machine.

Wirth [1976a], N., "Programming Languages: What To Demand and How To Assess Them," in *Symposium on Software Engineering*, Belfast, Ireland. What language should do for the user; a strong case for PASCAL.

Wirth [1976b], N., "Professor Cleverbyte's Visit to Heaven," private communication. A tongue-in-cheek tale of a heaven in which every possible feature of every possible language is implemented in a colossal computer, with such a large operating system that it breaks down 50 times per second (but recovers through elaborate mechanisms).

Wirth [1976c], N., *Algorithms + Data Structures = Programs*, Englewood Cliffs, NJ: Prentice-Hall. PASCAL textbook. Applications to data structures, files, sorting, recursive algorithms, dynamic information structures, language structures, and compilers. Contains a complete top-down definition of grammar and construction of a compiler for a small language (PL/0), including transformation of syntax graphs into program structures, checking for validity, error recovery, scanning, and code generation for an Algol-class stack machine.

Wirth [1976d], N., *Portable Pascal Compiler*. Available on request from Professor Wirth*, this is a complete Pascal compiler in magnetic tape form, written in itself, that can be adapted to a variety of different machines. It generates P-code, which can be assembled or interpreted on a variety of machines.

---

*Prof. Dr. Niklaus Wirth
Institut für Informatik
ETH Zürich
Clausinsstrasse 5
CH-8006   Zürich

Wirth [1978], N., K. Jensen, *Pascal User Manual and Report,* New York: Springer-Verlag, 1978. Concepts, examples, and formal definitions of a core Pascal supported by most implementations of the language.

YACC [1978], *YACC: Yet Another Compiler-Compiler,* Johnson, S. Murray Hill, NJ: Bell Laboratories. May be found among the user documentation for the Unix operating system.

INDEX